SOCIAL INSURANCE
and
ECONOMIC SECURITY

SOCIAL INSURANCE
and
ECONOMIC SECURITY

Fourth Edition

GEORGE E. REJDA, Ph.D., CLU

V. J. Skutt Professor of Insurance
University of Nebraska-Lincoln

Prentice Hall, Englewood Cliffs, New Jersey 07632

Library of Congress Cataloging-in-Publication Data

Rejda, George E.
    Social insurance and economic security / George E. Rejda. — 4th ed.
       p.   cm. — (The Prentice-Hall series in security and insurance)
    Includes bibliographical references and index.
    ISBN 0-13-816158-5
    1. Social security—United States. 2. Economic security—United
States. I. Title. II. Series.
HD7125.R37 1991
368.4′00973—dc20   90-38682
                                            CIP

Editorial/production supervision and
   interior design: *Carol Burgett*
Cover design: *Franklyn Graphics*
Prepress buyer: *Trudy Pisciotti*
Manufacturing buyer: *Robert Anderson*

 © 1991, 1988, 1984, 1976 by Prentice-Hall, Inc.
A Division of Simon & Schuster
Englewood Cliffs, New Jersey 07632

Printed in the United States of America

10 9 8 7 6 5 4 3 2 1

ISBN 0-13-816158-5

PRENTICE-HALL INTERNATIONAL (UK) LIMITED, *London*
PRENTICE-HALL OF AUSTRALIA PTY. LIMITED, *Sydney*
PRENTICE-HALL CANADA INC., *Toronto*
PRENTICE-HALL HISPANOAMERICANA, S.A., *Mexico*
PRENTICE-HALL OF INDIA PRIVATE LIMITED, *New Delhi*
PRENTICE-HALL OF JAPAN, INC., *Tokyo*
SIMON & SCHUSTER ASIA PTE. LTD., *Singapore*
EDITORA PRENTICE-HALL DO BRASIL, LTDA., *Rio de Janeiro*

CONTENTS

PREFACE

The academic response to earlier editions of this textbook has been gratifying. The text is widely used in social insurance and economic security courses in universities and colleges throughout the United States. It is also used by the Society of Actuaries in its actuarial science program. The fourth edition builds on the earlier editions and, it is hoped, is an improved product. Social insurance programs are enormously complex. The fundamental objective underlying the writing of the fourth edition, however, remains the same—I have attempted to write a textbook from which students can learn and professors can teach. I have attempted to simplify as much as possible the complex social insurance laws and regulations so that students can assimilate the fundamentals of social insurance in an easily understandable manner.

The fourth edition is designed for a one-semester course in social insurance at either the graduate or undergraduate level. It can also be used profitably in courses that emphasize public assistance and welfare programs, public and private income maintenance programs, labor economics, collective bargaining, and employee benefits.

Like the earlier editions, the text emphasizes social insurance as a major technique for meeting and alleviating the problems of economic insecurity. Although two chapters are devoted to poverty and public assistance programs in the United States, the central thrust of the book is devoted to an analysis of Social Security, unemployment insurance, and workers' compensation. The major principles, characteristics, and current issues surrounding these three important programs are discussed in considerable depth. Each major cause of economic security is examined, and the appropriate social insurance program and current issues surrounding the program are then analyzed in some detail.

CHANGES IN THE FOURTH EDITION

The substantive changes in the fourth edition are summarized as follows:

- The text is completely updated to reflect recent changes in Social Security, unemployment insurance, workers' compensation, and public assistance.

- Chapter 3 has been completely rewritten to reflect the impact of premature death on the different types of families in the United States, including single-parent households, two-income earners, traditional families, blended families, and sandwich families.

- Chapter 4 is an up-to-date treatment of the economic problem of old age, which includes an analysis of the current financial position of the aged. New programs such as reverse mortgages, long-term care insurance, and elder-care benefits are discussed in some detail.

- Chapter 5 is completely updated to reflect recent changes in the OASDI program.

- Chapter 6 now includes an analysis of the impact of the Social Security program on the federal budget, including the impact of the OASDI surplus on the federal deficit and use of the surplus to increase national saving.

- Chapter 7 includes an up-to-date analysis of the current financial position of the Social Security program.

- Chapter 8 has been substantially rewritten to reflect new developments in the rapidly changing health care field. The problems of the escalation in health care costs, inadequate access to medical care for many Americans, and health care cost containment are discussed in some depth.

- Chapter 9 discusses the present Medicare program after the Medicare Catastrophic Coverage Act of 1988 was repealed. The chapter also discusses the new method for reimbursing physicians under Medicare. The new system determines fees based on a "resource-based relative-value scale" that will gradually replace the present method of reimbursing physicians based on their customary, prevailing, and reasonable fees.

- Chapters 11 and 12 on workers' compensation have been completely updated to reflect current laws and problems in the workers' compensation field.

- The material on unemployment insurance has been expanded. Unemployment insurance programs have serious problems, and significant reforms are needed. A new chapter on unemployment insurance problems and issues has been added.

- Chapter 16 includes a discussion of the impact of social insurance programs in reducing poverty based on new research findings. The chapter also has an up-to-date discussion of the AFDC program based on the relatively new Family Support Act of 1988. This new act is designed to reform and improve the AFDC program.

- Chapter 18 includes a discussion of the burden of Social Security taxes and whether or not the tax is regressive, as is commonly believed. New research data suggest that, based on total income, the Social Security tax is progressive up to the eighth decile and then regressive thereafter. Moreover, based on new research findings, the burden of social insurance taxes on low-income groups has not increased significantly, as is commonly believed.

ACKNOWLEDGMENTS

A successful textbook is never written alone. I owe a heavy intellectual debt to numerous social insurance scholars, educators, government officials, and political representatives for their kind and gracious assistance. Persons who read part or all of the fourth edition, offered valuable comments and advice, or sent materials and reports include the following:

- Linden N. Cole, F.S.A., education actuary, Society of Actuaries
- Sen. James J. Exon (D., Nebr.)
- David Durbin, director of research, National Council on Compensation Insurance
- Roger Day, Department of Labor, State of Nebraska
- George C. Kahlandt, Department of Social Services, State of Nebraska
- Dr. Michael J. McNamara, assistant professor of insurance, University of Rhode Island
- Robert J. Myers, former chief actuary, Social Security Administration

Special thanks are given to Robert J. Myers, former chief actuary of the Social Security Administration. Robert Myers is widely recognized as the world's leading authority on social insurance programs. He graciously reviewed all of the chapters in the fourth edition, as well as the second and third editions. As a result of his keen eye and sharp pen, the fourth edition is an improved product. In addition, I would like to thank Sen. James J. Exon (D., Nebr.) for his prompt assistance in sending me numerous government documents dealing with social insurance programs. Government documents are a rich and fertile source of new ideas, and Senator Exon was extremely gracious in honoring my requests for government documents. Also, I would like to thank my typist, Suzie Sybouts, for her prompt and accurate typing assistance.

Finally, as tradition demands, all errors or omissions in the text are due solely to the author. The views expressed in the text do not necessarily reflect the viewpoints of the persons whose help I am gratefully acknowledging.

George E. Rejda, Ph.D., CLU
V. J. Skutt Professor of Insurance
University of Nebraska-Lincoln

ECONOMIC SECURITY AND INSECURITY

People have always sought security and protection from those forces that have threatened their security. In prehistoric times, people were concerned with physical protection against the brute forces of nature. As civilization progressed, the quest for security has become more sophisticated, involving numerous social, political, international, and economic techniques.

Security has many faces and dimensions. Since life is full of uncertainty and surrounded by complex threatening forces, the concept of security can be analyzed from several disciplines, including philosophy, sociology, psychiatry, political science, and economics. A complete analysis of security, however, is a burdensome, if not impossible, task. Thus, the concept must be narrowed. In this text, primary emphasis will be devoted to economic security, with specific emphasis on social insurance as a technique for combating insecurity.

In this chapter, we shall treat the following fundamental concepts: (1) nature of economic security, (2) nature of economic insecurity, (3) causes of economic insecurity, (4) meaning of social security and social insurance, and (5) methods for attacking economic insecurity.

NATURE OF ECONOMIC SECURITY

A human being's *total welfare* is the sum of a large number of different elements. Although the concept of total welfare cannot be broken up in the sense that one can attribute parts of the whole to the various elements from which that welfare is obtained, it is clear that a large part of our total welfare is derived from things obtainable with money.[1] *Economic security, which is part of our total welfare, can be defined as a state of mind or sense of well-being by which an individual is relatively certain that he or she can satisfy basic needs and wants, both present and future.* The phrase "basic needs and wants" refers to a person's desire for food, clothing, housing, medical care, and other necessities. When a person is relatively certain that both present and future needs and wants can be satisfied, then he or she may experience a sense of well-being. This sense of well-being, which results from satisfaction of human needs and wants, is dependent on the use of economic goods and services. An individual must have access to goods and services to attain economic security. It is obvious, therefore, that in a highly industrialized economy, economic security is closely related to income maintenance. The more income a person has—whether from money wages, public or private transfer payments, or the ownership of property—the greater is the level of economic security that is possible.

In analyzing the preceding concept of economic security, several points are worth noting. First, we saw that the receipt of income is a key factor in attaining economic security. The income, however, must be *continuous.* A person must have some reasonable expectation that his or her income will continue into the future so that future needs and wants will be satisfied. If the income is lost or significantly reduced, economic security is threatened.

Second, *real income* must be emphasized. Real income refers to the goods and services that can be purchased with money income. If real income increases, an improvement in economic security is possible. For example, if consumer prices increase 20 percent and money income increases 30 percent, real income is increased, and greater economic security is possible. But if both money income and prices increase at the same rate, real income is unchanged, and economic security is not enhanced.

Third, for most people, economic security also requires the receipt of income that is *above the poverty or subsistence level* of living. *Poverty can be defined as an insufficiency of material goods and services, whereby the basic needs of individuals or families exceed their means to satisfy them.* Poverty can be crudely measured by the various poverty thresholds established by the Bureau of the Census. In 1987, the poverty income threshold for a four-member family was $11,611. Based on this measure, the Bureau of the Census has estimated that 32.5 million persons, or 13.5 percent of the population, were living in poverty.[2] In contrast, mean cash family income during the same period was $29,487, an amount substantially above the poverty threshold. Thus, millions of Americans currently are not economically secure, because their incomes are below poverty levels.

Finally, economic security is *relative to the standard of living enjoyed by others.*

---

[1]S. G. Sturmey, *Income and Economic Welfare* (London: Longmans, Green, 1959), p. 2.

[2]U.S. Congress, House, Committee on Ways and Means, *Background Material and Data on Programs within the Jurisdiction of the Committee on Ways and Means* (Washington, D.C.: U.S. Government Printing Office, 1989), pp. 941–942, 986.

As that standard of living changes over time, the concept of economic security must also change. The nation's social mores, cultural background, educational level, and stage of economic development also influence the concept of economic security. As these factors change over time, the expectations of consumers and families will also change, in turn resulting in a changing concept of economic security.

NATURE OF ECONOMIC INSECURITY

Economic insecurity is the opposite of economic security; that is, the sense of well-being or state of mind that results from being relatively able to satisfy both present and future needs and wants is lacking. Instead, there is considerable worry, fear, anxiety, and psychological discomfort. The need for money is a constant problem.

Economic insecurity can be caused by a person's losing his or her income, or being forced to assume excessive or additional expenses, or earning an insufficient income. Economic insecurity may also be experienced if there is uncertainty regarding the continuation of future income. Thus, economic insecurity consists of one or more of the following: (1) loss of income, (2) additional expenses, (3) insufficient income, and (4) uncertainty of income.[3]

Loss of Income

Regardless of whether the income loss is relative or absolute, economic insecurity is present when the worker's income is lost. In such a case, unless the worker has sufficient financial assets, past savings, or other sources of replacement income, basic needs and wants cannot be satisfied. Moreover, the continuous consumption of goods and services above the poverty line may be difficult because of the income loss.

Additional Expenses

Economic insecurity can also result from additional expenses such as medical bills. For example, a person may be injured and unable to work. In addition to income loss, he or she may incur additional expenses because of substantial hospital, medical, or surgical bills. Or a family head may have a dependent who sustains a serious accident or illness that requires a substantial sum of money. Unless the worker has adequate past savings, health insurance, or other sources of funds on which to draw, economic insecurity is aggravated because of the additional expenses.

---

[3]C. Arthur Williams, Jr., John G. Turnbull, and Earl F. Cheit, *Economic and Social Security*, 5th ed. (New York: John Wiley & Sons, 1982), pp. 1–2.

Insufficient Income

Economic security is also present if a person is employed but earns an insufficient income, that is, if total income during the year is less than the amount needed to satisfy the person's basic wants and needs. The worker may be employed full time throughout the entire year, but economic insecurity is still the result if the level of income does not permit him or her to satisfy the basic necessities.

As noted earlier, millions of Americans are economically insecure because of poverty. The viewpoint that people are poor because they cannot find employment, or because they have some mental or physical defect that makes employment difficult, is not entirely correct. Many poor workers are steadily employed and work regularly throughout the entire year, but their incomes are insufficient to provide for their basic needs and wants.

For example, in 1987, 60 percent of all poor families with children were families in which someone worked during the year. Twenty-five percent of all poor families with children were families with one or more full-time worker equivalents.[4] Thus, earnings from work alone are not always sufficient for meeting the worker's basic needs and wants.

Uncertainty of Income

Economic insecurity may also be present if the worker, although employed, is uncertain of the future continuation of present income. For example, a highly paid space engineer may become fearful and apprehensive because the firm did not receive an expected government contract. In such a case, the worker experiences a form of economic insecurity because of the uncertainty of future income.

In the highly industrialized American economy, a chronic fear of unemployment may create considerable anxiety for the worker, because, although the economy provides the worker with a relatively high standard of living, it also threatens the feeling of economic security. The worker sells his or her labor in the marketplace and depends on the receipt of money wages. The basic feeling of security may be destroyed if the worker believes that his or her services will not be demanded in the future or that wages will be significantly reduced in the future; in such cases, economic insecurity is present because of the uncertainty of future income.

The preceding analysis, however, must be carefully qualified. The relative certainty of future income by itself does not contribute to economic security if the income a person actually receives is insufficient to satisfy his or her basic needs and wants. A person may be relatively certain that present income will continue into the future, but he or she may not experience economic security if

---

[4]*Background Material and Data on Programs within the Jurisdiction of the Committee on Ways and Means,* 1989, pp. 949–952. A full-time worker equivalent equal to one is defined as from 1,750 hours worked during the year up to 2,080 hours worked during the year.

the income is insufficient for satisfying basic needs and wants. For example, assume that an aged person with no other source of income receives a retirement benefit of $500 monthly from a public pension. Although the person is relatively certain that the pension will continue for as long as he or she lives, economic security is impossible because the income is insufficient. In short, it is not merely the relative certainty of future income that makes a person economically secure, since the income may be insufficient; it is the continuous receipt of an adequate income that enables a person to enjoy economic security.

CAUSES OF ECONOMIC INSECURITY

Numerous elements cause economic insecurity. The major causes include (1) premature death of the family head, (2) old age, (3) poor health, (4) unemployment, (5) substandard wage, (6) inflation, (7) natural disasters, and (8) personal factors.

Premature Death of the Family Head

Premature death can be defined as death of a family head with unfulfilled financial obligations—such as dependents to support, a mortgage to be paid, or children to educate. Premature death causes economic insecurity because of the loss of income to the dependents. If the family lacks additional sources of income or has insufficient financial assets to replace the lost income, financial hardship may result. The family may also incur sizable additional expenses because of burial costs, estate and death taxes, expenses of last illness, and funds to pay off outstanding installment debts. In addition, a large unpaid mortgage may still be outstanding, and funds may be needed to educate the children. Certain noneconomic costs are also incurred, such as emotional grief and pain of the surviving dependents and the loss of counseling and guidance for the children.

Finally, premature death can create economic insecurity only if the deceased has dependents and dies with unsatisfied financial obligations. Thus, the death of a child aged 7 is not regarded as being premature in the economic sense.

Old Age

Old age is another important cause of economic insecurity. An estimated 31.9 million persons, or 12.4 percent of the population, were age 65 or older in 1990. The actual number of aged persons is expected to increase sharply to 60.9 million in 2025, or about 20 percent of the population.[5] Many of them will experience considerable economic insecurity during their old age.

---

[5]*Background Material and Data on Programs within the Jurisdiction of the Committee on Ways and Means,* 1989, Table 1, p. 910.

Old age can cause economic insecurity because of the loss of earned income. When older workers retire, they lose their work earnings. Unless they have accumulated sufficient financial assets on which to draw or have access to other sources of income, such as a public or private pension, they will be exposed to economic insecurity.

Many aged persons also experience economic insecurity because of insufficient income. Most aged persons are not poor. However, in 1987, 12.2 percent of those aged 65 and over were living in poverty.[6] For these persons, considerable economic insecurity was present.

In addition, some aged persons experience economic insecurity because they are in poor health and incur sizable medical expenses. In particular, some elderly patients require long-term custodial care in nursing homes, and the financial burden for this type of care is staggering. Long-term care in nursing homes often exceeds $30,000 annually, and Medicare and most private health insurance plans do not cover long-term care. The result is that the limited assets of many elderly patients in nursing homes are quickly depleted. The aged must then seek financial assistance from their children or apply for welfare benefits under the Medicaid program.

Finally, some aged persons experience economic insecurity because of early retirement and inadequate income, an erosion of real income because of inflation, high property taxes, and exploitation. These problems will be discussed in greater detail in Chapter 4 when the economic problem of old age is analyzed.

Poor Health

Poor health is another important cause of economic insecurity. A serious illness or injury can create serious financial problems for the disabled person. Two major problems are present if the sickness or injury is severe and prolonged. First, medical expenses must be paid. In 1987, about one in eight Americans was admitted into a community hospital, and an average person saw a physician 5.4 times. The cost of a hospital stay is expensive. In 1987, the average cost of a stay in a community hospital was $3,850.[7] Although most Americans have some type of health insurance to cover their medical bills, a large number of persons are uninsured some time during the year. In early 1987, 37 million persons were uninsured, or about 15.5 percent of the population, up from 12.3 percent in 1977.[8] The problem of the uninsured is a serious problem that will be discussed in greater detail in Chapter 8.

---

[6]Ibid., p. 915.

[7]Health Insurance Association of America, *Source Book of Health Insurance Data, 1989* (Washington, D.C.: Health Insurance Association of America, 1989), pp. 43, 80, 82.

[8]*A Profile of Uninsured Americans, Research Findings 1*, National Medical Expenditures Survey, Department of Health & Human Services, Public Health Service, National Center for Health Services Research and Health Care Technology Assessment, (DHS Publication No. [PHS] 89–3443), September 1989, p. 4.

Second, a severe illness or injury also results in the loss of earned income. In cases of long-term disability, there is a substantial loss of earned income, medical expenses are still being incurred, savings often are depleted, employee benefits may be lost or reduced, and someone must care for the disabled person. Unless there is adequate replacement income from other sources during the period of disability, considerable economic insecurity is present.

The probability of becoming disabled before age 65 is much higher than is commonly believed, especially at the younger ages. Slightly more than one in three persons now age 25 will be disabled for six months before reaching age 65, and about one in seven will be disabled for five years.[9]

Unemployment

Unemployment can also cause economic insecurity. Unemployment can result from a deficiency in aggregate demand, technological and structural changes in the economy, seasonal factors, or frictions in the labor market. Regardless of the cause, economic insecurity can be present in at least four ways. First, unemployment causes the worker to lose his or her earned income. Unless there is replacement income from other sources (such as unemployment insurance) or past savings on which to draw, the worker will be economically insecure. Second, because of economic reasons, the worker may work only part time. Since work earnings are reduced, the income may be inadequate to maintain the worker and his or her family. Third, unemployment causes economic insecurity because of the uncertainty of income. Because of seasonal elements, the worker may be unemployed for a certain period each year. Finally, some groups experience considerable difficulty in finding new jobs. These groups include older workers, disadvantaged members of minority groups, handicapped workers, and the hard-core unemployed. Also, some older workers, beyond age 45 or 50, have an extended duration of unemployment, and the hard-core unemployed may be out of work for months or even years. Economic insecurity is present to a considerable degree for workers within these categories.

Substandard Wage

A substandard wage that is paid over an extended period can also cause economic insecurity. A substandard wage is any wage that is below some specified minimum necessary for workers to support themselves and their families. A careful distinction must be made between a substandard wage and an insufficient income. A substandard wage refers to a *wage rate* so low that the workers cannot adequately support themselves and their families if they are paid at that rate for any extended period. The federal minimum wage of $4.25 per hour is

---

[9]National Underwriter Company, *Why Disability Protection is Vital for You* (Cincinnati, Ohio: National Underwriter Company, 1989), p. 4.

an example of substandard wage. If a family head with several dependents is paid only the federal minimum wage for any extended period, the worker and his or her family will be living in poverty. On the other hand, insufficient income means that the *absolute amount of income* received during some time period is inadequate in terms of the worker's basic needs and wants. The substandard wage is the cause, and insufficient income is the result. If the worker is paid a substandard wage for any extended period, he or she will be living in chronic poverty.

It should be pointed out that insufficient income may be attributable to causes other than a substandard wage—for example, seasonal unemployment, poor health, or mental or physical defects that render a person incapable of employment. In all cases, the insufficient income leads to economic insecurity.

A case in point can illustrate the distinction between a substandard wage and insufficient income. Assume that a male dishwasher with three dependents works full time the entire year in a restaurant and earns $6 per hour. His annual income is $12,480, which is below the poverty line for a four-member family. If he has no other income, he may find it extremely difficult to support himself and his family. The low wage ($6.00) is the causal factor leading to insufficient income, which in turn gives rise to economic insecurity.

On the other hand, the wage rate may be more adequate, but the worker may still have an insufficient income because of other factors. For example, assume that a female factory worker with three dependents earns $12 per hour and works 40 hours per week. If, because of a severe recession, she loses her job after working 26 weeks, her total annual income is also $12,480, the same income received by the dishwasher. In both cases, economic insecurity is present because of insufficient income. The insufficient income of the dishwasher is attributable to a substandard wage, whereas with the factory worker, it is due to cyclical unemployment.

Inflation

As we stated earlier, if consumer prices increase at a faster rate than money income, real income declines and economic security is threatened. The United States at times has been plagued by severe inflation. A rapid increase in prices tends to hurt those workers whose wages lag behind the increase in prices. In particular, the working poor are severely hurt by rapid inflation, at least in the short run, because the money wages they receive may increase less rapidly than consumer prices. Food and energy costs may rise substantially, and the working poor are then confronted with the unpleasant dilemma of spending relatively more of their limited incomes on food and utilities simply to survive. Considerable economic insecurity is the result.

Natural Disasters

Floods, hurricanes, tornadoes, earthquakes, forest and grass fires, and other violent natural disasters can result in a loss of millions in property damage, as well as numerous deaths. During 1987, a total of 24 catastrophes affected parts of 27 states. A severe windstorm resulted in $150 million of insured losses in Illinois. In December 1987, a severe storm battered areas in nine states and caused insured property losses of some $115 million. A severe earthquake in southern California in 1987 caused an estimated $358 million of property damage. About 2,299 persons were left homeless, and more than 10,400 buildings were damaged in the Los Angeles-Pasadena-Whittier area.[10] In addition, a severe earthquake in San Francisco, California, in 1989 caused billions of dollars of property damage to both commercial and residential structures. Most homeowners did not carry earthquake insurance.

Natural disasters cause financial insecurity because of the considerable loss of human lives and a resultant loss of income to the stricken families. In addition, many property damage losses are either uninsured or underinsured, causing substantial additional expenses.

Personal Factors

In some cases, people are primarily responsible for their own economic insecurity. Some are poorly motivated, lack drive and ambition, and have little desire to improve themselves economically. Others are spendthrifts and are indifferent to a personal savings program of investments and private life insurance. Still others are apathetic to education and its importance in improving their economic status. Finally, some people lack the foresight and wisdom to provide for potential risks that could cause economic insecurity.

Personal factors are especially important in certain major social problems that cause economic insecurity to individuals and families. Widespread divorce, physical and psychological addiction to hard drugs, and the excessive use of alcohol all contribute to economic insecurity.

Divorce. Divorce is an important cause of economic insecurity for many divorced women. No-fault divorce laws often are an economic disaster for mothers of minor children. Based on a study of about 2,500 court cases in Los Angeles and San Francisco, Leonore Weitzman, a sociologist at Stanford University, found that divorced women with minor children experienced a 73 percent decline in their standard of living in the first year following a divorce. In contrast, during the same period, divorced men experienced an average increase of 42 percent.[11] She concluded that the decline in the standard of living was due to several factors. First, under the equal-division-of-property law in California, the home is often sold to meet the equal division requirement, which disrupts the family at a time that stability is needed. Before no-fault divorce laws were passed,

[10]Insurance Information Institute, *Insurance Facts 1988–1989 Property/Casualty Fact Book*, (New York: Insurance Information Institute, 1988), pp. 76–78.

[11]Leonore J. Weitzman, *The Divorce Revolution* (New York: The Free Press, 1985), pp. ix–xxiv. See also Peter Uhelberg, Teresa Cooney, and Robert Boyd, "Divorce for Women after Midlife," *Journal of Gerontology*, Vol. 45, No. 1 (January 1990), pp. S3–S11.

divorced women with children usually received the house, which may not be true today.

Second, divorce courts may not give sufficient attention to new forms of property that can be described as "career assets," such as future increases in earnings based on education and skills, health insurance, and private pensions.

Finally, most divorced women do not receive alimony payments. Child support payments generally are inadequate since they are often less than the average amount received by welfare mothers; there is no cost-of-living adjustment; and a high proportion of fathers default on their child support payments. The overall result is great economic insecurity for many divorced women with children.

Recent research studies also show that divorce often has a devastating financial impact on the standard of living of children whose parents have separated or divorced. Suzanne Bianchi of the Census Bureau and Edith McArthur of the National Center for Education Statistics examined the financial situation of about 8,000 children in households over a 32-month period. They found that total family income declined immediately by about one-third after the divorce or separation; also, after adjusting for smaller family size, per capita income declined by about 17 percent. Moreover, little lost income was recouped in subsequent months from welfare or child support payments.[12] Thus, children in divorced households are likely to experience greater economic insecurity than children in intact two-parent households.

Finally, divorce also has a severe emotional impact on the children. Research studies show that many children of divorced parents are hurt and bewildered, experience considerable anger, underachieve in school, and have problems with relationships years after the divorce occurred.

Alcohol and Drugs.   Addiction to alcohol or drugs is another personal factor that can cause considerable economic insecurity. Alcoholism is one of the most serious public health problems in the United States today. Approximately 12.1 million adults have one or more symptoms of alcoholism, an increase of 8.2 percent since 1980.[13] Thousands of Americans die each year in alcohol-related automobile accidents. Homicides, drownings, suicides, and serious health problems can develop before drinkers reach the state of addiction or chronic use.

In addition, drug addiction is rampant in the United States. Millions of Americans habitually use marijuana, cocaine, crack, heroin, and other drugs. In particular, cocaine is a powerful and expensive addictive drug that can cause serious health problems and death. The cost of supporting a cocaine habit ranges from $200 to $3,000 weekly, and users pay the additional price of damaged health, career, and personal life.

Physical and psychological addiction to alcohol or drugs causes economic insecurity because such addiction often results in poor health, inability to hold a

---

[12]*The Wall Street Journal,* April 17, 1989, p. B1.

[13]*Facts about Alcohol,* Alcoholism and Drug Abuse Council of Nebraska, n.d.

job, broken families, child abuse, crime, and the overall deterioration in the quality of life in many neighborhoods. In addition, the additional expense of supporting an expensive alcohol or drug habit and the resulting loss of income to the family often results in serious financial problems and great economic insecurity.

This concludes our discussion of economic insecurity. Let us next consider the concept of "social security."

MEANING OF SOCIAL SECURITY

Social security programs are part of the overall economic security programs in the United States, but are narrower in scope. There is no universal agreement on the meaning of social security; nevertheless, fairly widespread agreement exists regarding the chief characteristics of the programs. First, social security programs are established by government statute. Second, the programs generally provide individuals with cash payments that replace at least part of the income loss from old age, disability and death, sickness and maternity, unemployment, and occupational injuries. Family allowances and statutory programs that provide medical care (other than public health services) are also considered social security programs.

Social security programs can be distinguished by the major approaches used to provide cash payments and services. These approaches include (1) social insurance, (2) social assistance, (3) universal or demogrant programs, and (4) public provident funds.[14]

Social Insurance

General Characteristics. Social insurance is a part of social security. Social insurance programs are not financed primarily out of the general revenues of government, but are financed entirely or in large part by special contributions from employers, employees, or both. These contributions are usually earmarked for special funds that are kept separate from ordinary government accounts; the benefits, in turn, are paid from these funds. In addition, the right to receive benefits is ordinarily either derived from or linked to the recipient's past contributions or coverage under the program, and the benefits and contributions generally vary among the beneficiaries, according to their prior earnings. Most social insurance programs are compulsory; certain categories of workers and employers are required by law to pay contributions and participate in the programs. Finally, qualifying conditions and benefit rights are usually prescribed

---

[14]U.S. Department of Health and Human Services, Social Security Administration, Office of Research, Statistics, and International Policy, *Social Security Programs throughout the World, 1987*, Research Report No. 61 (Washington, D.C.: U.S. Government Printing Office, 1988), pp. vii–viii.

exactly in the statutes, leaving little room for administrative discretion in the award of benefits.

Definition of Social Insurance. Because of conceptual and practical difficulties, the task of defining social insurance is a complicated if not impossible task. Moreover, after defining it, there is still the problem of determining those programs that can be called social insurance and excluding those that fall outside the definition. After careful study and discussion, the Committee on Social Insurance Terminology of the American Risk and Insurance Association has defined social insurance as follows:

> A device for the pooling of risks by their transfer to an organization, usually governmental, that is required by law to provide pecuniary or service benefits to or on behalf of covered persons upon the occurrence of certain predesignated losses under all of the following conditions:

> 1. Coverage is compulsory by law in virtually all instances.
> 2. Except during a transition period following its introduction, eligibility for benefits is derived, in fact or in effect, from contributions having been made to the program by or in respect of the claimant or the person as to whom the claimant is a dependent; there is no requirement that the individual demonstrate inadequate financial resources, although a dependency status may need to be established.
> 3. The method for determining the benefits is prescribed by law.
> 4. The benefits for any individual are not usually directly related to contributions made by or in respect of him or her but instead usually redistribute income so as to favor certain groups such as those with low former wages or a large number of dependents.
> 5. There is a definite plan for financing the benefits that is designed to be adequate in terms of long-range considerations.
> 6. The cost is borne primarily by contributions which are usually made by covered persons, their employers, or both.
> 7. The plan is administered or at least supervised by the government.
> 8. The plan is not established by the government solely for its present or former employees.[15]

This definition indicates clearly that although social insurance is similar to private insurance in several respects, it does possess some unique characteristics normally not found in private insurance. Failure to recognize these similarities and differences has led to much error and confusion regarding the desirability of economic security programs. The unique characteristics of social insurance will be analyzed in Chapter 2.

The Committee on Social Insurance Terminology considers the following programs to be social insurance because they fall under the preceding definition:

---

[15]*Bulletin of the Commission on Insurance Terminology of the American Risk and Insurance Association*, Vol. 1, No. 2 (May 1965), and Vol. 2, No. 2 (July 1966).

1. Old-Age, Survivors, Disability, and Health Insurance
2. Unemployment Insurance
3. Workers' Compensation
4. Compulsory Temporary Disability Insurance
5. Railroad Retirement System
6. Railroad Unemployment and Temporary Disability Insurance

The following programs are *not* social insurance, because they do not satisfy that definition:

1. *Civil Service Retirement System.* This is not social insurance because the plan was established by the government solely for its own employees.
2. *National Service Life Insurance.* This program is not compulsory; in addition, it was established by the government solely for its present or former employees.
3. *Federal Crop Insurance.* The program is not compulsory.
4. *Public Assistance.* The individual must demonstrate that he or she has inadequate financial resources; a formal means test must be satisfied; and finally, the cost is not borne directly by employers and their employees.
5. *Veterans' Benefits.* The plan is financed entirely out of general revenues; it was established by the government solely for its former employees; and some benefits require that the applicant's income be below a specified level.

Social Assistance

Social assistance is another approach to social security. Social assistance programs—often referred to in different countries as public assistance, national assistance, old-age assistance, unemployment assistance, social pensions, and so on—provide cash payments and other benefits to individuals. These programs have several common features. The benefits are usually confined to low-income or poor recipients; the benefits are normally granted only after an investigation of the recipient's financial resources and needs; the benefit amount is commonly adjusted to the recipient's financial resources and needs; and the benefits are usually financed entirely out of the general revenues of government.

In the United States, public assistance, or "welfare," is used to provide cash income and other benefits to poor people who are not covered under social insurance programs. Public assistance is also used to supplement social insurance benefits that may be inadequate for people whose other financial resources are small or nonexistent, or for those with special needs. Public assistance programs are treated in greater detail in Chapters 16 and 17.

Universal or Demogrant Programs

Universal or demogrant programs are programs that provide flat cash benefits to citizens or residents without regard to the recipient's income, employment, or wealth. The benefits are usually financed out of general revenues and are applied universally to persons who are residents for a specified number of years. Demogrants include old-age pensions to persons over a certain age; pensions to surviving spouses, disabled workers, and orphans; and family allowances to families with a specified number of children. Most social security programs that have universal pensions also have a second-tier program that is earnings related.

Examples of universal or demogrant programs include flat pensions to people age 65 and over in Canada and family allowances to families with two or more children in France.

Public Provident Funds

Public provident funds typically are compulsory savings programs in which contributions are regularly withheld from the earnings of employees and are matched by the contributions of employers. Provident funds typically are used in developing countries. The joint contributions are credited to the account of each employee in a special fund. The funds accrue interest and are later repaid to the employee at retirement or upon the occurrence of certain events such as a pension to surviving dependents.

An example of a provident fund is the provident fund system in Indonesia. Each insured worker contributes 1 percent of earnings into the fund; the employer contributes 1.5 percent of payroll plus 0.5 percent of payroll for death benefits. A lump sum benefit is paid at age 55 or under age 55 if the worker is totally disabled. The benefit can also be paid as a survivor benefit if the deceased is insured and under age 55 at the time of death.

THE ATTACK ON ECONOMIC INSECURITY

A wide variety of public and private techniques are used in the United States to attack economic insecurity. Some aim at preventing economic insecurity by reducing or eliminating a cause of it. Other approaches are designed to alleviate the undesirable financial consequences after a loss occurs. Some techniques entail highly formalized public or private insurance programs, while other measures are very informal. Table 1-1 presents a list of selected programs and techniques that have been used in the United States to combat economic insecurity.

Private Economic Security Programs

The individual and family can be protected against economic insecurity through the purchase of individual life, health, property, and liability insurance. Savings can be accumulated to meet the financial impact of economic insecurity. Individual retirement account benefits may be available; property may be sold or used as collateral for loans; assistance may be available from friends, relatives, or private welfare agencies; earnings of other family members may be available; free treatment at hospitals may be obtained by the poor. Finally, the person may be able to improve his or her job skills, thus enhancing future income.

TABLE 1-1 Selected Programs and Techniques Used in the United States to Combat the Problem of Economic Insecurity

I. PRIVATE PROGRAMS AND TECHNIQUES

Individual	Employer

A. Private insurance:
  1. Life insurance and annuities
  2. Health insurance (including disability income payments)
  3. Property and liability insurance
B. Private savings
C. Individual retirement accounts
D. Property for sale or use as loan collateral
E. Assistance from children, relatives, and private welfare agencies
F. Earnings of other family members
G. Charity programs at hospitals
H. Improvement in job skills
	A. Pensions (including widow pensions)
	B. Group insurance:
	  1. Life
	  2. Health (including disability income and paid sick leave)
	C. Guaranteed annual wage
	D. Severance pay
	E. Supplementary unemployment benefits
	F. Employee profit-sharing plans, thrift plans, and Section 401(k) plans
	G. Employment stabilization techniques
	H. Keogh plans for the self-employed

II. PUBLIC PROGRAMS AND TECHNIQUES

A. Social insurance:
1. Old-Age, Survivors, Disability, and Health insurance
2. Unemployment insurance
3. Workers' compensation
4. Compulsory temporary disability insurance
5. Railroad Retirement System
6. Railroad Unemployment Insurance Act

B. Public assistance:
1. Supplemental Security Income for the Aged, Blind, and Disabled
2. Aid to Families with Dependent Children
3. Medicaid
4. General Assistance

C. Selected economic welfare legislation:
1. Fair Labor Standards Act
2. Occupational Safety and Health Act of 1970
3. Employee Retirement Income Security Act of 1974 (ERISA)
4. Full Employment and Balanced Growth Act of 1978
5. National Flood Insurance Act
6. Age Discrimination in Employment Act Amendments of 1978

D. Government policies:
1. Stimulation of economic growth
2. Monetary policy to stabilize output and employment
3. Fiscal policy to stabilize output and employment

E. Other programs:
1. Veterans' benefits
2. Civil Service Retirement System
3. Federal Employees' Retirement System
4. Services for children
5. Food stamps
6. Public housing
7. Mental health programs
8. Vocational rehabilitation
9. Crime compensation plans
10. Energy assistance programs
11. Subsidized student loans
12. Low-interest housing loans

The worker and family are also protected against economic insecurity through various group insurance programs of private firms. The employer may provide a private pension. Group life, health, and disability income benefits may be available. The firm may have a program for a guaranteed annual wage, severance pay, supplementary unemployment benefits, employee profit-sharing plan, and Section 401(k) plan. The firm may also utilize employment stabilization techniques to maintain and stabilize its employment. Finally, self-employed persons may establish a Keogh plan for the self-employed.

Public Economic Security Programs

In the public sector, government combats economic insecurity in several ways. First, social insurance and public assistance are used to alleviate the economic insecurity resulting from the social perils described earlier. Second, through the use of full-employment policies designed to counter cyclical unemployment, the government attempts to deal with a major source of economic insecurity. Monetary and fiscal policies are also used to promote economic growth and maintain full employment. Finally, the government may attack economic insecurity through specific legislation designed to deal with an important social problem. For example, the Fair Labor Standards Act attempts to deal with the problem of substandard wages through minimum-wage provisions; Medicare benefits under OASDHI are designed to meet the economic problem of high medical expenses for the aged; and the Supplemental Security Income program is designed to provide cash payments to aged, blind, and disabled persons who are poor.

AREAS OF AGREEMENT IN ECONOMIC SECURITY PROGRAMS

Considerable discussion and heated controversy often arise concerning the enactment or expansion of economic security programs. A person's attitude toward existing programs and proposed legislation may be biased because of economic, political, philosophical, and religious beliefs. To think objectively about economic security issues, let us delineate those areas where some agreement generally exists regarding them. These areas of general agreement can be stated as principles.[16]

Principle of Subsidiarity

One fundamental problem in economic security programs is to determine the extent of government and individual responsibility. That is, society must decide

---

[16]Herbert S. Denenberg et al., *Risk and Insurance* (Englewood Cliffs, N.J.: Prentice-Hall, 1964), pp. 517–518.

whether a given social problem should be solved by government or by the individual. The principle of subsidiarity provides a guide to the problem. This principle states that a higher government unit should not perform the tasks that can be effectively performed by a lower unit. This means that in the area of economic security, government should perform only those tasks that cannot be performed efficiently by the people themselves. Moreover, if government intervention is necessary, it should be done first at the local level, then at the state level, and finally at the federal level. The principle of subsidiarity promotes the desirable qualities of personal initiative, freedom, and self-reliance in solving social problems. Excessive reliance on the federal government can discourage flexibility and innovation at the local level.

Principle of Sovereignty of Demand

Critics of economic security programs often deplore the movement of the federal government into economic security areas. However, in a democratic society, government actions usually reflect the will of the people. The principle of sovereignty of demand illustrates this idea; it is stated as follows: democratic government does essentially what the citizens want it to do. In effect, this principle is an application of the majority rule and holds that, in the long run, the desires of the citizenry will be reflected in the passage of legislation reflecting their wishes. If certain economic security programs are desired, the citizenry will tend to vote for political representatives who will support these programs.

Principles of Loss Prevention and Rehabilitation

It is generally agreed that activities that minimize losses or reduce loss severity, such as rehabilitation of disabled workers, are highly desirable in economic security programs.

Society benefits in several ways through loss prevention and rehabilitation activities. First, the gross national product is increased. If a worker is disabled and unemployed, the goods and services that he or she could have produced are lost forever. In addition, if a potential economic loss is prevented or its severity reduced, the economic burden of risk on society is reduced. Finally, rehabilitation of the disabled by surgery, physical restoration, occupational training, physiotherapy, and job placement is also necessary in a viable economic security program. The family's income can still continue, and economic security is thereby enhanced.

Principle of Diversity

The principle of diversity states that no single approach should be used to solve the economic security problems in the United States. Various approaches and techniques are employed that supplement and complement each other. For example, a federal-state program of unemployment insurance is designed to help meet the financial problems of the unemployed. But unemployment itself may be reduced by expansionary monetary and fiscal policies of the federal government. And job-training programs can provide people with skills the modern economy demands.

The point is that numerous approaches are used to attack economic insecurity, and it is generally agreed that the advantages of diverse programs generally outweigh the disadvantages. On the other hand, excessive economic security programs can result in substantial costs, overlapping programs, administrative inefficiencies, and considerable waste.

SUGGESTIONS FOR ADDITIONAL READING

MYERS, ROBERT J. *Social Security,* 3rd ed., Chap. 1. Homewood, Ill.: Richard D. Irwin, 1985.

RENO, VIRGINIA P., AND SUSAN GRAD. "Special Anniversary Feature: Economic Security, 1935–85," *Social Security Bulletin,* Vol. 48, No. 12 (December 1985), pp. 5–20.

"Social Security Programs in the United States," *Social Security Bulletin,* Vol. 52, No. 7 (July 1989), pp. 2–79.

U.S. DEPARTMENT OF HEALTH AND HUMAN SERVICES, SOCIAL SECURITY ADMINISTRATION, OFFICE OF RESEARCH, STATISTICS, AND INTERNATIONAL POLICY. *Social Security Programs throughout the World,* 1987, Research Report No. 61. Washington, D.C.: U.S. Government Printing Office, 1988.

WILLIAMS, C. ARTHUR, JR., JOHN G. TURNBULL, AND EARL F. CHEIT. *Economic and Social Security,* 5th ed., Chap. 1. New York: John Wiley & Sons, 1982.

2

BASIC PRINCIPLES
OF SOCIAL INSURANCE

A multitude of errors in thinking surround our social insurance programs. This confusion is due largely to a misunderstanding of the principles, nature, and objectives of social insurance. Comparisons with private insurance are often improperly made. It is important, therefore, to analyze the basic principles and characteristics of social insurance programs so that these programs can be viewed in their proper perspective.

In this chapter, we shall consider the following fundamental concepts: (1) basic principles and characteristics of the OASDI program, (2) desirability of a voluntary OASDI program, (3) whether the OASDI program can properly be called insurance, (4) comparison of social insurance with private insurance, (5) comparison of social insurance with public assistance, and (6) economic objectives of social insurance.

BASIC PRINCIPLES AND CHARACTERISTICS OF OASDI

The basic principles and characteristics of social insurance programs can be illustrated by examining the OASDI portion of the total OASDHI program.[1]

---

[1]For an extensive discussion of social insurance principles and characteristics, see Robert J. Myers, *Social Security*, 3rd ed. (Homewood, Ill.: Richard D. Irwin, 1985), pp. 3–32. See also C. Arthur Williams, Jr., John G. Turnbull, and Earl F. Cheit, *Economic and Social Security*, 5th ed. (New York: John Wiley & Sons, 1982), Chap. 1.

OASDI refers to the monthly retirement, disability, and survivor benefits that are paid under the program. (When Medicare is included, it is customary to refer to the Social Security program as OASDHI.) The following discussion of social insurance principles, however, generally will be limited only to the OASDI portion of the total Social Security program.

Compulsory Program

With few exceptions, OASDI coverage is compulsory. This principle has been consistently followed since the passage of the original Social Security Act in 1935. A compulsory program makes it easier to protect the population against certain social risks, such as premature death of the family head, insufficient income during retirement, or long-term disability. By a compulsory program, a basic floor of income protection to the masses can be more easily achieved, and both healthy and unhealthy people can be covered. A social insurance program covering only unhealthy lives on a massive scale would be extremely costly and would be difficult to implement. Finally, the OASDI program is a large social insurance system because of its compulsory nature, and a large system has an advantage over smaller systems. Since fewer random and accidental fluctuations in experience are likely to occur, the necessity of providing margins in contingency reserves is reduced.

Minimum Floor of Income

The OASDI program provides only a minimum floor of income protection against the various risks covered. Traditional philosophy in the United States says that the individual is primarily responsible for his or her own economic security, and if government assistance is necessary, only a minimum benefit should be paid. People are expected to supplement government economic security programs with their own personal programs of savings, investments, and insurance.

The concept of a minimum floor of income is difficult to define precisely, and some disagreement exists concerning the minimum and maximum benefits that should be paid. Generally speaking, there are three views regarding the minimum floor.[2] First, one extreme view is that the minimum should be so low as to be virtually nonexistent. Second, the other extreme says that it should be high enough to provide a comfortable standard of living by itself, with no consideration given to other economic security programs provided by private or group methods (private insurance, group insurance, private pensions). Third, a middle view is that the minimum income should, in combination with other income and financial assets, be sufficient to maintain a reasonable standard of living for the vast majority of people. Any residual group whose basic needs are then still unmet would be provided for by supplementary public assistance.

[2]Myers, *Social Security,* p. 26.

Social Adequacy Rather than Individual Equity

The OASDI program emphasizes the payment of benefits based on social adequacy rather than individual equity.[3] *Social adequacy means that the benefits paid provide a certain standard of living to all contributors. Individual equity means that contributors receive benefits directly related to their contributions; in technical terms, the actuarial value of the benefits is closely related to the actuarial value of the contributions.* The OASDI program provides benefits on a basis falling between complete social adequacy and complete individual equity, with heavy emphasis on the former.

The social adequacy principle results in the payment of OASDI benefits that are heavily weighted in favor of certain groups, such as the lower-income groups, people with large families, and those who were near retirement when first covered by the OASDI program. The actuarial value of the benefits received by these groups exceeds the actuarial value of their contributions; this means that they receive relatively larger benefits compared with their contributions than other groups.

The purpose of the social adequacy principle is to provide a minimum floor of income to all groups. If certain groups received OASDI benefits actuarially equal to the value of their contributions (individual equity principle), the benefits paid would be so small for some groups (for instance, lower-income groups) that the objective of providing a minimum floor of income to everyone would not be achieved.

Although the OASDI program and other social insurance programs emphasize social adequacy, private insurance stresses the individual equity principle. Losses are pooled, and people with roughly the same loss-producing characteristics are grouped into the same class and pay roughly equal premiums. Private insurance is voluntary and must be built on equity between different classes of insureds. It is considered inequitable to have one relatively homogeneous group of insureds pay a large part of the loss costs for another group whose loss-producing characteristics are substantially different. Furthermore, once people in the first category become aware that they could save money by being treated as independent, financially self-contained units, they would tend to drop their insurance.

However, the OASDI program and other social insurance programs are different in character and have different functions. Since social insurance programs generally are compulsory, they are aimed at providing society with some protection against major social risks. The benefit structure is designed to provide society with a minimum floor of income so that people do not become wards of society. It is only after this objective is achieved that any remaining funds can be

---

[3]The classic paper in the professional literature on the social adequacy principle is Reinhard A. Hohaus, "Equity, Adequacy, and Related Factors in Old-Age Security," in William Haber and Wilbur J. Cohen, eds., *Social Security: Programs, Problems, and Policies* (Homewood, Ill.: Richard D. Irwin, 1960), pp. 61–63.

considered available for providing additional benefits based on individual equity.[4]

Methods of Providing Socially Adequate Benefits. Several methods are used to provide socially adequate OASDI benefits.[5] First, as stated earlier, the benefit formula is heavily skewed in favor of the lower-income groups. The benefit rate applied to the lower portion of wages is higher than the rate applied to the higher portion. This allows the lower-income groups to receive proportionately larger benefits compared with their contributions than do the upper-income groups.

Second, when dependents' benefits are paid, the recipient with a large family receives relatively higher OASDI benefits than does one with no dependents.

Third, OASDI cash benefits are annually adjusted for inflation to maintain the real purchasing power of the benefits. Since the beneficiaries receive increased benefits for which they have not paid, the social adequacy principle is again reflected in the payment of benefits.

Finally, social adequacy is emphasized by favoring initial older workers who were near retirement when first covered by the OASDI program. In establishing a social insurance plan, a problem often arises regarding the adequacy of benefits for people near retirement. If the individual equity principle were closely followed, it would be difficult to provide socially adequate benefits.

This situation is not unique to social insurance. When private pension plans are initially established, the benefits for older workers near retirement may be inadequate if they are based only on future service with the company. A future service benefit is that portion of a participant's retirement benefit that relates to the period of credited service after the effective date of the plan. Since future service alone will not provide adequate benefits to workers who are near retirement when the plan is first installed, many private pension plans give credit for past service. A past service benefit is that portion of the retirement benefit that relates to the period of credited service *before* the effective date of the plan. Since older workers generally receive credit for past service, the actuarial value of their benefits may exceed the actuarial value of their contributions. Also, private pension benefits may be increased for those already retired when the cost of living rises. This again reflects an application of the social adequacy principle in private pensions, since the retired participants generally do not pay for the higher benefits.

Redistribution-of-Income Effect. Emphasis on the social adequacy principle in the OASDI program results in a redistribution of income. As stated earlier, certain groups receive benefits that actuarially exceed the value of their

---

[4]Ibid.

[5]Margaret S. Gordon, *The Economics of Welfare Policies* (New York and London: Columbia University Press, 1963), p. 56.

contributions. In effect, these groups (lower-income groups, people with large families, and older retired workers) are undercharged for their benefits, and other groups (such as younger workers) are overcharged. This redistributes income, by taking away income from one group and giving it to another. The redistribution-of-income effect under the OASDI program is an important economic issue that will be analyzed later in Chapter 18.

Benefits Loosely Related to Earnings

OASDI benefits are loosely related to earnings. This means that some relationship exists between individual equity and social adequacy; and in general, the higher the worker's average covered earnings, the greater will be the benefits. The relationship between higher average earnings and higher benefits is loose and disproportionate, but it does exist.

The payment of higher benefits because of higher earnings can be defended in several ways.[6] First, the free enterprise system stresses economic rewards to the individual based upon personal talents and initiative, and this principle is reflected in the OASDI program. A worker who earns a higher income because of personal efforts is rewarded with larger OASDI benefits.

Second, relating benefits to earnings takes into consideration different standards of living, diverse economic conditions, and price levels in various parts of the country. Generally speaking, work earnings establish the worker's standard of living and income level at retirement. If flat benefits were paid to everyone, the amount paid to some workers could equal or exceed their preretirement earnings, whereas the same amount paid to those who had worked at higher income levels would not provide them with meaningful economic security.

Finally, some argue that relating benefits to earnings is desirable because the OASDI benefits are a form of "deferred wage," and the benefit payments are merely an extension of the wage contract. From the employer's viewpoint, OASDI contributions are costs involved in obtaining labor; these contributions can be looked upon as deferred wages to be received by workers in the future. From the employee's viewpoint, the OASDI contributions amount to income earned but withheld, to be received in the future when he or she retires or becomes unemployed because of disability. Thus, according to this view, it is logical to award the worker higher OASDI benefits because of higher earnings.

The preceding theory, however, is faulty because it would impede the attainment of economic security for the lower-income groups. Strict adherence to the principle of relating benefits to earnings would mean that the benefits received by the lower-paid worker, being only a percentage of his or her already low wages, would be inadequate to provide even a modest standard of living. Carried to its logical conclusion, an OASDI program based upon the deferred-

---

[6]Eveline M. Burns, *Social Security and Public Policy* (New York: McGraw-Hill, 1956), pp. 38–41.

wage theory would imply a restricted program that is limited to workers whose earnings were high enough so that the benefits (some fraction of high earnings) would meet the workers' demand for security. Society would still have the problem, however, of providing economic security to the lower-paid workers.

Rights to Benefits with No Needs Test

OASDI benefits are paid as a matter of right without a formal demonstration of need. Although need is clearly recognized in the program,[7] a needs or means test is never required. A needs test is used in public assistance, in which applicants must demonstrate that their income and financial assets are insufficient to maintain themselves or their families. Under the OASDI program, however, recipients have a right to the benefits with no such demonstration of need, assuming that they fulfill the eligibility requirements.

Contractual Right. The right to OASDI benefits clearly is not a contractual right, because no formal contract exists between the insureds and the government. In the *Nestor* case, the Supreme Court held that the right to OASDI retirement benefits was not comparable to that of the holder of an annuity contract, whose right to benefits was based on contractual premium payments.[8] A contractual right can be modified only by agreement between two parties, so the right to OASDI benefits is not contractual, since Congress can alter, amend, and repeal the benefits without the insured's consent.

Earned Right. Another view is that the right to OASDI benefits is an earned right, because the recipient has contributed to and has paid for the benefits throughout his or her lifetime, or someone has contributed on the recipient's behalf. This view of an earned right is misleading for several reasons. First, the payment of OASDI taxes by itself does not give the person an unequivocal right to benefits, since other eligibility conditions must also be fulfilled.

Second, many who are eligible for benefits have contributed little or nothing to the program. One example would be the 3 million people age 65 and over who were never covered under OASDI or the Railroad Retirement System but were blanketed in for hospital insurance benefits under the 1965 amendments.

Finally, low-income groups that receive socially adequate benefits have not strictly "earned" the right to benefits, because the actuarial value of their benefits substantially exceeds the actuarial value of their modest tax contributions.

---

[7]For example, a retired person with dependents has a greater need for income than does the person with no dependents. Thus, higher benefits are paid to retired workers with dependents.

[8]*Flemming v. Nestor*, 363 U.S. 603 (1960).

Statutory Right. This is probably the correct view regarding the right to OASDI benefits.[9] A statutory right can be enforced in the courts; and individuals can and do sue to enforce their right to benefits. This is a powerful right, because specific benefits established by statute must be paid to an eligible recipient and cannot be withheld or reduced because of administrative discretion.

It should be pointed out, however, that Congress can alter, amend, or repeal any provision of the Social Security Act if public policy so demands. In the *Nestor* case, the Supreme Court ruled that, although there were substantial property rights involved in the benefits, Congress could modify the benefits in any reasonable way, but that there was protection under the Constitution against arbitrary change on the part of Congress. This means that any modification of benefits by Congress, even in a downward direction, is constitutional as long as there are sound reasons for it.

Benefits Based on Presumed Need

OASDI benefits are also based upon presumed need. Presumed need means OASDI benefits are never automatically paid, but are paid only when certain events occur and all eligibility requirements are met. For example, retirement benefits are never automatically paid at age 65, but only upon retirement. In this case, the gainfully employed worker is presumed not to need the benefits, since he or she has not lost any earned income. However, the retired worker, who has lost his or her work earnings, is presumed to need the benefits.

Failure to recognize that benefits are based on presumed need has led to errors in thinking. For example, critics of the OASDI earnings test[10] argue that the right to receive benefits is fictitious, since the benefits are not automatically paid upon attainment of the normal retirement age, despite years of compulsory contributions. Although a statutory right to benefits exists, this right is contingent upon fulfillment of certain conditions set down in the law. Since the benefits are based on presumed need, they are not paid if the worker is gainfully employed and work earnings exceed some maximum limit as defined in the law.

Self-supporting Contributory Principle

Another important principle of the OASDI program, adopted by Congress in 1950 and still followed today, is that the OASDI program generally should be financially self-supporting from the payroll tax contributions of employers, employees, and the self-employed, interest on the trust fund investments, and revenues from the taxation of part of the OASDI benefits.

The contributory-financing principle is justified on several grounds.

---

[9]Arthur J. Altmeyer, *The Formative Years of Social Security* (Madison: University of Wisconsin Press, 1966), pp. 227–228.

[10]See Chapter 5 for an explanation of the retirement or earnings test.

First, because employers, employees, and the self-employed contribute to the program, they are made aware of the relationship between the benefits received and the contributions paid and that increased benefits will generally require increased tax contributions. For example, just as few people relate the taxes on gasoline and tires to the federal program for highway improvement, it is doubtful that the covered worker would relate the taxes paid to the benefits received if the OASDI contributions were based on something other than earnings (such as a sales tax). However, workers *are aware* that part of their earnings are deducted for OASDI benefits and that higher benefits will require higher tax contributions.

Second, the contributory principle also encourages a more responsible attitude on the part of covered workers. They know that their benefits and those of their families are made possible by OASDI contributions, and this knowledge gives them a greater personal interest in the soundness of the program.

Third, the contributory principle also encourages a more responsible attitude on the part of elected representatives. Any social insurance program can be changed by legislative action; such legislative action in a democracy ultimately depends upon the voters. If the voters are contributors, as well as the ultimate decision makers regarding the program, a more responsible attitude will be taken by their elected representatives with regard to the program.

Finally, almost all gainfully employed workers contribute to the OASDI program; this has an important psychological appeal, which results in widespread acceptance of the program.[11] The protected groups feel greater psychological security in the coverage provided, and at the same time, the program is less susceptible to unsound changes because of political pressure groups.

No Full Funding

Although private pensions stress full funding, it is not necessary for social insurance programs to be fully funded. A fully funded program means that the value of the accumulated assets under the plan will be sufficient to discharge all liabilities for the benefit rights accrued to date under the plan. For example, the OASDI trust fund balance on September 30, 1988, totaled $104.2 billion. To be fully funded, a trust fund of $5.74 trillion would have been required.

A fully funded program is considered unnecessary for several reasons. First, the program is expected to operate indefinitely and will not terminate in the predictable future. Since it will not terminate, full funding is unnecessary. Second, since the program is compulsory, new entrants will always enter the program and pay taxes to support it. Third, the taxing powers of the federal government can be used to raise additional revenues through the payroll tax if the program has financial problems. Finally, from an economic viewpoint, full

---

[11]A discussion of the advantages of the contributory principle and other principles followed in the OASDI program can be found in Charles I. Schottland, *The Social Security Program in the United States,* 2nd ed. (New York: Appleton-Century-Crofts, 1970).

funding is undesirable. Full funding would require substantially higher OASDI tax contributions for many years in the future, which would be deflationary and could result in higher unemployment. In contrast, private pension plans must emphasize full funding, since private pension plans can and do terminate. Thus, to protect the pension rights of active and retired workers, private plans should be fully funded.

Benefits Prescribed by Law

In the OASDI program and other social insurance programs, the benefits are prescribed by law, with the administration or supervision of the plan performed by government. In all social insurance programs, the benefits or benefit formulas are established by statute, as are the eligibility requirements. Although the OASDI program is administered by the federal government, the level of administration in other social insurance programs may be state or local.

Plan Not Established Solely for Government Employees

The OASDI and other social insurance programs can be distinguished from other government insurance programs. A social insurance program is established by the government not solely for its own employees, but for the solution of a social problem that requires government intervention. A plan established only for government employees is not social insurance because the government is acting like any other employer in providing fringe benefits to employees.

SHOULD THE OASDI PROGRAM BE MADE VOLUNTARY?

The fact that the OASDI program is generally compulsory makes the program repugnant to many people who believe that they are coerced into participating. The right to live one's life in freedom, as long as the rights of others are not impaired, is a well-established American principle. The compulsory nature of the OASDI program appears to violate this principle.

Proposals for a voluntary OASDI program are not new. In the report prepared by the Committee on Economic Security to President Roosevelt prior to the enactment of the Social Security Act in 1935, a voluntary system of old-age annuities was proposed in addition to a compulsory system.[12] The government would sell deferred life annuities to individuals, similar to those issued by private companies, on a cost basis. In consideration for the premiums paid at specific ages, the government would guarantee a definite income to the purchaser of the annuity, starting at age 65 and continuing throughout his or her lifetime.

---

[12]U.S. Committee on Economic Security, *Social Security in America* (Washington, D.C.: U.S. Government Printing Office, 1937), p. 214.

The proposal for voluntary annuities was not included in the original Social Security Act. It was dropped because it appeared to compete with private insurers and because the experience of foreign nations indicated the ineffectiveness of voluntary methods in meeting the economic problem of old age.[13]

Arguments for a Voluntary OASDI Program

Powerful arguments are advanced for a voluntary OASDI program. The most important emphasize the following: (1) expansion of economic freedom, (2) greater flexibility with private insurance, (3) restriction of government, and (4) equity to younger workers.

Expansion of Economic Freedom. One argument is that economic freedom is diminished by a compulsory program because the number of individual decisions is reduced. A person with a given amount of income can make a certain number of decisions regarding the spending of the income. The fact that OASDI contributions (taxes) are involuntarily taken away reduces the number of decisions regarding disposition of the worker's income, thereby reducing economic freedom. Under a voluntary program, however, the individual decides whether to participate. Since the number of his or her decisions is increased, economic freedom is enhanced.

It is difficult to determine whether a compulsory program reduces economic freedom. Generally speaking, the meaning of economic freedom depends upon individual value judgments regarding politics, philosophy, economics, religion, and the role of the federal government in providing economic security. In the last analysis, each person must decide whether a compulsory OASDI program reduces economic freedom. However, two guidelines are helpful in analyzing the problem.

First, given the present institutional framework and value judgments that now prevail in the United States, a truly voluntary OASDI program is difficult, if not impossible. A truly voluntary program must allow the individual three major choices: (1) to participate in the present OASDI program, (2) to purchase an annuity from a private insurer, or (3) not to participate in any program, either public or private. All three options must be present to have a truly voluntary program.

Some take the position that people should be required either to participate in the OASDI program or to purchase annuities from private insurers.[14] In

---

[13]Wilbur J. Cohen, *Retirement Policies under Social Security* (Berkeley: University of California Press, 1957), p. 4.

[14]For example, Milton Friedman argues that government should not be given a monopoly in the sale of annuities, but should compete with private insurers. A person would not be compelled to buy an annuity from the government, but would be given the option to buy one from a private company. If purchased privately, the person would include a copy of the premium receipts with the income tax return to show that he or she had provided for his or her own security. See Milton Friedman, *Capitalism and Freedom* (Chicago: University of Chicago Press, 1962), p. 186. See also Wilbur J. Cohen and Milton Friedman, *Social Security: Universal or Selective?* Rational Debate Series (Washington, D.C.: American Enterprise Institute, 1972).

this case, they would be given two choices. A compulsory program would still exist, however, because people would still be compelled to purchase either a government or a private annuity. A truly voluntary program would allow a third choice: that of not participating in any program, public or private.

Of course, some people might not purchase any annuities and thus not provide for their own economic security. But "true freedom" implies that people should be free to make their own mistakes, and if they should willingly decide against participation in any program, they should then suffer the consequences of that decision. This would mean that society should not assist them in any way, and for all practical purposes, the imprudent would starve. But this is the nub of the problem. A philosophy has developed in the United States that people should not be allowed to starve—regardless of how imprudent and undeserving of aid they might be. This implies that public assistance should be made available to the imprudent and that society, through general taxation, should assume that burden.

For the most part, society would prefer that the imprudent should provide for their own economic security (at least in part) through compulsory participation in the OASDI program, or else through the purchase of private annuities. Since the decision of not participating in any program would be absent, the number of individual decisions would be reduced from three to two; thus, a truly voluntary program would be conceptually difficult to attain.

Second, if economic freedom is reduced for those who make the compulsory contributions, it is expanded for those who receive these contributions as benefit payments. The people receiving them will have an increase in their income, thereby increasing the number of personal decisions they have on how to spend their income. Thus, there may be a net gain in economic freedom—the increase in freedom for the recipients of benefits may exceed the loss of freedom because of the involuntary contributions.

Greater Flexibility with Private Insurance.   Another argument for a voluntary program is that private insurance provides greater flexibility. This argument has considerable merit. Private insurance permits an insured to select diverse types of benefits in terms of individual needs, dependents, ability to pay, and financial goals. The OASDI program, however, is relatively inflexible. The insured is not given a choice of benefits or benefit amounts, since these are prescribed by law, and he or she cannot select coverages to conform to individual needs and financial goals.

Restriction of Government.   Another argument is that a voluntary program may curb the encroachment of government into the private sector and thereby foster the free enterprise system. The OASDI program is viewed as a threat to the survival of private insurance, and this threat is reduced by a voluntary program.

Equity to Younger Workers.   A final argument for a voluntary system is that the present OASDI program is unfair to younger workers, since new

OASDI entrants will receive benefits that are actuarially less than the actuarial value of the combined employer-employee tax contributions, and new workers entering the program in the future will be cheated.

The argument that the OASDI program cheats younger workers and is a "bad buy" is an important issue that merits careful analysis. It will be treated in greater detail in Chapter 6, when the controversial problems and issues surrounding the OASDI program are analyzed.

Arguments against a Voluntary OASDI Program

The major arguments against a voluntary OASDI program are more convincing than are the arguments for it. The major arguments against a voluntary program are (1) greater probability of adverse selection, (2) more difficulty in achieving minimum economic security, (3) financial disruption of the present program, and (4) inability of lower-income groups to purchase private insurance.

Greater Probabilty of Adverse Selection. Adverse selection is any process by which the exercise of choice by insureds leads to higher than average loss levels. Without adequate controls, the people who obtain insurance tend to be those who need it most—those with a greater probability of loss than the average.

A voluntary system could increase adverse selection for several reasons. First, as indicated earlier, OASDI benefits are largely paid on the basis of social adequacy rather than individual equity. In private insurance, individual equity considerations require that each insured must be charged a rate that closely reflects the probability of occurrence and the probable severity of loss to which he or she is exposed. This is not true in social insurance, where an absence of complete individual equity in the rating structure arises out of the social desirability of providing a minimum floor of income to groups most in need of the protection. The result is that some groups are overcharged while other groups are undercharged. If the program became voluntary, the overcharged groups might withdraw and provide for their own economic security by insuring with private insurers, where individual equity considerations prevail. Since it is the more desirable insureds that would withdraw because of the rate inequity (primarily younger, healthy workers), the contributions collected from the remainder (less desirable risks) might be insufficient to pay socially adequate benefits to those most in need of the protection. Thus, it might become necessary to increase contribution rates to pay adequate benefits. But the contribution rate increase could easily cause others to withdraw from the program. This process would continue until the only people covered by the OASDI program are the worst risks, with the final contribution rate quite high. On the other hand, if contribution rates were not increased, it would be difficult to provide socially adequate benefits. It is only by having a compulsory OASDI program that an inequitable rate structure can be maintained for any extended period to provide socially adequate benefits.[15]

Second, adverse selection might increase if, because of underwriting standards, private insurers could offer the insurance at lower premiums to potential insureds. People in poor health, in extrahazardous occupations, or with poor moral character might be unable to purchase private insurance, or be able to obtain it only by the payment of higher premiums. Thus, company underwriting procedures would eliminate some persons who may have an immediate loss, and by their elimination, private insurers would be able to offer the protection at a lower cost. From a loss viewpoint, private companies might insure only the more desirable individuals, and only the less desirable would be left for the OASDI program to insure. Since the program would then consist of a relatively larger number of less desirable or substandard insureds, higher loss levels would result. It would be inconceivable for OASDI to apply private insurer underwriting standards, since this would defeat the basic objective of providing a minimum floor of income protection to all. A compulsory program avoids the problem of underwriting and covers both desirable and undesirable insureds, with a reduction in adverse selection as a result.

Finally, a compulsory program reduces the problem of overinsurance. The problems of overinsurance and profiting from insurance are well known in the private insurance industry. But in a compulsory program with the benefits fixed by law, those who are in a position to have a loss cannot select additional amounts of insurance. Because of competition from private insurers, however, a voluntary program might force the OASDI program to offer additional benefits. Once this occurred, the probability of adverse selection might increase; without some type of underwriting controls, people in poor health, near retirement, or with large families might select additional coverages.

More Difficulty in Achieving Minimum Economic Security. A voluntary program may make it more difficult for society to achieve a minimum level of economic security. First, some people might neither participate in the OASDI program nor purchase private insurance, thereby exposing themselves to possible economic insecurity. A compulsory OASDI program currently covers most of the population and provides some protection against the risks of premature death, old age, and disability. A voluntary program could dilute this wide base of protection.

Second, some people who purchase private insurance benefits in lieu of participation in the OASDI program might decide later to cancel their policies or

---

[15]See O. D. Dickerson, *Health Insurance*, 3rd ed. (Homewood, Ill.: Richard D. Irwin, 1968), pp. 468–469, for a discussion of an inequitable rating structure and adverse selection. See also "Nature and Functions of Old-Age and Survivors Insurance," in William Haber and Wilbur J. Cohen, eds., *Readings in Social Security* (Englewood Cliffs, N.J.: Prentice-Hall, 1948), pp. 258–259.

let them lapse. This problem does not arise in a compulsory program, since, with few exceptions, they must participate.

Third, some argue that the OASDI program should not cover the wealthy because they do not need the benefits. In this case, the principle of subsidiarity is violated by compelling the wealthy to participate when they can provide for their own economic security; the government should not do those things that individuals can do for themselves.

Although the subsidiarity principle is clearly violated by requiring the wealthy to participate, coverage can be justified on both theoretical and practical grounds. If the premise is accepted that society should provide some economic security to everyone, the rich would have to show that they can provide for their own economic security. In effect, they would have the burden of demonstrating that their income and assets are sufficiently large to justify exclusion from the OASDI program. In this case, a *negative means test* would be introduced into the program. But it would be wrong in principle to require a needs test in social insurance, regardless of the form of the test, and the principle of not requiring a needs test in the OASDI program would be violated.

Moreover, technical problems may make it administratively difficult to determine the level of income and assets necessary for persons to be considered "wealthy" and therefore eligible for exclusion under OASDI. Furthermore, the wealthy always face the risk of losing their wealth at some future date because of conditions over which they have no control. Many rich people saved and provided for their retirement needs in the 1920s, only to see their financial assets decline sharply or become worthless as a result of the Great Depression of the 1930s. A compulsory OASDI program assures the wealthy of at least a minimum base of economic security if financial misfortune should occur.

Finally, if the wealthy can elect out, other groups may demand the same right, thereby weakening the entire program. Except for constitutional or administrative reasons that justify voluntary participation, minimum economic security can be achieved with greater certainty by a compulsory program.

Financial Disruption of the Present Program. The OASDI program could be exposed to serious financial disruption by a voluntary scheme. As stated earlier, a truly voluntary program would allow currently covered workers the right of withdrawal. Many people have contributed to the OASDI program for years, and refunds would have to be made. Since the trust funds are not fully funded, they are insufficient for providing refunds to all who might desire to withdraw. Congress would then be forced to increase taxes to raise the additional sums for refunds; if Congress were unwilling to do this, the possibility exists (although slight) that the present OASDI program could default on its obligations. On the other hand, if the OASDI program were still compulsory for those currently covered, but made voluntary for new entrants who ordinarily would be covered, a truly voluntary program would not exist.

In any event, a severe financial disruption could take place if the OASDI program were made voluntary.

Inability of Lower-Income Groups to Purchase Private Insurance. A final argument against a voluntary plan is that the lower-income groups might be unable to afford private insurance (assuming that they preferred private coverage to OASDI) because of insufficient incomes. On the other hand, a compulsory OASDI program provides certain advantages to the lower-income groups. As we have seen, the benefit formula is heavily weighted in their favor. In addition, some lower-income workers may be uninsurable or substandard by private standards. Thus, private insurance may be unavailable to them, or may be obtainable only by the payment of higher premiums, which they may be unable to afford. Protection is available to these people, however, under a compulsory OASDI program.

IS THE OASDI PROGRAM INSURANCE?

Disagreements concerning the meaning of *insurance* have formed the basis of serious debate among economists, insurance scholars, legal technicians, and private insurance practitioners. The controversy becomes even more intense when the OASDI program is analyzed as a form of insurance. One position, generally presented by economists, is that the OASDI program should not be considered insurance since the program is compulsory, contracts are not issued, the actuarial relationship between benefits and contributions is imprecise, a redistribution of income is heavily stressed, certain groups are heavily subsidized, and the compulsory tax contributions are not the same as private insurance premiums. Instead, these economists view OASDI as a massive government income maintenance program for promoting national economic security through the imposition of compulsory payroll taxes.

This viewpoint is misleading and incorrect. Its proponents generally ignore the important insurance elements of pooling, fortuitous losses, risk transfer, and indemnification. It is true, however, that the OASDI program differs from private insurance in several respects. The OASDI program can be correctly viewed as a form of social insurance, which contains both (1) private insurance elements and (2) a strong welfare element.

Private Insurance Elements

Insurance can be defined in a way that includes or excludes the OASDI program, depending on the definition adopted. After careful study, the Commission on Insurance Terminology of the American Risk and Insurance Association has defined insurance as follows:

> Pooling of risks of fortuitous losses by transfer of such risks to insurers who agree to indemnify insureds for such losses, to provide other pecuniary benefits on their occurrence, or to render services connected with the risks.[16]

---

[16]*Bulletin of the Commission on Insurance Terminology of the American Risk and Insurance Association,* Vol. 1, No. 4 (October 1965), p. 1.

Although this definition may be unacceptable to some insurance scholars, it forms a suitable basis for determining whether OASDI is a true form of insurance. Several critical elements in the definition are worthy of discussion. They are (1) pooling, (2) fortuitous losses, (3) risk transfer, and (4) indemnification.

Pooling. Private insurance utilizes the pooling technique for meeting risk. Pooling, or combination, is a technique by which a large number of homogeneous exposure units are combined or grouped so that the law of large numbers can operate to provide a substantially accurate prediction of future losses. In addition, pooling involves the spreading of losses over the entire group. The losses of individuals exposed to certain risks are pooled or averaged, and average loss is substituted for actual loss. Thus, pooling implies the prediction of future losses with some accuracy and the spreading of these losses over the group.

Because of complex sociological, economic, and demographic variables, the social insurance actuary has a more difficult task of predicting future losses than does the private insurance actuary. The law of large numbers is of little practical value in predicting future long-run OASDI experience because of the difficulty of computing the standard deviations of the many variables on which the cost estimates are based. Although OASDI experience can be predicted rather closely for the short-term future, cost estimates and anticipated future losses may prove to be quite different because of the large compounding effects of variations in the many factors involved.

It is questionable, however, whether application of the law of large numbers is necessary for a true insurance program. In an exhaustive analysis of the meaning of insurance, Irving Pfeffer argues that no line of insurance is able to meet the complete set of tests implied by the law of large numbers, because the universe of insurance experience is constantly changing with respect to the economic and social environment, so past loss experience may not have the same relevance with respect to future loss experience. For some insurance lines, the requirements for applying the law of large numbers can generally be fulfilled, but for other lines, few requisites can be met. Thus, Pfeffer argues that application of the law of large numbers is a *sufficient* condition for insurance, but not a *necessary* condition.[17] To the extent, however, that future short-run OASDI experience can be closely estimated by application of the law of large numbers, the OASDI program can legitimately be called insurance.

Although the law of large numbers is difficult to apply to long-run future OASDI experience, nevertheless, the pooling device involves the spreading of losses over the entire covered group. For example, the loss of earned income because of mandatory retirement can be viewed as a loss attributable to a social risk. If OASDI retirement benefits are payable, a person can recoup part of the income loss. In effect, the loss experienced by a retired person is spread

---

[17]Irving Pfeffer, *Insurance and Economic Theory* (Homewood, Ill.: Richard D. Irwin, 1956), p. 43.

over and paid for by the group that has not yet suffered any loss—those not yet retired and still making OASDI contributions. Thus, the OASDI program utilizes the pooling technique.

Some insurance scholars take the position that pooling is unnecessary for a true insurance scheme.[18] However, pooling or combination of risks, when it does exist, constitutes a legitimate insurance scheme, even though it is not a necessary condition for insurance. Since the pooling technique can be applied to the OASDI program, the program can be called a true form of insurance.

Fortuitous Loss. Private insurance also involves the pooling of fortuitous losses. Fortuitous losses are unforeseen and unexpected, and ideally, they should be accidental and outside the insured's control. Most OASDI losses are fortuitous and outside the individual's control. For example, the family may experience economic insecurity because of the family head's premature death, or the worker may be exposed to financial hardship because of permanent disability. These losses are largely fortuitous and unforeseen. Thus, both private insurance and the OASDI program treat fortuitous losses.

Risk Transfer. Risk transfer is another technique for handling risk. In private insurance, a pure risk is transferred to the insurer, which is in a stronger financial position to pay losses than the individual is. Risk transfer also takes place in the OASDI program. The risks associated with premature death, old age, and disability are shifted, at least partly, from the individual to the OASDI program. If the position is taken that only transfer of a pure risk is necessary to constitute insurance, then the OASDI program fulfills this requirement.

Indemnification. Private insurance indemnifies the insured for losses. Indemnification means compensation to the victim of a loss, in whole or in part, by payment, repair, or replacement. The OASDI program also involves indemnification for losses. Survivor benefits restore, at least partly, the family's share of the deceased family head's income; retirement benefits restore part of the earned income that is lost when a worker retires; and disability benefits indemnify people for accidental injuries or serious diseases. Thus, both private and social insurance indemnify insureds for losses.

Welfare Element

The welfare element in the OASDI program generally can be defined as the receipt of unearned benefits; that is, the benefits received by certain groups, such as the aged, have little or no actuarial relationship to the value of their OASDI tax contributions.

The welfare element in the OASDI program is derived from the principle of social adequacy, whereby some groups receive benefits that exceed the

---

[18]Ibid., p. 185.

actuarial value of their tax contributions. The relationship between the benefits received and the average monthly earnings on which the tax contributions are paid is loose and tenuous. As stated earlier, the social adequacy principle is reflected in the benefit formula in which the benefits are heavily weighted or skewed in favor of lower-income groups. In contrast, the insurance element can be defined as that portion of the benefits paid that have some actuarial relationship (in the private sense) to the covered person's average earnings and the payroll tax contributions paid on those earnings. The relation between the benefits received and the contributions paid, of course, is not as close as that found in private insurance. Nevertheless, some relation exists.

In summary, the OASDI program appears to meet the definition of insurance adopted by the Commission on Insurance Terminology and can be considered a form of insurance. Two critical elements normally found in any insurance program—pooling and risk transfer—are present in the OASDI program. From this viewpoint, the OASDI program is insurance. But it should not be viewed as pure insurance, since a strong welfare element is also embodied in the benefit structure.

SOCIAL INSURANCE COMPARED WITH PRIVATE INSURANCE

Much confusion between social and private insurance arises from the application of private insurance standards to social insurance. Social and private insurance are quite different in character and content, and identical performance standards should not be used to judge them. Also, they do not have identical goals; therefore, they cannot be compared by the same standards of success.

As an example of the error of *noncomparable performance standards,* a Honda motorbike and a Rolls Royce automobile are both machines; but if the same efficiency test, such as gasoline mileage, is used to evaluate them, the motorbike would be judged a superior machine—a dubious conclusion at best. The error of noncomparable performance standards has been committed. Likewise, one cannot compare the standards of social insurance and private insurance. True, they are similar, since both are forms of insurance. But social insurance differs from private insurance in many respects.[19]

Applying private insurance standards to social insurance is also inappropriate because the *fallacy of composition* may nullify such comparisons. What is true for private insurance may be incorrect when applied to social insurance. For

---

[19]The major similarities and differences between private insurance and social insurance can be found in Myers, *Social Security,* Chaps. 1 and 2; Williams, Jr., Turnbull, and Cheit, *Economic and Social Security,* pp. 8–15; Ray M. Peterson, "Misconceptions and Missing Perceptions of Our Social Security System (Actuarial Anesthesia," *Transactions of Society of Actuaries,* Vol. 11 (March 1960), pp. 812–851; and C. A. Kulp, "Social and Private Insurance—Contrasts and Similarities," in H. Wayne Snider, ed., *Readings in Property and Casualty Insurance* (Homewood, Ill.: Richard D. Irwin, 1959), pp. 27–35. The following discussion is based on these sources.

example, private insurance stresses individual equity, whereas social insurance must emphasize the social adequacy principle. The fallacy of composition is committed if one contends that because private insurance stresses individual equity, social insurance must also stress individual equity rather than social adequacy in the payment of benefits.

Similarities

First, as noted earlier, both social and private insurance are based on risk transfer and the widespread pooling of definite risks. Second, both provide for specific and complete descriptions of all conditions relating to coverage, benefits, and financing. Third, both require precise mathematical calculations of benefit eligibility and amounts. Fourth, both require contributions and the payment of premiums sufficient to meet the estimated costs of the programs. Fifth, both provide predetermined benefits not based upon demonstrated need. Finally, both benefit society as a whole in providing economic security.

Differences

The major differences between social and private insurance may be listed as follows:

SOCIAL INSURANCE	PRIVATE INSURANCE
1. Compulsory	Voluntary
2. Minimum floor of income protection	Larger amounts available, depending on individual desires and ability to pay
3. Emphasis on social adequacy (welfare element)	Emphasis on individual equity (insurance element)
4. Benefits prescribed by law that can be changed (statutory right)	Benefits established by legal contract (contractual right)
5. Government monopoly	Competition
6. Costs difficult to predict	Costs more readily predictable
7. Full funding not needed because of compulsory contributions from new entrants and because the program is assumed to last indefinitely	Must operate on fully funded basis without reliance on new entrants' contributions
8. No underwriting	Individual or group underwriting
9. Widespread differences of opinion regarding objectives and results	Opinions generally more uniform regarding objectives and results
10. Investments generally in obligations of federal government	Investments mainly in private channels
11. Taxing power readily available to combat erosion by inflation	Greater vulnerability to inflation

The first three items in this comparison are self-explanatory and have already been explored. In the fourth, we see that social insurance benefits are prescribed by laws that can be changed; a statutory right to benefits exists. However, private insurance benefits are established by a legal contract enforceable in the courts; a contractual right to benefits exists. In social insurance, a contract is unnecessary. The terms are established by law and by interpretative regulations, and emphasis is placed on administrative regulations to carry out the intent of the law. This is considered a virtue and not a defect, because it is difficult to provide precise answers in the statutes for every conceivable set of circumstances. On the other hand, private insurance is competitive, and people cannot be coerced into purchasing the coverage; thus, the contractual terms must be stated clearly in the contract when it is first written. Finally, the virtues of a legally enforceable contract in private insurance may be overemphasized in providing economic security. Even though a contract exists, the protection may be inadequate, unsound, unreliable, or excessively costly. Some private insurance contracts are cancelable, the terms can be altered, or premiums can be increased (there are cancelable contracts, optionally renewable contracts, and guaranteed renewable contracts). In the last analysis, the economic security provided by a private contract depends upon the continued existence and financial strength of the insurer. If the company becomes bankrupt, the economic security provided by the legal contract may be lost.

Also, government usually has a monopoly in social insurance, whereas competition from other insurers prevails in private insurance. A monopolistic government carrier may be sound public policy. Since the programs are normally compulsory, competitive selling costs can be eliminated or reduced by a monopoly carrier; moreover, the public may consider it undesirable for profit to accrue to private insurers because of a compulsory program made possible by government.[20]

Another difference is that prediction of costs in social insurance is more difficult and less precise than in private insurance. The social insurance actuary is required to make rate and reserve calculations for risks whose insurability may be questionable (for instance, unemployment). Moreover, the actuary must work with economic, demographic, and sociological variables, such as births, deaths, marriages, employment, unemployment, disability, retirement, average wage levels, benefit levels, interest rates, and numerous additional factors that make prediction of costs difficult.

In addition, social insurance programs may not be fully funded, whereas private insurance and private pension plans stress fully funded programs. And underwriting selection procedures are not generally employed in social insurance, whereas they are applied to individuals or groups in private insurance. Underwriting is inappropriate in social insurance because the objective is to provide a base of economic protection for all; this means that most of the population should be covered. In private insurance, however, underwriting is necessary because the objective is to insure *profitable* risks.

---

[20]Workers' compensation insurance is a major exception to a government monopoly in social insurance. Although most state workers' compensation laws are compulsory, the benefits are generally underwritten by private insurers. Thus, profits could accrue to private insurers.

Another difference is that in social insurance, serious disagreement may exist concerning the method of financing, benefit levels, eligibility requirements, periods to be covered, the role of government, and numerous other factors. Opinions and objectives regarding private insurance programs are more uniform.

Also, the investments of the various social insurance trust funds are confined to the obligations of the federal government. In private insurance, investments in private securities are emphasized. (In some foreign countries, however, social insurance investments may be made in private securities.)

Finally, the government's taxing powers can more readily overcome the impact of inflation on social insurance programs. During inflationary periods, social insurance benefits may be increased, thereby providing the recipient some relief against higher prices. In private insurance, the benefits may be fixed and therefore more vulnerable to inflation.

SOCIAL INSURANCE COMPARED WITH PUBLIC ASSISTANCE

Although clear-cut differences between social insurance and public assistance are difficult to define precisely, certain dissimilarities appear. They are in the following areas: (1) prediction of eligibility requirements and benefit amounts, (2) demonstration of need, (3) method of financing, (4) number of participants, and (5) stigma attached to benefits.

Prediction of Eligibility Requirements and Benefit Amounts

Benefit amounts are generally predictable in social insurance. However, with the exception of the Supplemental Security Income (SSI) program, which guarantees a minimum income to needy aged, blind, and disabled persons, the benefit amounts are more difficult to predict in public assistance. In public assistance, the recipient's benefit is based on the extent of demonstrated need, and among the various states, there is considerable variation in the concept of need, the amount of income and assets allowed a recipient, and the prevailing standard of living and financial resources. Thus, with the exception of the SSI program, prediction of benefit amounts in public assistance is more difficult. For these reasons, workers seldom consider the availability of public assistance benefits in their financial plans.

Demonstration of Need

Social insurance programs never require a needs test; public assistance always involves a needs or income and assets test. Applicants for benefits must show that their income and assets are below certain specified levels. The public assistance benefit is based on the extent of *demonstrated need,* in contrast to the *presumed need* on which social insurance is based. Also, social insurance is based on *average need*, whereas public assistance is based on *individual need*. As a result, public assistance may be necessary to supplement social insurance to provide for emergencies and special needs.

Method of Financing

Social insurance benefits are normally financed out of specifically ear-marked taxes. However, public assistance benefits are usually financed out of the general revenues of government, and these are usually derived from a more progressive tax system than the one used to finance social insurance.

Also, in public assistance, the benefit recipient does not make specific contributions to the program before he or she is eligible for benefits, and there is no relation between the benefits received and the contributions made, since the funds are normally derived from general revenues.

Number of Participants

All those participating in social insurance programs are the insureds; only a small percentage of the participants will actually be beneficiaries at any given time. However, the direct participants in public assistance programs are only the people who receive benefits. Thus, more people are involved in social insurance than in public assistance.

Stigma Attached to Benefits

No stigma is attached to the receipt of social insurance benefits, since recipients have a statutory right to them, without showing need, if the eligibility requirements are met. Many eligible people, however, fail to apply for welfare benefits because of the needs test, which they consider repugnant and degrading. Since no stigma is attached to social insurance benefits, relatively few eligible participants refuse to make a claim.

ECONOMIC OBJECTIVES OF SOCIAL INSURANCE

From an economic viewpoint, social insurance programs have several important objectives: (1) to provide basic economic security to the population, (2) to prevent poverty, (3) to provide stability to the economy, and (4) to preserve important values.

Provide Basic Economic Security to the Population

The primary objective of social insurance is to afford basic economic security to most people against the long-range risks of premature death, old age, sickness and disability, and unemployment. As indicated in Chapter 1, these events cause economic insecurity because of the loss of income and additional expenses. Social insurance programs should provide a layer or a base of income protection to the population. In this context, basic economic security means that the social insurance benefit, along with other sources of income and other financial assets, should be sufficiently high to provide a minimum standard of living to the great majority of the population.

Prevent Poverty

By their operations, social insurance programs prevent a considerable amount of poverty. For example, although this is not the sole aim of the OASDI program, it does prevent a relatively large proportion of aged persons from sinking into poverty. In 1986, 14 percent of the aged units 65 or older whose families received OASDI benefits were living in poverty. If OASDI benefits had not been paid, 51 percent would have been counted poor.[21]

Provide Stability to the Economy

Another objective of social insurance is to enhance and contribute to the nation's economic stability. This means that the programs should influence consumption, saving, and investment in a desirable way and should tend to move in a desired countercyclical direction against the business cycle. For example, unemployment insurance benefits are sensitive to business downswings and tend to pump funds into the economy during periods of unemployment, thereby bolstering and maintaining personal income and consumption. In addition, the methods of financing of the programs should contribute to economic stability.

Although economic stability considerations are important in social insurance, they must never overshadow and override its primary objective: providing basic economic security to individuals and families against the widespread social risks confronting them. Economists generally tend to evaluate the various programs in terms of their macroeconomic impact on the economy and view this primary objective as secondary.

Preserve Important Values

A final objective of social insurance is to promote and not stifle the desirable qualities of personal incentives, initiative, and thrift. Many social insurance programs embody the concept that a person's economic security should arise out of work, and they relate the worker's right to benefits, the benefit amount, and the benefits received by the family to work earnings. Thus, basing eligibility on a demonstration of work and paying variable benefits related to the worker's wage

---

[21]Susan Grad, *Income of the Population 55 or Older, 1986,* Social Security Administration, Office of Policy, Office of Research and Statistics (June 1988), Table 53, p. 101.

appear to fit in well with our system of economic incentives. Moreover, social insurance benefits are paid regardless of income received from savings, private pensions, and financial investments. Thrift is thereby promoted, since the worker is encouraged to augment the basic layer of protection by a personal program of savings, investments, and private insurance.

The social insurance technique is an important device in providing economic security. Need is prevented as a result of the work and contributions of the worker and the contributions of his or her employer. This approach fits in well with our generally accepted system of economic values and personal incentives. Because social insurance is geared to a conservative value system, it has the stability that comes from widespread appeal and acceptance.[22]

SUGGESTIONS FOR ADDITIONAL READING

BALL, ROBERT M. *Social Security Today and Tomorrow.* New York: Columbia University Press, 1978.

BROWN, J. DOUGLAS. *An American Philosophy of Social Security: Evaluation and Issues.* Princeton, N.J.: Princeton University Press, 1972.

COHEN, WILBUR J., AND MILTON FRIEDMAN. *Social Security: Universal or Selective?* Washington, D.C.: American Enterprise Institute, 1972.

ELDRED, GARY W. "Social Security: A Conceptual Alternative." *The Journal of Risk and Insurance,* Vol. 47, No. 2 (June 1981).

MYERS, ROBERT J. *Social Security,* 3rd ed., Chap. 1. Homewood, Ill.: Richard D. Irwin, 1985.

"Social Security Programs in the United States," *Social Security Bulletin,* Vol. 52, No. 7 (July 1989), pp. 2–79.

WILLIAMS, C. ARTHUR, JR., JOHN G. TURNBULL, AND EARL F. CHEIT. *Economic and Social Security,* 5th ed. New York: John Wiley & Sons, 1982.

WITTE, EDWIN E. "The Objectives of Social Security." In Robert J. Lampman, ed., *Social Security Perspectives.* Madison, University of Wisconsin Press, 1962.

---

[22]Robert M. Ball, "Some Reflections on Selected Issues in Social Security," in *Old-Age Income Assurance, A Compendium of Papers on Problems and Policy Issues in the Public and Private Pension System, Part I: General Policy Guidelines,* Subcommittee on Fiscal Policy of the Joint Economic Committee, 90th Cong., 1st sess. (Washington, D.C.: U.S. Government Printing Office, 1967), pp. 49–51.

3

PROBLEM OF PREMATURE DEATH

In this chapter, we begin our study of the first of several economic problems that can cause great economic insecurity—the problem of premature death. Premature death has declined in importance as a cause of economic insecurity because of improvements in medical science and a longer life expectancy. Nevertheless, it merits serious study because family heads can and do die prematurely. As a result, surviving family members may experience a decline in their standard of living and financial insecurity. More specifically, in this chapter, we shall examine the following important areas: (1) meaning of premature death, (2) economic impact of premature death on the family both before and after death, and (3) techniques for meeting the problem of premature death.

MEANING OF PREMATURE DEATH

Premature death can be defined as death of a family head with unfulfilled financial obligations, such as dependents to support, children to educate, a mortgage to be paid off, and other installment debts. In this sense, the death of a family head can be considered premature if it occurs before age 70. Most family heads retire before age 70, employment opportunities after that age are limited, the children are grown, and financial obligations such as mortgage or car payments are likely to be paid off. Finally, in general, premature death can cause economic insecurity only if the deceased family head has dependents or dies with large unsatisfied financial obligations. Thus, the death of a child aged 7 is not regarded as being premature in the economic sense.

Costs of Premature Death

Numerous costs, both economic and noneconomic, are associated with premature death. First, the human life value is lost to the family; the family's share of the deceased's future income is lost forever. Second, additional expenses may be incurred because of burial costs, expenses of last illness, probate costs, estate and inheritance taxes, and the forced liquidation of assets. Third, the family may be uncertain regarding the continuation and amount of future income. Fourth, because of insufficient income, some families may sink into poverty and require public assistance or other welfare payments. Finally, certain noneconomic costs are also incurred, such as the emotional grief of surviving dependents and loss of a role model, counseling, and guidance for the children during the critical formative years.

Loss of Human Life Value

The loss of human life value by premature death can be enormous, especially if death occurs at a relatively young age. *The human life value can be defined as the present value of the family's share of the deceased breadwinner's earnings.* In its simplest form, the human life value can be calculated by the following steps:

1. Estimate the individual average annual earnings over his or her productive lifetime.
2. Deduct federal and state income taxes, Social Security taxes, life and health insurance premiums, and the costs of self-maintenance. The remaining amount is used for the family.
3. Determine the number of years from the person's present age to the contemplated age of retirement.
4. Using a reasonable discount rate, determine the present value of the family's share of earnings for the period determined in step 3.

For example, assume that a family head, age 30, has two dependents. The worker earns $40,000 annually and plans to retire at age 65. (For sake of simplicity, assume earnings remain constant.) Of this amount, $15,000 goes toward federal and state taxes, life and health insurance premiums, and the worker's personal needs. The remaining $25,000 is used to support the family. Using a conservative discount rate of 6 percent, the present value of $1 payable for 35 years is $14.50. Therefore, the worker has a human life value of $362,500 ($25,000 × $14.50 = $362,500). This sum represents the family's share of the deceased's future income, which is lost forever by premature death. The illustration clearly indicates that the loss of the human life value is a monumental loss.

Causes of Death

It is also worthwhile to examine the major causes of death in the United States. Table 3-1 shows the major causes of death in 1985 for all ages and for selected

TABLE 3-1 Deaths and Death Rates by Age and Sex, 1985

CAUSE	NUMBER OF DEATHS[1]			DEATH RATES[2]		
	Total	*Male*	*Female*	*Total*	*Male*	*Female*

All Ages

All Causes	2,086,440	1,097,758	988,682	**874.0**	**945.0**	**806.6**
Heart disease	771,169	398,208	372,961	323.0	342.8	304.3
Cancer	461,563	246,914	214,649	193.3	212.6	175.1
Stroke (cerebrovascular disease)	153,050	60,780	92,270	64.1	52.3	75.3
Accidents	**93,457**	**64,160**	**29,297**	**39.1**	**55.2**	**23.9**
Motor-vehicle	45,901	32,443	13,458	19.2	27.9	11.0
Falls	12,001	6,392	5,609	5.0	5.5	4.6
Drowning	5,316	4,411	905	2.2	3.8	0.7
Fires, burns	4,938	3,008	1,930	2.1	2.6	1.6
Poison (solid, liquid)	4,091	2,872	1,219	1.7	2.5	1.0
Chronic obstructive pulmonary disease	74,662	46,596	28,066	31.3	40.1	22.9
Pneumonia	67,615	33,159	34,456	28.3	28.5	28.1
Diabetes mellitus	36,969	15,263	21,706	15.5	13.1	17.7
Suicide	29,453	23,145	6,308	12.3	19.9	5.1
Chronic liver disease, cirrhosis	26,767	17,244	9,523	11.2	14.8	7.8
Atherosclerosis	23,926	9,062	14,864	10.0	7.8	12.1
Nephritis and nephrosis	21,349	10,551	10,798	8.9	9.1	8.8
Homicide	19,893	15,066	4,827	8.3	13.0	3.9

15 to 24 Years

All Causes	**37,935**	**28,162**	**9,773**	**95.9**	**141.1**	**49.9**
Accidents	**19,161**	**14,791**	**4,370**	**48.4**	**74.1**	**22.3**
Motor-vehicle	14,277	10,680	3,597	36.1	53.5	18.4
Drowning	1,346	1,232	114	3.4	6.2	0.6
Firearms	479	430	49	1.2	2.2	0.3
Poison (solid, liquid)	427	308	119	1.1	1.5	0.6
Fires, burns	380	244	136	1.0	1.2	0.7
Suicide	5,121	4,267	854	12.9	21.4	4.4
Homicide	4,772	3,767	1,005	12.1	18.9	5.1

25 to 44 Years

All Causes	**117,667**	**80,848**	**36,819**	**159.5**	**220.8**	**99.0**
Accidents	**25,940**	**20,438**	**5,502**	**35.2**	**55.8**	**14.8**
Motor-vehicle	15,034	11,403	3,631	20.4	31.1	9.8
Poison (solid, liquid)	2,385	1,881	504	3.2	5.1	1.4
Drowning	1,547	1,384	163	2.1	3.8	0.4
Falls	1,057	906	151	1.4	2.5	0.4
Fires, burns	929	644	285	1.3	1.8	0.8
Cancer	20,026	9,344	10,682	27.1	25.5	28.7
Heart disease	15,539	11,538	4,001	21.1	31.5	10.8

(continued)

TABLE 3-1   *(Continued)*

CAUSE	NUMBER OF DEATHS[1]			DEATH RATES[2]		
	Total	Male	Female	Total	Male	Female

45 to 64 Years

All Causes	**403,114**	**251,031**	**152,083**	**897.3**	**1,169.7**	**648.1**
Cancer	138,829	74,883	63,946	309.0	348.9	272.5
Heart disease	132,610	94,399	38,211	295.2	439.9	162.8
Stroke (cerebrovascular disease) ...	16,910	9,126	7,784	37.6	42.5	33.2
Accidents	**15,251**	**10,915**	**4,336**	**33.9**	**50.9**	**18.5**
Motor-vehicle	6,885	4,682	2,203	15.3	21.8	9.4
Falls	1,639	1,198	441	3.6	5.6	1.9
Fires, burns	965	662	303	2.1	3.1	1.3
Poison (solid, liquid)	678	389	289	1.5	1.8	1.2
Ingestion of food, object	658	426	232	1.5	2.0	1.0
Chronic obstructive pulmonary disease	12,901	7,541	5,360	28.7	35.1	22.8
Chronic liver disease, cirrhosis	12,506	8,499	4,007	27.8	39.6	17.1

65 to 74 Years

All Causes	**482,646**	**283,017**	**199,629**	**2,837.4**	**3,786.2**	**2,093.9**
Heart disease	183,733	112,709	71,024	1,080.1	1,507.8	745.0
Cancer	142,542	81,113	61,429	838.0	1,085.1	644.3
Stroke (cerebrovascular disease) ...	29,129	14,783	14,346	171.2	197.8	150.5
Chronic obstructive pulmonary disease	25,149	16,062	9,087	147.8	214.9	95.3
Diabetes mellitus	10,159	4,499	5,660	59.7	60.2	59.4
Pneumonia	9,828	6,121	3,707	57.8	81.9	38.9
Accidents	**8,583**	**5,077**	**3,506**	**50.5**	**67.9**	**36.8**
Motor-vehicle	3,014	1,685	1,329	17.7	22.5	13.9
Falls	1,641	963	678	9.6	12.9	7.1
Surgical, medical complications ..	701	366	335	4.1	4.9	3.5
Ingestion of food, object	635	349	286	3.7	4.7	3.0
Fires, burns	590	344	246	3.5	4.6	2.6

[1]Deaths are for 1985. Data are from National Center for Health Statistics, Public Health Service, U.S. Department of Health and Human Services. The all causes and accident totals for each age group include deaths not shown separately.
[2]Deaths per 100,000 population in each age group. Rates are averages for age groups, not individual ages.

Source: *Accident Facts, 1988 Edition* (Chicago: National Safety Council, 1988), pp. 8–9.

ages. When all ages are considered, the major causes of death are heart disease, cancer, stroke, and accidents. However, when premature death at the younger ages is considered, the major causes of death are dramatically different. The major causes of death for younger persons ages 15 to 24 are accidents, primarily motor vehicle accidents, suicide, and homicide. In particular, suicide and homicide are important causes of death at the younger ages and vividly highlight the mental unrest and violence experienced by young people today.[1] Many of the deaths at the younger ages are alcohol- or drug-related.

---

[1]Suicide data based on cause-of-death certification may be grossly understated because of reluctance

When the age group 25 to 44 is considered, the leading causes of death are motor vehicle accidents, cancer, and heart disease, while for the older age group, 45 to 64, the major causes of death are cancer, heart disease, strokes, and accidents. Cirrhosis of the liver is also an important cause of death for this group, which reflects the increasing incidence of alcoholism at the older age.

Chances of Dying Prematurely

The chances of dying prematurely have declined over time because of break-throughs in medical science, improvements in public health and sanitation, and increased economic growth and development. However, those chances are generally higher than is commonly believed, especially at the younger ages. The chances at various selected ages of dying before age 65 are as follows:[2]

age 20	22 out of 100
age 30	21 out of 100
age 40	19 out of 100
age 50	16 out of 100
age 60	8 out of 100

ECONOMIC IMPACT OF PREMATURE DEATH ON THE FAMILY

Any analysis of premature death must first consider the changing composition of the family. In addition, any analysis of premature death must also consider the financial impact on the family both *before* a terminally ill family head dies and *after* death occurs.

Changing Family Composition

The composition of the family has changed over time. As a result, the financial impact of premature death on the family is not uniform but is more severe for certain categories of families than for others.

Single People. The number of single people has increased dramatically in recent years. Young adults are postponing marriage, and many young and middle-aged adults are single because of divorce. In addition, older persons are finding themselves single once again because of the death of their spouse. The single population age 18 and older increased from 38 million in 1970 (28 percent of all adults) to 66 million in 1988 (37 percent of all adults).[3]

---

to admit the suicidal intent of friends and relatives and the difficulty in recognizing suicide under certain circumstances. For example, some automobile deaths involving only the driver are reported as accidents, when suicide is the actual cause of death.

[2]Kenneth Black, Jr., and Harold Skipper, Jr., *Life Insurance,* 11th ed. (Englewood Cliffs, N.J.: Prentice-Hall, Inc., 1987), Table 1-1, p. 5.

[3]U.S. Department of Commerce, Bureau of the Census, *Studies in Marriage and the Family, Singleness in America, Single Parents and Their Children, Married-Couple Families with Children,* Current Population Reports, Special Studies, Series P-23, No. 162, June 1989, p. 1.

In general, the death of a single adult who has no dependents to support or outstanding financial obligations is not likely to cause a problem of economic insecurity for others.

Single-Parent Families.   The number of single-parent families with children under age 18 has also increased dramatically. Between 1970 and 1987, the number of single-parent families with children under age 18 increased sharply from 3.8 to 9.2 million, or an increase of 142 percent.[4]

The decline in the incidence of two-parent families is especially pronounced for black families. *The proportion of white families maintained by two parents decreased from 90 percent in 1970 to 78 percent in 1987. However, the proportion of black families maintained by two parents declined sharply from 64 percent in 1970 to 42 percent in 1987.*[5]

In addition, most single-parent families are headed by a female. In 1987, 88 percent of all single-parent families with children under age 18 were maintained by the mothers. In contrast, only 12 percent of the single-parent families were maintained by the fathers.[6] The large number of families with female heads can be explained by the fact that the mothers have never married, or the fathers are absent because of divorce, separation, or death.

Premature death of the family head in a single-parent family can cause great economic insecurity for the children. An unprecedented number of children now live in single-parent homes, and many do not receive any financial support from the other parent, or the support is inadequate. *By 1988, nearly one out of every four children in the United States lived in a family where the mother never married, or the father was absent because of divorce, separation, or death.*[7]

In addition, 47 percent of the female-headed families with children and no husband present were poor in 1987, compared with only 8 percent of male-present families.[8] Premature death of the family head can only aggravate and intensify the poverty and economic insecurity that the children are already experiencing.

Traditional Families.   The traditional family has been characterized as a family where only the father works, and the mother remains at home to care for the children. The traditional family has declined in relative importance over time, and the number of married women with children who are now working has increased dramatically. In 1977, both the husband and wife worked in slightly over half (51.8 percent) of all married-couple families with children. However, in

---

[4]U.S. Congress, House, Committee on Ways and Means, *Background Material and Data on Programs within the Jurisdiction of the Committee on Ways and Means* (Washington, D.C.: U.S. Government Printing Office, 1989), p. 829.

[5]Ibid.

[6]Ibid., pp. 829–830.

[7]Ibid., p. 632.

[8]Ibid., p. 953.

1987, both the husband and wife worked in two-thirds (66.8 percent) of such families.[9]

Premature death can cause great economic insecurity in families with children where only the father works. In most cases, the husband dies first. Because of a longer life expectancy, the majority of married women with children will survive their husbands by several years. Because of premature death of the husband, widows who are not in the labor force must often adjust their standard of living downward, and the period of financial adjustment can be painful. Most husbands die with outstanding financial obligations and debts and own insufficient amounts of life insurance to reduce or prevent this financial readjustment. Some widows who are not in the labor force may be required to work to supplement the family's income, and this can create additional problems. Efforts to work full time, especially when there are preschool children, often result in a severe drain on the widow's time, energy, and nervous system. In addition, intense emotional grief may aggravate the problem.

Two-Income Earners. The traditional family has been largely replaced by families with children in which both the husband and wife work. Years ago, it was customary for women to stay at home to care for the children. This is no longer the case. There has been a dramatic increase in the proportion of women with children who are now in the labor force. *In March 1960, only 39 percent of the married women with children age 6 or over were in the labor force. In March 1988, this figure increased sharply to about 73 percent.[10]* The proportion of married women with children who are in the labor force has increased because women wish to pursue their own professional careers. Also, many married mothers are forced to work in order to maintain the family's standard of living.

In two-income families with children, the death of one income earner can cause considerable economic insecurity. The combined income of both spouses allows the family to maintain a much higher standard of living than if only one spouse works. If a working spouse dies, the standard of living may be reduced if the deceased has inadequate life insurance, or replacement income from other sources is inadequate.

However, in the case of a married working couple without children, premature death of one income earner is unlikely to cause economic insecurity. The other income earner is already in the labor force and is supporting himself or herself. Moreover, children-free career couples do not have the problem of providing an expensive college education for the children. Thus, although the death of one working spouse can cause serious emotional problems and grief for the surviving spouse, premature death is not likely to cause economic insecurity.

Blended Families. The number of blended families has also increased. A blended family is one in which a divorced or surviving husband or wife with

---

[9]Ibid., p. 848.
[10]Ibid., Table 16, p. 849.

children remarries, and the new mate also has children. Both spouses may be working and in the labor force at the time of remarriage.

Death of a working spouse in a blended family can cause considerable economic insecurity to the surviving dependents. Blended families with several children from two marriages are often faced with the problem of high child-rearing costs and other living expenses that accompany large families. The death of one working spouse can result in a reduction in the family's standard of living since the family's share of that income is lost. Moreover, in many blended families, older children are present from the previous marriage, and additional children are born out of the new marriage. As a result, both spouses are faced with expenses that extend over a longer time period than for other families. As a consequence, funds for the children's college education or for retirement may be limited. The premature death of a working spouse in a blended family can only aggravate the financial problems of the surviving spouse in such a situation.

Sandwich Families. A sandwich family is one in which a son or daughter with children must also support an elderly parent or parents. The middle generation is "sandwiched" between the younger generation (children) and the older generation (parents).

Premature death of a working spouse in a sandwich family can also cause considerable economic insecurity. Both children and parent(s) depend on the son or daughter for financial support. Premature death causes a loss of financial support and exposes the surviving dependents to economic insecurity.

This concludes our discussion of the changing composition of the family. Let us next consider the impact of premature death on the family before death occurs.

Impact Before Death Occurs

Premature death can strike without warning. A family head may die suddenly from a heart attack, automobile accident, plane crash, drowning, homicide, or other cause. However, in the majority of cases, a family head who is terminally ill is sick or disabled over a period of months or years before death finally occurs. During this period prior to death, the family often experiences a serious disruption of normal living patterns, reduced employment opportunities, a decline in family income, and substantial medical expenses. In addition, many spouses are inadequately prepared when a premature death occurs. Thus, any analysis of premature death must also consider the financial impact on the family before a terminally ill family head dies, as well as after death occurs.[11]

---

[11]This section is based on several sources. See Lynn Caine, *Being a Widow* (New York: William Morrow, 1988); Lynn Caine, *Widow* (New York: William Morrow, 1974); Philip B. Springer, "Health Care Coverage of Survivor Families with Children: Determinants and Consequences," *Social Security Bulletin*, Vol. 47, No. 2 (February 1984), pp. 3–16; U.S. Department of Health and Human Services, Social Administration, Office of Research and Statistics, *Preliminary Findings from the 1978 Survey of*

Disruption of Normal Living Patterns. When a family head is terminally ill, the family's normal living patterns are often seriously disrupted. One spouse may have to perform the household duties formerly performed by the other. Family meals may be irregular, which further disrupts the normal household schedule. If the terminally ill family head is hospitalized and there are small children, the other spouse must hire a babysitter in order to visit. In addition, the healthy spouse may have intense negative feelings of resentment, anger, guilt, or loneliness. Finally, there may be a serious lack of open communication between the couple concerning the illness.

Reduced Employment Opportunities. A serious health problem can also reduce the employment opportunities for a family head. Opportunities for promotion and advancement in a position may be limited; the number of hours of work may be reduced; the worker may be forced to shift to a less demanding but lower-paying job; the impairment may be so severe that the worker must retire early; and there is a complete loss of earned income to the family if the worker cannot work at all.

Decline in Family Income. An extended duration of terminal illness or disability often results in a decline in family income, or if family income does not decline, it may increase less rapidly because of the impairment. The decline in family income can be especially severe in two-income families if one working spouse is terminally ill, since the replacement income from all sources may restore only part of the lost earnings. For example, a full five-month waiting period is required before a terminally ill family head qualifies for OASDI disability benefits, and the benefits restore only part of the lost earnings. The 1982 New Beneficiary Survey of new disabled-worker beneficiaries and families revealed that about one-third of the married-couple families had an average total income of less than $1,000 monthly; the median total monthly income of married disabled men and their families was only $1,230, which was less than half of the income received by the noninstitutionalized population ages 25–64.[12]

Moreover, replacement income from private sources is likely to be inadequate for many families. Short-term group disability income plans restore only part of the lost earnings; long-term disability benefits are available to only a small fraction of the labor force; and most workers are seriously underinsured in the

---

Survivor Families with Children by Robert I. K. Hastings and Phillip B. Springer, Research Statistics Note No. 12 (November 7, 1980); Tim Sass, "Demographic and Economic Characteristics of Nonbeneficiary Widows: An Overview," *Social Security Bulletin*, Vol. 42, No. 11 (November 1979); Life Underwriter Training Council and Life Insurance Agency Management Association, *The Widows Study*, Vol. 1, *The Onset of Widowhood* (Hartford, Conn.: Life Underwriter Training Council and Life Insurance Agency Management Association, 1970); and *The Widows Study*, Vol. 2, *Adjustments to Widowhood: The First Two Years* (Hartford, 1971). See also Elisabeth Kubler-Ross, *On Death and Dying* (New York: Macmillan, 1969). See also Julian Abbott, "Knowledge of Social Security: Survivor Families with Young Children," *Social Security Bulletin*, Vol. 46, No. 12 (December 1983), pp. 3–13.

[12]Michael D. Packard, "Income of New Disabled-Worker Beneficiaries and Their Families: Findings from the New Beneficiary Survey," *Social Security Bulletin*, Vol. 50, No. 3 (March 1987), p. 13.

event of an extended illness. For example, American workers lost $45.6 billion in earnings from short-term nonoccupational sickness or injury in 1983. Of this amount, $16.4 billion, or only about 36 percent, was restored from private and individual and group disability income insurance, public funds, sick leave, government insurance programs, and income from other programs.[13] The proportion of earned income restored by long-term disability income plans during a long illness is undoubtedly much lower. Only 13 percent of all persons with private insurance had coverage under a long-term disability income plan in 1987.[14]

In addition, a terminally ill person may lose a considerable amount of income because of the loss of employee benefits. Employee benefits are an important part of the total wage package and, on average, account for about 39 percent of payroll.[15]

The loss of employee benefits can be substantial. The average value of all employee benefits per employee in 1987 was $10,708.[16] If full vesting has not been attained, a terminally ill person can lose part or all of his or her pension benefits; the pension benefit may also be reduced, since the benefit amount in most pension plans is related to the length of employment; employer contributions under a profit-sharing or thrift plan may be lost; and unless there is some provision for continuing group insurance during a long illness, group life and health insurance benefits may also be lost.

Finally, if the decline in family income is especially severe, some families may fall into poverty. For example, one study of 825 married-couple households in which the husband died before 1979 showed that 14.2 percent of the wives were living in poverty prior to their husband's death.[17] *Thus, it is clear that, for some families, economic insecurity from insufficient income can occur long before a family head actually dies.*

Substantial Medical Expenses. Some families with a terminally ill family head also incur catastrophic medical expenses that can aggravate the problem of economic insecurity. Only a relatively small proportion of all families incur catastrophic expenses during any given year. An earlier 1982 study (excluding the aged and poor) showed that only 5 percent of the families reported medical expenses exceeding $5,000; however, one half of 1 percent of the families had

---

[13]*Source Book of Health Insurance Data, 1986 Update* (Washington, D.C.: Health Insurance Association of America), Table 2.3, p. 12.

[14]*Source Book of Health Insurance Data, 1989* (Washington, D.C.: Health Insurance Association of America), p. 8.

[15]U.S. Chamber Research Center, *Employee Benefits, 1988 Edition* (Washington, D.C.: U.S. Chamber of Commerce, 1988), p. 5.

[16]Ibid.

[17]Daniel A. Myers, Richard V. Burkhauser, and Karen C. Holden, "The Transition from Wife to Widow: The Importance of Survivor Benefits to Widows," *The Journal of Risk and Insurance*, Vol. 54, No. 4 (December 1987), p. 754.

more than $20,000 in medical expenses.[18] If the family lacks major medical health insurance, it is exposed to considerable economic insecurity during an extended terminal illness of a family head.

In addition, many families with related children have no health insurance coverage. People in married-couple families with related children accounted for 29 percent of the nonaged uninsured.[19] Families in this category with a terminally ill family head are exposed to great economic insecurity if sizable medical expenses are incurred prior to death.

Inadequate Preparation for Death. Another part of the problem is that many spouses are inadequately prepared for a premature death. Financial planning prior to the death of a family head is often inadequate and incomplete. A family head may die without a will; the couple may not have discussed the need for life insurance protection and investment of the policy proceeds; in families where only one spouse handles the family funds, the surviving spouse may have difficulty in money management; and many surviving spouses have inadequate knowledge of OASDI survivor benefits prior to the deceased's death.[20] Thus, many surviving spouses are inadequately prepared to become widows or widowers.

In summary, for many families, economic insecurity from premature death does not occur suddenly but may begin long before a family head actually dies. In the professional literature on economic insecurity, the risks of premature death, catastrophic medical costs, and unemployment generally are analyzed separately. It must be recognized, however, that all three risks may be simultaneously present in the premature death problem, and any attack on premature death must also consider protection against the other risks that simultaneously accompany the problem.

Impact After Death Occurs

After the death occurs, the surviving spouse is often confronted with problems of loneliness and grief, payment of final expenses and inadequate life insurance proceeds, and a reduction in the family's income.

Loneliness and Grief. The surviving spouse often experiences intense emotional suffering and grief. Many surviving spouses indicate that loneliness is

---

[18]*Source Book of Health Insurance Data, 1982–1983* (Washington, D.C.: Health Insurance Association of America), p. 46.

[19]*Background Material and Data on Programs within the Jurisdiction of the Committee on Ways and Means,* 1989, p. 277.

[20]Many widows have inadequate knowledge of survivor benefits under the OASDI program. Only about 23 percent of all widows correctly answered eight or more of the ten questions asked concerning the OASDI program. See Abbott, "Knowledge of Social Security, Survivor Families with Young Children," p. 3.

the most serious problem they must face. Most feel a deep sense of loss and lack of companionship after the death of their husbands or wives. A painful period of psychological readjustment is often necessary. During this readjustment period, many spouses feel bitter, angry, and numb. In addition, the children may experience considerable guilt feelings and remorse after a parent dies.

Inadequate Life Insurance.   A terminally ill family head often owns an inadequate amount of private life insurance. In many cases, a family head may die uninsured, or the amounts paid to the family are abysmally low. This is particularly true if an older family head dies. Household heads ages 55–64 owned only an average of $47,900 of individual and group life insurance in 1984,[21] which represents about two years of disposable income to the family. If OASDI survivor benefits are not available to an older surviving spouse because she or he is not caring for any eligible children under age 16, the standard of living may have to be reduced.

Reduction in Income.   Families can also experience a substantial reduction in income and living standards after a family head dies. This is especially true for many older surviving spouses who are not in the labor force at the time the family head dies, and the amount of life insurance proceeds, if any, is inadequate. To receive OASDI survivor benefits, a surviving spouse must be age 60 or older, be age 50 or older and disabled, or have eligible children under age 16 in his or her care. Most older surviving spouses are widows because of a longer life expectancy. Older widows under age 60 generally are ineligible for monthly OASDI benefits because they are not disabled, or the children are grown. As a result, older widows under age 60 who are not in the labor force at the time a family head dies can experience severe economic insecurity since the major source of income is cut off. Of the 2.2 million nonmarried women ages 55–61 who were not OASDI beneficiaries, 23 percent were living in poverty in 1986.[22] The majority of women within this group are widows.

In summary, after the family head dies, two important problems clearly stand out: loneliness and grief, and insufficient income for many families. It is clear that premature death can cause considerable economic insecurity.

MEETING THE PROBLEM OF PREMATURE DEATH

Numerous techniques can be used to meet the problem of premature death. Some techniques are appropriate only before the family head actually dies, while other approaches become operational after death occurs.

---

[21]*1988 Life Insurance Fact Book,* (Washington, D.C.: American Council of Life Insurance), p. 38.
[22]Social Security Administration Office of Policy, Office of Research and Statistics, *Income of the Population 55 or Older, 1986* (June 1988), Table 51, p. 97.

Before Death Occurs

Some important techniques for meeting the problem of premature death before death occurs include (1) loss prevention, (2) hospice care, and (3) support groups. Let us briefly examine each of these techniques.

Loss Prevention. Loss prevention is the ideal technique for meeting the risk of premature death. Both private and public loss-prevention activities can reduce the probability of death. Traditional private loss-prevention methods include health education, medical research, accident prevention, and individual medical examinations. Loss-prevention techniques are highly desirable for reducing the incidence of high-risk diseases, such as heart attacks, cancer, diabetes, and strokes. The physician seeks clues indicating that an otherwise healthy person will later contract a high-risk disease. For example, a blood test can reveal the future possibility of emphysema, which might be prevented by not smoking; a high cholesterol level may indicate the individual is in a high-risk group with respect to a heart attack. Other tests, such as multiphasic screening, are designed to detect symptoms in an otherwise healthy person that indicate a high probability of dying from a certain disease. Preventive measures can then be prescribed.

Loss prevention offers great potential for reducing the problem of premature death in the future. In this respect, the United States has made considerable progress in reducing the death rate from heart disease. The reduction is due largely to improvements in medical science and changing life styles that can be appropriately described as loss-prevention techniques. New medical techniques that can reduce the number of deaths from heart attacks include clot-dissolving therapy, angioplasty, and open heart surgery. In addition, Americans have a greater awareness of the importance of physical fitness and aerobic exercise, weight control, low-fat diets, cessation of smoking, moderation in drinking, stress management, hypertension control, and cholesterol testing. As a result, the death rate from heart disease has decreased significantly over time. In 1960, 28.9 percent of the natural causes of death in the United States population were caused by ischemic heart disease and other myocardial insufficiencies. In 1987, this percentage declined to 24.1 percent, or a decline of about 17 percent.[23] The United States clearly has made considerable progress in reducing premature death from heart diseases by loss-prevention techniques.

In addition, public loss-prevention activities can also reduce the probability of premature death. These activities include public health and sanitation measures, reduction of air and water pollution, control of communicable diseases, regulation of food and drugs, highway and occupational safety programs, early detection of childhood diseases, and many other techniques.

---

[23]*1988 Life Insurance Fact Book,* p. 100.

Hospice Care.   Hospice care is another effective approach to premature death. *A hospice is a program that provides for the medical relief of pain and supportive services to terminally ill persons and assistance to their families in adjusting to the patient's illness and death.*[24] The basic objective is to make the dying patient as comfortable as possible and to help the family cope with the stress. Hospices are aimed primarily at assisting terminally ill cancer patients and their families.

The hospice concept had its origin in homes established by religious orders during the Middle Ages in Europe whereby traveling pilgrims received lodging and care as they traveled throughout the Holy Land. The hospice concept later developed into programs of personal attention and care for the sick and dying poor. A hospice program has the following characteristics:

1. The patient and family are considered the unit of care, not just the patient.
2. An interdisciplinary team provides physical, psychological, and spiritual assistance to the patient and family and provides for an overall coordinated plan of care.
3. Physical pain is controlled by appropriate medication, but no heroic efforts are made to cure the patient.
4. Bereavement follow-up services are available to the family to help family members overcome the emotional suffering associated with the patient's death.

As an approach to meeting the problem of premature death, hospices have several advantages. First, physical pain is controlled, especially for terminally ill cancer patients. In addition, terminally ill patients are given emotional support and assistance in accepting their illness and imminent death. This assistance is especially helpful to dying patients who are still in the denial stage. Second, supportive services are provided to the patient's family both before and after death to reduce the emotional pain, suffering, and grief. Finally, hospice care has the potential for lowering the cost of dying and medical care provided to terminally ill patients. The programs are designed so that the patient can die at home, or care is provided in lower-level facilities, such as an inpatient hospice facility, rather than in a more expensive hospital or nursing home. Also, hospices are heavily staffed with volunteer workers, which reduces the cost of dying.

Support Groups.   Support groups such as "Make Today Count" are another approach to premature death. A person who is terminally ill periodically meets with other people who are terminally ill or have serious health problems. Common problems are discussed. The intent is to share common experiences, strength, and hope with each other so that facing death is easier. For example, many hospitals have support groups for terminally ill cancer patients who meet periodically to discuss common problems faced by all cancer patients.

Many communities also have grief programs for surviving spouses and family members who have recently experienced the death of a close family

---

[24]General Accounting Office, *Hospice Care—A Growing Concept in the United States,* Report to the Congress of the United States (Washington, D.C.: U.S. Government Printing Office, 1979), p. 1.

member. Surviving family members meet periodically to discuss common problems and feelings associated with the death of a loved one, such as guilt, loneliness, resentment, anger, depression, and similar feelings. The grief programs enable surviving family members to adjust more quickly to the death of a loved one and work through the grieving process more easily. The stress and pain that accompany the death of a close family member can be dealt with more effectively by discussing common problems with others who have also experienced the death of a loved one.

After Death Occurs

Numerous techniques are also available to reduce the economic insecurity that can result from premature death. The major techniques include the following: (1) OASDI survivor benefits, (2) private life insurance and private pension benefits, (3) employment earnings, (4) investment income, (5) relatives, friends, and charities, and (6) public assistance and other miscellaneous sources of income.

OASDI Survivor Benefits. OASDI survivor benefits are extremely important in reducing economic insecurity from premature death. Along with employment earnings, they are an important source of income to surviving spouses with eligible children under age 16 in their care. The benefits include both monthly income payments and a nominal funeral benefit. The monthly benefits help to maintain the family's standard of living and prevent financial hardship.

Although the OASDI program provides an important layer of income protection, the economic position of some surviving spouses is still precarious. As we noted earlier, not all widows receive monthly benefits. Many widows are ineligible for monthly benefits because they are under age 60 and have no eligible children in their care. Or they may work and earn an income in excess of the earnings test limitation, which results in a reduction or termination of their monthly benefits. Also, some younger widows may remarry, thereby losing their benefits. Finally, a small number of widows fail to apply for benefits, or the deceased husband had insufficient work experience to qualify for benefits.

The problem of an older widow without children is especially difficult. Since OASDI monthly cash benefits may not be available and other sources of income may be inadequate, the older widow must find a job. Employment opportunities may be limited because of her age, because she lacks highly paid skills, or because of an ineffective job search. An older widow with limited employment opportunities may find it extremely difficult to attain meaningful economic security.

Private Life Insurance. Both individual and group life insurance are excellent techniques for attacking the problem of premature death. Private individual life insurance, however, is not being used to the maximum extent possible. Most family heads die underinsured, with only a small fraction of their human life values insured. Many family heads fail to recognize that as their family needs change over time, the amount of life insurance coverage should also change. The amount of life insurance carried often is inadequate because of rapid increases in inflation, upgrading of aspirations, increases in productivity and real wages, and substantial improvements in the nation's standard of living. Failure to upgrade the amount of life insurance is especially prevalent among older family heads who purchased their insurance many years prior to their death. Life insurance agents should attempt to sell more life insurance to the over-40 market, which undoubtedly contains a large proportion of family heads who need significantly larger amounts of life insurance than they currently own. More aggressive selling to this market could do much to reduce future economic insecurity from premature death.

Although individual life insurance can significantly reduce economic insecurity from premature death, certain limitations must be recognized. Life insurance may not be available if the family head is uninsurable; the lower-income groups most in need of protection lack the ability to pay for large amounts of insurance; and insureds often receive poor advice from agents concerning the type of insurance to purchase. In many cases, substantial amounts of term insurance can be justified for younger family heads whose need for protection is great but whose income is limited. Many family heads are persuaded to purchase the more expensive types of life insurance, such as an ordinary life or 20-payment life policy, and are substantially underinsured as a result. In addition, many family heads have inadequate knowledge of life insurance and believe they have no need for additional coverage. Finally, agents often give inadequate service and advice to their clients with respect to the use of settlement options, life insurance programming, and the disposition and investment of policy proceeds.

Group life insurance also offers great potential in reducing economic insecurity from premature death. Most employers provide some group life insurance benefits to their workers. Group insurance has the advantages of low-cost protection, mass coverage, and the availability of insurance even if the worker is substandard or uninsurable. The coverage is normally available without evidence of insurability if the employee applies before or during his or her eligibility period.

Present group life insurance, however, has two major disadvantages that limit its effectiveness in attacking economic insecurity from premature death. First, the amount of group life insurance on an employee's life is relatively low. The average amount of group life insurance on an employee was only $34,479 in 1988, which generally is inadequate for most families.[25] Second, as in the case of individual life insurance, most beneficiaries do not receive group insurance proceeds in the form of monthly income. The family needs both continuous and adequate monthly replacement income after the family head's death to maintain

---

[25] *1989 Life Insurance Fact Book, Update,* p. 16.

its previous standard of living. Although group life insurance settlement options generally are available, they are seldom used.

There is a great need for group life insurance benefits to be paid as monthly income to the survivors for an extended period. Moreover, the monthly income should be related to the worker's salary and family needs. In this respect, Survivor Income Benefit Insurance (SIBI) offers tremendous potential in reducing economic insecurity from premature death. SIBI benefits are paid only if a qualified survivor exists, such as a surviving spouse. In addition, there is no lump-sum payment. The benefits, which are related to the worker's earnings, are paid in equal monthly installments. The monthly earnings generally are a maximum of 20–25 percent of the worker's monthly earnings or may be a flat dollar amount. The benefits are paid to the surviving spouse until she or he remarries, dies, or attains a certain age, such as 62. If children's benefits are included, they are paid until the youngest unmarried child attains a certain age, such as age 19. Benefits can be paid longer to unmarried children who are still in school.[26] SIBI benefits, along with monthly OASDI survivor benefits, practically guarantee that the family can maintain its former standard of living after the worker's death.

Private Pension or Profit-Sharing Death Benefits. Death benefits may also be available to surviving dependents under a qualified private pension or profit-sharing plan. In a contributory pension plan, the accumulated value of the employee's contributions can be paid to the surviving spouse. The account balance under a profit-sharing or thrift plan can also be paid. Also, in a fully insured individual pension plan, such as a retirement income contract, a death benefit is paid equal to $1,000 for each $10 of monthly income, or the cash value if greater. Group permanent pension plans also provide death benefits.

In addition, as a result of the Retirement Equity Act of 1984 (REA), the surviving spouse of a retired worker is now entitled to a survivor annuity under a qualified pension plan. The retirement benefit paid to the retired worker must be in the form of a *qualified joint-and-survivor annuity.* This means that the surviving spouse of a retired worker must receive a benefit that is not less than 50 percent of the amount payable when both the retired worker and spouse were alive.

A preretirement survivor annuity must also be made available to the surviving spouse of a worker with vested rights who dies before retirement. However, if the worker dies before the plan's early retirement age (such as age 55), the preretirement survivor benefit does not have to be paid until the worker would have reached the plan's early retirement age. Thus, the benefit is computed as if the worker separated from service on the date of death, survived until the early retirement age, and then retired with a joint-and-survivor annuity in force.

The joint-and-survivor annuity is automatic and mandatory unless the

---

[26]Jerry S. Rosenbloom and G. Victor Hallman, *Employee Benefit Planning,* 2nd ed. (Englewood Cliffs, N.J.: Prentice-Hall, 1986), pp. 60–61.

employee elects not to provide his or her spouse with a qualified survivor annuity. However, the employee's spouse must agree in writing to waive the required benefit.[27]

The joint-and-survivor annuity option has great potential in reducing economic insecurity for surviving spouses. One study of 825 married-couple households in which the husband died before 1979 showed that about 17 percent of the widows were living in poverty. However, if the joint-and-one-half life annuity option had been used, the poverty rate would have been reduced to about 8 percent.[28]

Employment Earnings.   Employment earnings are also important in attacking economic insecurity from premature death. Many surviving spouses with children are already in the labor force prior to the death of their husband or wife; others may reenter the labor force after the husband or wife dies. A surviving spouse who can work after the husband or wife's death is more likely to maintain or improve his or her previous standard of living. In some cases, the surviving spouse has no choice but to work if the OASDI survivor benefits, private pensions, or other income maintenance programs are insufficient for meeting the family's needs. And working has the additional advantage of helping the spouse to overcome his or her loneliness and grief.

A surviving spouse, however, faces two major obstacles if she or he wishes to reenter the labor force after the death of the other spouse. First, there may be preschool children present who require someone to care for them. If the mother or father attempts to work by placing the children in a day care center or by hiring a babysitter, substantial additional expenses are incurred, which reduce the family's income.

Second, if a surviving spouse has work earnings that exceed the limit allowed by the OASDI earnings test, she or he will lose part or all of the monthly survivor benefits. As a result, the incentive to work may be reduced. The OASDI earnings test is a highly controversial issue that will be discussed in greater detail in Chapter 6.

Investment Income.   Investment income can also supplement the family's income after the death of a family head. However, most surviving spouses do not accumulate sizable assets prior to the death of a husband or wife, especially if death occurs at an early age. Investment income generally accounts only for a small fraction of total income received by the family. Income from assets accounted for only 9 percent of the total aggregate income received by aged units 55–61 in 1986.[29]

---

[27]Ibid., pp. 65–66.

[28]Myers, Burkhauser, and Holden, "The Transition from Wife to Widow: The Importance of Survivor Benefits to Widows," p. 756.

[29]*Income of the Population 55 or Older, 1986*, Table 47, p. 93.

Relatives and Friends. Relatives and friends can also help meet the problem of premature death. Gifts of money can be given. This type of financial assistance, however, is generally ineffective as a long-run solution to economic insecurity from premature death. Most families need adequate and continuing income to attain meaningful economic security, and few friends or relatives are financially able to provide continuous financial assistance to a bereaved family. Temporary assistance, however, in the form of gifts and loans can be especially valuable until other income is received, and temporary financial aid from relatives and friends can be extremely helpful during this period.

Private Charities. Private charities—churches, labor unions, fraternal organizations, and charitable institutions such as the Salvation Army—may also provide temporary financial assistance to surviving spouses with children. The effectiveness, however, of private charities in reducing economic insecurity from premature death is limited. As in the case of relatives and friends, the amount of aid that private charities can provide is limited. Few of them are financially able to provide continuous income payments to a large number of surviving spouses. In addition, some surviving spouses with children who need financial help find it repugnant to appeal to private charities for assistance. Most spouses do not consider charity an acceptable solution to their need for continuous and adequate income.

Public Assistance. Public assistance benefits may also be available to some surviving spouses and their children; however, these benefits are relatively unimportant in meeting the problem of premature death. One study of non-beneficiary aged units ages 55–61 revealed that only 4 percent of the units received public assistance in 1986.[30]

Increased dependence on public assistance is an ineffective solution to the problem of premature death. Some surviving spouses are reluctant to apply for public assistance because of the stigma attached to the benefits. Also, the needs test and stringent eligibility and categorical requirements will disqualify many spouses who apply for benefits. Finally, if aid is received, the income generally is insufficient for meeting the full needs of the family; unfulfilled needs make it difficult to attain economic security, because a reasonable standard of living is not being attained.

Other Sources of Income. The family may also be eligible to receive monthly income payments from other public programs, including veterans' benefits, civil service death benefits, railroad retirement death benefits, and workers' compensation if the death is related to the job. Also, a surviving spouse may receive funds from the sale of the deceased's business interest or from the sale of certain household possessions no longer needed.

---

[30]Ibid., Table 3, p. 8.

SUGGESTIONS FOR ADDITIONAL READING

CAINE, LYNN. *Being a Widow.* New York: William Morrow, 1988.

HASTINGS, ROBERT I. K., AND PHILIP B. SPRINGER. *Preliminary Findings from the 1978 Survey of Survivor Families with Children.* U.S. Department of Health and Human Services, Social Security Administration, Office of Research and Statistics, Research and Statistics Note No. 12, November 7, 1980.

KUBLER-ROSS, ELISABETH. *Living with Death and Dying.* New York: Macmillan, 1981.

———. *On Death and Dying.* New York: Macmillan, 1969.

LIFE UNDERWRITER TRAINING COUNCIL AND LIFE INSURANCE AGENCY MANAGEMENT ASSOCIATION. *The Widows Study,* Vol. 1, *The Onset of Widowhood.* Hartford, Conn.: Life Underwriter Training Council and Life Insurance Agency Management Association, 1970.

———. *The Widows Study,* Vol. 2, *Adjustment to Widowhood: The First Two Years.* Hartford, Conn.: Life Underwriter Training Council and Life Insurance Agency Management Association, 1971.

MYERS, DANIEL A., RICHARD V. BURKHAUSER, AND KAREN C. HOLDEN. "The Transition from Wife to Widow: The Importance of Survivor Benefits to Widows," *The Journal of Risk and Insurance,* Vol. 54, No. 4 (December 1987), pp. 752–759.

ROSENBLOOM, JERRY S., AND G. VICTOR HALLMAN. *Employee Benefit Planning,* 3rd ed. Englewood Cliffs, N.J.: Prentice-Hall, 1991.

SASS, TIM. "Demographic and Economic Characteristics of Nonbeneficiary Widows: An Overview," *Social Security Bulletin,* Vol. 42, No. 11 (November, 1979).

SILVERMAN, PHYLLIS R. *Widow-to-Widow.* New York: Springer Publishing Co., 1986.

UPSON, NORMA S. *When Someone You Love Is Dying.* New York: Simon & Schuster, 1986.

U.S. DEPARTMENT OF COMMERCE, BUREAU OF THE CENSUS. *Studies in Marriage and the Family, Singleness in America, Single Parents and Their Children, Married-Couple Families with Children.* Series P-23, No. 162. Washington, D.C.: U.S. Government Printing Office, 1989.

PROBLEM
OF OLD AGE

Although the United States is a relatively young nation, about 32 million persons, or 12 percent of the total population, are age 65 and over. Many retired people are exposed to considerable economic insecurity in their old age because of insufficient income. Other workers retire early because of technological change and automation, plant shutdowns, poor health, or desire for more leisure. As a result, they are spending a relatively larger proportion of their adult lives in retirement, and the incomes they receive may be insufficient for providing them with a reasonable standard of living. Millions of older Americans also live in poverty, and the problem of poverty among aged women who are divorced, separated, or widows is particularly acute. Furthermore, many retired workers experience serious financial problems or poor health and spiraling medical expenses, high property taxes, inadequate low-cost housing, inflation, inadequate transportation, exploitation, and abuse. Suicide rates for the aged have also increased. Finally, some older workers experience difficulty in finding jobs because of arbitrary age discrimination.

In this chapter, we shall analyze each of the preceding problems in greater detail under three general areas: (1) nature of the old-age problem, (2) employment problems of older workers, and (3) techniques for attacking the economic problem of old age.

NATURE OF THE OLD-AGE PROBLEM

The economic problems of old age consist of the loss of earned income because of retirement, a lengthening period of retirement, insufficient income, erosion of real income, and additional expenses, including medical expenses and property taxes. In addition, many aged persons are physically, mentally, and financially abused by relatives and other people. We shall deal more specifically with these problems by considering the following: (1) loss of earned income because of retirement, (2) longer retirement period, (3) insufficient income during retirement, (4) poor health, (5) heavy property taxes, (6) inflation, (7) other financial problems, and (8) abuse of the elderly.

Loss of Earned Income Because of Retirement

Loss of earned income because of retirement is an important cause of economic insecurity. Unless retired workers have adequate replacement income from the OASDI program, private pensions, and personal investments, they will be exposed to considerable economic insecurity during retirement.

In the past, mandatory retirement by employers has been an important cause of economic insecurity for some older workers since they lost their earned income. Employers defended a mandatory retirement age, such as age 65, on the grounds that older workers could be retired in a dignified fashion; a uniform retirement policy applied to all workers; employers were relieved of the problem of permitting certain older workers to continue working while asking others to retire; and employment and promotion opportunities were increased for younger workers.

Mandatory retirement today, however, is less important as a cause of economic insecurity in old age. This is true for two reasons. First, as a result of a 1986 amendment to the Age Discrimination in Employment Act, the vast majority of employees in private firms and state and local government cannot be forced to retire at any retirement age. With certain exceptions, it is now illegal for employers to require workers to retire at some stated retirement age, such as age 70. As a practical matter, however, the vast majority of employees retire long before age 70. Only 16 percent of the male and 7 percent of the female workers age 65 or older were actually participating in the labor force in 1986. The labor force participation rates for this group in 2000 are projected to be only about 10 and 5 percent, respectively.[1]

Second, and more importantly, workers who are retiring today do so voluntarily and are not forced by their employers to do so. This has not always been the case. In 1968, 57 percent of nonemployed men age 65 or older who received OASDI retired-worker benefits indicated that retirement was initiated by the employer; only 22 percent was employee initiated. However, by 1982, employer-initiated retirement declined to 20 percent, while employee-initiated retirement increased sharply to 63 percent.[2] In addition, most workers who

---

[1]U.S. Congress, House, Committee on Ways and Means, *Background Material and Data on Programs within the Jurisdiction of the Committee on Ways and Means* (Washington, D.C.: U.S. Government Printing Office, 1989), Table 7, p. 487.

[2]Virginia P. Reno and Susan Grad, "Economic Security, 1935–85," *Social Security Bulletin*, Vol. 48, No. 12 (December 1985), Table 20, p. 18.

voluntarily retire do so because of the desire for leisure or for other reasons and not because of poor health. New OASDI beneficiaries generally view themselves as being in good health. One study revealed that two-thirds of the newly retired OASDI beneficiaries reported no health-related work limitations and no moderate or severe functional limitations.[3] In short, mandatory retirement as a cause of economic insecurity has declined over time.

Although much of the current retirement is initiated by employees, it is a mistake to view retirement as not being an important cause of economic insecurity in old age. Most workers retire early, and for many of them, they are faced with the problem of insufficient income during a longer retirement period. Let us consider next the problem of a longer retirement period.

Longer Retirement Period

A longer retirement period is another part of the economic problem of old age. Workers are spending a relatively longer period of their adult lives in retirement and a relatively shorter period in productive employment. Because of a shorter period of productive earnings, the average worker may not be able to save enough during his or her working years to maintain a reasonable standard of living during the longer retirement period.

The relatively longer retirement period and shorter working period can be explained by the strong trend toward early retirement, an increase in life expectancy at the older ages, and a longer period of formal education.

Trend toward Early Retirement.   In recent years, there has been a distinct trend toward early retirement, which reduces the period of productive earnings and increases the length of the retirement period. Only 67 percent of the male workers and 42 percent of the female workers ages 55–64 were working or seeking work in 1986.[4] Since private pension benefits are often actuarially reduced for early retirement, some early retirees have insufficient incomes during retirement. In addition, very few private pensions are automatically adjusted for inflation each year. As a result, inflation can gradually erode the real incomes of workers who have retired early, which also aggravates the problem of insufficient income.

Workers retire early for a variety of reasons.[5] First, many workers are dissatisfied with their jobs and want to retire. Second, the availability of early retirement benefits under the OASDI program and private pension plans encourages many older workers to retire early; those workers who can look forward to substantial private pension benefits are more likely to retire early.

---

[3]Michael Packard, "Health Status of New Retired-Worker Beneficiaries: Findings from the New Beneficiary Survey," *Social Security Bulletin*, Vol. 48, No. 2 (February 1985), p. 5.

[4]*Background Material and Data on Programs within the Jurisdiction of the Committee on Ways and Means,* 1989, Table 7, p. 487.

[5]See Herbert S. Parnes, "The Retirement Decision," in *The Older Worker* (Madison: Industrial Relations Research Association, University of Wisconsin, 1988), pp. 115–150.

Third, other workers retire because of poor health, technological change and automation that permanently displaces workers, layoffs and plant closings, and labor union and management pressures.

Fourth, the average total incomes of married working couples initially may not be significantly reduced by early retirement, which encourages some workers to retire early. There has been an increase in two-income families in which one spouse remains employed while the other spouse retires. The loss of earned income can be partially offset by private pension and OASDI benefits.

Finally, in order to reduce labor costs, many corporations are restructuring by reducing permanently the size of their work force. Firms frequently encourage older workers to retire early by offering a substantial cash bonus or by reducing the early retirement pension by less than the full actuarial equivalent. This policy is often referred to as an *open window retirement policy* by which the early retirement window is opened to older employees with long periods of service.

Impact of Early Retirement. The trend toward early retirement and a subsequent increase in the retirement period compound the problem of economic insecurity in old age. First, whether compulsory or voluntary, early retirement makes it more difficult for some workers to receive an adequate income during retirement. *Early retirement may reduce the amount of accumulated savings, since the period of productive earnings is shortened, with the result that the worker may be unable to save a sufficient amount to provide for income during the longer retirement period.*

For example, assume that a male worker works W years and lives in retirement for R years. If interest is ignored and the worker desires to maintain the same standard of living after retirement as he had before, he must save R/W of his earnings. If the worker enters the labor force at age 20 and retires at age 70, and assuming a retirement period of 13 years, he must save 13/50, or 26 percent, of his preretirement income to maintain the same standard of living after retirement as he had before. On the other hand, if he retires early, at age 60, he can expect to live about 20 years in retirement, so to maintain his average consumption, he must save 20/40 of his preretirement income, or 50 percent, disregarding interest. Although higher average real income during the working years may increase, the increase may be insufficient to offset the increase in the average length of retirement and the shrinkage in the working lifetime of an individual.

In addition, as we noted earlier, if workers retire early, their public and private pension benefits generally are actuarially or otherwise reduced. As a result, the early retirement pension by itself may be seriously inadequate for maintaining a reasonable standard of living during the retirement period.

Still another part of the problem is that some workers who retire early lose their employer-financed group health insurance. Some financially troubled firms have filed for bankruptcy and have terminated or substantially reduced group health insurance benefits for retired workers. Unlike private pension plans, the costs of health insurance benefits for retired workers generally have not been advance funded. As a result, many firms are experiencing a significant increase in group health insurance costs as the number of retired workers continues to increase. The costs of providing health insurance coverage to retired workers are substantial. The General Accounting Office estimates that American corporations had total liabilities of $402 billion for retiree health benefits in 1988.[6] As a result, an increasing number of firms are reducing or eliminating insurance coverage for retired workers, or the retired workers are being asked to pay a larger share of the cost. The financial impact on the early retiree's budget can be substantial.

In addition, some retired workers who lose their group health insurance are uninsurable. Others go uninsured or are forced to pay relatively high premiums for individual coverage. For example, a retired male worker age 59 lost his group health insurance coverage. His monthly pension was only $443, out of which he had to pay a monthly premium of $180 for an individual policy with less coverage than he had while working.[7] In short, some workers who retire early may be confronted with substantial additional expenses if individual health insurance has to be purchased.

Finally, because of the relative reduction in the labor force from early retirement, there is a loss of experienced labor that comes at a time when relatively fewer younger people are entering the labor force.[8]

Increase in Life Expectancy. The longer retirement period is also explained by an increase in life expectancy. Although most of the increase in life expectancy has occurred at the younger ages, there has been an increase as well at the older ages. For example, the life expectancy of a male age 65 increased from 11.9 years in 1940 to 14.9 years in 1988.

Longer Period of Formal Education. A longer period of formal education is a final reason for the increase in the period of retirement. A highly industrialized economy requires a skilled labor force, which necessitates a longer period of formal education, and a longer period of formal education necessarily delays entry into the labor force, thereby reducing the period of productive earnings. The need for a more highly educated labor force and the growth of child labor legislation have both increased the average age of entry into the labor force. The higher entry age reduces the proportion of an average worker's lifetime that can be considered economically productive, thereby increasing the proportion that can be considered economically nonproductive. Thus, in a high-

---

[6]United States General Accounting Office, *Employee Benefits: Companies' Retiree Health Liabilities Large, Advance Funding Costly* (Washington, D.C.: United States General Accounting Office, 1989), p. 4.

[7]Clare Anberry, "Broken Promises: Retirees Learn to Live without Pension Benefits," *The Wall Street Journal*, July 28, 1986, p. 25.

[8]See Dan Cordtz, "Gray Drain," *Financial World* (January 24, 1989), pp. 26–30. Cordtz discusses early retirement and whether the nation can afford it.

**TABLE 4-1   Size of Total Income Received by the
Aged 65 and Over, 1988**

	PERCENT OF UNITS
Under $5,000	14.1%
$5,000–9,999	27.8
$10,000–14,999	17.1
$15,000–19,999	12.4
$20,000–24,999	7.9
$25,000–29,999	5.6
$30,000–34,999	3.9
$35,000–39,999	3.1
$40,000–44,999	1.7
$45,000–49,999	1.2
$50,000 or more	5.5
Median income	$12,173

Source: Susan Grad, *Income of the Population Aged 65 and
Over,* Social Security Administration, Office of Research and
Statistics, Washington, D.C., March 9, 1990. The data shown
were presented by Susan Grad in testimony to the Advisory
Council on Social Security, March 9, 1990.

ly industrialized economy, the average person spends a relatively shorter period
preparing economically for a relatively longer retirement period.

Insufficient Income

Some aged persons also experience considerable economic insecurity because of
insufficient income. The incomes received often are insufficient for providing
them with a reasonable standard of living.

  Size of Income. It is a mistake to assume that all retired persons are
financially wealthy; it is equally wrong to assume that the aged as a group are
poor. *The aged are an economically diverse group, and the incomes received are far from
uniform.* This can be illustrated by Table 4-1 and Figure 4-1, which show the total
income received by the aged 65 and over in 1988. The data show that some aged
persons experience considerable economic insecurity. *Fourteen percent of the aged
units had incomes under $5,000 in 1988.* At the other extreme, a small proportion
of the aged has attained a substantially higher standard of living. *About 6 percent
of the aged units had incomes of $50,000 or more. The median income of all aged units was
approximately $12,000.*[9]

---

[9]Income data should be interpreted with caution, since there often is a significant underreporting of
actual income received.

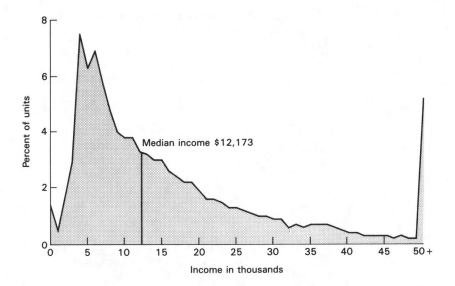

FIGURE 4-1 Size of Total Income Received by the Aged 65 and Over, 1988

Source: Susan Grad, *Income of the Population Aged 65 and Over,* Social Security Administration, Office of Research and Statistics, Washington, D.C., March 9, 1990.

The diversity in incomes among the aged can also be illustrated by comparing the total income received by selected groups of aged persons. Table 4-2 and Figure 4-2 show that married couples, aged persons under age 70, and whites are much better off financially than their counterparts. The median income of married couples was more than two-and-one-half times higher than the median income received by nonmarried persons. Many equivalence scales indicate that two persons need only one-fourth to one-third more income than one person. In addition, the median income of the aged 65–69 was two times higher than the income received by the aged 85 and over, and the median income of whites was considerably higher than the income received by Hispanics and blacks.

Source of Income. It is also important to analyze the various sources of income received by the aged to determine their relative importance. Figure 4-3 shows that the income of the aged in 1988 came largely from four major sources: Social Security, income from assets, work earnings, and pensions. These four sources accounted for 97 percent of the total income received by the aged. Social Security benefits were the most important and accounted for 38 percent of the total income received. Income from assets was the second most important source and accounted for 25 percent of the total income received. Work earnings and pensions each accounted for 17 percent of the total income received.

TABLE 4-2 **Median Total Income of the Aged 65 and Over, 1988**

	MEDIAN INCOME
Married	$20,305
Nonmarried	7,928
Aged 65–69	15,733
Aged 70–74	13,739
Aged 75–79	10,794
Aged 80–84	8,863
Aged 85+	7,830
White	13,117
Hispanic	7,266
Black	6,303

Souce: Susan Grad, *Income of the Population Aged 65 and Over,* Social Security Administration, Office of Research and Statistics, Washington, D.C., March 9, 1990.

FIGURE 4-2 **Median Total Income of the Aged 65 and Over, 1988**

Source: Susan Grad, *Income of the Population Aged 65 and Over,* Social Security Administration, Office of Research and Statistics, Washington, D.C., March 9, 1990.

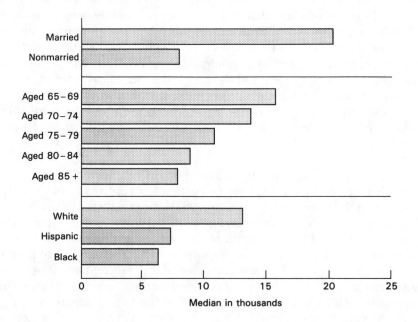

Median in thousands

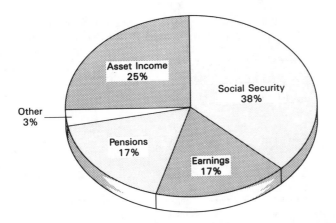

FIGURE 4-3   Share of Income Received by the Aged 65 and Over, 1988

Source: Susan Grad, *Income of the Population Aged 65 and Over,* Social Security Administration, Office of Research and Statistics, Washington, D.C., March 9, 1990.

Relative Importance of Each Income Source.   It is also important to consider the relative importance of each source of income to the aged. Table 4-3 and Figure 4-4 show the share of income received from major sources of income by income level for 1988.

The importance of each source of income to the aged differs significantly for the high- and low-income aged. Social Security and public assistance are the major sources of income for the low-income aged with incomes under $5,000. In contrast, asset income is the most important source of income for the high-income aged with incomes of $20,000 or more. Work earnings are the second most important source of income to this group. Social Security benefits and pension income are the third and fourth most important sources of income, respectively, to this group.

Assets of the Aged.   A complete analysis of the financial situation of the aged must also consider the total assets that they own. Although work earnings may terminate or be reduced at retirement, accumulated financial assets can be used to offset the loss of income. Financial assets can provide a cushion during retirement for emergencies and can also be used to supplement any retirement income.

Table 4-4 shows the net worth position of aged and nonaged households for 1984 (latest available data).[10] *The median net worth including equity in the home is*

---

[10]Net worth is defined as wealth less unsecured debt. Wealth consists of equity in an owner-occupied home, motor vehicles, business and professional property, real estate, and financial assets. Unsecured debt includes credit card and store bills; doctor, dentist, hospital, and nursing home bills; loans from financial institutions and individuals; and education loans.

TABLE 4-3 Relative Importance of Each Income Source to the Aged 65 and Over by Income Level, 1988

	UNDER $5,000	$20,000 OR MORE
Social Security	79%	23%
Asset Income	4	32
Pensions	3	20
Earnings	−1	24
SSI	14	0
Other	1	1

Source: Susan Grad, *Income of the Population Aged 65 and Over,* Social Security Administration, Office of Research and Statistics, Washington, D.C., March 9, 1990.

$59,680 for aged households and $32,600 for all households. Two points are worth noting in Table 4-4. First, the aged 65 or older as a group have a median net worth that is higher than the net worth of all other age groups except for the age 55–64 group. Second, it is a mistake to assume that the net worth position is satisfactory for all aged households. *There is a wide dispersion in wealth among the aged. Some aged have little or no wealth. Twenty percent of the aged households have a net worth that is negative or under $10,000. At the other extreme, 6 percent of the aged households have a net worth of $250,000 or more.*

Net worth also includes nonliquid assets that are not readily available for consumption purposes, such as equity in the home and the value of an automobile. Thus, a complete analysis of the financial position of the aged also must consider the value of any financial assets, such as checking and money market accounts, bonds, stocks, or IRAs. Financial assets can provide supplemental

FIGURE 4-4 Relative Importance of Each Income Source to the Aged 65 and Over by Income Level, 1988

Source: Susan Grad, *Income of the Population Aged 65 and Over,* Social Security Administration, Office of Research and Statistics, Washington, D.C., March 9, 1990.

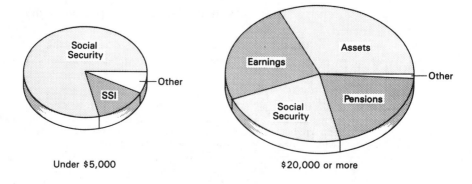

Under $5,000 $20,000 or more

TABLE 4-4 Percentage Distribution of Households by Net Worth and Age of Householder, 1984

NET WORTH	All ages	AGE					AGED 65 OR OLDER		
		Under 25	25–34	35–44	45–54	55–64	Total	65–74	75 or older
Total number of households (in millions)	86.9	5.7	20.1	17.4	12.6	12.9	18.2	10.7	7.5
Total percent	100	100	100	100	100	100	100	100	100
Negative or $0	11	26	17	10	8	5	7	7	6
$1–$9,999	21	55	35	18	12	11	13	11	15
$10,000–$24,999	12	12	18	13	11	8	9	9	10
$25,000–$49,999	15	4	14	18	14	14	16	15	17
$50,000–$99,999	20	2	10	21	25	26	26	26	25
$100,000–$249,999	16	1	4	15	22	27	24	25	23
$250,000 or more	4	(¹)	1	4	7	10	6	7	4
Median	$32,600	$2,160	$8,100	$35,500	$56,500	$72,460	$59,680	$62,060	$54,620

¹Less than 0.5 percent.

Source: Daniel B. Radner, "Net Worth and Financial Assets of Age Groups in 1984," *Social Security Bulletin,* Vol. 52, No. 3 (March 1989), Table 1, p. 5.

income during retirement and also provide a cushion during financial emergencies.

In general, the financial asset position of the majority of aged persons is far from satisfactory. Table 4-5 shows the distribution of financial assets by age of the household head for 1984. *The median value of financial assets is only $11,000 for households age 65 or older and $2,600 for all households.* In addition, there is also a wide dispersion in financial assets owned by the elderly. A large proportion of aged households have little or no financial assets. *Almost half of the aged households owned less than $10,000 in financial assets.* At the other extreme, 8 percent of the aged households owned financial assets of $100,000 or more.

There are several reasons for the unsatisfactory financial asset position of some retired workers. First, some workers are unaware of their future retirement needs and undersave for their old age. Second, many workers experience extended periods of unemployment during their working careers, which deplete their financial assets. Third, early retirement has increased, which reduces the period of productive employment. As a result, total potential earned income is reduced, and the amount of income that is available for saving is also reduced. Fourth, many retired workers are employed at low wages during their working careers and are unable to save substantial amounts for their old age. Finally, inflation, high income taxes, poor health or personal misfortune, and the influence of advertising also help to explain the relatively low financial asset position of many retired workers.

Poverty among the Aged. It is also worthwhile to determine the extent of poverty among the aged. In 1987, 32.5 million Americans or 13.5 percent of the population were living in poverty. The incidence of poverty, however, is somewhat lower for the aged as a group. However, the incidence of poverty is significantly higher for minority groups, especially elderly women. The following illustrates the extent of poverty in 1987 for selected categories of aged persons.[11]

	PERCENT OF TOTAL
Total population poor	13.5%
Age 65 and over poor	12.2
Black men, heads of households, age 65 and over poor	18.7
Black men, unrelated individuals, age 65 and over poor	42.2
White men, heads of households, age 65 and over poor	5.0
White men, unrelated individuals, age 65 and over poor	15.6
Black women, wives, age 65 and over poor	19.5
Black women, unrelated individuals, age 65 and over poor	62.8
White women, wives, age 65 and over poor	4.7
White women, unrelated individuals, age 65 and over poor	21.9

Finally, a serious problem of poverty exists for a large proportion of aged women who are divorced, separated, or widowed. In 1987, 26 percent of

---

[11]*Background Material and Data on Programs within the Jurisdiction of the Committee on Ways and Means,* 1989, Table 6, p. 915.

TABLE 4-5 Percentage Distribution of Households, by Financial Assets and Age of Householder, 1984

FINANCIAL ASSETS	All ages	AGE — Under 25	25–34	35–44	45–54	55–64	AGED 65 OR OLDER — Total	65–74	75 or older
Total	100	100	100	100	100	100	100	100	100
$0	15	26	19	13	13	12	12	13	11
$1–$999	24	46	34	26	19	14	13	13	13
$1,000–$9,999	30	25	34	34	32	23	23	21	26
$10,000–$24,999	13	3	8	13	14	17	15	16	14
$25,000–$49,999	8	1	3	7	10	14	14	15	13
$50,000–$99,999	7	(1)	1	4	7	11	15	14	16
$100,000 or more	4	(1)	1	2	4	8	8	8	7
Median[2]	$2,600	$350	$800	$2,160	$4,150	$10,000	$11,000	$11,900	$10,100

[1] Less than 0.5 percent.
[2] For all households in the group.

Source: Daniel B. Radner, "Net Worth and Financial Assets of Age Groups in 1984," *Social Security Bulletin*, Vol. 52, No. 3 (March 1989), Table 2, p. 6. Because of rounding, the sum of the columns may not total 100.

the divorced or separated women and 20 percent of the widows age 65 and over were living in poverty.[12]

Comparison of the Aged and Nonaged.   It is also worthwhile to compare the financial position of the aged and nonaged to determine if the aged are better or worse off financially. Two problems arise when the incomes of the aged are compared with the nonaged. First, aged households typically are smaller in size than nonaged households; thus, an adjustment for the number of household members is necessary. Second, the aged receive preferential tax treatment; thus, a comparison of incomes on an after-tax basis also is necessary.

There adjustments are reflected in Table 4-6, which shows the average amount of income per household member on a before-and-after tax basis for various age groups for 1980 and 1986. In general, the average income per household member of aged households compares favorably with nonaged households. *The average after-tax income per household member in households headed by older persons age 65 and over is greater than the average after-tax income of household members in households headed by younger individuals ages 15 through 44.* However, if we drop down to the age 60–64 group, which includes a large proportion of early retirees, the relative income position improves sharply. *The average after-tax income of household members in households headed by older persons ages 60–64 is greater than the average after-tax income of all nonaged household members.* In short, on an after-tax basis, the average income of older persons compares very favorably with average income received by younger persons.

Finally, it is also worthwhile to compare the net worth and financial asset position of the aged and nonaged. Table 4-7 shows the median net worth and financial assets of aged and nonaged households for 1984 (latest available data). Except for the age 55–64 group, the age 65 and over group has a higher median net worth than any other age group. In addition, we noted earlier that the financial assets owned by the elderly are relatively low. *Nevertheless, the median financial assets owned by the age 65 and over group are still higher than any other age group.*

Summary.   Based on the preceding analysis, the financial position of the aged can be summarized as follows:

1. The aged as a group are neither wealthy nor poor but are an economically diverse group. In 1988, 14 percent of the aged units had incomes under $5,000, while about 6 percent received $50,000 or more. The median income was slightly in excess of $12,000.
2. The major sources of income to the aged are Social Security, income from assets, work earnings, and pensions. These four sources accounted for 97 percent of the total income received by the aged in 1988.
3. There is a wide dispersion in wealth among the aged. Twenty percent of the aged households have a net worth that is negative or under $10,000. In contrast, 6 percent of the aged households have a net worth of $250,000 or more.

---

[12]Ibid., Table 7, p. 916.

TABLE 4-6 Mean Real Income Before and After Taxes per Household Member, 1980 and 1986

	1980[1] INCOME PER HOUSEHOLD MEMBER		TAXES AS A PERCENT OF INCOME	1986 INCOME PER HOUSEHOLD MEMBER		TAXES AS A PERCENT OF INCOME	AFTER TAX PERCENT CHANGE 1980–86
	Before taxes	After taxes		Before taxes	After taxes		
Age of householder:							
15–24	$ 8,419	$ 6,855	18.6%	$ 7,865	$ 6,452	18.0%	−5.9%
25–29	9,601	7,492	22.0	10,206	7,953	22.1	6.2
30–34	9,276	7,091	23.6	10,184	7,775	23.7	9.6
35–39	9,302	6,983	24.9	10,750	8,082	24.8	15.7
40–44	9,709	7,272	25.1	11,699	8,771	25.0	20.6
45–49	10,853	8,093	25.4	12,993	9,639	25.8	19.1
50–54	11,890	8,846	25.6	13,861	10,293	25.7	16.4
55–59	13,596	10,076	25.9	14,259	10,673	25.1	5.9
60–64	12,830	9,882	23.0	14,211	10,872	23.5	10.0
65 and over	9,638	8,381	13.0	11,285	9,574	15.2	14.2
All households	10,272	7,936	22.7	11,552	8,894	23.0	12.1

[1]In 1986 dollars.

Source: U.S. Congress, House, Committee on Ways and Means, *Background Material and Data on Programs within the Jurisdiction of the Committee on Ways and Means* (Washington, D.C.: U.S. Government Printing Office, 1989), Table 19, p. 931.

4. The financial assets accumulated by the majority of aged persons are relatively low. The median value of financial assets was only $11,000 in 1984, which excludes equity in the home.

5. The incidence of poverty among the aged is less than for the total population. However, the incidence of poverty for aged minority groups and for aged women who are divorced, separated, or widowed is significantly higher than for the total population.

6. On an after-tax basis, the average income per household member in households headed by older persons age 60 and older compares favorably with younger households. The aged generally have attained a median net worth and financial asset position superior to that of the nonaged.

TABLE 4-7 Median Net Worth and Financial Assets for Aged and Nonaged Households, 1984

AGE OF HOUSEHOLDER	MEDIAN NET WORTH	MEDIAN FINANCIAL ASSETS
Under 25	$2,160	$350
25–34	8,100	800
35–44	35,500	2,160
45–54	56,500	4,150
55–64	72,460	10,000
Age 65 or older	59,680	11,000

Source: Calculated from Daniel B. Radner, "Net Worth and Financial Assets of Age Groups in 1984," *Social Security Bulletin,* Vol. 52, No. 3 (March 1989), Table 1, p. 5 and Table 2, p. 6.

Poor Health

Another part of the problem of old age is that older Americans as a group are in poorer health than the general population. Older people see physicians more frequently, are more likely to become disabled, and have longer hospital stays. The health problems of the aged can be broken down into two categories: (1) chronic conditions and (2) long-term care.

Chronic Conditions.   Many older people have one or more chronic conditions that require continuing medical treatment. Some common chronic conditions are arthritis, hearing impairments, heart disease, diabetes, cataracts, high blood pressure, and deformity or orthopedic impairment. Although covered by Medicare, some older persons have difficulty in paying their medical bills. Medicare pays considerably less than the full cost of care, and many elderly must pay sizable amounts out-of-pocket because of a chronic health condition.

In addition, some aged persons experience extreme depression and commit suicide. After years of decline, the suicide rate is rising for older Americans in the United States. Older Americans commit suicide more frequently than adolescents, and the suicide rate is more than 50 percent higher than that of the general population. Experts believe that the increase in the suicide rate is due to lack of money; rapid urbanization and technological change that can make some older people feel useless; merger-related forced retirements; cutbacks in pensions and benefits; increased acceptance of the idea that terminally ill people should be able to take their own lives; and growth of right-to-die groups, such as the Hemlock Society.[13]

Long-term Care.   Many elderly persons face serious financial problems because they need long-term care in a nursing home. Approximately 1.3 million elderly persons, or 5 percent of the elderly population, resided in nursing homes in 1985. When broken down by age, residents age 85 and older comprise the largest group (46 percent), followed next by those age 75–84 (39 percent), and finally by those age 65–74 (15 percent). Older nursing home residents also are predominantly female (almost 77 percent) because of a longer life expectancy and the greater probability of a person in poor health and with no spouse present to enter a nursing home.[14]

Most older residents in nursing homes are there because of incontinence, severe dementia (memory loss and memory disorders), immobility from a hip fracture or arthritis, and senility. In addition, many nursing home residents have Alzheimer's disease. More than 2.6 million persons in the United States have Alzheimer's disease, and half the cases occur after age 80.

---

[13]Earl C. Gottschalk, Jr., "Ending It All: After Years of Decline, Suicide Rate Is Rising among Elderly in U.S.," *The Wall Street Journal,* July 30, 1986, p. 1.

[14]*Background Material and Data on Programs within the Jurisdiction of the Committee on Ways and Means,* 1989, p. 232.

The cost of long-term care in a nursing facility is staggering. Many skilled nursing facilities charge $35,000 or more annually for care. The Medicare program provides only limited assistance in paying for long-term care. Care in a skilled nursing facility is limited to a maximum of 100 days, and custodial care is excluded altogether. Some aged may qualify for assistance under the Medicaid program. However, Medicaid is not a satisfactory solution since a stringent means test must be met, and the eligibility requirements are complex. Most aged do not qualify for long-term care under the Medicaid program unless they are willing to spend down their assets so that a means test can be met. Thus, it is not surprising that many aged persons are reduced to poverty because of the cost of long-term care. The Joint Economic Committee states that one-third of the near-poor elderly are reduced to poverty by their out-of-pocket expenses for medical care, including the cost of long-term care.[15]

Finally, the involuntary relocation of the frail elderly to nursing homes is traumatic and often results in death. Several research studies indicate that the mortality rate among the elderly increases sharply before and after a physical move.[16]

Heavy Property Taxes

Although a large proportion of aged homeowners have their homes paid for by the time they retire, the property taxes they must pay can be a heavy financial burden. The result is that some aged homeowners on limited incomes must give up their homes or liquidate some financial assets to pay these taxes. In many cases, the low-income aged are unable to locate suitable alternate housing at rents they can afford to pay.

In addition, many retired aged, especially the low-income and poverty-stricken aged, do not own their homes but must rent. The property taxes are merely shifted from the landlords to the tenants in the form of higher rents. Although aged homeowners may receive personal income tax relief because of property tax deductions, aged renters cannot take advantage of this deduction even though they are paying the property taxes in the form of higher rents. In recognition of the heavy property tax burden on the aged, most states today provide for full or partial property tax relief to low-income aged homeowners.

Inflation

A rapid increase in consumer prices can also cause considerable financial hardship to the aged. The costs of food, housing, clothing, medical care, and energy

---

[15]*A Staff Report Summarizing the Hearings on "The Future of Health Care in America,"* Prepared for the Subcommittee on Education and Health, Joint Economic Committee, October 2, 1989, p. iv.

[16]Statement of James Thorson, professor of gerontology, University of Nebraska at Omaha, before the legislature's Health and Human Services Committee, as reported in the *Omaha World Herald,* January 29, 1986, p. 24.

have substantially increased over time. Because of more limited income, the aged tend to spend a higher proportion of their income on food, compared with the general population.

In addition, medical expenses have increased sharply over time. Although the aged have considerable protection against catastrophic medical expenses under the Medicare program, certain important expenditures are excluded. Medicare covers less than half of the total medical expenses incurred by the aged. In particular, prescription drugs outside of hospitals, eyeglasses and hearing aids, and false teeth—items necessary for their health and well-being—are not covered, and their purchase can cause a serious dent in the budget of a low-income household. Finally, long-term custodial care in nursing homes is also excluded from Medicare. Thus, rapid inflation in medical costs can also erode the economic security position of the aged.

Other Financial Problems

The aged are subject to other financial problems that add to their economic insecurity. Low-cost housing generally is in short supply. Lack of adequate transportation is another problem: many aged persons cannot afford automobiles, and public transportation may be inadequate, especially in smaller communities. And the aged are often exploited by unscrupulous entrepreneurs, who promote land sales or home repairs, and by deceptive health insurance advertising.

Abuse of the Elderly

A final part of the problem of old age is abuse of the elderly. An increasing number of aged persons report being abused. The abuse can be in the form of neglect, physical abuse, financial exploitation, emotional abuse, or sexual abuse. One estimate is that one in 25 older adults is abused.[17] In 1988, 140,000 cases of abuse of older persons were reported nationally, up 10 percent from 1987. It is estimated, however, that only one in 14 cases is reported.[18] Most abusers are adult children or other relatives, spouses, providers of services, friends, and neighbors. In many cases, the abusers have serious personal problems, such as drug or alcohol addiction, money problems, mental illness, or unemployment. In some cases, the abusers, such as an adult son or daughter, may have been the victims of violence in their youth.

This concludes our discussion of the nature of the economic problem of older age for workers who have retired. Let us next consider the employment problems of older workers who are near retirement.

---

[17]Barbara Metzler, "Increasing Number of Elderly Being Abused," *Lincoln Journal*, August 12, 1989, p. 11.
[18]Ibid.

EMPLOYMENT PROBLEMS OF OLDER WORKERS

The economic problems of old age cannot be separated from the employment problems of older workers. The economic insecurity experienced by some aged people can be traced directly to the employment problems they experienced prior to their retirement. Thus, many older workers carry into old age the economic insecurity problems, including the loss of income and insufficient income, that they were experiencing for years prior to their actual retirement.

Although age 65 is thought to mark the beginning of old age, the employment problems of workers over 45 must also be considered. This age usually marks the beginning of an increase in withdrawals from the labor force, a decline in weekly and annual earnings, a lengthening of the duration of unemployment, and an increase in part-time work and part-time workers. These factors tend to increase in importance for subsequently older age groups. The employment problems of older workers can be summarized as follows.[19]

1. *Declining Labor Force Participation Rate.* The labor force participation rate declines after age 45 and declines even more rapidly as older workers approach age 65. The declining labor force participation rate for older workers is due to voluntary retirement, availability of private pensions and Social Security benefits, poor health and the availability of disability payments, dislocated older workers who cannot find jobs and retire, and the desire for leisure.

2. *Longer Duration of Unemployment.* Although older workers have lower unemployment rates, the duration of unemployment is considerably longer. Older workers have seniority rights and are less likely to leave their jobs voluntarily, which helps explain the lower unemployment rates. If older workers become unemployed, however, the duration of unemployment is usually longer than for younger workers.

3. *Age Discrimination in Employment.* Age discrimination in employment also exists. The Equal Employment Opportunity Commission receives numerous age discrimination complaints, which are a significant part of its overall caseload. Male workers complain about the refusal of firms to hire older workers and discrimination in employee benefits. Female workers complain about denials of promotion, training, and wage increases.

4. *Obsolescence in Job Skills.* Earnings of full-time workers generally increase until age 50 and then level off. This can be partly explained by the obsolescence in job skills of many older workers. Older workers near retirement generally have fewer financial incentives to participate in training programs that would upgrade their work skills.

5. *Dislocated Older Workers.* Many older workers have permanently lost their jobs because of competition from foreign countries, structural changes in basic industries such as automobiles and steel, shifts from manufacturing jobs to service jobs, and massive layoffs during the 1981–82 recession. Many plants have closed,

---

[19]See National Commission for Employment Policy, *Older Workers: Prospects, Problems and Policies, 9th Annual Report* (Washington, D.C.: National Commission for Employment Policy, 1985). See also Michael E. Borus, Herbert S. Parnes, Steven H. Sandell, and Bert Seidman, eds., *The Older Worker* (Madison: Industrial Relations Research Association, University of Wisconsin, 1988).

or permanent reductions in the work force have been made. As a result, the local economy may be depressed, and job opportunities at high wages for displaced older workers may be limited.

6. *Displaced Homemakers.* Displaced homemakers are older women who have spent most of their adult lifetime as homemakers and are suddenly forced to enter the job market because of divorce or death of their husbands. Displaced homemakers generally lack marketable skills for high-paying jobs and must often accept lower-paying positions.

7. *Older Minority Workers.* Older minority workers have serious labor market problems. A labor market problem is a combination of a low-income job and unemployment or underemployment. Older blacks and Hispanics are more likely to have labor market problems than white workers.

8. *Health Problems.* Older workers have more health problems than younger workers. The earnings of health-impaired individuals usually decline relative to other workers as age increases. Also, poor health is a reason for early retirement.

9. *Less Mobility.* Older workers are less mobile than younger workers. Older workers are less likely to move voluntarily from one job, residence, or occupation to another. The unwillingness to relocate geographically to another area often makes it difficult for them to find new jobs. Older workers often prefer to remain in high unemployment areas rather than relocate because of homes, families, friends, and emotional attachment to the area.

ATTACKING THE ECONOMIC PROBLEM OF OLD AGE

Numerous private and public techniques are currently used to meet the economic problem of old age. We shall consider the most important approaches: (1) continued employment, (2) retirement planning programs, (3) Social Security benefits, (4) private pensions and other government pension plans, (5) individual retirement accounts, (6) Supplemental Security Income, (7) Age Discrimination in Employment Act of 1967, (8) tax relief, and (9) new techniques.

Continued Employment

Studies indicate that many older workers have a definite need for additional income and wish to continue working, at least on a part-time or intermittent basis. It is worthwhile, therefore, to examine some employment policies that can be applied as alternatives to complete retirement for older workers.

Part-time Employment. Part-time employment beyond age 65 is a valuable technique for meeting the economic problem of old age. Part-time employment permits many older persons to work and supplement their limited retirement incomes. Poor health or the desire for leisure may make full-time work relatively unattractive to older workers; however, many of them can work part time and can make a valuable contribution to the sustaining and strengthening of our economic system. The income from part-time employment often means the difference between a poverty level and a relatively higher standard of living.

Gradual Retirement. Gradual retirement is another approach to the economic problem of old age. Under this concept, employment is not abruptly terminated by retirement; instead, partial employment and partial retirement are combined so that older workers can obtain the advantages of both continued employment and retirement.

Numerous approaches to gradual retirement are possible. First, the older worker can be given an extended leave in the last year or longer time off each year for a period of three to five years prior to retirement. Or the worker may be permitted to transfer to less demanding work or to part-time employment; many firms can accommodate older workers in this manner without a formal designation of the workload as gradual retirement.

Finally, for professional workers and executives, gradual retirement may take the form of rehiring them after retirement on a temporary basis, to perform specific jobs for which their talents qualify them. The older employees benefit, since they can accept work on terms that suit them. And management also benefits, since the younger workers can be promoted, yet the employer can retain the services and skills of valuable employees; in addition, management can provide employment only for those workers considered valuable.

Retirement Planning Programs

To help prepare a worker for eventual retirement, many firms today provide some form of preretirement training program or advice to retiring workers. The programs provide useful information to workers about to retire, usually covering such topics as financial planning for retirement, money management, physical aspects of aging, mental health in later years, increasing retirement income, housing and nutrition problems, living arrangements in later life, and the use of leisure time.

Postretirement adjustment is often closely related to the preretirement training. Older workers are seldom aware of the extensive changes that will occur after retirement. The decision to retire may present a considerable amount of uncertainty, and the necessary adjustments to retirement are more easily made if these uncertainties are removed. Counseling by trained experts in gerontology can often make the difference between successful and unsuccessful retirement.

Social Security Benefits

Both OASDI retirement benefits and Medicare benefits are extremely important in promoting economic security for the aged. The retirement benefits reduce the problem of the loss of earned income from retirement, while the Medicare program helps meet the problem of additional expenses in old age because of high medical costs.

OASDI Retirement Benefits. As we noted earlier, OASDI retirement benefits are the most important single source of income to most aged persons. The benefits provide an important base of income protection to the elderly. OASDI benefits are especially important in reducing poverty among the aged. In 1986, 14 percent of the aged units 65 or older whose families received OASDI benefits were counted poor. If OASDI benefits had not been paid, the percentage counted poor would have increased sharply to 51 percent.[20]

Medicare Benefits.   Almost all aged Americans have health insurance protection under the Medicare program, which relieves them and their children of a major portion of the financial burden of poor health in their old age. But since older persons under age 65 are generally ineligible for these benefits, and since many older workers retire early, the problem of medical expenses for those within the early retirement category can be especially acute. The Medicare program is analyzed later in Chapter 9, when the economic problem of poor health among the aged is discussed in greater detail.

Private Pensions and Other Government Pension Plans

Private pensions and other government pension plans are also important for meeting the problem of economic insecurity during retirement, especially for those workers with average or above-average earnings. Pension plans have an important macroeconomic impact on the economy. The pension contributions are an important source of private savings; they affect economic growth; and pension fund investments have an enormous influence on the financial markets and concentration of economic power. Finally, pension plans have a significant impact on the redistribution of income, labor mobility, early retirement, and employment opportunities for older persons.

Although private pensions and other government retirement programs provide an additional layer of income to retired persons, fewer than half of the aged receive benefits from these programs. In 1987, only 41 percent of the units with all members age 65 or over reported receiving income from a pension plan (other than OASDI and Railroad Retirement).[21] However, for those persons who receive a second pension in addition to OASDI, their average monthly incomes are substantially higher than those persons who have no source of income other than OASDI. For example, during the third quarter of 1984, the mean monthly income for OASDI beneficiaries with no other source of income was only $372. However, for persons who received both OASDI benefits and a private pension,

---

[20]Susan Grad, *Income of the Population 55 or Older, 1986,* Social Security Administration, Office of Policy, Office of Research and Statistics (June 1988), Table 53, p. 101.

[21]*Background Material and Data on Programs within the Jurisdiction of the Committee on Ways and Means,* 1989, Table 13, p. 923.

the mean monthly income was $826, or 122 percent higher.[22] Thus, the receipt of a second pension often makes the difference between living in poverty and a higher standard of living.

Private Pension Problems. Although pension plans have great potential for reducing economic insecurity among the aged, certain problems must be resolved. They include the following:[23]

1. LACK OF COVERAGE. The most serious problem facing retirement programs today is the lack of pension coverage for millions of workers. Only 46 percent of the full-time private sector employees were participating in an employer-financed pension plan in 1988.[24] Workers who are not covered are largely employees in small firms, in nonunion retail trade and service industries, and in agriculture.

In addition, large numbers of women are not covered by pension plans. Many women enter and leave the labor force several times during their working careers because of family responsibilities, and they often are not employed long enough to qualify for a pension. Also, many married women are employed in low-wage trade and service industries, where the pension coverage is incomplete.

The President's Commission on Pension Policy believes that the proportion of the labor force covered by private pension plans will not increase significantly in the future under current policies. The lack of pension coverage in many small business firms is the major reason why growth in private pension plans is expected to stagnate. Pension plans are costly, and small firms frequently have narrow profit margins and operate in a highly competitive environment. Thus, because of cost, many small firms cannot afford to install pension plans.

2. LOWER BENEFITS FOR WOMEN. In addition to incomplete coverage, women are more likely to receive lower private pension benefits than men. During the third quarter of 1984, the mean monthly private pension benefit paid to women was only $221, which was 50 percent lower than the corresponding benefit paid to men ($442) during the same time period.[25] This difference can be explained by both the lower earnings of women when compared with male earnings and the shorter average period of coverage. Women are more likely than men to be working in lower-paying occupations, and their earnings increase less rapidly than men's earnings. Also, as we noted earlier, women are in and out of the labor force more frequently than the men because of family

[22]*Social Security Bulletin*, Vol. 49, No. 3 (March 1986), Table 3, p. 21.

[23]See President's Commission on Pension Policy, *Coming of Age: Toward a National Retirement Income Policy* (Washington, D.C.: President's Commission on Pension Policy, 1981).

[24]John R. Woods, "Pension Coverage among Private Wage and Salary Workers: Preliminary Findings from the 1988 Survey of Employee Benefits," *Social Security Bulletin*, Vol. 52, No. 10 (October 1989), p. 2.

[25]*Social Security Bulletin*, Vol. 49, No. 3 (March 1986), Table 2, p. 20.

responsibilities. Since private pension benefits are related to work earnings and length of service, women generally receive lower monthly benefits than men. Thus, other factors being equal, economic insecurity for older women is likely to be higher because of an inadequate pension.

3. LIMITED PROTECTION AGAINST INFLATION. Most pension plans provide limited protection against inflation. The result is that the real purchasing power of the benefits declines during a period of rapidly rising prices. For example, a 10 percent annual inflation rate will reduce the real purchasing power of a $500 monthly benefit to $195 in 10 years. Although most private pension plans have adjusted benefits for inflation within the past decade, the average adjustment was considerably less than the rate of inflation.

The primary obstacle to full protection against inflation is cost. An inflation hedge of 1 percent annually will increase the cost of the plan by about 10 percent. Thus, because of prohibitive costs, most pension plans do not provide complete protection against inflation.

4. PROBLEMS IN ACCUMULATING PENSION FUNDS. Pension plans control significant amounts of financial assets. In late 1989, pension fund assets totaled $2.6 trillion.[26] Numerous public policy questions, largely unresolved, are associated with this vast pool of funds. These problems include the recapture of excess pension assets by employers whose pension plans are actuarially overfunded; the legal ownership of pension funds; whether employees should have greater participation in determining how pension funds are invested; the parties that should have the legal right to vote the common stock shares of companies in which the funds are invested; whether pension funds should be invested in programs to achieve certain "social goals," such as assuring human rights, providing housing to pension plan members, improving human relations, and protecting the environment; the impact of pension policy on the level and allocation of capital in the economy; and the relationship between pension fund investments and concentration of economic power because of investments in large firms. These questions are not completely resolved at the present time and are beyond the scope of the text. Nevertheless, they are important public policy questions that must be answered if pension plans are to function effectively as economic security tools in the future.

5. ABUSES IN DISABILITY INCOME. Several problems are also caused by the lack of coordination between disability income and retirement programs. The President's Commission on Pension Policy points out that, in some cases, disability programs are misused as old-age retirement programs, while in other cases, the opposite is true—retirement programs are being misused as disability programs. For example, some workers take early retirement when they should be retiring under a disability program. This is especially true under the OASDI program. As we pointed out earlier, many persons retire early because of poor

---

[26]"The Power of the Pension Funds," *Business Week* (November 6, 1989), p. 154.

health and apply for early retirement benefits. They really should be receiving benefits under a private disability income program or, if they qualify, under the disability income portion of the OASDI program. Since they retire early, their retirement benefits are actually reduced, which often results in inadequate retirement income.

Individual Retirement Accounts

An individual retirement account (IRA) also can provide supplementary retirement income to retired persons. Prior to 1987, anyone with earned income could establish an IRA and make an annual tax deductible contribution of up to $2,000 ($2,250 with a nonworking spouse). The amounts contributed were fully deductible for federal income tax purposes. The investment income on the contributions also accumulated income tax free.

However, as a result of the tax reform law of 1986, eligibility for a fully deductible IRA contribution is reduced significantly. In general, there are three classes of workers:

1. Workers not covered by an employer-sponsored pension plan can make annual IRA contributions that are fully deductible up to the maximum limit of $2,000 ($2,250 with a nonworking spouse). The same holds true for workers who are covered under a pension plan but have an adjusted gross income of $25,000 or less ($40,000 for couples).
2. Workers covered by a pension plan who have an adjusted gross income between $25,000 and $35,000 (between $40,000 and $50,000 for couples) receive a partial IRA deduction. As income increases, the maximum IRA contribution is reduced. For example, a single person earning $30,000 could make a tax deductible IRA contribution of up to $1,000.
3. Workers with an adjusted gross income of $35,000 or more ($50,000 for couples) can make an annual IRA contribution of up to $2,000 but receive no income tax deduction on the amounts contributed. However, the investment income accumulates income tax free until withdrawn.

Since the federal income tax advantages of an IRA plan are substantially reduced, the new tax law discourages additional saving for retirement by middle-income and upper-income taxpayers. The new law, however, has little or no impact on low-income workers who need all of their income just to survive. Thus, the problem of providing additional income to low-income persons not covered under a pension plan still remains.

Supplemental Security Income

The aged may also be eligible for monthly income benefits under the Supplemental Security Income (SSI) program for the aged, blind, and disabled. The SSI program, which became effective in January 1974, replaced the former state-federal public assistance programs of Old-Age Assistance, Aid to the Blind, and Aid to the Permanently and Totally Disabled.

As of January 1990, the SSI program guaranteed a minimum monthly income of $386 to an eligible individual with no other source of income and $579 to a couple. To qualify for benefits, an aged applicant must be 65 or over and meet the needs test. The limits are $2,000 in financial assets for an individual and $3,000 for a couple. In determining eligibility, a home is excluded, regardless of its value. Also excluded are personal and household goods with an equity value of up to $2,000, an automobile with a current market value of up to $4,500, and up to $1,500 in burial funds ($3,000 for a couple).

The SSI program is part of the overall system of public assistance in the United States. The SSI program is analyzed in greater detail in Chapters 16 and 17.

Age Discrimination in Employment Act of 1967

The federal Age Discrimination in Employment Act of 1967 is also designed to reduce the economic problem of old age. The law prohibits employers, employment agencies, and labor unions from discriminating against older workers in hiring, discharge, compensation, and other terms of employment. With certain exceptions, the original act applied to workers between ages 40 and 65. The act was later amended in 1977 to extend protection against age discrimination in employment to workers up to age 70 and eliminated the upper age limit entirely for most federal workers.

The act was again amended in 1986, and mandatory retirement at any age was prohibited. Certain groups were temporarily excluded from the act for seven years, such as police officers, firefighters, prison guards, and tenured academic faculty.

Despite the existence of the Age Discrimination in Employment Act, numerous older workers still report age discrimination. Although hard data on actual age discrimination are difficult to obtain, complaints from older workers indicate that age discrimination is still present. Common violations reported include illegal advertising, refusal to hire, and refusal to promote. Stronger law enforcement by both the federal and state governments undoubtedly can do much to reduce future age discrimination in employment.

Tax Relief

Various tax relief programs may benefit retired workers. Under the personal income tax, the aged receive favorable tax treatment, such as an additional standard deduction for persons age 65 or older (generally $800 if single and $650 if married), retirement income credit for low-income persons, and favorable income tax treatment when a home is sold. Also, the state may provide property tax relief or a homestead exemption. The tax relief may be in the form of a reduction in the assessed value of the home or a tax credit or tax rebate, usually on the income tax return.

New Techniques

Several new techniques are emerging that should reduce the economic problem of old age. They include reverse mortgages, elder-care benefits, and long-term care insurance.

Reverse Mortgages. Although many aged have relatively low money incomes, they frequently own their homes or have a large equity in them. Some financial institutions are now making reverse mortgages available to aged home-owners. *A reverse mortgage is a financial instrument by which aged homeowners can convert part of the equity in their homes into a steady stream of income while still living in the homes.* A mortgage loan is obtained on the home, which is used to liquidate the equity in the home. For example, a homeowner would obtain a mortgage loan from a financial institution equal to a certain percentage of the home, such as 75 percent. The loan can be for life or for a fixed period. The interest rate can be fixed or variable. As the monthly payments accumulate, the amount of the loan increases. The mortgage loan must be paid off at some future date when the homeowner dies or at the expiration of the fixed term. At that time, the house is sold and the loan paid off, or the loan is renegotiated.

Some reverse mortgages have a provision for shared appreciation by which the lender is entitled to part of the appreciation in the value of the home instead of a fixed interest rate on the loan. For example, if the original loan is equal to 30 percent of the home's value, the lender is entitled to 30 percent of the increase in value from the date of the loan until the home is sold.

The Department of Housing and Urban Development (HUD) initiated a pilot program of reverse mortgages in 1989. Under the pilot program, HUD will insure reverse mortgages that fall into the following three categories:

- Tenure loans in which the homeowner receives a fixed monthly amount for as long as he or she occupies the house as a principal residence.
- Term loans that have a definite repayment rate, such as five or 10 years.
- Line-of-credit loans that allow homeowners to borrow the equity in the home in an amount and frequency of their own choosing, up to some maximum limit.

For example, a 75-year-old widow with a $100,000 debt-free house, 10 percent interest, and no appreciation sharing would qualify for lifetime monthly payments of $357. The maximum monthly payments would be $510 on a 10-year term loan and $812 on a five-year loan.[27] The monthly payments would be larger by sharing future appreciation with the lender.

Reverse mortgages have great potential for reducing economic insecurity during the period of retirement since additional income is paid to older homeowners. However, on the negative side, reverse mortgages have several important disadvantages that must be recognized. First, reverse mortgages are

---

[27]Kenneth Harney, "Reverse Mortgages Set to Aid Older Homeowners," *Sunday World Herald,* June 18, 1989, p. 4-F.

complex financial instruments that are difficult to understand. Second, older retired persons as a group are reluctant to go into debt, and reverse mortgages are not likely to appeal to large numbers of older retired homeowners. Third, reverse-mortgage borrowers face the risk of giving too much away in shared appreciation in those geographical areas where real estate inflation is occurring. Fourth, the fixed monthly payments can be quickly eroded during a period of rapid inflation. Finally, if a term loan is too short, the homeowner may outlive the loan and be forced to sell the house while he or she is still alive.

Elder-Care Benefits. Employees often must care for aged parents or older relatives. Employees may provide financial help or provide assistance in eating, bathing, dressing, and other household duties if the parent or relative is sick. As a result, some employees may experience severe emotional and physical stress, job performance may decline, and overtime may be refused. Some employees are forced to quit their jobs, and others refuse promotions or transfer to a new location. In addition, because of labor mobility, some employees are hundreds of miles away from the home of an ailing parent or relative, which aggravates the problem. The substantial increase of working women with children who are in the labor force also aggravates the problem, since women are the traditional caregivers for sick parents or relatives. In many cases, a working woman with her own family to raise can experience severe emotional, physical, and financial stress in caring for an aged parent or relative.

To assist employees who must care for older adults, employers increasingly are establishing elder-care programs that provide some assistance. Although elder-care programs vary among employers, common benefits include flexibility in work hours, extended and generous leaves of absence, job sharing, employee assistance programs, flexible spending accounts that allow employees to pay for certain elder-care benefits with before-tax dollars, and counseling and referral services. As a result, the needed care can be provided more easily, stress is reduced, and job performance is improved.

Long-Term Care Insurance. A growing number of insurers are now making available long-term care policies that provide coverage for nursing home care, home care, and other benefits. A 1988 survey indicated that the number of insurers selling long-term care contracts has increased sixfold from 1984 to 1988, and the number of persons who purchase the coverage is increasing. In addition, the quality of the newer long-term policies has improved significantly. More than nine out of 10 policies require no prior hospitalization before nursing home care is covered; all policies are guaranteed renewable; more than 70 percent of the policies provide a means by which the coverage can be increased to compensate for inflation; and 40 percent offer coverage for adult day care.[28] Custodial care is also covered in many policies.

---

[28]"Long-Term Care Insurance: Market Trends," *Benefits Quarterly,* Vol. 5, No. 4 (Fourth Quarter 1989), p. 92.

Although long-term care insurance can reduce the crushing financial burden from an extended stay in a nursing home, the policies are expensive to purchase. Annual premiums for an aged couple can easily cost $2,000 or more annually. Thus, many aged persons with limited incomes cannot afford the coverage. Moreover, the existence of a preexisting medical condition may be grounds for rejection.

SUGGESTIONS FOR ADDITIONAL READING

AARON, HENRY J., "Costs of the Aging Population: Real and Imagined Burdens." In Henry J. Aaron, ed., *Social Security and the Budget, Proceedings of the First Conference of the National Academy of Social Insurance*. Lanham, Md.: The National Academy of Social Insurance and University Press of America, 1990, pp. 51–61.

ANDREWS, EMILY S., AND OLIVIA S. MITCHELL. "The Current and Future Role of Pensions in Old Age Economic Security," *Benefits Quarterly*, Vol. 2, No. 2 (Second Quarter 1986), pp. 26–35.

BODIE, ZVI. "Pensions as Retirement Income Insurance." *Journal of Economic Literature*, Vol. 38, No. 1 (March 1990), pp. 28–49.

BORUS, MICHAEL E., HERBERT S. PARNES, STEVEN H. SANDELL, AND BERT SEIDMAN, EDS. *The Older Worker*. Madison: Industrial Relations Research Association, University of Wisconsin, 1988.

GRAD, SUSAN. "Income and Assets of Social Security Beneficiaries by Type of Benefit," *Social Security Bulletin*, Vol. 52, No. 1 (January 1989), pp. 2–10.

———. "Income Change at Retirement," *Social Security Bulletin*, Vol. 53, No. 1 (January 1990), pp. 2–10.

PACKARD, MICHAEL D., AND VIRGINIA P. RENO. "A Look at Very Early Retirees," *Social Security Bulletin*, Vol. 52, No. 3 (March 1989), pp. 16–29.

PALMER, BRUCE A. "Tax Reform and Retirement Income Replacement Ratios." *The Journal of Risk and Insurance*, Vol. 56, No. 4 (December, 1989), pp. 702–725.

RADNER, DANIEL B. "Net Worth and Financial Assets of Age Groups in 1984," *Social Security Bulletin*, Vol. 52, No. 3 (March 1989), pp. 2–15.

ROSS, MYRON H., ED. *The Economics of Aging*. Kalamazoo, Mich.: W. E. Upjohn Institute for Employment Research, 1985.

SCHULTZ, JAMES H. *The Economics of Aging*, 4th ed. Dover, Mass.: Auburn House Publishing Company, 1988.

UNITED STATES GENERAL ACCOUNTING OFFICE. *Retirement before Age 65: Trends, Costs, and National Issues*. Washington, D.C.: United States General Accounting Office, 1987.

WACHTER, SUSAN M., ED. *Social Security and Private Pensions, Providing for Retirement in the Twenty-first Century*. Lexington, Mass.: Lexington Books, 1988.

WILLIAMS, C. ARTHUR, JR., JOHN G. TURNBULL, AND EARL F. CHEIT. *Economic and Social Security*, 5th ed., Chap. 2. New York: John Wiley & Sons, 1982.

OLD-AGE, SURVIVORS, DISABILITY, AND HEALTH INSURANCE

The Old-Age, Survivors, Disability, and Health Insurance (OASDHI) program is the most important public program in the United States for attacking economic insecurity from premature death and old age. It also provides valuable protection against the loss of earnings from disability and high medical expenses for the aged and long-term disabled. Almost all workers today are working in occupations covered by the OASDHI program.

In this chapter, we shall be primarily concerned with the current provisions of the OASDI portion of the total program. In particular, we shall consider the following: (1) development of the Social Security Act, (2) covered occupations, (3) determination of insured status, (4) amounts and types of benefits, (5) loss or reduction of benefits, (6) taxation of benefits, and (7) financing and administration.

DEVELOPMENT OF THE SOCIAL SECURITY ACT

Changing Structure of the Economy

The present program had its genesis in the Social Security Act of 1935.[1] The enactment of the act was partly the result of the changing social and economic conditions in the United States prior to 1935.

---

[1]The history of the development of the Social Security Act of 1935 can be found in Committee on Economic Security, *Social Security in America: The Factual Background of the Social Security Act as Summa-*

Before 1870, the United States was predominantly an agricultural economy, which made it possible for many individuals to become financially self-sufficient and provide for their own economic security. A rapidly growing population, an abundance of natural resources, and an open frontier offered economic opportunities to workers and their families. The shift from a predominantly rural to a highly industrialized economy, however, created new risks for the workers. They became dependent on money wages and the sale of their services in the labor markets, and any event that interrupted their incomes, such as old age, unemployment, occupational injuries, or disease, could lead to destitution and poverty. Workers were no longer self-sufficient, but had to depend on a viable economy for jobs and their economic security.

During the early development of the United States, many cities and towns provided some assistance to poor individuals and families, although the aid, often consisting of the poor relief system and almhouses, was in many cases grudgingly given. As the economy continued to expand, many states enacted laws that provided some financial assistance to widows and orphans. In the 1920s, a few states also provided financial help to the poor, under old-age assistance and programs for aid to the blind. Also, after 1900, both the federal government and the states began to enact workers' compensation legislation. By 1929, most states had passed laws covering occupational injuries to workers. Finally, retirement programs for teachers, police, firefighters, and military personnel were also established.

The enactment of social insurance programs in the United States, however, lagged behind those in foreign nations. Although Germany established an old-age pension program in 1889 and Great Britain did so in 1909, the United States did not enact such a national program until 1935. The lagging development can be explained by the great American stress on rugged self-individualism, by the unconstitutionality of some early social insurance laws, by the relatively high wages paid before the depression of the 1930s, and by the lack of strong support by some labor unions.

The Great Depression

The Great Depression of the 1930s underscored the need for massive federal action to meet the problem of economic insecurity from old age, unemployment, premature death, and disability. Widespread unemployment, hunger, poverty, and wasted human resources highlighted the need for corrective federal legislation to reduce the economic distress from the severe depression.

The Townsend Plan, proposed in 1934, also focused attention on this need. Under the plan, each citizen age 60 or over would receive a monthly pension of $200, which had to be spent within 30 days, and the recipient could not engage in any employment. A 2 percent transaction tax was proposed to

rized from Staff Reports to the Committee on Economic Security (Washington, D.C.: U.S. Government Printing Office, 1937). See also "Social Security Programs in the United States," *Social Security Bulletin,* Vol. 52, No. 7 (July 1989), pp. 2–19.

finance the plan. The Townsend Plan was never enacted, however, primarily because of the financing problem, concerns about the incidence of the tax, possible inflationary effects, and the fact that $200 was such a relatively high benefit compared with prevailing wage levels. Finally, the 2 percent tax would have been insufficient for the funding of benefits.[2]

Enactment of the Social Security Act

President Franklin D. Roosevelt created the Committee on Economic Security in 1934 to study the problem of economic insecurity and make suggestions for legislation. The committee's report, submitted in 1935, culminated in the passage of the Social Security Act on August 14, 1935. The original act provided for a compulsory federal program of old-age benefits for workers in industry and commerce, a federal-state program of unemployment insurance, and federal grants-in-aid to the states for old-age assistance, aid to the blind, and aid to dependent children. In addition, the act established federal grants to the states for maternal and child health services, services for crippled children, public health services, and vocational rehabilitation.

The original act provided only retirement benefits at age 65 for most workers in industry and commerce. Since then, the program has been changed and liberalized several times. In 1939, survivor benefits were added. In the 1950s, coverage was broadened to include most self-employed persons, household and farm employees, members of the armed services, ministers, and most state and local government employees. In 1956, disability insurance was added to cover the loss of earnings from total disability. In 1965, the Medicare program was enacted to provide hospital and medical insurance for the aged. In 1972, legislation was enacted that automatically increased benefits based on specific changes in the Consumer Price Index and extended the Medicare program to disabled beneficiaries who had been on the roll for at least 24 months. In 1977, tax contributions were substantially increased and the method for computing monthly cash benefits was also changed. In 1980, disability income benefits for younger workers and maximum family disability income benefits were both reduced. In 1981, the minimum monthly primary benefit of $122 was initially eliminated and later restored to certain existing beneficiaries.

In addition, based on the recommendations of the National Commission on Social Security Reform, sweeping legislative changes were made in the Social Security program in 1983. The changes in the law were designed to restore financial stability to the Social Security program both in the short run and long-term future. The 1983 legislation provided for numerous changes, including mandatory coverage of newly hired federal employees, acceleration of scheduled tax rate increases, taxation of part of the benefits for upper-income persons, and a higher normal retirement age that will be gradually phased in in the

---

[2]For an historical description of the Townsend Plan, see Arthur J. Altmeyer, *The Formative Years of Social Security* (Madison: University of Wisconsin Press, 1966), pp. 9–11, 105–106, 242–243.

future. Finally, the Medicare Catastrophic Coverage Act of 1988 was enacted into law to cover catastrophic medical expenses incurred by the elderly. The act was later repealed in 1989.

In the following section, we shall briefly examine the major provisions of the current Social Security program.

COVERED OCCUPATIONS

Employees in Private Firms

The Social Security program is a compulsory program that covers virtually all gainfully employed workers in private firms. As a result, the workers are building valuable protection against the loss or reduction of earnings because of retirement, disability, or death.

Federal Civilian Employees

All civilian employees of the federal government hired after 1983 are covered on a compulsory basis. Federal civilian employees who were hired before 1984 are covered under the Civil Service Retirement System and are not required to contribute to the OASDI program. However, they must contribute to the Hospital Insurance portion of the Medicare program. Also, they are allowed to switch over to the new Federal Employees Retirement System established for new employees hired after 1983 and then be covered by both OASDI and Hospital Insurance.

Employees of Religious, Charitable, and Educational Nonprofit Organizations

Employees of religious, charitable, and educational nonprofit organizations are covered on a compulsory basis if they are paid $100 or more in a year. However, church organizations that object to the payment of Social Security taxes based on religious principles can irrevocably elect not to be covered. In such a case, the employees are considered to be self-employed persons and must pay OASDHI taxes on their earnings.

State and Local Government Employees

State and local government employees can be covered by a voluntary agreement between the state and federal government. In addition, if the employees are covered under an existing retirement plan, the majority of them must agree to be covered under Social Security. However, state and local government employees hired after March 1986 are compulsorily required to pay the Hospital Insurance tax under the Medicare program.

Self-employment

Self-employed people are covered on a compulsory basis if their net profits are at least $400 during the year. This includes self-employed professionals, such as physicians, dentists, and attorneys.

Farm Operators

Self-employed farmers are covered if their net annual earnings are at least $400. There is an alternate reporting system based on gross income for low-income farmers.

Farm Workers

Farm workers are covered if they receive $150 or more in cash wages by any employer during the year, or are employed by an employer who pays at least $2,500 in wages in a calendar year. Farm work performed by foreign workers who are lawfully admitted on a temporary basis is not covered.

Household Workers

Household workers are covered if they receive cash wages of $50 or more in a calendar quarter from any employer.

Employees Receiving Tips

The tip income of employees receiving cash tips of $20 or more in a month from one employer is also covered. The employee must report the tips to the employer and pays a Social Security tax on them. The employer must also pay a matching tax contribution on the tips.

Ministers

Ministers are automatically covered unless they elect out because of conscience or religious principles. Those electing out must file an exemption form. Although ministers may be working as employees, they report their income and pay tax contributions as if they were self-employed.

Members of a religious order who have taken a vow of poverty can also be covered under the Social Security program if the order irrevocably agrees to cover them on an employer-employee basis.

Military Service and Wage Credits

Persons on active duty in the military service in 1957 or later are covered by the Social Security program and earn wage credits the same way that civilian employees do. However, additional noncontributory wage credits for military services are also granted. The additional wage credits vary by time periods. Wage credits of $160 monthly are granted under certain conditions for active military service from September 16, 1940, through 1956. For 1957 through 1977, a wage credit of $300 is granted for each calendar quarter in which the person had any active duty basic pay. Finally, for 1978 and later, a wage credit equal to $100 for each $300 of active duty pay is granted for each year of active duty up to a maximum credit of $1,200 annually.

Railroad Employment

Railroad workers subject to the Railroad Retirement Act are not required to pay Social Security taxes. However, because of certain coordinating provisions, railroad employees can obtain coverage under the Social Security program under certain conditions. These provisions are discussed later in Chapter 19.

Foreign Employment

An American employer (not just corporations) must provide coverage for U.S. citizens and residents who are working outside the United States. The employer can elect such coverage for U.S. citizens and residents who are employed by a foreign affiliate outside the United States if the American employer has at least a 10 percent interest in the foreign affiliate. Once such an election is made, it cannot be revoked.

Excluded Occupations

Certain occupations are excluded from coverage. With the exception of certain designated states, police officers with their own retirement system are excluded. Other occupations that are excluded include student nurses; students working in educational institutions; students performing domestic services for college fraternities, sororities, and clubs; newspaper carriers under age 18; and children under age 18 employed by their parents in an unincorporated business. However, work performed by a parent in a son or daughter's business is covered. Also, household work by a parent for a son or daughter may be covered under certain conditions.

DETERMINATION OF INSURED STATUS

Before you or your family can receive benefits, you must have credit for a certain amount of work in covered employment. For 1990, covered employees and the self-employed receive *one quarter of coverage* for each $520 in covered annual earnings.[3] No more than four quarters of coverage can be credited for the year.

---

[3]The amounts required for a quarter of coverage were $500 in 1989, $470 in 1988, $460 in 1987, $440 in 1986, $410 in 1985, $390 in 1984, $370 in 1983, $340 in 1982, $310 in 1981, $290 in 1980,

The amount of covered earnings needed for a quarter of coverage will automatically increase in the future as average wages increase.

To become eligible for the various benefits, you must attain an insured status. There are three principal types of insured status: (1) fully insured, (2) currently insured, and (3) disability insured. Retirement benefits require a fully insured status. Survivor benefits require either a fully insured or currently insured status; however, certain types of survivor benefits require a fully insured status. Disability benefits require a disability insured status.

Fully Insured

You are fully insured if you meet one of the following tests: (1) you have 40 quarters of coverage or (2) you have one quarter of coverage for each year after 1950 (or after age 21, if later) up to the year you die, become disabled, or attain age 62, whichever occurs first. A minimum of six quarters is required under the second test. For example, if you work during high school, college, or later, you are fully insured after acquiring 40 quarters of coverage or 10 years of work. You are then fully insured for life even though you never work again in covered employment.

A fully insured status can also be obtained under the second test. For example, a worker who attains age 62 in 1990 needs 39 quarters of coverage to be fully insured. All workers eventually will need 40 quarters of coverage to be fully insured for retirement benefits.

Finally, as a result of the 1983 amendments, newly covered older employees of nonprofit organizations can acquire more easily a fully insured status with fewer quarters of coverage. Persons age 55 and over who were, on January 1, 1984, employees of nonprofit organizations to whom coverage has been extended as a result of the 1983 legislation are fully insured if they have the following quarters of coverage acquired after 1983:

AGE ON JANUARY 1, 1984	QUARTERS OF COVERAGE REQUIRED
60 or over	6
59	8
58	12
57	16
55 or 56	20

The purpose of the special rule is to make it easier for newly covered older employees of nonprofit organizations to qualify for Social Security retirement benefits.

$260 in 1979, and $250 in 1978. Before 1978, an employee earned one quarter of coverage if he or she had been paid $50 or more in a calendar quarter. Self-employed persons received four quarters of coverage if they had net earnings of $400 or more in a year. The quarters of coverage can be counted any time they are earned (e.g., before age 22, after age 62, or before 1951).

Currently Insured

A currently insured status is easy to attain. You are currently insured if you have at least six quarters of coverage out of the last 13 quarters ending with the quarter of death, disability, or entitlement to retirement benefits.

Disability Insured

You are insured for disability benefits if you are fully insured and have at least 20 quarters of coverage out of the last 40 quarters ending with the quarter in which the disability occurs.

Special rules apply to younger workers and to the blind to make it easier for them to qualify for disability income benefits. If you are between the ages of 24 and 31, you must have quarters of coverage in half the time between your twenty-first birthday and the time that you became disabled. If you are under age 24, you need only six quarters of coverage out of the last twelve quarters. Blind persons are required only to have a fully insured status; they are not required to meet the recent work test requirement that applies to other disability applicants.

BENEFIT AMOUNTS

Primary Insurance Amount

All monthly income benefits are based on the worker's *primary insurance amount* (PIA), which is the monthly amount paid to a retired worker at the normal retirement age (currently age 65) or to a disabled worker. The primary insurance amount, in turn, is based on the worker's average indexed monthly earnings (AIME).

Average Indexed Monthly Earnings

Prior to the 1977 amendments to the Social Security Act, a technical flaw existed in the provision for computing initial benefits. During a period of inflation, the benefit table was adjusted upward to reflect the price inflation. In addition, since wages tend to increase during inflationary periods, higher wages would also result in higher future benefits. As a result, under certain economic conditions (such as those that prevailed in the mid-1970s), some workers retiring in the future would have received retirement benefits that exceeded 100 percent of their earnings in the year prior to retirement, and long-run costs would have sharply increased. To correct this flaw, the AIME method for determining benefits was developed.

The wage-indexing method is designed to ensure that monthly cash benefits will reflect changes in wage levels over the worker's lifetime so that the benefits paid initially will have a relatively constant relationship to the worker's earnings before age 62, disability, or death. The result is that the workers who retire today and workers who will be retiring in the future will have about the same proportion of their earnings replaced by Social Security retirement benefits.

To illustrate the principle of wage indexing, the worker's actual earnings after 1950 are updated (indexed) to reflect the increase in average annual wages through the second year before the worker reaches age 62, becomes disabled, or dies, whichever occurs first. *Earnings are indexed by multiplying the actual earnings for the year being indexed by the ratio of average wages in the second year before the worker reaches age 62 (or, if earlier, becomes disabled or dies) to average wages in the year being indexed.* For example, assume that Joseph retired at age 62 in 1989. The significant year for setting the index factor is the second year before he attains age 62 (1987). If Joseph's actual wages were $3,000 in 1956, this amount is multiplied by the ratio of the average annual wage in 1987 to the average annual wage in 1956. Thus, Joseph's indexed earnings for 1956 are $15,649.46. This can be summarized as follows:

$$
\begin{array}{c} \$3,000 \\ \text{(actual earnings} \\ \text{in 1956)} \end{array} \times \frac{\begin{array}{c}\$18,426.51 \\ \text{(average annual} \\ \text{wages in 1987)}\end{array}}{\begin{array}{c}\$3,532.36 \\ \text{(average annual} \\ \text{wages in 1956)}\end{array}} = \begin{array}{c} \$15,649.46 \\ \text{(indexed earnings} \\ \text{for 1956)} \end{array}
$$

This procedure is carried out for each year in the measuring period except that earnings for and after the indexing year are counted in actual dollar amounts. The adjusted earnings are then used to determine the worker's primary insurance amount. A more detailed explanation of the AIME method can be found in the appendix at the end of this chapter.

Primary Insurance Amount Formula

After the worker's AIME is computed, a weighted formula is used to determine the primary insurance amount. Based on the 1990 benefit formula, which applies to persons who first become eligible for retirement benefits or eligibility benefits in 1990, or who die in 1990 before becoming eligible for benefits, the PIA is determined as follows:

90 percent of the first $356 of AIME
+
32 percent of the next $1,789 of AIME
+
15 percent of the AIME above $2,145

The result is then rounded down to the next lower multiple of ten cents if not already a multiple of ten cents.

The formula is adjusted annually for new cohorts. The bend points (dollar amounts) in the formula are adjusted each year to reflect changes in average wages in the national economy. In addition, the benefit amount resulting from application of the formula is subject to the automatic cost-of-living provisions for the year of attainment of age 62 (or prior death or disability) and after.

The benefit formula weights the benefits heavily in favor of low-income persons. This is a reflection of the social adequacy principle discussed earlier. The formula also reflects the principle of relating monthly cash benefits to the worker's earnings. As the worker's average indexed monthly earnings increase, the primary insurance amount also increases, but not proportionately to the increase in earnings.

Table 5-1 provides examples of monthly benefits paid to various beneficiaries as of January 1990.

Automatic Cost-of-Living Adjustment

The monthly cash benefits are automatically adjusted each year for measurable (0.1 percent) increases in the cost of living, which maintains the real purchasing power of the benefits. Whenever the Consumer Price Index (CPI) on a quarterly basis increases from the third quarter of the previous year to the third quarter of the present year, the benefits are automatically increased by the same percentage. The benefit increase applies to the December benefit that is payable in early January. For example, the January 1990 benefit payments reflected a 4.7 percent increase based on the cost-of-living provision.

Financial Stabilizer. To protect the trust funds during adverse economic conditions, a financial stabilizer is now built into the system. *Whenever the trust fund ratio at the beginning of the year (ratio of combined OASDI trust fund assets to estimated outgo over the next 12 months) falls below 20 percent, the cost-of-living increase for December of that year is limited to the lower of (1) the increase in the CPI or (2) the increase in average wages.*

If one or more of the benefit increases is based on the increase in

TABLE 5-1 Examples of Monthly OASDI Benefits January 1990

TYPE OF BENEFICIARY	MONTHLY BENEFIT
Average monthly benefit, retired worker	$566
Maximum monthly benefit to a person retiring at age 65	975
Aged couple, both receiving benefits	966
Widowed mother and two children	1,173
Aged widow living alone	522
Disabled worker, spouse, and children	975
All disabled workers	555

Source: Social Security Administration.

average wages, a "catch up" benefit increase will be made in any year the combined trust fund balance reaches 32 percent of expected expenditures.

The financial stabilizer will help protect the trust funds during periods of adverse economic conditions in which the trust funds may be relatively low, and the CPI is increasing more rapidly than average wages.

Delayed Retirement Credit

To encourage working beyond the normal retirement age, a delayed retirement credit is available. Under previous law, the worker's primary insurance amount was increased 3 percent for each year of delayed retirement ($\frac{1}{4}$ of 1 percent monthly) beyond the normal retirement age (currently age 65) and up to age 70. However, beginning in 1990, the delayed retirement credit will gradually be increased in the future from 3 to 8 percent.

The increase in the delayed retirement credit law applies to all workers who attain age 62 after 1986. For workers attaining age 65 in 1990–1991, the delayed retirement credit is $3\frac{1}{2}$ percent ($\frac{7}{24}$ of 1 percent monthly). The credit will gradually be increased until it reaches 8 percent ($\frac{2}{3}$ of 1 percent monthly) for people who reach the normal retirement age in 2009 (then age 66).

Finally, if the worker's earnings are high enough during the years of delayed retirement, his or her average indexed monthly earnings will also be increased, which will further increase the benefits. The higher AIME will increase the PIA that is used to determine benefits for the workers and family members. However, the delayed retirement credit applies only to the benefits paid to the *worker and, subsequently, to the surviving spouse*. The annual percentage increases under the delayed retirement credit do not increase the benefits paid to other family members.

Minimum Benefit

There is no regular benefit amount for workers who attain age 62 or become disabled or die before age 62 after 1981. However, one exception is that certain members of religious orders who have taken a vow of poverty will continue to qualify for a minimum benefit (a basic PIA of $122 monthly) if they first become eligible for benefits before 1992.

Special Minimum Benefit

A special minimum benefit can be paid to low-income workers who have been covered under the Social Security program for more than 10 years. The purpose of the special minimum benefit is to enable low-income workers with a long history of coverage (but with earnings above a certain level) to receive higher benefits.

As of January 1990, the special minimum benefit is approximately $21.88 monthly for each year of coverage above 10 years and up to 30 years.

Thus, the special minimum benefit at age 65 for a worker with 30 years of work is $437.60 monthly. However, most people are already receiving regular benefits that are much higher than the special minimum benefit. The automatic cost-of-living provisions discussed earlier also apply to the special minimum benefit.

Maximum Family Benefits

There is a maximum limit on the monthly benefits that can be paid to the family based on the earnings record of one person. Maximum family benefits are based on the worker's primary insurance amount and are generally higher for retirement and survivor benefits than for disability benefits. The maximum family benefit for persons who reach age 62 in 1990 or who die in 1990 before age 62 is based on the following formula:

150 percent of the first $455 of the PIA
+
272 percent of the PIA over $455 through $656
+
134 percent of the PIA over $656 through $856
+
175 percent of the PIA over $856

However, for disabled persons, the maximum family benefit is the *lower* of (1) 85 percent of the worker's AIME (or actual PIA if higher) or (2) 150 percent of the PIA.

Whenever the total monthly benefits payable to all beneficiaries on the basis of one earnings record exceed the maximum allowed, each dependent's or survivor's benefit is proportionately reduced (but not the worker's benefit) to bring the total within the maximum. In determining the total monthly benefits based on a single earnings record, a benefit payable to a divorced spouse is not included, except for a surviving divorced spouse who qualifies for benefits because he or she is caring for a child of the deceased worker whose benefit must be included in determining the maximum family benefit.

Elimination of Windfall Benefits
from Noncovered Employment

The law also eliminates windfall benefits for certain persons who receive pensions from noncovered employment. Because of the heavy weighting in the benefit formula—originally designed to help low wage earners—substantial windfall benefits were often paid to workers who had a long history of employment in noncovered employment but worked only a relatively short period under Social Security.

The benefit formula is changed for certain persons who receive pensions based on noncovered employment. The 90 percent factor that is now applied to average earnings in the first band of the benefit formula is reduced to

40 percent for persons first becoming eligible in 1990 or later (with graded-in amounts for those first becoming eligible in 1986–1989). This change is designed to eliminate the payment of windfall benefits in the future to persons who have a long period of work in noncovered occupations but have only a short history of work covered by Social Security.

To minimize the impact of this provision on people with small pensions from noncovered employment, the law guarantees that the reduction in Social Security benefits will not exceed one-half of the pension amount that is based on noncovered work after 1956.

Finally, certain persons are excluded from this provision. They include the following:

- Persons reaching age 62 before 1986
- Persons who were eligible for such pensions before 1986
- Disabled worker beneficiaries disabled before 1986
- Federal employees who were compulsorily covered by Social Security on January 1, 1984
- Persons employed on January 1, 1984, by nonprofit organizations that were not covered by Social Security before 1984
- Workers covered under Social Security for 30 or more years (For workers with 21 to 29 years of coverage, the percentage in the first band increases incrementally from 45 percent for 21 years of coverage to 85 percent for 29 years of coverage.)

TYPES OF BENEFITS

OASDHI benefits can be classified into four major categories: (1) retirement benefits, (2) survivor benefits, (3) disability benefits, and (4) Medicare benefits. Our discussion generally will be limited to retirement and survivor benefits. Disability benefits and the Medicare program are discussed in Chapter 9, where the role of social insurance programs in meeting the health care problem in the United States is examined.

Retirement Benefits

Retirement benefits provide an important layer of income protection to retired workers and their families. Without these benefits, economic insecurity and poverty among the aged would be substantially increased.

Normal Retirement Age.   The normal retirement age is the age at which full unreduced benefits can be received. The normal retirement age is presently age 65, but it will gradually increase to age 67 in the future. For persons attaining age 62 in 2000, the normal retirement age will be increased by two months to age 65 and two months. For persons who attain age 62 in each succeeding year, the normal retirement age will be increased by two additional months until it reaches age 66 for persons who attain age 62 in 2005. The normal retirement age will then be maintained at age 66 for persons who attain age 62 through 2016. Beginning in 2017, for persons who attain age 62, the normal retirement age will again be increased two months each year until it reaches age 67 for persons who attain age 62 in 2022 and later. Table 5-2 shows the future increases in the normal retirement age.

It is important to note that the eligibility age for Medicare benefits is not changed. Aged persons will continue to remain eligible for Medicare at age 65.

Early Retirement Age. Workers and their spouses can elect to retire early at age 62 with actuarially reduced benefits. Currently, the benefit that would be paid at age 65 is reduced by $\frac{5}{9}$ of 1 percent for each month the person is under age 65. Thus, a worker retiring early at age 62 receives 80 percent of the full primary insurance amount. If a person retires early and works after early retirement and benefits are withheld because of the earnings test (discussed later), they are automatically recomputed at age 65 (as to the reduction factor) in recognition of the period when there were earnings.

The actuarial reduction in benefits for early retirement at age 62 will gradually be increased from 20 percent to 30 percent in the future when the higher normal retirement age provisions become effective. The reduction for early retirement will be equal to the present reduction factor ($\frac{5}{9}$ of 1 percent) for the first 36 months, plus a new reduction factor of $\frac{5}{12}$ of 1 percent for each additional month. Thus, if a worker retires at age 62 when the normal retirement age is 66, the actuarial reduction will be 25 percent (20 percent under present law + 5 percent additional), and only 75 percent of the PIA will be paid. If the worker retires at age 62 when the higher retirement age of 67 is in effect,

TABLE 5-2 Future Social Security Normal Retirement Age

YEAR OF BIRTH	YEAR OF ATTAINMENT OF AGE 62	NORMAL RETIREMENT AGE
1937 and before	1999 and before	65
1938	2000	65, 2 mo.
1939	2001	65, 4 mo.
1940	2002	65, 6 mo.
1941	2003	65, 8 mo.
1942	2004	65, 10 mo.
1943–54	2005–16	66
1955	2017	66, 2 mo.
1956	2018	66, 4 mo.
1957	2019	66, 6 mo.
1958	2020	66, 8 mo.
1959	2021	66, 10 mo.
1960 and later	2022 and later	67

Source: U.S. Congress, House, Committee on Ways and Means, *Background Material and Data on Programs within the Jurisdiction of the Committee on Ways and Means* (Washington, D.C.: U.S. Government Printing Office, 1989), Table 4, p. 9.

the actuarial reduction will be 30 percent, and only 70 percent of the PIA will be paid.

Retired Worker.   A retired worker can receive a monthly benefit equal to the primary insurance amount at the normal retirement age if certain eligibility requirements are met. The worker must be fully insured and not earn an income in excess of the maximum permitted by the earnings test.

As noted earlier, the worker can retire earlier at age 62 with actuarially reduced benefits.

Spouse of Retired Worker.   A monthly cash benefit can also be paid to the spouse of a retired worker if she or he is at least age 62 and has been married to the retired worker for at least one year. The spouse's benefit at the normal retirement age or older is 50 percent of the retired worker's PIA. Reduced benefits can be paid as early as age 62. Currently, the spouse's benefit is reduced $\frac{25}{36}$ of 1 percent for each month under age 65. Thus, if the spouse of a retired worker receives benefits at age 62, the benefit is equal to 75 percent of the amount payable at age 65.

It should be noted that the present age of 65 for a full spouse's benefit will also be increased in the future in the manner described earlier for worker benefits. However, early retirement benefits will continue to be available at age 62, but there will be a greater actuarial reduction in the future when the higher normal retirement age provisions become effective.[4]

In addition, a divorced spouse is also eligible to receive retirement benefits based on the worker's earnings if he or she is at least age 62 and the marriage has lasted at least 10 years.

Finally, a wife (or husband) who has worked may be eligible for retirement benefits based on her own earnings and those of her husband as well. However, she does not receive two full benefits. *If her PIA as a retired worker is at least 50 percent of the PIA of the retired worker, she receives benefits based only on her own earnings. However, if the retired-worker PIA is smaller than 50 percent of her husband's PIA, she receives her own retirement benefit plus any excess of the other benefit over her own benefit—in effect the larger of the two.* For example, assume that Mary has a PIA of $400 and her husband has a PIA of $700; both retire at age 65. In this case, she receives a monthly benefit of $400. However, if her PIA at age 65 is only $300, she would receive a monthly benefit of $350, which consists of her own benefit ($300) plus the difference between that benefit ($300) and the higher wife's benefit ($350). The total benefits, however, are paid in only one check. As

---

[4]The reduction factors will change from the present 75 percent at age 62 to 70 percent when the normal retirement age is 66 and to 65 percent when the normal retirement age is 67. In the latter case, the reduction factor will be 70 percent at age 63 and 75 percent at age 64, with graded-in amounts at the older ages up to age 67. See Robert J. Myers, "Sweeping Social Security Legislation Enacted," *Meidinger Social Security News* (Spring 1983) for additional information.

a general rule, if the wife has worked in covered employment over an extended period, the retirement benefit based on her own earnings will be higher than the benefit payable based on her husband's earnings.

Unmarried Children under Age 18. Monthly benefits can also be paid to unmarried children of a retired worker who are under age 18 (or under 19 if full-time elementary or high school students). The monthly benefit to each child is 50 percent of the PIA.

Grandchildren are also eligible for benefits based on a grandparent's earnings if they are supported by and are living with the grandparent and the children's parents have died or are totally disabled.[5]

Unmarried Disabled Children. Unmarried disabled children age 18 or over are eligible for benefits based on the retired worker's earnings if they were severely disabled before age 22 and continue to remain disabled. The benefit is 50 percent of the PIA.

Spouse with Dependent Children under Age 16. A spouse at any age can receive a benefit equal to 50 percent of the PIA if he or she is caring for an eligible child under age 16 (or a child of any age who was disabled before age 22) who is receiving a benefit based on the retired worker's earnings. The mother's or father's benefit terminates when the youngest child reaches age 16 (unless he or she is caring for a disabled child who became disabled before age 22).

Survivor Benefits

Social Security survivor benefits provide considerable protection against economic insecurity because of premature death. The benefits are also inflationproof because of the automatic cost-of-living provisions.

Unmarried Children under Age 18. Survivor benefits can be paid to unmarried children under age 18 (or under 19 if full-time elementary or high school students). The deceased parent must be either fully or currently insured. The benefit for each child is 75 percent of the deceased's PIA. In addition, grandchildren (or great-grandchildren) may be eligible for benefits based on a grandparent's earnings if the requirements described earlier in the case of retirement benefits are met.

Unmarried Disabled Children. An unmarried son or daughter age 18 or over who was severely disabled before age 22 and who continues to be disabled is also eligible for survivor benefits. The benefit is 75 percent of the PIA. The deceased parent must be either fully or currently insured.

---

[5]This statement also applies to great-grandchildren.

Surviving Spouse with Children under Age 16.   A widow, widower, or surviving divorced mother or father is entitled to a monthly benefit if he or she is caring for an eligible child under age 16 (or disabled) who is receiving a benefit based on the deceased worker's earnings. The deceased must be either fully or currently insured. The monthly benefit is 75 percent of the PIA, and it is paid until the youngest child reaches age 16 (unless the parent is caring for a disabled child).

Surviving Spouse Age 60 or Over.   A surviving spouse age 60 or over is also eligible for survivor benefits. The deceased must be fully insured. Currently, the monthly benefit at age 65 or over is 100 percent of the PIA (plus any delayed retirement credits that the spouse had earned). Reduced benefits can be paid as early as age 60, but the benefits are permanently reduced by $\frac{19}{40}$ of 1 percent for each month under age 65. Thus, a surviving spouse age 60 would receive only 71.5 percent of the PIA (plus any delayed retirement credits the deceased spouse had earned). A surviving divorced spouse age 60 or older is also eligible for survivor benefits if the marriage lasted at least 10 years.

Disabled Widow or Widower, Ages 50–59.   A disabled widow, widower, or surviving divorced spouse who is age 50 or older can also receive survivor benefits under certain conditions. First, the person must be disabled at the time of the worker's death or must become disabled within seven years after the worker's death or within seven years after the mother's or father's benefits end. Second, the deceased worker must also be fully insured. Third, the disabled person must be unable to engage in any gainful activity, which is a more severe test of disability than that applied to other disability beneficiaries. Finally, a surviving divorced spouse must have been married to the deceased spouse for at least 10 years.
Benefits for a disabled widow(er) age 50–59 are computed using the same reduction factor that applies to an aged widow(er) at age 60. Thus, a disabled widow(er) age 50–59 receives benefits equal to 71.5 percent of the PIA. There is no further reduction for entitlement before age 60.

Dependent Parents.   Dependent parents age 62 and over can also receive benefits based on the deceased's earnings. The deceased worker must be fully insured. The benefit paid to each parent is 75 percent of the PIA. If there is only one parent, the benefit is 82.5 percent of the PIA.

Lump-Sum Death Benefit.   A lump-sum death benefit of $255 can be paid when the worker dies. The benefit, however, is paid to a spouse living with the worker at the time of death. If the spouse does not meet that condition, the benefit is payable if she or he is eligible for a widow or widower's benefit for the month in which the worker died (not available to divorced spouses). If there is no eligible spouse to receive the benefit, it is then paid to the children who are eligible for monthly benefits in the month of death. Earlier law permitted payment of the death benefit directly to a funeral home or to other persons responsible for the funeral. This is no longer the case.

Other Benefit Provisions

The 1983 amendments resulted in some minor liberalization of benefits that generally affect *certain surviving divorced and disabled spouses*. They include the following:

1. Benefits payable to a disabled surviving spouse age 50–59 and to a divorced, disabled surviving spouse age 50–59 are no longer terminated if she or he remarries before age 60.
2. Benefits payable to a divorced surviving spouse age 60 or over are no longer terminated if she or he remarries after attaining age 60.
3. A divorced spouse age 62 or over who has been divorced for at least two years can receive benefits based on the earnings of a former spouse who is eligible for retirement benefits even though the former spouse has not retired or applied for benefits. This provision helps divorced women who do not qualify for benefits based on their own earnings and are unable to obtain benefits based on the former husbands' earnings because the husbands are still working. The requirement that the divorce must be in effect for at least two years is intended to discourage divorce solely for the purpose of becoming entitled to benefits or to avoid the earnings test.
4. Benefits can be paid to the illegitimate child of a disabled worker for the first month in which the child satisfies all entitlement conditions even though the acknowledgment, court decree, or order establishing parenthood occurs later than the first day of the month.
5. Benefits can be paid retroactively for one month to an aged widow or widower who files an application for actuarially reduced benefits in the calendar month following the month the spouse died. This provision is an exception to the rule that bars the payment of retroactive benefits before an application is filed if the retroactive benefits would result in the reduction of future benefits. This provision facilitates the payment of benefits in those situations where death occurs late in the month, and the widow(er) is under the normal retirement age and fails to apply for benefits until the following month.
6. A worker who is disabled before age 31 and then recovers and shortly thereafter becomes disabled again will find it easier to qualify for disability income benefits. (See Chapter 9.)
7. All gender-based distinctions in the Social Security law are eliminated by making all of the provisions applicable to both sexes. However, this change has no real effect because almost all such distinctions based on sex had already been overturned by the courts.

LOSS OR REDUCTION OF BENEFITS

Social Security benefits can be terminated or reduced under certain conditions. The following section describes the major situations that can result in a loss or reduction of benefits.

General Situations

Mothers and fathers lose their benefits when they are no longer caring for an eligible child under 16 (or are no longer caring for a disabled child over age 16). Children generally lose their benefits when they reach age 18, with the exceptions that benefits are payable if they are attending elementary or high school, or become disabled before age 22. Death or recovery from disability also causes the benefits to terminate. In addition, OASDI benefits to convicted felons are suspended while in prison. The benefits are also suspended if the person is deported because of conviction for a crime or because of conviction for certain crimes committed against the United States, such as treason or espionage. Finally, benefits generally terminate if the beneficiary marries a person who is not receiving dependents' or survivor benefits. One exception is a widow or widower who remarries after age 60.[6]

Earnings Test

The Social Security program has an earnings test (retirement test) that can result in a loss of monthly cash benefits. If a beneficiary has earnings in excess of some maximum limit, he or she will lose some or all of the benefits. *The purposes of the earnings test are to restrict the monthly cash benefits only to those persons who have lost their earned income and to hold down the costs of the program.*

In 1990, beneficiaries ages 65 through 69 can earn a maximum of $9,360 with no loss of benefits. A different exempt amount applies to beneficiaries under age 65. In 1990, beneficiaries under age 65 can earn $6,840 with no loss of benefits. The annual exempt amounts will automatically increase each year to keep pace with increases in average wages.

Benefits are withheld if the beneficiary's earnings exceed the annual exempt amount. *For beneficiaries ages 65 through 69, $1 in benefits is withheld for each $3 of earnings above the exempt amount. However, for beneficiaries under age 65, $1 in benefits is withheld for each $2 of earnings above the exempt amount.* These rules can be made clearer by the following examples:

Example 1.   James, age 66, is a retired engineer who returns to work as a part-time consultant and earns $25,000 in 1990. The annual exempt amount for 1990 is $9,360. James will lose $5,213 in retirement benefits.

Example 2.   Mary, age 63, is a retired nurse who is persuaded by a director of nursing in a hospital to work part-time. She earns $15,000 in 1990. The annual exempt amount in 1990 for workers under age 65 is $6,840. Mary will lose $4,080 in retirement benefits.

---

[6]There are other exceptions as well. Disabled surviving spouses age 50–59 and disabled divorced surviving spouses age 50–59 can remarry before age 60 without losing benefits. Also, divorced surviving spouses age 60 or over can remarry without losing benefits.

The earnings test has three major exceptions. First, persons age 70 and older can earn any amount and receive full benefits. Second, the earnings test does not apply to investment income, dividends, interest, rents, pensions, or annuity payments. The purpose of this exception is to encourage private savings and investments to supplement the Social Security benefits. Finally, a special monthly earnings test is used for the *initial year of retirement* if it produces a more favorable result than the annual test. Under this special test, the monthly exempt amount is one-twelfth of the annual exempt amount. Thus, for the initial year of retirement, regardless of total earnings for the year, full benefits are paid to a beneficiary who neither earns more than the monthly exempt amount ($780 in 1990 for persons age 65 through 69 and $570 for those under age 65) nor performs substantial services in self-employment. The purpose of the special monthly test is to pay full retirement benefits, starting with the first month of retirement, to the worker who retires during the year after having had substantial earnings. Otherwise, the worker would lose some or all of the benefits for months after retirement if the earnings were in excess of the maximum allowed under the annual test.

The earnings test is a highly controversial issue that is analyzed in greater detail in Chapter 6.

Government Pension Offset

If a spouse or surviving spouse who is receiving Social Security benefits as a dependent or survivor is also receiving a pension based on government employment not covered by Social Security on the last day of employment, the Social Security benefit is reduced in an amount equal to two-thirds of the public pension. The offset does not apply to workers whose government job is covered by OASDI on the last day of employment.

The purpose of the government offset is to reduce the problem of windfall benefits, or double dipping, by which a person working in noncovered government employment could otherwise receive a sizable pension based on that employment and also Social Security benefits as a dependent or surviving spouse.

TAXATION OF SOCIAL SECURITY BENEFITS

Part of the Social Security benefits (and Railroad Retirement Tier 1 benefits) is now subject to federal income taxation. Beginning in 1984, up to half of the Social Security benefits is included in the gross income of beneficiaries whose modified adjusted gross income exceeds certain base amounts. The base amounts are $25,000 for a single taxpayer, $32,000 for married taxpayers filing jointly, and zero for married taxpayers filing separately.

In determining the amount of income that must be counted, the taxpayer must count his or her adjusted gross income under present law, plus all nontaxable interest income (such as interest from a municipal bond), plus half of the Social Security benefits. The total combined income is then compared with the base amount. *The amount of Social Security benefits that must be included in gross income is the lower of (1) half of the Social Security benefits or (2) half of the excess of the taxpayer's combined income over the base amount.* This can be made clear by the following examples:

(1)	Type of taxpayer ..	Single	Single	Couple	Couple	Couple
(2)	Adjusted gross income	$16,000	$23,000	$24,000	$28,000	$50,000
(3)	Tax-free interest income	0	0	0	3,000	2,000
(4)	Social Security	4,000	8,000	3,000	6,000	10,000
(5)	Sum of lines (2) plus (3) plus one-half of (4)	18,000	27,000	25,500	34,000	57,000
(6)	Base amount	25,000	25,000	32,000	32,000	32,000
(7)	Excess amount (line [5] minus [6])	−7,000	2,000	−6,500	2,000	25,000
(8)	Amount of Social Security which is taxed	$0	$1,000	$0	$1,000	$5,000

The taxes are collected by the Treasury Department as part of the federal income tax and are credited to the OASDI trust funds. The tax currently affects only middle- and upper-income beneficiaries. In 1989, an estimated 17 percent of all OASDI beneficiaries paid taxes on part of their benefits. The taxes collected accounted for about 2 percent of the total benefits paid under the program.[7]

FINANCING

The OASDI program is financed by a payroll tax paid by employees, employers, and the self-employed; interest income on the trust fund investments; and revenues derived from the taxation of part of the OASDI benefits. In addition, the general revenues of the federal government are also used in certain situations to fund the benefits.[8]

---

[7]U.S. Congress, House, Committee on Ways and Means, *Background Material and Data on Programs within the Jurisdiction of the Committee on Ways and Means* (Washington, D.C.: U.S. Government Printing Office, 1989), Table 13, p. 26.

[8]General revenues of the federal government are used to pay the costs of noncontributory wage credits for military service, payments to noninsured persons age 72 and over, the federal government's share of Supplementary Medical Insurance premiums, and the costs of covering certain

Payroll Tax

A covered worker pays a payroll tax on earnings up to some specified maximum limit, and the amount is matched by an identical contribution from the employer. In 1990, a covered worker paid a tax rate of 7.65 percent on a maximum taxable earnings base of $51,300. The maximum taxable earnings base is adjusted annually based on changes in average wages in the national economy if benefits are increased according to the automatic cost-of-living provisions. Table 5-3 illustrates the payroll tax schedule both historically and under the provisions of current law.

The self-employed paid a tax contribution rate that is twice the combined employer-employee tax rate. The earnings base is the same as that used for employers and employees. From 1984 through 1989, the self-employed received a partial tax credit that reduced the effective tax rate. However, beginning in 1990, half of the payroll tax paid is deductible for federal income tax purposes. The special deduction is designed to treat the self-employed in much the same manner as employers and employees are treated for Social Security and income tax purposes.[9]

In 1990, based on current law, the self-employed paid a contribution rate of 15.3 percent on the maximum wage base of $51,300. Table 5-4 summarizes the tax contribution rates paid by the self-employed for 1980 and later years.

In addition, persons eligible for Medicare also pay a monthly premium for coverage under Part B of Medicare.

The tax contributions and premiums are deposited into federal trust funds. All sums needed for the various benefits and administrative expenses are paid out of the trust funds. The excess contributions not needed for current benefits and administrative expenses are invested in government securities. The trust funds are discussed in greater detail in Chapter 7.

This brief discussion is only a highlight of some important financing provisions. However, there are numerous controversial problems and issues associated with the financing of the Social Security program, including the future financial solvency of the program and the role of the trust funds in the

---

uninsured persons under the Hospital Insurance portion of the Medicare program. General revenues are also used to pay the interest on the government bonds held by the OASDHI trust funds. Also as a result of the 1983 amendments, the tax credit for employees (1984 only) and for the self-employed (1984–1989 only) is directly financed out of general revenues. In 1990, there is a general revenues subsidy (indirect) because a self-employed person is allowed to deduct 50 percent of the Social Security tax for federal income tax purposes.

[9]Beginning in 1990, the tax credit has been replaced by two new deductions that reduce the income tax liability for self-employed people. First, net earnings from self-employment are reduced by an amount equal to one half of the total self-employment tax. This is similar to the way employees are treated under the law since the employer's share of the total Social Security tax is not considered income to the employee. Second, half of the self-employment tax can be deducted as a business expense. This is similar to the deduction allowed to employers on the Social Security taxes they pay for their employees.

TABLE 5-3 Selected Payroll Tax Rate and Wage Base Levels, Historically and Under Current Law

	WAGE BASE	CONTRIBUTION RATE, EMPLOYER/EMPLOYEE EACH			
		Total	OASI	DI	HI
1937	$3,000	1.0%	1.0%	....	
1950	3,000	1.5	1.5	....	
1955	4,200	2.0	2.0	....	
1959	4,800	2.5	2.25	0.25%	....
1966	6,600	4.2	3.5	.35	0.35%
1970	7,800	4.8	3.65	.55	.60
1974	13,200	5.85	4.375	.575	.90
1978	17,700	6.05	4.275	.775	1.00
1979	22,900	6.13	4.33	.75	1.05
1981	29,700	6.65	4.70	.65	1.30
1982	32,400	6.70	4.575	.825	1.30
1984	37,800	[1]7.00	5.20	.50	1.30
1985	39,600	7.05	5.20	.50	1.35
1986	42,000	7.15	5.20	.50	1.45
1987	43,800	7.15	5.20	.50	1.45
1988	45,000	7.51	5.53	.53	1.45
1989	48,000	7.51	5.53	.53	1.45
1990	51,300	7.65	5.60	.60	1.45
1991–99	([2])	7.65	5.60	.60	1.45
2000 and after	([2])	7.65	5.49	.71	1.45

[1]A tax credit of 0.3 percent of taxable wages was allowed in 1984 against the tax paid by employees, so that the effective employee withholding rate was 6.7 percent.
[2]Subject to automatic increase.

Source: U.S. Congress, House, Committee on Ways and Means, *Background Material and Data on Programs within the Jurisdiction of the Committee on Ways and Means* (Washington, D.C.: U.S. Government Printing Office, 1989), Table 1, p. 67.

TABLE 5-4 Current Law Social Security Payroll Tax Rates for Self-Employed Individuals, by Individual and Combined Trust Funds, 1980 and After

CALENDAR YEAR	OASI	DI	OASDI COMBINED	HI	OASDHI COMBINED
1980	6.2725%	.7775%	7.05%	1.05%	8.10%
1981	7.0250	.9750	8.00	1.30	9.30
1982	6.8125	1.2375	8.05	1.30	9.35
1983	7.1125	.9375	8.05	1.30	9.35
1984	10.4000	1.0000	11.40	2.60	[1]14.00
1985	10.4000	1.0000	11.40	2.70	[1]14.10
1986–87	10.4000	1.0000	11.40	2.90	[1]14.30
1988–89	11.0600	1.0600	12.12	2.90	[1]15.02
1990–99	11.2000	1.2000	12.40	2.90	15.30
2000 and after	10.9800	1.4200	12.40	2.90	15.30

[1]Excludes tax credits, which equaled 2.7 percent in 1984, 2.3 percent in 1985, and 2.0 percent for the years 1986 through 1989.

Source: U.S. Congress, House, Committee on Ways and Means, *Background Material and Data on Programs within the Jurisdiction of the Committee on Ways and Means* (Washington, D.C.: U.S. Government Printing Office, 1989), Table 2, p. 68.

economy. These important issues are discussed in Chapter 7, when the financing provisions of the Social Security program are analyzed in greater detail.

ADMINISTRATION

The OASDI program is administered by the Social Security Administration, which is part of the U.S. Department of Health and Human Services. The Medicare program is administered by the Health Care Financing Administration, which is also part of the U.S. Department of Health and Human Services. Regional and district offices provide local residents with information and assistance in filing claims.

If you work in a covered occupation, you need a Social Security card. The number of your card is used to record your earnings. The earnings record is kept by the Social Security Administration at its central office in Baltimore, Maryland. You need only one Social Security card during your lifetime. If you lose your card, a duplicate card will be issued.

You should periodically check on your earnings to make sure that they are correctly reported. You can get a free form from any Social Security office for this purpose. This form can also be used to get an estimate of your future retirement benefits. If you should die or become disabled, the estimated survivor and disability benefits are also shown. The form is extremely valuable for personal financial planning purposes. It can be obtained from your local Social Security office or by dialing a toll-free number and requesting a copy.

APPENDIX

CALCULATION OF AVERAGE INDEXED MONTHLY EARNINGS (AIME)

The AIME can be calculated by the following steps:

1. Count the number of years after 1950 (or after age 21, if later) up to but not including the year the worker dies, becomes disabled, or attains age 62, whichever comes first. The number of years is the number of *computation elapsed years.*
2. Subtract 5 from the number of years determined in the first step. This has the effect of eliminating some years with little or no earnings. Also, years in which the worker has established a period of disability can be eliminated. At least two years must be included in the base for disability and survivor benefits. (However, special dropout rules now apply to younger disabled workers. See the discussion that follows.) The number of years remaining is the number of *computation years* that must be used in computing the AIME.
3. List the worker's actual covered earnings for all years after 1950 up to and *including* the year of death or the year *before* entitlement to retirement or disability benefits. (The year in which the person is first entitled to retirement or

disability benefits is not included for benefits payable until the next calendar year.) Do not count more than the following amounts:

1951–54	$ 3,600	1976	$15,300	1985	$39,600
1955–58	4,200	1977	16,500	1986	42,000
1959–65	4,800	1978	17,700	1987	43,800
1966–67	6,600	1979	22,900	1988	45,000
1968–71	7,800	1980	25,900	1989	48,000
1972	9,000	1981	29,700	1990	51,300[a]
1973	10,800	1982	32,400		
1974	13,200	1983	35,700		
1975	14,100	1984	37,800		

[a]Subject to an automatic adjustment for 1991 and later if benefits are automatically increased.

4. Index the actual earnings for each year before the indexing year. Earnings for any later year are not indexed.

5. From the list of indexed and nonindexed earnings (earnings in and after the indexing year), select the highest years of earnings equal to the number of years found in step 2. The years need not be consecutive. Add the earnings for the selected years and divide by the number of months in the computation years to determine the AIME.

These rules can be made clearer by referring to Table 1 in the Appendix, which shows the indexed earnings for minimum, average, and maximum wage earners who retire at age 62 in 1989. For example, assume that Sam is a *maximum* wage earner who retires when he attains age 62 on January 1, 1989. There are 38 elapsed years between 1951 and 1989, the year Sam attains age 62. Five years of low earnings can be dropped (1954, 1962–1965). Thus, in computing Sam's AIME, the highest 33 years must be selected. The indexing year is 1987. Total indexed earnings for the 33 highest years are $986,291. When this sum is divided by 396, Sam's AIME is $2,490. (All remaining cents are dropped.) The AIME is then used to determine Sam's primary insurance amount. Based on the 1989 benefit formula, Sam's PIA is $917.60. However, since Sam retired early at age 62, the PIA is actuarially reduced. His PIA, however, will be increased annually based on the cost-of-living escalator provisions.

Finally, special rules now apply to younger disabled workers with respect to the number of years they can drop in determining their average monthly earnings. For disabled workers who first become entitled to disability benefits in July 1980 and later, the following rules apply:

WORKER'S AGE	NUMBER OF DROPOUT YEARS
Under 27	0
27 through 31	1
32 through 36	2
37 through 41	3
42 through 46	4
47 and over	5

TABLE 1   **Earnings Histories for Hypothetical Workers Age 62 in 1989
(Rounded to nearest dollar)**

YEAR	NOMINAL EARNINGS			INDEXING FACTOR	INDEXED EARNINGS		
	Minimum[1]	Average[2]	Maximum[3]		Minimum	Average	Maximum
1951 ..	$1,560	$2,799	$3,600	6.5829	$10,269	[4]$18,427	$23,698
1952 ..	1,560	2,973	3,600	6.1973	9,668	[4]18,427	22,310
1953 ..	1,560	3,139	3,600	5.8694	9,156	[4]18,427	21,130
1954 ..	1,560	3,156	3,600	5.8392	9,109	[4]18,427	[4]21,021
1955 ..	1,560	3,301	4,200	5.5814	8,707	[4]18,427	23,442
1956 ..	1,993	3,532	4,200	5.2165	10,396	18,427	21,909
1957 ..	2,080	3,642	4,200	5.0598	10,524	18,427	21,251
1958 ..	2,080	3,674	4,200	5.0157	10,433	18,427	21,066
1959 ..	2,080	3,856	4,800	4.7789	9,940	18,427	22,939
1960 ..	2,080	4,007	4,800	4.5984	9,565	18,427	22,073
1961 ..	2,184	4,087	4,800	4.5088	9,847	18,427	21,642
1962 ..	2,392	4,291	4,800	4.2938	10,271	18,427	[4]20,610
1963 ..	2,461	4,397	4,800	4.1910	10,314	18,427	[4]20,117
1964 ..	2,600	4,576	4,800	4.0265	10,469	18,427	[4]19,327
1965 ..	2,600	4,659	4,800	3.9553	10,284	18,427	[4]18,985
1966 ..	2,600	4,938	6,600	3.7313	9,701	18,427	24,627
1967 ..	2,886	5,213	6,600	3.5344	10,200	18,427	23,327
1968 ..	3,293	5,572	7,800	3.3071	10,890	18,427	25,796
1969 ..	3,328	5,894	7,800	3.1264	10,405	18,427	24,386
1970 ..	3,328	6,186	7,800	2.9786	9,913	18,427	23,233
1971 ..	3,328	6,497	7,800	2.8361	9,439	18,427	22,122
1972 ..	3,328	7,134	9,000	2.5830	8,596	18,427	23,247
1973 ..	3,328	7,580	10,800	2.4309	8,090	18,427	26,254
1974 ..	3,883	8,031	13,200	2.2945	8,910	18,427	30,287
1975 ..	4,368	8,631	14,100	2.1349	9,325	18,427	30,103
1976 ..	4,784	9,226	15,300	1.9971	9,554	18,427	30,556
1977 ..	4,784	9,779	16,500	1.8842	9,014	18,427	31,089
1978 ..	5,512	10,556	17,700	1.7456	9,622	18,427	30,897
1979 ..	6,032	11,479	22,900	1.6052	9,682	18,427	36,758
1980 ..	6,448	12,513	25,900	1.4725	9,495	18,427	38,139
1981 ..	6,968	13,773	29,700	1.3379	9,322	18,427	39,735
1982 ..	6,968	14,531	32,400	1.2681	8,836	18,427	41,085
1983 ..	6,968	15,239	35,700	1.2091	8,425	18,427	43,167
1984 ..	6,968	16,135	37,800	1.1420	[4]7,958	18,427	43,168
1985 ..	6,968	16,823	39,600	1.0953	[4]7,632	18,427	43,376
1986 ..	6,968	17,322	42,000	1.0638	[4]7,412	18,427	44,679
1987 ..	6,968	18,427	43,800	1.0000	[4]6,968	18,427	43,800
1988 ..	6,968	[5]19,205	45,000	1.0000	[4]6,968	19,205	45,000

[1]Worker with earnings equal to annualized Federal minimum wage.
[2]Worker with earnings equal to the SSA average wage index.
[3]Worker with earnings equal to the Social Security maximum taxable earnings.
[4]Dropout years.
[5]Estimate based on Alternative II-B assumptions in 1988 Trustees Report.

Source: U.S. Congress, House, Committee on Ways and Means, *Background Material and Data on Programs within the Jurisdiction of the Committee on Ways and Means* (Washington, D.C.: U.S. Government Printing Office, 1989), Table 5, p. 10.

However, a disabled worker under age 37 can have an additional dropout year for each year that he or she had no earnings and had a child under age 3 living in the same household. However, for such persons, the total number of all dropout years—regular and child care—is limited to two. The purpose of this special insured-status provision is to correct an inequity in the payment of OASDI disability income benefits. Previously, younger disabled workers could drop out five years of low or no earnings. This often resulted in a higher PIA for younger workers since the benefits may have been based on only a few years of recent high earnings.

SUGGESTIONS FOR ADDITIONAL READING

ALTMEYER, ARTHUR J. *The Formative Years of Social Security.* Madison: University of Wisconsin Press, 1966.

BROWN, J. DOUGLAS. *The Genesis of Social Security in America.* Princeton, N.J.: Princeton University, Industrial Relations Section, 1969.

COMMERCE CLEARING HOUSE. *Social Security Benefits 1989—Including Medicare.* Chicago: Commerce Clearing House, 1989.

COMMITTEE ON ECONOMIC SECURITY. *Social Security in America: The Factual Background of the Social Security Act as Summarized from Staff Reports to the Committee on Economic Security.* Washington, D.C.: U.S. Government Printing Office, 1937.

MYERS, ROBERT J. *Social Security,* 3rd ed. Homewood, Ill.: Richard D. Irwin, 1985.

SOCIAL SECURITY DIVISION, MERCER-MERDINGER-HANSEN, INC. *1990 Guide to Social Security and Medicare.* Louisville, Ky.: William M. Mercer-Merdinger-Hansen, Inc., December 1989.

"Social Security Programs in the United States," *Social Security Bulletin,* Vol. 52, No. 7 (July 1989), pp. 2–79.

U.S. CONGRESS, HOUSE, COMMITTEE ON WAYS AND MEANS. *Background Material and Data on Programs within the Jurisdiction of the Committee on Ways and Means.* Washington, D.C.: U.S. Government Printing Office, 1989.

WILLIAMS, C. ARTHUR, JR., JOHN C. TURNBULL, AND EARL F. CHEIT. *Economic and Social Security,* 5th ed., Chaps. 3 and 4. New York: John Wiley, 1982.

WITTE, EDWIN E. *The Development of the Social Security Act: A Memorandum on the History of the Committee on Economic Security and Drafting and Legislative History of the Social Security Act.* Madison: University of Wisconsin Press, 1962.

6

PROBLEMS AND ISSUES
IN THE OASDI PROGRAM

Numerous problems and issues are associated with the OASDI program. Some issues are highly controversial, especially those resulting from recent changes in the law. In this chapter, we shall examine some important issues associated with the OASDI portion of the total program. Medicare issues are discussed later in Chapter 9. Because of their importance and timeliness, financing issues and the financial condition of the trust funds are discussed separately in Chapter 7. More specifically, the following areas will be discussed: (1) coverage issues, (2) higher retirement age, (3) adequacy of benefits, (4) earnings test, (5) taxation of benefits, (6) treatment of women, (7) treatment of younger workers, (8) effect of Social Security on private saving, (9) attitudes of Americans toward the OASDI program, and (10) Social Security surplus and the federal budget.

COVERAGE ISSUES

The OASDI program is a nearly universal system, since more than 95 percent of the nation's workers are covered at the present time. Thus, the social goal of a base of income to the population has largely been attained. The major groups that are excluded or have less than complete coverage include (1) the vast majority of federal civilian employees hired before 1984 who have their own retirement plan, (2) certain state and local government employees, (3) low-paid farm and domestic workers, (4) self-employed persons with extremely low earnings, and (5) certain family employment. Railroad workers are covered under their own program.[1]

Federal Civilian Employees

Most federal civilian employees who were hired before 1984 are covered under the Civil Service Retirement System (CSRS). One problem currently is the lack of close coordination between OASDI and CSRS. As a result, there are serious gaps in protection for workers who have been covered under both systems.

Employees who die or become disabled shortly after terminating their federal service have no carry-over protection from their years of federal service. Disabled workers also do not have any disability protection if they have an insufficient number of quarters to qualify for OASDI coverage. Finally, the majority of workers who terminate federal employment prior to retirement withdraw their CSRS contributions and do not receive retirement benefits based on federal employment.

All new federal civilian employees hired after 1983 are now covered under the OASDI program on a compulsory basis; they also have a supplementary retirement system (Federal Employees Retirement System). The extension of coverage to new federal employees has two major advantages. First, the gaps-in-protection problem is reduced. Federal employees who leave government employment still retain their coverage for survivor and disability benefits, and their retirement benefits are likely to be higher. Second, compulsory coverage of new federal employees improves the long-run solvency of the OASDI program.

State and Local Government Employees

About 28 percent of the employees of state and local government are not covered under the OASDI program.[2] Most of them can be covered by a voluntary agreement between the state and federal government. In addition, if there is an existing staff retirement program, a majority of employees must agree to be covered under the OASDI program. Once a state or local government provides coverage, all new employees thereafter are automatically covered. Also, except for some states, police officers with their own retirement plan are excluded from coverage. Finally, some states have split system provisions. Under these provisions, the state or local government has the option of extending OASDI coverage to employees who are covered under an existing retirement system by dividing the system into two parts. One part consists of employees who desire OASDI

---

[1]However, the OASDI and Railroad Retirement programs are coordinated by certain coordinating provisions. See Chapter 19 for further details.

[2]U.S. Congress, House, Committee on Ways and Means, *Background Material and Data on Programs within the Jurisdiction of the Committee on Ways and Means* (Washington, D.C.: U.S. Government Printing Office, 1989), Table 3, p. 69.

coverage, and the other part includes those members who do not desire coverage, provided, however, that new members of the retirement system coverage group must also be covered under the OASDI program.

As a result of legislation enacted in 1986, state and local government employees hired after March 1986 are now required to pay the HI portion of the total OASDHI tax. However, additional legislation is needed to cover them under the OASDI portion of the total program.

Compulsory coverage of state and local government would have two major advantages: (1) the gaps-in-protection problem discussed earlier would be reduced and (2) the additional tax revenues would improve the financial solvency of the program.

Other Excluded Groups

The remaining excluded groups do not appear to be a major problem at the present time. The number of low-paid farm and domestic workers and self-employed persons with low earnings is relatively small. Also, there are serious administrative difficulties in trying to extend additional OASDI coverage to these groups.

Also excluded are newspaper carriers under age 18 and employment of a child under age 18 in an unincorporated business. However, children are likely to obtain coverage in other occupations as they grow older.[3]

HIGHER RETIREMENT AGE

When the Social Security Act was enacted in 1935, age 65 was selected as the normal retirement age for full benefits. However, there was no scientific, social, or gerontological basis for selection of that age as the normal retirement age. The Committee on Economic Security believed that age 60 was too low and age 70 too high for normal retirement; consequently, age 65 was considered to be the most acceptable retirement age.[4]

At the present time, the normal retirement age for full benefits is still age 65. However, the normal retirement age for full benefits will gradually be increased in the future to age 66 in 2009 and to age 67 in 2027. Early retirement will still be permitted at age 62, but the actuarial reduction in benefits for workers at age 62 will gradually be increased from 20 to 30 percent (from 25 percent to 35 percent for spouses). Medicare benefits for the aged are still available at age 65.

---

[3]Robert J. Myers, *Social Security,* 3rd ed. (Homewood, Ill.: Richard D. Irwin, 1985), pp. 435 and 438.
[4]Wilbur J. Cohen, *Retirement Policies under Social Security* (Berkeley and Los Angeles: University of California Press, 1957), p. 24.

Reasons for a Higher Retirement Age

Several demographic, financial, and economic reasons justify a higher normal retirement age in the future. They include the following:

1. INCREASE IN LIFE EXPECTANCY. A higher retirement age is justified because the life expectancy of older workers is expected to increase in the future. It is estimated that, under the intermediate actuarial estimates, the life expectancy for males at age 65 in the year 2000 will be about 3.7 years higher than it was in 1940 when the Social Security program was in its infancy. The life expectancy for females is estimated to be 6.2 years higher.[5] Thus, since older workers are expected to live longer in the future, a higher retirement age can be justified.

2. SUBSTANTIAL IMPROVEMENT IN LONG-RANGE FINANCIAL SOLVENCY. A higher retirement age will substantially improve the future financial solvency of the OASDI program. Prior to enactment of the 1983 amendments, the OASDI program was expected to develop a serious long-range actuarial deficit. The Office of the Actuary in the Social Security Administration estimated that the long-range actuarial deficit of the OASDI trust funds over the 75-year valuation period from 1983 to 2057 would have been 2.09 percent of taxable payroll.[6] The long-term deficit was due to the increased number of retired persons in the future as the "baby boom" generation retires; to the wage-indexed benefit structure that guarantees to future retirees increased real benefits that will reflect general increases in the standard of living over their working careers; and to inadequate long-term financing in previous congressional actions.[7]

However, as a result of the new higher retirement age of 67 in the future, the long-term financial solvency of the OASDI program has been substantially improved. The long-term financial condition of the Social Security program is discussed in greater detail in Chapter 7.

3. INCREASE IN DEMAND FOR OLDER WORKERS. A higher retirement age is also justified on the grounds that there will be an increase in the demand for older workers in the future. Because of declining birth rates, the proportion of younger workers in the labor force is expected to decline in the future. Thus, it is argued that the demand will increase for older workers who will be better trained and educated than older workers today. A higher retirement age will encourage older workers to continue working, and employers can profitably take advantage of their skills and experience.

---

[5]Alice Wade, *Social Security Area Population Projections: 1989*, Actuarial Study no. 105, Social Security Administration, June 1989, Table 10, p. 14.

[6]U.S. Congress, House, Committee on Ways and Means, *Social Security Act Amendments of 1983*, Report 98–25, Part 1, 98th Cong., 1st sess., March 4, 1983, p. 65.

[7]Ibid.

Arguments against a Higher Retirement Age

Several counterarguments are offered against a higher future retirement age. They include the following:

1. EQUIVALENT TO A REDUCTION IN BENEFITS. It is argued that the increase in the retirement age from 65 to 67 is equivalent to a reduction in benefits, since the benefits will be paid over a relatively shorter period. However, in opposition to this argument, proponents of a higher retirement age point out that the increase in life expectancy in the future will more than offset the higher retirement age of 67 so that total benefits paid to a typical retired worker need not decline.

2. HARMFUL TO MINORITY WORKERS. It is also argued that a higher retirement age will be harmful to minority workers (blacks, Hispanics, and native Americans) who have lower life expectancies than does the general population. Thus, it is argued that many minority workers will die before age 67 and never receive any retirement benefits.

3. HARMFUL TO OLDER WORKERS WITH HEALTH PROBLEMS. Another argument against a higher retirement age is that older workers with health problems will be harmed. It is argued that many older workers in poor health may not be able to qualify for OASDI disability income benefits; thus, they will be forced to remain in the labor force for a longer period to collect full retirement benefits. Also, although older workers in poor health will still have the option of retiring early at age 62, they will be faced with a larger actuarial reduction in their benefits. Under the new law, the actuarial reduction in benefits at age 62 will gradually be increased from 20 to 30 percent of the worker's PIA in the future.

4. REDUCTION IN JOB OPPORTUNITIES FOR YOUNGER WORKERS. A higher future retirement age is also opposed on the grounds that job and promotion opportunities for younger workers will be reduced. It is argued that the United States economy historically has experienced few periods of full employment and that chronic unemployment and periodic recessions will continue in the future. If older workers retire before or at age 65, their jobs become available for younger workers. Moreover, the argument that labor shortages in the future will increase the demand for older workers is greeted with skepticism, since critics point out that relatively high unemployment rates will continue in the future. If the labor shortage does not materialize, large numbers of older persons who lose their jobs in a recession will be forced into early retirement with lower benefits (reduction of 30 percent at age 62 instead of 20 percent); thus, the higher retirement age of 67 will only exacerbate the unemployment problems of older workers in the future.

ADEQUACY OF BENEFITS

The adequacy of the monthly cash benefits is another important issue that merits some discussion. We noted in Chapter 2 that the OASDI program is designed to provide only a minimum floor of income. However, there is considerable disagreement concerning the meaning of a "minimum floor of income." Whether OASDI benefits are adequate depends on the measure of adequacy that is selected.

Replacement Rate

There are several measures of adequacy that can be used to evaluate the level of OASDI retirement benefits. One commonly used measure of benefit adequacy is the replacement rate. *The replacement rate is the ratio of the worker's initial OASDI retirement benefits to earnings in the year prior to retirement.* The replacement rate can be based on either gross earnings or on net earnings after making an adjustment for taxes and work-related expenses. The replacement rate is an extremely useful concept, since it indicates the extent to which OASDI retirement benefits permit retired workers to maintain a standard of living reasonably close to the standard of living they have attained prior to retirement.

Retired workers typically have their mortgages paid off, their children are grown, and they do not have work-related expenses that younger workers usually have. Also, payroll taxes are not paid on OASDI benefits. Thus, retired workers do not need 100 percent of their gross earnings replaced to maintain their previous standard of living.

Table 6-1 shows the gross replacement rates under the OASDI program for a minimum, average, and maximum wage earner from 1940 through 2000. The replacement rates are based on the primary insurance amounts for workers who retired at age 65 after full-time careers with steady earnings. The minimum earner is a worker who earns only the federal minimum wage; the average earner is a worker who has average earnings in the economy (as recorded by the Social Security earnings index); and the maximum earner is a worker who has earnings equal to the maximum OASDI wage base. *The gross replacement rate in 1990 was 77 percent for a minimum earner, about 43 percent for an average earner, and 24 percent for the maximum earner.* If a retired worker has a spouse age 65 or older, she or he can receive 50 percent of the worker's primary insurance amount. Thus, for a minimum-wage married couple, the replacement rate may be close to or slightly in excess of 100 percent.

Based on the replacement rate concept, OASDI benefits generally are adequate for most minimum-wage earners. However, OASDI benefits are not adequate for most average- and maximum-wage earners with no other source of income. However, an important principle must be stressed at this point. *The OASDI program is not designed to provide for the full replacement of earnings, but only to provide a minimum floor of income.* Retired workers are expected to provide addi-

**TABLE 6-1 Social Security Replacement Rates, 1940–2000
(in percent)**

| CALENDAR YEAR | REPLACEMENT RATES[1] | | |
	Minimum Earner	Average Earner	Maximum Earner
1940	39.8%	26.3%	16.5%
1950	42.8	19.7	21.2
1960	45.0	33.3	29.8
1965	40.0	31.4	32.9
1970	42.7	34.3	29.2
1975	59.5	42.3	30.1
1976	57.9	43.7	32.1
1977	57.2	44.8	33.5
1978	62.7	46.7	34.7
1979	60.4	48.1	36.1
1980	64.0	51.1	32.5
1981	68.5	54.4	33.4
1982	63.8	48.7	28.6
1983	63.7	45.8	26.4
1984	62.4	42.9	23.7
1985	63.8	40.9	22.8
1986	65.7	41.2	23.1
1987	67.6	41.3	22.6
1988	71.2	40.9	23.1
1989	76.0	41.9	24.1
1990	77.4	42.8	24.4
2000	72.9	41.4	25.5

[1]Monthly PIAs in year of entitlement at age 65, expressed as percent of earnings in year prior to entitlement. Projections for 1988 and later are based on the Intermediate II-B assumptions of the 1988 OASDI Trustees' Report.

Source: U.S. Congress, House, Committee on Ways and Means, *Background Material and Data within the Jurisdiction of the Committee on Ways and Means* (Washington, D.C.: U.S. Government Printing Office, 1989), Table 8, p. 14.

tional amounts of income from their own resources, such as private pension, savings, investments, and insurance. The OASDI benefits, however, provide a solid base of income protection to average and maximum income workers who obviously need additional amounts of income during retirement to maintain their previous standard of living.

In addition, retired workers often have other sources of income to supplement their OASDI retirement benefits. *The vast majority of the aged have other sources of income.* For example, about 17 percent of the units with all members age 65 or over had some work earnings; 41 percent had retirement pensions other than OASDI and Railroad Retirement; and 71 percent had income from assets.[8]

---

[8]*Background Material and Data on Programs within the Jurisdiction of the Committee on Ways and Means,* 1989, Table 13, p. 923.

Finally, average- and upper-income workers should be expected to provide for more of their economic security in old age. They are more likely to be covered by private or government pensions and have greater amounts of personal savings and investments to supplement their OASDI benefits. Also, average- and upper-income workers are more likely to have individual retirement accounts (IRAs). Also, the relatively low replacement rates for maximum-income earners should not be viewed with alarm, since these persons generally have substantial amounts of investment and retirement income from other sources; part of the OASDI benefits is still income tax free, which is of considerable importance to upper-income beneficiaries. Finally, low-income beneficiaries whose OASDI benefits are inadequate may be eligible for supplemental income under public assistance (discussed later).

OASDI Benefits and Poverty

Another measure of benefit adequacy is the extent to which OASDI benefits keep aged persons out of poverty. OASDI benefits have a powerful impact in reducing poverty among aged beneficiaries. *In 1986, 14 percent of the aged units 65 or older whose families received OASDI benefits were counted poor. Without OASDI benefits, 51 percent of the aged units would have been counted poor.*[9] The OASDI benefits are particularly powerful in reducing poverty for aged black and Hispanic beneficiaries.

OASDI Benefits and Public Assistance

Another measure of benefit adequacy is to examine the proportion of aged beneficiaries who are forced to apply for supplemental public assistance benefits to meet their basic needs. Low-income workers whose OASDI retirement benefits are inadequate are often eligible for additional monthly cash benefits under the Supplemental Security Income (SSI) program for the aged, blind, and disabled. However, since only about 7 percent of all aged units 65 or older receive SSI benefits, OASDI retirement benefits can be considered reasonably adequate in keeping people off welfare.[10]

EARNINGS TEST

The earnings (retirement) test is another controversial issue in the OASDI program, and numerous views exist regarding its nature and purpose. Under the earnings test, OASDI benefits are withheld if earned income exceeds the max-

---

[9]Susan Grad, *Income of the Population 55 or Older, 1986*, Social Security Administration, Office of Policy, Office of Research and Statistics (June 1988), Table 53, p. 101.

[10]Ibid., Table 1, p. 1.

imum annual exempt amount. For beneficiaries ages 65–69, $1 of benefits is withheld for each $3 of earnings above the exempt amount. For beneficiaries under age 65, $1 of benefits is withheld for each $2 of excess earnings above the exempt amount. Several groups, including Congress, the Social Security Administration, labor unions, and consumer organizations, have debated, often bitterly and heatedly, the arguments for and against the test. Although several bills have been introduced to abolish the test, Congress has chosen to move toward liberalization of the test rather than its abolishment. And although proponents of the earnings test wish to retain it, they are not necessarily opposed to its liberalization.

Arguments in Support of the Earnings Test

Several arguments are advanced for retention of the earnings test. They include the following:

1. INSURANCE AGAINST THE LOSS OF EARNED INCOME.   One argument for retention of the test is that the OASDI program insures against the loss of earned income; if work earnings are not lost, the benefits should not be paid, and the retirement test is necessary to implement this purpose.

One risk insured against is the loss of earned income because of retirement at a specified age and not merely the *attainment* of a certain age. That is, the OASDI program is a retirement program and not merely an annuity program. If the benefits were automatically paid at some stated retirement age to workers with substantial work earnings, they would be receiving benefits even though they had not lost their earned income and the event being insured against had not occurred. The earnings test is necessary as an objective measure for determining whether the loss of earned income has occurred from retirement.

2. SUBSTANTIAL INCREASE IN COST.   Elimination of the earnings test will substantially increase the cost of the OASDI program in the short range. It is estimated that elimination of the earnings test for beneficiaries ages 65–69 would increase the cost of the program by about $24 billion for 1989–1993.[11]

It should be noted, however, that costs will increase only over the short range if the earnings test is abolished. After the delayed retirement credit reaches 8 percent for each year of delayed retirement in the future, the earnings test for workers over the normal retirement age (currently age 65) will be effectively eliminated. Under present law, a delayed retirement credit is available for each month of delayed retirement beyond the normal retirement age and up to age 70. For workers attaining age 65 in 1990–1991, the delayed retirement credit is $3\frac{1}{2}$ percent per year ($\frac{7}{24}$ of 1 percent monthly). The delayed retirement credit will increase gradually to 8 percent per year ($\frac{2}{3}$ of 1 percent monthly) in 2009 for

---

[11]Congressional Budget Office, Congress of the United States, *The Social Security Earnings Test and Options for Change,* Staff Working Paper (September 1988), Table 2, p. 26.

workers who delay retiring beyond the normal retirement age (then age 66). It is important to note that when the delayed retirement credit reaches 8 percent, it will be the approximate actuarial equivalent of the increase in benefits from a cost standpoint. Thus, once the delayed retirement credit reaches 8 percent, it makes no difference from a cost standpoint if the benefits are paid automatically at the normal retirement age (earnings test is abolished) or if the worker delays taking the benefits and receives instead a delayed retirement credit.

3. BENEFITS PAID TO UPPER-INCOME WORKERS. Elimination of the earnings test would result in the payment of additional benefits to upper-income workers who have not retired. For example, in 1986, 63 percent of the beneficiaries who had benefits withheld because of the earnings test earned $32,000 or more.[12] If the earnings test were repealed, most of the benefits would be paid to upper-income beneficiaries with incomes exceeding $32,000. Thus, instead of helping low- and middle-income workers, elimination of the earnings test would benefit largely those upper-income workers who have not yet retired.

4. EXPANSION OF EMPLOYMENT OPPORTUNITIES. It is also argued that the retirement test keeps older workers out of the labor force and expands employment opportunities for younger workers. This argument is a carry-over from the lack of employment opportunities for younger workers during the 1930s and may not be relevant during periods of full employment when labor is relatively scarce. However, during periods of high unemployment, employment of the aged may be less important than the loss of job opportunities for younger workers, and arguments for rationing jobs in favor of the young have greater validity.

5. RELATIVELY FEW PERSONS AFFECTED. A final argument for retention of the earnings test is that relatively few persons are affected. In 1986, only 600,000 persons, or less than 10 percent of the persons ages 65 through 69 who were eligible for OASDI benefits, had their benefits reduced because of the earnings test.[13] The other 90 percent either did not work or had earnings below the exempt amount. Thus, it is argued that since relatively few beneficiaries are affected by the test, it should be retained.

The preceding statistic, however, should be interpreted with caution since it tells us nothing about the number of older workers who would continue working or reenter the labor force if the earnings test were abolished. There is considerable evidence that suggests some workers may deliberately hold down their work earnings to avoid being penalized by the earnings test. Thus, work incentives may be significantly reduced by the test. This is an important point that will be discussed in greater detail later in the chapter.

---

[12]*Background Material and Data on Programs within the Jurisdiction of the Committee on Ways and Means,* 1989, Table 10, p. 19.

[13]Ibid., p. 18.

Arguments against the Earnings Test

Several persuasive arguments are presented against the earnings test. They include the following:

1. OPPRESSIVE TAX ON WORK EARNINGS ABOVE THE EXEMPT AMOUNT. Critics argue that the earnings test should be abolished because it results in an oppressive tax on work earnings above the maximum exempt amount. The beneficiary who works will lose OASDI benefits if his or her earnings are above the maximum exempt amount and must also pay Social Security taxes on the work earnings. The loss of benefits because of the earnings test can be viewed as a tax. In addition, a federal and state income tax must also be paid on the work earnings. Thus, when all taxes and the loss of benefits are considered, the marginal tax rate on the excess earnings may be inordinately high.

For example, assume that the beneficiary is in the 15 percent federal income tax bracket and earns an additional $1,000 above the exempt amount in 1990. Also assume that the state income tax is 4 percent. *A beneficiary under age 65 would net only $233.50, which is equivalent to a marginal tax rate of about 77 percent for earnings above the exempt amount. A beneficiary age 65–69 would net only $400.17, which is equivalent to a marginal tax rate of about 60 percent.*[14] This can be illustrated by the following:

	BENEFICIARIES UNDER AGE 65	BENEFICIARIES AGES 65–69
Earnings above the exempt amount	$1,000.00	$1,000.00
Loss of benefits because of the earnings test	−500.00	−333.33
Social Security tax	− 76.50	− 76.50
Federal income tax	−150.00	−150.00
State income tax	− 40.00	− 40.00
Net earnings =	$ 233.50	$ 400.17
Marginal tax rate =	76.65%	59.98%

The marginal tax rates are considerably higher than those shown above for self-employed persons, for beneficiaries who also must pay a federal income tax on their OASDI benefits, and for workers in the 28 or 33 percent income tax bracket. Thus, under the circumstances, few workers will want to work since the additional take-home pay is substantially reduced.

---

[14]The true marginal tax rates are somewhat lower than those indicated. For beneficiaries under age 65, the benefits are actuarially increased at age 65 to take into account the withholding of benefits because of the earnings test. Also, the rates shown do not reflect the impact of the delayed retirement credit on beneficiaries over the normal retirement age. The true marginal tax rate would be somewhat lower because of the increase in benefits for those months in which benefits are withheld because of the earnings test. Because most beneficiaries do not consider these factors in their decision to work or not work, they are ignored in the analysis.

2. DAMPENING OF WORK INCENTIVES.   It is also argued that the earnings test should be abolished because it strikes at the very heart of the work ethic embodied in the OASDI program and results in a dampening of work incentives. Some studies suggest that work incentives are reduced for some workers whose earnings are approaching the annual exempt amount.[15] Some workers may deliberately hold down their work earnings to avoid being penalized by the earnings test. Critics of the test argue that the OASDI program is based on work, and in general, as work earnings increase, OASDI cash benefits will also increase. However, as we noted earlier, work efforts for some workers may be reduced as earned income approaches the annual exempt amount. Thus, work incentives are dampened, which conflicts with the work ethic embodied in the program.

In addition, the earnings test is illogically applied. Persons age 70 and over can earn any amount and still receive full benefits. In effect, the law encourages some older workers age 70 and over to reenter or remain in the labor force, since they are not penalized if they earn more than the maximum allowed. Thus, the law encourages older workers to work when they are least able to work because of poor health, but it discourages employment at a younger age when workers are more capable of working if their health permits.

3. DISCRIMINATION AGAINST EARNED INCOME.   It is also argued that the earnings test is unfair, since it discriminates against earned income in favor of nonearned or investment income. As we noted in Chapter 5, income from savings, investments, insurance, pensions, rents, royalties, and similar types of income are not subject to the earnings test. The purpose of this exemption is to encourage persons to save for their old age and for other contingencies. If the OASDI cash benefits were reduced or terminated because of investment income or private insurance, individual saving for old age and thrift would be discouraged.

However, critics argue that it is illogical to exempt investment income from the earnings test but not earned income. Work earnings reduce economic insecurity and also make it possible for a worker to save for retirement and other needs. If the exemption of investment income from the earnings test is justified on the grounds that saving is encouraged and economic security is enhanced, it follows logically that earned income should also be exempt from the earnings test on the same grounds. *Stated differently, why should one dollar of investment income be treated more favorably than one dollar of work earnings, especially when most of the investment income is received by upper-income persons?* Indeed, one can argue that a

---

[15]For example, see Aldona Robbins and Gary Robbins, *Paying People Not to Work: The Economic Cost of the Social Security Retirement Earnings,* NCPA Policy Report no. 42 (Dallas, Tex.: The National Center for Policy Analysis, 1989). See also Anthony J. Pellechio, *The Social Security Earnings Test, Labor Supply Distortions, and Foregone Payroll Tax Revenue, Working Paper 272* (Washington, D.C.: National Bureau of Economic Research, 1978); U.S. Congress, House, Committee on Ways and Means, *President's Proposals for Revision in the Social Security System,* Hearings before the Committee on Ways and Means, 90th Cong., 1st sess., on H.R. 5710, 1967, Part 1, p. 319; and U.S. Department of Health, Education and Welfare, Social Security Administration, Office of Research Statistics, *The Effects of the 1966 Retirement Test Changes on the Earnings of Workers Aged 65–72,* Note No. 1 (January 30, 1970).

dollar of work earnings should be treated more favorably, since working and the receipt of earned income are consistent with the work ethic embodied in the Social Security program, and Social Security payroll taxes are also paid on the earned income. In contrast, investment income can be received while not working and is not subject to Social Security payroll taxes.

4. COMPLEX AND COSTLY TO ADMINISTER.   Critics also argue that the earnings test is complex and costly to administer and also encourages some beneficiaries to cheat. Thus, it is argued that elimination of the test would hold down administration expenses, since the earnings test would no longer have to be administered and policed. Also, there would be no need for some beneficiaries to cheat to avoid the loss of benefits. Sen. Robert Dole (R., Kans.) maintains that the Social Security Administration must use 8 percent of its employees just to police the income levels of senior citizens.[16]

5. EARNED RIGHT TO BENEFITS.   Some critics argue that the earnings test should be eliminated and the benefits automatically paid at the normal retirement age (now 65) because the worker has purchased and paid for the benefits and so has earned the right to them at that age. This argument is fallacious on several grounds. First, currently retired workers have paid only a small fraction of the true actuarial costs of their OASDI benefits, so they have not strictly earned the right to them. Second, the benefits are paid on the basis of a statutory right to them, not on the basis of an earned right. Finally, although younger workers, who contribute throughout their entire working lifetimes, have a more defensible claim to benefits on the basis of an earned right, it does not follow that they should receive them automatically at a certain age because they have earned them. Retirement benefits are never paid automatically at a certain specified age since other eligibility requirements must also be fulfilled.

Proposals for Changing the Earnings Test

Several proponents have been made to change the earnings test so that the loss of benefits from excess earnings is less severe. One recent proposal passed by the Senate would increase the annual exempt amount for people ages 65–69 to $10,560. For the first $5,000 of excess earnings, benefits would be reduced only $1 for each $4 of excess earnings above the exempt amount; any additional excess earnings would then be subject to the regular $1 for $3 reduction rule. The automatic adjustment provisions would apply only to the annual exempt amount, and the $1 for $4 reduction rule would continue to apply to the first $5,000 of excess earnings.

The two-tier proposal would make the earnings test even more complex and difficult to administer and police. However, work incentives may be expanded slightly for low- and moderate-income beneficiaries since the marginal tax rate on the first $5,000 of excess earnings would be only 25 percent.

---

[16]*Hiawatha Daily World* (Kansas), April 20, 1989.

Robert Myers, former chief actuary of the Social Security Administration, has also recommended that the earnings test should be abolished for persons who delay retirement beyond the normal retirement age. However, to encourage people to work, the benefits would be increased by a delayed retirement credit of 8 percent for each year of delayed retirement. As stated earlier, the delayed retirement credit will be gradually increased in the future to 8 percent for those workers who reach the normal retirement age in 2009 (then age 66). Under the Myers proposal, the delayed retirement credit of 8 percent would be moved up to the present to encourage working. In addition, a continuing education campaign would be undertaken to inform workers of the advantages of deferring benefits beyond the normal retirement age (including better income design and possibly more favorable income tax treatment of benefits).

TAXATION OF OASDI BENEFITS

A portion of the OASDI benefits must be included in the taxable income of taxpayers whose adjusted gross incomes, when combined with tax-exempt interest and 50 percent of their benefits, exceed certain dollar thresholds.

The taxation of benefits is a sensitive and important issue in view of the widespread taxpayers' revolt in recent years. Persuasive arguments are presented by both those who support and those who are opposed to the taxation of benefits.

Arguments in Support of the Taxation of Benefits

Several arguments are used to justify the taxation of OASDI benefits. They include the following:

1. SUBSTANTIAL INCREASE IN REVENUES. Taxation of part of the benefits provides substantial amounts of additional revenue needed to maintain the financial solvency of the system. Taxation of OASDI benefits in fiscal 1990 generated an estimated $4.5 billion of income for the OASDI and DI trust funds, or 1.5 percent of total 1990 financing.[17]

2. TAXATION OF UPPER-INCOME PERSONS. It is also argued that the taxation of benefits affects only upper-income beneficiaries. In 1989, 5.8 million persons, or only about 17 percent of all OASDI beneficiaries, were affected by the taxation of OASDI benefits. Most of the individuals or couples who were taxed had annual incomes of $30,000 or more (see Table 6-2).

However, the claim that the taxation of OASDI benefits affects only upper-income individuals is misleading. The dollar thresholds of $25,000 for a single person and $32,000 for a married couple are not indexed. Thus, as

---

[17]*Background Material and Data on Programs within the Jurisdiction of the Committee on Ways and Means,* 1989, Table 11, p. 86.

TABLE 6-2   Effect of Taxing Social Security Benefits, by Income Class, 1989

LEVEL OF INDIVIDUAL OR COUPLE INCOME[1]	PERSONS 65 AND OVER		ALL RECIPIENTS		AGGREGATE AMOUNT OF SOCIAL SECURITY BENEFITS (IN BILLIONS OF DOLLARS)	AGGREGATE AMOUNT OF TAXES ON BENEFITS (IN BILLIONS OF DOLLARS)	TAXES AS A PERCENT OF BENEFITS
	Number (in thousands)	Number Affected by Taxation of Benefits[2] (in thousands)	Number of Social Security Beneficiaries[3] (in thousands)	Number Affected by Taxation of Benefits (in thousands)			
Less than $10,000	9,124	0	11,560	0	$ 53.7	0	0.0%
$10,000 to $15,000	4,290	0	5,184	0	30.8	0	0.0
$15,000 to $20,000	3,483	0	4,094	0	25.7	0	0.0
$20,000 to $25,000	2,884	0	3,518	0	22.2	0	0.0
$25,000 to $30,000	2,278	122	2,751	167	17.5	(4)	0.1
$30,000 to $40,000	3,161	927	3,612	1,180	23.3	$0.4	1.7
$40,000 to $50,000	1,657	1,430	1,810	1,710	12.3	.7	5.5
$50,000 to $100,000	2,119	1,891	2,224	2,217	15.0	1.9	12.8
At least $100,000	663	549	567	567	3.9	.6	15.5
All	29,659	4,919	35,319	5,840	$204.4	$3.6	1.8%

[1] Cash income (based on income of tax filing unit), plus capital gains realizations.
[2] Some elderly individuals do not receive Social Security benefits and are thus not affected by taxation of benefits.
[3] Includes beneficiaries under and over age 65.
[4] Less than $50 million.
Note: Aggregate benefits and revenues are understated by about 10 percent because of benefits paid abroad, deaths of recipients before the March CPS interview, and exclusion of institutionalized beneficiaries. The number of beneficiaries is also understated.

Source: U.S. Congress, House, Committee on Ways and Means, *Background Material and Data on Programs within the Jurisdiction of the Committee on Ways and Means* (Washington, D.C.: U.S. Government Printing Office, 1989), Table 13, p. 26. The data are derived from the Congressional Budget Office and are based on the Current Population Survey (CPS).

average earnings and OASDI benefits continue to increase in the future, the majority of beneficiaries will pay taxes on part of their OASDI benefits.

3. BENEFITS UNDER OTHER RETIREMENT SYSTEMS NOW TAXABLE.   It is argued that OASDI benefits should be taxed because benefits under other retirement systems are taxable to the extent that they exceed a worker's after-tax contributions. Also, taxing part of the OASDI benefits improves equity in taxation by treating more equally nearly all forms of retirement income and other income designed to replace part of the worker's lost wages (such as unemployment compensation).

4. WINDFALL BENEFITS NOW BEING PAID.   Taxation of benefits for upper-income individuals is also justified on the grounds that present beneficiaries are receiving large windfall benefits, since they have paid only a small proportion of the actuarial cost of their benefits. The typical retired person receives back in benefits all Social Security tax contributions in less than two years.

5. MORE EQUITABLE TREATMENT OF YOUNGER PEOPLE.   By taxing benefits, younger people are treated more fairly, since the present generation of upper-income beneficiaries also shares in the current cost of the program.

Arguments against the Taxation of Benefits

Those opposed to the taxation of OASDI benefits offer several powerful counterarguments in support of their position. They include the following:

1. ESTABLISHES A NEEDS TEST ON BENEFITS.   A well-established principle in the OASDI program is that a needs test is not required in order for a person to receive benefits. It is argued that this principle is violated by taxing benefits, since an indirect needs test is introduced into the program. In effect, upper-income beneficiaries are being told they do not need OASDI benefits because of their incomes; therefore, they should be taxed on part of the benefits.

2. PENALIZES THE THRIFTY.   It is also argued that people who are thrifty and save for their old age are penalized the most by taxing benefits and that the taxation of benefits discourages savings. People who receive tax-exempt interest must now count this income in determining whether their combined income exceeds the base amount. Thus, the attractiveness of tax-exempt investments to some upper-income beneficiaries may be reduced in the future. Also, the present method of taxing benefits is viewed as a subtle and indirect way of taxing income that is now exempt from federal taxation (such as interest from municipal bonds).

3. COMPLEX AND DIFFICULT TO UNDERSTAND.   The present method of taxing benefits is also considered complex and difficult for taxpayers to understand. Thus, it is argued that the taxing provisions add to the complexities of the already complex Internal Revenue Code and represent a dramatic departure

from the movement toward a more simplified and understandable federal income tax code.

    4. HEAVY TOTAL TAX BURDEN ON THE ELDERLY. Critics of the present system of taxation also argue that the elderly as a group are the most heavily taxed group in our society. We noted earlier the relatively high marginal tax rates that can result from application of the earnings test. However, when the taxation of OASDI benefits is also combined with the loss of benefits under the earnings test, the federal and state income tax, and the Social Security payroll tax, the overall tax burden on some older workers can be excessively high.

    A recent study by the National Center for Policy Analysis that was widely quoted in the national media showed that marginal tax rates for older beneficiaries who work can easily exceed 70 or 80 percent when all of the aforementioned factors are taken into account. Under certain conditions, the study also showed that marginal tax rates for some workers can even exceed 100 percent.[18] Thus, the taxation of benefits when combined with other taxes and the loss of benefits under the earnings test can discourage older persons from working. This is unfortunate since society is deprived of the experience, skills, and talents of older workers. In addition, growth in the labor force is slowing down, and labor shortages are appearing in parts of the economy. The combined impact of the taxation of earned income and OASDI benefits along with the loss of benefits under the earnings test can aggravate such shortages since older retired beneficiaries have little financial incentive to reenter the labor force.

TREATMENT OF WOMEN

The treatment of women under the OASDI program is another important issue. Women often complain bitterly about the inequities that they perceive to exist in the present program. Let us briefly examine this important issue.

Inequitable Treatment of Women

One problem involves the payment of retirement benefits to a working wife. Under the law, the wife can receive a retirement benefit based on either her own earnings or those of her husband, and the retirement benefit based on her husband's earnings is often higher than the one based on her own. She may have lower covered earnings because of irregular or part-time employment, years of little or no earnings because of family responsibilities, or employment in low-paying occupations. Thus, a working wife often receives a retirement benefit that is no larger than the one received by the nonworking wife, and she may feel that her tax contributions for OASDI retirement benefits are wasted.

---

[18]John C. Goodman and A. James Meigs, *The Elderly: People the Supply-Side Revolution Forgot*, NCPA Report No. 135 (Dallas, Tex.: The National Center for Policy Analysis, 1989).

A second problem is that a working couple may receive lower total OASDI retirement benefits than another couple with the same earned income. For example, assume that Jim is an accountant who retires at age 62 in 1989 with average indexed monthly earnings of $2,000. Jim's nonworking wife is also age 62. Bob and Mary, however, work full time in a factory, and both retire at age 62 in 1989 with identical average indexed monthly earnings of $1,000 each. Based on the benefits payable in January 1989, and ignoring the automatic adjustment provisions, the following benefits would be paid:

ONE EARNER	(AIME)	MONTHLY RETIREMENT BENEFITS
Jim	$2,000	$669
Wife	—	313
Total	$2,000	$982

TWO EARNERS	(AIME)	MONTHLY RETIREMENT BENEFITS
Bob	$1,000	$413
Mary	1,000	413
Total	$2,000	$826

Jim and his nonworking wife receive total monthly retirement benefits of $982. However, even though Bob and Mary together have the same average indexed monthly earnings as Jim, they would only receive total monthly benefits of $826, or about 16 percent less than Jim and his nonworking wife.

Women may also receive inequitable treatment if a divorce occurs. Nationally, for each two marriages, on average, there is one divorce. Under present law, eligibility for the retirement benefits based on the spouse's earnings terminates at divorce unless the marriage has lasted at least 10 years. When the couple gets a divorce, the wife may lose her right to a wife's or widow's benefit and be inadequately protected. In effect, her previous income contribution to the home and family would be wiped out if she loses her right to OASDI benefits after a divorce occurs.

Counterarguments against the Inequitable Treatment of Women

Several counterarguments are offered in opposition to the commonly held viewpoint that women, especially married women with children, receive inequitable treatment under the OASDI program. First, it is argued that a working wife receives valuable survivor and disability insurance protection while she is working. Second, the weighted benefit formula and the dropping of the five lowest years of earnings in computing the retirement benefit offset, to a considerable degree, the loss of earnings because of family responsibilities and relatively low covered earnings of women. Third, there is no actuarial reduction in benefits because women live longer than men. Finally, a working wife may be able to retire earlier than her husband based on her own earnings. If she did not work and acquire a fully insured status, this valuable right would be lost.

Proposals for Eliminating Inequities against Women

Several proposals have been made to eliminate the possible inequities against women under the OASDI program. They include the following:

1. GIVE CREDIT FOR CHILD CARE YEARS. The National Commission on Social Security recommended that the special minimum benefit for long-term low-wage earners should be changed to allow credit for up to 10 years for child care and the number of creditable years would be increased from 30 to 35. A child care year is one in which the worker has a child age 6 and under and did not earn sufficient income to obtain a year of coverage. This change would increase the benefits for about one in five retired women, and most of the benefit increase would go to persons whose benefits under present law are below the poverty threshold.

2. INCLUDE SOCIAL SECURITY BENEFITS IN PROPERTY SETTLEMENT. There is an increasing tendency for the divorce courts to grant a divorced spouse rights of entitlement to private pension benefits. In view of this trend, *the National Commission on Social Security recommended that a plan should be developed to include entitlement to OASDI benefits, along with other property, when property is divided in a divorce.* The commission believes that any disposition of property rights should take into account the existence of OASDI benefits.

3. SHARE THE COMBINED EARNINGS. Under this approach, the worker's benefits would be based on his or her earnings while single and on the combined earnings of both persons after marriage. At retirement, each person would receive a benefit based on one-half of the combined earnings. If a divorce occurred, each would receive one-half of the combined earnings credits, regardless of how long the marriage had lasted. One disadvantage of this approach, however, is that the division of credits at the time of divorce would reduce the benefits for both the higher-paid spouse and any future family of that person. Thus, under this approach, benefits would increase for some persons and be reduced for others.

To determine the feasibility of some type of earnings sharing approach to benefits, the 1983 amendments required the U.S. Department of Health and Human Services to study and develop a program for the sharing of earnings by the spouses during the period of their marriage. The study showed that women generally would receive higher benefits under an earnings sharing system, but many individual women and most men would receive lower benefits.[19]

---

[19]"Report on the Earnings Sharing Implementation Study," *Social Security Bulletin*, Vol. 48, No. 3 (March 1985), p. 31.

IS THE YOUNGER WORKER TREATED FAIRLY UNDER THE OASDI PROGRAM?

One of the most controversial and complex issues in the OASDI program is whether a young worker receives his or her money's worth in terms of contributions and benefits. It is argued that the OASDI program is a "bad buy" for the younger worker, since the actuarial value of the *combined employer-employee tax contributions* will exceed the actuarial value of the benefits he or she will receive. Thus, some critics say that younger workers are "cheated" and that they should be allowed to purchase protection from private insurers. Let us examine the argument that the OASDI program is inequitable to younger workers.

Illustrative Studies

Several researchers have attempted to compare the value of the OASDI protection with the OASDI tax contributions to determine whether the younger worker receives his or her money's worth under the program.[20] Most of the studies have concentrated on only the retirement and survivor portions of the OASDI program. *In addition, the studies often assume that the employer's portion of the total tax should be made completely available for the individual worker; that is, both the employer's portion and the employee's portion should be used to provide benefits for the individual employee.* This is a key point and one that we shall return to later. Let us first examine an earlier study by the 1979 Advisory Council on Social Security that addresses the equity question in terms of benefit/tax ratios.

Advisory Council on Social Security Study. Table 6-3 illustrates the benefit/tax ratios for a hypothetical group of workers who retired at age 65 in 1979. The benefit/tax ratio is defined as the present value of the OASDI benefits that workers can expect to receive in the future divided by the present value of the OASDI taxes they can expect to pay (under 1979 law). *A ratio exceeding 1 indicates that the present value of expected future benefits exceeds the present value of expected future employee taxes to be paid. A ratio above 2 indicates that the present value of future benefits exceeds the present value of expected combined employer-employee taxes.*

Table 6-3 shows the enormous bargain and windfall benefits that current beneficiaries now enjoy. The present value of the benefits paid to single workers

---

[20]See Robert J. Myers and Bruce D. Schobel, "A Money's-Worth Analysis of Social Security Retirement Benefits," *Transactions,* Society of Actuaries, Vol. 35, 1983, pp. 533–561. For earlier studies, see Orlo Nichols and Richard G. Schreitmueller, *Some Comparisons of the Value of a Worker's Social Security Taxes and Benefits,* Social Security Administration, Office of the Actuary, Actuarial Note 95 (April 1978); Shirley Scheibla, "Anti-Social Security: The System Is Inflationary and Loaded with Inequities," *Barron's,* January 21, 1974, pp. 3 and 16–18; John A. Brittain, *The Payroll Tax for Social Security* (Washington, D.C.: The Brookings Institution, 1972), Chap. VI; and Elizabeth Deran, "Some Economic Effects of High Taxes for Social Insurance," *Old Age Income Assurance, Part III: Public Programs,* A Compendium of Papers on Problems and Policy Issues in the Public and Private System, Subcommittee on Fiscal Policy of the Joint Economic Committee, 90th Cong., 1st sess., 1967 (Washington, D.C.: U.S. Government Printing Office, 1967), pp. 181–201.

TABLE 6-3   Benefit/Tax Ratios for Hypothetical Workers Retiring at Age 65 in 1979

WORKER	BENEFIT/TAX RATIO
Single male, maximum earner	4.97
Single male, average earner	5.51
Single male, low earner	7.07
Single female, maximum earner	6.21
Single female, average earner	6.88
Single female, low earner	8.82
Married male worker with dependent spouse, maximum earner	9.19
Married male worker with dependent spouse, average earner	10.18
Married male worker with dependent spouse, low earner	13.06

Note: The ratio is computed using only OASI employee contributions.

Source: *Reports of the 1979 Advisory Council on Social Security,* Committee on Ways and Means, U.S. House of Representatives (Washington, D.C.: U.S. Government Printing Office, 1980), Table 3, Chap. 3.

with average earnings who retired in 1979 is more than five times as great as their *own* contributions for Old-Age and Survivor's Insurance. Low-income wage earners with dependent spouses will receive benefits with a present value equal to about 13 times the value of their *own* contributions. However, the benefit/tax ratios for future beneficiaries will be substantially lower than the ratios attained by present beneficiaries, as will be pointed out later.

Myers' Study.   Robert J. Myers, former chief actuary of the Social Security Administration, also has provided valuable information concerning the treatment of younger workers under the program based on the 1983 amendments.[21] His analysis considers only the employee's part of the OASI total tax. DI taxes and HI taxes are not counted since it is assumed that the worker has paid for the DI and HI protection with the taxes. The analysis also ignores the value of survivor benefits under the program for death before age 65 and the substantial forfeiture that could occur if a single worker with no dependents dies before retirement.

Table 6-4 shows the benefit/tax ratios for male workers who entered the labor force at age 25 in 1985 and will retire at age 67 in 2027. The male worker with maximum covered earnings pays OASI taxes with an accumulated value of $922,038. The present value of the benefits at age 67 is $1,257,340.[22] Thus, the benefit/tax ratio is 1.36, which is significantly lower than the ratios illustrated in the 1979 Advisory Council on Social Security study for persons retiring at age 65 in 1979 (see Table 6-3). If the worker has an eligible spouse the same age with no benefits based on his or her own earnings, the benefit/tax ratio is 2.50.

---

[21]Myers, *Social Security,* pp. 462–465 and 478–483.

[22]Myers, *Social Security,* p. 482. It is assumed that wages increase $5\frac{1}{2}$ percent annually, the CPI increases 4 percent annually, and the interest rate is 6 percent.

TABLE 6-4   **New Male Workers Entering the Labor Force at Age 25
and Retiring at Age 67 in 2027: Benefit/Tax Ratios**

MAXIMUM EARNER

Accumulated value of employee OASI taxes at age 67 in 2027	$ 922,038
Present value of benefits at age 67 in 2027 (male worker, age 67)	$1,257,340
Benefit/tax ratio	1.36

MARRIED COUPLE

Accumulated value of employee OASI taxes at age 67 in 2027	$ 922,038
Present value of benefits at age 67 in 2027 (married couple both age 67)	$2,305,075
Benefit/tax ratio	2.50

Source: Based on Robert J. Myers, *Social Security,* 3rd ed. (Homewood, Ill.: Richard D. Irwin, 1985), pp. 481–482.

Criticisms of the "Bad Buy" Argument

The allegation that the younger worker is "cheated" under the OASDI program because the actuarial value of the total tax contributions often exceeds the value of the benefits can be criticized on several grounds: (1) imputation of the employer's contribution to a specific individual, (2) failure to make adjustments for other benefits, (3) doubtful assumptions used, and (4) noncomparable forms of insurance.

Imputation of the Employer's Contribution to a Specific Individual. Almost all empirical studies attempting to show that the OASDI program is a "bad buy" for younger workers use contribution figures that include the employer's portion of the tax; that is, the value of the *entire combined employer-employee contribution* is measured against the value of the retired employee's benefit. This is clearly an unreasonable assumption.

The employer's portion of the total tax contribution is often interpreted incorrectly in one of two ways: either as a private insurance premium that is segregated solely for the employer's own employees or as a general tax. A more correct interpretation of the employer's contribution is somewhere between these two extremes. The employer's contribution is neither a private insurance premium (and thus available only for a specific employee) nor a general tax for general government purposes. It properly should be considered as a social insurance premium for all covered employees. *More specifically, the employer's contribution is considered to be pooled for the general benefit of all covered persons and is not earmarked for the benefit of any specific person.*[23]

This condition is necessary to achieve the objectives of a social insurance program. When such a program is first started, some people are already near retirement. Also, certain groups such as low-income people are unable to pay the full actuarial cost of their benefits. In order to provide socially adequate benefits,

[23]See Myers, *Social Security,* pp. 453–454 and 462–465.

full benefits must be paid to these people when they retire, even though the actuarial value of the protection provided them exceeds the actuarial value of the contributions made by them or on their behalf. However, someone must pay for these "windfall" benefits. And their cost can be viewed conceptually as being paid by the *pooled employers' contributions.*[24] Thus, the employer's contribution should not be viewed as being made completely available for the individual employee on whose behalf the contribution is made, since the employer's contribution is pooled for the general benefit of all covered persons.

The use of the employer's contribution under the OASDI program is not unique. In a contributory private pension plan, the employer's contribution is used in similar situations. For example, workers who are close to retirement when they are first covered receive past service credits so that their retirement benefits will be more adequate, and they can retire in a socially acceptable manner. Thus, these workers also receive windfall benefits for which someone must pay. And once again, the employer's contributions are used for this purpose. Also, if the private pension plan is liberalized with increased benefits, part of the employer's contribution pays for the greater value of the past service credits.

Robert Myers, former chief actuary of the Social Security Administration, claims that the employer's contribution belongs to the system as a whole and not to any specific employee. Although the burden of the employer's contribution is ultimately borne by the workers in the form of lower wage increases or higher prices for goods and services, it does not fall on the wage earners in exact proportion to the earnings on which the tax is paid. The incidence of the tax depends on many complex factors. Therefore, he concludes, the employer's tax should not be viewed as a matching contribution that is credited to each employee on the basis of the tax the employee pays.[25] Based on the preceding viewpoint, the younger worker is not cheated in terms of the total combined employer-employee contribution, since he or she is not entitled to the benefits based on the entire employer's contribution.

Finally, those who think that most or all of the employer's contributions should be assigned to a specific individual also base their argument on the grounds of greater individual equity in the OASDI program. However, if such a proposal were carried out, it would be impossible to pay benefits based on the social adequacy principle without substantial general revenue contributions. For example, the weighted benefit formula significantly favors low-income groups who receive benefits that substantially exceed the actuarial value of their contributions. Part of the employer's contribution can be viewed as being used to cover this deficit. This results in potentially lower benefits for younger workers than they would otherwise receive if the entire employer-employee contribution had been earmarked for them; but this is justified because the OASDI program is social insurance. If most or all of the employer's contribution were used to

---

[24]See the statement by Robert J. Myers on this point in *President's Proposals for Revision in the Social Security System*, pp. 330–332.

[25]*President's Proposals for Revision in the Social Security System*, pp. 330–331.

provide greater individual benefits for a specific worker (individual equity), it would be difficult to pay socially adequate benefits to the lower-income groups, who are unable to pay the full actuarial cost of their protection, and they would then receive relatively smaller OASDI benefits, based on their smaller contributions. Thus, the program would not achieve the basic objective of providing a minimum floor of income protection to all.

Counterargument. The preceding viewpoint that the employee's tax should not be imputed or assigned to the individual worker is rejected by many economists. For example, some economists argue that the employer's contribution should be included in the cost of the worker's retirement benefits since a payroll tax paid by the employer is shifted to the employees in the form of lower wages. The employer's portion of the combined OASDI tax increases the firm's labor costs and reduces the demand for labor. As this effect spreads over all firms, the level of money wages falls (or increases less than it otherwise would). In effect, the worker pays not only his or her part of the total tax but the employer's part as well. Thus, tax payments by the employer should be included in analyzing the cost of the worker's OASDI pension.[26]

Criticism of the Myers position is further buttressed by the argument presented by John Brittain.[27] Brittain is concerned with the cost of the tax to the individual worker and not to the system as a whole. He argues that if the employer's tax is paid by the employees as a group, it must also be paid by them as individuals, and it is better, says Brittain, to make an imperfect imputation (allocation of the employer's tax to individuals) that is roughly right than one that is precisely wrong. Thus, he would also include the employer's contribution in determining the true cost of the worker's OASDI retirement benefits.

Lack of Adjustments for Other Benefits. In many studies that conclude the OASDI program is a bad buy, adjustments for other OASDI benefits are often lacking. In many cases, the amount of the retirement benefit is compared with the amount of an annuity that could be purchased from a private insurer with equivalent taxes. This is an improper comparison, since the tax contributions also pay for survivor and disability income benefits and Hospital Insurance benefits under the Medicare program.

The contribution for disability income (DI) insurance should be eliminated in comparing the OASDI retirement benefit with a private annuity because it is assumed that the worker has received disability protection prior to retirement. The hospital insurance tax (HI) also should not be considered since the worker has purchased Medicare protection with the taxes. However, an adjustment for survivor benefits under the program should be made because the insured has coverage for a certain amount of survivor benefits before reaching

---

[26]Statement of Colin D. Campbell in *President's Proposals for Revision in the Social Security System*, Part 3, p. 1,389.

[27]John A. Brittain, in *Old Age Income Assurance*, Part III, *Public Programs*, pp. 112–114.

retirement age. Failure to make these adjustments can result in serious bias. In addition, the cost of private retirement benefits should also be adjusted for inflation. OASDI cash benefits are automatically adjusted for inflation based on the consumer price index. Most private pension benefits are not automatically adjusted for inflation. However, for comparability purposes, any private retirement benefits should be priced out on the basis of an automatic increase in benefits that is about 2 percent less than the interest rate used.[28] If this adjustment is made, the private benefits that can be purchased with the equivalent Social Security taxes are much lower than would otherwise be the case.

Based on Doubtful Assumptions. Another criticism of the various studies that compare the OASDI program with private insurance is that these studies are often based on doubtful assumptions. For example, it is often assumed that if the total combined OASDI tax contributions were instead given to the worker, he or she could obtain superior protection from a private insurer. However, in the absence of a compulsory OASDI program, it is highly unlikely that the employer would make available to the individual worker an amount equal to the employer's contribution, which the worker could then add to his or her own contributions. The employer's contribution could be used instead to increase the firm's profit margin, to reduce prices, or both. It could also be used to provide other fringe benefits for the workers. Then, too, some employers might be more willing to contribute to the OASDI program rather than grant a wage increase equal to the employer's tax, because they believe that such a policy could save them charitable obligations later on or that the OASDI program is worthy of support.

Second, the studies that compare the OASDI program with private insurance are often based on the implicit assumption that if the employees were given the equivalent of the combined OASDI tax contributions, they would buy private annuities from private companies. There is no reason to believe that all employees would do this, even if given the opportunity. This is especially true of the lower-income groups, who would probably spend the equivalent of the combined taxes for their present consumption needs rather than save the money for their future retirement.

Finally, the studies are usually based on the assumption that the workers now covered under the OASDI program can obtain equal protection from private insurers. This viewpoint is incorrect because private insurers have underwriting standards that screen out the undesirable risks because of occupation, age, health, and similar factors. So even if the entire combined OASDI contribution were made available to the workers to purchase private individual insurance, some workers would be unacceptable to private insurers and would have to obtain their protection from the OASDI program, which would then experience serious adverse selection.

---

[28]Robert J. Myers, private correspondence with the author. See also Myers, *Social Security,* p. 307.

Noncomparable Types of Insurance.   Another problem is that many of the studies that attempt to compare the Social Security program with private insurance are not based on a true comparison between the value of the Social Security package of benefits and that available from private insurers. No private plan can provide protection completely identical to the protection now provided under the total OASDHI program. The OASDHI program provides retirement, survivor, disability, and Medicare benefits. Private insurance plans do not provide all these coverages in one package. Indeed, even if they did, they would have to charge rates that covered administration, marketing, payment of commissions, and similar expenses. Thus, to buy from a private insurer something comparable to the OASDHI program, even if it were available, would cost more than the values indicated in many of the studies.

Evaluation of the "Bad Buy" Issue

Based on the realistic assumption that the employer's contributions belong to the system as a whole and are not earmarked for specific individuals, the evidence indicates that *average young new entrants* receive their money's worth in terms of their own contributions. However, if total combined employer-employee taxes are considered (not entirely valid for the reasons indicated earlier), that statement is not true.

Finally, when one considers that the cash benefits are automatically adjusted for inflation; that the OASDI program eliminates or reduces the financial support that children would have to make to support their parents; that there is no individual underwriting; and that the value of the survivor protection for young families with children is substantial,[29] the vast majority of younger worker will receive their money's worth under the program.

EFFECT OF SOCIAL SECURITY ON PRIVATE SAVING

Another controversial issue is the effect of the Social Security program on private saving. Critics argue that the Social Security program has reduced private saving; thus, the amount of savings available for new capital formation is reduced.

The Social Security program can both reduce and increase private saving, but the empirical evidence is inconclusive. The Social Security program can *reduce private saving,* since the need to save for retirement is reduced. The retirement benefits can be viewed as a form of Social Security wealth, which reduces the need to save for retirement and accumulate personal wealth. However, the Social Security program can also *increase private saving;* the Social Security pro-

---

[29]For example, assume that a husband age 29 in 1984 has a wife age 25 and newborn twins. Also assume that he earned $35,700 in 1983 and $37,800 in 1984. The present value of the survivor benefits if he should die in 1984 is $320,000. See Myers, *Social Security,* p. 684.

gram encourages early retirement and indirectly stimulates saving, since a worker who retires early must provide for a longer retirement period. *Thus, the Social Security wealth effect or substitution effect tends to reduce private saving, while the early retirement effect tends to increase private saving.*

Researchers have attempted to measure the impact of the Social Security program on private saving, but the studies conflict and are largely inconclusive.[30] Martin Feldstein argued that the Social Security program has substantially reduced personal saving and capital formation in the United States.[31] However, in a paper presented at the annual meeting of the American Economics Association, Selig Lesnoy and Dean Leimer discovered a fundamental flaw in Feldstein's computer program and, upon its correction, concluded that the Social Security program did not reduce private saving. However, after correcting the error and providing new evidence, Feldstein still maintained that the Social Security program reduced private saving. After examining Feldstein's new evidence, Lesnoy and Leimer concluded that Feldstein's new evidence provided only weak empirical support that the Social Security program reduces private saving.[32]

In summary, the effect of the Social Security program on private saving is inconclusive. The weight of the time series evidence does not support the proposition that the Social Security program has significantly depressed private saving in the United States.[33] The various studies can be criticized since they often fail to consider that people save for reasons other than for retirement, such as saving for an emergency, vacation, new car, or to leave a bequest; therefore, even if saving for retirement is reduced by Social Security, saving for other purposes can dilute this effect. Also, the life cycle model explaining personal saving may be inadequate. The life cycle model assumes that individuals have a clear vision of their economic future, which takes into consideration lifetime earnings, interest rates, family composition, and tastes for consumption; individuals then make rational and complex decisions during their lifetime with respect to spending and saving. Many social scientists, however, are skeptical that individuals are willing or even able to make such decisions.[34] In addition, the various studies fail to consider that the children may have to support their parents in the absence of Social Security, thereby reducing their saving. Finally, the studies fail to consider that in the absence of Social Security, massive public

---

[30]For a summary of the various studies, see Selig D. Lesnoy and Dean R. Leimer, "Social Security and Private Saving: Theory and Historical Evidence," *Social Security Bulletin*, Vol. 48, No. 1 (January 1985), pp. 14–30; and George F. Break, "The Economic Effects of the OASI Program," in Felicity Skidmore, ed., *Social Security Financing* (Cambridge, Mass.: M.I.T. Press, 1981), pp. 59–71.

[31]Martin Feldstein, "Social Security, Induced Retirement, and Aggregate Capital Formation," *Journal of Political Economy* (September–October 1974), pp. 906–926.

[32]For an extensive analysis of their position, see Lesnoy and Leimer, "Social Security and Private Saving: Theory and Historical Evidence," pp. 19–28.

[33]Ibid., p. 28.

[34]Ibid., pp. 16–17.

assistance programs probably would be needed and would have to be financed by taxes, which would reduce private saving.

ATTITUDES OF AMERICANS TOWARD THE OASDI PROGRAM

Another important issue is whether Americans are satisfied or dissatisfied with the OASDI program. The OASDI program has been under heavy attack in recent years, and it is important to determine if the public currently has confidence in the program.

An important concern of most Americans is whether the OASDI program will pay promised benefits in the future. Although the various polls indicate growing confidence in the financial ability of the OASDI program to pay future benefits, only about half of the adult population believes that the federal government will pay the benefits it has promised to pay. In particular, younger Americans have less confidence in the OASDI program than older Americans. The results of the various polls are summarized as follows:[35]

1. A 1979 poll conducted by Peter D. Hart for the National Commission on Social Insurance showed that 62 percent of the nonretired Americans expressed little or no confidence that funds would be available to pay benefits.
2. A 1981 Lou Harris and Associates poll for the National Council on Aging showed that 65 percent of those polled had hardly any confidence that the present program will pay them benefits when they retire.
3. A June 1981 poll by CBS and the *New York Times* showed that 54 percent of the American public had doubts that the program will provide full benefits for their retirement. Seventy-five percent of the younger respondents ages 25–34 expressed doubts about the program.
4. A 1982 Gallup poll for the U.S. Chamber of Commerce showed that 63 percent of employed Americans expressed fears that they might not receive any OASDI benefits when they reach retirement age. A 1983 poll by CBS and the *New York Times* showed that only 27 percent of the public believed that the OASDI program will have the money to pay benefits when they retire.
5. A 1985 poll by Yankelovich, Skelly, and White for the American Association of Retired Persons showed that confidence had increased over earlier surveys. Only 52 percent of the respondents had little or no confidence in the OASDI program; however 67 percent of the younger respondents ages 25–34 had little or no confidence in the program. However, the Yankelovich survey also showed that 92 percent of the American public believed that the OASDI program had been very successful or somewhat successful.
6. A 1988 survey for the American Council of Life Insurance showed that for the first time in years, fears about the OASDI program had declined. Overall, 49 percent of the respondents stated they were very confident or somewhat confident in the future of the program, up from a low of 32 percent in 1982.

---

[35]Robert M. Ball, "Public Confidence in Social Security," in National Academy of Social Insurance, *Social Insurance Update*, No. 8 (August 1989).

Although the Board of Trustees of the OASDI program has indicated that the program is financially sound in its recent annual reports, only about half of the adult population believes that the federal government will deliver on its promises. Thus, prominent national experts on the OASDI program believe that continuing research is necessary to determine the causes of relatively low public confidence and the actions that might be taken to increase public confidence in the program.[36]

SOCIAL SECURITY AND THE FEDERAL BUDGET

Another important and timely issue is the impact that the "OASDI surplus" has on the federal budget. *The OASDI surplus refers to the excess of income over outgo, which is invested in government bonds.* Prior to 1983, the OASDI program experienced a serious cash-flow problem. To correct the problem, the 1983 amendments provided for a significant increase in OASDI tax rates, and other measures were adopted to restore the long-run financial solvency of the program. As a result, OASDI trust fund assets have increased substantially in recent years and are expected to increase to sizable levels in the future. Actual OASDI trust fund assets totaled $163 billion at the end of calendar 1989. Based on the intermediate set of actuarial assumptions (alternative IIB), the combined OASI and DI trust funds are expected to accumulate rapidly to a peak contingency fund ratio of 476 percent of annual outgo in the year 2014. After that time, the fund ratio is estimated to decline until the funds are exhausted in 2043.[37] The combined OASDI trust funds will eventually decline because of the continuing high level of outgo for the "baby boomers" who will be retiring at that time. The high level of outgo will continue even after the baby boomers pass from the scene.

The substantial OASDI annual surpluses have a significant impact on the federal budget, and certain problems have emerged. These problems center on the following: (1) impact of the OASDI surplus on the federal deficit, (2) whether a large trust fund is desirable, and (3) using the surplus to increase national saving.

Impact of the OASDI Surplus on the Federal Deficit

The federal government has incurred substantial deficits in recent years. Under the Gramm-Rudman-Hollings law, the federal government must have a balanced budget by the end of fiscal 1993, as measured by the deficit-reduction

[36]For example, see Ball, "Public Confidence in Social Security."

[37]The Board of Trustees, Federal Old-Age and Survivors Insurance and Disability Insurance Trust Funds, *1990 Annual Report of the Board of Trustees of Federal Old-Age and Survivors Insurance and Disability Insurance Trust Funds* (Washington, D.C.: U.S. Government Printing Office, 1990), p. 2. The *contingency fund ratio* is the amount in the trust funds at the beginning of the year, including advance tax transfers for January, divided by that year's expenditures. Thus, if the trust fund ratio is 50 percent, the amount in the fund represents about six months' outgo. At the beginning of 1990, the OASDI fund ratio was about 74 percent.

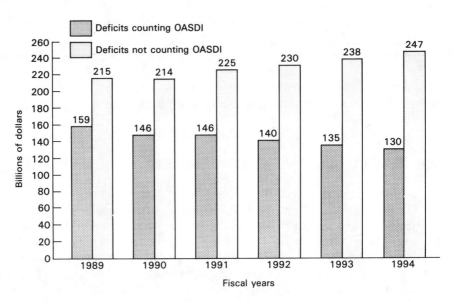

FIGURE 6-1   **Federal Budget Deficits With and Without OASDI**

Source: U.S. Congress, House, Committee on Ways and Means, *Background Material and Data on Programs within the Jurisdiction of the Committee on Ways and Means* (Washington, D.C.: U.S. Government Printing Office, 1989), Chart 1, p. 75.

target. Under this law, although the operations of the OASDI program are not included in the unified budget of the federal government, they are used in computing the deficit-reduction target. As a result, in computing the target, surplus OASDI receipts offset a substantial portion of the deficits that the federal government actually incurs in its other activities. *The overall result is that the actual federal deficit as shown by the target is understated significantly by including the OASDI surplus.* If the operations of the OASDI program were removed from the target measurements, the federal budget deficits would be shown to be significantly higher (see Figure 6-1).

Critics argue that the OASDI program should be removed from the budget target computations because it masks or hides the true deficit from the public. In addition, critics argue that the OASDI surplus will be needed in the future to pay the retirement benefits of the large numbers of "baby boomers" who will be retiring in the future. At the present time, this surplus is viewed as being used to finance deficits in other parts of the federal budget and is not set aside for future retirees. Thus, critics argue that when the baby boomers retire, Congress will have to raise taxes to redeem the trust fund assets that will be needed at that time to pay retirement benefits. Critics believe that a key question must be answered: How will the federal government obtain and allocate the financial resources needed to keep its future commitments to the trust funds? This question is largely unanswered at the present time.

Desirability of a Large Trust Fund

Another related issue is the political and economic desirability of a large trust fund. The major advantage of a sizable trust fund is that larger amounts of interest income can be earned on the invested assets. As a result, assuming the trust fund is not depleted, the contribution rate will ultimately be lower than it would be if the benefits were financed by pay-as-you-go financing. Thus, the financial burden on the future generation of workers will be reduced.

However, many social insurance experts believe that a large trust fund is undesirable. Robert Myers, former chief actuary of the Social Security Administration, believes that it is illogical to build up a huge trust fund over the next 20 to 25 years to finance the retirement benefits of the baby boomers, only to have the fund drawn down to exhaustion after the buildup period. Myers believes that current payroll tax rates should be reduced to slow the growth in the OASDI trust funds. The tax rates would then be increased starting in 2015 when the baby boomers begin to retire. As a result, the undesirable "roller coaster" effect under present law would be replaced by a slower but steadier growth in the trust funds.[38]

In addition, it is also argued that a large trust fund allows politicians to increase the benefits excessively (which will make financing the system when the baby boomers retire just that much more difficult); the availability of large amounts of money may lead to excessive government spending; and the large trust fund investments will absorb most or all of the government bonds that represent the national debt.[39]

Using the Surplus to Increase National Saving

Another related issue is whether the OASDI surplus can be used to increase national saving. The United States has experienced relatively low rates of national saving, net investment, and economic growth in recent years when compared with other industrial countries. In addition, the federal government has experienced large federal deficits. Financing the deficits has diverted funds away from the private sector that could have been used for new economic investments that would increase productivity and economic growth. Thus, federal deficits are a drain on national saving. However, a surplus in the federal budget adds to national saving. As federal debt is repaid, funds become available for private investment, and economic growth and productivity can be increased.

Some economists argue that the present OASDI surplus presents a unique opportunity to increase national saving in the United States.[40] An in-

---

[38]Robert J. Myers, "Social Security and the Federal Budget: Some Mirages, Myths, and Solutions," *Journal of the American Society of CLU and ChFC*, Vol. 43, No. 2 (March 1989), p. 61.

[39]Ibid., p. 59.

[40]For an excellent analysis of this argument, see Henry J. Aaron, Barry P. Bosworth, and Gary

crease in national saving would result in an increase in new economic investment, increased productivity, and more rapid economic growth. As a result, the financial burden on future workers will be reduced when the baby boomers begin to retire.

There is considerable disagreement among economists, however, concerning the impact that the OASDI surplus has on national saving. One viewpoint is that the OASDI surplus will not increase national saving unless the rest of the federal budget is approximately in balance. This is presently not the case. Economists who hold this view argue that the OASDI surplus is now being used to finance other current operations of the federal government that are incurring deficits and that the surplus funds are now being used to finance current consumption rather than productive economic investments. Thus, it is argued that the current OASDI surplus will not materially increase national saving unless there is an approximate balance between revenues and outlays in other parts of the federal budget.

A counterargument is that the OASDI surplus can increase national saving even if the federal budget is unbalanced. It is argued that the sale of government bonds to the trust funds reduces the amount of bonds that the Treasury would otherwise have to sell to private investors. Thus, private investors have more financial resources available to invest in stocks and bonds that represent new economic investment. As a result, the OASDI surplus indirectly finances a higher rate of private capital formation.[41]

SUGGESTIONS FOR ADDITIONAL READING

AARON, HENRY J., ED. *Social Security and the Budget, Proceedings of the First Conference of the National Academy of Social Insurance.* Lanham, Md.: The National Academy of Social Insurance and University Press of America, 1990.

AARON, HENRY J., BARRY P. BOSWORTH, AND GARY BURTLESS. *Can America Afford to Grow Old? Paying for Social Security.* Washington, D.C.: The Brookings Institution, 1989.

BALL, ROBERT M. "Public Confidence in Social Security," *Social Insurance Update,* National Academy of Social Insurance, No. 8 (August 1989).

———. *Social Security: Today and Tomorrow.* New York: Columbia University Press, 1978.

BERNSTEIN, MERTON C., AND JOAN BRODSHAUG BERNSTEIN. *Social Security: The System That Works.* New York: Basic Books, 1988.

CONGRESS OF THE UNITED STATES, CONGRESSIONAL BUDGET OFFICE. *The Social Security Earnings Test and Options for Change,* Staff Working Paper, September 1988.

GARNER, C. ALAN. "The Social Security Surplus—A Solution to the Federal Budget Deficit?" *Economic Review,* Federal Reserve Bank of Kansas City (May 1989), pp. 25–39.

HONIG, MARJORIE, AND CORDELIA REIMERS. "Is It Worth Eliminating the Retirement Test?" *The American Economic Review, Papers and Proceedings,* Vol. 79, No. 2 (May 1989), pp. 103–107.

KOITZ, DAVID S. *The Social Security Surplus: A Discussion of Some of the Issues.* CRS Report for Congress. Washington, D.C.: Congressional Research Service, November 21, 1988.

Burtless, *Can America Afford to Grow Old? Paying for Social Security* (Washington, D.C.: The Brookings Institution, 1989).

[41]For a discussion of this viewpoint, see Martin Feldstein, "Social Security Can Build a National Trust," *The Wall Street Journal,* April 25, 1990, p. A18.

MUNNELL, ALICIA H. "The Social Security Surpluses and National Saving," *Social Insurance Update*, National Academy of Social Insurance, No. 64 (September 1988). See also Robert J. Myers. "The Social Security Surpluses and National Savings: A Rejoinder and Supplementation," *Social Insurance Update*, National Academy of Social Insurance, No. 3 (October 1988).

MYERS, ROBERT J. *Social Security*, 3rd ed., Chap. 5. Homewood, Ill.: Richard D. Irwin, 1985.

———. "Social Security and the Federal Budget: Some Mirages, Myths, and Solutions," *Journal of the American Society of CLU and ChFC*, Vol. 43, No. 2 (March 1989), pp. 58–63.

REJDA, GEORGE E. "A Reexamination of the Controversial Earnings Test under the OASDI Program." *Benefits Quarterly*, Vol. 6, No. 1 (Third Quarter 1990).

———. "An Analysis of the Social Security Retirement Test," *CLU Journal*, Vol. 30, No. 3 (July 1976), pp. 57–64.

———. "Coverage Issues under the Social Security Program," *Journal of Pension Planning & Compliance* (November 1979), Vol. 5, No. 6, pp. 499–519.

———. "Should the Social Security Earnings Test Be Abolished?" *Journal of Pension Planning & Compliance*, Vol. 9, No. 2 (April 1983), pp. 121–131.

———. "Taxation of Social Security Benefits: A Critical Evaluation," *Benefits Quarterly*, Vol. 1, No. 2 (Second Quarter 1985), pp. 30–35.

———, AND JAMES R. SCHMIDT. "The Impact of Social Security and ERISA on Private Pension Contributions," *The Journal of Risk and Insurance*, Vol. 51, No. 4 (December 1984), pp. 640–651.

———, AND JAMES R. SCHMIDT. "The Impact of the Social Security Program on Private Pension Contributions," *The Journal of Risk and Insurance*, Vol. 46, No. 2 (December 1979), pp. 636–651.

———, JAMES R. SCHMIDT, AND MICHAEL J. MCNAMARA. "The Impact of Social Security Tax Contributions on Group Life Insurance Premiums," *The Journal of Risk and Insurance*, Vol. 54, No. 4 (December 1987), pp. 712–720.

ROBBINS, ALDONA, AND GARY ROBBINS. *Paying People Not to Work: The Economic Cost of the Social Security Retirement Earnings Limit*, NCPA Policy Report No. 142. Dallas, Tex.: The National Center for Policy Analysis, September 1989.

ROBERTSON, A. HAEWORTH. *The Coming Revolution in Social Security*. McLean, Va.: Security Press, 1981.

UNITED STATES GENERAL ACCOUNTING OFFICE. *Social Security, The Trust Fund Reserve Accumulation, the Economy, and the Federal Budget*. Washington, D.C.: United States General Accounting Office, 1989.

WACHTER, SUSAN M., ED. *Social Security and Private Pensions, Providing for Retirement in the Twenty-First Century*. Lexington, Mass.: Lexington Books, 1988.

7

FINANCING
THE OASDHI PROGRAM

The OASDHI program is the major economic security program for almost all Americans, and it must be soundly financed to pay the promised benefits. In this chapter, we shall examine the financing principles and operations of both the OASDI and Medicare programs. In particular, the following areas will be discussed: (1) OASDI financing principles; (2) nature, purposes, and investments of the trust funds; (3) concepts of actuarial soundness; (4) financial condition of OASDI; (5) financial condition of Medicare; and (6) other viewpoints concerning the future financial solvency of the program.

FINANCING PRINCIPLES

The financing principles that are followed in the financing of OASDI benefits include the following: (1) partial-reserve financing, (2) no full funding, (3) actuarially sound program, and (4), some individual equity considerations.[1]

---

[1]The basic financing principles and considerations underlying the Social Security program can be found in Robert J. Myers, *Social Security*, 3rd ed. (Homewood, Ill.: Richard D. Irwin, 1985), Chaps. 4, 5, 8 and 10. See also The Board of Trustees, Federal Old-Age and Survivors Insurance and Disability Insurance Trust Funds, *1990 Annual Report of the Board of Trustees of the Federal Old-Age and Survivors Insurance and Disability Insurance Trust Funds* (Washington, D.C.: U.S. Government Printing Office,

Partial-Reserve Financing

To finance the monthly cash benefits, two basic approaches and numerous variations between them are possible. One approach is pay-as-you-go or current-cost financing. *Current-cost financing* is essentially a pay-as-you-go system, plus the maintenance of a relatively small contingency fund that can be drawn down during temporary periods when income and outgo are not in balance. The element of prepayment is not present, and a large reserve fund is not accumulated. As we stated earlier, only a relatively small contingency fund is maintained that can be used during temporary periods when income and outgo are not in balance.

The second approach is *full-reserve financing*, which emphasizes a fully funded program and can be viewed as a prepayment system of financing. All benefits are paid or are financed during the years prior to their receipt. Under this approach, the dollar amount of all payments into the fund, when added to the investment income from the fund's assets, is sufficient for paying all guaranteed or promised benefits.

The OASDI program is neither a completely unfunded program nor one financed on the basis of full-reserve financing and full funding. Instead, the program is presently financed on the basis of partial-reserve financing. *Partial-reserve financing* means that the payroll tax schedule under present law is sufficient not only for the payment of current benefits and expenses but also for the payment of future benefits and expenses as well. Under partial-reserve financing, a large fund is building up so that benefits and expenses in the distant future can be paid in a timely manner. The reserve fund that is building up is substantially higher than a contingency or emergency fund that can be drawn down during temporary periods when outgo exceeds income, such as during a business recession.

During most of the 1960s and 1970s, the OASDI program in practice was financed based on pay-as-you-go or current-cost financing. However, the 1977 amendments, and more importantly the 1983 amendments, departed from the principle of current-cost financing. As we noted in Chapter 6, the OASDI program experienced a serious cash flow problem prior to 1983. To correct the problem, the 1983 amendments significantly increased OASDI payroll tax rates in the short run and reduced benefit outgo over both the short run and long range to restore the long-run solvency of the program. As a result, the OASDI trust funds have increased significantly in recent years and will accumulate to sizable levels in the future.

1990); The Board of Trustees, Federal Hospital Insurance Trust Fund, *1990 Annual Report of the Board of Trustees of the Federal Hospital Insurance Trust Fund* (Washington, D.C.: U.S. Government Printing Office, 1990); and The Board of Trustees, Federal Supplementary Medical Insurance Trust Fund, *1990 Annual Report of the Board of Trustees of the Federal Supplementary Medical Insurance Trust Fund* (Washington, D.C.: U.S. Government Printing Office, 1990). The author drew heavily on these sources in preparing this chapter.

No Full Funding

The OASDI program is not fully funded. A *fully funded program* means that if the program should terminate, the value of the accumulated assets under the plan are sufficient to discharge all liabilities for the benefit rights accrued to date under the plan.

A fully funded program is considered unnecessary for several reasons. First, since the program is expected to continue indefinitely and will not terminate in the predictable future, full funding is considered unnecessary. Second, since the program is compulsory, new entrants will always enter the program and pay taxes to support it. Third, the taxing and borrowing powers of the federal government can be used to raise additional revenues if the program has financial problems. Finally, from an economic viewpoint, full funding is undesirable; full funding requires substantially higher payroll taxes for many years, which could be deflationary and cause substantial unemployment.

In contrast, private pension plans must emphasize full funding, since private pension plans can and do terminate. Thus, to protect the pension rights of active and retired workers, private pension plans should be fully funded.

Actuarially Sound Program

Congress has consistently indicated that the OASDI program should be actuarially sound. This is important because it is the major economic security program for most Americans, and if it fails to provide the promised benefits, economic security would be jeopardized for many persons.

The term "actuarial soundness" has different meanings, and whether the program is actuarially sound depends on the definition that is adopted. We shall analyze this important issue later in the chapter.

Some Individual Equity Considerations

Although the monthly cash benefits are paid largely on the basis of the social adequacy principle, there is some consideration of individual equity in the program's structure. This means that the tax paid by younger workers entering the program should not be so high that it could purchase greater protection from private insurers. This principle has been reaffirmed many times by social insurance students, although it was never set forth in any of the congressional committee reports underlying the 1950 and subsequent amendments.

SOCIAL SECURITY TRUST FUNDS

Nature of the Trust Funds

The Social Security program is financed through four separate trust funds. The Federal Old-Age and Survivors Insurance Trust Fund (OASI) was established in 1940, the Federal Disability Insurance Trust Fund (DI) in 1956, and the Federal

Hospital Insurance Trust Fund (HI) and Federal Supplementary Medical Insurance Trust Fund (SMI) in 1965.

The major sources of revenues to the OASI and DI programs are payroll taxes, interest on the trust fund assets, and revenues derived from the federal income tax on part of the monthly benefits paid to upper-income persons. The major sources of revenue to the Medicare program are HI payroll taxes and SMI monthly premiums. In addition, the general revenues of the federal government are also used to finance a large part of the SMI program.

All tax contributions are collected by the Internal Revenue Service and deposited into the general fund of the Treasury (except for amounts received under state agreements for covered wages paid prior to January 1, 1987, which were paid to the Social Security Administration). The Internal Revenue collections are then appropriated to the trust funds on an estimated basis. Periodic adjustments are later made to the extent that the estimates differ from the amounts of contributions actually paid based on the reported earnings.

Estimated contributions are credited to the trust funds on the first day of the month. Since the estimated contributions are credited on the first day of the month instead of throughout the month as the contributions are actually received, the trust funds are required to pay interest to the general fund to reimburse it for the interest lost because of the advance transfers. The net effect of this provision is to make funds available to pay benefits, which are normally paid on the third of the month.

All funds not needed to pay current benefits and administrative expenses are invested in interest-bearing obligations of the federal government. The trust fund assets cannot be used for any other purposes.

Purposes of Trust Funds

The trust funds serve three useful purposes. First, they provide some interest income, which helps to reduce the program's cost. Second, the trust funds are available as contingency reserves to help meet any deficiency in contribution income during periods of economic recessions or other periods when outgo exceeds income. Finally, the trust funds help to establish greater public confidence in the program.

Investments of Trust Funds

Any excess funds not needed currently to pay benefits and administrative costs can be invested (1) in interest-bearing obligations of the federal government, (2) in obligations guaranteed as to principal and interest by the United States, and (3) in certain federally sponsored agency obligations. The trust funds can invest either in public issues that are available to all investors in the open market or in special public debt obligations issued exclusively for purchase by the trust funds. The special issues have fixed maturities and bear interest equal to the average market yield at the end of the preceding month on all marketable interest-bearing obligations of the United States not due or callable for at least four years after that date. In the past, almost all investments have been in special issues.

Some observers argue that the trust funds should be allowed to invest in other than government securities and guaranteed obligations, while others believe that the present investment policies are sound and should not be changed. Thus, it is important to analyze the major arguments for and against the present investment practices of the trust funds.

Maintaining Present Investment Policies. Several arguments are advanced for maintaining present trust fund policies limiting the investments to securities issued or guaranteed by the federal government.[2] First, since the Social Security program is designed for all of society, the trust funds must be confined to safe investments and not to speculative ventures that might impair the solvency of the programs, and U.S. government securities are the safest form of investment available.

Second, departing from the present investment policies would directly involve the trust funds in the operations of the private economy or in the affairs of state and local government. The trust funds have relatively large amounts available for investment, and if these funds were invested in bonds or stocks of private firms, the federal government could control part of the free enterprise economy, thus, in effect, letting in socialism through the back door. In addition, investing in the securities of state and local governments would involve the federal government in affairs that are beyond the scope of the program.

Third, for the trust funds to obtain an adequate rate of interest with reasonable safety, the federal government would have to establish a rating organization to evaluate the various securities. If the investments were indiscriminately made, there would be serious danger of the loss of capital and reduction of investment income. However, establishing some type of rating organization for private securities would again involve the federal government in the private economy.

Changing the Present Investment Policies. It is argued that the trust funds should be allowed to invest in securities that represent social goods, such as hospitals, highways, public housing, schools, dams, and similar projects that yield large and widespread benefits to society as a whole.

There is little doubt that such investments by the trust funds would have a beneficial impact on the economy—for example, in projects designed to reduce poverty, such as public housing, special schools for the disadvantaged, slum clearance projects, and so on. In addition, the trust funds could provide loans to business firms to locate in poverty areas and provide employment opportunities to the hard-core unemployed poor. It must be recognized, however, that there are dangers involved in such an approach. Investing in securities representing social goods would involve public funds, and decisions would have to be made

---

[2]Myers, *Social Security,* p. 374.

regarding the priority of investments. Such decisions in regard to public funds, many feel, should be made by Congress rather than by the trust fund managers, since investments in social goods affect the economic welfare of the nation, and the elected representatives of the people should be the ones to determine what is best for the country.

Another argument is that the trust funds should be allowed to invest in private securities to obtain higher yields than are currently provided by government securities. This argument is somewhat defective on several grounds. Interest earnings provide only a relatively small part of the total income of the program. Thus, higher-yielding private securities would have only a small impact on the total income of the program, given the present funding policy. In addition, higher-yielding private securities have greater risk, whereas government securities are noted for their safety. Finally, the potentially higher return must be weighed against the disadvantage of having the federal government heavily involved in the private sector of the economy.

Erroneous Trust Fund Views

The nature of the trust funds is often misunderstood. For sake of convenience, these erroneous views can be classified as follows: (1) double taxation, (2) fictitious trust funds, and (3) an increase in the national debt from trust fund investments.

Double Taxation. Critics charge that fraud is being perpetrated upon the American people since they are taxed twice in the financing of benefits. First, covered employees, employers, and the self-employed are taxed to pay benefits to those currently eligible to receive them. Second, the excess of the taxes collected over the amount needed to pay current benefits and expenses is invested in interest-bearing obligations of the federal government, and the government must tax the general public a second time to pay the interest on these obligations and also to repay the principal.

The double-taxation argument is fallacious. It is true that the federal government must levy taxes to pay the interest on the bonds held by the trust funds and to redeem the bonds. However, these taxes are not levied for the specific purpose of paying benefits; rather, they are levied to meet the general costs of the federal government. If the trust funds did not exist, the funds needed for general government purposes would have to be borrowed from other sources, and taxes would still have to be raised to pay the interest and principal on these borrowed funds.

Fictitious Trust Funds. Some critics claim that the trust funds are fictitious, since the securities held by them are merely IOUs issued by the federal government to itself. This argument is also erroneous. When the trust funds invest in government bonds, the trust funds are the lenders, and the Treasury is the borrower. The trust funds receive federal securities as evidence of the loans.

These securities are in turn liabilities (part of the national debt) of the U.S. government, which must pay interest on them and must repay the principal when they are redeemed or mature. The bonds are redeemed when the trust funds require cash for disbursement.

In addition, the special obligations issued directly to the trust funds are backed by the full faith and credit of the United States. Interest on the securities held by the trust funds and the proceeds from the redemption of such securities are credited to and form a part of each trust fund. Thus, the argument that the trust funds are fictitious is completely erroneous.

Increase in National Debt. Another specious argument is that trust fund investments in federal obligations, which represent the national debt of the federal government, increase the size of the debt. However, the national debt increases only if the expenditures by the federal government during a given fiscal year are greater than the revenues received during the same period. When a deficit occurs, the Treasury must borrow funds to meet the deficit through the sale of federal securities, which increases the size of the national debt. However, the purchase of federal obligations by the trust funds does not increase the amount of money the Treasury must borrow. If the trust funds did not exist and were not available as a source from which to borrow, the Treasury would have to borrow the same amount from other sources; it is only that the purchaser of the government obligations is a public agency rather than a private investor.

CONCEPTS OF ACTUARIAL SOUNDNESS

Actuarial soundness refers to the ability of the plan to deliver the promised benefits. Some critics claim that the Social Security program is actuarially unsound and on the verge of financial bankruptcy. Whether this is true depends, of course, on the definition of actuarial soundness that is adopted.[3]

Deficit for Present Members

One concept of actuarial soundness that normally applies to private pension plans is the *deficit for present members. Under this definition, a plan is actuarially sound if the existing trust fund plus the present value of future contributions are sufficiently high to pay future benefits to those already on the rolls (and to their survivors), and to the survivors of previously deceased persons who have not reached the minimum eligibility age for survivor benefits.* Based on the concept of a closed group, there would be no new entrants into the program, and present members would continue to contribute and accumulate benefit rights.

If this definition is used, the OASDI program is *not* actuarially sound.

---

[3]The various definitions of actuarial soundness that can be applied to the OASDI program can be found in Myers, *Social Security,* pp. 350–357.

Based on this definition, an earlier study indicated that the OASDI trust fund was short by $5.1 trillion as of September 30, 1983. This means that, based on the closed group concept, an additional $5.1 trillion (plus the appropriate interest earnings thereon) would have been needed to pay future benefits to people on the rolls and to their survivors, and to the survivors of previously deceased members who had not reached the minimum eligibility age for survivors benefits.[4]

Although the OASDI program is not actuarially sound based on the definition just given, it does not follow that the benefit rights of covered individuals are in jeopardy. That stringent definition, which is normally used in private pensions, is clearly inappropriate for the OASDI program for several reasons. First, the error of noncomparable performance standards is committed. As we saw in Chapter 2, social insurance and private insurance differ in character, content, and objectives, and so it is wrong in principle to apply identical performance standards to them. The unfunded accrued liabilities for the present group of covered workers is based on the incorrect comparison of the OASDI program to a private insurer selling individual whole life insurance policies. The private company must stress a fully funded program in order to have sufficient funds on hand to fulfill the terms of the contracts for present policyowners and also to pay off policyowners if they should surrender their policies and demand their cash values.

Second, since it is assumed that the OASDI program will operate indefinitely in the future, it is reasonable to consider both the benefits promised the future entrants and the contributions that will be paid by them and their employers, in determining whether the program can meet its financial obligations to covered individuals and families. Thus, a fully funded program is unnecessary, since the contributions of the workers of the future and their employers can be relied on.

Third, because the OASDI program is compulsory, those entering the labor force in the future, and their employers, must pay the tax contributions whether or not they are willing to participate in the program. So it is again reasonable to consider the contributions of the new entrants and their employers in determining whether the OASDI program is actuarially sound. In contrast, private companies, which cannot assume that new policyowners will always join the company, must emphasize full funding.

Finally, this definition is based on a closed-group concept, whereby only present members are considered. This is clearly invalid, since it is assumed that new entrants will participate in the OASDI program because it is compulsory and will operate indefinitely.

Most actuaries generally agree that the severe definition of actuarial soundness described earlier should not be applied to the OASDI program. Thus, the concept of the deficit for present members is only a theoretical exercise and is not of true significance to the OASDI program in the long run.

---

[4]Ibid., p. 354.

Pay-As-You-Go Financing

A less severe definition can be used to determine if the OASDI program is actuarially sound, by evaluating it in terms of *pay-as-you-go financing.* Pay-as-you-go financing in this context means that annual receipts and annual disbursement should be approximately equal. The OASDI program can be considered actuarially sound under this system if the income from the future contribution schedule is seen to approximate closely the estimated future disbursements year by year.

FINANCIAL CONDITION OF THE OASDI PROGRAM

Regardless of the definition of actuarial soundness used, the OASDI program must be adequately financed to pay all promised benefits. Let us next examine the current and future financial condition of the OASDI program.[5]

Current OASDI Financial Operations

During 1989, about 132 million workers contributed to the OASDI program. At the end of September 1989, 39 million persons were receiving monthly OASDI benefit payments. Administrative expenses represented about 1.1 percent of benefit payments in fiscal 1989.

Income to the OASDI trust funds in fiscal 1989 was $284.9 billion, while outgo was $232.5 billion. Thus, the assets of the OASDI trust funds increased by $52.4 billion. A summary of the OASDI financial operations in fiscal 1989 is shown in Table 7-1.

Actuarial Status of the OASDI Program

Economic and Demographic Assumptions. The law requires the Board of Trustees to make actuarial cost projections over the next 75 years for the OASDI program. Future OASDI income and outgo will depend on numerous economic and demographic factors, including economic growth, inflation, unemployment, fertility, and mortality. Economic factors affect the level of workers' earnings and OASDI benefits, while demographic factors affect the number of people making contributions and receiving benefits.

The estimates in the 1990 report were prepared based on four alternative sets of economic and demographic assumptions. One set (alternative I) is based on optimistic assumptions. Two sets are designated as "intermediate" (al-

---

[5]This section is based on the *1990 Annual Report of the Board of Trustees of the Federal Old-Age and Survivors Insurance and Disability Insurance Trust Funds* (Washington, D.C.: U.S. Government Printing Office, 1990), pp. 1–10. To maintain technical accuracy, relevant parts of this report are reprinted in their entirety in this section.

TABLE 7-1   Summary of OASDI Financial Operations
in Fiscal 1989 (Billions)

Trust fund assets at end of fiscal year 1988	$104.2
Income during year:	
Contributions	270.8
Revenue from taxation of benefits	3.8
Net interest	10.3
Total income	284.9
Outgo during year:	
Benefit payments	227.1
Administrative expenses	2.4
Transfer to Railroad Retirement program	2.9
Total outgo	232.5
Net increase in assets during year	52.4
Trust fund assets at end of fiscal year 1989	156.7

Note: Totals may not equal sums of components, due to rounding.

Source: *1990 Annual Report of the Board of Trustees of the Federal Old-Age and Survivors Insurance and Disability Insurance Trust Funds* (Washington, D.C.: U.S. Government Printing Office, 1990), p. 3.

ternative II-A and alternative II-B). Somewhat more robust economic growth is assumed for alternative II-A than alternative II-B. A final set is based on pessimistic assumptions (alternative III).

Measures of Actuarial Status. For purposes of determining the adequacy of the trust funds and the financial status of the OASDI program, several measures of actuarial status are commonly used.

No single measure is used to assess the actuarial status of the OASDI funds. Short-range measures usually focus on the adequacy of reserves available to pay benefits. Long-range measures usually focus on the balance between income and outgo during the projection period as well as the adequacy of the reserves.

The ***contingency fund ratio*** is the usual measure of the OASDI program's ability to pay benefits on time in the near future. *The **contingency fund ratio** is the amount in the trust funds at the beginning of the year, including advance tax transfers for January, divided by that year's expenditures.* Thus, if the trust fund ratio is 50 percent, the amount in the fund represents about 6 months' outgo. A ratio of at least 8 to 9 percent is required to pay benefits at the beginning of each month. At the beginning of 1990, the fund ratio for OASDI was about 74 percent.

In analyzing the actuarial status of OASDI for the next 75 years, several different measures are commonly used. *The annual **income rate** is the combined OASDI employee-employer contribution rate scheduled in the law, plus the income from taxation of benefits, expressed as a percentage of taxable payroll. The annual **cost rate** is the annual outgo expressed as a percentage of taxable payroll.* The annual balance, which is the difference between the annual income rate and the annual cost rate, measures the adequacy of funding in each year of the long-range projection period. If the difference is negative, the annual balance is a deficit. The level and pattern of annual positive balances and annual deficits during various periods of time within the next 75 years measure the financial strength of the program over such periods.

The **actuarial balance** *for the 75-year long-range projection period, is the difference between the summarized estimated income rate and the summarized estimated cost rate.* If this actuarial balance is negative, the program is said to have an actuarial deficit. Such a deficit is a warning that future changes may be needed in the program's financing or benefit provisions, although it does not present a complete picture without the other measures of financing discussed here.

Short-Range Financing (1990–94).   Estimates for the next 5 years are used to assess the adequacy of OASDI financing in the short range. In this period, the numbers of persons receiving OASDI benefits can be estimated fairly accurately. Changes in the national economy, however, which are difficult to predict, can have major effects on income and outgo.

The actuarial estimates shown in the 1990 report indicate that the combined assets of the OASI and DI Trust Funds will be sufficient to pay OASDI benefits on time throughout the 5-year period and for may years thereafter, based on all four sets of assumptions. The contingency fund ratio for the combined funds is estimated to reach at least 150 percent by the beginning of 1994 under both alternatives II-A and II-B. In addition, the estimates based on alternatives I, II-A, and II-B indicate that the OASI and DI programs, separately, can operate satisfactorily for many years. During the next 9 years, however, if experience is very adverse, such as under alternative III, the assets of the DI Trust Fund could decline to such a low level that financial problems would occur.

Figure 7-1 shows the OASDI contingency fund ratio for 1989 and the estimated OASDI ratios for 1990–94, on the basis of all four sets of assumptions. The fund ratios for the combined trust funds are estimated to increase each year.

Long-Range Financing (1990–2064).   Long-range 75-year estimates for OASDI indicate the trend and general range of the program's future financial status. During this long-range period, income and outgo are greatly affected by demographic, as well as economic, conditions. Most of the beneficiaries during the next 75 years have already been born, so that their numbers are projected mainly from the present population. The numbers of workers involved in these projections, however, depend largely on future birth rates, which are subject to more variability.

Several important demographic trends are anticipated, which will raise the proportion of the aged in the population during the next 75 years. First, because of the large number of persons born in the two decades after World War II, rapid growth is expected in the aged population after the turn of the century. Second, assumed declines in death rates would increase the numbers of aged

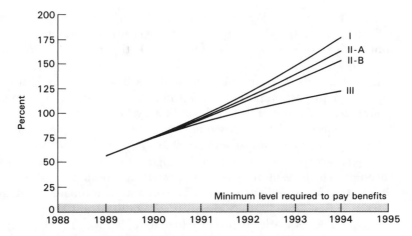

FIGURE 7-1   Contingency Fund Ratio at the Beginning of the Year

Source: *1990 Annual Report of the Board of Trustees of the Federal Old-Age and Survivors Insurance and Disability Insurance Trust Funds* (Washington, D.C.: U.S. Government Printing Office, 1990), Chart A, p. 6.

persons more gradually, but on a permanent basis. At the same time, birth rates, which began to decline in the 1960s and are assumed to remain relatively low in the future, would hold down the numbers of young people.

Figure 7-2 shows the long-range trend in the number of covered workers per OASDI beneficiary. (The term "beneficiary" includes not only retired workers, but also disabled workers, spouses, children, and survivor beneficiaries.) Based on the intermediate assumptions, this ratio is estimated to decline

FIGURE 7-2   Number of Covered Workers per Beneficiary

Source: *1990 Annual Report of the Board of Trustees of the Federal Old-Age and Survivors Insurance and Disability Insurance Trust Funds* (Washington, D.C.: U.S. Government Printing Office, 1990), Chart B, p. 7.

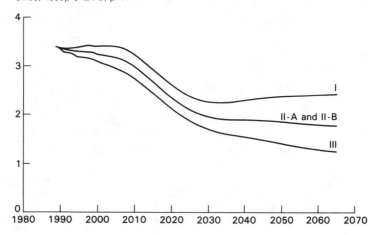

gradually from 3.4 in 1989 to 3.0 in 2010. From 2010 to 2030, the estimated ratio falls rapidly to 2.0 as the number of beneficiaries increases more rapidly than the number of covered workers. After 2030, the ratio is estimated to decline gradually.

Figure 7-3 shows the estimated OASDI income and cost rates for the long-range projection period. *During the first three decades of this period, the estimates indicate that the income rate will generally exceed the cost rate, resulting in substantial positive balances each year. Beginning about 2020, the reverse is true for all but the optimistic assumptions, with the cost rate exceeding the income rate, thus resulting in substantial deficits.* These positive balances and deficits do not reflect interest earnings, which result in trust fund growth continuing for about 10 years after the first actuarial deficits occur. The cost rate is estimated to increase rapidly after the first half of the 75-year projection period, primarily because the number of beneficiaries is projected to increase more rapidly than the number of covered workers.

Figure 7-4 shows the projected OASDI contingency fund ratios for the 75-year period. *The ratio rises steadily and reaches 476 percent in 2014, based on the intermediate alternative II-B assumptions; then the ratio declines until the combined funds are exhausted in 2043.* The importance of the trust funds' accumulation of reserves is emphasized by Figure 7-4. As Figure 7-4 shows, the build-up in the reserves will be needed later on to pay benefits to the increasing numbers of retired persons who were born in the high birth-rate years from the mid-1940s to the mid-1960s.

Table 7-2 presents a comparison of the annual income and cost rates for the 75-year long-range projection period, based on the four sets of assumptions. The figures are expressed as percentages of taxable payroll.

FIGURE 7-3   OASDI Income Rates and Cost Rates

Source: *1990 Annual Report of the Board of Trustees of the Federal Old-Age and Survivors Insurance and Disability Insurance Trust Funds* (Washington, D.C.: U.S. Government Printing Office, 1990), Chart C, p. 8.

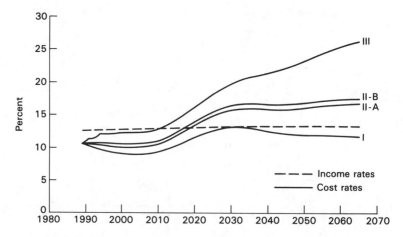

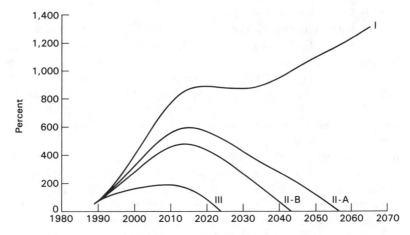

FIGURE 7-4   Long-Range Contingency Fund Ratio

Source: *1990 Annual Report of the Board of Trustees of the Federal Old-Age and Survivors Insurance and Disability Insurance Trust Funds* (Washington, D.C.: U.S. Government Printing Office, 1990), Chart D, p. 9.

The long-range OASDI actuarial deficit of 0.91 percent of taxable payroll, based on the intermediate II-B assumptions, results from an income rate of 13.04 percent of taxable payroll over the 75-year period (including beginning trust fund balances) and a cost rate of 13.95 percent over the period. *In the absence of other changes, the long-range actuarial balance will tend to worsen slowly in future annual reports, as the valuation period moves forward and additional distant years of deficit are included in the valuation.* The actuarial deficits in the later years of the 75-year projection period are caused primarily by the demographic trends described above, in combination with a flat contribution rate schedule.

> ***Summary.***   *The trust funds are expected to continue growing for many years into the future. Based on intermediate assumptions, the combined trust funds are estimated to reach a level of about 4 to 6 times annual outgo in the next 20 to 30 years. Even if future experience is very adverse, the combined funds are estimated to increase to*

TABLE 7-2   Income Rate, Cost Rate, and Actuarial Balance
for the 75-Year Long-Range Projected Period

ASSUMPTIONS	INCOME RATE	COST RATE	ACTUARIAL BALANCE
Optimistic I	12.91	11.15	1.76
Intermediate II-A	13.01	13.32	−.31
Intermediate II-B	13.04	13.95	−.91
Pessimistic III	13.19	17.06	−3.87

Note: Income rate, cost rate, and actuarial balance are defined in the text.

Source: *1990 Annual Report of the Board of Trustees of the Federal Old-Age and Survivors Insurance and Disability Insurance Trust Funds* (Washington, D.C.: U.S. Government Printing Office, 1990), p. 10.

nearly 2 times annual outgo during the next 15 to 20 years. However, under such adverse conditions, the assets of the DI Trust Fund could decline to such a low level that financial problems with that fund would occur before the end of this decade. Thus, the DI program needs careful monitoring in the short range.

The long-range 75-year estimates indicate that, under the intermediate assumptions, the OASDI program will experience about 25 to 30 years of positive annual balances, with continuing annual deficits thereafter. *Based on the intermediate alternative II-B assumptions, the OASDI program has a future deficit of 0.91 percent of taxable payroll, which is 0.21 percent larger than in the 1989 report.* The deficit of 0.91 percent results from an estimated income rate of 13.04 percent of taxable payroll over the 75-year projection period (including beginning trust fund balances), which is 93.5 percent of the estimated 13.95-percent cost rate. The program has traditionally been considered to be adequately financed over the next 75 years when the long-range income rate is between 95 percent and 105 percent of the long-range cost rate. However, because the estimates based on the same assumptions indicate that the program is solvent for the next 20 to 30 years, the Trustees did not recommend that any immediate action be taken to change either the financing or the benefit provisions for the OASDI program. The Board recommended, however, continued extensive study of possible ways to address the long-range deficits, as well as the implications of the expected large buildup of the trust funds.

As stated earlier, during the first part of the long-range projection period, the combined OASI and DI Trust Funds are expected to accumulate rapidly to a peak fund ratio of 476 percent of annual outgo in the year 2014, based on the alternative II-B assumptions. Thereafter, the fund ratio is estimated to decline until the funds are exhausted in 2043, or 3 years earlier than estimated in the 1989 report. *Thus, according to the alternative II-B estimates, the OASDI program will have enough funds to cover expenditures for more than 50 years into the future.*

For OASI and DI, separately, the long-range actuarial balances, based on the alternative II-A assumptions, are deficits of 0.15 percent and 0.16 percent of taxable payroll, respectively. Based on the alternative II-B assumptions, the programs have actuarial deficits which are 0.69 percent and 0.22 percent of taxable payroll, respectively. *Because of the size of the DI deficit, relative to its cost rate, the DI program needs careful monitoring in the long-range period, as well as in the short-range period.*

FINANCIAL CONDITION OF MEDICARE

There are two basic programs under Medicare: (1) Hospital Insurance (HI) pays for inpatient hospital care and other related care provided to the aged 65 and over and to the long-term disabled; (2) Supplementary Medical Insurance (SMI) pays for physicians' services, outpatient hospital services, and other medical expenses incurred by the aged 65 and over and by the long-term disabled.

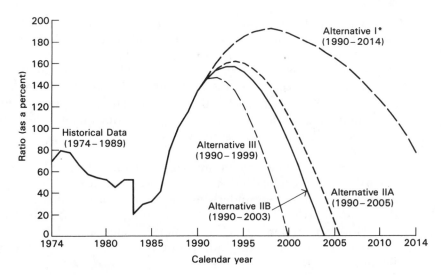

FIGURE 7-5   Short Term HI Trust Fund Ratios

*The trust fund is depleted in 2018 under alternative I.

Note: The trust fund ratio is defined as the ratio of assets at the beginning of the year to disbursements during the year.

Source: *1990 Annual Report of the Board of Trustees of the Federal Hospital Insurance Trust Fund* (Washington, D.C.: U.S. Government Printing Office, 1990), Figure 1, p. 6.

In this section, we shall briefly examine the current financial condition of the HI and SMI programs.[6]

Hospital Insurance

Actuarial Status of HI Trust Fund. *Because of soaring health care costs and inadequate financing, the HI trust fund is expected to develop serious financial problems in the years ahead.* This can be illustrated by Figure 7-5, which shows the historical HI trust fund ratios for recent years and projected ratios under the four sets of assumptions. Under both sets of intermediate assumptions, the trust fund ratio (ratio of assets at the beginning of the year to disbursements during the year) is projected to increase until 1994 and then decline steadily until the fund is completely exhausted shortly after the turn of the century. Under the optimistic set of assumptions (alternative I), the HI trust fund is projected to remain solvent throughout the first 25-year period, with trust fund exhaustion occurring in 2018. However, under the pessimistic set of assumptions (alternative III),

---

[6]This section is based on the *1990 Annual Report of the Board of Trustees of the Federal Hospital Insurance Trust Fund* (Washington, D.C.: U.S. Government Printing Office, 1990), pp. 1–12, and the *1990 Annual Report of the Board of Trustees of the Federal Supplementary Medical Insurance Trust Fund* (Washington, D.C.: U.S. Government Printing Office, 1990), pp. 1–7. To maintain technical accuracy, relevant parts of this report are reprinted in their entirety in this section.

the HI trust fund ratio is projected to increase to a level of about 146 percent in 1992 and then decrease rapidly until the fund is exhausted in 1999.

Table 7-3 shows the 75-year actuarial balance of the HI programs as published in the 1988 and 1990 reports. As Table 7-3 indicates, the projections in the 1990 report show that the HI fund will be depleted a few years earlier than in the 1988 report under the intermediate assumptions, with a larger change in the year of depletion occurring under the optimistic assumptions and no change at all under the pessimistic assumptions.

Summary. The present financing schedule for the HI program is sufficient to ensure the payment of benefits over the next 13 to 15 years if the intermediate assumptions underlying the estimates are realized, with trust fund exhaustion occurring in 2005 and 2003 under alternatives II-A and II-B, respectively. However, under the more pessimistic alternative III, the fund is exhausted in 1999. Under the more optimistic alternative I, the trust fund is exhausted in 2018.

There are currently over four covered workers supporting each HI enrollee. This ratio will begin to decline rapidly early in the next century. By the middle of that century, there will be only about two covered workers supporting each enrollee. Not only are the anticipated reserves and financing of the HI program inadequate to offset this demographic change, but under all but the most optimistic assumptions, the trust fund is projected to become exhausted even before the major demographic shift begins to occur. *Exhaustion of the HI trust fund is projected to occur shortly after the turn of the century under the intermediate assumptions, and could occur as early as 1999 if the pessimistic assumptions are realized.*

The Board noted that promising steps have already been taken to reduce the rate of growth in payments to hospitals, including the implementation of prospective payment and diagnosis-related groups. Initial experience under the prospective payment system for hospitals suggests that this payment mecha-

TABLE 7-3 Status of the Hospital Insurance Trust Fund

ALTERNATIVE ASSUMPTIONS	YEAR IN WHICH THE TRUST FUND IS EXHAUSTED AS PUBLISHED IN THE		75-YEAR ACTUARIAL BALANCE[1] OF THE HI PROGRAM AS PUBLISHED IN THE	
	1988 Report	*1990 Report*	*1988 Report*	*1990 Report*
I (optimistic)	2044	2018	−0.15%	−0.75%
II-A (intermediate)	2008	2005	−2.11	−2.83
II-B (intermediate)	2005	2003	−2.35	−3.26
III (pessimistic)	1999	1999	−6.63	−8.35

[1]The actuarial balance in the 1988 report was computed on an average-cost basis. For 1990, it is computed on a level-financing basis. For details, see the "Actuarial Status of the Trust Fund" section in the 1990 report. The actuarial balance is the difference between the average contribution rate and program expenditures (computed on a level-financing basis).

Source: *1990 Annual Report of the Board of Trustees of the Federal Hospital Insurance Trust Fund* (Washington, D.C.: U.S. Government Priting Office, 1990), Table III, p. 9.

nism is effective in constraining the growth in hospital payments and improving the efficiency of the hospital industry. Efforts focused on improving the efficiency and reducing the costs of the health care delivery system need to be continued, in close combination with mechanisms that will assure that the quality of health care is not adversely affected.

Because of the magnitude of the projected actuarial deficit in the HI program and the probability that the HI trust fund will be exhausted shortly after the end of this century, the Board recommended early corrective action to avoid the need for later, potentially precipitous changes. The Board, therefore, urged Congress to take early remedial measures to bring future HI program costs and financing into balance, and to maintain an adequate trust fund against contingencies.

Supplementary Medical Insurance

The SMI program essentially is yearly renewable term insurance financed from premium income paid by the enrollees and from income contributed from general revenue. This means that the SMI program is financed on an accrual basis with a contingency margin, and, therefore, the SMI trust fund should always be somewhat greater than the claims that have been incurred by enrollees but not yet paid by the program. The trust fund holds all of the income not currently needed to pay benefits and related expenses. The assets of the fund may not be used for any other purpose; however, they may be invested in certain interest-bearing obligations of the U.S. Government.

Financing of the SMI program is established annually on the basis of standard monthly premium rates (paid by or on behalf of all participants) and monthly actuarial rates determined separately for aged and disabled beneficiaries on which general revenue contributions are based. Prior to the 6-month transition period (July 1, 1983, through December 31, 1983) these rates were applicable in the 12-month periods ending June 30. Beginning January 1, 1984, the annual basis was changed to calendar years. Monthly actuarial rates are equal to one-half the monthly amounts necessary to finance the SMI program. These rates determine the amount to be contributed from general revenues on behalf of each enrollee. *Based on the formula in the law, the government's contribution effectively makes up the difference between twice the monthly actuarial rates and the standard monthly premium rate.* In 1989, general revenue contributions accounted for about 70 percent of all SMI income.

Table 7-4 shows the historical and projected operations of the SMI trust fund through 1992. As can be seen, income has exceeded disbursements for most of the historical years. The financing for calendar 1990 was established to maintain aged assets and to decrease disabled assets while reducing the assets overall. As a result, in calendar 1990, disbursements are projected to exceed income, and the trust fund balance is projected to decrease through calendar 1990.

The financial status of the SMI program depends on both total net assets

TABLE 7-4 Estimated Progress of Supplementary Medical Insurance Trust Fund (Cash Basis) Calendar Years 1990–1992 and Actual Data for 1967–1989 (In millions)

CALENDAR YEAR	INCOME				DISBURSEMENTS			BALANCE IN FUND AT END OF YEAR[3]
	Premiums from Enrollees	Government Contributions[1]	Interest and Other Income[2]	Total Income	Benefit Payments	Administrative Expenses	Total Disbursements	
Historical:								
1966	$ 322	$ 0	$ 2	$ 324	$ 128	$ 75	$ 203	$ 122
1967	640	933	24	1,597	1,197	110	1,307	412
1968	832	858	21	1,711	1,518	184	1,702	421
1969	914	907	18	1,839	1,865	196	2,061	199
1970	1,096	1,093	12	2,201	1,975	237	2,212	188
1971	1,302	1,313	24	2,639	2,117	260	2,377	450
1972	1,382	1,389	37	2,808	2,325	289	2,614	643
1973	1,550	1,705	57	3,312	2,526	318	2,844	1,111
1974	1,804	2,225	95	4,124	3,318	410	3,728	1,506
1975	1,918	2,648	107	4,673	4,273	462	4,735	1,444
1976	2,060	3,810	107	5,977	5,080	542	5,622	1,799
1977	2,247	5,386	172	7,805	6,038	467	6,505	3,099
1978	2,470	6,287	299	9,056	7,252	503	7,755	4,400
1979	2,719	6,645	404	9,768	8,708	557	9,265	4,902
1980	3,011	7,455	408	10,874	10,635	610	11,245	4,530
1981	3,722[4]	11,291[4]	361	15,374	13,113	915	14,028	5,877
1982	3,697[4]	12,284[4]	599	16,580	15,455	772	16,227	6,230
1983	4,236	14,861	727	19,824	18,106	878	18,984	7,070

1984	5,167	959	23,180	19,661	891	20,552	9,698
1985	5,613	1,243	25,106	22,947	933	23,880	10,924
1986	5,722	1,141	24,665	26,239	1,060	27,299	8,291
1987	7,409[5]	875	31,844	30,820	920	31,740	8,394
1988	8,761[5]	861	35,825	33,970	1,260	35,230	8,990
1989	12,263[6]	1,219[6]	44,334[6]	38,294	1,489[6]	39,783[6]	13,541[6]
Projected: Alternative A:							
1990	11,125	1,285	44,865	43,643	1,460	45,103	13,303
1991	11,781	1,216	49,482	48,938	1,543	50,481	12,304
1992	12,406	1,076	56,146	55,862	1,628	57,490	10,960
Alternative B:							
1990	11,125	1,285	44,865	43,643	1,460	45,103	13,303
1991	11,781	1,216	49,489	48,956	1,539	50,495	12,297
1992	12,445	1,076	56,226	55,940	1,622	57,562	10,961

[1]The payments shown as being from the general fund of the Treasury include certain interest-adjustment items.

[2]Other income includes recoveries of amounts reimbursed from the trust fund which are not obligations of the trust fund and other miscellaneous income.

[3]The financial status of the program depends on both the total net assets and the liabilities of the program.

[4]Section 708 of Title VII of the Social Security Act modified the provisions for the delivery of Social Security benefit checks when the regularly designated delivery day falls on a Saturday, Sunday, or legal public holiday. Delivery of benefit checks normally due January, 1982 occurred on December 31, 1981. Consequently, the SMI premiums withheld from the checks ($264 million) and the general revenue matching contributions ($883 million) were added tot he SMI trust fund on December 31, 1981. These amounts are excluded from the premium income and general revenue income for CY 1982.

[5]Delivery of benefit checks normally due January, 1988 occurred on December 31, 1987. Consequently, the SMI premiums withheld from the checks ($692 million) and the general revenue matching contributions ($2,178 million) were added to the SMI trust fund on December 31, 1987. These amounts are excluded from the premium income and general revenue income for CY 1988. (Refer to footnote 4)

[6]Includes the impact of the Medicare Catastrophic Coverage Act of 1988 (Public Law 100-360).

Source: *1990 Annual Report of the Board of Trustees of the Federal Supplementary Medical Insurance Trust Fund* (Washington, D.C.: U.S. Government Printing Office, 1990), Table 6, p. 28.

and liabilities. Therefore, it is necessary to examine the incurred experience of the program, since this experience determines the actuarial rates discussed earlier and also forms the basis of the concept of actuarial soundness as it relates to the SMI program.

Actuarial Soundness of the SMI Program. The concept of actuarial soundness, as it applies to the SMI program, is closely related to the concept as it applies to private group insurance. The SMI program is essentially yearly renewable term insurance that is financed from premium income paid by the enrollees, from income contributed from general revenue, and from interest payments on the trust fund assets.

In testing the actuarial soundness of the SMI program, it is not appropriate to look beyond the period for which the enrollee premium rates and level of general revenue financing have been established. The primary tests of actuarial soundness, then, are that: (1) assets and income for years for which financing has been established be sufficient to meet the projected benefits and associated administrative expenses incurred for that period and (2) assets be sufficient to cover projected liabilities that will have been incurred by the end of that time but will not have been paid yet. Even if these tests of actuarial soundness are not met, the program can continue to operate if the trust fund remains at a level adequate to permit the payment of claims as presented. However, to protect against the possibility that cost increases under the program will be higher than assumed, assets should be sufficient to cover the impact of a moderate degree of variation between actual and projected costs.

The primary tests for actuarial soundness and trust fund adequacy can be viewed by direct examination of absolute dollar levels. In providing an appropriate contingency or margin for variation, however, there must also be some relative measure. *The relative measure or ratio used for this purpose is the ratio of the assets less liabilities to the following year's incurred expenditures.* Figure 7-6 shows this ratio for historical years and for projected years under the intermediate assumptions (alternative B), as well as high (pessimistic) and low (optimistic) cost sensitivity scenarios.

Financing in calendar 1990 was established to maintain aged assets and to decrease disabled assets while reducing the overall relative level of the excess of assets over liabilities. In addition, the Omnibus Budget Reconciliation Act of 1989 was enacted on December 19, 1989, after the financing had been established for calendar 1990. As a net result, the excess of assets over liabilities is expected to decrease by December 31, 1990.

Summary. The Board of Trustees concluded that SMI financing established through December 1990 is sufficient to cover projected benefits and administrative costs through that time period. The financing is sufficient to maintain a level of trust fund assets that is adequate to cover the impact of a moderate degree of variation between actual costs and projected costs. *Thus, the SMI program can be said to be actuarially sound.*

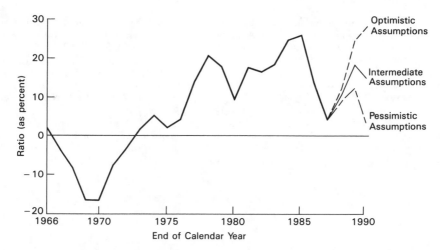

FIGURE 7-6 **Actuarial Status of the SMI Trust Fund**

Note: The actuarial status of the SMI trust fund is measured by the ratio of the end of year surplus or deficit to the following year incurred expenditures.

Source: *1990 Annual Report of the Board of Trustees of the Federal Supplementary Medical Insurance Trust Fund* (Washington, D.C.: U.S. Government Printing Office, 1990), Figure 2, p. 6.

Although the SMI program is financially sound, the Board noted with concern the rapid growth in the cost of the program. Growth rates have been so rapid that outlays of the program have nearly doubled in the last five years. For the same time period, the program grew 40 percent faster than the economy as a whole. This growth rate shows no sign of significantly abating despite recent efforts to control the cost of the program. The Board recommended that Congress continue to work to curtail the rapid growth in the SMI program.

SUGGESTIONS FOR ADDITIONAL READING

BALL, ROBERT M. "Why the Social Security Tax Should Not Be Reduced." National Academy of Social Insurance, *Social Insurance Update,* Update No. 13 (May 1990), pp. P-5–P-7.

BOARD OF TRUSTEES, FEDERAL HOSPITAL INSURANCE TRUST FUND. *1990 Annual Report of the Board of Trustees of the Federal Hospital Insurance Trust Fund.* Washington, D.C.: U.S. Government Printing Office, 1990.

BOARD OF TRUSTEES, FEDERAL OLD-AGE AND SURVIVORS INSURANCE AND DISABILITY INSURANCE TRUST FUNDS. *1990 Annual Report of the Board of Trustees of the Federal Old-Age and Survivors Insurance and Disability Insurance Trust Funds.* Washington, D.C.: U.S. Government Printing Office, 1990.

BOARD OF TRUSTEES, FEDERAL SUPPLEMENTARY MEDICAL INSURANCE TRUST FUND. *1990 Annual Report of the Board of Trustees of the Federal Supplementary Medical Insurance Trust Fund.* Washington, D.C.: U.S. Government Printing Office, 1990.

MYERS, ROBERT J. *Social Security,* 3rd ed. Homewood, Ill.: Richard D. Irwin, 1985. Chaps. 4, 5, 8, and 10.

———. "Social Security: Its Future Financial Viability and Desirability." *Journal of the American Society of CLU & ChFC,* Vol. XL, No. 6 (November 1986), pp. 44–48.

———. "Social Security's Health Is Really Robust." *Benefits Quarterly,* Vol. V, No. 4 (Fourth Quarter 1989), pp. 85–86.

————. "Social Security under the Moynihan Proposal Is Responsibly Financed." National Academy of Social Insurance, *Social Insurance Update*, Update No. 13 (May 1990), pp. P-1–P-4.

————. "Will Social Security Have Another Financing Crisis Soon?" *Benefits Quarterly*, Vol. I, No. 1 (First Quarter 1985), pp. 22–25.

————. "Without Social Security—Then What?" *Benefits Quarterly*, Vol. II, No. 1 (First Quarter 1986), pp. 55–58. See also, "Author's Reply" in the same issue by A. Haeworth Robertson.

ROBERTSON, A. HAEWORTH. "Is the Current Social Security Program Financially Feasible in the Long Run?" *Benefits Quarterly* Vol. I, No. 3 (Third Quarter 1985), pp. 36–42.

————. "Is the Current Social Security Program (of OASI, DI, HI, and SMI Benefits) Financially Feasible in the Long Run?" *Journal of the American Society of CLU and ChFC*, Vol. XL, No. 6 (November 1986), pp. 52–57.

————. "1989 Trustees Report on Social Security's Financial Health: Good News for the Elderly, Bad News for the Young." *Benefits Quarterly*, Vol. VI, No. 1 (First Quarter 1990), pp. 1–5.

8

PROBLEM OF
POOR HEALTH

Poor health can cause great economic insecurity. An unexpected illness or accident can result in the loss of earnings and can create substantial medical expenses. Unless the disabled person has adequate health insurance or other sources of income to meet these expenditures, economic insecurity will be present.

The problem of poor health can be examined from two perspectives. First, it can be analyzed from the viewpoint of the individual, since poor health can create enormous financial problems. A person who is experiencing a long-term disability will lose a substantial amount of earned income and employee benefits, catastrophic medical expenses may be incurred, and other losses may be experienced. Second, from the broader perspective of the economy, the impact of poor health on the economy must also be recognized. This latter approach requires an analysis of the entire system of health care in the United States and current problems within the system.

In this chapter, we shall analyze the problem of poor health in some detail. In particular, the following areas will be examined: (1) problem of disability, (2) problem of health care in the United States, and (3) attacking the problem of poor health. Our comments will be confined largely to *nonoccupational disability and disease*. The problem of job-related accidents and disease merits special attention, and *occupational disability* is discussed later in Chapter 11.

PROBLEM OF DISABILITY

Millions of Americans are disabled and in poor health. In 1987, 32 million people, or 13.5 percent of the U.S. civilian noninstitutional population, reported a limitation of activity because of one or more chronic health conditions. Of that number, 22 million persons reported a limitation of their major activity. Moreover, in a typical year, about one in eight Americans will be admitted into a community hospital, and an average person will visit a physician 5.4 times during the year.[1]

A person who is disabled, especially someone who is experiencing a long-term disability, is faced with the following problems: (1) loss of earned income, (2) payment of medical expenses, (3) loss of employee benefits, (4) depletion of savings, and (5) other expenses. In addition, there is the loss of the disabled person's services to the firm.

Loss of Earned Income

A major cost of disability is the loss of earned income. Unless the disabled person has replacement income from disability income insurance, or income from other sources, he or she will be economically insecure. Many working Americans seldom think about the financial consequences of long-term disability. However, the probability that a worker will become disabled is much higher than is commonly believed, especially at the younger ages (see Table 8-1). *Slightly more than one in three persons age 25 will be disabled for six months before reaching age 65. About one in seven will be disabled for five years.*

If a disabled worker cannot work, the loss of earned income can result in great economic insecurity. It is clearly evident, however, that most workers are not adequately protected against the loss of earned income during a period of disability. American workers lost $45.6 billion in earnings from short-term non-occupational sickness or injury in 1983. Of this amount, $16.4 billion, or only about 36 percent,[2] was restored from private individual and group disability income insurance, public funds, sick leave, government insurance programs, and income from other programs. The proportion of earned income restored during a period of long-term disability is undoubtedly much lower.

Payment of Medical Expenses

A disabled person may also incur substantial medical expenses. Medical expenses can be classified into three major categories: (1) normal or budgetable, (2) larger than normal, and (3) catastrophic.[3] *Normal or budgeted expenses* are

[1]Health Insurance Association of America, *Source Book of Health Insurance Data, 1989* (Washington, D.C.: Health Insurance Association of America, 1989), pp. 70, 80, 82.

[2]*Source Book of Health Insurance Data, 1986 Update,* Table 2.3, p. 12.

[3]Glenn L. Wood, Claude C. Lilly, III, Donald S. Malecki, Edward E. Graves, and Jerry S. Rosen-

TABLE 8-1 **Probability of Becoming Disabled before Age 65**

AGE	FOR 6 MONTHS	FOR 1 YEAR	FOR 2 YEARS	FOR 5 YEARS
25	34%	27%	22%	15%
30	33	26	22	15
35	33	26	21	15
40	32	25	21	15
45	30	24	20	14
50	28	23	19	14

Source: *Why Disability Protection Is Vital for You* (Cincinnati, Ohio: The National Underwriter Co., 1989), p. 4.

expenses that the family can pay out of its normal income and include routine visits to physicians, small drug purchases, and similar small expenses. These routine expenses seldom cause severe financial problems to most families.

Larger than normal expenses are medical expenses that exceed the normal or budgetable expenses. If they occur (such as major surgery), they can cause a substantial drain on the family's income. These expenses are typically met by purchasing private health insurance or by using the family's accumulated savings. However, if the family has no insurance or is inadequately insured, the financial burden can be severe, especially if a family member is hospitalized. For example, in 1987, the average hospital stay in a community hospital was 7.2 days, and the average cost of a stay was $3,850.[4]

The most severe type of medical expense is a *catastrophic medical bill.* However, only a relatively small proportion of families incur catastrophic medical expenses during any given year. A 1982 study (excluding the aged and poor) revealed that only 5 percent of the families reported medical expenses exceeding $5,000; one-half of 1 percent of the families had more than $20,000 in medical expenses.[5]

Although the frequency of catastrophic claims is relatively small, the persons involved may experience great economic insecurity if they are not adequately insured for a catastrophic loss. Fortunately, the majority of Americans have major medical health insurance protection. In 1987, 181 million people were covered under a major medical plan.[6]

Loss of Employee Benefits

Another cost of disability is the loss of employee benefits during a period of disability. Employee benefits are an important part of the total wage package. The average payment in 1988 was 37 percent of payroll and $10,750 for each

bloom, *Personal Risk Management and Insurance*, 4th ed., Vol. I (Malvern, Pa.: American Institute for Property and Liability Underwriters, 1989), p. 41.

[4]*Source Book of Health Insurance Data, 1989*, p. 43.

[5]*Source Book of Health Insurance Data, 1982–1983*, p. 46.

[6]*Source Book of Health Insurance Data, 1989*, p. 8.

employee.[7] Thus, during a long-term disability, the loss of employee benefits can be substantial.

The loss of employee benefits can take several forms. Disabled persons can lose their pension benefits, or the benefits may be reduced, since the pension benefit at normal retirement often depends on the length of service. Employer contributions under a profit-sharing or thrift plan may also be lost during a period of disability. Also, unless there is some provision for continuing group insurance during a period of disability, group life and health insurance protection may be lost.

Depletion of Savings

Another cost of disability is the depletion of family savings. A prolonged terminal illness can often deplete the family's liquid savings. Because of medical expenses not covered by insurance, or other expenses associated with the disability, the family's savings can be reduced or even exhausted before a terminally ill family head actually dies. Also, a long-term disability can result in both a reduction in income and failure to realize a future growth in income, which makes it more difficult for the family to accumulate future additional savings and financial assets.

Other Expenses

Other expenses not covered by insurance may also be incurred during a long-term disability. Someone may have to be hired to care for the disabled person; transportation expenses to receive medical care may be incurred; there may be a reduction or loss of income to a working spouse who may have to take off work to care for the disabled person; and baby-sitting expenses may be incurred to visit a disabled person who is hospitalized. These indirect costs of disability can have a substantial financial impact on the family when the family head is experiencing a long-term disability.

Loss of Services to the Firm

A final cost of disability is the loss of the disabled person's services to the firm. When a person is disabled, the output attributable to that person's services during the period of disability is lost forever. If the disabled person is a key person, there may be a substantial reduction in the firm's profits. Also, the owner of the firm may become disabled, and his or her economic value to the firm may be substantially reduced. Finally, the cost to the firm because of short-term sickness or accidents to other employees can be substantial. In 1987, employed workers age 18 and older lost an average of 3.1 work days from acute condi-

---

[7]U.S. Chamber of Commerce, *Employee Benefits 1989 Edition* (Washington, D.C.: U.S. Chamber of Commerce, 1989), p. 2.

tions.[8] Since most firms have sick leave or short-term disability income plans to cover such disabilities, the cost of these plans must also be considered when the problem of disability is analyzed.

PROBLEM OF HEALTH CARE IN THE UNITED STATES

The health of Americans has improved remarkably over time. Death rates have declined; life expectancy has increased; certain diseases, such as polio and diphtheria, have almost disappeared; and the use of miracle drugs has greatly reduced the danger from pneumonia and other infectious diseases. The overall health levels have improved because of rising incomes; improvements in nutrition, housing, sanitation, and education; rapid advancements in medical science; and introduction of new technological innovations, such as magnetic resonance imaging (MRI), CAT scanners, organ transplants, and kidney dialysis machines. However, despite this progress, the present system is confronted with several major problems. They include (1) soaring health care costs, (2) inadequate access to medical care, (3) uneven quality of care, (4) waste and inefficiency, and (5) ineffective financing.

Soaring Medical Costs

Total spending on health care in the United States and the cost of specific types of medical services have both increased sharply in recent years. Let us first consider total health care expenditures.

Total Health Care Expenditures.   Total expenditures on health care in the United States have soared in recent years. Total expenditures on health care increased from about $42 billion in 1965, or about 6 percent of the gross national product, to $539.9 billion in 1988, or 11.1 percent of the gross national product, up from 10.7 percent in 1987 and almost double since 1965. In 1988, the health outlays amounted to $2,124 per person, or a 100 percent increase in per capita spending since 1980.[9] If health care costs continue to skyrocket, it is estimated that health care will consume more than 15 percent of the nation's gross national product in 2000.[10]

The sharp increase in health expenditures over time can be explained by general price inflation, population growth, aging of the population, increased use of medical services and changes in the types of medical services, changes in

---

[8]*Source Book of Health Insurance Data, 1989*, Table 6.4, p. 75. A work-loss day is a day on which a currently employed person, 17 years of age and over, did not work at least half of his or her normal workday because of a specific illness or injury.

[9]U.S. Department of Health and Human Services, *HHS News*, May 3, 1990.

[10]*Medical Alert, A Staff Report Summarizing the Hearings on "The Future of Health Care in America,"* Prepared for the Subcommittee on Education and Health, Joint Economic Committee, October 2, 1989, p. 22.

consumption per capita, and other factors. Figure 8-1 shows in greater detail the nature of national health expenditures and sources of payment for 1988.

Comparison with Foreign Countries.   The United States spends more on health care than any other country in the world. This can be illustrated by Figure 8-2, which shows health expenditures of selected nations as a percentage of their gross domestic product. The United States ranks first, Sweden is second, and the United Kingdom ranks last.

FIGURE 8-1   The Nation's Health Dollar in 1988

Note: Other private includes industrial inplant health services, philanthropy, and privately financed construction. Other personal health care includes dental, other professional services, home health, drugs, and durable medical equipment. Other spending is for program administration and the net cost of private health insurance, government public health, research, and construction.

Source: U.S. Department of Health and Human Services, *HHS News,* May 3, 1990.

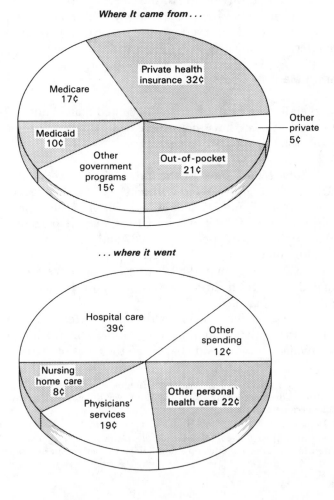

Where It came from . . .

. . . where it went

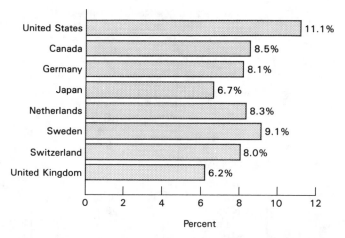

FIGURE 8-2   Health Expenditures as Percent of Gross Domestic Product, 1986 (Selected Countries)

Source: Health Insurance Association of America, *Source Book of Health Insurance Data, 1989* (Washington, D.C.: Health Insurance Association of America, 1989), p. 48.

Although the United States leads the world in the amounts spent on health care, the country has a dismal record with respect to certain key health indicators. In particular, infant mortality rates in the United States are much higher than in many foreign countries. The United States ranked twentieth in infant mortality in 1986 (see Table 8-2).

The high infant mortality rate can be partly explained by the fact that many pregnant women, especially poor unmarried pregnant women who reside in poverty areas, receive late or no prenatal care before their babies are born. Many poor pregnant women are not covered by private health insurance and often delay seeing a physician after they become pregnant. Other poor women may be unaware that prenatal care is available under the Medicaid program or else fail to apply for coverage under the program. In addition, many physicians will not treat Medicaid patients because the program often pays less than the full cost of care. The result is further delay. Consequently, because of the delay in seeing a physician, many pregnant women have babies who are born with serious health problems. Another aggravating factor is that some pregnant women are severely addicted to drugs or alcohol. As a result, their babies are often born with severe health problems and die shortly after birth.[11]

Comparison with Consumer Price Index.   The costs of specific medical services have also increased sharply over time. In particular, physician's fees, hospital rooms, and prescription drugs outpaced the overall inflation rate in the

---

[11]See Sonia L. Nazard, "Life and Death, High Infant Mortality Is a Persistent Blotch on Health Care in U.S.," *The Wall Street Journal,* October 19, 1988, p. 1 and A8.

TABLE 8-2   Infant Mortality Rate—1986
(Deaths per 1,000 births)

COUNTRY	1986	RANK
Iceland	5.1	1
Japan	5.5	2
Sweden	5.9	3
Finland	6.3	4
Netherlands	6.4	5
Switzerland	6.8	6
Canada	8.0	7
France	8.0	8
Denmark	8.4	9
Norway	8.5	10
Germany	8.6	11
Ireland	8.7	12
Spain	9.4	13
United Kingdom	9.5	14
Belgium	9.7	15
Australia	9.9	16
Italy	10.1	17
New Zealand	10.2	18
Austria	10.3	19
United States	10.6	20
Greece	12.2	21
Portugal	15.8	22
Average	8.8	—

Source: Subcommittee on Education and Health, Joint Economic Committee, *Medical Alert: A Staff Report Summarizing the Hearings on "The Future of Health Care in America,"* October 2, 1989, Table 3, p. 28.

economy in 1988 (see Table 8-3). The reasons for the sharp increase in medical care costs are complex and involve an analysis of numerous factors. These factors are discussed in the following section.

Reason for Increase in Medical Costs.   The sharp increase in medical costs can be explained by several factors. They include the following:

- *Increase in Demand.* There has been an increase in demand for medical care over time because of an increase in population, rising real per capita incomes, and greater health awareness by consumers. Also, the proportion of aged persons in the total population has increased, which has increased the demand for medical care.
- *Growth in Private Health Insurance.* The rapid growth of private health insurance has also increased the demand for medical care, especially for services provided by hospitals. Health insurance reduces the net price of care that the patient must pay out of his or her pocket. Patients may demand more expensive services when a large part of the cost is paid by health insurance. Also, the increased use of

TABLE 8-3 Annual Changes in Consumer Price Index, Selected Years

CALENDAR YEAR	ALL ITEMS	ALL MEDICAL CARE ITEMS	PHYSICIANS' FEES	DENTISTS' FEES	HOSPITAL ROOM	DRUGS AND PRESCRIPTIONS	
						Prescription Drugs	Over-the-Counter Drugs
1979	11.3	9.3	9.2	8.4	11.4	7.7	7.4
1980	13.5	10.9	10.6	11.8	13.1	9.2	10.2
1981	10.4	10.8	11.0	9.6	14.9	11.5	12.4
1982	6.2	11.6	9.4	7.7	15.7	11.7	10.8
1983	3.2	8.7	7.7	6.7	11.3	11.0	7.5
1984	4.3	6.2	6.9	8.1	8.3	9.6	6.2
1985	3.6	6.2	5.8	6.3	5.9	9.5	5.4
1986	1.9	7.5	7.3	5.6	6.0	8.6	4.9
1987	3.7	6.6	7.4	6.7	7.2	8.0	5.3
1988	4.1	6.5	7.2	6.8	9.2	7.9	5.5

Source: Health Insurance Association of America, *Source Book of Health Insurance Data, 1989* (Washington, D.C.: Health Insurance Association of America, 1989), Table 5.12, p. 59.

health insurance has induced hospitals to improve their services and provide much more expensive and sophisticated care.[12]

- *Tax Subsidy of Private Health Insurance.* It is argued that favorable income tax treatment of private health insurance has also contributed to the increase in medical costs. Employer contributions are income tax deductible and are not taxable income to the employees. As a result, employers and employees through collective bargaining often choose the more costly and comprehensive forms of health insurance, which increases further the demand for medical care.

- *Increased Utilization of Services.* Consumers are now using medical services more frequently than in the past, which also increases the cost of health care. Higher incomes permit more spending on health care. Also, the growing trend toward specialization in medical care creates a demand for specific medical services and treatment that did not previously exist. In addition, as a result of improvements in medical care, consumers tend to rely more on health care providers, expect a higher level of care, and utilize medical services with greater frequency.[13]

- *Higher Wage and Nonwage Costs.* Wages and salaries account for more than 60 percent of the operating cost of a typical hospital, and hospital prices have risen because of higher wage costs. Wages have increased because of a shortage of registered nurses and because of collective bargaining agreements with the employees. In addition, the costs of new construction, food, drugs, and other medical supplies have also increased and must be reflected in higher prices charged for health care.

- *New Technology.* The costs of new technology and highly specialized equipment have increased sharply over time. This includes CAT scanners, electronic fetal monitoring equipment, magnetic resonance imaging (MRI), coronary bypass operations, and kidney dialysis machines. As the cost of new technology increases, hospital costs have also increased. Some experts believe that new technology and new applications of existing technology or increased use of existing technology may account for as much as 25 percent of the dramatic increase in health care costs over the past two decades.[14]

- *Diffusion of Responsibility for Cost Containment.* It is argued that the root cause of inflation in health care costs is a faulty third-party reimbursement system and diffusion of responsibility for cost containment. More than three-fourths of the nation's medical bills are paid by private insurers, federal, state, and local governments, and other third parties not directly involved in setting the price for that care. *This often results in a diffusion of responsibility for holding down the costs of health care.* For example, patients who are hospitalized may not be concerned about cost, since group health insurance plans typically pay 80 percent or more of the cost of hospitalization. Physicians may not be unduly concerned about cost, since they do not personally pay for the various tests, procedures, and other services that they prescribe for their patients. Also, hospital administrators can pass higher operating costs on to the patients because of a relatively inelastic demand for hospital services. The higher costs ultimately must be borne by the patients in the form of increased health insurance premiums, which in turn aggravates the inflationary spiral.

---

[12]Martin Feldstein, "The High Cost of Hospitals—And What to Do about It," *The Public Interest,* No. 48 (Summer 1977), pp. 41–42.

[13]"Health Care Benefits: A Look at the Past with an Eye to the Future," *Newsletter,* Martin E. Segal Company, Vol. 33, No. 2 (July 1989).

[14]*Medical Alert, A Staff Report Summarizing the Hearings on "The Future of Health Care in America,"* p. 29.

- *Attitudes of Patients.* The various attitudes of patients also drive up the cost of health care. Patients today demand the best and most sophisticated medical care available; they believe that more tests and procedures are better than less; they expect to be treated for every medical condition; they generally believe that all procedures or treatments are cures; and many patients refuse to accept responsibility for maintaining their health.

- *Price Inflation.* The overall effects of general price inflation that have characterized the American economy have also contributed to the increase in health care costs. Hospitals, physicians, and other suppliers of medical care must pay more for supplies, equipment, health personnel, and other services provided to patients. Because of the overall higher costs from inflation alone, hospitals and physicians must periodically raise their prices and fees to cover these costs.

- *Government Regulation.* It is argued that excessive government regulation is a major contributor to skyrocketing health care costs. Health care providers must contend with a vast number of complex federal and state laws, much of which increases the costs of health care.

- *Medicare and Medicaid.* Medicare and Medicaid pour billions of dollars into the health care delivery system each year. This results in a great increase in the demand for medical care and causes prices to rise. In 1987, outlays for personal health care by Medicare and Medicaid totaled almost $131 billion. These two programs paid about 30 percent of all personal health care expenditures in the nation in 1987.[15]

- *Increases in Medical Malpractice Premiums.* Medical malpractice insurance premiums paid by physicians have increased sharply over time. Malpractice premiums increased from $2.5 billion in 1983 to $4.7 billion in 1985, or a sharp increase of 88 percent.[16] As a result, physicians have been forced to increase their fees.

- *Defensive Medicine.* Defensive medicine is another reason why health care costs have increased. The fear of medical malpractice lawsuits has forced physicians to practice defensive medicine, which often results in unnecessary diagnostic tests or longer than necessary hospital stays. The Joint Economic Committee states that the practice of defensive medicine adds an estimated $10.6 billion to annual medical costs.[17]

- *Cost Shifting.* Group health insurance premiums have increased substantially in recent years. Part of the increase can be explained by cost shifting by health care providers to patients with private health insurance. Physicians and hospitals frequently inflate their medical bills to recover the costs not paid by Medicare and Medicaid and also to recover the costs incurred in treating poor or uninsured patients. In particular, billions of dollars of costs have been shifted by the federal government to employers and insurers because of cutbacks in the Medicare and Medicaid programs. In addition, it is estimated that the uninsured are responsible for as much as 70 percent of the unreimbursed costs that are shifted to providers and insurers.[18]

- *Mandated Benefits.* Most states require health insurance plans to cover certain specific diseases or groups, such as coverage of newborn infants, alcoholism,

---

[15]"National Health Expenditures, 1987," *Health Care Financing Review,* Vol. 10, No. 2 (Winter 1988), Table 4, p. 116.

[16]*Medical Alert, A Staff Report Summarizing the Hearings on "The Future of Health Care in America,"* p. 44.

[17]*Medical Alert, A Staff Report Summarizing the Hearings on "The Future of Health Care in America,"* p. 44.

[18]*Source Book of Health Insurance Data,* p. 12.

psychologists, chiropractors, or physically and mentally handicapped persons. The mandated benefits increase the utilization of medical services and drive up costs.

- *Faulty Reimbursement Methods.* The methods for reimbursing health care providers are faulty and ineffective. In particular, the fee-for-service method for reimbursing physicians encourages physicians to perform more services or provide more costly care. The result is an increase in health care costs. The financing of health care is an important issue that will be discussed in greater detail later in the chapter.

Inadequate Access to Medical Care

Another serious problem is that millions of Americans find that access to high-quality medical care is often difficult. Delays in seeing a physician and long periods of waiting for an appointment are common. Certain groups frequently experience serious problems in receiving high-quality medical care. They include (1) uninsured persons, (2) poor people, (3) pregnant women, (4) rural residents, and (5) AIDS victims.

Uninsured Persons. Large numbers of people do not receive adequate medical care because they are uninsured. *In early 1987, 37 million people were uninsured, or about 15.5 percent of the population, up from 12.3 percent in 1977.*[19] The groups with serious gaps in health insurance coverage include the following:[20]

- *Employed Workers and Their Families.* Almost 16 percent of the working population and their families under age 65 were uninsured in 1987. The uninsured workers typically worked in low-wage or part-time jobs, in seasonal or temporary jobs, in smaller firms, or were self-employed.
- *Young Adults.* In 1987, 30 percent of young adults between ages 19 through 24 were uninsured. Young people in this age group who are not full-time students typically are excluded from the group health insurance plans of their parents but often are employed in jobs that do not provide any health insurance.
- *Unmarried Adults.* A large proportion of unmarried adults have no health insurance. In 1987, 25 percent of all single and never-married persons were uninsured. Twenty-one percent of the persons who were divorced were uninsured, and 25 percent of the separated were also uninsured.
- *Families without a Working Adult.* In 1987, about 29 percent of the persons uninsured under age 65 lived in families without a working adult.
- *Blacks and Hispanics.* In 1987, 22 percent of the blacks and about 32 percent of the Hispanics were uninsured. In contrast, only 12 percent of the whites had no health insurance.

---

[19]*A Profile of Uninsured Americans, Research Findings 1,* National Medical Expenditures Survey, Department of Health and Human Services, Public Health Service, National Center for Health Services Research and Health Care Technology Assessment (DHS Publication No. [PHS] 89–3443), September 1989, p. 4.

[20]This section is based on ibid., Table 1, p. 6, and Table 3, p. 8.

For many uninsured Americans, the only available source of medical care is *treatment in a hospital emergency room*. As a result, many emergency rooms in public hospitals are used to provide nonemergency treatment, which places severe stress on both medical personnel and physical facilities. In addition, health care from emergency rooms does not provide for routine examinations or preventive care. Also, in some parts of the country, even access to emergency care is limited. For example, in Miami, there is only one public hospital for the entire city.[21] Finally, even when medical care is available from a clinic in a public hospital, it may take weeks to get an appointment, and patients often must wait hours before they are treated by a physician. Clearly, medical care provided by hospital emergency rooms or clinics in public hospitals for uninsured and poor people is a temporary stopgap measure at best and cannot be viewed as a viable solution to the health care problem faced by many Americans.

Poor People.   Many poor people in the United States also have difficulty in receiving high-quality medical care. Medicaid is a major welfare program that is designed to cover the medical expenses incurred by the poor. However, a means test is required, and the eligibility standards are strict. Although their incomes are below the poverty line, many poor people are not covered by Medicaid. *In 1986, according to preliminary findings by the Urban Institute, one-third of all noninstitutionalized, low-income persons were not covered by the Medicaid program.*[22] Many poor people fail to qualify because their incomes and cash resources are too high; they are not aware of the program and fail to apply; the forms are too complex and difficult to fill out; or they are too embarrassed to apply for charity.[23]

In addition, even if the poor are covered by Medicaid, access to medical care often is difficult. Many physicians refuse to treat welfare patients because Medicaid often pays less than the full cost of care. Also, access to long-term care in some areas is limited because of a shortage of nursing home beds. Since Medicaid frequently pays less than the full cost of care in many states, nursing homes with limited beds tend to restrict the number of new Medicaid patients who are admitted. Nursing homes with a limited number of beds typically give priority to private-pay patients who are more profitable.

Finally, poor people who receive medical care but are unable to pay may find themselves subject to lawsuits by hospitals that provided care. For example, in a two-month period in the District of Columbia, 872 suits were filed by hospitals against people who received care. On an annual basis, that would represent over 5,000 suits in only one jurisdiction.[24] Obviously, hospitals in poverty areas do not have the financial resources to provide unlimited medical

---

[21]*Medical Alert, A Staff Report Summarizing the Hearings on "The Future of Health Care in America,"* p. 4.
[22]Spencer Rich, "Ignorance, Fear Keep Millions Off Welfare," *Washington Post,* June 26, 1989.
[23]Ibid.
[24]*Medical Alert, A Staff Report Summarizing the Hearings on "The Future of Health Care in America,"* p. ii.

care without reimbursement to every poor or uninsured person. However, critics argue that all Americans should have access to high-quality care regardless of their ability to pay.

Pregnant Women. As we noted earlier, many pregnant women who are uninsured or not covered by Medicaid frequently receive late or no prenatal care. As a result, many babies are born with serious health problems. In particular, certain high-risk groups delay in seeing a physician or receive no prenatal care at all. This group includes unmarried pregnant teen-agers, black and Hispanic women, women with less than a high school education, and women with incomes less than 150 percent of the federal poverty line.[25]

As we noted earlier, some pregnant women delay in receiving prenatal care because they are uninsured or not covered by Medicaid. Others cannot find a physician who will treat them. In particular, as a result of the increase in medical malpractice lawsuits, many physicians no longer will provide prenatal care and deliver babies. The result has been a significant reduction in the availability of obstetrical care in many parts of the country, especially in rural areas. For example, 44 percent of the counties in Georgia and 30 percent of the counties in Colorado no longer have a family practice physician or obstetrician who will provide obstetrical services.[26] Moreover, even in those areas where obstetrical services are available, physicians tend to limit the number of high-risk pregnancies they will treat.

Rural Residents. Rural residents frequently face serious problems in receiving high-quality medical care because of a shortage of physicians in those areas. Although an absolute shortage of physicians nationally does not exist, many small towns and rural communities have no physicians. In 1985, there were 552,716 active physicians in the United States, up from 279,212 in 1970.[27] This represented a sharp increase of about 98 percent since 1970. However, the physicians are not sprinkled uniformly over the entire population, but instead tend to practice medicine in large metropolitan areas. The District of Columbia, New York, Massachusetts, Maryland, and Connecticut have the highest ratio of nonfederal physicians to the civilian population; rural and sparsely populated states contain relatively fewer physicians. The lowest ratio of physicians to the population is in Alaska, Arkansas, Idaho, Mississippi, South Dakota, and Wyoming.[28] As a result, many rural residents have great difficulty in receiving high-quality care because of a shortage of physicians.

---

[25]U.S. Congress, House, Committee on Ways and Means, *Background Material and Data on Programs within the Jurisdiction of the Committee on Ways and Means* (Washington, D.C.: U.S. Government Printing Office, 1989), p. 844.

[26]*Medical Alert, A Staff Report Summarizing the Hearings on "The Future of Health Care in America,"* p. 46.

[27]*Background Material and Data on Programs within the Jurisdiction of the Committee on Ways and Means,* 1989, p. 269.

[28]Ibid., Table 16, pp. 270–271.

AIDS Victims.   Many persons with AIDS (acquired immune deficiency syndrome) also have serious problems in receiving adequate medical care. The AIDS epidemic is one of the worst public health disasters in the nation's history. There is no known cure, and the disease is usually fatal. Since 1981, more than 87,300 cases of AIDS have been reported, and an estimated 1.5 million Americans are infected with the AIDS virus.[29] AIDS patients typically are shunned by private insurers and by many physicians and health care providers.

Uneven Quality of Health Care

Another problem is the uneven quality of health care. Americans generally have access to the highest-quality medical care in the world. Unfortunately, the quality of medical care is not uniform throughout the nation but varies widely depending on the physician, hospital, and geographical location of treatment.

Most physicians provide safe and competent medical care to their patients. However, several studies show that the medical care provided by some physicians is inappropriate, unnecessary, or of low quality. *First, many surgical operations performed each year are unnecessary.* For example, 900,000 Caesarean operations were performed in the United States in 1986, and at least half of them were unnecessary. In addition, 250,000 Americans have a coronary bypass operation each year, which makes Americans four times more likely to have bypass surgery than Western Europeans. However, 60 percent to 80 percent of the patients who have bypass surgery gain no increase in life expectancy beyond what they would have attained by medical management of their condition; the cost of the unnecessary bypass operation is over $5 billion annually.[30] Finally, another study showed that 20 percent of the implantations of permanent pacemakers were not justified, and another 36 percent were of questionable value.[31]

Second, medical treatment for the same condition varies widely depending on geographical location. For example, residents in New Haven, Connecticut, are twice as likely to undergo coronary artery bypass surgery than residents in Boston, Massachusetts. In one community in Maine, almost 70 percent of the women have had a hysterectomy by age 70, while the hysterectomy rate is only 20 percent in another community. In Vermont, only 8 percent of the children in one community have had a tonsillectomy operation, while almost 70 percent of the children in another community have had a tonsillectomy operation.[32]

In addition, the substantial increase in medical malpractice lawsuits is another indication that some physicians provide low-quality medical care to their patients. In four

---

[29]*Source Book of Health Insurance Data, 1989,* p. 80.

[30]*Medical Alert, A Staff Report Summarizing the Hearings on "The Future of Health Care in America,"* p. 31.

[31]William C. Hsiao, Peter Braun, Daniel Dunn, and Edmund R. Becker, "Resource-Based Relative Values: An Overview," *The Journal of the American Medical Association,* Vol. 260, No. 16 (October 28, 1988), p. 2,347.

[32]*Press Release No. 15,* Subcommittee on Health, Committee on Ways and Means, U.S. House of Representatives, May 11, 1989.

years from 1981 to 1985, the number of claims filed against physicians tripled from 3.2 per 100 physicians to 10.1 per 100 physicians.[33]

Medical malpractice lawsuits have increased for several reasons.[34] First, according to some experts, there is a disturbing level of improper or negligent medical care provided by some physicians. Second, medical malpractice lawsuits have escalated because of unrealistic patient expectations; when patient expectations are high, failure to fulfill them often results in a lawsuit. Third, Americans increasingly believe in the philosophy of entitlement, which means that if a person has an unsuccessful or even damaging operation, he or she should be entitled to collect even though the physician may not be negligent. Finally, there has been a deterioration in the physician-patient relationship. The result is that patients are more willing to sue than formerly.

As we noted earlier, the fear of medical malpractice lawsuits has forced many physicians to practice defensive medicine, which often results in unnecessary diagnostic tests or longer-than-necessary hospital stays. Defensive medicine is another reason why health care costs have increased. Also, because of the fear of lawsuits, many physicians have abandoned certain high-risk medical specialties such as obstetrics and gynecology.

Waste and Inefficiency

The health care industry consists of hospitals, physicians, dentists, pharmaceutical firms, and other health professionals and activities. The Joint Economic Committee recently issued a report highly critical of the health care industry because of considerable waste and inefficiency.[35] Defects include the following:

- *Excessive Waste.* It is estimated that as much as $125 billion annually or $1 out of every $4 spent on health care is wasted. The money is spent on unnecessary tests and medical procedures, including diagnostic tests, X-rays, drugs, and unnecessary surgery.
- *Overutilization of Expensive Technology.* Many experts believe that new technology is overutilized or used inappropriately, which also increases the cost of health care. New technology such as CAT scanners and magnetic resonance imaging (MRI) provide diagnostic information that could not be obtained previously or could be obtained only with risk to the patient. However, the inappropriate use of new technology is an important factor that increases the cost of health care. Examples of inappropriate use are situations where the technology is used in ignorance, the procedure is of marginal value to the patient, or conclusive studies have not been conducted.

---

[33]*Medical Alert, A Staff Report Summarizing the Hearings on "The Future of Health Care in America,"* p. 44.

[34]Charles P. Hall, Jr., "Medical Malpractice Problem, *Annals of the American Academy of Political and Social Science,* Vol. 443 (May 1979), p. 82.

[35]This section is based largely on *Medical Alert, A Staff Report Summarizing the Hearings on "The Future of Health Care in America."*

- *Excessive Paperwork.* The paperwork created by a pluralistic system of health care in the United States adds a $20 surcharge for each $100 spent on health care.
- *Duplication of Expensive Equipment.* There is considerable duplication of expensive equipment and new technology, such as the purchase of expensive CAT scanners by several hospitals in the same city. Also, many hospitals have overbuilt, and there is a large surplus of beds in many communities.

In addition, there are numerous obstacles to a free market that can promote greater efficiency in the delivery of health care services. The medical care sector in the economy generally is characterized by limited price competition. Physicians and hospitals usually do not engage in price competition, and consumers generally have inadequate knowledge concerning the prices of medical services. Fees are seldom discussed, and most patients are incapable of determining the quality of care that they receive. Finally, the present system is geared to sickness and not health; there are few incentives to prevent an illness or diagnose it early.

Ineffective Financing

It is also argued that the financing of health care is ineffective and aggravates many of the problems analyzed earlier. Critics point out the following problems:

1. BASED ON ABILITY TO PAY.   The present system is based largely on the person's ability to pay and not on the basis of health needs. Thus, it is argued that some Americans with health problems do not receive treatment because they cannot pay for it. An earlier study for the Robert Wood Johnson Foundation indicated that about one million persons were refused medical care by hospitals because of financial reasons in 1982.[36]

2. FEE-FOR-SERVICE DEFECTS.   It is argued that the traditional fee-for-service method of compensating physicians often works in a perverse way. Under this system, the more services physicians provide, the higher are their incomes. As a result, some surgical operations are unnecessary, and other medical services are often provided that are not needed. Also, physicians have little incentive to provide less costly forms of treatment under this system. Finally, there is no incentive to physicians to spend time talking with patients about good health habits and preventive care.

3. DISTORTIONS IN MEDICAL CARE.   It is argued that the present system results in a distortion in medical care. For example, because specialists earn higher incomes and work shorter hours, most medical school graduates enter specialty fields and abandon general practice; because consumers in the suburbs

---

[36]*Press Release No. 2*, U.S. House of Representatives, Committee on Ways and Means, January 15, 1987.

are better able to pay for specialists, physicians tend to practice in the suburbs, thereby exacerbating the shortages of physicians in rural and inner-city areas.

4. DEFECTS IN PRIVATE HEALTH INSURANCE.   In addition to contributing to the inflation in health care costs, it is argued that private health insurance has other serious defects. First, as we noted earlier, 37 million Americans have no health insurance coverage. Some 70 million more are underinsured.[37] Second, some individual health insurance policies sold are of doubtful quality, including limited accident policies, cancer policies, and hospital indemnity contracts. Third, many contracts still tend to encourage hospitalization instead of less costly forms of care. Fourth, although group health insurance provides comprehensive benefits and pays 80 percent or more of the cost of hospitalization, a major limitation of group insurance applies to unemployed workers. Unemployed workers generally lose their group health insurance benefits during an extended layoff. During the severe recession years of 1981 and 1982, 5.3 million laid-off workers lost their coverage under an employer-based health benefits plan.[38] Although laid-off employees and their dependents now have the option of remaining in the employer's plan for 18 months after being laid off, they must pay 102 percent of the premium. Many laid-off workers cannot afford to pay the entire premium plus 2 percent, and they drop their insurance. Finally, some persons are overinsured and profit from insurance when they are sick or disabled.

ATTACKING THE PROBLEM OF POOR HEALTH

A wide variety of techniques and approaches are used to meet the problem of poor health. Let us first consider the problem of disability.

Meeting the Problem of Disability

The major approaches for meeting the problem of nonoccupational disability are (1) disability income benefits; (2) sick leave plans; (3) social insurance benefits; (4) Supplemental Security Income program for the aged, blind, and disabled; (5) health insurance pools for the uninsurable; and (6) vocational rehabilitation.

Disability Income Benefits.   Disability income benefits from private insurers and other sources provide for the partial replacement of income as a result of sickness or accidents. These coverages include individual and group

---

[37]*Medical Alert, A Staff Report Summarizing the Hearings on "The Future of Health Care in America,"* p. 4.

[38]U.S. Senate, *Health Insurance for the Unemployed,* Hearings before the Subcommittee on Finance, 98th Cong., 1st sess. (Washington, D.C.: U.S. Government Printing Office, 1983), pp. 4–5.

disability income plans from private insurers, paid sick leave plans, and other plans.

1. INDIVIDUAL DISABILITY INCOME INSURANCE. The individual policies provide weekly or monthly cash payments to a person who is totally disabled from an accident or sickness; residual disability benefits may also be paid.[39] The insured has a choice of benefit periods, which typically range from 13 to 52 weeks, 2, 5, 10, or 20 years, up to age 65, or even for life. The policies are usually sold with a waiting period that normally ranges from 7 to 90 days. Many policies also contain a waiver-of-premium provision, by which premiums are waived if the insured is totally disabled for at least 90 days.

2. GROUP DISABILITY INCOME INSURANCE. There are basically two types of group disability plans: short-term and long-term.

The majority of employers provide *short-term disability income benefits* to their employees. The benefits are paid for relatively short periods, typically 13 weeks to 2 years. A common benefit period is 26 weeks. Most plans have a 3- to 7-day waiting period for sickness to discourage malingering and excessive absenteeism, while accidents are usually covered from the first day of disability.

Most short-term plans cover only *nonoccupational disability*, which means that an accident or sickness must occur off the job. (Job-related disabilities are covered by workers' compensation plans.) Disability is usually defined in terms of the worker's *own* occupation. The amount of the weekly or monthly benefit is typically equal to some percentage of the worker's normal earnings, such as two-thirds.

Many employers also provide *long-term disability* income benefits. These plans pay benefits for longer periods, which typically range from two years to age 65 or even for life.

A dual definition of total disability is typically used in long-term plans. For the first two years, disability is defined as the inability of the insured to perform all duties of his or her occupation. After that time, the worker is considered disabled if he or she is unable to work in any occupation reasonably fitted by training, education, and experience. Also, in contrast to short-term plans, long-term plans usually cover both *occupational and nonoccupational disability*.

The maximum monthly benefits are usually limited to 50 to 70 percent of the employee's normal earnings. Since long-term plans are designed largely for average and upper-income employees and executives, monthly benefits of $3,000, $4,000, or even higher are commonly paid.

Most plans have a waiting period of four to six months before benefits are payable. To provide proper benefit design and hold down costs and to reduce malingering and moral hazard, Social Security and workers' compensa-

---

[39]A residual disability benefit is a pro rata disability income benefit that is paid if the worker's earnings are reduced because of an accident or sickness. The amount paid is based on the proportion of earnings reduced.

tion benefits are taken into consideration, and the long-term benefit is reduced accordingly. Finally, many plans provide for a limited *annual cost-of-living adjustment* and a *pension accrual benefit,* which provides for a pension contribution so that the disabled person's normal pension benefit remains intact.

Sick Leave Plans. Many firms have formal sick leave plans that pay the employee's full salary during an initial period of disability. For example, the firm may pay the disabled person's full salary for three weeks, and then 50 percent of salary for eight additional weeks. Another approach is to give the workers one day of sick leave for each month worked.

Sick leave plans have two major limitations. First, they are designed largely for short-term disabilities and are not normally used to pay a disabled person's wages during a long-term disability. Second, sick leave plans may be abused by the employees who tend to use sick leave days because they are available. It is not uncommon for some workers to fake an illness each month and take one or two days off at the employer's expense.

Social Insurance Benefits. Monthly disability income benefits may be payable to disabled workers under the disability income portion of the OASDI program. To receive benefits, the disabled worker must be disability insured, satisfy a five-month waiting period, and meet the definition of disability stated in the law.

In addition, five states,[40] Puerto Rico, and the railroad industry have temporary disability insurance laws that pay cash benefits to insured workers who are unemployed because of sickness or injury.

The OASDI disability income program and state temporary disability insurance laws are treated in greater detail in Chapter 9.

Supplemental Security Income Program. A disabled person who can satisfy a means test may be eligible for monthly benefits under the Supplemental Security Income (SSI) program for the aged, blind, and disabled. The SSI program is a welfare program that guarantees a minimum monthly income of $386 to an eligible individual with no other source of income and $579 to couples as of January 1, 1990. A means test must be satisfied to receive benefits. Financial resources are limited to $2,000 for an individual and $3,000 for a married couple. Certain resources are not counted, such as the value of the home, personal and household goods with an equity value of up to $2,000, an automobile used for essential transportation or worth $4,500 or less, and up to $1,500 in burial funds ($3,000 for a couple).

Health Insurance Pools for the Uninsurable. A number of states have created special health insurance pools that provide health insurance to people who have difficulty in getting insured because of a medical condition. The basic

---

[40]California, Hawaii, New Jersey, New York, and Rhode Island.

objective is to make health insurance available to uninsurable persons. Applicants generally must show they have been refused health insurance elsewhere before they are accepted.

To illustrate, under Nebraska's plan, a resident who is rejected for health insurance by a licensed insurer within the last six months, or is offered a policy that contains a restrictive rider for a preexisting condition within the last six months, or is offered comparable coverage at a higher rate can apply for coverage from the state pool. Major medical insurance can be purchased with a lifetime maximum limit of $500,000. The policyowner has the choice of a $250, $500, or $1,000 annual deductible. The plan pays 80 percent of the cost after the deductible is met. The policyowner pays the remaining 20 percent up to a maximum of $5,000 per year. Premiums are significantly higher than under individual plans (e.g., $1,648 annually for a 40-year-old woman in Omaha with a $500 deductible). Losses in excess of the premiums paid are pooled among the health insurers doing business in the state based on the amount of business conducted in Nebraska. The companies in turn can deduct the assessments from the premium taxes paid to the state. The result is that the taxpayers are indirectly paying the excess costs incurred by the pool.

State pools have the major advantage of making health insurance available to uninsurable persons. The major disadvantage is that many uninsured persons cannot afford to pay the significantly higher premiums that are charged.

Vocational Rehabilitation. Vocational rehabilitation can also be used to rehabilitate disabled workers for meaningful employment. All states have vocational rehabilitation agencies that provide counseling, financial assistance, and special training programs to disabled workers to enable them to return to productive employment. Society benefits from rehabilitation, since the overhead costs of caring for disabled workers are reduced. Disabled workers who are successfully rehabilitated also benefit, since their self-esteem is enhanced, income is being received, and economic security is promoted.

Meeting the Problem of Health Care

Several approaches are used to meet the problem of health care in the United States, and several new techniques have been introduced to attack the problem on all fronts. They include (1) private health insurance, (2) extension of group health insurance to terminated employees, (3) new cost-containment methods to hold down increases in medical costs, and (4) improving the access to medical care.

Private Health Insurance. Private health insurance protection can be obtained from several major sources. They include the following: (1) commercial insurers, (2) Blue Cross and Blue Shield plans, (3) self-insurance by employers, (4) health maintenance organizations (HMOs), and (5) preferred provider organizations (PPOs).

1. COMMERCIAL INSURERS. Many employees and dependents are covered for their medical expenses under conventional group health insurance plans sponsored by employers. The major coverages include hospital expense insurance, surgical expense insurance, physicians' expense insurance, major medical insurance, short-term and long-term disability income plans, and dental expense plans. Group medical expense insurance is sold primarily by life and health insurers, but coverage is also available from some property and liability insurers. However, because of heavy underwriting losses, numerous insurers have withdrawn from the health insurance market in recent years. Although approximately 700 insurers write group health insurance, over half of the coverage is now written by only about 30 insurers.[41]

2. BLUE CROSS AND BLUE SHIELD PLANS. Blue Cross and Blue Shield plans are prepayment plans that provide coverage primarily for hospital expenses, physician services, major medical expenses, and other covered services. In recent years, most Blue Cross and Blue Shield plans have merged into single entities. In mid-1987, 50 plans jointly wrote Blue Cross and Blue Shield benefits. However, 13 separate Blue Cross plans and 15 separate Blue Shield plans were in operation.[42]

Blue Cross plans provide hospital benefits to covered members. These plans generally provide *service benefits* rather than cash benefits to the subscribers. For example, most plans cover the full cost of a semiprivate room in the hospital. Payment usually is made directly to the hospital or other providers of care rather than to the subscriber.

Blue Cross plans consist of individual, family, and group membership. Most members are in group plans. However, Blue Cross plans actively compete for business in the individual markets. The benefits generally are broad and comprehensive. In addition to daily room and board benefits, Blue Cross plans typically provide outpatient services for accidental injury and surgery, diagnostic testing, physical therapy, kidney dialysis, and chemotherapy. Preadmission testing is also covered in most plans. Finally, most Blue Cross plans also offer supplemental major medical coverage for a catastrophic injury or illness.

Blue Shield plans are prepayment plans that provide coverage for physicians' and surgeons' fees and other medical costs. Two major methods are used to reimburse physicians. The first method is to pay physicians and other suppliers of care on the basis of their *usual, customary, and reasonable charges*. The second method of payment is the *indemnity approach* where a fixed dollar amount is paid for medical care; predetermined cash benefits are paid for a listed schedule of procedures.

Finally, many Blue Cross and Blue Shield plans also sponsor health

---

[41]Burton T. Beam, Jr., and John J. McFadden, *Employee Benefits*, 2nd ed. (Homewood, Ill.: Richard D. Irwin, 1988), p. 146.
[42]Ibid., p. 147.

maintenance organizations (HMOs) and preferred provider organizations (PPOs). HMOs and PPOs are discussed later in the chapter.

3. SELF-INSURANCE BY EMPLOYERS. Self-insurance by employers is widely used to provide health insurance benefits to employees. *Self-insurance* (also called self-funding) means that the employer pays part or all of the group health insurance benefits provided to employees. Self-insurance plans have grown rapidly in recent years. Relatively few employees were enrolled in self-insurance plans in 1977. However, in 1987, nearly 60 percent of the nation's employees with employer-sponsored conventional health insurance were enrolled in plans that self-insure in some capacity.[43]

Self-insurance plans are usually established with stop-loss coverage and an administrative-services-only (ASO) contract. *Stop-loss* coverage means that excess claims over a certain maximum dollar limit are paid by a commercial insurer. An *administrative-services-only (ASO) contract* is an arrangement by which the insurer or some independent organization handles the administration of claims, pays benefits, and performs other administrative functions for a fee.

Self-insurance has several advantages for an employer.[44] First, substantial cost savings may be possible from savings in commissions, state premium taxes, risk charge, and insurer's profit. Second, cash flow can be improved since the funds needed to pay claims can be retained by the employer and earn interest until needed to pay claims. Finally, self-insured plans are often exempt from state-mandated benefit laws.

4. HEALTH MAINTENANCE ORGANIZATIONS (HMOs). A health maintenance organization (HMO) is an alternative to traditional health insurance. *An HMO can be defined as an organized system of health care that provides comprehensive health services to its members for a fixed, prepaid fee.* The number of employees covered by HMOs has grown rapidly. In 1987, nearly 30 million people were enrolled in HMOs, up sharply from 6 million in 1976.[45]

There are two basic types of HMOs.[46] First, under a *group practice plan* (also called a staff model), physicians usually are employed by the HMO or an organization that contracts with the HMO and are paid a salary. Most HMOs have a closed panel of physicians, and members are limited in their choice of physicians associated with the plan. The physicians typically are general practitioners or family practice specialists and other medical specialists who practice medicine as a group and share facilities. Most HMO subscribers are covered under group practice plans.

The second type of HMO is an *individual practice association plan* (IPA). An IPA is an open panel of physicians who work out of their own offices. The

[43]Steven DiCarlo and Jon Gabel, "Conventional Health Insurance: A Decade Later," *Health Care Financing Review,* Vol. 10, No. 3 (Spring 1989), p. 86.

[44]Beam, Jr., and McFadden, *Employee Benefits,* pp. 237–238.

[45]*Source Book of Health Insurance Data, 1989,* p. 7.

[46]Beam, Jr., and McFadden, *Employee Benefits,* pp. 154–155.

individual physicians contract with the HMO to treat members based on an agreed-upon fee schedule or on the capitation basis (flat amount for each member). To encourage physicians to be cost conscious, a bonus may be paid if the plan experience is better than expected.

HMOs have certain characteristics that distinguish them from traditional private health insurance and Blue Cross-Blue Shield service plans.[47] *First, the HMO has the responsibility for organizing and delivering comprehensive health services to its members.* The HMO owns or leases medical facilities, enters into agreements with hospitals and physicians to provide medical services, hires ancillary personnel, and has general managerial control over the various services provided.

Second, the HMO provides broad comprehensive health services to its members. Most services usually are covered in full, with relatively few maximum limits on individual services. Covered services typically include the full costs of hospitalization, all necessary medical services for acute care, surgeons' and physicians' fees, maternity care, laboratory and X-ray services, outpatient services, special-duty nursing, and numerous other services. All office visits to HMO physicians are also covered, either in full or at a nominal charge for each visit.

Third, a member of an HMO pays a fixed prepaid fee (usually paid monthly) and is provided with a wide range of comprehensive health services. However, some HMOs charge a nominal fee for certain services, such as office visits or prescription drugs. The payment of an annual fixed fee is an important advantage to the member, since it eliminates any financial barriers to needed medical care and assures a wide range of health services.

Fourth, some persons may become dissatisfied with the medical care provided by HMOs. *Therefore, the members generally have the opportunity each year to elect to remain in the HMO or participate in a group health insurance plan, including Blue Cross and Blue Shield.* The objective is to offer the members an alternative to the HMO in the event they become dissatisfied, thereby conforming to the traditional concept of freedom of choice.

Finally, in group practice HMOs, physicians are not usually compensated based on fee for service. Some physicians are employees of the HMO and are paid an *annual salary.* The *capitation method* is another approach. This means that a medical group of physicians and other health care professionals engage in the group practice of medicine. The medical group receives income for the health services provided in the form of a fixed monthly charge for each member, which is often referred to as a capitation charge. The medical group then pays its physicians any way it wishes, such as with a salary. Since the medical group is charged for the costs of hospitalization, it may provide financial incentives for physicians to achieve lower hospital utilization rates. These financial incentives include profit-sharing schemes, bonuses, and shares in the net earnings at the end of the year.

---

[47]See Jerry S. Rosenbloom and G. Victor Hallman, *Employee Benefit Planning*, 2d ed. (Englewood Cliffs, N.J.: Prentice-Hall, 1986), pp. 87–91, 166–179.

Several advantages are claimed for HMOs. They are summarized as follows:

a. *Broad Comprehensive Care*. The major advantage is that broad comprehensive care is provided to the members. There are fewer gaps in coverage; service benefits are provided; relatively few exclusions are present; and deductibles and coinsurance generally are not emphasized; however, many HMOs place limits on the amount paid for the treatment of alcoholism and drug addiction.

b. *Loss Prevention*. Many loss prevention services are typically provided to keep the members healthy. They include multiphasic screenings, regular physical examinations, access to medical specialists, well-child care, eye exams, prenatal and postnatal maternity care, and immunizations. There is a strong incentive to treat a disease in its early stage to promote a prompt recovery.

c. *Convenience*. There may be fewer administrative problems since the members do not have to file claim forms. Also, members may save time in receiving medical care. Since a full range of comprehensive services is available from one organization, often at a single location, the patient may not have to visit numerous specialists in different locations, and time is saved.

d. *Access to Care*. The members have access to medical care at night or over the weekend as opposed to the situation under the solo-practice approach, where the family's physician may be unavailable during those times.

However, critics of HMOs point out certain disadvantages. They include the following:

a. *Financial Problems*. Some HMOs have failed, and many are in financial difficulty. The start-up costs are substantial, and many HMOs are too small to achieve substantial economies of scale. From an optimum viewpoint, an HMO should have at least 20,000 members. Many HMOs are well below this figure.

b. *Restriction on Right to Select Physicians*. Another disadvantage is that the freedom to select an individual physician is restricted. Many HMOs have a closed panel of physicians, and the member must choose among those available in the group. Some members feel that the medical care provided to them is too impersonal, and a close physician-patient relationship is difficult to attain.

c. *Care Outside the Area*. There is also the problem of receiving medical care outside of the geographical area of the HMO. Most HMOs pay only for emergency care provided outside of the immediate geographical area served by the HMO.

d. *Quality of Care*. It is also argued that the quality of medical care is not as high as that provided by the physicians engaged in solo practice. It is argued that emphasis on cost savings under an HMO could result in a reduction in the quality of medical care. Some members may not receive prompt hospitalization when necessary, outpatient services may be rushed, and in some HMOs, a member may wait a long time to get an appointment.[48]

5. PREFERRED PROVIDER ORGANIZATIONS (PPOS). A preferred provider organization (PPO) is another approach for holding down health care costs. *A*

---

[48]For example, see Michael Wels Hirschorn, "Cost Cutting Methods by HMOs Increase Patient Dissatisfaction, Report Suggests" *The Wall Street Journal,* August 20, 1986, p. 7; and Michael Wels Hirschorn, "Medical Discord: Some Doctors Assail Quality of Treatment Provided by HMOs," *The Wall Street Journal,* September 16, 1986, p. 1.

PPO can be defined as an arrangement in which employers or insurers contract with health care providers to provide health services to the group members at discounted fees. Under this arrangement, the employer or insurer negotiates a contract with certain physicians, hospitals, pharmacists, and other health care providers to provide health care services to the group members at discounted fees. In return, the health care providers are promised prompt payment and an increased volume of business. To encourage patients to use the PPO providers, deductibles and coinsurance charges are reduced or waived. Also, the member may be charged a lower fee for certain routine treatments or offered increased benefits such as preventive health care.

PPOs should not be confused with HMOs. There are two important differences between them.[49] First, PPOs do not provide medical care on a prepaid basis. The PPO providers are paid on a fee-for-service basis as their services are used. However, as we stated earlier, the fees charged are below the provider's regular fee. Second, unlike an HMO, employees are not required to use the PPO, but have freedom of choice each time they need care. However, as we stated earlier, employees have a financial incentive to use PPO providers, since deductibles and coinsurance charges are reduced or waived.

PPOs offer major advantages to employers and insurers, employees, and health care providers. Employers and insurers benefit since medical services are provided to employees at discounted fees; thus, health care costs can be held down. Employees benefit since they usually have a greater choice of providers than under an HMO, and deductible and coinsurance charges are reduced or waived. Finally, health care providers benefit since they are paid promptly and are assured access to a larger group of patients.

Extension of Group Health Insurance to Terminated Employees. Workers who lose their jobs often lose their group health insurance benefits. This is particularly true for workers who are laid off during recessions. During the 1981–1982 recession, numerous laid-off workers and their dependents lost their group health insurance benefits.

A federal law (Consolidated Omnibus Budget Reconciliation Act, or COBRA) enacted in 1985 requires many employers to offer group health insurance benefits to terminated employees, their spouses, and dependent children. This law applies to employers and to state and local government agencies that employ 20 or more workers. The federal government and churches are exempt.

Under this law, terminated employees have the option of continuing their group health insurance protection for up to 18 months if they are voluntarily or involuntarily terminated from their jobs or their hours are reduced. Persons who want the group benefits must pay 102 percent of the group rate. The extra 2 percent goes to the employer for administrative expenses.

In addition, the employee's spouse and dependents can continue to be covered for up to three years if the employee dies, is legally separated or di-

---

[49]Beam, Jr., and McFadden, *Employee Benefits*, p. 160.

vorced, becomes eligible for Medicare protection, or has a dependent child who reaches the maximum age for coverage.

For example, an older male worker was 18 months short of eligibility under the Medicare program. His wife was two years younger. Although he had open-heart surgery for a heart condition, insurers still considered him a high risk. Individual health insurance for both persons would cost $960 monthly. However, by remaining in the group plan of his former employer, he and his wife were covered for a monthly premium of $250. Thus, the premium savings over the 18-month period until he qualified for Medicare was $12,780.[50]

Reducing Medical Costs. To meet the problem of spiraling medical costs, employers and health insurers have introduced a wide variety of new approaches and techniques to reduce medical costs. They include the following:

- *Preadmission Testing.* A patient may be scheduled for surgery or for admission into a hospital. Various tests are given on an outpatient basis before the patient is admitted into the hospital. In most cases, one or two days of hospital room and board charges can be eliminated. Thus, the insurer's claim costs can be reduced.
- *Second Opinions.* Many surgical operations are unnecessary. Many group plans pay for a second opinion where the patient consults another physician to determine if surgery is needed. The objective is to reduce unnecessary surgery. Some plans now require second opinions for certain operations.
- *Outpatient Surgery.* Plans now pay for surgery where the patient enters a hospital as an outpatient for surgery. The patient does not remain in the hospital, but recovers at home after the surgery is performed. Thus, hospital costs are reduced.
- *Ambulatory Surgical Centers.* Many plans now pay for ambulatory surgery where the patient enters a facility other than a hospital for minor surgery, or the surgery may be performed in the physician's office.
- *Home Health Care.* An employee may be discharged early from a hospital to recover at home. A typical home health care plan covers part-time nursing in the home; physical, occupational, or speech therapy; and medical equipment used in the home. The cost of care at home is less expensive than care provided in the hospital. Thus, this benefit is valuable in reducing hospitalization costs.
- *Nursing Home Coverage.* Plans now pay for medical care in a less costly nursing home or extended-care facility if the employee is disabled from an accident or illness.
- *Claim Audits.* Hospitals frequently make mistakes in billing patients. Under a claim audit, independent auditing forms are used to verify hospital bills and to avoid duplicate charges. Substantial savings have been realized.
- *Additional Benefits for Outpatient Surgery or Treatment.* The deductible and coinsurance charges are frequently waived if the patient has outpatient surgery or treatment for less serious ailments.
- *Fee Negotiation.* Some physicians or hospitals may overcharge their patients. Many insurers have their own medical-cost staff personnel who deal directly with physicians and hospitals to ensure that their charges are fair and reasonable.
- *Hospice Coverage.* Many insurers now cover hospice care where the cost of treat-

---

[50]*Sunday World-Herald,* August 10, 1986, p. 2-M.

ing terminally ill patients is substantially lower than traditional forms of treatment.

- *Prospective Payment System.* Under a prospective payment system (PPS), the amounts that will be paid to hospitals or other providers for medical care are negotiated in advance. If actual costs are below the negotiated charge, the hospital or provider can retain the profit. If actual costs, however, rise above the predetermined fixed amount, the hospital or provider must absorb the extra cost. Thus, there is a strong financial incentive to keep costs down.

- *Wellness Programs.* Many firms have initiated wellness programs by which employees are encouraged to exercise regularly, change their diets, reduce their weight, eliminate smoking, and drink moderately. Many firms have constructed special exercise facilities for the employees and encourage the regular use of these facilities.

- *Employee Assistance Programs.* Many firms also have special treatment and counseling programs for employees who have drinking or drug problems. The fundamental purpose of a wellness program is to keep employees healthy by promoting a healthy life style. Thus, medical costs can be held down.

- *Hospital Certification.* Before a patient enters a hospital for surgery, approval by the insurer or employer is required. The intent is to reduce unnecessary surgery and hospitalization.

- *Case Management.* Case management refers to expensive or difficult medical cases that are monitored by a case manager, such as a registered nurse. The case manager works closely with the attending physician and family to determine if less costly but acceptable alternatives are available.

Although cost-containment techniques have the potential for holding down increases in the cost of medical care, many employers are disappointed since the expected reduction in cost often is not realized. For example, second opinions for surgery often are not cost effective because, in the great majority of cases, the second physician agrees with the first. Thus, the surgery is performed anyway, but the examination fee of the second physician must also be paid. In addition, some employers do not have an accurate accounting system that accurately measures the costs and benefits of a wellness program. The result is that some firms cannot determine accurately the financial payoff, if any, from a wellness program.[51] Finally, many employers find that the expected savings from preferred provider organizations (PPOs) have not been realized.[52]

Improving the Access to Medical Care

If high-quality medical care is to be made available to all Americans, some significant changes must be made in the present health care delivery system.

---

[51]Marvin S. Katzman and Kenneth J. Smith, "Not Many Firms Know What They Are Getting for Their Occupational Health Promotion Program Expenditures," *Benefits Quarterly*, Vol. 5, No. 1 (First Quarter 1989), pp. 42–50.

[52]David L. McDaniel, "Can PPOs Ever Work?" *Benefits Quarterly*, Vol. 5, No. 4 (Fourth Quarter 1989), p. 68.

Several proposals have been made to make access to medical care easier. They include the following:

- *National Health Insurance.* The Joint Economic Committee generally supports enactment of a national health insurance plan that would provide high-quality and affordable health care to all Americans.[53] The United States and South Africa are the only Western industrialized countries that do not have a universal health insurance plan for the entire population. National health insurance is a sensitive and highly controversial issue that will be discussed in Chapter 10.

- *Extension of Medicaid.* In the absence of national health insurance, some experts recommend an extension of Medicaid to cover those groups most in need of care. In particular, Medicaid eligibility requirements would be relaxed so that more poor people are covered. In 1987, 30 percent of the uninsured had family incomes below the poverty line.[54] In addition, Medicaid programs would also be extended to cover a larger number of pregnant women and children.

- *High-Risk Pools for the Uninsurable.* At least 15 states have established high-risk pools for persons who are uninsurable or substandard in health. All states would be encouraged to develop high-risk pools to make health insurance available to individuals who have been turned down for insurance by private insurers.

- *Employer-Mandated Health Insurance.* Massachusetts has enacted legislation that encourages employers, especially smaller employers, to provide health insurance to employees as a way of covering some of the uninsured. A number of other states are also considering similar proposals. In addition, Sen. Edward Kennedy has introduced legislation that would require most employers in the United States to provide health insurance benefits to the workers. The primary objective of these proposals is to make health insurance available to the large number of employed workers who have no health insurance. Most of the uninsured population under age 65 are employed workers and their families. The issue of employer-mandated health insurance is an important topic that will be discussed in greater detail in Chapter 10.

- *Long-Term Care.* Critics argue that access to long-term care is limited under the present system. Medicare provides only a maximum of 100 days of care in a skilled nursing facility, and custodial care is excluded altogether. Medicaid is not a satisfactory solution since many aged fail to qualify because of a stringent means test and complex eligibility requirements. In addition, private long-term policies are too expensive for many aged to purchase, and preexisting medical conditions often are grounds for rejection. Thus, a new approach is needed.[55]

  Robert Ball, former commissioner of the Social Security Administration, has suggested a new approach that would combine both social insurance and private insurance.[56] A new social insurance program would provide basic home care, respite care, and long-term care in a nursing facility. Care in a nursing facility would be limited to one year for beneficiaries without spouses or dependents.

[53]*Medical Alert, A Staff Report Summarizing the Hearings on "The Future of Health Care in America,"* p. vi.

[54]*Source Book of Health Insurance Data, 1989,* p. 11.

[55]For an excellent discussion of the numerous approaches to long-term care, see Alice M. Rivlin and Joshua M. Wiener, with Raymond J. Hanley and Denise A. Spence, *Caring for the Disabled Elderly, Who Will Pay?* (Washington, D.C.: The Brookings Institution, 1988). This book is reviewed by Robert J. Myers in *Benefits Quarterly,* Vol. 5, No. 3 (Third Quarter 1989), pp. 83–84.

[56]Robert M. Ball, with Thomas N. Bethell, *Because We're All in This Together* (Washington, D.C.: Families U.S.A. Foundation, 1989).

Both deductibles and copayments would be required. Private insurance would be purchased to cover the deductibles and copayments and whatever is not covered by the social insurance program. Medicaid would pay for the deductibles and copayment charges incurred by the poor. The new program would be financed by an increase in Social Security taxes and by deductibles and copayments.

SUGGESTIONS FOR ADDITIONAL READING

BALL, ROBERT M., WITH THOMAS N. BETHELL. *Because We're All in This Together.* Washington, D.C.: Families U.S.A. Foundation, 1989.

BEAM, BURTON T., JR., AND JOHN F. MCFADDEN. *Employee Benefits,* 2nd ed., Chaps. 7–13. Homewood, Ill.: Richard D. Irwin, 1988.

BUTLER, STUART M., AND EDMUND F. HAISLMAIER, EDS. *Critical Issues, A National Health System for America.* Washington, D.C.: The Heritage Foundation, 1989.

DANZON, PATRICIA M., MARK V. PAULY, AND RAYMOND S. KINGTON. "The Effects of Malpractice Litigation on Physicians' Fees and Incomes." *The American Economic Review,* Vol. 80, No. 2 (May 1990), pp. 122–127.

Driving Down Health Care Costs: Strategies and Solutions. Greenvale, N.Y.: Panel Publishers, Inc., 1990.

FRECH, H. E., III, ED. *Health Care in America, the Political Economy of Hospitals and Health Insurance.* San Francisco, Calif.: Pacific Research Institute for Public Policy, 1988.

Health Insurance Coverage of Retired Persons, Research Findings 2. National Medical Expenditures Survey, Department of Health and Human Services, Public Health Service, National Center for Health Services Research and Health Care Technology Assessment. Rockville, Md.: Public Health Service, September 1989.

A Profile of Uninsured Americans, Research Findings 1. National Medical Expenditures Survey, Department of Health and Human Services, Public Health Service, National Center for Health Services Research and Health Care Technology Assessment. Rockville, Md.: Public Health Service, September 1989.

RIVLIN, ALICE M., AND JOSHUA M. WIENER, WITH RAYMOND J. HANLEY AND DENISE A. SPENCE. *Caring for the Disabled Elderly, Who Will Pay?* Washington, D.C.: The Brookings Institution, 1988.

ROSENBLOOM, JERRY S., AND G. VICTOR HALLMAN. *Employee Benefit Planning,* 3rd ed., Englewood Cliffs, N.J.: Prentice-Hall, 1991.

SCHRAMM, CARL J., ED. *Health Care and Its Cost.* New York: W. W. Norton and Company, Inc., 1987.

SLOAN, FRANK A. "Experience Rating: Does It Make Sense for Medical Malpractice Insurance?" *The American Economic Review,* Vol. 80, No. 2 (May 1990), pp. 128–133.

STROSBERG, MARVIN A., I. ALAN FEIN, AND JAMES D. CARROLL, EDS. *Rationing of Medical Care for the Critically Ill.* Washington, D.C.: The Brookings Institution, 1989.

SUBCOMMITTEE ON EDUCATION AND HEALTH, JOINT ECONOMIC COMMITTEE. *Medical Alert: A Staff Report Summarizing the Hearings on "The Future of Health Care in America,"* October 2, 1989.

9

SOCIAL INSURANCE
AND THE PROBLEM
OF POOR HEALTH

Social insurance programs are also used to meet the problem of poor health in the United States. These programs provide some protection against the loss of income and crushing medical expenses from a serious disability or illness. The major social insurance programs that provide some protection are the following: (1) OASDI disability benefits, (2) Medicare, (3) temporary disability insurance, and (4) workers' compensation. Since workers' compensation deals specifically with occupational injuries and disease, it merits special attention and is analyzed later in Chapter 12.

OASDI DISABILITY BENEFITS

Disability often occurs suddenly, and in many cases, the disabled worker loses several years of productive earnings. Relatively few workers have sufficient financial resources on which to draw during a period of long-term disability. In recognition of the possibility of such a crushing impact, disability benefits were first added to the OASDI program (then called OASI) in 1956. The program has been broadened and liberalized several times since its inception.

Eligibility Requirements

A disabled worker generally must fulfill three major requirements to receive disability benefits. He or she must (1) be disability insured, (2) satisfy the definition of disability stated in the law, and (3) fulfill a full five-month waiting period.

Disability Insured. To acquire a disabled-insured status, a person age 31 or older must be fully insured and have at least 20 quarters of coverage out of the last 40 calendar quarters, ending with the quarter in which the disability occurs.

A person age 24 through 30 must have worked under Social Security for only half the time between age 21 and the time he or she becomes disabled. If under age 24, a person needs only 6 quarters of coverage out of the last 12 quarters, ending with the quarter when the disability began. These rules make it easier for younger persons to qualify for disability benefits.

The law also makes it easier for certain disabled workers who recover and then become disabled a second time to requalify for benefits. If a person becomes disabled *before* age 31, recovers, and then becomes disabled again at age 31 or older, he or she may not need 20 quarters of coverage to be eligible for benefits. A person needs quarters of coverage for only half the time between age 21 and the time he or she becomes disabled. However, the period in which the person was previously disabled does not count. This provision provides some relief to those disabled workers who otherwise would not qualify for disability benefits because they did not work long enough after recovering from an earlier disability to meet the 20-out-of-40 quarters insured status test.

Finally, the blind are exempt from the requirement of demonstrating a recent attachment to the labor force (i.e., the 20-out-of-the-last-40 quarters requirement). They can qualify for benefits if they are only fully insured. They are not required to meet the substantial recent work test requirement that applies to other disability applicants.

Definition of Disability. A strict definition of disability is used in the OASDI program. *The worker must have a medically determinable physical or mental condition that (1) prevents him or her from engaging in any substantial gainful work and (2) is expected to last (or has lasted) at least 12 months or is expected to result in death.* The impairment must be so severe that the worker not only is unable to perform his or her previous work but cannot, considering the worker's age, education, and work experience, engage in any substantial gainful work that exists in the national economy. It is not necessary for the work to be full time to be considered substantial; part-time work can be so considered. A job does not have to exist in the immediate area where the disabled worker resides, nor does a specific job vacancy have to be available. The worker does not have to be assured of being hired if he or she applies for the job. Jobs must exist in significant numbers, however, in the region where the worker resides or in several regions of the country.

Finally, if the worker earns $500 monthly (net of impairment-related work expenses), he or she would be considered as engaging in substantial gainful activity and therefore not disabled.

If the worker is unable to work at his or her regular job, but can engage in other work that is substantial and gainful, the disability claim will not be allowed. (However, special rules apply to blind persons, as discussed later.) The following are examples of some conditions that ordinarily are severe enough to be considered disabling:

1. Loss of use of both arms, both legs, or an arm and a leg
2. Total inability to speak
3. Progressive cancer that is not controlled or cured
4. Serious loss of kidney functions
5. Progressive diseases that result in the loss of a leg or render it useless
6. Severe arthritis that severely limits the use of the hands
7. Diseases of the heart, lungs, or blood vessels that result in serious loss of heart or lung reserve, with breathlessness, fatigue, or pain
8. Serious disease of the digestive system, resulting in weakness, anemia, and malnutrition
9. Brain damage with severe loss of judgment, intellect, or memory
10. Mental illness that results in an inability to get along with others, marked reduction of activities and interests, and deterioration in personal health

The preceding definition of disability has two major exceptions. First, special rules apply to the blind. If the vision is not better than 20/200 even with corrective lenses, or if the visual field is 20 degrees or less, the worker is considered blind.

The special provisions for blind people include the following:

1. Average monthly earnings of $780 or less in 1990 are not considered substantial gainful work. This monthly amount will increase in future years.
2. A blind person ages 55 through 64 is considered disabled if he or she cannot perform work requiring skills or abilities comparable to those required by the work the person did regularly at any time in the past. This definition of disability is more liberal than that for younger blind persons.
3. If the worker's earnings are too high to receive disability income benefits, he or she is still eligible for a disability "freeze." This means that future benefits, which are based on average earnings, will not be reduced because of relatively lower earnings in those years in which the worker is blind.

Second, a more stringent test of disability applies to disabled widows, widowers, and surviving divorced spouses. These persons can receive reduced monthly benefits as early as age 50 based on the work earnings of the deceased spouse. However, a stricter test of disability is applied to them. They are considered disabled if they cannot engage in *any gainful activity* (rather than "substantial gainful activity" that applies to disabled workers). Other factors, such as age, education, and previous work experience, cannot be considered in determining whether the person is disabled as they would ordinarily be in disabled worker cases.

Five-Month Waiting Period. The disabled worker must also meet a five-month waiting period. Benefits begin after a waiting period of five full calendar months. Therefore, the first payment is for the sixth full month of disability, payable on the third day of the seventh month.

A new waiting period is not required if the worker becomes disabled a second time within five years after the benefits terminate because of recovery or return to work. These benefits begin with the first full month in which the worker is considered disabled. In the case of disabled widows, widowers, or persons disabled before age 22, the rule is the same, except that a seven-year period is used instead of five.

Disability Benefits

Four major disability benefits are available under the OASDI program: (1) disability income benefits, (2) disability freeze, (3) Medicare benefits for the disabled, and (4) vocational rehabilitation services.

Disability Income Benefits. The monthly disability income benefit payable to an eligible disabled worker is equal to the worker's primary insurance amount at the time of disability, except in those cases where an actuarial reduction applies.

The major groups who are eligible to receive OASDI disability income payments are the following:

1. DISABLED WORKER. A disabled worker under the normal retirement age can receive a benefit equal to 100 percent of the primary insurance amount. He or she must be disability insured, meet the definition of disability, and satisfy a five-month waiting period.

2. SPOUSE OF A DISABLED WORKER. The spouse of a disabled worker at any age can receive benefits if he or she is caring for a child who is under age 16 or became disabled before age 22 and is receiving benefits based on the disabled worker's record. If there are no eligible children, the spouse must be at least age 62 to receive benefits.

3. UNMARRIED CHILDREN. Unmarried children under age 18 (or under 19 if a full-time student in an elementary or secondary school) are also eligible for benefits based on the disabled worker's earnings.

4. PERSONS DISABLED SINCE CHILDHOOD. A person who becomes disabled before age 22 can receive disability benefits if one of the parents is entitled to retirement or disability benefits or dies after being covered for a sufficient length of time under the OASDI program. The person disabled before age 22 does not need OASDI work credits to receive benefits. The payments are based on the earnings of the parent and continue for as long as the child remains disabled and unmarried and the parent's eligibility continues. In addition, there is no waiting period for a person disabled before age 22 who qualifies based on the wage record of a parent.

5. DISABLED WIDOW OR WIDOWER.   A disabled widow or widower, or a surviving divorced spouse under certain circumstances, can receive reduced benefits as early as age 50–59 (otherwise, not eligible until age 60, with reduced benefits then too). The disability must begin either before the spouse's death or within seven years thereafter. A disabled surviving divorced wife or husband may receive benefits based on the earnings of the former spouse only if the marriage lasted at least 10 years.

The monthly benefits are paid until the disabled worker reaches the normal retirement age, dies, or recovers from the disability. If the medical condition improves so that the person can perform substantial gainful work, the monthly benefits will terminate. However, the payments are continued for a three-month adjustment period that includes the month in which the disability ceased and two additional months.

Amount of Monthly Benefits.   The monthly benefits are based on the worker's average indexed monthly earnings. Depending on age, up to five years of low (or no) earnings can be dropped in computing the disabled worker's primary insurance.[1] The average monthly benefit for a disabled worker in early 1990 was $555.

There is also a maximum limit on family benefits. The maximum monthly benefit that can be paid to a disabled worker with one or more eligible dependents is limited to the *smaller* of (1) 85 percent of the worker's average indexed monthly earnings (or 100 percent of the primary insurance amount if larger) or (2) 150 percent of the primary insurance amount. This limitation does not affect the worker's benefit, but it may affect the payments to the family.

The purpose of the family limitation is to prevent some disabled workers with dependents from receiving disability income benefits that exceed their average after-tax earnings prior to the disability. Thus, profiting and malingering during a period of disability are discouraged.

Offset for Other Disability Payments.   If a disabled person is also receiving workers' compensation benefits or other disability payments from certain federal, state, or local government plans, the maximum monthly benefit to the

---

[1] The actual number of dropout years is determined by the disabled worker's age according to the following schedule:

AGE	NUMBER OF DROPOUT YEARS
Under 27	0
27 through 31	1
32 through 36	2
37 through 41	3
42 through 46	4
47 and over	5

A disabled worker under age 37 can have an additional dropout year for each year that he or she had no earnings and had a child under age 3 living in the same household. However, for such persons, the total number of all dropout years (regular and child care) is limited, in practice, to two.

worker or family is limited to 80 percent of the worker's average current earnings. In determining average current earnings, all earnings covered by the OASDI program, including those above the maximum taxable wage base, can be counted. Private insurance benefits, however, are not counted under this provision.

Trial Work Period.   Benefits are also paid during a nine-month trial work period. The purpose of the trial period is to determine if the disabled worker is capable of working. The months in the trial work period need not be consecutive. In general, only those months that the disabled person earns over $200 or works over 15 hours in self-employment are counted as trial work months.

After the trial work period, a decision is made concerning the disabled person's ability to do *substantial gainful work.* If the person is considered able to work, benefits will continue for an additional three months and then terminate. If the disabled person cannot perform substantial gainful work, the disability benefits will continue.

The worker's earnings are a major factor in determining whether the work activity is substantial and gainful. For 1990, if the worker's gross wages average more than $500 monthly ($780 if blind), he or she generally would be considered capable of doing substantial gainful work and would not be considered disabled.

Finally, certain impairment-related work expenses can be deducted from earnings for purposes of determining whether the worker is performing substantial gainful work. Items generally deductible include medical devices and equipment (such as a wheelchair), attendant care, and drugs and services required because of the impairment.

Disability Freeze.   A disability freeze is the second benefit. A disability freeze means that periods of disability of at least five months' duration can be excluded for purposes of determining insured status and average indexed monthly earnings. To qualify for the disability freeze, the worker must be disability insured and also meet the definition of disability for the monthly cash benefits.

The purposes of the disability freeze are to prevent workers from losing their insured status during a period of disability or from having future benefits reduced because of little or no earnings during the period of disability.

Medicare for the Disabled.   The third benefit is Medicare for the disabled. Medicare benefits are available to disabled persons under 65 who have been entitled to monthly disability benefits for 24 months or more (they need not be continuous or during the same period of disability). Also, insured workers and their dependents who need kidney dialysis treatment or a kidney transplant because of permanent kidney failure are eligible for Medicare. However, it is not required that these persons receive monthly disability benefits.

If the monthly cash payments are terminated because the disabled person can return to substantial gainful work, and if the person has not completely recovered from the disability, Medicare coverage generally can continue for 39 months after the trial work period.

Finally, if a disabled worker previously covered under Medicare recovers, and then becomes disabled a second time within five years after the cash benefits stop (seven years for disabled widows, widowers, and adults disabled from childhood), the Medicare coverage is resumed when the monthly benefits start again. A new 24-month waiting period is not required. If the worker earlier did not complete the 24-month waiting period for Medicare, any months in which he or she received monthly disability benefits during the first period of disability can be counted toward meeting this requirement in the second period of disability.

Vocational Rehabilitation Services. Vocational rehabilitation services are the fourth disability benefit. Disabled persons are considered for possible rehabilitation by the state vocational rehabilitation agency even if the claim is not approved. Vocational rehabilitation services include counseling and guidance, medical or surgical help, and job training and placement.

If the claim is approved, acceptance of vocational rehabilitation services will not prevent the disabled person from receiving monthly cash benefits. However, if a disabled person who is entitled to benefits refuses counseling, training, or other services without good cause, he or she will lose the monthly benefits.

Financing

The OASDI disability income program is financed primarily by a payroll tax, which is paid by employees, employers, and the self-employed. The contribution rate for 1990 is 0.60 percent of covered earnings up to the maximum Social Security wage base for both employers and employees; the self-employed pay 1.2 percent on the same wage base.

Administration

The Social Security Administration is responsible for the payment of disability income benefits. However, the actual determination of disability is made by the Disability Determination Services (DDS) office in the state. A physician and a disability evaluation specialist will evaluate all relevant facts in a particular case. The disabled person must provide medical evidence from physicians, hospitals, and other sources concerning the severity of the condition and the extent to which it prevents working. The DDS specialists may also request medical information from physicians, hospitals, clinics, or institutions where the person has been treated. The applicant for disability benefits may also be required to take a special examination or test.

If the claim is approved, the disabled person will receive a written notice from the Social Security Administration that shows the amount of monthly benefits and the date the payments start. Each claim generally is reviewed every three years to verify that the person is unable to work because of the disability. New medical evidence may be required, or a person may be asked to undergo a special examination or test.

If the claim is denied, the notice must indicate the reason for denial. The worker has the right to appeal the decision. The appeal process will be discussed in greater detail later in the chapter.

Problems and Issues

OASDI disability income benefits were paid to 2.9 million disabled workers and 1.2 million spouses and children of such workers in November 1989.[2] Although the benefits provide considerable economic security to disabled workers and their families, certain problems must be resolved.

Large Number of Initial Claims Denied. A fundamental objective of social insurance programs is to provide a base of protection against certain risks that can result in great economic insecurity, including the risk of long-term disability. This objective is not being met at the present time since a large number of initial disability claims are denied. *Of the 1.5 million initial application decisions by state agencies in fiscal 1988, 64 percent of the disability claims were denied.*[3] Many claims are denied because the applicants do not meet the strict definition of disability in the OASDI program and are considered capable of working in substantial gainful activity. Other claims are denied because the applicants are not disability insured, do not meet the recent work test requirement, or fail to meet other eligibility requirements. In short, the majority of applicants may be sick enough that they want to file a claim but not sick enough to qualify initially for benefits. Since most disabled workers do not have adequate individual or group disability income protection for a long-term disability, they must rely primarily on the OASDI program for income. However, many of them will experience considerable economic insecurity because of the denial of OASDI benefits.

Strict Definition of Disability. The definition of disability is another issue that merits some discussion. As we noted earlier, the definition of disability in the OASDI program is strict. Partial disability is not recognized, and the fact that applicants cannot work at their former jobs is not sufficient. If they are capable of working at other jobs available anywhere in the nation, and not just in their own labor market areas, they are not considered disabled.

The definition of disability also imposes a severe hardship on older disabled workers. Disabled younger workers have a greater potential for suc-

---

[2]*Social Security Bulletin*, Vol. 53, no. 2 (February 1990), p. 27.

[3]U.S. Government, House, Committee on Ways and Means, *Background Material and Data on Programs within the Jurisdiction of the Committee on Ways and Means* (Washington, D.C.: U.S. Government Printing Office, 1989), Table 4, p. 51.

cessful retraining and adjustment to a different line of work. However, this is not true for many older workers who often withdraw from the labor force because of poor health. They may be considered incapable of working at their regular jobs, but not at some other job, since they are not totally disabled. As a practical matter, however, they are often unable to find another job but do not qualify for OASDI disability benefits because they are considered capable of working in some substantial gainful activity.

Several proposals have been made that would liberalize the definition of disability for disabled workers age 55 and over. Disability would be defined in terms of the worker's occupation or occupational skills, which would be more liberal than the general disability definition. For example, older workers would be considered disabled if they cannot engage in any substantial gainful activity that requires skills or abilities similar to those required in jobs in which they have previously worked with some regularity over a substantial period of time.

Waiting Period. The length of the waiting period is another issue. Two waiting periods have relevance to the disability income program. They are (1) regular five-month waiting period for disability income benefits, and (2) two-year waiting period to qualify for Medicare benefits.

1. FIVE-MONTH WAITING PERIOD. As stated earlier, a disabled worker must satisfy a full five-month waiting period to qualify for benefits. Thus, a person disabled on December 15 is not eligible for benefits until June, and the first check is not paid until July.

An earlier Advisory Council on Social Security has recommended that the waiting period should be shortened to three months. Several reasons underlie this recommendation.[4] Disabled persons and their families generally face financial hardship as soon as their earnings terminate; medical expenses are greatest during the initial months of disability, and savings may be rapidly depleted; and reducing the waiting period may encourage rehabilitation to begin sooner, since disabled persons come in contact sooner with the state rehabilitation agency.

However, because of the increased cost of the recommendation, availability of short-term disability benefits from employers (over two-thirds of the labor force has short-term sick pay coverage), and difficulty in predicting the duration of disability soon after it occurs, Congress to date has not changed the present waiting period.

2. TWO-YEAR WAITING PERIOD FOR MEDICARE. We noted earlier that disabled workers who are entitled to OASDI disability benefits for at least two years also are eligible for Medicare benefits. The two-year period is designed to hold down costs, avoid overlap and duplication with private health insurance, and

---

[4]Advisory Council on Social Security, *Report of the 1979 Advisory Council on Social Security,* Committee on Ways and Means, U.S. House of Representatives (Washington, D.C.: U.S. Government Printing Office, 1980), Chap. 6.

provide assurance that some insurance protection will be available to persons with severe and long-lasting disabilities. However, there is some evidence that the two-year waiting period may be too long, and a shorter waiting period is needed. Health care utilization by disabled OASDI beneficiaries is higher during the first two years of entitlement than in subsequent years. Also, death rates are higher during the waiting period, and some of the sickest disabled beneficiaries die during the waiting period.[5] For example, with respect to cancer, more than half of the disabled persons who are entitled to disability income benefits because of cancer die before becoming eligible for Medicare.[6] Many victims of AIDS also die within two years. Thus, although the two-year period holds down costs, it also results in the denial of Medicare benefits to truly sick persons at a time when their medical needs are greatest.[7]

Recency-of-Work Requirement. The recency-of-work requirement is another issue that merits some consideration. A disabled person must meet a recent work requirement, which is designed to limit benefits only to workers who have a recent attachment to the labor force. A person may satisfy the definition of disability but have the claim disallowed because of failure to meet this test. A worker age 31 or older must be fully insured and have coverage for 20 out of the last 40 quarters to qualify for disability benefits. In this respect, a worker under age 24 is treated more favorably, since he or she needs only one and a half years of work in the three-year period ending when the disability begins.

The recency-of-work provision is clearly inequitable to some women and to others who work intermittently. Women who stop working to care for their children are often denied disability benefits despite the fact that they may have worked previously for a substantial number of years. Also, the recency-of-work requirement may also result in a denial of benefits to some disabled persons who formerly were regular workers, but whose working ability has been gradually reduced over a period of time because of a progressive impairment. The result is that some workers who have paid into the OASDI program for many years fail to qualify for benefits because they cannot meet the recency-of-work requirement.

Uneven Administration. Another important issue is the uneven administration of the disability income program by the states. There is considerable evidence that the determination of disability is not being done on a uniform basis throughout the country. The various state agencies have interpreted and applied the standards and regulations for determining disability in a variety of ways. The result is that some states are more liberal while others are more conservative in determining whether a person is disabled. For example, an earlier study showed that in fiscal 1980, about 67 percent of the initial disabled worker claims in the

---

[5]James Lubitz and Penelope Pine, "Health Care Use by Medicare's Disabled Enrollees," *Health Care Financing Review*, Vol. 7, No. 4 (Summer 1986), p. 29.

[6]Ibid., p. 30.

[7]Ibid.

United States were turned down. However, the rejection rate ranged from a low of about 53 percent in Rhode Island to a high of about 76 percent in Arkansas.[8]

The lack of national uniformity among the states is also evident in the appeals process. There are several stages in the appeals process when a claim is denied. The claimant can first ask the state agency to reconsider its decision; if dissatisfied, the claimant can then request a hearing before an administrative law judge (ALJ). If still dissatisfied, the ALJ decision can be appealed to an appeals council; the final stage is court action in the U.S. District Court.

There is considerable evidence that many disabled persons who are initially denied benefits are truly disabled. A large proportion of initial decisions that are appealed are reversed by administrative law judges in the appeals process. The reversal rate at the ALJ hearing level was 59 percent in fiscal 1988 (that is, judged in favor of the applicant).[9] It is argued that the high reversal rate is partly due to errors in the initial determination of disability by the various state agencies. Critics claim that medical reports favorable to a claimant are often ignored by the state agencies and that the medical evidence on which the agencies rely often is of doubtful quality. This often results in a reversal of the denied claim by an administrative law judge when the claim is appealed.

MEDICARE

The Medicare program is designed to meet the problem of medical expenses of the aged and disabled. The 1965 amendments to the Social Security Act established a basic compulsory hospital insurance plan for the aged and a related voluntary supplementary medical insurance plan. Medicare benefits first began in July 1966, with the exception of posthospital care benefits in an extended-care facility, which were first covered in January 1967. The Medicare program currently consists of two major programs: (1) Hospital Insurance and (2) Supplementary Medical Insurance.[10]

Hospital Insurance

Hospital Insurance (HI), or Part A of the Medicare program, is a basic plan that covers major inpatient hospital services and related posthospital care for most of the aged.

---

[8]U.S. Congress, House, *Status of the Disability Insurance Program,* Committee on Ways and Means, Subcommittee on Social Security, 97th Cong., 1st sess. (Washington, D.C.: U.S. Government Printing Office, 1981), Table 11, p. 81.

[9]*Background Material and Data on Programs within the Jurisdiction of the Committee on Ways and Means,* 1989, Table 4, p. 51.

[10]A complete description of the Medicare program can be found in U.S. Department of Health and Human Services, Health Care Financing Administration, *The Medicare Handbook* (Baltimore, Md.: Health Care Financing Administration, 1990). The handbook is published annually.

Coverage. Almost all people are eligible for HI benefits at age 65. Also, certain persons under age-65 can receive benefits. The major groups covered for HI include the following:

1. People age 65 or older who are eligible for monthly OASDI or Railroad Retirement benefits are eligible for HI benefits, whether retired or not.
2. Disabled beneficiaries under age 65 are also eligible for benefits if they have been entitled to OASDI disability benefits for at least 24 months. The months need not be continuous.
3. Persons are eligible at any age for HI benefits if they need maintenance dialysis or a kidney transplant for permanent kidney failure and (1) they are insured or are receiving monthly benefits under Social Security or the Railroad Retirement system or (2) they have worked long enough in federal employment. Also, the covered person's wife, husband, or child may be eligible for benefits if he or she needs maintenance dialysis or a transplant. However, only the family member who has permanent kidney failure is eligible for Medicare protection. Coverage begins with the third month after the patient first begins maintenance dialysis treatment. The three-month waiting period does not apply to persons who enter self-dialysis programs.
4. All federal employees must pay the HI portion of the Social Security tax. Federal employment counts toward eligibility for HI protection in the same way that work covered by Social Security counts. Federal employees are eligible for HI benefits at age 65, before age 65 if they are disabled and meet the requirements of OASDI beneficiaries, or at any age if they have permanent kidney failure.
5. New state and local government employees hired after March 31, 1986 are mandatorily covered for HI and must pay the HI tax. Extension of HI coverage to state and local government employees is justified on the grounds that most of them will qualify for Medicare either through a second job or through their spouse.

Persons who are not insured for HI benefits can voluntarily enroll in the HI program and pay a monthly premium. The basic HI premium is $175 monthly for 1990. Also, to be eligible for voluntary HI, the person must enroll for Supplementary Medical Insurance and pay the monthly premium.

HI Benefits. HI provides several basic benefits; they include (1) inpatient hospital care, (2) skilled nursing facility care, (3) home health care, and (4) hospice care.

1. INPATIENT HOSPITAL CARE. Inpatient hospital care is provided for up to 90 days for each benefit period. A *benefit period* begins when the person first enters the hospital and ends when he or she has been out of both a hospital and a skilled nursing facility for 60 consecutive days. For benefit periods beginning in 1990, the patient must pay an initial deductible of $592 for the first 60 days plus a coinsurance payment of $148 daily from the sixty-first through the ninetieth day. The inpatient deductible and coinsurance charges are automatically adjusted each year to reflect changes in hospital costs.

If the patient is still hospitalized after 90 days, a *lifetime reserve* of 60 additional days can be used. In 1990, a daily coinsurance charge of $296 must be paid for each day of lifetime reserve used. Lifetime reserve days cannot be renewed. Once a patient uses a reserve day, he or she can never get it back.

In addition, care in participating psychiatric hospital is limited to a maximum of 190 days during the patient's lifetime. Once the patient has received 190 days of care in a psychiatric hospital, Medicare will not pay for any additional days of care.

Covered hospital services include a semiprivate room, meals, regular nursing services, operating and recovery room costs, hospital costs for anesthesia services, intensive care and coronary care, lab tests, X-rays, medical supplies and appliances, inpatient drugs, rehabilitation services, and preparatory services relating to kidney transplant surgery.

Payments for inpatient hospital services are determined in advance under a *prospective payment system*. Under this system, hospital care is classified into diagnosis-related groups (DRGs), and a single payment amount is paid for each type of care depending on the diagnosis group in which the case is placed. Thus, a flat uniform amount is paid to each hospital for the same type of care or treatment. (However, the amount paid varies by urban and rural facilities.)

The purpose of the DRG system is to create financial incentives to encourage hospitals to operate more efficiently. Hospitals are allowed to keep payment amounts that exceed their costs, but they are required to absorb any costs in excess of the DRG flat amounts.

2. SKILLED NURSING FACILITY CARE. Inpatient care in a skilled nursing facility is also covered. A skilled nursing facility is a special facility that has the staff and equipment to provide skilled nursing care or rehabilitation services and other related health services. Most nursing homes in the United States are not skilled nursing facilities, and many skilled nursing facilities are not certified by Medicare.

The patient must be hospitalized for at least three days to be eligible for coverage in a skilled nursing facility, and confinement must be for medical reasons. Custodial care is not covered. A maximum of 100 days of coverage is provided. The first 20 days are paid in full. For the next 80 days, the patient must pay a daily coinsurance charge ($74 in 1990). No benefits are available after 100 days of care in a benefit period.

Covered services in a skilled nursing facility include a semiprivate room, meals, regular nursing services, rehabilitation services, drugs, medical supplies, and appliances. As stated earlier, custodial care is not covered; the patient must require skilled care and not merely assistance in eating, bathing, or taking the right medicine.

3. HOME HEALTH CARE. Home health care services can be provided in the patient's home by visiting nurses, physical therapists, speech therapists, and other health professionals. HI covers an unlimited number of home health visits if certain conditions are met. These conditions are as follows: (1) the care needed includes part-time skilled nursing care, physical therapy, or speech therapy; (2) the patient must be confined in the home; (3) a plan of treatment is estab-

lished by the patient's physician; and (4) the home health care agency providing the services is participating in Medicare.

4. HOSPICE CARE.   Hospice care for terminally ill beneficiaries can also be provided for up to 210 days if the hospice is certified by Medicare. The beneficiaries can elect hospice care instead of other Medicare benefits, except for the services of the attending doctor and for treatment of conditions not related to the terminal condition. Emphasis is on pain reduction, control of symptoms, and counseling, but not curative treatment. Covered hospice care includes nursing care, therapies, medical social services, homemaker-home health aide services, outpatient drugs for pain relief, and respite care.

During a hospice benefit period, HI pays the full cost of all covered services, with the exception that the patient must pay *part of the cost of outpatient drugs and inpatient respite care.*[11] The patient pays 5 percent of the cost of outpatient drugs up to a maximum of $5 for each prescription. Also, the patient pays 5 percent of the cost of respite care, not to exceed five consecutive days, but not more than the initial hospital deductible for a period of hospice care.

Supplementary Medical Insurance

Supplementary Medical Insurance (SMI), or Part B of Medicare, is a voluntary program that pays for physicians' services and a variety of other medical services and supplies that are not covered by the HI program. Most services needed by persons with permanent kidney failure are covered only by SMI.

Coverage.   Except for the disabled, most people become eligible for SMI benefits when they first attain age 65. Persons entitled to HI benefits are automatically enrolled for SMI benefits unless they voluntarily refuse the coverage. The automatic enrollment also applies to the disabled under age 65 when they qualify for HI benefits after receiving cash benefits for 24 months. Eligible people age 65 or over who are not eligible for either monthly OASDI or Railroad Retirement benefits can voluntarily enroll for SMI benefits without first being covered for HI benefits.

Some persons, however, are not automatically enrolled but must apply for SMI coverage. They include the following:

1. Persons who plan to work after age 65.
2. Persons age 65 and over who are not eligible for HI benefits.
3. Persons with permanent kidney failure.
4. Disabled widows or widowers between ages 50 and 65 who are not receiving disability checks (because, although disabled and eligible for disability benefits for at least 24 months, they are receiving some other type of benefit—such as a mother's or widow's benefit—because it is equal or larger in size).

---

[11]Respite care is a short-term inpatient stay that may be necessary in order to provide temporary relief to the person who regularly assists with home care. Inpatient respite care is limited each time to stays of no more than five days in a row.

5. Persons who live in Puerto Rico or outside the United States.

6. Persons eligible for Medicare on the basis of federal employment.

Enrollment Period. There is an *initial* enrollment period of seven months for SMI benefits. This period begins three months before the month the individual first becomes eligible for SMI coverage and ends three months after that date.

If a person declines to participate in SMI during the initial enrollment period, he or she can enroll during a general enrollment period, which is the first three months of each year. However, the protection will not start until the following July, and the monthly premium will be 10 percent higher than the basic premium for each full year of delay for those who fail to enroll at the first opportunity. These requirements are necessary to protect the program from adverse selection because of people who decide against enrolling when healthy but seek protection when their health deteriorates.

SMI Benefits. SMI provides four basic benefits: (1) doctors' services, (2) outpatient hospital services, (3) home health visits, and (4) other medical and health services.

1. DOCTORS' SERVICES. The services of doctors are covered in the doctor's office, hospital, or elsewhere. Medical supplies furnished in the doctor's office, services of the office nurse, and drugs that are administered as part of the patient's treatment are also covered. If surgery is recommended, the cost of a second opinion by another doctor is also covered.

Services of dentists generally are not covered. However, Medicare now covers the services of a dentist if the same kind of service is covered when a physician provides it. Also, if the person requires hospitalization because of dental surgery, Medicare will cover the hospital stay even though the dental procedure itself is not covered.

Certain services of podiatrists are covered (such as treatment of plantar warts). Also, if an optometrist provides examination services for aphakia (absence of the natural lens of the eye), Medicare covers the optometrist's services. Finally, limited services of chiropractors are covered. Treatment by means of manual manipulation of the spine is covered, but only to treat a subluxation demonstrated by X-ray to exist.

2. OUTPATIENT HOSPITAL SERVICES. Outpatient hospital services for diagnosis and treatment are also covered, such as care in an emergency room or outpatient clinic in a hospital. Laboratory tests, X-rays, and diagnostic hospital services as an outpatient are also covered.

3. HOME HEALTH VISITS. An unlimited number of home health visits are also provided, such as physical or speech therapy. It is not necessary for the patient to be hospitalized first to be covered for home health care visits under either Part A or Part B.

4. OTHER MEDICAL AND HEALTH SERVICES. Other medical and health care services are covered, including ambulance transportation, prosthetic devices, diagnostic testing prior to a hospital stay, medical equipment such as a wheelchair, home dialysis equipment and supplies, outpatient physical therapy and speech pathology services, outpatient psychiatric services, and X-ray and radiation treatment.

SMI pays 80 percent of the approved charges for covered medical services after the patient pays a $75 calendar-year deductible. However, there are several exceptions to the general rule. They include the following:

- *Physical and occupational therapy services* in the therapist's office or patient's home are limited to a maximum of $750 for each of these two types of services during any one year.
- *Home health services* are paid on a 100 percent basis (except for the purchase or rental of certain durable medical equipment) and are not subject to the annual deductible or copayment charges.
- *Outpatient treatment of mental illness* is covered under special rules. Medicare ordinarily pays only 50 percent of the recognized charges. However, Medicare will pay 80 percent of the recognized outpatient charges if the patient requires admission to the hospital without the treatment.
- SMI pays 100 percent of the approved charges for *pneumococcal vaccine and its administration.*
- There is no cost sharing for *outpatient clinical diagnostic tests or laboratory tests* performed by hospitals and independent laboratories that are Medicare certified and by physicians who accept assignments. All physicians furnishing such services *must* accept assignments, or else no benefits are payable.

Reimbursement of Physicians. The reimbursement of physicians under Part B of Medicare is complex. Physicians are now reimbursed based on their customary, prevailing, and reasonable charges. However, beginning in 1992, a new "resource-based relative-value scale" method will be used to determine the payments made to physicians under Part B.

1. APPROVED OR REASONABLE CHARGES. SMI payments are not based on the doctor's or supplier's actual charge but rather on "reasonable charges," which are the amounts actually approved by the Medicare carrier. Because of the method of computing approved charges and because of high rates of inflation, the charges approved are often *less* than the actual charges of doctors and suppliers. However, SMI pays only 80 percent of the approved charge, even if it is less than the actual charge.

When a Medicare claim is reimbursed on a reasonable charge basis, the carrier compares the actual charge shown on the claim with the customary and prevailing charges for that service. *The charge approved by the carrier will be the lowest of the customary charge (the charge most frequently made by the doctor or supplier for each item or service); the prevailing charge (based on all the customary charges in the locality for each type of service); or the actual charge.*

2. RESOURCE-BASED RELATIVE-VALUE SCALE. Because of the rapid increase in physician fees, Congress enacted into law in late 1989 a new method for reimbursing physicians called a "resource-based relative-value scale." The new system will gradually be phased in over a five-year period beginning January 1, 1992. Under the new system, higher fees will be paid to physicians involved in primary and preventive care (such as family practitioners and internists), and payments to specialists (such as surgeons and radiologists) will be reduced. The new system is designed to control the rapid increase in physician fees in recent years by placing limits on the amounts that Medicare will pay.

The basic features of the new reimbursement method are summarized as follows:

- Physician fees under Medicare would be based on a complex national fee schedule that determines fees based on the time and resources that physicians devote to each procedure, with a geographical adjustment factor.
- Physicians who do not accept assignments of Medicare claims are prohibited from charging patients more than 125 percent of the Medicare-approved fee in 1991, 120 percent in 1992, and 115 percent thereafter.
- Physicians are required to file all claims for Medicare patients after September 1, 1990, including claims for nonassigned services.
- A measure called "Medicare Volume Performance Standards" is used to give physicians a financial incentive to hold down the volume of unnecessary tests and procedures ordered. Under this measure, physician fees will be reduced if the cost of payments to all physicians exceeds a preset target.
- Physicians would be prohibited from referring patients to clinical laboratories in which the physician has a financial interest. Also, Medicare providers would be required to disclose ownership arrangements involving physicians.

The new method of reimbursing physicians is designed to improve Medicare and save money. The rationale underlying the new reimbursement method will be discussed in greater detail later in the chapter.

Method of Payment. The physician or supplier can be paid under the *assignment method*. Under this method, the physician agrees to accept the approved charge by the Medicare carrier as the total charge for the service. The Medicare carrier then pays the physician 80 percent of the approved charge, after subtracting any part of the $75 deductible that the patient has not met. The physician can bill the patient only for the remaining 20 percent of the approved charge and for any part of the $75 deductible not met. However, the patient can be billed for any services that Medicare does not cover.

If the physician does not accept an assignment, Medicare pays the patient 80 percent of the approved charge (after subtracting any part of the $75 deductible not met). The physician can bill the patient for the actual charge of the services provided. However, as we noted earlier, if a physician does not accept an assignment, he or she is prohibited from charging a patient more than 125 percent of the approved Medicare fee in 1991, 120 percent in 1992, and 115 percent thereafter.

Medicare Exclusions

Certain medical services and supplies, such as the following, are excluded under Medicare:

- Acupuncture
- Chiropractors' services except manipulation of the spine to correct a subluxation that can be demonstrated by X-ray
- Christian Science practitioners' services
- Custodial care, such as help with bathing, eating, and taking medicine
- Dentures and routine dental care
- Dialysis aides' services to assist in home dialysis (except under certain conditions)
- Eyeglasses and examinations to prescribe or fit eyeglasses
- First three pints of blood
- Full-time nursing care in the home
- Hearing aids and examinations to prescribe or fit hearing aids
- Homemaker services and meals delivered to the home
- Immunizations and vaccinations (other than pneumococcal vaccinations or hepatitis-B vaccine for certain beneficiaries)
- Injections that can be self-administered, such as insulin
- Lodging costs when an outpatient dialysis facility is not near the home
- Naturopaths' services
- Orthopedic shoes (except under certain conditions)
- Personal comfort items furnished at the patient's request, such as telephone, radio, or TV in the room
- Prescription drugs and medicines taken at home
- Private-duty nurses
- Private room
- Routine physical checkups and tests directly related to such examinations
- Services or supplies that are not necessary for the diagnosis or treatment of an illness or injury

Care Outside the United States

Medicare generally does not pay for medical care received outside the United States (note that Puerto Rico, the Virgin Islands, Guam, American Samoa, and the Northern Mariana Islands are part of the United States). However, there are three situations where care in a qualified Canadian or Mexican hospital is covered:

1. The individual is in the United States when an emergency occurs, and a Canadian or Mexican hospital is closer than the nearest U.S. hospital that can provide emergency medical services.
2. The individual lives in the United States, and a Canadian or Mexican hospital is closer to the person's home than the nearest U.S. hospital that can provide the needed care, regardless of whether or not an emergency exists.

3. If the person is in Canada and is traveling by the most direct route between Alaska and another state, emergency care that requires the individual to be admitted to a Canadian hospital is also covered.

Medicare Catastrophic Coverage Act of 1988

Our discussion of Medicare would not be complete without a brief discussion of the Medicare Catastrophic Coverage Act of 1988, which has since been repealed. In 1988, Congress enacted legislation that provided considerable protection against a catastrophic loss to Medicare beneficiaries. The new legislation provided unlimited hospital coverage after an initial deductible; an annual maximum cap on outlays to physicians; 150 days of coverage in a skilled nursing facility; expansion of home health care, respite, and hospice benefits; new coverage of mammography screening; and other benefits. The benefits were financed by an increase in the Part B premium ($4 monthly in 1989) and by a new supplemental premium ($22.50 surcharge for each $150 of federal income tax liability up to a maximum of $800 in 1989).

The new catastrophic act was short lived. Congress repealed the act in late 1989 because of strong and vocal opposition from the aged. The aged objected because they had to pay the entire cost of the program; the new legislation duplicated benefits they already had; and long-term care in a nursing home was not provided. As a result of these objections, the act was repealed in 1989. Thus, the aged presently have inadequate protection against a catastrophic loss under the Medicare program.

Medigap Insurance

Because of the various deductibles, coinsurance, exclusions, and limits on benefits, the Medicare program does not pay all medical expenses incurred by covered persons. Thus, many private insurers sell Medicare supplement or Medigap policies to provide additional benefits. However, Medigap policies often do not cover drugs or custodial care in nursing homes, or at best provide only limited coverage.

Medigap policies that meet certain minimum federal standards are certified with a special seal by the federal government, which indicates that the policy is federally approved.

The policy must avoid duplicate coverage and pay at least certain minimum benefits. A buyer's guide and policy outline must be furnished, and certain solicitation standards must also be met. The policy also must have a minimum loss ratio, which means that aggregate losses for all contracts must be at least equal to 60 percent of the premiums.

Although the majority of Medicare beneficiaries have Medigap policies, the policies vary widely in quality and costs. A recent General Accounting Office report on 92 commercial Medigap contracts and six Blue Cross–Blue Shield plans indicates that many commercial Medigap contracts are of low quality and do not provide significant supplementary protection to the elderly. Most of the Medigap contracts sold by commercial insurers had loss ratios below 60 percent in 1987; in contrast, the six Blue Cross–Blue Shield plans had an average loss ratio of 104 percent during the same period.[12]

In addition, some unethical insurance agents often prey on the fears of the elderly by selling them Medigap policies that duplicate Medicare coverage. It is estimated that 4 million Medicare beneficiaries may have two or more Medigap policies that duplicate Medicare coverage.[13]

Finally, many older people believe erroneously that a Medicare supplement policy will pay 100 percent of the medical costs not covered by Medicare. This is clearly not the case. For example, assume that a doctor charges an older person $1,000 for a surgical operation and that Medicare determines the approved amount to be $900. Assume that the annual Part B deductible of $75 has already been met. Medicare would pay 80 percent of the approved charge of $900, or $720. A typical Medicare supplement policy would pay 20 percent of the *approved charge* (not actual charge), or $180. The patient would still have to pay $100 out of pocket, which is the difference between the doctor's actual charge and Medicare's approved amount. However, if the doctor accepts an assignment of the claim, the extra payment can be avoided. Many insurers are now making available Medicare supplement policies that will pay most or all of the actual covered charges that are not paid by Medicare. However, these plans are expensive and often beyond the ability to pay of a Medicare beneficiary.

Medicare as a Secondary Payer

In certain situations, Medicare is the secondary payer of health care costs. This means that certain other types of insurance are considered primary, and Medicare is the secondary payer. Medicare is the secondary payer in the following situations:

1. Employers with 20 or more employees are required to offer workers age 65 or older and the spouses age 65 or older of workers of any age the same health insurance benefits that are provided to younger employees. If the older worker or spouse accepts the employer's health care plan, Medicare is the secondary payer. However, an older worker or spouse has the right to reject the employer's plan and retain Medicare as the primary payer.

2. If certain disabled beneficiaries under age 65 are covered under an employer's health plan or the health plan of an employed family member, Medicare is the secondary payer. This provision applies to group health plans of employers that employ 100 or more workers. However, under certain conditions, employees of smaller firms and their dependents may also be covered.

---

[12]United States General Accounting Office, *Medigap Insurance: Effects of the Catastrophic Coverage Act of 1988 on Benefits and Premiums* (Washington, D.C.: United States General Accounting Office, 1989).

[13]Spencer Rich, "Health Insurance Supplements Cheating Elderly, Panel Told," *The Washington Post,* April 27, 1989, p. A8.

3. Medicare is the secondary payer if the beneficiary has a work-related injury or illness that is covered by workers' compensation or by federal black lung benefits.
4. Medicare is the secondary payer for up to one year for beneficiaries who are eligible for Medicare solely on the basis of end-stage renal disease and are covered under a group health plan.
5. Medicare is also the secondary payer in those cases where automobile medical or no-fault insurance or any liability insurance is available as the primary payer.

The purpose of this provision is to hold down the costs of the program by having the Medicare program pay as excess insurance rather than provide primary coverage.

Financing of Medicare

Part A (HI) and Part B (SMI) are financed differently. The major financing provisions of each part are discussed in the following section.

Hospital Insurance. HI is financed largely by a payroll tax paid by covered employers, employees, and the self-employed, plus a relatively small amount of general revenues. In 1990, the HI payroll tax contribution rate for covered employees and employers was 1.45 percent of covered earnings up to the maximum Social Security wage base. The self-employed paid 2.90 percent on the same wage base. All contributions are deposited into a separate Hospital Insurance Trust Fund. Finally, as we stated earlier, persons who voluntarily elect HI coverage must pay a monthly premium ($175 in 1990).

Supplementary Medical Insurance. The SMI program is financed by the monthly premiums paid by covered individuals and by the general revenues of the federal government. The SMI monthly premium was $28.60 in 1990. All SMI premiums, along with the federal government's contributions, are deposited in the Supplementary Medical Insurance Trust Fund. All SMI benefits and expenses are paid out of this fund.

Administration of Medicare

The Health Care Financing Administration (HCFA), which is part of the U.S. Department of Health and Human Services, has the primary responsibility of administering the Medicare program.

Hospital Insurance. The HCFA enters into agreements with Blue Cross associations, private insurers, and state agencies to act as fiscal intermediaries in the administration of the HI program. Although a provider of care can deal directly with the federal government, in almost all cases, it usually selects its own fiscal intermediary to process claims. The fiscal intermediary receives bills from the hospital, skilled nursing facility, or home health agency and determines the amount to be paid. The providers of medical services are reimbursed on the basis of reasonable cost, and the fiscal intermediary is reimbursed for reasonable administrative costs. The intermediary receives the funds from the federal government and is also responsible for the auditing of the records of the providers of service.

To determine whether the medical service provided to Medicare beneficiaries is necessary and proper, peer review organizations (PROs) have been established. PROs consist of practicing physicians in local areas who determine whether the health care services provided are medically necessary and reasonable, are provided in the most economical setting, and meet professional quality standards.[14]

Supplementary Medical Insurance.   The HCFA also has the responsibility for administering the SMI program. Contracts are entered into with private insurance carriers—including Blue Shield plans, private health insurers, group prepaid practice plans, or state agencies—to serve as administrative agents. The carriers determine the reasonable charges and allowable payments and also disburse and account for SMI funds.

Problems and Issues

Although the Medicare program provides considerable protection, certain problems and issues have emerged that require certain changes.

Financial Burden to the Aged.   Medicare increasingly is becoming a heavy financial burden to the aged, especially for those who live in poverty or are members of low-income groups. Medicare paid only about 49 percent of the total health care expenditures incurred by the aged 65 or over in 1984.[15] This low percentage can be explained by the numerous exclusions, deductibles, cost-sharing provisions, and limits on approved charges. In addition, a large proportion of the total medical expenses incurred by the aged is due to a long-term stay in a nursing home. Medicare provides limited coverage for care in a nursing home, and custodial care is excluded altogether.

1. *Catastrophic Medical Expenses.* A large proportion of Medicare beneficiaries incur catastrophic medical expenses during the year. In 1986, 22 percent of the elderly spent 15 percent or more of their incomes on medical care, and another 21 percent spent 10 to 15 percent of their incomes for medical care. Since nearly half of the Medicare beneficiaries have annual incomes under $10,000, out-of-pocket expenses for medical care can be a financial catastrophe. Although the Medicare program spent over $70 billion on health care in 1986, the aged also

---

[14]Commerce Clearing House, *1986 Medicare Explained* (Chicago: Commerce Clearing House, 1986), p. 167.
[15]*Background Material and Data on Programs within the Jurisdiction of the Committee on Ways and Means,* 1989, Table 16, p. 230.

had out-of-pocket medical expenses of $30 billion, not including the cost of long-term care.[16]

2. *Long-Term Care Burden.* Expenditures for long-term care are an increasing burden for many older Americans. Estimated spending for nursing home care in fiscal 1985 was about $36 billion. Of this amount, about 45 percent was paid by private sources. Almost all of the private expenditures were paid directly by consumers out-of-pocket. Less than 2 percent was paid by private insurance.[17]

Medicare is not a program for funding long-term care in nursing homes. The emphasis instead is on acute care. At present, Medicare coverage in a skilled nursing facility is limited to a maximum of 100 days.

3. *Extra Charges on Unassigned Claims.* Extra charges on unassigned claims are a heavy financial burden on Medicare beneficiaries. Under current law, physicians and other Part B providers have the option of accepting or refusing assignment of a Medicare claim. If an assignment is accepted, the physician submits the claim directly to Medicare and bills the patient for the standard 20 percent coinsurance payment. No extra charges are permitted when the physician accepts an assignment. However, if the physician refuses to accept an assignment of a Medicare claim, the physician bills the patient and may charge more than the Medicare-approved fee (subject, however, to certain limits as mentioned earlier). During 1987, extra charges on Part B services exceeded $3 billion, and 700,000 elderly incurred extra charges in excess of $1,000.[18]

Soaring Medicare Costs. Another serious problem is that Medicare costs are increasing at an alarming rate. HI and SMI disbursements increased from $35 billion in fiscal 1980 to about $88 billion in fiscal 1988,[19] or a sharp increase of 151 percent. These higher expenditures can be partly explained by the increased number of aged and disabled beneficiaries who are covered by Medicare, by the overall effects of price inflation, and by the rapid increase in physician fees.

In addition, SMI costs are escalating at a rapid rate. Growth rates have been so rapid that SMI outlays have nearly doubled within the last five years. During the same time period, the SMI program grew 32 percent faster than the economy as a whole.[20] The SMI growth rate shows no sign of slowing despite efforts to control program costs.

Finally, a large and growing proportion of SMI costs is financed out of general revenues. As we noted earlier in Chapter 7, general revenue contributions in 1989 accounted for about 70 percent of total SMI income.

---

[16]*Press Release No. 2,* Committee on Ways and Means, U.S. House of Representatives, January 15, 1987.

[17]*Background Material and Data on Programs within the Jurisdiction of the Committee on Ways and Means,* 1989, Table 25, p. 244.

[18]*Press Release No. 12,* Subcommittee on Health, Committee on Ways and Means, U.S. House of Representatives, April 30, 1987.

[19]*Background Material and Data on Programs within the Jurisdiction of the Committee on Ways and Means,* 1989, Table 15, p. 152.

[20]The Board of Trustees, Federal Supplementary Medical Insurance Trust Fund, *1989 Annual Report of the Board of Trustees of the Federal Supplementary Medical Insurance Trust Fund* (Washington, D.C.: U.S. Government Printing Office, 1989), p. 8.

To control Medicare costs, Congress has introduced a wide variety of cost-containment techniques, which include setting maximum limits on the amounts paid for specific medical services, reducing hospital reimbursement rates, limiting the fees of physicians not accepting assignments, establishing a prospective payment system (PPS), enacting a new resource-based relative-value scale for paying doctors, and numerous other budget-cutting proposals. It is beyond the scope of the text to discuss these measures in detail; however, it is worthwhile to examine the financial impact of the new prospective payment system on hospitals and the new resource-based relative-value scale for paying physicians.

Impact of Prospective Payment System on Hospitals. Another important issue is to analyze the impact of the prospective payment system (PPS) on inpatient hospital care. Under this system, inpatient hospital care is classified into 477 diagnosis-related groups, and a flat amount is paid to each hospital for the same type of care. The payments, however, are adjusted for rural and city hospitals, teaching hospitals, care provided the poor, and certain other factors. The prospective payment system is designed to slow the explosive growth in Medicare costs and to eliminate the problem of the payment of substantially different amounts to hospitals for the same type of care.

The new system was gradually phased in over a four-year period from October 1, 1983, to October 1, 1987. Although experience is limited, some evidence indicates that the prospective payment system is successful in holding down hospital costs. Some preliminary conclusions based on the first three years of PPS experience are as follows:[21]

1. *Declining Hospital Stays.* Hospital stays for Medicare beneficiaries have declined. The average length of stay for all Medicare patients in short-stay hospitals decreased by 3.5 percent in fiscal 1986. Hospital stays decreased 17 percent since the implementation of PPS. However, the decline in the average length of stay under PPS appears to be leveling off.

2. *Decrease in Hospital Admissions.* Medicare short-term stays decreased for the third consecutive year in fiscal 1986. During the first three years under PPS, admissions declined by a total of 11.3 percent and admissions per Medicare enrollee by 15.9 percent.

3. *Higher Profits.* Despite falling occupancy rates, many hospitals report higher profits under the new system. On average, hospitals received Medicare payments that were considerably higher than their costs during the first two years under PPS. However, the trend in payment margins appears to have turned downward during the third year. The distribution of payment margins, however, is uneven. Urban hospitals, large hospitals, and major teaching hospitals have much higher payment margins than rural hospitals, smaller hospitals, and nonteaching hospitals.

---

[21]This section is based largely on Stuart Guterman et al., "The First 3 Years of Medicare Prospective Payment: An Overview," *Health Care Financing Review,* Vol. 9, No. 3 (Spring 1988), pp. 67–77. See also Louise B. Russell, *Medicare's New Hospital Payment System: Is It Working?* (Washington, D.C.: The Brookings Institution, 1989).

4. *Favorable Impact on Medicare Expenditures.* The new system appears to be holding down increases in patient hospital payments. The real annual rate of increase in inpatient benefit payments during the first three years of PPS was 3.5 percent, down from 7.1 percent in the five years immediately prior to the enactment of the Tax Equity and Fiscal Responsibility Act of 1982 (TEFRA).

5. *Shift Away from Inpatient Hospital Treatment.* Medical and surgical services provided under Part B of Medicare appear to be shifting away from inpatient treatment toward office visits and outpatient treatment.

Although the prospective payment system has slowed the growth in Medicare spending, two negative elements have surfaced. First, critics argue that the quality of medical care may be declining because some Medicare patients are discharged early. This would be particularly important in those cases where the hospital's actual costs are approaching the flat DRG payment. As a result, a sick patient may be discharged early. However, some researchers believe that the prospective payment system to date has not resulted in a reduction in the quality of care.[22]

Second, the prospective payment system may be partly responsible for the closing of a large number of rural hospitals. Since 1984, 159 rural hospitals in the United States have closed their doors.[23] As a result, older Medicare beneficiaries residing in rural areas must seek health care elsewhere. Critics believe that the prospective payment system is a major contributing factor to the worsening financial position of many rural hospitals. Rural hospital administrators argue that Medicare pays rural hospitals 12 to 13 percent less than city hospitals.[24] The lower payments are based on the assumption that wage costs and other input costs are lower for rural hospitals. However, hospital administrators argue that this is not the case.

In addition, rural hospitals typically have a higher proportion of older Medicare patients than city hospitals. Rural hospitals also have fewer patients, and, therefore, fewer economies of scale are possible. As a result of the combined effects of lower PPS payments and a higher proportion of older Medicare patients, many rural hospitals found that their costs exceeded revenues and were forced to shut down.

Reimbursement of Physicians. The reimbursement of physicians under the new resource-based relative-value scale method discussed earlier is another important issue that merits discussion. In this section, we shall briefly examine the rationale underlying the development of this new system.

The new method of paying doctors was enacted into law because of the rapid increase in physician fees in recent years. Medicare payments to physicians are the fastest growing component of the Medicare program. Moreover, physician expenditures under Medicare are growing much faster than the general

[22]Russell, *Medicare's New Hospital Payment System: Is It Working?* pp. 84–85.

[23]*Press Release No. H-17,* Committee on Finance, United States Senate, April 17, 1989.

[24]Ibid.

economy. *Between 1975 and 1987, physician expenditures per Medicare enrollee grew an annual compound rate of 15 percent, which was almost double the growth rate of 7.9 percent in per capita gross national product.*[25] About half of the increase in physician expenditures per Medicare enrollee was due to an increase in prices, while the other half was due to an increase in the volume of physician services.[26]

A related concern was that some Medicare payments to physicians were wasteful, and the funds were not spent effectively. As we noted earlier in Chapter 8, many surgical operations are unnecessary. For example, one study showed that 20 percent of the implantation of permanent pacemakers was not justified.[27]

In addition, some physicians believed that current Medicare payment schedules were inequitable based on the amount of time spent with a patient. In particular, office visits were reimbursed at a much lower rate than surgery. For example, a hernia repair may require one hour of time, and the surgeon may receive a fee of $750. However, a family-practice physician would receive a fee of only $25 for an office visit of 15 minutes; total fees for one hour of time spent with four patients would be only $100. Thus, there were wide disparities in fees based on the same amount of time spent with a patient.

As we noted earlier, physicians are reimbursed under Medicare based on their customary, prevailing, and reasonable (approved) charges. This method is frequently referred to as the CPR method. Experts have criticized the CPR method on the grounds that it is extremely complex; payments made to physicians are unpredictable; and the CPR method is inflationary since the payments are based on a physician's past fees, which gives physicians an incentive to raise fees.[28]

In view of the wide disparity in fees for the time spent with patients and defects in the CPR method, Congress commissioned a study by Harvard University to determine how physicians could be reimbursed based on the amount of work or resources spent on specific medical services.[29] To measure work, researchers used four variables: time, mental effort, technical skill, and stress. Data were obtained from approximately 3,200 physicians. A simulation study of Medicare outlays for 1986 based on the proposed reimbursement method showed that general practitioners and family-practice physicians would receive substantially higher fees, while surgeons would receive lower fees. The simulation study

---

[25]William C. Hsiao, Peter Braun, Daniel Dunn, and Edmund R. Becker, "Resource-Based Relative Values, An Overview," *The Journal of the American Medical Association,* Vol. 260, No. 16 (October 28, 1988), p. 2347.

[26]Ibid.

[27]Ibid.

[28]Glenn Ruffenbach, "Big Changes Proposed for Doctors' Fees," *The Wall Street Journal,* September 9, 1988, Section 2, p. 19.

[29]The reimbursement method is based on a resource-based relative-value scale (RBRVS). It is described in detail in Hsiao, Braun, Dunn, and Becker, "Resource-Based Relative Values, An Overview," pp. 2347–2353. Other articles on the same topic also appear in this issue.

showed that fees for office visits could rise by 70 percent, while some surgical fees could drop by 60 percent.[30]

In response to the continued escalation in physician fees and the Harvard study, Congress enacted a new resource-based relative-value scale system for paying doctors. We have already discussed the basic features of this new system, and further treatment is not needed here.

When fully implemented, the new reimbursement system should result in certain advantages.[31] First, if the amounts paid for certain surgical procedures, such as coronary bypass surgery, are reduced, surgeons will have less incentive to operate when other less costly procedures are available. Second, since office visits will be compensated at higher rates, physicians will be encouraged to spend more time with their patients. Finally, the wide disparity in fees among physicians based on the time spent with patients will be reduced.

TEMPORARY DISABILITY INSURANCE

Five states, Puerto Rico, and the railroad industry have compulsory temporary disability insurance laws (also called cash sickness insurance) that partly identify covered workers for the loss of wages caused by a temporary nonoccupational disability or by maternity.[32] Rhode Island enacted the first temporary disability law in 1942, California and the railroad industry in 1946, New Jersey in 1948, New York in 1949, Puerto Rico in 1968, and Hawaii in 1969.

Temporary disability laws are designed to pay short-term weekly cash benefits to covered workers who are temporarily disabled because of nonoccupational accident or disease. Benefits also can be paid to eligible unemployed workers who become sick or disabled while unemployed. In this section, we shall discuss the major features of the state programs and Puerto Rico. The railroad industry program is discussed later in Chapter 18.

Covered Workers

In these jurisdictions with temporary disability insurance laws, most commercial and industrial wage and salary employees in private industry are covered under the programs. However, certain occupations are excluded, or coverage is less than complete. The excluded groups generally are domestic employees, family workers (child, spouse, or parent of the employer), government employees, and

---

[30]William C. Hsiao, Peter Braun, Nancy L. Kelly, and Edmund R. Becker, "Results, Potential Effects, and Implementation Issues of the Resource-Based Relative-Value Scale," *The Journal of the American Medical Association*, Vol. 260, No. 16 (October 28, 1988), p. 2429.

[31]Ruffenbach, "Big Changes Proposed for Doctors' Fees," p. 19.

[32]This section is based largely on "Social Security Programs in the United States," *Social Security Bulletin*, Vol. 52, No. 7 (July 1989), pp. 37–41.

the self-employed. However, Hawaii covers government employees, and Rhode Island covers hospital employees. Agricultural workers are covered in varying degrees in California, Hawaii, New Jersey, and Puerto Rico. California also allows self-employed persons to elect coverage voluntarily.

Methods for Providing Protection

Several methods are used to provide temporary disability benefits to covered workers. They are (1) monopoly state fund, (2) competitive state fund, (3) private insurance, or (4) self-insurance.

In Rhode Island, a monopoly state fund provides benefits to all covered workers; all covered employers must pay into the fund, and all benefits are paid directly out of the fund. The employer can provide additional supplemental benefits if desired.

Benefits are also available from a state fund in California, New Jersey, and Puerto Rico. However, employers can contract out of the state fund by purchasing group insurance from a commercial insurer, by negotiating an agreement with a union or employees' association, or by self-insuring. Coverage in the state fund is automatic unless the employer or employees have a substitute private plan that meets certain statutory standards and is approved by the administrative agency.

New York and Hawaii require employers to provide their own disability plan for covered workers. Employers can purchase group insurance from a commercial insurer, enter into an agreement with the employees or a union to establish a benefit plan, or self-insure the benefits. New York also has a competitive state fund from which the benefits can be purchased. In addition, both New York and Hawaii have special funds that pay benefits to workers who become disabled while unemployed and to disabled workers whose employers fail to provide the required benefits. Finally, in those jurisdictions where private plans can be substituted for the state plan, certain statutory standards must be fulfilled.

Eligibility Requirements

Four eligibility requirements must be satisfied to receive benefits. The claimant must (1) meet certain earnings or employment requirements, (2) be disabled as defined in the law, (3) not have disqualifying income, and (4) satisfy a waiting period.

Earnings or Employment Requirements. The claimant must have a certain amount of past employment or qualifying wages to receive benefits. The purpose of this requirement is to limit benefits only to persons who have demonstrated a substantial attachment to the labor force. The amount of required earnings or employment generally is similar to the requirements for unemployment insurance benefits but may be less stringent in certain cases.

In addition, in most jurisdictions with private plans, employees are immediately covered upon employment or after a short probationary period of one to three months. If employment is terminated, after a specified period, workers generally lose their private plan coverage and must look to a state-created fund for protection.

Disability Requirements.   A disabled worker must meet the definition of disability as stated in the law. *Disability generally is defined as the inability to perform regular or customary work because of a physical or mental condition.* New Jersey and New York, however, impose stricter requirements for disability during unemployment. Four jurisdictions (Hawaii, New Jersey, New York, and Puerto Rico) exclude disabilities caused by willfully self-inflicted injuries or injuries sustained in the performance of illegal acts. Finally, all jurisdictions pay full benefits for a disability due to pregnancy.

Disqualifying Income.   The claimant also must not be receiving any disqualifying income. All jurisdictions restrict the payment of benefits if the claimant is receiving workers' compensation. New York does not pay any benefits if the injury is job-related even if workers' compensation benefits are not paid. The other jurisdictions do not pay for disabilities covered by a workers' compensation law. However, there are certain exceptions. The laws usually allow benefits to be paid in those cases where the workers' compensation benefits are for partial disability or for previously incurred work disabilities. Also, California pays the difference in benefits if the temporary disability benefit is higher than the workers' compensation benefit.

In addition, all jurisdictions provide that claimants cannot receive temporary disability benefits for a week in which unemployment compensation benefits are being paid. Finally, some jurisdictions place restrictions on the payment of disability benefits if sick-leave payments are being received.

Waiting Period.   A waiting period of seven consecutive days is required before the disability benefits are paid. In California and Puerto Rico, the waiting period is waived from the day of confinement in a hospital. In New Jersey, the weekly benefit is paid for the waiting period after disability benefits are paid for three consecutive weeks. Finally, in Rhode Island, the waiting period applies only to the first sickness in a benefit year.

Benefits.   In general, weekly cash benefits are paid to eligible disabled workers that are designed to replace at least half of the weekly wage loss for a certain period, subject to certain minimum and maximum limits. As of September 1988, the maximum weekly amount ranged from $104 in Puerto Rico to $252 in Rhode Island.[33] However, in three states, the maximum weekly benefit

---

[33]Ibid., p. 39.

is recomputed annually so that it equals a certain percentage of the state's average weekly wage in covered employment (66⅔ percent in Hawaii, 53 percent in New Jersey, and 70 percent in Rhode Island). The maximum duration of benefits payable per disability or per year is 26 to 39 weeks. In Hawaii, New York, and Puerto Rico, benefits are paid over a uniform duration to all claimants who qualify. In the other jurisdictions, the length of time that benefits are paid varies, depending on base period earnings or length of time in covered employment.

Financing. Temporary disability income benefits are financed by a payroll tax on covered wages. Covered employees are required to contribute to the program in all six jurisdictions. In addition, with the exception of Rhode Island and California, where the employees pay the entire cost, covered employers must also contribute to the program.

Administration

In four jurisdictions (California, New Jersey, Puerto Rico, and Rhode Island), temporary disability insurance programs are administered by the same agency that administers the unemployment insurance law. Under these four programs, the unemployment insurance agency collects contributions, maintains wage records, determines eligibility, and pays benefits to workers under the state-operated funds. In New York, however, the program is administered by the workers' compensation board and in Hawaii, by the Department of Labor and Industrial Relations.

Claims of disabled workers who are covered by private plans are filed with and paid by the employer, by the insurance company, or by the union health and welfare fund which operates the private plan. The state agency exercises general supervision over the private plans, establishes standards of performance, and adjudicates disputes.

Disabled persons must be under the care of a physician, and the first claim must be supported by medical certification of the disability. (In California and Hawaii, the claimant may be in the care of an authorized religious practitioner of the claimant's faith.) The physician's certification must include a diagnosis, date of treatment, an opinion as to whether the disability prevents the claimant from doing his or her customary work, and an estimate of the date when the claimant is expected to return to work. Claimants who are dissatisfied with the claim decision have the right to appeal under all state laws.

Problems and Issues

One important issue is the proper balance between private insurers and state funds. The private insurance market for temporary disability benefits has been declining relative to the state funds. In California, coverage under private plans declined from 47 percent in 1955 to 6 percent in 1982. In New Jersey, the private plans declined from 62 percent to 28 percent during the same period.[34] The major reason for the sharp decline is that private insurers cannot compete effectively with the state funds under current benefit and financing provisions.

Private insurers in California found it difficult to compete with the state fund because of unfavorable legal requirements, which included periodic statutory liberalization of benefits. Also, regulations that were adopted earlier in 1961 prevented private insurers from covering only selected low risks based on age, sex, and wage levels. These regulations, originally intended to reduce adverse selection against the state fund, have hindered the operations of private insurers in California and have made it difficult for them to compete with the state fund so they have gradually lost most of their market.

The adequacy of benefits is another important issue. Because of restrictions on coverage, exclusions of certain groups, waiting periods, and statutory limits on benefits, the programs fall short of providing substantial economic security to workers who have nonoccupational disabilities. Although more than four-fifths of the employees in private industry are covered in the six jurisdictions with temporary disability insurance plans, some groups are excluded or have less than complete protection. Domestic employees generally are excluded. Government employees generally are not eligible for temporary disability income benefits, although hospital employees are covered in Rhode Island and government employees in Hawaii. Thus, to the extent that these groups have less than complete protection, the goal of universal short-term income protection for nonoccupational disabilities is not being attained.

Finally, temporary disability insurance plans restore only a small fraction of the total wages lost during periods of nonoccupational disability. In 1983, the plans restored only about 28 percent of the total wages lost by workers in private industry who were covered by temporary disability insurance laws.[35]

SUGGESTIONS FOR ADDITIONAL READING

COMMERCE CLEARING HOUSE. *1989 Medicare Explained.* Chicago: Commerce Clearing House, 1989.

———. *1989 Social Security Explained.* Chicago: Commerce Clearing House, 1989.

GUTERMAN, STUART ET AL. "The First 3 Years of Medicare Prospective Payment: An Overview," *Health Care Financing Review,* Vol. 9, No. 3 (Spring 1988), pp. 67–77.

HSIAO, WILLIAM C., PETER BRAUN, DANIEL DUNN, AND EDMUND R. BECKER. "Resource-Based Relative Values," *The Journal of the American Medical Association,* Vol. 260, No. 16 (October 22, 1988), pp. 2347–2353.

RUFFENBACH, GLENN. "Big Changes Proposed for Doctors' Fees," *The Wall Street Journal,* September 9, 1988, p. 19.

RUSSELL, LOUISE B. *Medicare's New Hospital Payment System, Is It Working?* Washington, D.C.: The Brookings Institution, 1989.

SOCIAL SECURITY DIVISION, MERCER-MEIDINGER-HANSEN, INC. *1990 Guide to Social Security and Medicare.* Louisville, Ky.: William M. Mercer-Meidinger-Hansen, Inc., December 1989.

---

[34]Robert J. Myers, *Social Security,* 3rd ed. (Homewood, Ill.: Richard D. Irwin, 1985), p. 918.

[35]Daniel N. Price, "Cash Benefits for Short-Term Sickness: Thirty-five Years of Data, 1948–83," *Social Security Bulletin,* Vol. 49, No. 5 (May 1986), Table 4, p. 11.

U.S. Congress, House, Committee on Ways and Means. *Background Material and Data on Programs within the Jurisdiction of the Committee on Ways and Means.* Washington, D.C.: U.S. Government Printing Office, 1989. This volume is published annually and contains current information on the DI and Medicare programs.

U.S. Department of Health and Human Services, Social Security Administration, Health Care Financing Administration. *Your Medicare Handbook.* Washington, D.C.: U.S. Government Printing Office, 1990.

NATIONAL HEALTH INSURANCE

With the exception of South Africa, the United States is the only industrialized country in the Western world that does not have some form of national health insurance covering its citizens. Such a plan has been proposed to solve the health care problems in the United States.

National health insurance is a delicate and sensitive issue, involving consumers, the medical profession, state and federal government, labor unions, and private health insurers. There has been considerable discussion and analysis of the various proposals, which has provided considerable insight concerning the desirability of national health insurance in the United States. In this chapter, we shall consider the following topics: (1) arguments for national health insurance, (2) criteria for an effective plan, and (3) national health insurance proposals.

ARGUMENTS FOR NATIONAL HEALTH INSURANCE

Several important arguments are advanced for the enactment of some type of national health insurance plan in the United States. They include the following: (1) basic right of all citizens to medical care, (2) large number of uninsured persons, (3) reformation of the health care delivery system, and (4) inferior medical care received by the poor.

Basic Right to Medical Care

Proponents of national health insurance argue that all citizens should have a basic right to medical care and that a national plan would ensure equitable treatment by providing access to high-quality care to all.

The right of every citizen to a basic education is often cited as a parallel to support a plan for national health insurance. Regardless of ability to pay, each citizen is entitled to a public elementary and high school education. In contrast, it is argued that medical care generally is available only to those who can afford it, and since many citizens cannot, they may not receive the medical care they require. Thus, according to the argument, medical care should be considered a social good, available to all citizens, and a national health insurance plan would ensure that availability.

The public education analogy is a slippery concept that must be carefully analyzed. The right to medical care and the right to public education involve subtle differences. First, public education involves compulsory school attendance until a stated age and the observance of state laws regarding education. In contrast, with few exceptions, a citizen cannot be forced by law to undergo medical treatment even if it is necessary to correct a serious health condition.[1]

Second, the government does not pay for other necessary goods and services for people who can afford them. For example, the government provides money for food, shelter, and clothing to the poor under public assistance programs; but although these goods are absolutely essential, the government would be abusing its power if it made food, clothing, and shelter available to all citizens, regardless of their ability to pay. Consequently, it is argued that since most Americans can afford medical care, as evidenced by the widespread ownership of private health insurance, a federal subsidy to all citizens for medical care, regardless of their ability to pay, is unnecessary and unsound.

Despite these philosophical hang-ups, however, it is generally agreed that all citizens should have access to medical care and that the lack of ability to pay for it should not be a barrier.

Large Number of Uninsured Persons

Another argument for national health insurance is the large number of persons in the United States who are presently uninsured for health care. A National Medical Expenditures Survey revealed that 37 million people were uninsured in early 1987, or about 15.5 percent of the population, up from 12.3 percent in 1977.[2] In addition, another 70 million were underinsured.[3]

---

[1] Robert D. Eilers and Sue S. Moyerman, eds., *National Health Insurance: Proceedings of the Conference on National Health Insurance* (New York: Tax Foundation, 1971), p. 263.

[2] *A Profile of Uninsured Americans, Research Findings 1*, National Medical Expenditures Survey, Department of Health and Human Services, Public Health Service, National Center for Health Services Research and Health Care Technology Assessment (DHS Publication No. [PHS] 89–3443), September 1989, p. 4.

[3] *Medical Alert, A Staff Report Summarizing the Hearings on "The Future of Health Care in America,"*

The uninsured groups generally are workers who are employed by smaller firms that are not unionized, that hire seasonal workers, or employ relatively large numbers of low-wage employees; individuals who are not in the labor force and cannot afford to pay the higher premiums for individual coverage; persons who are substandard in health and cannot obtain private protection; and low-income persons who are not covered by Medicaid. Also, some self-employed individuals are uninsured because of difficulty in paying health insurance premiums. Thus, it is argued that national health insurance is needed to cover the large number of persons who have no protection.

Reformation of the Health Care Delivery System

We noted earlier in Chapter 8 that the present health care delivery system is marred by numerous defects, including rapid inflation in medical costs, inadequate access to medical care, considerable waste and inefficiency, ineffective financing, and large numbers of people without health insurance. Thus, it is argued that a new system of national health insurance under government sponsorship is necessary to correct these defects, especially the reduction of waste and inefficiency. Critics argue that the present system must be reformed by a new system of national health insurance. Some proposals would simply build on the present system; others would radically modify the present system. We will examine several national health insurance proposals later in the chapter.

Inferior Medical Care Received by the Poor

It is also argued that national health insurance is needed because the poor receive inferior medical care. Low-income groups are in relatively poorer health than is the general population; many poor persons have inadequate access to high-quality medical care because of their inability to pay; and many physicians are unwilling to practice in poverty areas or treat welfare patients. Finally, it is argued further that any new system should not be limited only to the poor, since they may be stigmatized by the use of such services; instead a new national health insurance system should be created to cover all citizens.

CRITERIA FOR EFFECTIVE NATIONAL HEALTH INSURANCE

An effective national health insurance program should ideally aim at correcting each of the defects in the present health care delivery system. Competent researchers who have studied national health insurance generally agree that the following requirements should be fulfilled: (1) universal coverage, (2) compre-

Prepared for the Subcommittee on Education and Health, Joint Economic Committee, October 2, 1989, p. ii.

hensive benefits, (3) effective financing, (4) effective cost controls, (5) consumer and provider acceptance, and (6) efficient administration.[4]

Universal Coverage

Universal coverage of the population is necessary for an effective national health insurance plan. No one who desires coverage should be excluded. The goal of economic security for the nation is more easily achieved when the entire population is protected against the risk of financial ruin from poor health and the inability to pay for medical care.

In addition, the goal of universal protection should not be defeated by stringent eligibility requirements that limit entry into the plan. In other words, no one should be excluded because of age, sex, geographical location, social class, income, race, religion, or political beliefs. And preexisting conditions should not be used to limit entry into the plan.

Comprehensive Benefits

An effective national health insurance plan should provide comprehensive health benefits to consumers. It should offer inpatient hospital care, physical services, prenatal care, extended facility and nursing home care, rehabilitation services, prescription drugs, and prosthetic devices.

In addition, the plan should stress preventive care and health maintenance programs, such as health education and the formation of good health habits with respect to smoking, drugs, obesity, and accident prevention. It should provide for the early detection, screening, and treatment of certain diseases that are best treated when diagnosed in their early stages—for instance, glaucoma, hypertension, and breast and cervical cancer.

Effective Financing

A sound national health insurance plan should establish an effective financing system for health care. The financing of costs should be done in a way that is fair to all, with the cost burden distributed equitably among the various segments of the population.

Methods of Financing. Various combinations of premiums, payroll

---

[4]A discussion of the various issues can be found in Stuart M. Butler and Edmund F. Haislmaier, eds., *Critical Issues, A National Health System for Americans* (Washington, D.C.: The Heritage Foundation, 1989); Martin S. Feldstein, "A New Approach to National Health Insurance," Institute for Contemporary Studies, *New Directions in Public Health Care: An Evaluation of Proposals for National Health Insurance* (San Francisco: Institute for Contemporary Studies, 1976), Chap. 9; Herman M. Somers and Anne R. Somers, "Major Issues in National Health Insurance," *Milbank Memorial Fund Quarterly*, Vol. 1, No. 2, Part 1 (April 1972), pp. 177–209; and Eilers and Moyerman, eds., *National Health Insurance: Proceedings of the Conference on National Health Insurance.*

taxes, general revenues, and tax credits can be used to finance the costs of national health insurance, and deductibles and coinsurance can be used as cost-sharing devices.[5]

1. PREMIUMS. The participants in the plan could be charged a specific premium, as in private health insurance, thus offering the advantage of an identifiable cost to the consumer. The disadvantage of this approach is that a uniform premium for all participants would be burdensome to the poor. This could be overcome by grading the premium downward according to income, but such a method would introduce a form of needs test into the program. It would also identify the poor and possibly result in two separate insurance programs, with a splintering of the insured population as a result.

2. PAYROLL TAXES. A specific payroll tax to finance national health insurance would have the advantage of ease of collection, restraint on costs, and an increasing source of revenue as the economy grows. However, relying exclusively on a payroll tax has certain disadvantages. Both employers and employees might protest the significant increase in payroll taxes necessary to fund a national health insurance plan.

In addition, an increase in payroll taxes would fall heavily on the working poor; the tax has the additional disadvantage of being a flat percentage of earnings up to some maximum amount that makes no allowance for family size; and in the long run, the employees would pay not only their portion of the total payroll tax, but that of employers as well, in the form of higher prices, lower wages, or both.

3. GENERAL REVENUES. To finance all or part of the cost of national health insurance, the federal government could make a contribution out of its general revenues for that purpose. Since the bulk of federal general revenue funds is derived from the personal and corporate income tax, and these taxes are more progressive than a flat payroll tax, the result would be to shift more of the cost burden of a national health insurance plan to the middle- and upper-income groups.

One major obstacle, however, to the use of general revenues is that the federal government itself currently has no general revenues to spare. Thus, taxes would have to be increased to obtain the necessary funds. A tax increase, however, would be politically difficult to enact in view of sizable federal deficits and the present emphasis on achieving a balanced budget.

4. TAX CREDITS. If tax credits are used to finance a national health insurance plan, taxpayers would be allowed to deduct the premiums paid to the plan from their income tax liability. In effect, the taxes that would have been paid to the federal government would be used to finance the plan.

---

[5]For a discussion of these approaches, see Charles L. Schultze, Edward R. Fried, Alice M. Rivlin, and Nancy H. Teeters, *Setting National Priorities: The 1972 Budget* (Washington, D.C.: The Brookings Institution, 1971). See also Robert D. Eilers, *Financing Health Care: Past and Prospects* (Minneapolis: Federal Reserve Bank of Minneapolis, 1974).

5. DEDUCTIBLES AND COINSURANCE.   Two major advantages are claimed for the use of deductibles and coinsurance as cost-sharing provisions in a national health insurance plan: (1) they hold down costs, and (2) they reduce overutilization of benefits.

Research studies indicate that utilization of plan benefits declines when a substantial coinsurance requirement is introduced into the plan. One study of a national health insurance experiment by the Rand Corporation revealed that families who paid part of their medical expenses purchased up to 25 percent less medical care for their children than families whose medical expenses were entirely reimbursed. In the experiment, families were assigned to a free-care plan with no copayment requirement and to other plans with copayment requirements ranging from 25 percent to 95 percent. In the cost-sharing plans, reductions in utilization occurred across the board in such measures as total expenditures, number of doctor visits, and episodes of treatment (defined as one or more medical services related to a specific medical condition such as an ear infection with the follow-up visit). The study also revealed that the increased use of medical services under the free plan did not provide additional health benefits to the children and that children covered under the cost-sharing plans did not appear to suffer any adverse effects because of fewer visits to the doctor.[6]

In addition, a deductible must also be considered in the financing of national health insurance. Deductibles are extremely important, since they reduce the demand for health care and the cost of the plan. One study on the effect of deductibles on the demand for medical care indicated that demand is quite sensitive to variations in the deductible in the region of $50 and becomes steadily less sensitive as the deductible rises above $75. The demand for health care with a $200 deductible is estimated to be about 85 percent of demand in a plan with a $50 deductible; increasing the deductible to $500 reduces demand to only 72 percent; and increasing the deductible to $1,000 reduces demand an additional seven percentage points to 65 percent of the $50 level.[7]

Finally, the size of the deductible is extremely important in the overall cost of a national health insurance plan. As the deductible increases, total cost declines, since demand is reduced, and the insurance no longer covers some bills. One study showed that if a tax-financed national health insurance plan with a $50 deductible and 20 percent coinsurance costs $100 billion, the cost would decline to about $65 billion with a $200 deductible, and to around $20 billion with a $1,000 deductible.[8] Thus, a large deductible would have a powerful effect in reducing the total cost of national health insurance, which has resulted in keen

[6]"Rand Studies Insurance Impact on Health Care," *National Underwriter,* Life & Health Insurance ed., June 1, 1985, p. 40. See also Anne A. Scitovsky and Nelda M. Snyder, "Effect of Coinsurance on Use of Physician Services," *Social Security Bulletin,* Vol. 35, No. 6 (June 1972); and Blue Cross Association, *The Effects of Deductibles, Coinsurance, and Copayment on Utilization of Health Care Services—Opinions and Impressions from Blue Cross and Blue Shield Plans* (September 28, 1971).

[7]Jack P. Newhouse et al., "The Effect of Deductibles on the Demand for Medical Care Services," *Journal of the American Statistical Association,* Vol. 75, No. 371 (September 1980), p. 527.

[8]Ibid., p. 528.

interest in a catastrophic plan with a large deductible as the correct approach to national health insurance. Catastrophic health insurance is discussed later in the chapter.

Based on the preceding discussion, coinsurance and deductibles are suitable for middle- and upper-income families, but they can impose a substantial financial burden on low-income families. This can be avoided by eliminating coinsurance entirely from the national health insurance plan or by reducing downward the coinsurance percentage for low-income families. Another approach is a *stop-loss limit* by which 100 percent of all covered expenses are paid in full once out-of-pocket expenses exceed a certain amount, such as $500 or $1,000 annually for each individual. The stop-loss limit could also be graded by family income, with a smaller limit (or no limit) for low-income families. Finally, to avoid financial hardship to low-income families, the size of the deductible could also be graded by family income, with a smaller deductible (or no deductible) for low-income families.

Financing Criteria. A system for financing a national health insurance plan should also be judged by the following objectives:

1. ELIMINATION OF FINANCIAL BARRIERS. No one should be denied needed health care because of an inability to pay, and the financing system should not discourage or delay preventive care and treatment.

2. AVOIDANCE OF FINANCIAL HARDSHIP. No family or individual should be forced to bear an unusual financial hardship because of catastrophic medical expenses from an unpredictable illness or accident. The financing of the plan should clearly provide for the funding of large medical expenses to avoid financial hardship.

3. AVOIDANCE OF INITIAL SUBSTANTIAL TAX INCREASE. The financing plan should avoid an initial substantial tax increase to fund the program. A sharp tax increase may distort the supply of work effort and cause economic resources to be used inefficiently. Thus, a national health insurance plan that takes large amounts away from the public in the form of higher taxes and returns them in the form of health insurance benefits has a large hidden cost in the form of lower national income. In addition, a substantial tax increase is undesirable because it could cause taxpayers to revolt and reject the plan.

Effective Cost Controls

A sound national health insurance plan should also provide effective cost controls to encourage the efficient use of resources and discourage price inflation in medical care. The plan should encourage the use of low-cost facilities rather than expensive inpatient hospital care. It should provide effective cost controls for hospitals to moderate the forces that increase their costs, such as unnecessary duplication of equipment, unnecessarily high salaries, and increased personnel.

Physician cost controls should also be used to prevent higher fees and the over-charging of patients because of insurance. Finally, the financing method should encourage and foster cost-consciousness among physicians, hospital administrators, and patients.

Whether the federal government can develop effective cost controls that meet the preceding requirements is highly debatable. The experience of many government programs is not too encouraging in this regard. In particular, under both the Medicare and Medicaid programs, costs have soared, despite cost-containment efforts by the federal government. Without effective cost controls, however, the national health insurance plan is doomed to failure.

Acceptance by Consumers and Providers

An effective national health insurance plan must also be acceptable to both consumers and providers of health care. If consumers dislike the plan, there may be political opposition and lack of plan acceptance; and lack of cooperation or hostility by physicians and hospitals could severely cripple the success of the plan.

The following factors are generally considered important in gaining consumer acceptance: (1) consumers must participate in policy-making decisions and plan design; (2) all consumers must be eligible for coverage; (3) comprehensive health services must be available; (4) consumers must have access to medical services no matter where they are located; (5) the costs of the plan must be acceptable and not present substantial financial barriers to needed medical care; (6) quality controls concerning the medical care provided must be strictly enforced; and (7) the plan must provide for continued research into, and development of, new health care delivery models.[9]

For the plan to be politically acceptable to physicians and other suppliers of health care, certain other criteria are important: (1) federal control over the private practice of medicine must be kept to a minimum; (2) a pluralistic system is necessary, using both private health insurance and government agencies, rather than a single government monopoly for providing health care; (3) a variety of payment methods—fee for service, capitation, salary, and others—should be established; (4) consumer options and freedom in selection of physicians must be built into the plan; and (5) reorganization of health care and the introduction of new delivery models must be phased in gradually, without severely disrupting the present system.

It is obvious that these criteria will not be completely fulfilled, since some conflict with others. For example, effective cost controls may be acceptable to consumers but unacceptable to physicians if they feel that federal controls are seriously interfering with the private practice of medicine. In the last analysis,

---

[9]David A. Kindig and Victor W. Sidel, "Impact of National Health Insurance Plans on the Consumer," in Eilers and Moyerman, *National Health Insurance*, pp. 19–38.

any national health insurance plan will reflect political compromises and trade-offs among consumers, physicians, and government.

Efficient Administration

Efficient administration is a major policy question that must also be recognized when national health insurance proposals are being analyzed. Administrative procedures should not be unduly complex, costly, or inconvenient. Considerable attention is often devoted to the design of a new income maintenance plan or economic security program and the policy implications associated with it; but in far too many instances, inadequate attention is given to the administration of the plan. The result is that the plan objectives are not fulfilled. The administrative procedures can be bureaucratic, slow, and cumbersome, and the program then becomes inordinately expensive to administer. The administrative framework must also provide for flexibility and adaptability to changing circumstances because of rapidly changing health care technology.

Reorganization of Health Care. Any financing plan for national health insurance must also consider and encourage the reorganization of health care and the development of new health care delivery models. It must permit experimentation with health maintenance organizations, rural health care delivery models, and others. It would be disastrous to pour billions of new dollars into the present system, marred as it is by fragmentation, waste, inefficiency, ineffective cost controls, and other defects. Any new health insurance plan must permit the development of new models that are superior to the present system of health care.

Advance Preparation. Finally, the financing of national health insurance must allow for advance preparation—a gradual phase in of the new plan, and a setting up of administration well in advance of the plan's effective date. It is particularly important to avoid repeating the same mistakes associated with the introduction of Medicare and Medicaid. The supply of new medical resources was not substantially increased before the implementation of those programs. The result was a massive infusion of billions of new funds into an already-burdened health care delivery system, which further aggravated the inflation in medical costs that was occurring at that time. This mistake must not be repeated if a new national health insurance plan becomes operational.

NATIONAL HEALTH INSURANCE PROPOSALS

Numerous national health insurance proposals have been introduced into Congress over time. Other proposals have been introduced recently that would provide private health insurance to large numbers of uninsured persons. Although these latter proposals, strictly speaking, are not forms of national health insurance, they deal with an important issue and thus merit some discussion. For sake of convenience and ease of understanding, the various proposals can be grouped into the following categories: (1) centralized federal plan, (2) catastrophic health insurance, (3) proposals to stimulate competition, (4) U.S. Health Act of 1986, and (5) other recent proposals.[10]

Centralized Federal Plan

Under this approach to national health insurance, the major operations and financing of the health care delivery system would be centralized in the federal government. The Health Care for All Americans Act, sponsored by Sen. Edward Kennedy and Rep. Henry Waxman in 1979, is an example of a centralized federal program. The major features of their proposal are summarized as follows:

1. BASIC APPROACH.   Each resident in the United States would be covered under a universal national health insurance plan, with federal financing of coverage for the poor and near poor. Employers would be required to offer their employees a choice of approved health insurance plans, including an HMO plan. Private health insurers would be required to meet federal standards to participate in the plan.

The aged and eligible disabled persons would continue to be covered under the Medicare program. The poor and near poor would also be covered by the national health insurance plan for all mandated benefits; premiums for this group would be subsidized by the federal and state governments. All other persons, including the self-employed, could be covered by enrolling with private insurers.

2. BENEFITS.   Comprehensive benefits would be provided with full coverage of inpatient hospital services, physicians' services, home health services, X-rays, and lab tests. A catastrophic illness would also be covered, since there would be no arbitrary nonmedical limits on the number of hospital days or physicians' visits. The Medicare program would be upgraded and would also cover prescription drugs.

3. FINANCING.   The program would be financed primarily by wage-related premiums, Medicare payroll taxes and premiums, state payments for the poor, and federal general revenues. Employers would be required to pay premiums related to total wages. The premiums would be sufficient to pay the full cost of benefits. Employees could be required to pay up to 35 percent of the premium costs. Employers could receive tax credits or grants if their health

---

[10]A description of several national health insurance proposals can be found in U.S. Congress, House, *Summaries of Selected Health Insurance Proposals and Proposals to Restructure the Financing of Private Health Insurance,* Subcommittee on Health of the Committee on Ways and Means, 96th Cong., 2d sess. (Washington, D.C.: U.S. Government Printing Office, 1980). See also Robert J. Myers, *Social Security,* 3rd ed. (Homewood, Ill.: Richard D. Irwin, 1985), pp. 623–642.

insurance costs substantially increased because of the new law. To control costs, hospitals and physicians would be paid on the basis of prenegotiated amounts and would not be permitted to charge more than the health insurance plan pays. National, areawide, and state budgets would be established, and any increases would be tightly controlled.

A centralized federal plan of national health insurance has both desirable and undesirable features. The major advantage is that comprehensive health insurance benefits would be provided to all Americans, including those poor or uninsurable.

A centralized federal plan, however, has several obvious defects. First, the transfer of health care from the private to federal sector would result in a bureaucratic and cumbersome administration, complex regulations, and centralized authority. Health care is a rapidly changing field, which demands decentralization of authority and administrative flexibility.

Second, the centralized federal plan could cause serious harm to the present health care delivery system. Critics argue that the federal government would completely control all health care in the United States and that private insurers would be mere surrogates of the federal government.[11]

Finally, private health insurers would be adversely affected. If the federal government is the actual insurer under the plan, the role of private insurers in the health care industry would be substantially reduced. The number of private health insurers would decline; thousands of employees would lose their jobs; and state premium taxes would be reduced.

Catastrophic Health Insurance

Under this approach to national health insurance, it is assumed that most private health insurance plans are adequate but that the typical family needs additional protection against a catastrophic loss. Catastrophic losses are large, unpredictable medical expenses associated with a serious illness or injury. Expenses incurred from long-term care in a nursing home or similar institution are usually a major cause of a catastrophic loss, especially for the aged.

A relatively small proportion of families incur catastrophic medical expenses during the year. An earlier 1982 study by the Congressional Budget Office (excluding the aged and poor) indicated that only 5 percent of the families incurred medical expenses exceeding $5,000 and only one-half of 1 percent incurred medical expenses exceeding $20,000.[12]

Numerous catastrophic health insurance proposals have been introduced in Congress. The Catastrophic Health Insurance and Medical Assistance

---

[11]Statement of Dr. Lowell H. Steen, American Medical Association, in U.S. Congress, House, *National Health Insurance*, Vol. 2, Hearings before the Subcommittee on Health of the Committee on Ways and Means, 96th Cong., 2d sess., 1980, pp. 322–323.

[12]*Source Book of Health Insurance Data, 1982–83*, (Washington, D.C.: Health Insurance Association of America, 1983), p. 46.

Reform Act, introduced by Sen. Russell Long and Rep. Doug Walgren, is an example. The major features of their proposal are summarized as follows:

1. BASIC APPROACH. Major emphasis is on coverage of catastrophic medical expenses. Catastrophe health insurance would be provided to all citizens and legal residents through either (a) a federally administered plan for the unemployed, welfare recipients, the aged, and other groups; or (b) approved catastrophic insurance plans by employers and the self-employed. Employers would be required to provide catastrophic health insurance to all full-time employees and dependent family members. The coverage would continue for 90 days after the employee terminated his or her employment unless coverage is obtained from another plan. The unemployed, welfare recipients, aged, and all others not covered under an approved employer or self-employer plan would be covered under the public plan.

2. BENEFITS. The benefits would be similar to those under Medicare. Under the Catastrophic Plan, inpatient hospital care would be covered after 60 days of confinement, with an unlimited number of days of care thereafter. A $2,000 deductible would apply to physicians' fees and related services. After the hospital or medical deductible (60 days or $2,000) is satisfied, the individual would not pay anything for covered services. A separate Medical Assistance Plan would be developed for low-income persons.

3. FINANCING. The Catastrophic Plan would be financed by a 1 percent payroll tax paid by employers on the same wage base used in the OASDHI program. Employee contributions would not be allowed. An employer or self-employed individual who selects the private plan could deduct the premium from the 1 percent payroll tax liability. The Medical Assistance Plan would be financed by federal general revenues and state funds.

Catastrophic health insurance has both desirable and undesirable features. On the positive side, it is substantially less expensive than other more comprehensive national health insurance proposals. It also provides major medical insurance to millions of Americans who now have no protection against a catastrophic loss.

On the negative side, however, certain defects are readily apparent. First, the approach of covering only catastrophic expenses can be seriously questioned. Although it is highly desirable to cover a catastrophic loss by eliminating financial barriers to care, most individuals and families do not incur catastrophic medical expenses each year. Thus, relatively few people would qualify for benefits under a catastrophe-only plan.

Second, a catastrophe-only plan does nothing to correct the major defects that now exist in the health care delivery system. Instead, it could actually aggravate present problems. A catastrophe-only plan invites physicians, hospitals, and other suppliers of medical services to increase their fees and prices; there may be pressures placed on physicians to keep patients in the hospital until the trigger point of the deductible is reached; and a catastrophe plan does nothing to encourage use of the less costly types of medical care, such as home health care and ambulatory care.[13]

Proposals to Stimulate Competition

Proponents of greater competition in the health care field argue that the present methods for the payment of health care have interfered with the operation of natural market forces and have significantly contributed to the inflation in medical costs in recent years. More specifically, critics argue that the present system contributes to inflation in health care costs in the following ways: (1) third-party payments by private insurers and government programs (Medicare and Medicaid) insulate consumers from the real cost of health care; (2) fee-for-service reimbursement systems to doctors encourage them to increase the price and quantity of their services; (3) cost reimbursement to hospitals operates as a disincentive for institutions to restrain their costs; and (4) tax deductions and exclusions encourage employers and employees to choose more costly forms of health insurance.[14]

Proponents of greater competition believe that a number of changes are needed to stimulate competition in the health care industry and encourage greater cost-consciousness by consumers of health care. These changes include placing limits on the tax benefits presently provided for employer premium contributions, changes in the types of employer-based health insurance plans, and a voucher system for Medicare and Medicaid. It is argued that if consumers are given a choice of several health insurance plans, they will select the coverage that gives them adequate coverage at the lowest cost. The result is a reduction in demand for health care and greater price competition among private insurers. Finally, the proposals place competitive pressures on hospitals, physicians, and other providers to deliver health care services more efficiently and at lower cost.

Basic Elements in Pro-Competition Proposals.   The various proposals for promoting greater competition in the health care industry have several common elements. They include the following:

1. A LIMIT IS PLACED ON EMPLOYER CONTRIBUTIONS EXCLUDED FROM TAXATION.   Under present law, employer contributions for health insurance are not included in the employee's gross income for federal income tax purposes. It is argued that the present exclusion encourages employers and employees to choose health insurance plans that are more expensive than is necessary. By

---

[13]Statement of Melvin A. Glasser, Committee for National Health Insurance, in U.S. Congress, House, *National Health Insurance*, Vol. 2, Hearings before the Subcommittee on Health of the Committee on Ways and Means, 96th Cong., 2d sess., 1980, pp. 306–310.

[14]U.S. Congress, House, *Description of Proposals to Stimulate Competition in the Financing and Delivery of Health Care*, Subcommittee on Health of the Committee on Ways and Means, 97th Cong., 1st sess. (Washington, D.C.: U.S. Government Printing Office, 1981), p. 1. The following discussion is based on this source.

placing a limit on the amount of employer contributions that can be excluded, employees will be more cost-conscious, since excess employer contributions would be taxable income to the employees.

2. A REBATE OF CASH OR OTHER BENEFITS IS PROVIDED. An employee who selects a health insurance plan with a premium that is less than the employer's contribution would receive a rebate in cash or other benefits.

3. EMPLOYERS MUST OFFER A MULTIPLE CHOICE OF HEALTH INSURANCE PLANS TO THE EMPLOYEES. Employers would be required to make an equal contribution to each plan. The various plans would require the following coverages: (1) minimum benefit plan; (2) family coverage; (3) continuity of coverage in case of death, divorce, or change in employment; and (4) catastrophic coverage.

4. MEDICARE VOUCHERS WOULD BE PROVIDED. To promote competition, Medicare beneficiaries would be given vouchers to purchase qualified health plans from private insurers.

Illustrative Example. The Health Incentives Reform Act of 1981 is an example of a pro-competition proposal. The major features of his proposal are summarized as follows:

1. BASIC APPROACH. The Internal Revenue Code would be amended so that the employer's contributions toward a health or dental insurance plan that exceeded certain limits would be included in the employee's gross income. For example, the monthly limit might be $50 for an employee, $100 for an employee and spouse, and $125 for a family. The excluded amounts would be annually adjusted based on changes in the medical care component of the Consumer Price Index.

2. BENEFITS. Employers with 100 or more employees would be required to offer at least three health insurance options. Each option must include minimum benefits similar to Medicare; catastrophic coverage; continuity of coverage in the event of death, divorce, or separation from employment; and family coverage.

3. FINANCING. The employer would be required to contribute an equal amount toward each employee's health insurance plan. Contributions exceeding the prescribed limits would be taxable income to the employee. If an employee selects a health insurance plan that is less expensive than the employer's contributions, he or she would be given a rebate or other benefits. The rebate would be subject to income taxation.

As an approach to reforming health care in the United States, the pro-competition bills have both advantages and disadvantages.[15] On the positive

---

[15]An evaluation of the pro-competition bills can be found in Health Insurance Association of America, *Competition in the Health Care System: An Evaluation of the Pro-Competition Bills* (Washington, D.C.: Health Insurance Institute, 1981). The following discussion is based on this source.

side, the proposals are aimed at reformation of the present system by promoting greater price competition, more competitive markets, and greater consumer awareness. In addition, federal financing by payroll taxes and general revenues would not be required. Finally, increased competition among the providers of care will reduce pressures for cost-containment legislation and federal regulation of providers.

On the negative side, however, certain glaring defects are immediately apparent. First, placing a limit on nontaxable health insurance benefits will result in a substantial income tax increase for most covered workers. The expansion of group health insurance protection is the result of years of collective bargaining. Under the different proposals, covered employees would be faced with a substantial increase in the personal income tax.

Second, the proposed system of rebates can lead to strong adverse selection against the high-cost plan. Because of rebates, younger, healthier employees would tend to select the lower-cost plan, while unhealthy and older employees would select the higher-cost plan. This would lead to adverse selection against the high-cost plan.

Third, it is doubtful whether consumers can shop effectively for doctors and hospitals. Consumers generally cannot evaluate the quality and appropriateness of the medical care provided and generally will not challenge the doctor's orders on the type of care ordered. However, the pro-competition bills are based on the implicit assumption that consumers can evaluate the different types of care and will opt for low-cost care if financial incentives are provided.

Finally, it is argued that group health insurance is already intensely competitive. The requirement that the various options to employees must be plans of different carriers would only increase insurance marketing and administrative expenses and reduce the economies now inherent in group health insurance.

U.S. Health Act of 1986

One national health insurance proposal is the U.S. Health Act of 1986, which was introduced by Rep. Edward R. Roybal in the summer of 1986. The major features of the proposal are summarized as follows:[16]

1. BASIC APPROACH.   An all-purpose universal health insurance plan would provide both basic health insurance and catastrophic protection to every citizen and resident of the United States. Primary, acute, and long-term care would be provided as well as catastrophic protection.

2. BENEFITS.   Basic health care benefits would include inpatient and outpatient services, physicians' services, laboratory and X-rays, home health care, skilled nursing home care, prescription drugs, and other services. Catastrophic protection would also be provided. A beneficiary would be required to

---

[16]Mary Jane Fisher, "House Gets Comprehensive Health Care Bill," *National Underwriter*, Property & Casualty ed., July 18, 1986, p. 46.

pay 20 percent of the covered costs of health care, skilled nursing home care, and home health care costs up to $500 per year; for nonskilled long-term care, the cost-sharing charge would be 25 percent up to $1,000 each year.

3. FINANCING. The funds needed would come from several sources. They include an increase in the cigarette tax; beneficiary cost sharing; a surcharge on individual and corporate income taxes; an employer tax based on compensation; state revenues for funding one-half the cost of the poor; extension of the Medicare payroll tax to all income; a special premium paid by the aged to approximate the Part B Medicare premium; and savings generated by a prospective payment formula and by capitation.

The most obvious advantage of the proposal is the extension of national health insurance to the entire population, including the poor and uninsurable. In addition, catastrophic protection would also be provided. However, a major defect of the proposal is the complex method of financing. Funds would be derived from numerous sources, which may make it difficult for actuaries to estimate accurately the total amount of revenues that would be generated from all sources to fund the program.

Other Recent Proposals

Several recent proposals would extend private health insurance coverage to groups who are presently uninsured. These proposals technically are not forms of universal national health insurance. However, they merit some discussion because of the problem of the uninsured in the United States. Moreover, certain features in these proposals could be used in developing a prototype national health insurance plan for all Americans.

Employer-Mandated Health Insurance. Sen. Edward Kennedy and Rep. Henry Waxman have introduced legislation that would require most employers to provide minimum health insurance benefits to their workers. The proposed legislation would also provide coverage to virtually all Americans by 2000.

1. BASIC APPROACH. The proposal would require most employers to provide health insurance benefits that meet certain standards to most employees and their dependents. The proposal also provides for a public program financed with tax dollars that would make health insurance available to any American not covered by employment-based health insurance.

2. BENEFITS. The minimum package of benefits would include physician services, hospital services, diagnostic tests, prenatal and well-baby care, limited mental health coverage, and coverage for a catastrophic loss, with a $3,000 out-of-pocket limit. A $250 deductible per individual and $500 deductible per family would be required. A copayment charge of 20 percent would also be required. Limitation of coverage because of a preexisting condition would not be allowed. In addition, deductibles or copayments for prenatal and well-baby care would not be allowed.

As we noted earlier, all Americans not covered by employment-based health insurance would be assured of coverage by 2000. Based on budgetary considerations, the public program would be established in phases. The package of benefits would be the same as the private plan. The deductible and copayment amounts would be based on income, and poor individuals would pay no deductible or copayment charge. The states would administer the public plan under federal guidelines.

3. FINANCING. The private-employer plans would be financed by employer and employee contributions, deductibles, and copayment charges. The employee's share of premiums would be limited to a maximum of 20 percent. Employers would be permitted to make a pro rata contribution for part-time workers who work between 17.5 and 25 hours per week. Employees who work fewer than 25 hours weekly would be permitted to decline the coverage.

The Kennedy-Waxman proposal has both desirable and undesirable features. On the positive side, the proposal would provide health insurance to a large proportion of people who presently are uninsured. About two-thirds (23 million) of the 37 million persons who have no health insurance live in families in which at least one household member works full time. In addition, health insurance eventually would be made available to other Americans who have no employment-based health insurance.

The major objection to this proposal is that many employers may be unable to pay the cost of a group health insurance plan, especially smaller, marginal employers. Consequently, many smaller employers may employ fewer workers or reduce the number of hours worked by employees each week. Thus, the proposal could have a negative impact on employment.

Pepper Commission Proposal. In early 1990, a bipartisan congressional committee called the Pepper Commission endorsed a plan that would provide health insurance coverage to the uninsured and long-term care to the elderly and disabled.

1. BASIC APPROACH. Large employers with more than 100 employees would be mandatorily required to provide private health insurance to their employees or else contribute to a public plan that would provide health insurance to all employees and nonworking dependents. Smaller employers with 100 or fewer employees would be encouraged to provide health insurance coverage to the employees by tax credits and other subsidies.

A public health insurance plan would also be created that would replace Medicaid. The public plan—financed heavily by the federal government—would cover employees and dependents that contribute and nonworking individuals who buy in or are subsidized.

In addition, up to three months of care in a nursing home would be available to all Americans, regardless of age or ability to pay. Persons who need care beyond three months would be allowed to keep their home and a certain amount of assets. Home care assistance would also be provided to the severely disabled, such as assistance in dressing, bathing, and grocery shopping.

2. BENEFITS. The minimum benefit package would include primary and preventive care, physician and hospital care, and other services. Services would be subject to cost sharing, with subsidies for low income persons and limits on out-of-pocket spending. In addition, as noted earlier, nursing home care and home health care would also be provided.

3. FINANCING. Private health insurance plans would be financed by employers and employees. Employers would pay 80 percent of the premium, and employees would pay up to 20 percent. Alternatively, employers could contribute to the public plan and pay a premium based on a percentage of payroll.

To participate in the public plan, working individuals would pay a premium equal to a percentage of their wages. People with incomes below 100 percent of the poverty line and pregnant women and children under age six with incomes below 185 percent of the poverty line would pay nothing. The public plan would be heavily subsidized by the federal government. The states would also be required to make a contribution equal to their Medicaid expenditures.

The major advantage of the Pepper Commission is that all Americans would have access to health insurance from either a private or public plan. The major disadvantage, however, is cost. New federal expenditures in excess of $66 billion would be required. Congress did not seriously consider the Pepper Commission proposal because the commission did not offer specific recommendations on how the plan was to be financed.

American Medical Insurance Proposal. In 1990 the American Medical Association (AMA) presented a plan that would extend health insurance coverage to the uninsured. The proposal relies heavily on the private sector to accomplish its objectives.

1. BASIC APPROACH. Medicaid would be reformed to provide uniform and adequate benefits to all poor persons with incomes below the poverty level. Employers would be required to provide health insurance to all full-time employees and their families. Tax incentives would be provided and risk pools would be created to help smaller employers purchase health insurance for the employees at affordable rates. In addition, state risk pools would also be created to make health insurance available to the uninsured and to others who cannot afford individual coverage. Medicare would also be reformed by having the benefits prefunded by employees and employers during their working years; there would be no Medicare tax imposed on senior citizens; and Medicare vouchers would be provided so that health insurance could be purchased from private insurers. Long-term care financing would also be encouraged by tax incentives and by an asset protection program. Finally, health care costs would be reduced by reforming medical malpractice insurance to reduce the cost of malpractice insurance premiums and the practice of defensive medicine.

2. BENEFITS. A basic package of benefits would be required. Provisions excluding pre-existing conditions would be eliminated. Smaller employers

would not be required to provide state-mandated benefits. In addition, the state risk pools would provide a basic package of benefits at standard group rates.

3. FINANCING.   The self-employed could deduct 100 percent of the health insurance premiums paid. As stated earlier, the state risk pools would have standard group rates. Premium assistance would be provided to all persons not covered by employer plans who have incomes between 100 percent and 150 percent of the poverty level. A 100 percent tax deduction would be allowed individuals who purchase the insurance from the state pool. Medicare benefits would be prefunded by employees and employers prior to retirement. Long-term care subsidies would be provided individuals with incomes between 100 percent and 200 percent of the poverty level.

Although the AMA proposal addresses several national problems, it has numerous defects. Although the plan recommends a reduction in medical malpractice premiums, it says nothing about reducing the number of medical malpractice incidents by negligent physicians. In addition, employer costs would be substantially increased by the proposal. Finally, the proposal does not provide any cost estimates, nor does it provide specific recommendations (other than in vague, general terms) on how the recommendations are to be financed.

Outlook for National Health Insurance

Enactment of a universal national health insurance plan in the near future is highly unlikely. This is due to several factors. First, the size of the federal deficit is a strong deterrent to the enactment of national health insurance. To reduce the deficit, federal spending must be reduced. Under these circumstances, it is unlikely that a national health insurance plan will be enacted into law.

Second, private health insurance plans have been substantially upgraded and improved over time, especially group health insurance plans. Thus, public pressure for speedy passage of a national health insurance plan has been reduced.

Third, political pressures for enactment of a comprehensive national health insurance plan are not strong at the present time. Other critical national problems, such as reducing the federal deficit, reducing drug and alcohol abuse, and building a strong national defense have a higher priority in the minds of many politicians.

Finally, public confidence in the federal government's ability to operate efficiently large-scale programs has been seriously shaken by the soaring costs under Medicare and Medicaid and the overall mediocre record of many federal programs.

SUGGESTIONS FOR ADDITIONAL READING

AMERICAN MEDICAL ASSOCIATION. *Health Access America: The AMA Proposal to Improve Access to Affordable,* *Quality Health Care.* Chicago, Ill.: American Medical Association, 1990.

BUTLER, STUART M., AND EDMUND F. HAISLMAIER, EDS. *Critical Issues, A National Health System for America.* Washington, D.C.: The Heritage Foundation, 1989.

DAVIS, KAREN. "National Health Insurance: A Proposal." *The American Economic Review, Papers and Proceedings.* Vol. 79, No. 2 (May 1989), pp. 349–352.

FRECH, H. E., III, ED. *Health Care in America, The Political Economy of Hospitals and Health Insurance.* San Francisco, Calif.: Pacific Research Institute for Public Policy, 1988.

FRITZ, DAN. "What Universal Health Care in Massachusetts Means to Employers," *Compensation and Benefits Management,* Vol. 5, No. 3 (Spring 1989), pp. 173–177.

Health Insurance Coverage of Retired Persons, Research Findings 2. National Medical Expenditures Survey, Department of Health and Human Services, Public Health Service, National Center for Health Services Research and Health Care Technology Assessment. Rockville, Md.: Public Health Service, September 1989.

MYERS, ROBERT J. *Social Security,* 3rd ed., pp. 623–642. Homewood, Ill.: Richard D. Irwin, 1985.

PAULY, MARK V., ED. *National Health Insurance: What Now, What Later, What Never?* AEI Symposia Series, No. 80. Washington, D.C.: American Enterprise Institute, 1980.

THE PEPPER COMMISSION, U.S. BIPARTISAN COMMISSION ON COMPREHENSIVE HEALTH CARE. *Recommendations to the Congress by the Pepper Commission: Access to Health Care and Long-Term Care for all Americans,* One Hundred First Congress, 2nd. sess. (Washington, D.C.: U.S. Government Printing Office, 1990).

A Profile of Uninsured Americans, Research Findings 1. National Medical Expenditures Survey, Department of Health and Human Services, Public Health Service, National Center for Health Services Research and Health Care Technology Assessment. Rockville, Md.: Public Health Service, September 1989.

RAFFEL, MARSHALL W., ED. *Comparative Health Systems: Descriptive Analyses of Fourteen National Health Systems.* University Park, Pa.: Pennsylvania State University Press, 1984.

11

PROBLEM OF OCCUPATIONAL SAFETY AND HEALTH

Every year, thousands of workers in the United States die from job-related accidents because of unsafe working conditions or unsafe personal acts on the job. Large numbers of workers are also disabled for one or more days each year because of job-related injuries and disease. In addition to pain and suffering, disabled workers are confronted with the serious problems of the loss of earned income, payment of medical expenses, partial or permanent loss of bodily functions or limbs, and job separation. If the injury is particularly severe, the disabled worker must often undergo a traumatic financial, physical, and emotional readjustment, which can be especially hard on the younger workers who have several dependents and are deeply in debt.

Industrial accidents, however, are only a part of the occupational health and safety problem. Occupational disease is a growing problem. Because of new technology that often creates a dangerous industrial environment, many workers are now exposed to new chemical and physical hazards that did not previously exist. In addition, job stress is an increasing cause of occupational illness. Safety engineers were formerly concerned with the problem of industrial accidents and accident prevention. However, current emphasis is on the broader occupational health and safety problem, which includes the total working environment, plant safety, accident prevention, occupational disease, and all other factors that influence the worker's health.

In this chapter, we shall examine the important problem of occupational safety and health. In particular, we shall consider the following areas: (1) occupational accidents, (2) occupational disease, (3) the cost of occupational accidents and disease, and (4) solutions to the occupational health and safety problem.

PROBLEM OF OCCUPATIONAL ACCIDENTS

The annual toll of occupational accidents is staggering. In 1988, 10,600 workers died from job-related accidents. However, some safety experts believe data on work-related deaths may be substantially understated. Many job-related deaths are never reported because they are due to occupational diseases that have long latent periods and are difficult to attribute to occupational exposures. It is estimated that the number of job-related deaths could be as high as 100,000 annually, which is about twice that of traffic fatalities.[1]

In addition, the National Safety Council estimates that 1.8 million disabling injuries occurred in 1988.[2] These data, however, do not reflect the pain and suffering of the disabled workers or the anguish of their families. Job-related injuries also result in the loss of billions of dollars in wages each year and the diversion of scarce economic resources to the payment of workers' compensation benefits.

It is also worthwhile to examine the accident records of key industries. Based on data gathered by the National Safety Council and the Bureau of Labor Statistics, we know that certain industries are more hazardous than others. Table 11-1 provides information on incidence rates for key industries. Occupational injury incidence rates for each 100 full-time workers are shown for selected industries. Construction, manufacturing, agriculture (including forestry and fishing) and mining are dangerous industries in which to work. In contrast, employment in finance, insurance, real estate, and services is relatively safe.Although not shown in Table 11-1, there are also important differences among the various industries. Those industries with higher than average incidence rates include meat products, ship and boat building and repairing, lumber and wood products, sawmills and planing mills, millwork, and beverages.

Although certain industries have relatively high accident rates, the nation over time has made considerable progress in reducing work-related accidental death and injury rates. Between 1912 and 1987, accidental work deaths per 100,000 population declined 76 percent. An estimated 18,000 to 21,000 workers died from job-related accidents in 1912. However, with a labor force more than double and producing more than ten times as much, only 11,100 workers died in 1987.[3]

---

[1]Lawrence S. Bacow, *Bargaining for Job Safety and Health* (Cambridge, Mass.: MIT Press, 1980), p. 3.

[2]National Safety Council, *Accident Facts, 1989 Final Condensed Edition*, September 1989.

[3]Ibid., p. 32.

TABLE 11-1 Occupational Injury Incidence Rates Per 100 Full-Time Workers[a], by Industry, 1986 and 1987

INDUSTRY DIVISION	TOTAL CASES[b]		LOST WORKDAY CASES		NONFATAL CASES WITHOUT LOST WORKDAYS	
	1986	1987	1986	1987	1986	1987
Private Sector[c]	7.7	8.0	3.6	3.7	4.2	4.3
Agriculture, forestry, and fishing[c]	10.7	10.7	5.4	5.5	5.3	5.1
Mining	7.2	8.2	4.1	4.8	3.1	3.4
Construction	15.1	14.5	6.8	6.7	8.3	7.8
Manufacturing	10.2	11.3	4.5	5.0	5.7	6.3
Transportation and public utilities	8.1	8.3	4.8	4.9	3.3	3.4
Wholesale and retail trade	7.6	7.6	3.3	3.4	4.3	4.2
Finance, insurance, and real estate	2.0	1.9	0.9	0.9	1.1	1.1
Services	5.2	5.3	2.5	2.6	2.7	2.7

[a]Incidence rates are rates per 100 full-time employees, using 200,000 employee hours as the equivalent.
[b]Includes fatalities. Because of rounding, lost workday cases and nonfatal cases may not equal the number of total cases.
[c]Excludes farms with fewer than 11 employees.

Source: *News*, Bureau for Labor Statistics, U.S. Department of Labor, November 15, 1988, Table 4.

PROBLEM OF OCCUPATIONAL DISEASE

Some safety experts believe that occupational disease is increasingly becoming more important as a cause of occupational disability. Let us briefly examine the problem of occupational disease.

Widespread Problem

Occupational disease is widespread throughout the United States and can occur in virtually any occupation. In 1986, employers recognized or diagnosed about 137,000 new occupational disease cases according to the Bureau of Labor Statistics. Table 11-2 shows the distribution of these cases by industry. Manufacturing accounted for 61 percent of the cases. The services industry, trade, construction, transportation, and public utilities, agriculture, finance, and mining accounted for the remaining cases. In short, the data show that occupational disease can occur in almost any occupation.

It is also a mistake to assume that occupational disease is limited to only a small number of diseases. A wide variety of occupational diseases exists at the present time. Table 11-3 shows the various types of occupational diseases that are compensated by workers' compensation laws. The data again show that occupa-

TABLE 11-2 Number of Occupational Disease Cases
in the Private Sector, 1986 (in thousands)

INDUSTRY	NUMBER OF CASES
Manufacturing	83.6
Services	22.0
Trade[a]	11.8
Construction	5.8
Transportation and Public Utilities	5.4
Agriculture[b]	3.9
Finance[c]	2.6
Mining[d]	1.6
Private sector total[e]	136.8

[a]Trade includes wholesale and retail trade.
[b]Agriculture includes forestry and fishing. Data exclude farms with fewer than 11 employees.
[c]Finance includes insurance and real estate.
[d]Mining includes quarrying and oil and gas extraction.
[e]Excludes farms with fewer than 11 employees. Because of rounding, items do not equal the total.

Source: National Safety Council, *Accident Facts, 1988 Edition*, p. 46.

tional disease is not confined to a single disease or industry. For example, workers exposed to dusty working conditions in plants and elsewhere can develop various types of *dust disease*. Workers exposed to asbestos fibers can develop *asbestosis*, which is a latent form of lung cancer. Some coal miners have *black lung disease*, which is due to the inhalation of soft-coal dust and results in chronic coughing and shortness of breath. *Byssinosis* and *silicosis* are other crippling diseases that affect textile and cotton workers and also result in chronic coughing and shortness of breath. Other workers have serious *respiratory disorders* because of working conditions. Workers also can become sick and disabled because of *chemical or metal poisoning*, such as lead poisoning. Farm workers are exposed to *pesticides, herbicides, and fungicides*, which can cause serious occupational disease. In short, a wide variety of occupational diseases can disable the workers and cause serious economic insecurity.

Problem Areas

The problem of occupational disease is also aggravated by several problem areas that warrant special treatment.

1. NEW TECHNOLOGY. The United States is undergoing a technological revolution, with severe implications concerning the health of industrial workers. New technology often results in the use of new and potentially toxic chemicals that can cause occupational disease. For example, carcinogenic chemicals, arsenic, chromium, nickel, benzene, formaldehyde, epoxy resins, pesticides, and

TABLE 11-3 Occupational Disease Experience

DISEASE	% OF ALL OCCUPATIONAL DISEASE (O.D.) CLAIMS		AVERAGE INDEMNITY BENEFITS PER CASE	AVERAGE MEDICAL BENEFITS PER CASE	AVERAGE TOTAL BENEFITS PER CASE
	1984	1979	1984	1984	1984
Dust disease	6.52%	3.15%	$52,408	$1,545	$53,953
Asbestosis	15.41	1.83	4,731	1,771	6,502
Black lung	1.66	28.45	38,032	3,257	41,289
Byssinosis	0.00	0.04	—	—	—
Silicosis	9.10	2.17	8,378	410	8,788
Respiratory disorder	18.49	18.22	16,671	1,859	18,530
Poisoning, chemical	3.74	3.20	6,236	1,153	7,389
Poisoning, metal	7.44	1.14	1,850	2,865	4,715
Dermatitis	14.29	18.94	3,401	535	3,936
Mental disorders	10.72	5.52	16,720	2,407	19,127
Loss of hearing	1.16	3.31	24,121	1,510	25,631
Contagious diseases	2.37	3.97	1,748	350	2,098
Cancer	0.83	0.78	10,250	2,125	12,375
Other O.D.	8.27	9.28	18,771	3,030	21,801
All O.D. claims	100.00%	100.00%	$13,134	$1,696	$14,830
O.D. claims excluding black lung			$12,604	$1,662	$14,266

Source: Insurance Information Institute, *Insurance Facts 1988–89 Property/Casualty Fact Book* (New York: Insurance Information Institute, 1988), p. 101. Data are based on National Council on Compensation Insurance experience.

numerous other substances can threaten the worker's health. In addition, new technical processes and new sources of energy, such as atomic and ultrasonic energy, present great health hazards. Radioactive substances and radioactive machines can expose workers to radiation and potential occupational diseases.

2. EXPOSURE TO ASBESTOS. Thousands of workers are now disabled because of previous exposure to asbestos. Exposure to asbestos fibers and materials can result in latent lung cancer. The time gap can be as long as 50 years between the time of exposure and the emergence of the disease.

Workers who claim they are disabled because of previous exposure to asbestos have filed millions of dollars of lawsuits against companies that have produced asbestos products. As a result, numerous firms have declared bankruptcy or have sought protection under the federal bankruptcy code. Four manufacturers of asbestos, one of which has more than 16,000 asbestos liability claims exceeding $2 billion, already have filed for bankruptcy.[4]

3. JOB-RELATED STRESS. Job-related stress is another important cause of occupational disease. A study by the National Council on Compensation Insur-

---

[4]*1988–89 Property/Casualty Fact Book,* (New York: Insurance Information Institute, 1988), p. 101.

ance showed that the number of stress claims filed between 1980 and 1983 doubled, which accounted for 15 percent of all occupational disease claims during that period.[5] Workers can develop serious mental and physical problems because of stress associated with the job (such as those of police officers, firefighters, air traffic controllers). In addition, workers can become ill because of stress associated with terminations, transfers, demotions, layoffs, changes in duties, or criticism by supervisors. Also, fear of AIDS has resulted in some stress cases for nurses who treat AIDS victims.

4. VIDEO DISPLAY TERMINALS (VDTS). Exposure by workers to video display terminals (VDTs) is alleged to be another new cause of occupational disease. It is believed that some workers, especially pregnant women, who use word processors or office computers can become sick and disabled because of repeated exposure to the machines and from stress associated with their operation. The National Institute for Occupational Safety and Health found that VDT operators reported a higher level of stress than any other group of workers, including air traffic controllers.[6] Computer operators also have experienced eye strain, headaches, tension, and general malaise.

5. CUMULATIVE TRAUMA DISORDERS. Cumulative trauma disorders are a form of occupational disease that results from highly repetitive motions in the arm, hand, and wrist, such as those used by meatpacking plant workers. Cumulative trauma disorders were the most frequent occupational illness reported in 1986, with an estimated 45,500 cases nationally.[7]

Carpal tunnel syndrome is an example of a cumulative trauma disorder. Highly repetitive motions can cause severe nerve damage and a crippling of the hands, arms, and wrists. Workers most at risk are employed in meatpacking, food preparation, product fabrication, construction, mining, and clerical work. Butchers have the highest incidence rate of all occupations.

6. SUBSTANCE ABUSE ON THE JOB. The widespread use of drugs and alcohol on the job is another important occupational health and safety problem. According to the National Institute on Drug Abuse, one in five workers ages 18 to 25 and one in eight workers ages 26 to 34 use drugs on the job; 3 percent of the full-time work force uses cocaine.[8] The use of drugs and alcohol on the job results in an increase in job-related accidents, higher medical expense claims and insurance premiums, higher absenteeism rates, and decreased worker productivity.

The cost to employers because of substance abuse is substantial. One recent survey of the Fortune 1,000 companies showed that the costs of substance abuse ranged from 1 percent to 10 percent of payroll; the average cost of

---

[5]*National Underwriter,* Property and Casualty/Employee Benefits ed., May 16, 1988, p. 28.

[6]*National Underwriter,* Life and Health/Financial Services ed., February 22, 1988, p. 3.

[7]*Accident Facts, 1988 Edition,* p. 47.

[8]Steve Jordan, "Workplace Drug Use Common," *Sunday World Herald,* September 17, 1989, Section M, p. 1.

substance abuse by the respondents is estimated at approximately 3 percent of payroll.[9]

COSTS OF OCCUPATIONAL DISABILITY

The total physical, financial, psychological, and social costs of industrial accidents and occupational disease are gigantic. These costs fall heavily on disabled workers, business firms, and the economy.

Costs to Disabled Workers

Workers who are occupationally disabled and their families bear heavy burdens from a work-related injury or occupational disease. First, workers lose billions of dollars in lost wages each year because of occupational injuries and disease. Most workers' compensation claims, however, involve temporary total disability, and in many cases, the weekly income benefits restore less than half of the worker's total wage loss. In addition, a waiting period before cash benefits are payable typically must also be satisfied.

The family also bears a heavy burden from an occupational injury or disease. Besides their anguish, family members may experience considerable uncertainty concerning the future continuation of their income. This is particularly true if a family head dies as a result of a job-related accident or disease.

Costs to Business Firms

Business firms also incur heavy costs from industrial accidents and occupational disease. These costs can be classified into two major categories: insured and uninsured. *Insured costs* are the net premiums paid by the firm for workers' compensation insurance, or, if the firm is self-insured, the actual sums paid to disabled workers and their dependents under the state workers' compensation law, the amounts paid for medical care, and administrative costs.

The *uninsured costs* to a firm of occupational disabilities include the following:

- Lost production as a result of the accident
- Extra costs because of overtime
- Cost of wages paid to supervisors for their time lost from the accident
- Decreased output after the worker returns to work
- Cost of the learning period for a new worker hired
- Cost of investigation and accident reports.

---

[9]William M. Mercer Meidinger Hansen, *The Bulletin*, No. 164, February 1989.

The uninsured costs of an industrial accident are at least equal to the insured costs and, in many accidents, could substantially exceed them. In addition, workers' compensation insurance is experience rated, and depending on firm size, employers have a financial incentive to reduce accidents and their workers' compensation premiums. Thus, when both the insured and uninsured costs are considered, firms have a strong financial incentive to prevent or reduce industrial accidents and disease.

The loss of profits is still another way to measure the impact of work accidents on the firm. Every accident erodes the firm's profits. To offset even a modest $500 work-related accident, the firm must sell a surprisingly large amount of goods or services. An earlier study showed the dollar value of goods and services in 1982 that must be sold to offset a $500 work accident (see Table 11-4). Since most occupational injuries cost more than $500, the aggregate loss of profits to the firm is substantially higher.

TABLE 11-4   What Does a Work Accident Really Cost?

	DOLLAR VALUE		DOLLAR VALUE
Aerospace	$17,857	Instruments, photo goods	6,494
Amusements	6,849	Iron, steel	12,500
Automotive parts	10,638	Lumber, wood products	13,158
Baking	13,514	Machinery	9,804
Brewing	9,804	Meatpacking	21,739
Building, heating, plumbing equipment	8,772	Metal mining	1,984
Cement	7,937	Metal products	15,152
Chemical products	8,475	Nonferrous metals	9,615
Clothing, apparel	9,433	Office equipment, computers	5,319
Common carrier trucking	9,259	Paint, allied products	16,667
Construction	11,628	Paper, allied products	8,197
Dairy Products	13,889	Petroleum products, refining	9,804
Department, specialty stores	17,857	Printing, publishing	7,353
Distilling	9,434	Quarrying, mining	22,727
Drugs, medicines	5,208	Railroads	7,143
Electrical equipment, electronics	9,091	Restaurants, hotels	7,353
Electric power, gas	5,682	Rubber, allied products	16,129
Farm, construction, material handling equipment	8,475	Shoes, leather goods	11,364
		Soap, cosmetics	8,333
Food chains	41,667	Soft drinks	8,333
Food products	11,628	Stone, clay products	12,821
Furniture, fixtures	12,500	Sugar	8,929
Glass products	11,628	Telephone and communications	4,545
Hardware, tools	9,615	Textile products	20,000
Household appliances	15,152	Tobacco products	7,813
		Variety store chains	27,778
		Wholesale houses	17,241

Note: Dollar value of goods and services required to produce $500 profit is listed by industrial groups and is based on profit margin information published in 1982 by Citibank of New York for leading corporations reporting sales and income figures.

Source: American Mutual Insurance Alliance.

Costs to the Economy

The economy also bears a heavy burden from industrial accidents and occupational disease because they lead to a substantial loss of the gross national product. Lost output cannot be stored up; the goods and services that the disabled workers could have produced in the absence of industrial injuries are lost forever. The costs of damaged equipment, medical care, and lost wages are additional economic costs that must be recognized. The National Safety Council estimates that the dollar amount of lost wages, medical expenses, insurance administration costs, fire losses, and indirect costs of work accidents totaled $42.4 billion in 1987.[10] The true cost of industrial accidents, however, is understated since the preceding estimate does not include the value of property damage (other than fire) and indirect loss from fires.

SOLUTIONS TO OCCUPATIONAL DISABILITY

Effective programs and techniques must be undertaken to reduce the costs of job-related accidents and occupational disease. Three major approaches are (1) loss prevention, (2) the Occupational Safety and Health Act of 1970, and (3) workers' compensation.

Loss Prevention

Loss-prevention activities that reduce both the frequency and the severity of industrial accidents and occupational disease are the most effective solution to the problem of occupational safety and health. These programs attempt to determine the causes of occupational injuries and disease and then undertake corrective action.

There are two schools of thought among safety experts regarding the causes of work-related accidents.[11] The *engineering* approach stresses the importance of environmental factors and therefore calls for better design and construction of plants and equipment to prevent or reduce accidents. The *behavioral* approach, which is supported by educators and psychologists, places great emphasis on human factors, such as fatigue, boredom, sensory defects, alcoholism, and lack of motivation. Both the engineering and the behavioral approach will continue to be used in preventing future work-related accidents.

Objectives of Loss Prevention. Loss-prevention techniques have two major objectives: *humanitarian considerations* and *reduction of production costs*. Humanitarian considerations have as their primary purpose the prevention of personal

---

[10]*Accident Facts, 1988 Edition,* p. 34.

[11]National Commission on Workmen's Compensation Laws, *Report,* pp. 90–91. A detailed explanation of the various theories concerning the causes of accidents can be found in H. W. Heinrich, Dan Peterson, and Nestor Roos, *Industrial Accident Prevention,* 5th ed. (New York: McGraw-Hill, 1980), Chap. 2.

suffering or death. Effective safety programs can reduce pain and suffering and prevent permanent physical impairments. The humanitarian objective also includes the prevention of the loss of income from a work-related accident, since workers' compensation disability income benefits may be inadequate for some workers.

The objective of reducing production costs is also important, since, as we noted earlier, the uninsured costs of industrial accidents often equal or exceed the direct costs. By reducing both the insured and the uninsured costs, the firm can increase its profits, so it has a monetary incentive to make safety expenditures that reduce the frequency and severity of job-related accidents. From an economic viewpoint, a firm can profitably invest in safety programs until the last dollar spent on safety reduces the accident premium portion of wages by a dollar, or reduces the firm's liability in lawsuits by a dollar. The accident premium portion of the worker's wage refers to the extra wage that the firm must pay a worker to accept a job carrying the risk of accidents, instead of a job where accidents do not occur.[12]

Conflict between Maximum Profits and Optimal Safety. The firm's objectives of maximum profits and optimal safety can conflict with each other. Gordon, Akman, and Brooks point out clearly the nature of this conflict.[13] Industrial firms attempt to maximize their profits subject to various constraints or conflicting objectives, such as survival, growth rates, or individual goals. To be consistent with the objective of maximum profits, the optimal safety objective must be expressed in terms of reduced costs or productivity gains. The firm's maximum profit position, beyond which no additional profits can be realized from investment, production, or other courses of action, may conflict with the optimal safety point—the point beyond which no positive changes in employee safety can be accomplished by increased expenditures on safety programs. This conflict could arise when the gains in worker productivity from safety program expenditures have *decreasing returns* for the firm even though additional improvements in worker safety are possible. This conflict can be illustrated by the following hypothetical schedule of safety expenditures, gains in worker productivity, and additional injuries that can be prevented:

NUMBER OF SAFETY EXPENDITURES	AMOUNT OF ADDITIONAL SAFETY EXPENDITURE	ADDITIONAL INCREASE IN WORKER PRODUCTIVITY	ADDITIONAL DISABLING INJURIES PREVENTED
1	$100,000	$112,000	7
2	100,000	102,000	5
3	100,000	92,000	3

[12]See John F. Burton, Jr., and Monroe Berkowitz, "Objectives Other than Income Maintenance for Workmen's Compensation," *The Journal of Risk and Insurance,* Vol. 38, No. 3 (September 1971), pp. 345–346.

[13]Jerome B. Gordon, Allan Akman, and Michael Brooks, "Systems Analysis and Worker Safety and

It is profitable for the firm to make the first safety expenditure of $100,000, since the gain in worker productivity, expressed as a dollar amount, exceeds the amount spent on safety. The second expenditure of $100,000 yields an additional increase of $102,000 in worker productivity and an additional decrease in the number of disabling injuries. The firm that wishes only to maximize profits should stop investing in safety programs at this point, even though the number of disabling injuries can be further reduced. If the third expenditure of $100,000 is made, an additional three disabling injuries can be prevented, but additional worker productivity declines to $92,000. The conflict between maximum profit and optimal safety becomes readily apparent. If the firm wants to reduce further the number of disabling injuries at this point, it must be willing to accept a lower total profit.

Another possible conflict could arise if the dollar difference between safety program costs and productivity gains do not materialize, that is, if the productivity returns from safety programs are always less than the amounts invested in them. In this case, the safety programs may be subject to collective bargaining between the workers and the firm, or else reflected in federal and state legislation that would be a constraint on the firm's maximum profit position.

Occupational Safety and Health Act of 1970

The Occupational Safety and Health Act of 1970 (OSHA) is one of the most important forms of social legislation ever enacted into law. The enactment of OSHA was considered necessary for several reasons. Research in job-related accidents and occupational disease at the state and national levels was not keeping pace with the exploding technology that was creating new physical hazards for American workers. Occupational safety and health standards in many states were narrow, with wide diversity among the states regarding the standards and the extent to which they were enforced. Enforcement in most states was weak, and competent occupational health and safety experts were in short supply; moreover, few states had modernized their occupational health and safety laws to protect today's workers. Existing state occupational health programs had numerous defects, among which were lack of funds and personnel, low salary scales, lack of legislative support and concern regarding the health problems of workers, difficulties in filling staff vacancies, and lack of resources to identify statistically the nature of industrial health problems. Because of these defects, Congress responded by enacting the Occupational Safety and Health Act of 1970.

The basic purpose of the act is to provide safe and healthful working conditions for every worker in the United States by reducing hazards at his or her place of employment.[14] To fulfill this purpose, the act provides for mandato-

---

Health Programs," in U.S. Congress, Senate, Subcommittee on Labor, *Occupational Safety and Health Act,* 1970. Hearings before the Subcommittee on Labor of the Committee on Labor and Public Welfare, 91st Cong., 1st and 2d sess., 1969 and 1970, on S. 2193 and S. 2788, Part 1, pp. 226–228.

[14]For a detailed explanation of the original act, see Commerce Clearing House, *Occupational Safety*

ry health and safety standards, research in occupational health and safety, information regarding the causes and prevention of industrial accidents and disease, education for employees and employers, the training of occupational health and safety specialists, and assistance and encouragement to the states to develop effective occupational safety and health programs.

Coverage.   Coverage is broad. The act applies to all firms engaging in business that affects commerce among the states. No minimum number of employees is required, nor must a firm be engaged in interstate commerce. Agricultural firms are also covered. State and federal employees are excluded, but federal agencies must establish health and safety programs in accord with the act's standards.

Federal Safety and Health Standards.   One important provision gives the Secretary of Labor the authority to establish occupational safety and health standards. If a business firm violates a safety standard, the Secretary can issue a citation and notify the firm of a proposed penalty. If the firm objects to either the citation or the proposed penalty, it can appeal the case.

Inspections and Penalties.   Federal inspectors are authorized to inspect any factory, plant, establishment, construction site, or other area where work is performed. The inspection must be made during regular working hours and in a reasonable manner. Fines and penalties can be imposed for safety violations.

An important provision permits an employee to request a special inspection if he or she believes that an imminent danger exists or that there is a violation of a safety standard that threatens his or her safety or health. Business firms are expressly forbidden from discharging or discriminating against any employee who exercises this right.

Record Keeping.   Firms are required to maintain records and periodically issue reports concerning job-related deaths, injuries, and occupational disease. Also, the Secretary of Labor can issue regulations regarding the development of information on the causes and prevention of industrial accidents and disease. Finally, firms must maintain employee exposure records on employees who are exposed to toxic materials.

Evaluation.   OSHA has both desirable and undesirable features. First, on the positive side, OSHA has made the issue of job safety a major concern of business. Business firms have been forced to make a serious analysis of their safety programs. They must conform to federal safety and health standards or face substantial penalties.

---

and Health Act of 1970—Law and Explanation (Chicago: Commerce Clearing House, 1971), and U.S. Department of Labor, *A Handy Reference Guide, The Williams-Steiger Occupational Safety and Health Act of 1970* (Washington, D.C.: U.S. Government Printing Office, 1973).

Second, OSHA has also highlighted the problem of occupational disease. Knowledge about occupational disease has increased based on OSHA-sponsored research. Studies have been conducted concerning the dangers from prolonged exposure to asbestos, cotton dust, and various carcinogens that are often present in industrial plants. As a result, many hazardous substances and chemicals that threaten the workers' health are now identified and strictly controlled.

Finally, OSHA regulations now require employers to inform employees who handle hazardous chemicals and substances about the dangers involved. Under an earlier standard, some 13 million workers in manufacturing had to be informed about dangerous chemicals used on the job. In 1988, an estimated additional 33 million workers had to be informed about hazardous chemicals used on the job.[15] Employers are required to inform employees about dangerous chemicals through training, container labeling, and maintenance of safety data sheets. The new standard has the potential for increasing occupational safety and health, reducing workers' compensation costs, and increasing worker productivity.

On the negative side, however, OSHA has several undesirable features. First, OSHA has not significantly reduced accident rates in inspected firms. Several research studies concerning the impact of OSHA on accident frequency rates have concluded that accident rates of inspected firms have not been substantially reduced or that the reduction has been relatively minor.[16]

Second, the costs to business firms of complying with the OSHA requirements are high. There are three major costs to business firms.[17] Firms can be fined for noncompliance with OSHA regulations; firms have been forced to make certain capital investments in health and safety technology to comply with OSHA regulations; and health and safety regulations can impair worker productivity, such as proposed coke-oven emission standards that would have reduced coke production per worker by an estimated 29 percent.

Third, some research studies show that safety investments made in manufacturing because of the OSHA law cost substantially more than the benefits derived from these expenditures. Bartel and Thomas found that the costs of OSHA-induced safety investments in manufacturing were substantially greater than the benefits derived (reduction in lost workdays). If firms doubled the expenditures on safety investments, the lost workday rate would fall by only 2.1 percent.[18]

---

[15]John R. Angelo, "OSHA's New Rules: Case for Compliance," *National Underwriter*, Property and Casualty/Employee Benefits ed., August 15, 1988, p. 15.

[16]Bacow, *Bargaining for Job Safety and Health*, pp. 3–28.

[17]Ibid., p. 29.

[18]Ann P. Bartel and Lacy Glenn Thomas, "The Costs and Benefits of OHSA-Induced Investments in Employee Safety and Health," in John D. Worrall and David Appel, eds., *Workers' Compensation Benefits: Adequacy, Equity & Efficiency* (New York State School of Industrial and Labor Relations, Cornell University, Ithaca, N.Y.: ILR Press, 1985), p. 54. See also p. 15 in the same volume.

Finally, OSHA has been faced with a serious problem of reduced budgets in recent years, which severely limits the number of inspections that can be made. In 1988, OSHA employed only 1,125 inspectors which permitted the inspection of only a small fraction of the total plants in the United States. It is estimated that the inspection of each plant once a year would require 125,000 inspectors with a cost of about $14 billion.[19]

Workers' Compensation

Workers' compensation benefits are also available to disabled workers for job-related accidents or occupational disease. Since workers' compensation is a fundamental approach to occupational disability, it merits careful study, and we shall examine the current programs in Chapter 12.

SUGGESTIONS FOR ADDITIONAL READING

BACOW, LAWRENCE S. *Bargaining for Job Safety and Health.* Cambridge, Mass.: MIT Press, 1980.

BERKOWITZ, MONROE, AND M. ANNE HILL. *Disability and the Labor Market: Economic Problems, Policies, and Programs.* New York State School of Industrial and Labor Relations, Cornell University, Ithaca, N.Y.: ILR Press, 1986.

BURTON, JOHN F., JR., ED. *New Perspectives in Workers' Compensation.* New York State School of Industrial and Labor Relations, Cornell University, Ithaca, N.Y.: ILR Press, 1988.

LOFGREN, DON J. *Dangerous Premises: An Insider's View of OSHA Enforcement.* New York State School of Industrial and Labor Relations, Cornell University: ILR Press, 1989.

NATIONAL SAFETY COUNCIL. *Accident Facts, 1988 Edition.* Chicago: National Safety Council, 1988.

TROST, CATHY. "Occupational Hazard: A Much Maligned OSHA Confronts Rising Demands with a Reduced Budget," *The Wall Street Journal,* April 22, 1988, pp. 25R–26R.

WILLIAMS, C. ARTHUR, JR., JOHN G. TURNBULL, AND EARL F. CHEIT. *Economic and Social Security,* 5th ed., Chap. 6, pp. 189–192, and Chap. 7. New York: John Wiley, 1982.

WORRALL, JOHN D. *Safety and the Work Force: Incentives and Disincentives in Workers' Compensation.* New York State School of Industrial and Labor Relations, Cornell University, Ithaca, N.Y.: ILR Press, 1983.

———— AND DAVID APPEL, EDS. *Workers' Compensation Benefits: Adequacy, Equity & Efficiency,* Chaps. 2 and 5. New York State School of Industrial and Labor Relations, Cornell University, Ithaca, N.Y.: ILR Press, 1985.

---

[19]Cathy Trost,"Occupational Hazard: A Much-Maligned OSHA Confronts Rising Demands with a Reduced Budget," *The Wall Street Journal,* April 22, 1988, pp. 25R–26R.

WORKERS' COMPENSATION

Workers' compensation laws provide cash benefits, medical care, and rehabilitation services to workers who are disabled from work-related accidents or occupational disease and death benefits to the survivors of workers killed on the job. Workers' compensation laws exist in all states, the District of Columbia, American Samoa, Guam, Puerto Rico, and the U.S. Virgin Islands. Two federal workers' compensation laws also are in operation. The various workers' compensation laws differ widely with respect to coverage, adequacy of benefits, rehabilitation services, administration, and other provisions.

In this chapter, we shall analyze the various state workers' compensation laws, considering in particular the following areas: (1) development of state workers' compensation laws, (2) objectives and theory underlying them, (3) statutory provisions, (4) problems and issues in workers' compensation laws, and (5) recommendations for improvement.

DEVELOPMENT OF WORKERS' COMPENSATION

Workers' compensation was the first form of social insurance to develop in the United States. Its development can be conveniently analyzed in three stages: (1) the common law of industrial accidents, (2) the enactment of employer liability laws, and (3) the emergence of workers' compensation legislation.

Common Law of Industrial Accidents

The common law of industrial accidents was the first stage in the development of workers' compensation in the United States; its application dates back to 1837. Under the common law, workers injured on the job had to sue their employers and prove negligence before they could collect damages. The employer was permitted to use three common law defenses to block the worker's suit. They included the following:

- Under the *contributory negligence doctrine*, injured workers could not collect damages if they contributed in any way to their injuries.
- Under the *fellow servant doctrine*, an injured worker could not collect if the injury resulted from the negligence of a fellow worker.
- Under the *assumption-of-risk doctrine*, the injured worker could not collect if he or she had advance knowledge of the dangers inherent in a particular occupation.

As a result of these harsh defenses, relatively few disabled workers collected damages for their injuries. Lawsuits were expensive; the damage awards were small; legal fees had to be paid out of these small awards; and there was considerable uncertainty regarding the outcome of the lawsuit. The disabled worker had two major problems to solve: the loss of income from the disabling accident and the payment of medical expenses. Under the common law, these problems were largely unsolved, resulting in great economic insecurity and financial hardship to the disabled workers.

Enactment of Employer Liability Laws

Because of the deficiencies in the common law, most states enacted employer liability laws between 1885 and 1910.[1] These laws lessened the severity of the common law defenses and improved the legal position of the injured workers. For example, three states substituted the less severe doctrine of comparative negligence for contributory negligence; the fellow servant rule and assumption-of-risk doctrine were modified; employers and employees were denied the right to sign contracts that would relieve employers of legal liability for industrial accidents; and surviving dependents were allowed to sue in death cases.

Despite some improvements, however, the fundamental problems experienced by disabled workers still remained. The injured employee still had to sue the employer and prove negligence; the worker still had the problems of maintenance of income during disability and payment of medical expenses; and there were still long delays in securing court action, lawsuits were costly, and the legal outcome was uncertain.

---

[1] See C. Arthur Williams, Jr., *Insurance Arrangements under Workmen's Compensation*, U.S. Department of Labor, Wage and Labor Standards Administration, Bureau of Labor Standards, Bulletin No. 317 (Washington, D.C.: U.S. Government Printing Office, 1969), pp. 1–8.

Emergence of Workers' Compensation

The Industrial Revolution, which changed the United States from an agricultural to an industrial economy, caused a great increase in the number of workers who were killed or disabled in job-related accidents. Because of limitations on both the common law and the employer liability statutes, the states began to consider workers' compensation legislation as a solution to the growing problem of work-related accidents.

Workers' compensation laws existed in Europe in the 1880s, and by 1903, most European countries had enacted some type of legislation. But workers' compensation was slower to develop in the United States. Maryland passed such a law in 1902, but it was limited in application and was subsequently declared unconstitutional. The stimulus for enactment of state workers' compensation laws started in 1908, when the federal government passed a law covering certain federal employees, and by 1911, 10 states had passed workers' compensation laws. By 1920, all but six states had enacted such laws. Workers' compensation programs exist in all states today.

Workers' compensation is based on the fundamental principle of liability without fault. *The employer is held absolutely liable for the occupational injuries suffered by the workers, regardless of who is at fault.* The injured worker is compensated for his or her injuries according to a schedule of benefits established by law and does not have to sue the employer to collect benefits. The laws provide for the prompt payment of benefits to injured workers regardless of fault and with a minimum of legal formality.

OBJECTIVES OF WORKERS' COMPENSATION

Workers' compensation laws have five basic objectives: (1) broad coverage of employees for occupational injury and disease, (2) substantial protection against the loss of income, (3) sufficient medical care and rehabilitation services, (4) encouragement of safety, and (5) an effective delivery system for benefits and services.[2]

Broad Coverage for Occupational Injury and Disease

One basic objective of a modern workers' compensation law is to provide broad coverage of employees for occupational injury and disease. That is, the laws should cover most employees for all work-related injuries and occupational diseases.

Several reasons are often given to justify the exclusion of certain groups,

---

[2]National Commission on State Workmen's Compensation Laws, *The Report of the National Commission on State Workmen's Compensation Laws* (Washington, D.C.: U.S. Government Printing Office, 1972), pp. 35–40.

but many of these arguments break down after careful analysis. First, it is argued that some firms should be excluded because they are small, or have poor safety records, or are reluctant to bear the cost of workers' compensation benefits. However, the states have extended their workers' compensation laws to cover most firms without undue financial distress. And if the cost of covering certain excluded groups is high, then the disabled workers and society in general are bearing the costs of occupational injuries to these groups in the form of poverty or welfare payments. These costs should be charged to the firms and not to society.

Second, certain groups, such as household workers, are excluded because they lack political influence. This, of course, is very poor justification for their exclusion from a modern workers' compensation program. In addition, certain groups were formerly excluded because of the constitutional requirement of due process, which required some states to enact elective laws. The question of due process, however, has limited relevance for modern workers' compensation programs.

Third, some groups are excluded because of difficulties in administration. For example, certain employers, such as homeowners, who employ casual labor are frequently excluded, as are small farmers, because of the substantial administrative burdens and difficulty in informing these groups about the law.

Finally, it is argued that, because of the principle of the freedom to bargain, employers and employees should negotiate to determine how much protection against work-related accidents is desired, and thus to what extent the workers should be covered under workers' compensation. But many workers are not unionized and lack equal bargaining power with their employers, and few workers are in a position to determine accurately the probability of an occupational injury and the resulting economic loss. A mandatory workers' compensation law can protect these workers from possible poverty and destitution.

Substantial Protection against Loss of Income

The second basic objective of workers' compensation laws is that the benefits should replace a substantial proportion of the disabled worker's lost earnings. The measure of a worker's economic loss is the lifetime reduction in remuneration because of occupational injury or disease. Gross remuneration consists of basic wages and salaries, irregular wage payments, pay for leave time, and employer contributions for fringe benefits and Social Security benefits. *The measure of loss, however, is the difference in net remuneration before and after the work-related disability.* Net remuneration reflects taxes, job-related expenses, fringe benefits that lapse, and uncompensated expenses that result from the disability. This concept can be illustrated by Figure 12-1, which indicates the elements of gross and net remuneration before and after the disability.

The view that workers' compensation should restore a large proportion of the disabled worker's lost remuneration can be justified by two major considerations. First, workers' compensation is social insurance, not public assistance.

	BEFORE IMPAIRMENT		AFTER IMPAIRMENT
	Basic wages and salaries		Basic wages and salaries
+	Irregular wage payments	+	Irregular wage payments
+	Pay for leave time	+	Pay for leave time
+	Employer contributions for supplements	+	Employer contributions for supplements
=	*Total remuneration*	=	*Total remuneration*
−	Taxes	−	Taxes
−	Work-related expenses	−	Work-related expenses
		−	Expenses caused by injury or disease
=	*Net remuneration*	=	*Net remuneration*

FIGURE 12-1   Elements of Gross and Net Remuneration before and after the Disability
Source: National Commission on State Workmen's Compensation Laws, *Report*, p. 37.

Public assistance programs provide benefits based on a person's demonstrated need. Workers' compensation benefits, however, should be closely related to the worker's loss of present and future income and so should be considerably higher than a subsistence level of income. Second, in exchange for the workers' compensation benefits, disabled workers renounce their right to seek redress for economic damages and pain and suffering under the common law. Other social insurance programs, including Social Security and unemployment insurance, do not require the surrender of a valuable legal right in exchange for benefits.

As a practical matter, however, both minimum and maximum weekly cash payments must be established. A minimum benefit is necessary to keep the disabled worker off welfare; a maximum amount must be set because highly paid workers are in a position to provide for their own disability income insurance if the workers' compensation benefits are inadequate. A maximum limit is also necessary to constrain labor supply disincentives to work. Finally, some argue that a maximum limit on benefits is necessary to reduce employer costs; but this argument unfairly calls upon disabled workers who are highly paid to bear a higher proportion of their own lost remuneration.[3]

Sufficient Medical Care and Rehabilitation Services

Workers' compensation also has the objective of providing sufficient medical care and rehabilitation services to injured workers. The laws require the employer to pay medical, hospital, and surgical expenses, and other medical bills relating to the disability.

Vocational counseling, guidance, retraining, and other rehabilitation

---

[3]National Commission on State Workmen's Compensation Laws, *Report*, p. 37.

services are also provided to restore the injured worker to gainful employment. Disabled workers who can be returned to productive jobs can experience a feeling of well-being and worth as a result; and adequate and prompt rehabilitation services can reduce workers' compensation costs.

Encouragement of Safety

Workers' compensation programs also encourage safety and the development of sound safety programs. Experience rating is used to encourage firms to be safety-conscious and to make a determined effort to reduce industrial accidents, since firms with superior accident records pay relatively lower workers' compensation premiums. The end result is often an improvement in the competitive position of firms and industries with superior safety records. The laws allocate the costs of industrial accidents and occupational disease among those firms and industries responsible for them, so a firm or industry with a poor safety record may have to increase its prices, thereby losing some customers to other firms with lower rates of injury and disease. An individual firm with a poor safety record will generally have higher costs and lower profits, which weaken its competitive position.

Effective Delivery System

Finally, workers' compensation programs have the objective of providing an effective delivery system, by which the benefits and services are provided comprehensively and efficiently.

Comprehensive performance means that workers' compensation personnel should exist in sufficient numbers and quality to carry out the objectives of the program. High-quality performance is expected of employers, physicians, state courts, and workers' compensation insurers and agencies.

Efficient performance means that the services necessary to restore an injured worker are provided promptly, simply, and economically. Efficiency can be judged by comparing the workers' compensation program with similar activities outside the system.

THEORIES OF WORKERS' COMPENSATION

Several legal and economic theories are used to justify the existence of workers' compensation laws and the liability-without-fault principle on which the system is based.[4]

---

[4]Herman Miles Somers and Anne Ramsay Somers, *Workmen's Compensation* (New York: John Wiley, 1954), pp. 28–29.

Occupational Risk Theory

The occupational risk theory is based on the premise that each industry should bear the costs of its own occupational disabilities as a cost of production and that the costs of work-related injuries or disease should therefore be reflected in higher product prices.

The occupational risk theory is defective in several respects. First, it suggests that the workers do not bear any of the costs of industrial accidents. This is not correct. Since a workers' compensation insurance premium is based on the firm's payroll, its economic effects may be similar to those of a payroll tax; and research studies suggest that, in the long run, most payroll taxes are borne by labor.[5] To the extent that business firms view a workers' compensation premium as part of the total wage bill, the costs of industrial accidents, as reflected in the premiums paid, may be shifted backward to the workers in the form of lower wage increases.

Second, the occupational risk theory assumes that accident costs are shifted forward in the form of higher product prices. This might be difficult for a firm with a poor accident record if it is part of an industry where there is vigorous price competition, and the demand for the firm's product is elastic. Under these conditions, some accident costs may indeed be shifted backward to labor.

Finally, the typical worker bears a substantial proportion of the costs associated with an injury because of a waiting period, incomplete restoration of the total economic loss, and often inadequate rehabilitation services. These points are developed more fully later in the chapter.

Least Social Cost Theory

The least social cost theory is based on the concept that workers' compensation laws reduce economic losses from industrial accidents to a minimum. Firms have an incentive to reduce accidents because of the experience-rating provisions in the laws and because the uninsured costs often equal or exceed the insured costs of accidents.

Social Compromise Theory

The social compromise theory states that workers' compensation represents a balanced set of sacrifices and gains for both employees and employers. The injured workers are willing to exchange the right to a jury trial in a lawsuit and a

---

[5]For example, see Congress of the United States, Congressional Budget Office, *The Changing Distribution of Federal Taxes: 1975–1990* (Washington, D.C.: Congressional Budget Office, 1987), pp. 20–23. See also John A. Brittain, "The Incidence of Social Security Payroll Taxes," *The American Economic Review,* Vol. 59, No. 1 (March 1971), pp. 110–125.

potentially larger award for a smaller but certain disability benefit. The firms are willing to pay some claims where liability may not exist, but can escape expensive litigation and the payment of a potentially higher judgment if the injured employee won the suit.

STATE WORKERS' COMPENSATION LAWS

Workers' compensation provisions vary widely among the states. The variations are in the type of law, compliance with the law, covered occupations, eligibility requirements, types of benefits, second-injury funds, financing, and administration.[6]

Type of Law

Workers' compensation laws are either compulsory or elective. Under a compulsory law, each employer within its scope must comply with the law by providing the specified benefits. The law is also compulsory for employees.

Three states (New Jersey, South Carolina, and Texas) have elective laws, whereby the employer can either elect or reject the state plan. If the employer rejects the act and the injured worker sues for damages based on the employer's negligence, the employer is deprived of the three common law defenses of contributory negligence, fellow servant rule, and assumption of risk. Although most firms elect workers' compensation coverage, some do not, so some disabled employees are unable to collect benefits unless they sue for damages. Elective laws also permit the firms' employees to reject coverage, but they seldom do. Under most elective laws, it is presumed that both the employer and the employees elect coverage, unless a specific notice of rejection is filed prior to a loss.

Compliance with the Law

Employers can comply with the law by purchasing a workers' compensation policy, by self-insuring, or by obtaining protection from a monopoly or competitive state fund.

Most firms purchase a policy from a private insurer. The policy guarantees payment of the benefits that the employer is legally obligated to pay to the disabled workers. Self-insurance is permitted in 47 states. In addition, 28 states permit group self-insurance for smaller employers who collectively pool their workers' compensation loss exposures. However, the laws require firms to meet certain requirements before they can self-insure.

In eight jurisdictions, employers generally must insure in a monopoly

---

[6]For a detailed description of current state workers' compensation laws, see Chamber of Commerce of the United States, *Analysis of Workers' Compensation Laws, 1989 Edition* (Washington, D.C.: Chamber of Commerce of the United States, 1989).

state fund.[7] Monopoly state funds have been established for the following reasons: (1) workers' compensation is social insurance and private companies should not profit from the business, (2) monopoly state funds should have reduced expenses because of economies of scale and no sales effort, and (3) monopoly state funds have greater concern for the welfare of injured workers.

Thirteen states permit employers to purchase insurance from either private insurers or competitive state funds.[8] Competitive funds are established for the following reasons: (1) the fund provides a useful standard for measuring the performance of private insurers, (2) the states want to make certain that all employers can obtain the necessary protection, and (3) a competitive fund operates more efficiently if it faces competition from private insurers.[9]

Employers who do not meet the insurance requirements are subject to fines, imprisonment, or both. Also, some states enjoin the employer from doing business in the state until the insurance requirements are fulfilled.

Covered Occupations

In 1987, workers' compensation laws covered approximately 88.4 million workers or 87 percent of all wage and salary workers.[10] However, there is wide variation in coverage among the individual states. In 1984, actual coverage as a percentage of potential coverage ranged from a high of 100 percent in five jurisdictions (District of Columbia, Hawaii, Maine, Vermont, Wisconsin) to a low of 67 percent in Texas.[11]

Certain occupations are excluded or coverage is less than complete. The occupational groups most likely to be excluded from full workers' compensation coverage are farm workers, domestic employees, and casual employees. Farm workers are covered on the same basis as other employees in only 12 states.[12] In the other states, coverage for farm employees is usually excluded or restricted. In addition, most jurisdictions cover employees of state or local government on a compulsory basis. However, some states exclude specific groups (such as elected or appointed officials).

Some states also exempt employees of a nonprofit educational, charitable, or religious organization. Finally, in 14 jurisdictions, small firms with fewer than a specified number of employees (typically three to five) also are exempt

---

[7]Monopoly state funds exist in Nevada, North Dakota, Ohio, Washington, West Virginia, Wyoming, Puerto Rico, and the Virgin Islands.

[8]Competitive state funds exist in Arizona, California, Colorado, Idaho, Maryland, Michigan, Minnesota, Montana, New York, Oklahoma, Oregon, Pennsylvania, and Utah.

[9]Williams, *Insurance Arrangements*, pp. 135–136, 151–162.

[10]William J. Nelson, Jr. "Workers' Compensation: Coverage, Benefits, and Costs, 1987," *Social Security Bulletin*, Vol. 53, No. 4 (April 1990), pp. 3–4.

[11]John F. Burton, Jr., "National and State Workers' Compensation Coverage," *John Burton's Workers' Compensation Monitor*, Vol. 1, No. 8 (September 1988), Figure B, p. 3.

[12]William J. Nelson, Jr., "Workers' Compensation: 1980–84 Benchmark Revisions," *Social Security Bulletin*, Vol. 51, No. 7 (July 1988), p. 6.

from coverage. Railroad workers in interstate commerce and seamen in the U.S. merchant marine also are not covered by workers' compensation laws but instead are allowed to sue for damages under the Federal Employers' Liability Act; such employers are barred from using the common law defenses of contributory negligence, fellow servant rule, and assumption of risk.

Eligibility Requirements

Two major eligibility requirements must be met to receive workers' compensation benefits. First, the injured worker must work in a covered occupation. Second, the worker must have a job-related accident or disease. *This means that the injury or disease must arise out of and in the course of employment.* The courts have gradually broadened the meaning of this term over time. The following situations are usually covered under a typical workers' compensation law:

1. The employee is injured while performing specified duties at a specified location.
2. An employee who travels is injured while engaging in activities that benefit the employer.
3. The employee has a heart attack while lifting some heavy boxes.
4. The employee is on the premises and is injured while going to the work area.

Certain injuries, however, generally are not compensable under a workers' compensation law. An employee who is injured in an automobile accident going to or from work generally is not covered. Injury due to employee intoxication is usually not compensable, and self-inflicted injuries are also excluded.

The states also provide coverage of occupational disease. Most states earlier covered only certain occupational diseases. However, because of the growing number of chemicals and other substances that can cause occupational disease, it is impractical for the states to list each covered disease. Instead, a typical workers' compensation law today provides coverage for all occupational diseases.

Types of Benefits

Workers' compensation laws provide four principal benefits: (1) medical care, (2) disability income, (3) death benefits, and (4) rehabilitation services.

Medical Care. Medical care usually is covered in full without any dollar or time limits on the amount paid. Medical costs now account for 40 percent of workers' compensation benefits.[13]

---

[13]Nancy M. Schroeder, "Medical Cost Escalation Presents Major Challenge for Workers' Compensation System," *Workers' Compensation Report,* Alliance of American Insurers, Vol. 1, No. 2 (June 1989), p. 2.

Disability Income. Disability income benefits are payable after the disabled worker satisfies a waiting period that usually ranges from three to seven days. If the worker is still disabled after a certain number of days or weeks, most states pay benefits retroactively to the date of injury.

The weekly benefit amount is based on a percentage of the workers' average weekly wage, typically 66⅔ percent, and the degree of disability. Most states have minimum and maximum dollar limits on the weekly benefits. In addition, in most jurisdictions, the maximum weekly benefit is automatically adjusted each year based on changes in the state's average weekly wage. In 40 states, the maximum weekly cash benefit for temporary total disability cases now equals or exceeds 66⅔ percent of the statewide average weekly wage; of these states, 29 now pay a maximum weekly benefit of 100 percent or more of the statewide weekly wage.[14]

Four classifications of disability are generally used to determine the weekly benefit amount: (1) temporary total, (2) permanent total, (3) temporary partial, and (4) permanent partial.

1. TEMPORARY TOTAL. Most weekly disability income benefits are paid for temporary total disability. The employee is totally disabled but is expected to recover fully and return to work. As of January 1, 1989, maximum weekly temporary total disability benefits for states ranged from a high of $700 weekly in Alaska to a low of $198 in Mississippi.

2. PERMANENT TOTAL. Permanent total disability means that the employee is permanently and totally disabled and is unable to work in gainful employment. Most states pay lifetime benefits if the worker is permanently and totally disabled. As of January 1, 1989, maximum weekly permanent total disability benefits for the states ranged from a high of $700 in Alaska to a low of $198 in Mississippi.

3. TEMPORARY PARTIAL. Temporary partial disability means that the disabled worker has returned to work but is earning less than before and still has not reached maximum recovery. The weekly benefit is a percentage of the difference in earned wages before and after the injury (typically 66⅔ percent) up to the weekly maximum.

4. PERMANENT PARTIAL. Permanent partial disability means that the employee has a permanent impairment but is not completely disabled. An example is an employee who loses one eye in a job-related accident.

Permanent partial disability cases are of two types—scheduled and nonscheduled (or wage-loss). *Scheduled injuries are listed in the law and include the loss of an eye, arm, leg, hand, finger, or other member of the body.* In most states, the amount paid for a scheduled injury is determined by multiplying a certain number of weeks (based on the bodily member involved) by the weekly disability income benefit. For example, a worker in Nebraska who loses a hand can receive a

---

[14]U.S. Chamber of Commerce, *1989 Analysis of Workers' Compensation Laws*, p. viii.

maximum benefit of $42,875. Also, in most states the amount paid for a scheduled injury is in addition to the benefits paid during the healing period or while the worker is totally disabled.

Nonscheduled disabilities are of a more general nature and involve the loss of earning power to the body as a whole, such as a back or head injury that makes working difficult. The benefit paid for a nonscheduled injury generally is based on a wage-loss replacement percentage. The percentage is applied to the difference in earnings before and after the injury multiplied by a certain number of weeks. In some states, nonscheduled permanent partial disability benefits are based on a percentage of a total disability case.

Death Benefits. Death benefits are also payable if the worker is killed on the job. Two types of benefits are paid. First, a burial allowance is paid, ranging from $600 to $5,370. Second, cash income payments can be paid to eligible surviving dependents. A weekly benefit based on a proportion of the deceased worker's wages (typically $66\frac{2}{3}$ percent) is usually paid to a surviving spouse for life or until she or he remarries. Upon marriage, the widow or widower usually receives a lump-sum benefit, such as one or two years of payments. Benefits also can be paid to the children until age 16, 18, or later if the children are incapacitated. Many states, however, have amount or time limits on the maximum amount that can be paid.

Rehabilitation Services. Rehabilitation services are also available in all states to disabled workers to restore them to productive employment. In addition to weekly disability benefits, workers who are being rehabilitated are compensated for board, lodging, travel, books, and equipment. Training allowances are also paid in some states.

Second-Injury Funds

All states have second-injury funds. *The purpose is to encourage employers to hire handicapped workers.* If a second-injury fund did not exist, employers would be reluctant to hire handicapped workers because of the higher benefits that might have to be paid if a second injury occurs.

For example, assume that a worker with a preexisting injury is injured in a work-related accident. The second injury when combined with the first injury produces a disability greater than that caused by the second injury alone. Thus, the amount of workers' compensation benefits that must be paid is higher than if only the second injury had occurred. *The employer pays only for the disability caused by the second injury, and the second-injury fund pays for the remainder of the benefit award.*

As noted earlier, the fundamental purpose of second-injury funds is to encourage employers to hire handicapped workers. However, many employers are unaware of the existence of second-injury funds and how they operate and function. Thus, they may be reluctant to hire severely handicapped workers because of the possible adverse effect on their workers' compensation premiums.

Financing

Workers' compensation benefits are financed by employer premiums or by self-insurance payments based on the theory that the costs of job-related accidents or disease are part of the cost of production. However, a few states also have provisions for nominal contributions by covered employees for hospital and medical benefits.

The actual workers' compensation premium paid by employers is based on numerous factors, including the size of payroll, industry, occupation of covered employees, and industrial operations performed. Smaller firms are class rated. *Class rating means all employers in the same class pay the same workers' compensation rate.* Larger firms, whose annual workers' compensation premiums are at least $750, are subject to experience rating. *Experience rating means the class-rated premium is adjusted upward or downward depending on the employer's loss of experience and the statistical reliability of that experience.* Average workers' compensation rates at current rate levels in 37 states were $2.95 per $100 of covered payroll in October 1989.[15]

The purpose of experience rating is to encourage loss prevention by providing employers with a financial incentive to reduce job-related accidents or disease.

Finally, the costs incurred by the states in administering the workers' compensation laws and supervising insurance carriers, self-insurers, and the state funds are financed by legislative appropriations or by special assessments on insurance carriers and self-insurers.

Administration

Most states use a workers' compensation board or commission to administer workers' compensation claims. The law is administered either by an independent workers' compensation agency or by the same agency that administers the state's labor law. A few states use the courts to administer the claims. The court must either approve the settlement or, if the parties disagree, resolve the dispute.

To receive workers' compensation benefits, the injured worker must file a claim for benefits with the appropriate workers' compensation agency and give proper notice to the employer or insurer. Three principal methods are used to settle noncontested claims: (1) agreement, (2) direct-settlement, and (3) hearing.

Most states use the *agreement method* by which the injured worker and

---

[15]Data are from the Research Division, National Council on Compensation Insurance, New York, N.Y.

employer or insurer agree upon a settlement before the claim is paid. Some states use the *direct-settlement* system by which the employer or insurer pays benefits immediately to the injured worker upon notice of disability. Finally, under the *hearing method,* an industrial commission or board hears the case and must approve it before the claim is paid.

PROBLEMS AND ISSUES IN WORKERS' COMPENSATION

In 1972, the National Commission on State Workmen's Compensation Laws published a report highly critical of state programs. Since that time, state workers' compensation programs have been substantially improved. Weekly cash benefits have been substantially increased; medical care is covered in full; most states do not have numerical exemptions or elective laws; and restrictions on occupational disease are rapidly disappearing. Despite this progress, several important problems and issues are still present. The most important issues center on the following areas: (1) incomplete coverage, (2) cost of workers' compensation, (3) compensation for occupational disease, (4) permanent partial disability benefits, (5) inadequate rehabilitation, (6) increase in litigation, (7) administrative defects, (8) deregulation of workers' compensation rates, (9) increase in the residual market, and (10) impact of workers' compensation on safety.

Incomplete Coverage

State workers' compensation laws do not cover all workers. Because of elective laws, numerical exemptions, and exclusions or less than complete coverage of certain occupations, such as agricultural, domestic, and casual work, millions of workers have no protection under workers' compensation laws. Thirteen percent of all wage and salary workers were not covered by workers' compensation laws in 1987. This figure has remained roughly constant since 1980. Since a fundamental principle of social insurance is to provide income protection to all workers, the gap in coverage represents a serious deficiency.

Three states still retain their elective laws. However, it is difficult to justify elective laws. Many states enacted them because they feared that the courts would declare a compulsory law unconstitutional; but since the constitutionality of workers' compensation has been settled by the courts, this argument is no longer valid. However, in those states with elective laws, most employers elect workers' compensation benefits for their employees. If they fail to provide coverage, they lose the common law defenses in an employee tort action, and the employer may have to pay very large damages. In effect, the threat of a lawsuit for damages makes the workers' compensation law compulsory for most employers, even in states with elective laws.

In addition, numerical exemptions are seldom justified. Smaller firms generally lack the financial resources to protect injured workers unless the law compels them to carry workers' compensation insurance. Also, some uncovered workers cannot afford to initiate a successful damage suit against their employers for their injuries, so they may be exposed to serious economic insecurity if they are denied benefits because of numerical exemptions.

The exclusion of certain occupations represents another serious gap in coverage. Farm employment, for instance, which is one of the most hazardous occupations, is excluded from coverage in many states, or less than complete protection is provided. In addition to dangerous machinery, the workers are also exposed to pesticides, herbicides, fungicides, and defoliants. The need for protection is even greater in view of the risk of occupational disease from these chemicals.

Cost of Workers' Compensation

Workers' compensation costs have increased rapidly over time. Workers' compensation costs paid by employers as a percentage of covered payroll increased from 1.11 percent in 1970 to 2.06 percent in 1987 (see Table 12-1). The increase in costs was particularly sharp from 1970 through 1980. The rapid increase in cost during that period can be explained by (1) the substantial improvement in coverage and benefit levels under state workers' compensation laws, (2) the rapid increase in inflation that resulted in both higher wage increases and higher medical costs, and (3) the cost impact of the federal black lung program introduced in 1970.

Workers' compensation costs declined modestly in 1981–1984 (see Figure 12-2). However, since that time, workers' compensation costs have increased. One possible explanation for the relative decline in costs during the early 1980s is that workers' compensation insurers competed aggressively for business during that period because of historically high interest rates. Insurers attempted to increase their short-term cash flow that could be invested at high interest rates. However, when interest rates declined sharply in the mid-1980s, insurers could no longer cover their underwriting losses by increased interest from cash flow; thus, workers' compensation premiums had to be increased and workers' compensation costs also increased.[16] In addition, the recent increase in costs also reflects increases in average wages and medical costs and in the number of employed workers.[17]

Higher workers' compensation costs are harmful to employers since labor costs are increased; inflationary pressures in the economy may also increase; and smaller financially weak firms are faced with a heavier financial burden.

Escalation of Medical Costs. Another part of the cost problem is that medical costs have escalated in recent years. As we noted earlier, medical costs have increased to 40 percent of workers' compensation benefits and are the

---

[16]John F. Burton, Jr., "Benefits, Costs, and Coverage Continue to Increase," *John Burton's Workers' Compensation Monitor*, Vol. 1, No. 4 (April 1988), p. 2.

[17]Nelson, Jr., "Workers' Compensation: Coverage, Benefits, and Costs, 1987," p. 3.

TABLE 12-1 Workers' Compensation Benefits and Costs as Percentages of Covered Payroll

YEAR	BENEFITS PAID BY EMPLOYERS AS PERCENT OF COVERED PAYROLL	COST OF PROGRAM PAID BY EMPLOYERS AS PERCENTAGE OF PAYROLL	RATIO OF BENEFITS TO COSTS
1970	0.66	1.11	0.59
1971	0.67	1.11	0.60
1972	0.68	1.14	0.60
1973	0.70	1.17	0.60
1974	0.75	1.24	0.60
1975	0.83	1.32	0.63
1976	0.87	1.49	0.58
1977	0.92	1.71	0.54
1978	0.94	1.86	0.51
1979	1.01	1.95	0.52
1980	1.07	1.96	0.55
1981	1.08	1.85	0.58
1982	1.16	1.75	0.66
1983	1.17	1.67	0.70
1984	1.21	1.66	0.73
1985	1.30	1.80	0.72
1986	1.37	1.97	0.70
1987	1.43	2.06	0.69

Source: *John Burton's Workers' Compensation Monitor,* Vol. 3, No. 2 (March/April 1990), Table 1, p. 2.

largest single factor for rate increases in many states. Some factors contributing to the escalation of medical costs include technological advances, patient expectations regarding the results of medical care, and medical malpractice lawsuits that cause physicians to practice defensive medicine. In addition, injured claimants are not discouraged from seeking unnecessary medical care because there are no deductibles, coinsurance, or limits on care.[18] Finally, some physicians who have been financially squeezed because of increased restrictions on basic medical expense plans are providing extra and unnecessary medical care to workers' compensation patients.[19] As a result, medical costs have escalated in recent years.

Wide Variation in State Costs. Another important cost issue is the wide variation in state workers' compensation costs. One study of adjusted manual rates for 44 classes of employers in 11 states showed that average cost per $100 of payroll ranged from $0.554 in Indiana to $2.832 in California.[20] The wide

---

[18]Schroeder, "Medical Cost Escalation Presents Major Challenge for Workers' Compensation System," p. 2.

[19]James R. Schiffman, "Firms Try to Trim Fat in Workers' Comp Bills," *The Wall Street Journal,* June 30, 1989, p. B1.

[20]John F. Burton, Jr., and Timothy P. Schmidle, "Interstate Variations in Workers' Compensation Costs," *John Burton's Workers' Compensation Monitor,* Vol. 2, No. 1 (January 1989), Table 1, p. 2.

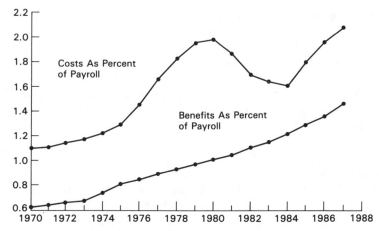

FIGURE 12-2 Costs and Benefits of Workers' Compensation, 1970–1987

Source: *John Burton's Workers' Compensation Monitor,* Vol 3, No. 2 (March/April), Figure A, p. 1.

variation in cost can be partly explained by the differences in benefit levels and industrial mix among the states. States with high costs generally pay relatively higher workers' compensation benefits and are highly industrialized.

The wide interstate variation in cost is an important issue because of the fear by some state legislators and government officials that employers in a high-cost state may move to a different state with lower costs and a more favorable business climate. Also, new employers may be unwilling to locate in a high-cost state. Thus, a high-cost state may find itself at a competitive disadvantage when compared with other states with lower costs. Do interstate workers' compensation cost differences influence employers in plant location? The general consensus among workers' compensation experts is that workers' compensation costs *alone* are not significant enough to play an important role in location decisions since they are less than 2 percent of payroll for many employers. However, when employers decide to move to another state, they will consider all important cost factors, such as state taxes, the quality of labor, business climate, as well as workers' compensation costs. Thus, when *combined with other cost factors,* employers will take workers' compensation costs into account in deciding where to locate.[21]

Compensation for Occupational Disease

One of the most critical problems at the present time is the compensation of disabled workers with an occupational disease. We noted earlier in Chapter 11 that thousands of workers die or become disabled each year because of the

[21]C. Arthur Williams, Jr., John G. Turnbull, and Earl F. Cheit, *Economic and Social Security,* 5th ed. (New York: John Wiley & Sons, 1982), p. 233.

effects of asbestos, cotton dust, benzene, vinyl chloride, radiation, and exposure from hazardous waste and other dangerous chemicals and substances. In addition, some workers are not even aware that they have been exposed nor do they know what can be done to minimize damage from the exposure.

The problem of compensating disabled workers with an occupational disease is aggravated by several additional factors: (1) long latency period, (2) problem of proving causality, and (3) barriers to recovery under workers' compensation.

Long Latency Period. The basic problem in occupational disease is the long latency period. It may take years for an occupational disease to disable a worker because of an earlier exposure to some dangerous chemical or substance. For example, in the case of workers who become disabled as a result of an earlier exposure to asbestos fibers, the period between the emergence of the disease or disabling symptoms can be as long as 50 years.

Problem of Proving Causality. Workers' compensation covers only a job-related accident or disease. There is also the problem of establishing causality or showing that the occupational disease is due to a unique job-related cause or causes. However, a disease can have several causes, both occupational and non-occupational in nature. For example, a worker who smokes and is also exposed to ionizing radiation on the job may develop lung cancer. Since both smoking and radiation can cause cancer, neither one can be considered a unique cause.

Barriers to Recovery under Workers' Compensation. In addition, there are barriers to recovery for occupational disease under some state workers' compensation laws.[22] First, the workers' compensation law may require that a claim be filed within a certain time period after the last work place exposure to the source of the disease. Second, the claim may be denied unless the worker has been employed and exposed to the hazard for a certain minimum period of time. Third, the law may require that a claim must be filed within a relatively short time period subsequent to the development of the disease, even if the worker is not presently disabled by the disease or even aware of it. In addition, there is considerable controversy as to whether the benefits paid should be at the levels in effect at the time of the exposure or at the generally higher benefit levels when the disease is later discovered. Also, it may be difficult to determine when the disease is contracted in the worker's employment history and which employer is responsible for the payment of benefits. Finally, even if a state has no artificial barriers to recovery, the claimant still has the formidable problem of proving causality. Even if expert medical and legal advice is available, the outcome is often uncertain and slow.

---

[22] Peter S. Barth, "On Efforts to Reform Workers' Compensation for Occupational Diseases," in James Chelius, ed., *Current Issues in Workers' Compensation* (Kalamazoo, Mich.: W. E. Upjohn Institute for Employment Research, 1986), pp. 332–333. See also Leslie I. Boden, "Problems in Occupational Disease Compensation," in Chelius, *Current Issues in Workers' Compensation,* pp. 313–325.

Solutions to the Problem. Several solutions have been proposed for compensating workers with an occupational disease, especially an asbestos-related disease. They include the following:

1. AMENDING WORKERS' COMPENSATION LAWS. Workers' compensation laws should be amended to extend the time period for filing claims, pay compensation benefits based on current levels, and provide for a more clear-cut identification of the responsible employer.

2. ASBESTOS CLAIM FACILITY. In 1985, some 50 insurers and asbestos manufacturers created a nonprofit organization that would settle asbestos claims outside of court. However, because of serious disagreements among the members over settling claims, the Asbestos Facility was later dissolved. A new Center for Claims Resolution was then created to resolve asbestos claims. The intent was to settle meritorious cases outside of the courtroom. In April 1989, the center had about 56,000 pending claims, down from 61,000 when the center was first formed.[23]

3. SPECIAL OCCUPATIONAL DISEASE FUNDS. Special occupational disease funds have been established in at least seven jurisdictions. The special funds provide compensation to workers who are disabled by chronic disease resulting from employment, especially long-latency diseases where the responsible employer is difficult to locate or identify.[24]

Permanent Partial Disability Benefits

One of the most pressing problems in workers' compensation benefits is the payment of benefits for a permanent partial disability. There are two principal problems in the payment of permanent partial disability benefits. First, there are wide variations from state to state. Most workers' compensation laws contain schedules that indicate the amounts paid for specific impairments; but these schedules cover only a small proportion of medically identifiable impairments. Also, the benefits for the specific impairments vary widely, depending on the state in which the injury occurred. The following sampling shows the maximum amounts that can be paid for certain listed impairments in selected states as of January 1989.

	LOSS OF ARM AT SHOULDER	LOSS OF ONE FOOT	LOSS OF ONE EYE
Wisconsin	$62,500	$31,250	$34,375
Arkansas	32,930	20,542	16,465
North Dakota	18,750	9,000	9,000

[23]*National Underwriter,* Property and Casualty/Risk & Benefits Management ed., April 17, 1989, p. 26.

[24]Lloyd W. Larson and John F. Burton, Jr., "Special Funds in Workers' Compensation," in John D. Worrall and David Appel, eds., *Workers' Compensation Benefits: Adequacy, Equity & Efficiency* (New York

Other illustrations are possible, but these should suffice. What the preceding data show is that indemnification for an impairment varies widely among the states, depending on their statutes and the courts' interpretation.

The second problem is the need to control permanent partial disability costs. Permanent partial disability benefits are the most expensive part of total benefit costs. Permanent partial disability accounted only for about 23 percent of all compensable cases in 1982. However, nearly 70 percent of all disability benefits were paid to workers whose permanent disability was partial.[25] Permanent partial disability benefits historically have been paid to workers with functional impairments regardless of their effect on earning capacity. As a result, permanent partial disability benefits frequently are paid to workers whose employment capacity is not affected by their injuries and who experience no wage loss at all. Thus, although the injury may not have affected the worker's earning capacity, the impairment benefit is still paid.

To control permanent partial disability costs, Florida enacted into law in 1979 an innovative *wage-loss concept. With few exceptions, the wage-loss concept bases benefits on the wages actually lost because of the injury.* To determine the amount of lost wages, the worker's actual current earnings are subtracted from 85 percent of the impaired employee's average monthly wage before the injury. The difference is then multiplied by 95 percent, and the result is the amount actually paid. This can be illustrated in the following example:[26]

Preinjury wage: $1,000 × 85%	$850
Postinjury wage:	−500
	350
	×.95
Actual benefit paid:	$332.50

Florida's wage-loss law has both positive and negative features. On the positive side, workers' compensation costs have decreased. Although workers' compensation costs prior to 1979 were almost double the national average, adoption of the wage-loss concept resulted in costs that are only about 25 to 30 percent above the national average.[27] On the negative side, however, the wage-loss law has resulted in an increase in complex legal issues that are not easily resolved. For example, one complex issue is the determination of the amount of

State School of Industrial and Labor Relations, Cornell University, Ithaca, N.Y.: ILR Press, 1985), p. 121.

[25]Nelson, "Workers' Compensation: 1980–84 Benchmark Revisions," Table 4, p. 9.

[26]"Florida's Bold Experiment in Cutting Worker Compensation Costs," *Journal of American Insurance*, Vol. 58, No. 2 (Summer 1982), pp. 22–23.

[27]John F. Burton, Jr., "The Wage-Loss Approach: Lessons from Florida," *John Burton's Workers' Compensation Monitor*, Vol. 1, No. 5 (May 1988), p. 2.

wage-loss benefits when the employer alleges that the worker's actual earnings after the injury are less than the worker is capable of earning.[28]

Inadequate Rehabilitation

Rehabilitation of disabled workers is another important issue. From a social and economic viewpoint, it is more desirable to rehabilitate disabled workers and return them to productive employment rather than to pay them workers' compensation benefits. Society benefits from their skills and talents, and the rehabilitated workers acquire a sense of dignity by returning to the labor force. In addition, workers' compensation costs can be substantially reduced by rehabilitation. A disabled worker at home can easily collect workers' compensation benefits that exceed a quarter of a million dollars during his or her lifetime. However, the payoff to the firm or workers' compensation insurer can be substantial if the disabled worker can be successfully rehabilitated. For example, one private insurance rehabilitation firm found that every dollar spent on rehabilitation can save as much as $10 in claim payments when a disabled worker is reemployed.

Although rehabilitation of disabled workers is a major objective of workers' compensation, several obstacles hinder the effective rehabilitation of disabled workers in many states. First, some states do not have a separate rehabilitation division within the workers' compensation agency. The agency, as the first official authority to become aware of the worker's injury, is in a good position to promote rehabilitation. Unless rehabilitation starts immediately after an injury, maximum physical restoration of the worker may be impossible. Lack of a rehabilitation division within the workers' compensation agency can mean that some handicapped workers do not receive prompt medical, vocational, and rehabilitation services for full restoration.

Second, some states do not provide adequate maintenance benefits during rehabilitation. A severely disabled worker may find it financially impossible to undergo physical and vocational rehabilitation when additional funds are required. Even if full workers' compensation benefits are paid during rehabilitation, the additional costs of travel, tuition, equipment, and other expenses may discourage rehabilitation. Maintenance benefits are essential for encouraging prompt rehabilitation.

Third, only a few states require mandatory rehabilitation as part of the benefit package. For example, Georgia makes rehabilitation compulsory for both employees and employers. If injured workers refuse rehabilitation after it is

---

[28]The legal complexities surrounding this issue are discussed in considerable detail in Burton, "The Wage-Loss Approach: Lessons from Florida." For other approaches to the problem of permanent partial disability, see Jack E. Nicholson, "Workers' Compensation: Permanent Partial Disabilities and a Proposal for Reform," *Benefits Quarterly,* Vol. 2, No. 2 (Second Quarter 1986), pp. 16–25; and John F. Burton, Jr., "Compensation for Permanent Partial Disabilities," in John D. Worrall, ed., *Safety and the Work Force* (New York State School of Industrial and Labor Relations, Cornell University, Ithaca, N.Y.: ILR Press, 1983), pp. 18–60.

considered appropriate, their workers' compensation benefits can be legally suspended or reduced. Although compulsory rehabilitation by the state is repugnant to many Americans, mandatory rehabilitation can be justified based on the social and economic benefits from rehabilitation.

Finally, existing workers' compensation laws may discourage some seriously disabled workers from rehabilitation. In cases where the degree of disability is in dispute, some injured workers fear that undergoing rehabilitation would show that their injuries are less serious than they contend. As a result, rehabilitation is discouraged, since the workers fear the loss of cash benefits if the degree of disability is changed by successful rehabilitation.

Increase in Litigation

Although workers' compensation is designed to reduce litigation, workers' compensation lawsuits have increased in many states. For example, in 1982, 26,853 workers' compensation claims in Florida were litigated. The number of lawsuits litigated increased sharply to 42,243 in 1987.[29] In addition, the involvement of attorneys in workers' compensation claims in Florida has also increased substantially.[30] Other states have experienced a similar increase in workers' compensation claims that are litigated.

Several reasons explain the increase in litigation. First, injured workers are often dissatisfied with their awards and seek higher benefits, especially if the award is paid in a lump sum. The injured worker often can obtain higher benefits through litigation. Once the award is made, the claimant usually returns to work at the same or higher wage.

Second, in a typical state, attorney fees are fixed for each controversy, which encourages *multiple claims* by the same claimant and attorney. The following is an example of how the present workers' compensation system encourages multiple claims by the same claimant and attorney.

> On January 1, 1966, a worker in an East Coast state suffered a low back injury. He filed his compensation claim on March 31 but the State Industrial Accident Board did not act until May 1. The claimant received his first check on May 15. When his pain continued, he was awarded permanent total disability, entitling him to two-thirds of his average weekly wage for life, subject to a $75 weekly maximum at that time.
>
> In 1975, pushed by inflation, the claimant consulted an attorney, who knew he could get more for his client. But using a series of controversies, each requiring a hearing, the attorney won for the claimant multiple permanent partial disability awards, totaling $600 a week, all paid simultaneously. *And the attorney received a fee for each controversy.* [italics added][31]

[29]S. James Brainerd, "Workers' Compensation Reform in Florida," *John Burton's Workers' Compensation Monitor,* Vol. 2, No. 7 (September/October 1989), p. 10.

[30]Ibid.

[31]Insurance Company of North America, *Insurance Decisions: What Ails Workers' Compensation?,* p. 1.

Third, to hold down premiums for workers' compensation insurance, some firms resist the payment of workers' compensation claims. Injured workers must then sue to receive benefits. The result is an increase in litigated claims.

Finally, lawsuits have increased because of *erosion of the exclusive-remedy doctrine.* Under this doctrine, employers agree to pay workers' compensation benefits without regard to fault in return for tort immunity in the form of an exclusive remedy defense. The injured worker has the right to receive statutory workers' benefits without proving negligence but in return gives up the right to sue the employer.[32] In short, workers' compensation benefits should be the sole and exclusive remedy available to injured workers.

The exclusive-remedy doctrine, however, has been eroded by court decisions in recent years. The result is that injured workers often can receive both workers' compensation benefits and a tort damage award based on negligence. Injured workers have been able to sue for damages based on the following legal doctrines:

1. INTENTIONAL INJURY. *Injured workers may be able to sue for damages if the employer intentionally causes the injury.* For example, in one case the employer ignored repeated warnings from the employees about dangerous chemicals. As a result, the injured employees were allowed to bring a direct action for damages against the employer.[33]

2. DUAL CAPACITY DOCTRINE. *Under this doctrine, the injured worker can sue the employer if the injury arises out of a relationship other than the employer-employee relationship.*[34] For example, if the employer produces a product that injures the worker in the course of employment, the injured worker can collect workers' compensation benefits as an employee and may be able to sue for damages as a consumer or user of a defective product. For example, assume that an employee is mowing the grass around the plant and is using a lawn mower manufactured by the company. If the worker is injured because of a defective mower, he or she can receive workers' compensation benefits and may be able to initiate a products liability lawsuit as a consumer or user of a defective product.

3. THIRD-PARTY-OVER CASES. *A third-party-over case is a claim by an injured worker against a third party who in turn sues the employer on the grounds of either contributory negligence or indemnity.*[35] For example, assume that a company is installing a machine and removes a protective guard at the employer's request. Assume that a worker is injured while using the machine without the protective guard. The injured worker sues the company that installed the machine. The installation company then sues the employer on the basis of contributory negli-

---

[32]"Interpreting Business Insurance Contracts," *The Risk Report,* Vol. 8, No. 7 (March 1986), p. 5.
[33]*Blankenship v. Cincinnati Milacrom Chem., Inc.,* 69 Ohio St. 2d 608, 433 N.E.2d 572 (1982).
[34]"Interpreting Business Insurance Contracts," p. 6.
[35]Ibid., p. 7.

gence. The result, however, is that the injured worker can receive both workers' compensation benefits and a tort damage award if his or her lawsuit is successful.

Administrative Defects

Inadequate administration of state workers' compensation laws is another deficiency. Some states are lax in the investigation and enforcement of coverage, supervision of claims and adjudication of contested claims, promotion of safety programs, and statistical analysis of the efficiency of workers' compensation insurers and state agencies.

In addition, labor unions charge that many states show little administrative concern for injured workers, since workers are inadequately informed about their compensation rights. Workers often receive compensation advice only from company supervisors or claims representatives. Also, workers' compensation insurers perform most administrative functions relating to the law. The insurer receives the claim, accepts or denies it, controls the payments, and terminates the benefits, often without adequate supervision by the state workers' compensation agency.

Claims supervision in many states is also inadequate. In many cases, an injured worker agrees to a lump-sum settlement or compromises his or her rights to full medical care under a compromise-and-release settlement, because the case is inadequately supervised by the state workers' compensation agency. Attorneys favor lump-sum awards because they generally provide a larger fee with greater certainty; employers also tend to favor lump-sum settlements because they terminate liability and reduce claims for additional compensation for aggravation of the injury. But lump-sum settlements are inconsistent with the workers' compensation objective of restoring lost wages on a systematic basis. Lump-sum settlements should be either forbidden or else confined to those special situations where they are in the best interest of the disabled worker, and then only after the workers' compensation agency has carefully supervised and approved the settlement after consultation with the rehabilitation agency.

Finally, many state workers' compensation agencies have inadequate budgets and staff. The quality of workers' compensation insurers varies widely. Although most insurers pay claims promptly, some do not, and although most settle claims fairly, some will try to persuade injured workers to settle for less than the full amount to which they are entitled. Because of inadequate budget and staff, many state workers' compensation agencies cannot adequately police claim settlements.

Deregulation of Workers' Compensation Rates

Another timely issue is whether workers' compensation rates should be deregulated. The central issue is whether workers' compensation rates should be established by a central rate-making organization, with all workers' compensation insurers required to use these rates (called prior-approval rating), or whether competitive rates should be determined based on free and open price competition in the marketplace (called competitive rating or open competition). In most states at the present time, workers' compensation insurers use the rates developed by the National Council on Compensation Insurance.

Prior-approval rating means that workers' compensation rates are determined for the various occupations and classes by the National Council on Compensation Insurance. These rates must be approved by state regulatory officials, and workers' compensation insurers must use these rates, subject to any rate deviations allowed under state law. It is argued that approved rating has worked well over time since rates are established for numerous occupations and trades that are ranked according to their risk or hazard level. The rates are based on a broad range of national loss data.

In contrast, competitive rating or open competition means that workers' compensation insurers are free to develop their own rates based on the competitive market system. A company would be free to establish and charge a particular rate without first obtaining approval of state regulatory officials. As of January 1, 1989, 12 states had open competition laws of one form or another in effect.

Supporters of the present system of approved rating argue that adoption of competitive rating will result in several adverse effects. They include the following:[36]

1. SAFETY MAY BE UNDERMINED. Emphasis on low workers' compensation rates may force companies to drop the additional expense of providing loss-control services and rehabilitation programs to firms. Since safety services may decrease, future workers' compensation claims could increase.

2. SMALL POLICYOWNERS WILL BE ADVERSELY AFFECTED. Critics also argue that under competitive rating, workers' compensation insurers would rate small firms on the basis of individual loss experience. Thus, smaller firms with a high loss potential would pay much higher premiums for their workers' compensation coverage than they are now paying.

3. SMALL INSURERS WOULD BE ADVERSELY AFFECTED. Under competitive rating, individual companies must have their own staff of experts to estimate the costs of any benefit changes in the state. Many insurers would have to hire additional persons with the necessary actuarial and underwriting expertise. Many smaller insurers would be confronted with a substantial increase in expenses and may lack the financial resources to develop their own rates. It is argued that ultimately many smaller companies would not be able to compete and would withdraw from the workers' compensation market. This would leave only a small number of large companies to write the coverage.

On the other hand, supporters of competitive rating point out certain

---

[36]Alliance of American Insurers, "Keeping Workers' Compensation Healthy: The Case for Approved Rating," *Journal of American Insurance*, Vol. 56, No. 4 (Winter 1980–1981), pp. 12–13.

advantages that will result from a competitive rating system. They include the following:[37]

1. PRICE COMPETITION WILL LOWER RATES. It is argued that, under approved rating, there is little incentive to reduce rates, even when loss experience is favorable. However, under competitive pricing, it is argued that there would be greater price competition, which would tend to lower rates. For example, Michigan's open competition law became effective in 1983. The law resulted in net savings to employers of about 30 percent in 1984. However, by 1985, savings had declined to 20 percent or less.[38]

2. GOVERNMENT INVOLVEMENT WOULD BE REDUCED. Since rates would not have to be approved by state regulatory officials, government involvement in the insurance industry would be reduced. This is consistent with the present national trend of reducing the role of government in the economy.

3. PRODUCT INNOVATION WOULD INCREASE. Eliminating the present system of administered pricing would stimulate the development of new programs and products in workers' compensation insurance. Thus, policyowners would have a greater opportunity to select their own combination of product, price, and service. In addition, insurers would be able to respond quickly to changing loss and loss experience.

At the present time, there is great emphasis on reducing the role of government in the economy, deregulation of key industries, and emphasis on free and competitive markets. Thus, there may be greater pressures placed on the states to pass open competition rating laws by which competitive rating based on the free market can prevail.

Increase in the Residual Market

Another important problem is the significant increase in the residual market. *The workers' compensation residual market refers to plans that provide insurance to high-risk employers who are unable to obtain insurance in the standard or normal markets.* Because of the nature of their business or loss experience, many high-risk employers are unable to obtain workers' compensation coverage from insurers on a voluntary basis. Examples include logging and lumber mills, where the probability of an occupational accident is considerably higher than the national average. High-risk employers can obtain workers' compensation insurance from a

---

[37]See J. Michael Low, "It's Time for Competitive WC Rating," *The National Underwriter*, Property & Casualty Insurance ed., August 28, 1981, pp. 29–31.

[38]John F. Burton, Jr., "Workers' Compensation: Evolving Issues and Expanding Perspectives," *John Burton's Workers' Compensation Monitor*, Vol. 1, No. 1 (January 1988), pp. 3–4. A counterargument is that under a prior-approval law, rates may be depressed because of the politics of state regulation and a regulatory lag and that competitive rating would actually increase prices. Research in the area of automobile insurance rates suggests this is the case. See J. David Cummins and Scott E. Harrington, "The Impact of Rate Regulation in U.S. Property-Liability Insurance Markets: A Cross Sectional Analysis of Individual Loss Ratios," *The Geneva Papers on Risk and Insurance*, No. 42 (January 1987).

workers' compensation assigned risk pool (also called workers' compensation reinsurance pool) in which workers' compensation insurers in the state are assigned their pro rata share of high-risk employers based on written premiums. The National Council on Compensation Insurance manages the assigned risk pool operations for 32 states through the National Workers' Compensation Reinsurance Pool. Collected premiums and incurred losses are determined on an individual state basis and apportioned to insurers based on the proportion of written premiums.

In recent years, the workers' compensation residual market has increased sharply. In 1985, about 6 percent of the countrywide premium was in the residual market in those states where the National Council managed the pool. In 1988, this figure ballooned to 19.6 percent of the total compensation market. States with the largest residual market shares in 1988 were Maine (82.3 percent), Rhode Island (51.5 percent), and Louisiana (43.3 percent).[39]

The major reasons for the swollen residual market are inadequate rates in many states, a decline in interest rates in the mid-1980s that reduced cash flow, and the reluctance of insurers to insure high-risk employers.[40] In particular, rates appear to be especially inadequate in those states with a large residual market (Maine, Rhode Island, Louisiana). Insurers cannot profitably insure certain firms at standard rates, so these firms are placed in the residual market where rates are considerably higher. Even so, the business in the residual market generally is unprofitable. In 1988, the residual market loss ratio was 114.8 percent, which produced an underwriting loss of nearly $1.5 billion. The residual market now requires 12 cents of each voluntary written premium dollar to subsidize the operating loss.[41] The residual market share is expected to remain high unless adequate rates and rate differentials for the residual market are obtained.

IMPROVING WORKERS' COMPENSATION

The National Commission on State Workmen's Compensation Laws concludes that workers' compensation programs are generally inadequate and inequitable, and it urges the states to incorporate several important recommendations in their workers' compensation laws. The essential recommendations are as follows:[42]

1. COMPULSORY COVERAGE. All elective laws should be abolished, and coverage should be compulsory for all employers.

---

[39]Data are from National Council on Compensation Insurance, New York, N.Y.

[40]Sharon Eisenberg and William F. Vieweg, "NWCRP Growth: An Unsavory Consequence of Inadequate Rates," *NCCI Digest*, Vol. 2, Issue 3 (September 1987), p. 37.

[41]Matthew A. Cantoni, Jr., "Understanding Workers Comp," *Independent Agent*, Vol. 85, No. 12 (August 1988), p. 12.

[42]National Commission on State Workmen's Compensation Laws, *Report*, pp. 14–27, 125–130.

2. NO NUMERICAL OR OCCUPATIONAL EXEMPTIONS. Numerical exemptions should be abolished, and all employers of one or more workers should be covered. Also, farm workers should be covered on the same basis as all other employees. Household and casual workers should be covered under workers' compensation at least to the extent that they are covered by Social Security. All government employees should also be covered. There should be no exemptions for any class of employees, including professional athletes and employees of charitable organizations.

3. FULL COVERAGE OF OCCUPATIONAL DISEASES. Present restrictions on occupational disease should be eliminated, and all occupational diseases should be fully covered.

4. FULL MEDICAL CARE AND REHABILITATION SERVICES. Medical care and physical-rehabilitation services should be provided without any limitations with respect to time or dollar amounts.

5. CHOICE OF FILING A CLAIM. A worker may travel in several states. The worker should have the option of filing a claim in the state where the injury occurs, where the worker is hired, or where employment is principally localized.

6. ADEQUATE TEMPORARY TOTAL DISABILITY BENEFITS. A worker who is temporarily and totally disabled should receive, subject to the maximum weekly benefit, a weekly benefit at least equal to 80 percent of the workers' spendable weekly earnings. The maximum weekly benefit should eventually be increased where it is at least 100 percent of the state's average weekly wage. Until the maximum state benefit exceeds 100 percent of the state's average weekly wage, the weekly benefit should be at least two-thirds of the worker's gross weekly wage.

7. ADEQUATE PERMANENT TOTAL DISABILITY BENEFITS. A worker who is permanently and totally disabled should receive benefits at least equal to two-thirds of the gross weekly wage. The maximum weekly benefit should be at least 100 percent of the state's average weekly wage. The benefits should be paid for life or for the duration of disability, without any limitations on time or total dollar amount. The definition of permanent total disability used by most states should be retained.

8. ADEQUATE DEATH BENEFITS. Surviving dependents should receive at least two-thirds of the deceased worker's gross weekly wage. The maximum weekly benefit should be at least 100 percent of the state's average weekly wage. The death benefits should be paid for life or until remarriage. In the event of remarriage, two years' benefit should be paid in a lump sum. The death benefits for a dependent child should be paid until age 18, or until age 25 if a full-time student.

The commission also made several less essential recommendations for improving state workers' compensation laws, including the following:

1. SHORTER WAITING PERIOD. To reduce the disabled worker's financial burden, all states should enact a waiting period of not more than three days, with retroactive benefits after two weeks or less of disability.

2. PROGRESSIVE INCREASE IN MAXIMUM WEEKLY BENEFIT. The maximum weekly benefit should be progressively increased to at least 200 percent of the state's average weekly wage.

3. NEW BASIS FOR CALCULATING BENEFITS. The weekly cash benefit should be equal to 80 percent of the worker's spendable weekly earnings. Spendable earnings are defined as gross earnings minus payroll taxes and job-related expenses, subject to a maximum weekly benefit. Under this approach, tax considerations or additional benefits for dependents would be unnecessary.

4. MINIMUM DEATH BENEFITS. Minimum weekly death benefits should be at least 50 percent of the state's average weekly wage.

5. COORDINATION WITH OTHER BENEFITS. Social Security benefits should continue to be reduced when workers' compensation benefits are paid for permanent and total disability. But in death cases, workers' compensation benefits should be reduced if the surviving family receives Social Security payments.

6. PROTECTION AGAINST EROSION OF BENEFITS. People who are receiving permanent total disability benefits should have their benefits increased over time in the same proportion as increases in the state's average weekly wage.

7. FREE CHOICE OF PHYSICIAN. A disabled worker should be allowed to select his or her own physician or choose from a panel of physicians approved by the workers' compensation agency.

8. BROAD COVERAGE UNDER SECOND-INJURY FUNDS. Second-injury funds should provide broad coverage for preexisting impairments, including epilepsy, polio, arthritis, and heart disease.

9. MEDICAL REHABILITATION DIVISION. Each state should establish a medical rehabilitation division within the workers' compensation agency to provide effective medical care and vocational rehabilitation services to disabled workers. Special cash maintenance benefits should be provided during the worker's rehabilitation.

10. TIME LIMIT FOR FILING CLAIMS. Time limits for filing claims should be liberalized. In the case of occupational disease, a substantial time period may elapse between exposure to a disease-causing substance and the worker's awareness of the disease.

11. MORE EFFECTIVE ADMINISTRATION. Each state should have a workers' compensation agency, which is staffed by full-time Civil Service employees and financed by assessments against insurers and self-insurers.

12. LIMIT ON LUMP-SUM SETTLEMENTS. Lump-sum settlements and compromise-and-release agreements, which terminate medical and rehabilitation benefits, should be used rarely, and only after the workers' compensation agency approves of the settlement.

How well have the states met the above recommendations? When the National Commission on Workmen's Compensation Laws first released its report, the commission made 19 essential recommendations. Fear of imposition of federal standards caused the states to move rapidly. As a result, the average state compliance score with respect to the 19 essential recommendations increased sharply from 6.9 in 1972 to 12.0 in 1980. Since that time, however, there has been little or no overall improvement. The average compliance score was only slightly higher (12.2) as of July 1988.[43]

Several reasons help explain the relative lack of progress. First, the states are not currently threatened with federal standards if workers' compensation programs are not improved. Second, state legislators are concerned that undue liberalization of workers' compensation would place the state at a competitive disadvantage with respect to the surrounding states; as a result, needed improvements in state programs have slowed. Finally, the severe 1981–1982 recession and depressed business conditions in some states in recent years undoubtedly have also slowed the growth of workers' compensation.

SUGGESTIONS FOR ADDITIONAL READING

APPEL, DAVID, AND PHILIP S. BORBA, EDS. *Workers' Compensation Insurance Pricing.* Boston, Mass.: Kluwer Academic Publishers, 1988.

BARTH, PETER S. *Workers' Compensation and Work-Related Illness and Diseases.* Cambridge, Mass.: MIT Press, 1980.

BERKOWITZ, MONROE, AND JOHN F. BURTON, JR. *Permanent Disability Benefits in Workers' Compensation.* Kalamazoo, Mich.: W. E. Upjohn Institute for Employment Research, 1987.

BERKOWITZ, MONROE, AND M. ANNE HILL, EDS., *Disability and the Labor Market: Economic Problems, Policies, and Markets,* 2nd ed. New York State School of Industrial and Labor Relations, Cornell University, Ithaca, N.Y.: ILR Press, 1989.

BURTON, JOHN F., JR., ED. *New Perspectives in Workers' Compensation.* New York State School of Industrial and Labor Relations, Cornell University, Ithaca, N.Y.: ILR Press, 1988.

———. "Workers' Compensation: Evolving Issues and Expanding Perspectives," *John Burton's Workers' Compensation Monitor,* Vol. 1, No. 1 (January 1988), pp. 1–20. *John Burton's Workers' Compensation*

Monitor is published ten times each year and provides valuable information and data on current issues.

CHAMBER OF COMMERCE OF THE UNITED STATES. *1990 Analysis of Workers' Compensation Laws.* Washington, D.C.: Chamber of Commerce of the United States, 1990.

CHELIUS, JAMES, ED. *Current Issues in Workers' Compensation.* Kalamazoo, Mich.: W. E. Upjohn Institute for Employment Research, 1986.

DUNNE, SEN. JOHN R. "Will the Workers' Compensation System Survive the Nineties?" *NCCI Digest,* Vol. 4, Issue 4 (December 1989), pp. 7–15.

HANSEN, RONALD W., PAUL W. MACAVOY, AND CLIFFORD W. SMITH, JR. "Compensation Alternatives for Occupational Disease and Disability," *The Journal of Risk and Insurance,* Vol. 56, No. 2 (June 1989), pp. 252–274.

MURRAY, MICHAEL L. "Workers' Compensation— A Benefit Out of Time," *Benefits Quarterly,* Vol. 1, No. 2 (Second Quarter 1985), pp. 8–15.

MYERS, ROBERT J. *Social Security,* 3rd ed., Chap. 14. Homewood, Ill.: Richard D. Irwin, 1985.

---

[43]John F. Burton, Jr., "State Workers' Compensation Laws: The Compliance Record," *John Burton's Workers' Compensation Monitor,* Vol. 1, No. 17 (July/August 1988), Figure A, p. 1.

NATIONAL COMMISSION ON STATE WORKMEN'S COMPENSATION LAWS. *The Report of the National Commission on State Workmen's Compensation Laws.* Washington, D.C.: U.S. Government Printing Office, 1972.

NELSON, WILLIAM J., JR. "Workers' Compensation: 1980–84 Benchmark Revisions," *Social Security Bulletin,* Vol. 51, No. 7 (July 1988), pp. 4–21.

———. "Workers' Compensation: Coverage, Benefits, and Costs, 1987," *Social Security Bulletin,* Vol. 53, No. 4 (April 1990), pp. 2–11.

WILLIAMS, C. ARTHUR, JR., JOHN G. TURNBULL, AND EARL F. CHEIT. *Economic and Social Security,* 5th ed., Chap. 7. New York: John Wiley & Sons, 1982.

WORRALL, JOHN D., ED. *Safety and the Work Force: Incentives and Disincentives in Workers' Compensation.* New York State School of Industrial and Labor Relations, Cornell University, Ithaca, N.Y.: ILR Press, 1983.

——— AND DAVID APPEL, EDS. *Workers' Compensation Benefits: Adequacy, Equity, & Efficiency.* New York State School of Industrial and Labor Relations, Cornell University, Ithaca, N.Y.: ILR Press, 1985.

13

PROBLEM OF UNEMPLOYMENT

Income maintenance is a critical element in the attainment of economic security. Most people depend on their work earnings as their major source of income. But widespread changes in business conditions, structural and technological changes, seasonal elements, and frictions in the labor market frequently interact to create unemployment for many groups; and the search for better jobs and geographical relocation also cause unemployment.

When earnings terminate from unemployment, unemployed workers can be exposed to economic insecurity in at least four ways. The first is obviously the loss of income. Unless the worker has replacement income from other sources (such as unemployment insurance) or past savings on which to draw, he or she will be economically insecure. Second, if, because of business conditions, the worker can work only part time, work earnings are reduced, and he or she may be unable to maintain a reasonable standard of living. Third, economic insecurity may result from the uncertainty of income. Because of seasonal elements, the worker may be unemployed for a certain period each year. A construction worker, for example, may experience some psychological discomfort as the layoff season approaches, because of uncertainty regarding the continuation of future income. Finally, some unemployed groups have difficulty in finding new jobs. These groups include some older workers, disadvantaged members of minority groups, and the hard-core unemployed. Older workers beyond age 50 often have an extended duration of unemployment, and the hard-core unemployed may be out of work for months or even years.

In this chapter, we shall analyze the nature of the unemployment problem in some detail, particularly in the following areas: (1) types of unemployment, (2) measurement of unemployment, (3) extent of unemployment in the United States, (4) underemployment of human resources, (5) groups affected by unemployment, and (6) approaches for reducing unemployment.

TYPES OF UNEMPLOYMENT

For purposes of prescribing appropriate public policy measures, some logical classification of unemployment is necessary. Although there is some disagreement on the meaning of full employment, it can be defined as an unemployment rate that does not exceed 5.5 to 6 percent.[1] A certain amount of unemployment is considered normal, since some workers are changing jobs and are therefore temporarily unemployed; other workers have jobs that are seasonal; and younger workers entering the labor force for the first time often have difficulty in finding initial employment. Thus, full employment does not mean that 100 percent of the labor force is employed.

Economists generally recognize the following types of unemployment: (1) cyclical unemployment, (2) technological unemployment, (3) structural unemployment, (4) frictional unemployment, and (5) seasonal unemployment.

Cyclical Unemployment

Cyclical unemployment (also called deficient-demand unemployment) is unemployment that results from a deficiency in aggregate demand; that is, total spending in the economy, or total aggregate demand for goods and services, is insufficient for generating an adequate number of jobs to provide full employment. This form of unemployment can be successfully attacked through appropriate monetary and fiscal policies—in particular, tax reductions—by which aggregate demand can be stimulated to generate additional jobs.

There is nothing inherent in the American economy that ensures sufficiently strong aggregate demand at all times to generate full employment; since World War II, the United States has experienced recessions in 1948 and 1949, 1953 and 1954, 1957 and 1958, 1960 and 1961, from 1973 through 1975, in January–July 1980, and in 1981 and 1982. At other times, aggregate demand can be excessive, especially during wartime periods, straining the economy's potential and generating inflationary pressures.

Variations in the major components of total aggregate demand—consumer spending, investment spending by business firms, and government

---

[1]Campbell R. McConnell and Stanley L. Brue, *Contemporary Labor Economics*, 2nd. ed. (New York: McGraw-Hill Book Co., 1989), p. 524. Economists earlier used a 4 percent unemployment rate. However, because of structural changes in the composition of the labor force, such as high teen-age unemployment, an unemployment rate of 5.5 percent or even 6 percent is now used as the measurement of full employment.

spending—often cause short-run fluctuations in the economy. Consumer spending is usually relatively stable and is closely related to household income, but occasionally it can be an independent source of economic instability. Since consumer spending accounts for more than 60 percent of the gross national product, small changes in consumer demand, especially in the areas of automobiles and other durable goods, can have a large impact on the economy.

The second component of aggregate demand—investment spending by business firms—can also cause economic instability. Firms invest in new plants, machinery, computers, and other equipment to modernize and expand their productive capacity. The decision to invest is influenced by numerous variables, including anticipated increases in demand, rate of current capacity utilization, relative costs of capital and labor, corporate cash flow, interest rates, borrowing costs, and taxes. The responses by business to these variables are not instantaneous, smooth, or readily predictable; and because the production of capital goods generally requires long lead times, these responses must be spread out over long periods. The overall result of these investment decisions is often sharp fluctuations in investment spending, which cause considerable instability to the economy.

Finally, sudden changes in federal spending can cause some instability in the economy, such as the rapid increase in defense expenditures during the Korean conflict, the rapid decline in 1953 and 1954, the large outlays for the Vietnam War period during the late 1960s, and the substantial cutbacks in federal spending by the Reagan administration in 1981 and 1982 instituted in order to balance the federal budget.

Technological Unemployment

Technological unemployment is unemployment that results from the displacement of workers by labor-saving machinery, by new production techniques, or by new management methods. Many workers seeking employment have migrated to urban centers, only to find that technological change has reduced the number of unskilled and semiskilled manufacturing jobs for which they could qualify. Also, technological change may result in the closing of obsolete plants and facilities, thereby causing severe economic distress to many communities.

Some people are fearful that technological change and automation are destroying jobs at a rapid rate and that unemployment will be permanently higher in the future. However, on the positive side, technological change and automation can have a beneficial effect on employment. Menial jobs are eliminated, and leisure is increased. Goods can be produced at lower cost, which increases the worker's real income. Although automation can eliminate jobs, it also creates new jobs in industries that manufacture automated equipment, and skilled workers are needed to maintain and repair complex machines and controls.

On the negative side, however, automation and technological change can create serious unemployment problems, at least in the short run. Automation can cause entire plants to become obsolete and can substantially alter the types of job skills demanded in the labor market. It can cause a massive displacement of workers in communities that are dependent on one industry for employment, such as closing an old plant that is inefficient and obsolete and building a new one in another area.

Structural Unemployment

Structural unemployment can be defined as unemployment that results from a mismatch between the skills required for the available jobs and skills possessed by workers seeking work. Structural unemployment can also occur from a mismatch between the geographical location of available jobs and job seekers.[2]

Several factors can cause structural unemployment. For example, increased imports of foreign automobiles have resulted in the displacement of thousands of workers in the automobile industry. The displaced workers generally lacked the skills needed for the jobs that were available, such as jobs in computer programming, health technology, and engineering. Thus, there is a mismatch between the skills required for the available jobs and the skills possessed by job seekers. The resulting unemployment is structural.

Other factors can also cause structural unemployment. Changes in demand for a particular good, the relocation of an industry, decline of an industry, or the exhaustion of a natural resource can also cause chronic unemployment in a given geographical area. Workers who live in depressed areas may be unwilling or unable to relocate to new areas with expanding employment opportunities. Finally, because of poor education, poor work habits and motivation, lack of work skills, poor health, and inadequate knowledge of job opportunities, many persons are unemployed for long periods of time.

Frictional Unemployment

Frictional unemployment refers to unemployment that can result from the changing of jobs. When workers are changing jobs, they may experience a short period of unemployment between jobs. Because of imperfections in the labor market, they cannot find work immediately even if jobs are available. They may not know of other jobs, or if they do, they may lack the necessary labor mobility to relocate quickly. Thus, they are temporarily unemployed because of an imperfect job search.

Seasonal Unemployment

Finally, seasonal unemployment can result from fluctuations in business activity because of weather, customs, styles, and habits. Agriculture and construction are two important seasonal industries, with wide swings in employment throughout the year.

---

[2]Ibid., p. 535.

MEASUREMENT OF UNEMPLOYMENT

Before appropriate public policy solutions for solving unemployment can be prescribed, the extent of unemployment must be measured. This involves consideration of basic labor force concepts. In addition, criticisms of unemployment statistics should be examined.

Basic Labor Force Concepts

The Bureau of the Census gathers monthly data on employment, unemployment, people outside the labor force, and other personal and occupational characteristics of the working population. The information is collected from a national sample of about 55,800 households to represent the U.S. population 16 years of age and older. The basic data are collected by the Census Bureau in its Current Population Survey, which is then turned over to the Bureau of Labor Statistics for analysis, interpretation, and publication. An explanation of terms used in these data is presented in the following sections.[3]

Employed Persons. *Employed persons* are all civilians who, during the survey week, worked as paid employees, in their own business, profession, or on their own farm, or who worked at least 15 hours without pay in a family business. It also includes persons who are temporarily absent from their regular jobs because of illness, vacation, labor-management dispute, or similar reasons.

Unemployed Persons. *Unemployed persons* are all civilians who did not work during the survey week but were available for work except for temporary illness and had looked for jobs within the preceding four weeks. Also counted as unemployed are persons who did not work at all but were available for work and (1) were waiting to be called back to a job after they had been laid off or (2) were waiting to start new jobs within the next 30 days.

Civilian Labor Force. The *civilian labor force* is the total of all civilians classified as employed or unemployed based on the preceding criteria. The *labor force* includes also all members of the armed forces stationed in the United States and abroad.

Unemployment Rate. The *unemployment rate* for all civilian workers is the number of unemployed as a percentage of the civilian labor force. Unemployment rates are also computed for different age groups in the labor force, based on sex, age, race, marital status, occupation, and other characteristics.

Not in the Labor Force. Persons *not in the labor force* are those who are not classified as employed or unemployed. They include retired persons, those

---

[3]The various definitions of labor force concepts can be found in U.S. Department of Labor, Bureau of Labor Statistics, *Employment and Earnings*, Vol. 36, No. 8 (August 1989), pp. 119–122.

engaged in their own housework, those not working while in school, those unable to work because of long-term sickness, those who are discouraged from seeking work because of personal or job market factors, and those who are voluntarily idle.

Criticisms of Unemployment Statistics

Although the preceding concepts are extremely useful in identifying the major characteristics of the unemployed, unemployment statistics are subject to some criticism. They include the following:[4]

1. THE TOTAL UNEMPLOYMENT RATE ALONE CAN BE MISLEADING. The total unemployment rate alone reveals little information and can be misleading. For example, in July 1989, the national unemployment rate was 5.2 percent. However, totals conceal as much as they reveal. The unemployment rate was even more serious than was indicated by the national unemployment rate. During the same period, the unemployment rate was 14.7 percent for teen-agers, 10.9 percent for blacks, and 9.0 percent for Hispanics. The point is that some groups have a greater incidence of unemployment than do others, and the total unemployment rate is misleading by itself.

2. THE TRUE UNEMPLOYMENT RATE IS UNDERSTATED. Unemployment data may understate the true unemployment rate in the economy, since certain groups are not counted in the official unemployment statistics. This includes workers who are discouraged by their efforts to find a job and drop out of the labor force. Also, because of economic reasons, some workers who are working only part time desire full-time employment. Although they are not working a full week (35 hours or more), they are counted as employed and not unemployed. In addition, many seasonal workers would like to work full time the entire year; however, if they are neither working nor seeking jobs during the survey week, they are not counted as part of the labor force. Finally, many people with physical handicaps desire to work, but they are unable to do so because of their disabilities.

3. THE TRUE IMPACT OF UNEMPLOYMENT IS EXAGGERATED. Unemployment data can also be criticized because they exaggerate the true impact of unemployment on the economy. For example, the economic burden and financial hardship of unemployment fall heavily on married men who must work to support their families. However, in July 1989, the unemployment rate for married men with a spouse present was only 2.7 percent—a relatively low figure that suggests that unemployment is not a major problem for this group. It is also argued that the relatively high unemployment rate for teen-agers should not be viewed with alarm, because most youths depend on their parents for their financial support; that many people are unemployed by deliberate choice; and

---

[4]The unemployment data cited are from U.S. Department of Labor, Bureau of Labor Statistics, *Employment and Earnings*, Vol. 36, No. 8 (August 1989).

that the duration of unemployment between jobs for most workers is relatively short.

UNEMPLOYMENT IN THE UNITED STATES

To determine the magnitude of the unemployment problem, let us examine the unemployment record in the United States and the economic and social costs of unemployment.

Extent of Unemployment

The volume of unemployment in the United States has fluctuated over time. Although many causal factors are associated with unemployment, the level of business activity is a critical element. During the Great Depression of the 1930s, when business activities were severely depressed, unemployment reached massive proportions. In 1933, about one in four workers in the civilian labor force was unemployed, often for considerable periods. However, unemployment rates have been far more moderate since that time, especially since World War II.

Table 13-1 shows the number of unemployed and the unemployment rates for selected years. Based on the concept of no more than 5.5 to 6 percent unemployment as full employment, the United States has experienced considerable unemployment from the mid-1970s to the late 1980s. However, since that time, the economy overall has experienced reasonably full employment.

TABLE 13-1   Unemployment in the United States: Selected Years

YEAR	LABOR FORCE[a] (MILLIONS)	UNEMPLOYED (MILLIONS)	UNEMPLOYMENT RATE (%)
1960	71.5	3.9	5.4
1962	7.27	3.9	5.4
1964	75.1	3.8	5.0
1966	77.9	2.9	3.7
1968	81.0	2.8	3.5
1970	84.9	4.1	4.8
1972	88.8	4.9	5.5
1974	93.7	5.2	5.5
1976	97.8	7.4	7.6
1978	103.9	6.2	6.0
1980	108.5	7.6	7.0
1982	111.9	10.7	9.5
1984	115.2	8.5	7.4
1986	119.5	8.2	6.9
1988	116.7	6.7	5.4
1989 (July)	119.1	6.5	5.2

[a]Labor force refers to the total labor force, including resident armed forces.

Source: *Employment and Earnings*, Vol. 36, No. 8 (August 1989), Table A-1, p. 6.

Reasons for Unemployment

Unemployment can also be measured by the immediate causes of unemployment. Unemployed persons can be classified into four categories. *Job losers* are persons whose employment ended involuntarily and immediately began looking for work and persons who lost their jobs by layoff. *Job leavers* are persons who quit or terminated their jobs voluntarily and immediately began looking for work. *Reentrants* are persons who previously worked at a full-time job lasting two weeks or more but were out of the labor force prior to looking for work. Finally, *new entrants* are persons who worked at a full-time job lasting two or more weeks.

As of July 1989, 6.5 million persons were unemployed. They were distributed according to the following categories:[5]

Job losers	44.3%
Job leavers	15.3
Reentrants	29.4
New entrants	11.0

The majority of workers lose their jobs because of layoffs or other economic reasons. A relatively small proportion of workers are unemployed because they voluntarily quit their jobs. However, reentrants and new entrants as a group experience considerable unemployment. This group consists of large numbers of women who frequently enter and leave the labor force and younger workers who are seeking their first jobs.

Duration of Unemployment

Some unemployed workers find jobs quickly and do not even fulfill the one-week waiting period that is required for collecting unemployment insurance benefits in most states. Others are unemployed for several months and eventually exhaust their unemployment benefits. Thus, the duration of unemployment must also be considered when evaluating the burden of unemployment.

In July 1989, 6.5 million workers, or 5.2 percent of the labor force, were unemployed. Fortunately, the duration of unemployment was relatively short for many workers. Forty-eight percent of the unemployed workers were out of work for less than five weeks.

It is misleading and incorrect, however, to assume that the duration of unemployment is inconsequential for all workers. Many are out of work for extended periods.

In July 1989, about 1.5 million workers were unemployed for 15 weeks or more. Of this total, about 626,000 workers had been looking for a job for 27 or more weeks.[6] The economic insecurity for many of the long-term unem-

---

[5]Ibid., Table A-41, p. 42.
[6]Ibid., Table A-40, p. 44.

ployed is severe. Many are excluded from unemployment insurance benefits, and even if covered, they may exhaust their benefits, deplete their savings, incur heavy debts, and experience other financial hardships.

Industries and Unemployment

Certain industries experience relatively higher unemployment rates than others. Manufacturing employment is greatly affected by business cycles, particularly in firms that manufacture durable goods that have wide fluctuations in consumer demand, such as automobiles and appliances. Workers in the high seasonal construction industry—both skilled craftsmen and laborers—experience high rates of unemployment, as do agricultural workers, especially farm laborers. Rural persons working in mines, forests, and fisheries experience irregular employment, poor working conditions, and relatively low wages. In sharp contrast are workers in finance, insurance, real estate, services, and government who have relatively little unemployment.

Location of Unemployment

Unemployment is not evenly distributed throughout the country. Certain communities experience substantially higher unemployment rates than the national savings. In June 1989, cities with unusually high unemployment rates included the following:[7]

McAllen-Edinburg-Mission, Texas	14.7%
Brownsville-Harlingen, Texas	12.7
Modesto, California	12.7
Flint, Michigan	10.0
Muskegon, Michigan	9.7
Shreveport, Louisiana	9.5

In addition, among the sections of any individual city, unemployment varies greatly. The rates are highest in urban poverty areas and decline as one moves out to the suburbs.

Costs of Unemployment

Widespread unemployment is costly to the economy, to individuals and families directly affected, and to society. These costs are both economic and noneconomic.

1. ECONOMIC COSTS.   Unemployment has some direct and real costs to the economy. First, there is the loss of gross national product that could have been produced if all economic resources had been fully employed. Because of

---

[7]Ibid., Table D-1, pp. 111–115. Data are preliminary and not seasonally adjusted.

underutilization of labor and high unemployment rates, the economy is not able to attain its full production potential, and the gross national product suffers. The loss in GNP can be considerable; for example, it is estimated that the GNP gap in 1983 (difference between actual and potential GNP) was about $290 billion, or about 9 percent of potential output.[8] Thus, because of a wasted work force, idle plant capacity, and high unemployment rates, the loss of gross national product can be an enormous cost to the economy.

Second, extended unemployment causes millions of person-years of labor to be lost forever. Labor is a perishable commodity, in the sense that it cannot be stored up. An hour of human labor, once lost because of unemployment, is lost forever.

Finally, extended unemployment retards economic growth. Vigorous economic growth is necessary for full employment and a higher standard of living. The economy does not attain its true growth potential if workers are unemployed or underutilized.

2. NONECONOMIC COSTS.   The noneconomic costs of unemployment fall heavily on individuals, families, and society. When people are unemployed for extended periods, skilled workers may experience some deterioration in their skills; others become depressed and have a negative attitude.

The cost to families is also heavy—in particular, to nonwhite minority families in urban slum areas. An earlier study by the National Advisory Commission on Civil Disorders showed that high unemployment rates in urban slums often cause serious family tensions and contribute to family breakdown.[9] During times of high unemployment, workers living within these poverty areas are seeking employment but are unable to find it; or the only jobs they can obtain are at the low end of the occupational structure and do not have the status to command the worker's self-respect or that of his or her family and friends.

Finally, prolonged unemployment can result in lower self-esteem; an increase in alcoholism, drug abuse, and divorce; child abuse; health problems; and deterioration of family life.

UNDEREMPLOYMENT OF HUMAN RESOURCES

Unemployment is only one form of underutilization of human resources; underemployment must also be considered. Wasted manpower is evident in the large numbers of workers who are working in jobs that do not utilize their full skills, those who are outside the labor force but still desire to work, and those involuntarily employed in part-time positions. Thus, underemployment can be classified into three major categories: (1) workers employed below their actual or potential

---

[8]Campbell R. McConnell, *Economics: Principles, Problems, and Policies,* 10th ed. (New York: McGraw-Hill, 1987), p. 176.

[9]The National Advisory Commission on Civil Disorders, *Report of the National Advisory Commission on Civil Disorders* (Washington, D.C.: U.S. Government Printing Office, 1968).

skill level, (2) people outside the labor force seeking work, and (3) involuntary part-time work.

Workers Employed Below Their Skill Level

The employment of workers below their actual or potential skill level is impossible to measure adequately; strictly speaking, there are relatively few people who are not underemployed to some extent. Underemployment can result from high unemployment that forces some workers to accept jobs where their skills are not completely utilized. Also, underemployment can result from racial and sex discrimination, poor education, inadequate diet, and inadequate medical care.

People Outside the Labor Force Seeking Work

Many people who are neither working nor actively seeking jobs would like to work. Many housewives with family responsibilities are prevented from working because they must care for their children. Illness and disability prevent some people from working in physically demanding jobs, and long-term disabilities dissuade some from even seeking work. Many are out of the labor force because of school attendance. And others do not look for work because they are discouraged and believe that it would be impossible to find it.

   The Department of Labor has made several studies on the number of people outside the labor force and their reasons for not seeking work. In the second quarter of 1989, 62.4 million persons were not in the labor force. Of this number, 5.3 million, or about 8.5 percent, wanted a job. The reasons for not working included ill health, school attendance, home responsibilities, and the belief that no work was available. These barriers to employment could be greatly reduced by improved health care, arrangements for child care, referral to suitable jobs, and other services. In particular, numerous workers drop out of the labor force because they think they cannot find jobs. Of the 5.3 million outside the labor force who wanted jobs in the second quarter of 1989, 869,000, or 16 percent, believed that they could not get a job.[10]

Involuntary Part-Time Work

Millions of workers who want to work full time are working part time because full-time jobs are unavailable, or because their regular workweek has been reduced below 35 hours for economic reasons (such as slack work, materials shortages, waiting to start a new job, or finding only part-time work). In July 1989, 5.5 million workers age 16 or over were working part-time because of economic reasons.[11]

---

[10]U.S. Department of Labor, Bureau of Labor Statistics, *Employment and Earnings*, Vol. 36, No. 7 (July 1989), Table A-53, p. 54.

[11]*Employment and Earnings*, Vol. 36, No. 8 (August 1989), Table A-28, p. 32. The data are not seasonally adjusted.

WHO ARE THE UNEMPLOYED?

The groups most prone to prolonged unemployment include the following: (1) black workers, (2) persons of Hispanic origin, (3) native Americans, (4) teenagers, (5) older workers, (6) families maintained by women, and (7) dislocated workers.

Black Workers

Although black workers have made substantial economic gains over time, their unemployment rate is still more than double that of white workers. In July 1989, the unemployment rate for blacks was 10.9 percent, while for white workers, it was only 4.6 percent.[12]

A major reason for the high unemployment rates for blacks is that many blacks work in low-skilled and low-paying occupations—as unskilled laborers, in semiskilled production jobs, or in service work—where higher unemployment rates often prevail. Their employment in these occupations is due in turn to other factors: for example, racial discrimination and discriminatory hiring practices, which keep them out of better jobs. In addition, blacks have higher school dropout rates and are therefore often inadequately educated. Inner city schools tend to be overcrowded, have inadequate facilities, and are often staffed by less qualified teachers. In the critical skills of verbal and reading ability, blacks often lag behind whites. The result is that relatively more black students drop out of school. Since high school dropouts generally lack the skills to enter the normal job market, they are forced into the lower-paying, low-status, unskilled occupations, where higher unemployment typically prevails.

Persons of Hispanic Origin

Hispanic workers are persons of Spanish origin, including Mexican Americans, Puerto Ricans, Cubans, South Americans, and others. Hispanic workers also have unusually high unemployment rates. In July 1989, the unemployment rate for Hispanic workers was 9 percent.[13]

Hispanic workers have high unemployment rates because of language barriers, inadequate education and work skills, and racial discrimination. Many are employed in low-status, low-paying jobs as laborers, service workers or domestics, or in semiskilled operations.

The educational system in the United States is oriented toward the culture of middle-class white society, as opposed to the distinct culture of Hispanic workers. Their inferior education is due in part to language and reading problems. When Spanish is often the only language spoken in the home, a student is handicapped in mastering the English language. Many students there-

---

[12]Ibid., p. 4.
[13]Ibid., p. 4.

fore perform poorly in school and drop out, which often results in considerable poverty, unemployment, and underemployment.

Native Americans

Native Americans are probably the most disadvantaged minority group in the nation. Many native Americans have health problems, are poorly educated, and often lack familiarity with the English language; as a result, they often have relatively few marketable skills, earn relatively low incomes, are handicapped by their culture when seeking jobs, and experience extremely high unemployment and underemployment rates. It is not uncommon for the unemployment rate for native Americans living on reservations to exceed 40 percent.

Reducing unemployment in this group is a monumental task. Many native Americans live on reservations that are remote from industrial centers where jobs are available; their traditional culture is not intrinsically job oriented and does not provide common incentives to work for pay similar to those confronting other American workers; and the assistance provided native Americans in the past has been inadequate for overcoming the serious obstacles they face.

Many native Americans migrate from the reservations into the cities, only to face similar problems of poor housing, inadequate schools, lack of marketable work skills, and high unemployment and underemployment rates. Because of their culture, many native Americans who migrate to the cities desire to maintain their communal and social separation from white society. Thus, the gap between them and the mainstream of society is widened, and the alienation is more severe. Also, the nature of native American life on the reservation often does not prepare them to be easily absorbed into city life. Consequently, high unemployment and underemployment rates, along with the grinding pressures of poverty, cause many native Americans to become disillusioned with city life and subsequently return to their reservations.

Teen-agers

Teen-agers also experience considerable unemployment. In July 1989, the unemployment rate for black teen-agers ages 16–19 was a monumental 27.4 percent, while for white teen-agers in the same age category, it was only 12.8 percent.[14]

Several factors help to explain the relatively high unemployment rates for teen-agers. First, the federal minimum wage has dissuaded many employers from hiring teen-agers, since it often exceeds their marginal revenue product. Second, many young persons remain in school to pursue a higher education and are frequently entering and leaving the labor force. Third, state child labor laws may restrict job opportunities for some young people. Finally, many teen-agers are unemployed because they consider the available jobs to be low paying and unattractive. Teen-agers who work in positions viewed as dead-end, low-paying

---

[14]Ibid., Table A-34, pp. 38–39.

jobs do not hesitate to quit, since comparable jobs may be easy to find, and unemployment is the result.

Older Workers

Older workers over age 50 often experience great difficulty in finding new jobs once they become unemployed. Seniority rights tend to protect the jobs of older workers, but once they lose their jobs, they are likely to remain unemployed for longer periods than are the younger workers. Although the unemployment rate for older workers is relatively low, the *duration of unemployment* is longer. For example, in July 1989, about 36 percent of the unemployed workers in the 55–64 age category were unemployed 15 or more weeks in contrast to 15 percent of the employees in the 20–24 age category.[15]

Older unemployed workers have a longer duration of unemployment for several reasons. First, older workers who lose their jobs because of automation and technological change often have work skills that are obsolete and not readily transferable, which makes it difficult for them to find new jobs.

Second, some older workers are relatively immobile and reluctant to relocate geographically. When employment opportunities are limited in the local community, many displaced older workers who have established homes in the community and made lifetime friendships find it extremely painful to relocate because of their homes and friends.

In many cases, older workers voluntarily retire instead of accepting unemployment or sporadic employment at low wages; some are discouraged in their attempts to find new jobs and voluntarily withdraw from the labor force; others are in poor health or are disabled, making it extremely difficult for them to maintain a full-time attachment to the work force.

Finally, as discussed in Chapter 4, age discrimination by employers and the reluctance of many firms to hire older workers are additional employment barriers.

Families Maintained by Women

The unemployment rate for female-headed families is also relatively high. In July 1989, the unemployment rate for women who maintained families was 8.7 percent.[16] The number of female-headed families has increased over time because of the increase in divorce, separation, and absence of the father from the home. Also, the number of unwed mothers has increased sharply in recent years. Most unwed mothers elect to keep and support their children. However, because unwed mothers typically lack marketable skills, they often experience considerable unemployment.

---

[15]Ibid., Table A-17, p. 24. The data are not seasonally adjusted.

[16]Ibid., Table A-39, p. 41.

Dislocated Workers

Dislocated workers also experience considerable unemployment. *Dislocated workers are workers with stable and lengthy work histories who are permanently laid off because of intense foreign competition, new technology, or continuing shifts in domestic consumption.* Because of these factors, millions of jobs have been permanently eliminated in manufacturing, mining, construction, transportation, public utilities, and other industries. Through no fault of their own, millions of workers with stable work records have lost their jobs permanently and are unlikely to be recalled back to work by their former employers.

A total of 9.7 million adult workers (age 20 or older) lost their jobs because of plant closings or relocations, slack work, or elimination of a position or shift between January 1983 and January 1988. Of this number, about 4.7 million or almost half were considered dislocated workers.[17]

By January 1988, 71 percent of the dislocated workers found new jobs. Fourteen percent were unemployed. The remaining 15 percent dropped out of the labor force.[18]

In many cases, the hours of work and wages paid are less favorable for dislocated workers who find new jobs. For those dislocated workers who were reemployed in January 1988, one in ten was employed on a part-time basis. *Moreover, among the dislocated workers who found full-time wage and salary jobs, 38 percent took pay cuts.*[19]

Finally, reemployment difficulties increase with age. In January 1988, only about 51 percent of the dislocated workers ages 55–64 were reemployed, while 77 percent of such workers ages 24–54 were working.[20] A large number of older workers left the labor force rather than continue looking for work.

APPROACHES FOR REDUCING UNEMPLOYMENT

Under the Employment Act of 1946, the federal government must take positive steps to promote maximum employment opportunities for people who are willing and able to work. Some specific approaches for reducing unemployment in the United States include the following: (1) monetary and fiscal policy, (2) automatic stabilizers, (3) improved labor market information, (4) employment and training programs, and (5) supply-side economics.

---

[17]U.S. Congress, House, Committee on Ways and Means, *Background Material and Data on Programs within the Jurisdiction of the Committee on Ways and Means* (Washington, D.C.: U.S. Government Accounting Office, 1989), p. 491.

[18]Ibid., Table 11, p. 494.

[19]Ibid., p. 493.

[20]Ibid., Table 11, p. 494.

Monetary and Fiscal Policy

Monetary and fiscal policy can be used by the federal government to stimulate aggregate demand and increase economic growth so that full employment can be attained.

Expansion of Aggregate Demand.   Expansion of aggregate demand is extremely important in reducing unemployment for several reasons. First, high levels of demand are necessary for the success of employment and training programs, since jobs may not be available at the end of training if the economy is in a recession. Second, an increase in the national unemployment rate affects large numbers of persons who would otherwise be competing for the available jobs; a one-percentage-point increase in the national unemployment rate results in more than 800,000 workers who are unemployed. Finally, an expansion of aggregate demand means tight labor markets, which improves employment opportunities for workers who are employed part time for economic reasons and also increases the wages of the working poor, thereby making it possible for them to work their way out of poverty.

Aggregate demand can be expanded by appropriate monetary and fiscal policy. *Monetary policy* refers to changes in the money supply and in the cost and availability of bank credit to achieve certain economic goals. *Fiscal policy* refers to changes in the level of taxes and government spending.

During a recession, the Federal Reserve would expand the money supply by following an easy money policy. The legal reserve ratio could be lowered; the discount rate would be reduced; and the Federal Reserve would buy bonds in the open market. Conversely, during an inflationary period, the Federal Reserve attempts to hold down the growth of the money supply by following a tight money policy. The legal reserve ratio could be raised; the discount rate would be increased; and the Federal Reserve would sell bonds in the open market.

Discretionary fiscal policy can also be used to stimulate aggregate demand so that full employment can be attained. During a recession, the federal government can reduce taxes, increase government spending, or both. Conversely, during an inflationary period, appropriate fiscal policy may require an increase in taxes, reduction in government spending, or both.

Limitations of Monetary and Fiscal Policy.   Many economists are critical of traditional monetary and fiscal policy as a tool for stabilizing the economy and reducing unemployment. They point out the following limitations:

1. MONETARY AND FISCAL POLICY IS A CRUDE STABILIZING TOOL.   Monetary and fiscal policy is a crude tool that cannot be applied with precision. The economic effects of a proposed policy change often cannot be accurately measured in advance; the need for a change in discretionary policy is recognized only

after a time lag; and economic forecasting is hazardous, since we do not know precisely where we are in the present business cycle.

2. POLITICAL CONSIDERATIONS MAY OVERSHADOW GOOD ECONOMICS. Good politics and sound economics often do not go together. Because of political considerations, appropriate fiscal policy may not be applied. For example, Congress is reluctant to increase taxes during an election year. Also, Congress is often slow to act with respect to a tax change and other stabilizing measures.

3. MONETARY AND FISCAL POLICY CAN BE DESTABILIZING. Monetary and fiscal policy is often destabilizing. For example, some economists believe that the tight money policy of the Federal Reserve during the first half of 1957 actually contributed to the subsequent 1957–1958 recession. Also, the tight money policy by the Federal Reserve contributed to the 1981–1982 recession.

4. TIME LAGS MUST BE CONSIDERED. There is also the problem of timing and time lags when monetary policy is changed. There may often be a time lag of 12 to 24 months before the full effects of a change in monetary policy are felt.

5. THE EFFECTS ON THE ECONOMY ARE NOT UNIFORM. The effects of changes in monetary and fiscal policy are not uniform throughout the economy. Certain industries are affected more severely than others. For example, as a result of the tight money policy followed by the Federal Reserve in 1980–1982, interest rates soared, and the prime rate exceeded 20 percent. Because of historically high mortgage interest rates, new housing starts declined, and unemployment in the construction industry increased sharply. Also, high interest rates were partly responsible for the sharp decline in new automobile sales, which had an adverse effect on employment in the automobile industry. Finally, state and local governments often face difficult financing problems when they attempt to borrow in tight money markets.

Automatic Stabilizers

Automatic stabilizers also reduce unemployment in the United States. *Automatic stabilizers* are elements built into the economy that tend to offset automatically any adverse fluctuations in economic activity. The stabilizers tend to bolster the incomes of households and business firms during business downswings and, conversely, to hold down the growth of income during business upswings.

The major automatic stabilizers are personal and corporate income taxes, unemployment insurance, welfare programs, and personal and corporate savings. Personal and corporate income taxes behave in a desirable countercyclical manner. During business downswings, incomes decline (or increase less rapidly), but income taxes decline proportionately more. Also, during business downswings, unemployment insurance benefits automatically increase in a desirable countercyclical manner. Welfare programs, such as food stamps and public assistance programs, also help some unemployed workers to maintain their consumption during business downswings. Finally, savings balances can be used to maintain consumption when workers are unemployed, and corporations can continue dividend payouts during recessions even though sales and profits are down.

Although the automatic stabilizers are effective in reducing the severity of recessions, they have several important limitations as countercyclical tools. First, although they moderate business downswings, they cannot by themselves generate a recovery. Other measures to promote full employment are also necessary. Second, the automatic stabilizers can cause a "fiscal drag" and make it more difficult for the economy to reach full employment. As the economy recovers and moves forward toward full employment, federal revenues increase, which acts as a fiscal drag by siphoning off income. Thus, aggregate demand is held down before full employment is reached, which makes it more difficult for the economy to attain full employment.

Finally, the effectiveness of unemployment insurance benefits as an automatic stabilizer has declined significantly over time. *Recent evidence provided by Gary Burtless shows that the countercyclical effects of unemployment insurance benefits are about 40 percent less than the earlier stimulus provided throughout the 1960s and 1970s.*[21] The reduced countercyclical effects can be explained by at least three reasons. First, relatively fewer unemployed persons now receive unemployment insurance benefits. For example, fewer than one in three unemployed persons received unemployment insurance benefits during an average month in 1988.[22] Second, the countercyclical effects provided by the extended benefits portion of the unemployment compensation program have been significantly reduced.[23] Finally, the taxation of unemployment benefits also reduces the countercyclical impact of unemployment insurance benefits.

Improved Labor Market Information

Some job seekers have comparatively little knowledge of the available jobs within their community or state. Frictional unemployment can be reduced by providing job seekers with more adequate information about job markets and available jobs. The Job Service, which is part of the U.S. Department of Labor, has offices in most major communities. The Job Service has three major functions. It attempts to match unemployed workers with the available jobs by providing employment assistance through local offices; unemployed workers who apply for unemployment insurance benefits must register for work at the local Job Service office; and the Job Service provides testing and counseling services to workers and conducts labor market surveys.

---

[21]Statement of Gary T. Burtless in U.S. Congress, House, Committee on Ways and Means, *Reform of the Unemployment Compensation Program,* Hearing before the Subcommittee on Public Compensation and Unemployment Compensation, 100th Cong., 1st sess., December 14, 1987, p. 125.

[22]Isaac Shapiro and Marion E. Nichols, *Unprotected: Unemployment Insurance and Jobless Workers in 1988* (Washington, D.C.: Center on Budget and Policy Priorities, 1989), p. vi.

[23]See Chapter 15 for details.

The Job Service also has a computerized job bank in many communities. Unemployed workers indicate their training, education, employment background, job skills, and career plans. This information is then matched with the available jobs within the community. By providing better information about jobs, frictional unemployment is reduced, and the workers' talents and skills can be better utilized.

Employment and Training Programs

Although monetary and fiscal policy can expand aggregate demand and increase economic growth, all groups do not share equally from that growth. Employment and training programs are also necessary for assisting persons who are structurally unemployed.

The fundamental objective of employment and training programs is to increase the employability of workers by providing them with basic and vocational education skills and on-the-job training. Many workers are unemployed because they lack job skills, are deficient in basic education, lack job market information, have social-psychological handicaps, or cannot work because of lack of transportation or child care facilities. Employment and training programs attempt to reduce or eliminate these employment barriers. Examples of employment and training programs are the Comprehensive Employment and Training Act of 1973 (CETA), Work Incentive Program (WIN), the Youth Training and Employment Program, and various apprenticeship programs.

Evaluation of Employment and Training Programs. How well have the various employment and training programs worked? Evaluation of the programs is mixed, and there is no unanimous consensus on the success of the various programs. Although some employment and training programs are reasonably successful in improving the job skills and earnings potential of some workers, especially minority and women workers, the programs overall have serious limitations in reducing total unemployment in the United States. They include the following:

1. THE PROGRAMS ARE EXPENSIVE AND SLOW. Complete and thorough training of unemployed workers takes a lot of money and time and, thus, cannot sharply reduce total unemployment in a relatively short period.

2. THE IMPACT ON TOTAL UNEMPLOYMENT IS SLIGHT. There is no strong evidence that shows that unemployment is substantially reduced or restrained by employment and training programs. Even if increased funding were available, it would take years to expand the programs to the level where total unemployment is significantly reduced.

3. JOBS MAY NOT BE AVAILABLE AT THE END OF TRAINING. Some trainees cannot find jobs at the end of training, since the economy may be in a recession. As we noted earlier, high levels of aggregate demand are necessary for the

success of employment and training programs. Most programs involve the private sector, and if aggregate demand is weak, jobs may not be available at the end of training. Also, those workers laid off in a recession would be competing with the graduates of employment and training programs for the available job.

4. THE RESULTS OF MANY PROGRAMS ARE DISCOURAGING. Under some programs, relatively few persons are enrolled, complete training, and are placed in jobs. For example, in fiscal 1986, 870,000 welfare recipients were new registrants in the Work Incentive Program (WIN) that provided work or training. During the same period, only 260,000 WIN enrollees found unsubsidized employment. In addition, only 130,000 individuals went off welfare completely because of employment.[24]

5. THERE IS CONSIDERABLE DUPLICATION AND OVERLAP OF PROGRAMS. The various employment and training programs overlap, are fragmented, and lack coordination. A comprehensive and uniform manpower policy must be developed to replace the numerous, fragmented, and piecemeal programs that now exist.

Supply-Side Economics

Supply-side economics is another approach for reducing unemployment in the United States. It is argued that traditional Keynesian economics, which emphasizes expansion of aggregate demand and government intervention in the economy to reduce unemployment, has not worked well, and new solutions to unemployment are necessary.

Basic Concepts in Supply-Side Economics. Supply-side economics is based on certain fundamental concepts. The most important are summarized as follows:[25]

1. HIGH TAX RATES DAMPEN WORK INCENTIVES. It is argued that taxes have increased substantially over time and that high marginal tax rates dampen both work incentives and incentives to invest. High taxes reduce the after-tax rewards to workers and business firms, making them less willing to work or invest in new capital goods and equipment.

2. MOST TAXES ARE SHIFTED FORWARD BY HIGHER PRICES. It is also argued that most taxes are incorporated in business costs and are shifted to consumers in the form of higher prices. This is especially true of sales, excise, and Social Security payroll taxes, which increase business costs and are passed on to consumers through higher prices. Thus, high taxes aggravate the problem of *cost-push inflation.*

---

[24]*Background Material and Data on Programs within the Jurisdiction of the Committee On Ways and Means,* 1989, Table 2, p. 521.

[25]McConnell, *Economics: Principles, Problems, and Policies,* pp. 325–329.

3. OVERREGULATION BY THE FEDERAL GOVERNMENT HAS ADVERSE EFFECTS ON PRODUCTIVITY AND COSTS. It is argued that federal regulations, laws, and directives have adverse effects on productivity and costs. Government regulation frequently protects the regulated firms from the rigors of competition. Also, the costs of complying with government regulations in the areas of occupational safety and health, pollution, equal access to job opportunities, and other areas have been enormous. The overall result is a substantial increase in costs to business firms and higher prices to consumers, which results in a stagnating and inefficient economy.

4. TAX CUTS STIMULATE ECONOMIC GROWTH AND REDUCE UNEMPLOYMENT. Supply-side economists believe that reducing personal and corporate income tax rates increases economic growth and reduces unemployment. By reducing taxes, consumers have more disposable income to spend and save. The supply-siders also believe that a large part of any across-the-board tax cut will be saved, especially by upper-income persons who do the bulk of the saving. The supply of savings will increase, and new economic investments will be forthcoming. In addition, tax cuts increase work incentives and expand aggregate demand. Finally, by reducing corporate income tax rates, the after-tax return on new economic investments is increased, thereby increasing the willingness of firms to invest in new capital goods.

Supply-side economists also believe that lower personal and corporate income tax rates need not necessarily reduce federal revenues. It is argued that by cutting marginal tax rates, work incentives will expand, incentives to invest will increase, and federal tax revenues will also increase. Thus, higher federal revenues could result even though tax rates are lower.

Supply-side concepts are clearly reflected in the Economic Recovery Tax Act of 1981 and the Tax Reform Act of 1986, which provided for massive tax cuts and a sharp reduction in marginal tax rates. In addition, under the Reagan administration, policies were followed to reduce government regulation and the growth of government in the private economy.

Criticisms of Supply-Side Economics. Many traditional economists are skeptical and have serious reservations about the effectiveness of supply-side economics in stimulating economic growth and reducing unemployment. Supply-side economics has been subject to numerous criticisms. Two major criticisms are the following:

1. FEDERAL DEFICITS HAVE INCREASED. It is argued that massive tax cuts have increased the size of the federal deficit. Although the incentive to work may increase as a result of the tax cuts, the loss of federal revenues is substantially greater than the increase in revenues that results from an increase in work incentives.

2. TAX CUT MAY NOT BE SAVED. Another criticism of supply-side economics is that a tax cut may not be saved. A basic assumption underlying supply-

side economics is that a large part of any tax cut will be saved. However, there is no assurance that most of the additional after-tax income will be saved and ultimately invested in capital goods. Most empirical studies conclude that changes in personal income tax rates have only a small effect on personal saving and new economic investment. For example, a 10 percent reduction in tax rates would increase personal saving by less than 3 percent. This would mean that the savings rate (an average of 5.7 percent annually over the past five years) would increase by no more than 0.2 percentage point. The additional saving would be equivalent to only about 0.2 percent of the gross national product.[26]

Moreover, even if every dollar of personal saving that resulted from a 10 percent tax cut were invested in plants and equipment, the impact on output and productivity would be small. If the tax cut and higher level of saving continued for five years, the potential increase in the gross national product would be less than 0.3 percent, and there would be only a negligible increase in productivity.[27]

SUGGESTIONS FOR ADDITIONAL READING

COOK, ROBERT F., CHARLES F. ADAMS, JR., AND V. LANE RAWLINS. *Public Service Employment: The Experience of a Decade.* Kalamazoo, Mich.: W. E. Upjohn Institute for Employment Research, 1985.

GERHART, PAUL F. *Saving Plants and Jobs.* Kalamazoo, Mich.: W. E. Upjohn Institute for Employment Research, 1987.

LEIGH, DUANE E. *Assisting Displaced Workers: Do the States Have a Better Idea?* Kalamazoo, Mich.: W. E. Upjohn Institute for Employment Research, 1989.

LEVITAN, SAR A., AND FRANK GALLO. *A Second Chance Training for Jobs.* Kalamazoo, Mich.: W. E. Upjohn Institute for Employment Research, 1988.

MCCONNELL, CAMPBELL R., AND STANLEY L. BRUE. *Contemporary Labor Economics,* 2nd ed., Chap. 18. New York: McGraw-Hill Book Company, 1989.

ZORNITSKY, JEFFREY, AND ADAM SEITCHIK. *From One Job to the Next: Worker Adjustment in a Changing Labor Market.* Kalamazoo, Mich.: W. E. Upjohn Institute for Employment Research, 1989.

---

[26]Council of Economic Advisers, *Economic Report of the President* (Washington, D.C.: U.S. Government Printing Office, 1981), p. 82.

[27]Ibid.

14

UNEMPLOYMENT INSURANCE

Unemployment insurance is a federal-state program that provides for partial income replacement during periods of short-term involuntary unemployment. All states pay benefits to temporarily unemployed workers in covered employment who are currently attached to the labor force and fulfill certain eligibility requirements. The benefits are paid as a matter of right, with no demonstration of need. Thus, covered workers receive some income while unemployed, and the aggregate unemployment benefits maintain purchasing power in the economy and cushion the economic impact in communities with large numbers of unemployed workers.

The unemployment insurance system in the United States consists of several distinct programs: a federal-state unemployment insurance program in all states, as well as the District of Columbia, Puerto Rico, and the Virgin Islands; a federal-state program of permanent extended benefits, which pays additional benefits during periods of high unemployment; a permanent unemployment insurance program for ex-service members; a program for federal civilian employees; and the Railroad Unemployment Insurance Act for railroad workers.

In addition, special unemployment insurance programs have been established for certain groups that experience high unemployment because of federal legislation or natural disasters. This includes workers who lost their jobs as a result of the expansion of imports, deregulation of airlines, consolidation of railroad carriers, and deinstitutionalization of treatment of mental patients.

In this chapter, we shall be primarily concerned with the regular federal-state unemployment insurance programs. The federal unemployment insurance programs for federal civilian employees, ex-service members, and railroad workers will be covered in Chapter 19. To limit the scope of treatment, the special employee protection programs will not be treated.[1] More specifically, the following areas will be covered: (1) development of unemployment insurance in the United States, (2) objectives of unemployment insurance, (3) state unemployment insurance provisions, (4) extended unemployment insurance benefits, (5) financing unemployment insurance, (6) administration, and (7) taxation of benefits.

DEVELOPMENT OF UNEMPLOYMENT INSURANCE

Prior to the enactment of the Social Security Act in 1935, only limited assistance was available to unemployed workers.[2] Some states had established work relief programs, which provided some assistance to the indigent; however, they were required to work or perform other public services in return for the aid. Private charities also gave some assistance, but their limited financial resources precluded payment of unemployment benefits for extended periods. Some labor unions also provided temporary assistance, but to relatively few recipients. A few firms had established private unemployment plans, but financing problems and massive unemployment during the depression of the 1930s made it difficult to provide extensive aid. Finally, a few states, including Wisconsin in 1932, considered or enacted unemployment insurance legislation. The Wisconsin law later served as the basis of the unemployment insurance provisions of the Social Security Act of 1935.

That act established a federal-state system of unemployment insurance, rather than one completely administered by the federal government because it was feared that a completely federal program would be unconstitutional. Also, because of disagreement concerning benefits, financing, administration, and other areas, it was believed that each state was best suited to develop its own unemployment insurance program and that state administration was more feasible than federal administration. Each state was free to develop its own program, subject to certain federal minimum standards.

The Social Security Act of 1935 encouraged the states to enact these programs through the use of a *tax offset*. A federal uniform tax was levied on the payrolls of covered employers—those that employed eight or more workers for

---

[1]A detailed discussion of the special unemployment insurance programs for certain groups can be found in National Commission on Unemployment Compensation, *Unemployment Compensation: Final Report* (Washington, D.C.: U.S. Government Printing Office, 1980), pp. 156–167.

[2]The historical development of unemployment insurance in the United States can be found in Daniel Nelson, *Unemployment Insurance: The American Experience, 1915–1935* (Madison: University of Wisconsin Press, 1969). See also U.S. Department of Health, Education and Welfare, Social Security Administration, *Social Security Programs in the United States* (Washington, D.C.: U.S. Government Printing Office, 1973), pp. 55–72, and "Social Security Programs in the United States," *Social Security Bulletin*, Vol. 49, No. 1 (January 1986), pp. 22–28.

20 or more weeks in a calendar year. If the state had an acceptable unemployment insurance program, 90 percent of the employers' tax could be deducted or offset and used by the state to meet its own unemployment problems instead of going to the federal government. The remaining 10 percent of the tax was paid to the federal government for administrative expenses incurred by both the federal government and state unemployment insurance systems. Employers in states without unemployment insurance laws would not have a competitive advantage over those in other states, because they would still have to pay the federal payroll tax, but their employees would be ineligible for unemployment insurance benefits. Thus, the states had a strong financial incentive to enact acceptable unemployment insurance laws, and by 1937, all states had done so.

The original tax in 1936 was 1 percent on the entire payroll of covered employers, 2 percent in 1937, and 3 percent in 1938. In 1939, an amendment limited the payroll tax to 3 percent of the first $3,000 per year for each covered worker. Since that time, the federal tax rate and taxable wage base have been increased several times. In 1983, the federal payroll tax was further increased to 3.5 percent of the first $7,000 of annual wages paid to each covered employee. As of January 1990, the federal payroll tax was 6.2 percent of the first $7,000 paid to each covered employee. However, if the state meets certain federal requirements, covered employers can receive a maximum tax credit of 5.4 percent of taxable wages. The remaining 0.8 percent is paid to the federal government and is used for administrative expenses; for financing the federal government's share of the extended-benefits program (covered later); and for maintaining a loan fund from which states can temporarily borrow when their accounts are depleted.

Each state must meet certain federal minimum standards if covered employers are to receive a tax offset against the federal tax and if the state is to continue receiving federal grants for administration. They include the following:

1. All unemployment taxes must be deposited in the Unemployment Trust Fund in the U.S. Treasury. Although the fund is invested as a whole, each state has a separate account, which is credited with its unemployment contributions and its share of investment earnings. All funds withdrawn from the unemployment fund must be used to pay unemployment compensation benefits or to refund amounts erroneously paid into the fund.

2. Benefits must be paid through public employment offices or other approved agencies.

3. The state cannot deny benefits to an otherwise eligible person who refuses to accept a new job because the job is vacant as a direct result of a labor dispute; or because the wages, hours, or conditions of work are substandard; or if as a condition of employment, the worker must join a company union or resign or refrain from joining a labor union.

4. Benefits are not payable in two successive benefit years to an individual who has not worked in covered employment after the beginning of the first benefit year.

5. Benefits cannot be denied to a person solely because he or she is taking part in an approved training program.

6. The only reasons for cancellation of wage credits or total benefit rights are discharge for work-connected gross misconduct or fraud.

7. Reduced state unemployment tax rates are permitted employers only on the basis of their unemployment experience.

8. Government entities and nonprofit organizations are permitted to finance the cost of benefits by reimbursing the fund for benefits paid to their former employees (instead of by paying unemployment taxes).

9. Benefits cannot be denied solely on the basis of pregnancy or termination of pregnancy.

10. Benefits are not payable during an off-season period on the basis of employment as a professional athlete or for an educational institution.

11. Benefits payable for unemployment after March 1980 must be reduced by the amount received from any public or private pension (including a primary OASDI retirement benefit and Railroad Retirement benefit). However, only the pension paid by the most recent (or chargeable) employer is considered. Also, the states are permitted to reduce benefits by less than a dollar-for-dollar basis to take into account the pension contributions paid by the worker into the pension plan from which the payments are made.

12. Claimants whose unemployment benefits have been denied must be given the right to appeal the decision by a fair hearing.

OBJECTIVES OF UNEMPLOYMENT INSURANCE

Unemployment insurance has both primary and secondary objectives. The primary objectives involve assistance to individual workers during periods of involuntary unemployment. The secondary objectives stress the promotion of economic efficiency and stability.[3]

Primary Objectives

The most important objectives of unemployment insurance deal with helping the unemployed worker; all other goals are secondary. For most workers, the duration of unemployment is relatively short, and unemployment assistance can be confined to the payment of weekly benefits. But in some cases, unemployment may be prolonged and involve vocational training and other adjustments; unemployment benefits can help support these workers during their readjustment period.

Provide Cash Payments during Involuntary Unemployment. *The most important objective is to provide cash payments to unemployed workers during periods of involuntary unemployment.* The major unemployment risk for most workers is a temporary layoff, so unemployment benefits are normally paid only for short

---

[3]Committee on Unemployment Insurance Objectives, *Unemployment and Income Security: Goals for the 1970's, A Report of the Committee on Unemployment Insurance Objectives Sponsored by the Institute* (Kalamazoo, Mich.: W. E. Upjohn Institute for Employment Research, 1969), pp. 14–22.

periods—typically a maximum of 26 weeks. Long-term unemployment and hard-core unemployment are generally considered outside the scope of unemployment insurance programs; other measures are necessary to help the long-term unemployed, including employment and training programs, retraining of dislocated workers, intensive counseling, and relocation.

Maintain the Worker's Standard of Living.   *Unemployment insurance also has the objective of maintaining to a substantial degree the unemployed worker's current standard of living.* This can be achieved by providing benefits that are adequate in amount and duration.

The worker's standard of living generally is determined by the amount of wages paid. Since it is assumed that temporarily unemployed workers will be recalled to their regular jobs or be reemployed in new jobs at about the same wage level, the unemployment benefits should be reasonably related to prior wages to maintain the worker's previous standard of living as nearly as possible.

Provide Time to Find Employment.   *Another important goal of unemployment insurance is to provide time so that the unemployed workers can find employment.* The benefits paid enable unemployed workers to find jobs consistent with their work skills and experience from previous employment. For example, a highly skilled machinist for an automobile manufacturer is not required to take a job as a day laborer during a temporary layoff caused by a model changeover. The benefits make it possible to be unemployed for a short period while waiting to be recalled to work.

Help Unemployed Workers Find Jobs.   *Unemployment insurance programs also help unemployed workers find new jobs.* They can be helped to locate job opportunities through close coordination with the appropriate labor force and employment service. If the workers are permanently displaced from their regular jobs, they should receive assistance in making a vocational readjustment or in overcoming other employment obstacles. If there is a communication problem, and the permanently displaced worker with marketable skills does not know how to find a new job, the agency administering the unemployment insurance program can provide information about job opportunities.

Secondary Objectives

The secondary objectives of unemployment insurance are the promotion of economic efficiency and stability. The broad economic goals are to stabilize the economy and to improve the utilization and allocation of labor resources.

Desirable Countercyclical Effects.   Unemployment insurance is an important automatic stabilizer. During business downswings, unemployment insurance benefits quickly increase, thereby bolstering personal income and consumption spending. This effect takes place whether the unemployment is confined to a local area or is widespread during a national recession.

Improved Allocation of Social Costs. Another objective is to allocate the social costs of unemployment by distributing them among the employers in some relation to their layoff experience. If the firms with high unemployment experience are charged with the costs of unemployment, these costs can be included in the costs of production, which can then be reflected in higher product prices. Resource allocation is thereby improved, to the extent that the social costs of unemployment are charged to the production of the particular goods and services that give rise to them.

Improving Labor Utilization. Unemployment insurance can promote greater economic efficiency and stability by encouraging unemployed workers to find appropriate jobs and, where necessary, helping them to improve their job skills.

Certain aspects of unemployment insurance indirectly promote better labor utilization. To reduce malingering and preserve work incentives, the benefits paid are below prevailing wage levels. Also, unemployment insurance recipients must register for work at the employment office, thus making possible their quicker reentry into the labor force.

Encourage Employers to Stabilize Employment. By the use of experience rating, unemployment insurance can encourage some employers to stabilize their employment. Some firms can do little to stabilize their employment patterns; for others, the amount of potential tax savings may be insufficient to induce them to reduce their unemployment. But evidence indicates that significant unemployment tax differentials exist among firms within an industry, reflecting differences in unemployment experience.[4] Thus, some firms can reduce their unemployment taxes through more aggressive efforts to stabilize employment.

Maintenance of Skilled Work Force. Finally, unemployment insurance contributes to a more stable labor supply by enabling employers to maintain their skilled or experienced work force during temporary interruptions of production. Because the benefits provide income during such periods, skilled workers are not forced to seek other jobs, and they are free to return when they are called back.

STATE UNEMPLOYMENT INSURANCE PROVISIONS

Although the states must meet the minimum federal standards described earlier, they are free to develop their own unemployment insurance programs. Each state determines coverage, eligibility requirements, and benefit amounts.[5]

---

[4]Committee on Unemployment Insurance Objectives, *Unemployment and Income Security*, p. 21.

[5]The basic characteristics of state unemployment insurance programs can be found in U.S. Department of Labor, Employment and Training Administration, *Comparison of State Unemployment Insurance*

Coverage

Most private firms, state and local governments, and nonprofit organizations are covered for unemployment benefits. A *private firm* must pay the federal unemployment tax if it employs one or more employees in each of at least 20 weeks during the current or preceding calendar year, or if it pays wages of $1,500 or more during any calendar quarter in the current or preceding calendar year.

Agricultural firms are covered if they have a quarterly payroll of at least $20,000 or employ 10 or more workers for at least one day in each of 20 different weeks during the current or prior year. *Domestic employment* in a private household is covered if the employer pays domestic wages of $1,000 or more in any calendar quarter during the current or prior year.

Nonprofit organizations of a charitable, educational, or religious nature are not subject to the federal unemployment tax, but the nonprofit organization must be covered under the state's program if it employs four or more people for at least one day in each of 20 different weeks during the current or prior year. The nonprofit organization has the right either to reimburse the state for the benefits paid or pay the unemployment tax under the state's law.

Many jurisdictions have extended coverage of nonprofit employees beyond that required by federal law. For example, 21 jurisdictions now cover nonprofit organizations that employ one or more workers (rather than four or more).

In addition most jobs in *state* and *local government* are also covered for unemployment benefits. Although the state and local governments are not subject to the federal unemployment tax, the state program must make unemployment benefits available to most state and local government employees.

In conclusion, as a result of federal legislation over time, most workers are now covered for unemployment insurance benefits. About 97 percent of all wage and salary workers, or about 85 percent of all employed persons, are employed in covered occupations.[6] Two major groups, however, are presently exempt from coverage—agricultural workers on small farms and most household employees. Coverage of agricultural employees and domestic workers is a highly controversial issue that will be discussed later in Chapter 15.

Eligibility Requirements

All states require covered unemployed workers to meet certain eligibility requirements to receive benefits. Unemployed workers typically must meet the following requirements: (1) earn qualifying wages or be employed for a specified

---

Laws, U.S. Department of Labor Employment and Training Administration, Unemployment Insurance Service, September 1989. The data are updated periodically.

[6]U.S. Congress, House, Committee on Ways and Means, *Background Material and Data on Programs within the Jurisdiction of the Committee on Ways and Means* (Washington, D.C.: U.S. Government Printing Office, 1989), p. 440.

period, (2) serve a waiting period in most states, (3) be able to work and be available for work, (4) actively seek work, and (5) be free of any disqualification.

Qualifying Wages and Employment. All states require the worker to earn a specified amount of wages, or work a certain period within his or her base period, or both. *The purpose of this requirement is to limit unemployment benefits to workers with a current attachment to the labor force.* The worker's *base period* is usually a 4-quarter or 52-week period preceding the benefit year. The *benefit year* is generally a 52-week period during which an individual claimant can receive benefits, subject to a maximum amount. In most states, the base period is the first four of the last five completed calendar quarters preceding the claim for unemployment benefits. Most states require employment in at least two quarters during the base year. In some states, the base period is 52 weeks closely preceding the claim for benefits.

The amount of wages that must be earned during the base period is stated in several ways. They include the following:

1. MULTIPLE OF WEEKLY BENEFIT OR HIGH-QUARTER WAGES. Some states express their earning requirement in terms of a specified multiple of the weekly benefit amount (commonly 30) or of high-quarter wages (commonly $1\frac{1}{2}$). For example, if the weekly benefit is $100, the worker needs qualifying wages of $3,000. If high-quarter wages are used, the worker must have earned in the base period $1\frac{1}{2}$ times the amount earned in the highest quarter of that period. In addition, most states using a multiple of the weekly benefit method have the additional requirement that the worker must have earned wages in at least two quarters. The purpose of this latter requirement is to eliminate the payment of benefits to part-time and low-paid workers whose average weekly earnings are less than the state's minimum benefit.

2. FLAT QUALIFYING AMOUNT. The amount of base-period wages can also be stated in terms of a flat qualifying amount of earnings. Some states using this method also require wages in more than one quarter to qualify for benefits. For example, Nebraska requires total base-period wages of at least $1,200 with at least $400 in each of two quarters to qualify for the minimum weekly benefit.

3. WEEKS OF EMPLOYMENT. Some states require that the claimant must have worked a certain number of weeks and earned at least a certain average or minimum amount of wages per week.

4. REQUALIFYING REQUIREMENTS. All states that have a time lag between the base period and benefit year require wages to be earned after the lag period for the purpose of qualifying for benefits in the second benefit year. The reason for this requirement is to prevent entitlement to benefits in two successive benefit years following a single separation from work.

Waiting Period. Most states require a one-week waiting period of total unemployment before benefits are payable. Some states compensate claimants for the initial waiting period if the unemployment exceeds a certain number of weeks, or the employee returns to work within a specified period.

The purposes of the waiting period are to eliminate short-term claims, hold down program costs, reduce administrative expenses, and provide time to process claims.

Able to Work and Available for Work.   To collect benefits, the unemployed worker must be both able to work—that is, physically and mentally capable of working—and available for work. One evidence of ability to work is the filing of a claim and registration for work at a public employment office; all states require a claimant to do this.

Availability means that the claimant is ready, willing, and free to work. Once again, registration for work at a public employment office provides some evidence of availability. If the unemployed person refuses suitable work or places substantial restrictions on the type of work he or she will accept, the worker may be considered not available for work and may be disqualified for benefits.

Actively Seeking Work.   Most states require claimants to seek work actively or make a reasonable effort to obtain it, in addition to registering for work at the local employment office.

Free of Disqualification.   The unemployed worker must also be free of disqualification. The major causes of disqualification in most states are voluntary separation from work, discharge for misconduct, refusal of suitable work, and participation in a labor dispute. The disqualification may include one or more of the following: (1) postponement of benefits for a certain period, (2) cancellation of benefit rights, or (3) a reduction in benefits otherwise payable.

The period of disqualification may be for a specific uniform period, for a variable period, or for the entire period of unemployment after the disqualifying act. Benefit rights, however, cannot be completely eliminated for the entire benefit year because of a disqualifying act other than discharge for misconduct or fraud, or because of disqualifying income.

The theory of denying benefits for a specified period is that, after a limited period, the worker's unemployment is attributable to labor market conditions rather than to the disqualified acts. Thus, he or she should not be punished further by the denial of benefits beyond that period.

1. VOLUNTARILY LEAVING WORK.   In all states, if a worker voluntarily quits without good cause, he or she is disqualified for benefits. If there is a good cause for leaving, however, the benefits are not denied. In many states, the meaning of "good cause" is restricted to reasons associated with the job, attributable to the employer, or involving fault on the part of the employer. The theory is that if the employer creates conditions of work that no reasonable person can tolerate, the worker's separation is involuntary, and he or she should then be compensated. On the other hand, if the worker quits for other reasons, he or she causes the unemployment and should not be eligible for benefits.

2. DISCHARGE FOR MISCONDUCT.   If a worker is discharged for misconduct, he or she typically will be disqualified according to the seriousness of the misconduct. For example, a worker may be discharged for continuous absence from work without notice, violation of company safety rules, or failure to observe reasonable obligations toward supervisors and fellow employees. Such reasons would call for relatively light penalties.

On the other hand, the worker may be discharged because of gross misconduct, such as an assault, committing a felony in connection with work, or dishonest or criminal acts. Many states provide for heavier penalties in these cases, such as cancellation of wage credits, entirely or partly.

3. REFUSAL OF SUITABLE WORK.   Most states have criteria to determine whether the claimant is refusing suitable work. These criteria include the degree of risk to the worker's health, safety, and morals; physical fitness and previous training, experience and earnings; length of unemployment and prospects for securing local work in the worker's usual occupation; and the distance to work from home.

4. LABOR DISPUTES.   All states have restrictions on the payment of benefits to workers who are unemployed because of a labor dispute. Some states, however, exclude certain labor disputes from these restrictions. Some pay benefits if the workers are unemployed because of a lockout by the employer; several pay benefits if the strike results from the employer's failure to conform to the provisions of a labor union contract or to the labor laws of the state; and most pay benefits to workers who are unemployed because of a strike if they are not participating in the labor dispute, financing it, or directly interested in it.

Unemployment during a labor dispute is generally disqualified for several reasons. First, strikes and lockouts are tactics of economic warfare in which the state should remain neutral. Payment of unemployment benefits to striking workers amounts in effect to a subsidy by the state and violates that neutral position. Second, the payment of benefits means that the employers are financing the strike, since the unemployment tax is paid entirely by them in most states. Finally, the denial of benefits is justified on the grounds that the workers are not involuntarily unemployed but have elected to exercise their right to strike.

5. OTHER CAUSES.   Certain groups are also disqualified from receiving unemployment insurance benefits. Students who are unavailable for work while attending school are generally disqualified in most states. Benefits cannot be paid to elementary and high school teachers, university professors, and other professional school employees during vacation periods or between school terms (provided there is reasonable assurance of reemployment after the vacation period). Also, benefits cannot be paid to illegal aliens or to professional athletes on the basis of employment as a professional athlete.

In addition, all states have special disqualification provisions covering fraudulent misrepresentation to obtain or increase the unemployment benefits.

All states also have provisions for recovering benefits paid to people who are not entitled to them.

Finally, a person may be disqualified or the benefits reduced if he or she is receiving certain types of disqualifying income, such as wages in lieu of notice, severance pay, worker's compensation for temporary partial disability, holiday pay, or back pay.

Benefit Amounts

Federal law does not establish benefit standards in the federal-state system of unemployment insurance. The benefits vary widely among the states, and diverse and complex formulas are used to determine benefits.

Weekly Benefit Amount. After a waiting period of one week in most states, a weekly cash benefit is paid for each week of total unemployment. The benefit paid varies with the worker's past wages within certain minimum and maximum dollar amounts.

Several methods are used to determine the weekly benefit amount. In most states, the weekly benefit amount is computed as a *fraction of the worker's high-quarter wages.* This fraction typically is one-twenty-sixth, which results in the payment of benefits equal to 50 percent of the full-time wage for workers with 13 full weeks of employment during their high quarter. For example, assume that Jane earns $300 weekly during her high quarter, totaling $3,900. Applying the fraction of one twenty-sixth to this amount gives her a weekly benefit of $150, or 50 percent of the full-time weekly wage. Some states use a weighted schedule to provide relatively higher benefits to low-paid workers.

Some states compute the weekly benefits as a *percentage of the worker's average weekly wages* in the base period or in part of the base period. For example, the weekly benefit may be 50 to 70 percent of the worker's average weekly wage, up to some statutory maximum.

Finally, a few states compute the weekly benefit as a *percentage of annual wages.* Most states employing this technique use a weighted schedule that provides relatively greater benefits to low-wage workers.

Minimum and Maximum Benefits. All states have minimum and maximum limitations on the weekly benefit amounts (see Table 14-1). In 1989, minimum weekly benefits for an unemployed worker ranged from $5 in Hawaii to $62 in Alaska. The maximum weekly benefit ranged from $96 in Indiana to $382 in Massachusetts. In fiscal 1988, the average national weekly benefit was $140, and the average duration was 13.3 weeks.[7]

A small number of states and the District of Columbia also provide for the payment of an additional unemployment benefit if eligible dependents are present. Eligible dependents typically include a nonworking spouse and children

---

[7]*Background Material and Data on Programs within the Jurisdiction of the Committee on Ways and Means,* 1989, p. 451.

TABLE 14-1 Amount and Duration of Weekly Benefits for Total Unemployment under the Regular State Programs

STATE	1989 WEEKLY BENEFIT AMOUNT[1]		1988 AVERAGE WEEKLY BENEFIT	1989 POTENTIAL DURATION (WEEKS)		1988 AVERAGE DURATION (WEEKS)
	Minimum	Maximum		Minimum	Maximum	
Alabama	$22	$145	$101	15	26	10
Alaska	38–62	188–260	157	16	26	16
Arizona	40	145	121	12	26	18
Arkansas	37	209	125	10	26	12
California	30	166	122	12	26	15
Colorado	25	214	158	13	26	13
Connecticut	15–22	234–284	176	26	26	11
Delaware	20	205	165	18	26	12
District of Columbia . . .	13	283	186	26	26	18
Florida	10	200	137	10	26	13
Georgia	37	165	127	9	26	9
Hawaii	5	239	166	26	26	14
Idaho	44	193	136	10	26	12
Illinois	51	187–244	151	26	26	17
Indiana	40	96–161	104	9	26	11
Iowa	26–31	174–214	148	11	26	12
Kansas	52	210	162	10	26	13
Kentucky	22	166	113	15	26	13
Louisiana	10	181	131	8	26	16
Maine	29–43	171–256	139	15	26	11
Maryland	25–33	205	157	26	26	13
Massachusetts	14–21	255–382	177	10	30	15
Michigan	59	263	182	15	26	21
Minnesota	38	254	181	10	26	15
Mississippi	30	145	100	13	26	12
Missouri	33	150	118	11	26	13
Montana	46	185	130	8	26	14
Nebraska	20	134	117	20	26	12
Nevada	16	184	145	12	26	13
New Hampshire	39	156	125	26	26	5
New Jersey	51	258	177	15	26	15
New Mexico	33	166	122	19	26	16
New York	40	180	143	26	26	17
North Carolina	19	228	131	13	26	8
North Dakota	43	183	133	12	26	13
Ohio	42	169–268	152	20	26	14
Oklahoma	16	197	142	20	26	13
Oregon	53	229	146	6	26	14
Pennsylvania	35–40	266–274	163	16	26	15
Puerto Rico	7	110	77	20	20	17
Rhode Island	48–58	240–300	163	12	26	12

(continued)

TABLE 14-1 *(Continued)*

STATE	1989 WEEKLY BENEFIT AMOUNT[1]		1988 AVERAGE WEEKLY BENEFIT	1989 POTENTIAL DURATION (WEEKS)		1988 AVERAGE DURATION (WEEKS)
	Minimum	Maximum		Minimum	Maximum	
South Carolina	20	147	109	15	26	9
South Dakota	28	140	121	18	26	12
Tennessee	30	155	104	12	26	11
Texas	34	210	159	13	26	15
Utah	14	208	157	10	26	13
Vermont	31	169	132	26	26	12
Virginia	56	176	133	12	26	9
Virgin Islands	30	160	116	14	26	11
Washington	57	209	151	16	30	15
West Virginia	24	225	142	26	26	15
Wisconsin	38	200	148	1	26	12
Wyoming	36	200	159	12	26	16

[1] A range of amounts is shown for those states that provide dependents allowances.
NA—Not available.

Source: U.S. Congress, House, Committee on Ways and Means, *Background Material and Data on Programs within the Jurisdiction of the Committee on Ways and Means* (Washington, D.C.: U.S. Government Printing Office, 1989), Table 7, pp. 451–452.

under a certain age, such as under age 16, 18, or 19 (or generally older if incapacitated).

Partial Unemployment. The states also have provisions for the payment of reduced unemployment benefits for partial unemployment. In most states, a worker is considered partially unemployed during a week of part-time work if the amount earned from the regular employer or from odd jobs is less than the weekly benefit amount. Some states consider a worker partially unemployed if he or she earns less than the weekly benefit plus an allowance either from odd jobs or from any source. The benefit paid for a week of partial unemployment is usually the weekly unemployment benefit less wages earned in the week, but with a specified amount of earnings disregarded in computing the benefit.

Duration of Benefits. All states have a limit on the amount of unemployment benefits that a claimant can receive during a benefit year, which is most commonly expressed as 26 times the weekly benefit amount. Thus, this provision determines the length of time the benefits are payable. The maximum duration of benefits is 26 weeks in virtually all states. However, not all claimants qualify for 26 weeks of benefits.

Ten states have a *uniform* duration of benefits for all unemployed workers. However, most states have a maximum duration of benefits that is *variable*, depending on the individual worker's wage credits or weeks of employment. The various formulas generally limit the maximum total benefits to a multiple of the weekly benefit amount or to a fraction of the base period wages, whichever is less. Almost all states with a variable duration have a maximum limit of 26 weeks.

Pension Offset. The weekly unemployment benefit must be reduced by the amount received from any public or private pension (including a primary OASDI retirement benefit and Railroad Retirement). However, only the pension paid by the most recent (or chargeable) employer is considered. In addition, the states are permitted to reduce the unemployment benefit by less than a dollar-for-dollar basis to take into account the pension contributions paid by the worker into the pension plan from which the payments are made.

EXTENDED UNEMPLOYMENT INSURANCE BENEFITS

Many workers exhaust their regular unemployment benefits during periods of high unemployment. The 1970 amendments established a permanent federal-state program of extended benefits (EB) to meet the problem. *Under the EB program, claimants can receive up to 13 additional weeks of benefits, or one-half the total amount of regular benefits, whichever is less. The overall duration on both regular and extended benefits is 39 weeks.* The cost of the EB program is financed equally by the federal government and the states.

State Trigger

The state's *insured unemployment rate* is used to trigger the payment of extended benefits in a particular state. *The insured unemployment rate is the ratio of unemployment insurance claims to total employment covered by unemployment insurance programs.* The insured unemployment rate is below the total unemployment rate, since some unemployed persons are not covered for unemployment benefits, have not met the eligibility requirements, or have exhausted their benefits.

Extended benefits can be paid whenever the state's insured unemployment rate (not seasonally adjusted) (1) averages 5 percent or more over a 13-week period and (2) is at least 20 percent higher than it was during the same period in the previous two years. When the 20 percent requirement is not being met, the state has the option of paying extended benefits when its insured unemployment rate reaches 6 percent, regardless of the insured unemployment rate in previous years. All but 13 states have adopted this second option.

After the "on" indicator is triggered, the extended-benefits program must remain in effect for at least 13 weeks. No state paid extended benefits during the first week of 1989.

Supplementary Extended Benefits

Because of the large number of unemployed workers who exhaust both regular and extended benefits during severe recessions, Congress on numerous occasions has enacted special programs to assist the long-term unemployed. Several special extended-benefits programs have been enacted in recent years.[8] The most recent was the Federal Supplemental Compensation Act of 1982 (modified in 1983) that provided benefits to people who had exhausted their rights to regular benefits and who had no rights to regular, extended, or additional benefits under any state or federal law. Under the program, unemployment benefits could be paid for additional weeks, varying in duration up to 14 weeks. The supplemental program ended in March 1985.

FINANCING UNEMPLOYMENT INSURANCE

Regular state unemployment insurance programs are financed by payroll taxes paid by covered employers on the covered wages of the employees. Five states also require the employees to contribute to the program (Alabama, Alaska, New Jersey, Pennsylvania, and West Virginia). All payroll taxes are deposited in the federal Unemployment Trust Fund. A separate account is established for each state, and unemployment benefits are paid out of each state's account.

In 1990, each covered employer paid a federal unemployment tax of 6.2 percent on the first $7,000 of annual wages paid to each covered worker. However, the employer can credit toward the federal tax any contributions paid under an approved state unemployment insurance program and any tax savings under an approved experience rating plan. However, the credit available to employers may be reduced if the state falls behind on the repayment of loans to the federal government that were obtained when the state's reserve for paying benefits became exhausted during periods of high unemployment.

The maximum employer credit is limited to 5.4 percent. The remaining 0.8 percent, including a temporary surcharge of 0.2 percent, is paid to the federal government. The tax revenues paid to the federal government are used for administrative expenses, for the federal government's share of the costs of extended benefits (50 percent), and for loans to states with depleted benefit reserves. The surcharge enacted in 1976 has been extended through 1990.

Finally, because of a desire to strengthen their unemployment reserves, the majority of states currently provide for a taxable wage base in excess of $7,000. In these states the 1989 taxable wage base ranged from $7,100 to $20,900.

---

[8]Those programs included the Temporary Unemployment Compensation Act (TUC) of 1958; Temporary Extended Unemployment Compensation Act (TEUC) of 1961; Extended Unemployment Compensation Act of 1970; Emergency Unemployment Compensation Act of 1971; Emergency Unemployment Compensation Act of 1974; Emergency Compensation and Special Unemployment Assistance Extension Act of 1975; and the Federal Supplemental Compensation Act of 1982 (modified in 1983).

Employee Contributions

Except in Alabama, Alaska, New Jersey, Pennsylvania, and West Virginia, employee contributions are not used to finance unemployment insurance programs. There are several reasons why most states do not require employee contributions: first, it is argued that employees should not contribute because they have no control over their unemployment; second, labor unions oppose employee contributions on the grounds that the contributions further reduce take-home pay and that employees already bear the tax burden as consumers in the form of higher prices; third, employers fear greater labor union demands for higher wages if employees contribute; finally, as the use of experience rating for employers increases, it is considered undesirable to develop a similar system for employee rates.

Experience Rating

All states have some type of experience rating by which individual employer contribution rates are based on their own experience. Experience rating is a highly controversial issue, and numerous arguments are advanced both for and against the concept.[9]

Arguments for Experience Rating. The arguments used to justify experience rating include the following: (1) stabilization of employment, (2) proper allocation of costs, and (3) greater employer interest and participation.

1. STABILIZATION OF EMPLOYMENT. It is argued that experience rating encourages firms to stabilize employment. This viewpoint is attributed to John R. Commons who believed that workers' compensation reduced industrial accidents, since employers were held responsible for the costs of such accidents. Likewise, experience rating in unemployment insurance would encourage some employers to reduce their unemployment if they were charged with its costs.

The viewpoint that experience rating causes firms to stabilize their employment is supported by several research studies that indicate that many firms attempt to reduce seasonal unemployment in response to experience rating.[10] Also, experience rating appears to have a positive effect in reducing short-term temporary layoffs. One study showed that an increase of one percentage point in the effectiveness of the maximum tax rate resulted in a decrease of 0.14 percent-

---

[9]See Joseph M. Becker, S. J., *Experience Rating in Unemployment Insurance: Virtue or Vice* (Kalamazoo, Mich.: W. E. Upjohn Institute for Employment Research, 1972), and William Haber and Merrill G. Murray, *Unemployment Insurance in the American Economy* (Homewood, Ill.: Richard D. Irwin, 1966), pp. 330–357.

[10]Terrence C. Halpin, "Employment Stabilization," *Unemployment Compensation: Studies and Research,* Vol. 2 (Washington, D.C.: U.S. Government Printing Office, 1980, p. 415.

age point in layoff unemployment (a 10 percent drop in the layoff unemployment rate for the 1976 sample used in the test).[11]

2. PROPER ALLOCATION OF UNEMPLOYMENT COSTS.   It is argued that experience rating results in the proper allocation of unemployment costs, since firms with high unemployment must pay higher contribution rates. Under a system of unemployment insurance, employers are considered responsible for the unemployment of their employees. If firms with high levels of unemployment are not charged the proper costs of unemployment benefits, then these costs must be partly paid by other firms. This is considered inequitable to firms that have lower levels of unemployment.

3. GREATER EMPLOYER INTEREST.   Finally, it is argued that experience rating encourages greater employer interest in unemployment insurance programs. Experience rating may cause some firms to have a greater interest in benefit levels and pending unemployment insurance legislation. Also, employers may have a greater interest in preventing the payment of dishonest claims and in the efficient administration of the program.

Arguments against Experience Rating.   The major arguments against experience rating include the following: (1) little control by firms over employment, (2) employer resistance to benefit increases, (3) inadequate trust fund income, and (4) automatic destabilizer.

1. LITTLE CONTROL OVER EMPLOYMENT.   It is argued that most unemployment is caused by a deficiency in aggregate demand, cyclical forces, and structural changes in the economy, factors over which firms have little control. In addition, firms in stable industries pay lower contribution rates even though they make no determined effort to stabilize their employment. Thus, it is said that firms with little control over unemployment should not be penalized by the payment of high rates.

2. EMPLOYER RESISTANCE TO BENEFIT INCREASES.   Another argument is that some business firms oppose the liberalization of unemployment benefits because of the higher contribution rates they must pay. Many firms evaluate proposed benefit increases in terms of their effect on experience rating and may lobby in the state legislatures to oppose these increases.

3. INADEQUATE TRUST FUND INCOME.   Critics of present financing methods oppose experience rating on the grounds that lower contribution rates provide inadequate income to the system. Thus, unemployment reserves may be depleted to dangerously low levels during periods of extended unemployment. Critics point out that many state unemployment programs are inadequately financed. For example, during the 1981–1982 recession, many states had drawn down their unemployment reserves to dangerously low levels. In addition, the average employer contribution rate declines during an extended period of pros-

---

[11]Ibid.

perity when the unemployment reserves should be building up rapidly. Thus, it is argued that experience rating causes the system to be underfinanced.

4. AUTOMATIC DESTABILIZER. Another argument against experience rating is that it is a destabilizer, since unemployment taxes increase during recessions when firms are least able to pay. Thus, the recession is aggravated because of the higher unemployment taxes that must be paid.

The empirical evidence, however, generally disproves the viewpoint that experience rating is a destabilizer.[12] These studies indicate that absolute unemployment taxes and unemployment insurance tax rates generally tend to move in the proper countercyclical direction.

There are three reasons why experience rating may not be a destabilizer. First, *absolute unemployment taxes* tend to decline (or increase less rapidly) during recessions, since workers are laid off and the payroll taxes paid by employers on their behalf cease.

Second, *unemployment insurance tax rates* do not automatically increase during a recession. There is usually a time lag of at least one year between the increased unemployment experienced by firms during a recession and the higher tax rates that must be paid under an experience-rating schedule. The state laws typically provide for the computation of unemployment tax rates for covered employers only once each year. Since the postwar recessions have been relatively short, the recession may be over before the higher tax rates from increased unemployment go into effect. Thus, the higher tax rates would tend to go into effect during the upswing of the cycle, which is the proper countercyclical direction.

Finally, any destabilizing features associated with experience rating are partly offset by the experience-rating provisions used by the states. The states typically use three years of payroll experience in their formulas when determining the firm's unemployment tax rate. The adverse financial impact of a year of high unemployment and lower payrolls, which would tend to increase the firm's tax rate, could be diluted by the favorable experience, if any, of the other two years.

Experience-Rating Provisions. The following section briefly describes the major features of experience-rating provisions.

1. REQUIREMENTS FOR EXPERIENCE RATING. Employers are required to meet certain federal and state requirements before they are eligible for experience rating. First, most states require new employers to have one to three years of unemployment experience before experience rating is used. Second, many states require a minimum balance in the unemployment fund before any reduced rates are allowed. The purpose of this solvency requirement is to make

---

[12]See George E. Rejda, "Unemployment Insurance as an Automatic Stabilizer," *The Journal of Risk and Insurance*, Vol. 33, No. 2 (June 1966), pp. 195–208, and Neil Anthony Palomba, *A Measure of the Stabilizing Effect of the Unemployment Compensation Program—With Emphasis on the Experience Rating Controversy,* Ph.D. Dissertation, University of Minnesota, 1968.

certain that the fund is adequate to pay benefits. Finally, many states provide for an increase in employer contribution rates when the fund falls below certain specified levels.

2. TYPES OF FORMULAS.   Five experience-rating formulas have been used: *the reserve ratio, benefit ratio, benefit-wage ratio, compensable separations,* and *payroll-decline formulas.* Although the formulas are complex and vary greatly, they have the common objective of establishing the relative experience of individual employers with respect to unemployment or benefit costs. Only the reserve-ratio method will be discussed, since it is used in the majority of states and is the most popular method for determining individual employer contribution rates.

The reserve-ratio system is essentially cost accounting. Each employer has an individual record, in which are recorded payroll amounts, tax contributions, and unemployment benefits paid. *The total benefits paid since the program became effective are subtracted from total employer contributions over that period. The balance is then divided by the employer's taxable payroll, which is usually an average of the last three years. The higher the reserve ratio, the lower the tax rate.* Thus, we have the following:

$$\frac{\text{Total employer contributions} - \text{Total benefits paid}}{\text{Taxable payroll (usually an average of the last three years)}} = \text{Reserve ratio}$$

The employer's contribution rate depends on the reserve ratio as well as the size of the state unemployment reserve fund. (A reduction in the overall reserve fund may require an alternate tax schedule involving higher rates.) As we stated earlier, the higher the reserve ratio, the lower the tax rate. However, the reserve-ratio method is designed to make certain that no employer receives a rate reduction unless the firm contributes more to the fund over the years than the workers receive in benefits. The following is an example of the reserve-ratio method:

POSITIVE RESERVE RATIO	CONTRIBUTION RATE
11.5% or more	0.1%
11.0–11.4	0.2
10.5–10.9	0.3
10.0–10.4	0.5
9.5–9.9	1.0
9.0–9.4	1.5
8.5–8.9	2.0
8.0–8.4	2.5
7.5–7.9	3.0
0.0–7.4	3.5

NEGATIVE RESERVE RATIO	CONTRIBUTION RATE
0.1–4.9	4.5
5.0–9.9	5.0
10.0% or more	5.4

3. OTHER FACTORS.   Various methods are used in experience rating to determine which employer should be charged with the benefits that an unemployed worker collects. A small number of states charge the *most recent employer*, on the theory that it has primary responsibility for the unemployment. Other states charge *base-period employers in inverse chronological order*. This method is based on the theory that responsibility for unemployment lessens with time. A maximum limit is placed on the amount charged to the most recent employer; when this limit is reached, the next most recent employer is charged, and so on. Most states, however, charge employers *in proportion to base-period wages*, because it is believed that unemployment results from general labor market conditions rather than from the separations of any single employer.

Noncharging-of-benefit provisions are used in most states. This means that certain unemployment costs are not charged to employers, such as benefits paid for appealed cases that are reversed and benefits paid following a period of disqualification for a voluntary quit, misconduct, or refusal of suitable work.

In many states, employers can obtain lower rates by voluntary contributions. The voluntary contribution increases the balance in the employer's account (in reserve-ratio states), and a lower rate results by which the employer saves more than the amount of the voluntary contribution.

Finally, provisions in all states specify the conditions under which the employer's experience can be transferred to another employer acquiring the business.

Unemployment Insurance Trust Fund

All unemployment insurance tax contributions are deposited in the Unemployment Trust Fund, which is administered by the Secretary of the Treasury. The fund is invested as a whole, but each state has a separate account, which is credited with the unemployment tax contributions collected by the states, plus the state's share of interest on investments. Trust fund balances are invested in securities of the federal government.

There are four special accounts in the Unemployment Trust Fund. First, the Employment Security Administration Account (ESAA) is used to pay for the administrative expenses of federal-state employment security programs. Second, the Extended Unemployment Compensation Account (EUCA) is used to pay the federal government's share of the Extended Benefits program. Third, states with depleted reserves can borrow from the Federal Unemployment Account (FUA); interest is charged on loans that are not repaid by the end of the fiscal year in which they are obtained. Finally, the Federal Employee Compensation Account (FECA) is used to pay benefits to federal civilian and military personnel. However, unlike the first three accounts that are financed by unemployment taxes, the FECA account is funded out of the general revenues of the federal government.

ADMINISTRATION

The federal law is administered by the Employment and Training Administration, Unemployment Insurance Service, in the U.S. Department of Labor.

Each state administers its unemployment insurance law by maintaining records, collecting taxes, determining eligibility, processing claims, and paying unemployment benefits. Each state is required to designate an employment security agency to perform these functions. Some states use an independent board or commission; some designate an independent department of state government, which reports directly to the governor; and some use the state department of labor or some other agency as the employment security agency.

The agencies operate through local employment offices, which process the claims and act as employment exchanges by providing job development and placement services. The unemployed worker normally registers for work at the public employment office. He or she usually files a weekly claim for benefits at the same office. In most cases, the claims may be filed by mail. Unless there is a good cause for late reporting, the worker must file for benefits within seven days after the week for which the claim is made. The employment security agency administering the program usually pays the benefits by check, but in some states, local offices also pay benefits.

The states must provide claimants who are denied benefits an opportunity for a fair hearing. The worker can appeal first to a referee or impartial tribunal and then to a board of review. If necessary, the board's decision can be appealed in the courts.

The employment security agency also administers the interstate agreements for workers who move to different states. There are special wage-combining agreements on behalf of workers who earn wages in two or more states.

TAXATION OF BENEFITS

Under an earlier law, only part of a recipient's unemployment insurance benefits was subject to the federal income tax. However, as a result of the Tax Reform Act of 1986, all unemployment insurance benefits are now taxable.

Table 14-2 shows the effects of taxing all unemployment insurance benefits in calendar 1989. The results overall show that taxation of unemployment benefits is highly progressive. About 15 percent of all benefits paid out were recovered by taxation. The table understates, however, the true financial impact because of significant underreporting by recipients. The total unemployment compensation benefits reported in the Current Population Survey (CPS) are equal to only about two-thirds of the total benefits paid out.

TABLE 14-2   Effect of Taxing Unemployment Compensation Benefits, by Income Class, 1989

LEVEL OF INDIVIDUAL OR COUPLE INCOME[1]	NUMBER OF RECIPIENTS OF UNEMPLOYMENT COMPENSATION (IN THOUSANDS)	NUMBER AFFECTED BY TAXATION OF BENEFITS (IN THOUSANDS)	TOTAL AMOUNT OF UNEMPLOYMENT COMPENSATION BENEFITS (IN BILLIONS OF DOLLARS)	TOTAL AMOUNT OF TAXES ON BENEFITS (IN BILLIONS OF DOLLARS)	TAXES AS A PERCENT OF TOTAL BENEFITS[3]
Less than $10,000	1,604	588	$ 2.2	$0.1	4.4%
$10,000 to $15,000	1,040	935	1.5	0.2	11.9
$15,000 to $20,000	938	906	1.3	0.2	16.2
$20,000 to $25,000	798	776	1.2	0.2	15.7
$25,000 to $30,000	767	764	1.1	0.2	16.6
$30,000 to $40,000	1,062	1,062	1.5	0.2	16.5
$40,000 to $50,000	579	579	0.9	0.2	19.2
$50,000 to $100,000	595	595	0.9	0.3	27.7
At least $100,000	37	37	0.1	(2)	30.1
All	7,421	6,242	$10.8	$1.6	14.5%

[1] Cash income (based on income of tax filing unit) plus capital gains realizations.
[2] Less than $50 million.
[3] Figures shown were calculated from the data used in the prior two columns before those data were rounded.

Note: Aggregate unemployment compensation benefits in the Current Population Survey (CPS) are equal to only about two-thirds of total benefits paid out. The number of recipients is also understated on the CPS.

Source: U.S. Congress, House, Committee on Ways and Means, *Background Material and Data on Programs within the Jurisdiction of the Committee on Ways and Means* (Washington, D.C.: U.S. Government Printing Office, 1989), Table 6, p. 450.

SUGGESTIONS FOR ADDITIONAL READING

MYERS, ROBERT J. *Social Security,* 3rd ed., Chap. 13. Homewood, Ill.: Richard D. Irwin, 1985.

NATIONAL FOUNDATION FOR UNEMPLOYMENT COMPENSATION & WORKERS' COMPENSATION. *Highlights of State Unemployment Compensation Laws.* Washington, D.C.: National Foundation for Unemployment Compensation & Workers' Compensation, January 1990.

PRICE, DANIEL N. "Unemployment Insurance, Then and Now, 1935–85," *Social Security Bulletin,* Vol. 48, No. 10 (October 1985), pp. 22–32.

"Social Security Programs in the United States," *Social Security Bulletin,* Vol. 52, No. 7 (July 1989), pp. 19–27.

U.S. CONGRESS, HOUSE, COMMITTEE ON WAYS AND MEANS. *Background Material and Data on Programs within the Jurisdiction of the Committee on Ways and Means.* Washington, D.C.: U.S. Government Printing Office, 1989. This volume is published annually and provides valuable data on the current operations of unemployment compensation programs.

U.S. DEPARTMENT OF LABOR, EMPLOYMENT AND TRAINING ADMINISTRATION, UNEMPLOYMENT INSURANCE SERVICE. *Comparison of State Unemployment Insurance Laws,* September 1989. The data are periodically updated.

WILLIAMS, C. ARTHUR, JR., JOHN G. TURNBULL, AND EARL F. CHEIT. *Economic and Social Security,* 5th ed., Chap. 12. New York: John Wiley & Sons, 1982.

15

PROBLEMS AND ISSUES IN UNEMPLOYMENT INSURANCE

Millions of unemployed workers must rely primarily on state unemployment compensation programs as their major source of income during periods of extended unemployment. State unemployment compensation programs, however, presently have serious defects that limit their effectiveness in reducing economic insecurity from involuntary unemployment.

In this chapter, we shall continue our discussion of unemployment insurance by examining several important problems and issues. More specifically, the following problems will be analyzed: (1) adequacy of benefits, (2) relatively small proportion of the unemployed who receive benefits, (3) greater difficulty in obtaining extended benefits, (4) harsh disqualifications, (5) exhaustion of benefits, (6) inadequate trust fund reserves in most states, (7) size of the taxable wage base, (8) reduction in the effectiveness of experience rating, (9) contest of claims by employers, (10) reinsurance, (11) decline in the effectiveness of unemployment insurance as an automatic stabilizer, and (12) improving unemployment insurance.[1]

ADEQUACY OF BENEFITS

One of the most controversial issues is the adequacy of weekly benefits. Ideally, the weekly benefits should be sufficiently high so that unemployed workers can maintain their previous standard of living.

---

[1]This chapter is based heavily on George E. Rejda and Kyung W. Lee, "State Unemployment Compensation Programs: Immediate Reforms Needed," *The Journal of Risk and Insurance*, Vol. 56, No. 4 (December 1989), pp. 649–669.

Average Wage Replacement Rate

One standard of benefit adequacy is that unemployment benefits should restore at least half of the average gross weekly wage in covered employment for the great majority of beneficiaries. This is based on the principle that most unemployed workers should not be faced with a substantial reduction in their previous standard of living, such as defaulting on a car loan or having a mortgage foreclosed.

The 50 percent replacement goal is a reasonable objective, but it is not being met in many states. *Under current laws, many unemployed workers receive benefits that are less than half of their wage.* This can be illustrated by Table 15-1 which shows the average wage replacement rate in the United States from 1971 through the third quarter of 1988. The average replacement rate has been roughly constant over time and was only 34 percent for the third quarter of 1988. Thus, many beneficiaries are not receiving benefits equal to half their wages at the present time.

The relatively low average replacement rate can be partly explained by the low statutory limits on maximum benefits in many states. As a result, high-wage earners have significantly lower replacement rates than the average rates shown.

TABLE 15-1   U.S. Average Wage Replacement Rate: Ratio of Average Weekly Benefit Amount to Average Weekly Wage 1971–1988

YEAR	FIRST QUARTER	SECOND QUARTER	THIRD QUARTER	FOURTH QUARTER	AVERAGE
1971	0.347	0.346	0.344	0.356	0.348
1972	.356	.356	.355	.361	.357
1973	.354	.350	.343	.354	.350
1974	.349	.349	.358	.365	.355
1975	.352	.358	.366	.377	.363
1976	.363	.362	.356	.366	.362
1977	.358	.351	.347	.362	.354
1978	.360	.351	.345	.357	.353
1979	.350	.345	.345	.362	.351
1980	.350	.358	.359	.363	.357
1981	.343	.346	.348	.363	.350
1982	.356	.362	.366	.377	.365
1983	.365	.364	.356	.357	.360
1984	.356	.355	.346	.357	.354
1985	.352	.350	.349	.359	.352
1986	.359	.361	.360	.363	.361
1987	.358	.358	.355	.357	.357
1988	.349	.344	.342	NA	NA

NA—Not available.

Source: U.S. Congress, House, Committee on Ways and Means, *Background Material and Data on Programs within the Jurisdiction of the Committee on Ways and Means* (Washington, D.C.: U.S. Government Printing Office, 1989), Table 17, p. 499.

Poverty Threshold

Another measure of benefit adequacy is to compare the state's average weekly unemployment benefit with the poverty threshold. The estimated national poverty level in 1988 for an unrelated individual under age 65 was $6,152 ($118.31 weekly). Most states presently pay benefits that are at least equal to the poverty level. *However, in 1988 eight states paid average weekly unemployment benefits for total unemployment that were below the poverty line.*[2]

The poverty threshold level of income, however, provides only a subsistence standard of living. Therefore, a more meaningful measure is 125 percent of the poverty threshold. *In 1988, 29 states paid average weekly unemployment benefits that were below 125 percent of the poverty line.* Thus, based on poverty thresholds, the standard of living attained by beneficiaries in many states during a period of total unemployment is relatively low.

After-Tax Value of the Benefits

Another measure of adequacy is the replacement rate after taxes for both benefits and earnings. A recent study by the House Ways and Means Committee shows the replacement rate of benefits and earnings on both a pre-tax and after-tax basis for low-wage and high-wage earners (see Table 15-2). A low-wage earner is assumed to earn $5.50 hourly ($11,400 annually), while a high-wage earner is assumed to earn four times the 1986 poverty threshold for a family of four ($44,812 annually). The unemployment benefits are those payable in January 1988.

In general, unemployment benefits on an after-tax basis appear adequate for most low-wage earners based on the 50-percent replacement rate standard discussed earlier. *On an after-tax basis, 48 states paid benefits that restored 50 percent or more of the incomes earned by low-wage earners.*

However, a different conclusion emerges when the after-tax replacement rate for high-wage earners is considered. *On an after-tax basis, no state paid benefits that replaced 50 percent or more of the incomes earned by high-wage earners.* The highest after-tax replacement rate was in Massachusetts (37 percent). In half of the states, the after-tax replacement rate was 25 percent or less.

In summary, based on the preceding standards, unemployment benefits generally are inadequate in most states. However, the true economic loss is understated, since the data do not consider the loss of valuable employee benefits, such as the loss of group life and health insurance, group disability income protection, employer contributions into the private pension, profit sharing or thrift and saving plan, Christmas or year-end bonus, and other employee benefits. The loss of employee benefits can be substantial if unemployment is pro-

---

[2]U.S. Congress, House, Committee on Ways and Means, *Background Material and Data on Programs within the Jurisdiction of the Committee on Ways and Means* (Washington, D.C.: U.S. Government Printing Office, 1989), Table 7, pp. 451–452 and Table 1, p. 941.

TABLE 15-2 Weekly UC Replacement Rates under Alternative Tax Treatment of UC and Earnings by State for Low-Wage and High-Wage Earners[1,2]

	AFTER-TAX BENEFITS/AFTER-TAX EARNINGS	PRE-TAX BENEFITS/PRE-TAX EARNINGS
Low-Wage Earner		
Massachusetts	0.80	0.73
Illinois	0.77	0.70
Michigan	0.76	0.69
Kentucky	0.75	0.69
Oregon	0.71	0.65
Rhode Island	0.71	0.65
Connecticut	0.70	0.64
Iowa	0.68	0.62
District of Columbia	0.67	0.61
New Jersey	0.66	0.60
Delaware	0.66	0.60
Colorado	0.66	0.60
Maryland	0.66	0.60
Maine	0.65	0.59
Missouri	0.64	0.59
Vermont	0.64	0.58
Pennsylvania	0.62	0.56
Indiana	0.61	0.56
Kansas	0.61	0.55
Alaska	0.60	0.55
Alabama	0.60	0.54
Nebraska	0.59	0.54
New Hampshire	0.59	0.53
Louisiana	0.58	0.52
Wyoming	0.57	0.52
West Virginia	0.57	0.52
Washington	0.57	0.52
Virginia	0.57	0.52
Texas	0.57	0.52
Oklahoma	0.57	0.52
Nevada	0.57	0.52
Hawaii	0.57	0.52
Georgia	0.57	0.52
Arizona	0.57	0.52
Wisconsin	0.55	0.50
Utah	0.55	0.50
South Dakota	0.55	0.50
South Carolina	0.55	0.50
Ohio	0.55	0.50
North Carolina	0.55	0.50

(continued)

TABLE 15-2 *(Continued)*

	AFTER-TAX BENEFITS/AFTER-TAX EARNINGS	PRE-TAX BENEFITS/PRE-TAX EARNINGS
New York	0.55	0.50
New Mexico	0.55	0.50
Mississippi	0.55	0.50
Minnesota	0.55	0.50
Idaho	0.55	0.50
Florida	0.55	0.50
Arkansas	0.55	0.50
Montana	0.54	0.49
California	0.50	0.45
Tennessee	0.48	0.44
North Dakota	0.44	0.40
High-Wage Earner		
Massachusetts	0.37	0.33
Pennsylvania	0.34	0.30
Minnesota	0.32	0.29
District of Columbia	0.32	0.29
Ohio	0.32	0.29
Connecticut	0.32	0.29
Michigan	0.31	0.28
New Jersey	0.31	0.28
Rhode Island	0.31	0.27
Illinois	0.30	0.27
West Virginia	0.29	0.26
Hawaii	0.29	0.26
Oregon	0.29	0.26
Colorado	0.28	0.25
Texas	0.27	0.24
Maryland	0.27	0.24
Washington	0.27	0.24
Louisiana	0.27	0.24
Delaware	0.26	0.24
North Carolina	0.26	0.24
Kansas	0.26	0.24
Arkansas	0.26	0.24
Utah	0.26	0.23
Florida	0.26	0.23
Wisconsin	0.26	0.23
Wyoming	0.26	0.23
Oklahoma	0.25	0.23
Idaho	0.24	0.22
Alaska	0.24	0.22
Montana	0.23	0.21
New York	0.23	0.21

(continued)

TABLE 15-2   *(Continued)*

	AFTER-TAX BENEFITS/AFTER-TAX EARNINGS	PRE-TAX BENEFITS/PRE-TAX EARNINGS
Iowa	0.23	0.21
North Dakota	0.23	0.21
Nevada	0.23	0.21
Maine	0.23	0.20
Virginia	0.22	0.19
California	0.21	0.19
Vermont	0.21	0.19
New Mexico	0.21	0.18
New Hampshire	0.20	0.18
Georgia	0.20	0.18
Kentucky	0.20	0.18
Tennessee	0.19	0.17
South Dakota	0.18	0.16
Missouri	0.18	0.16
Arizona	0.17	0.16
Nebraska	0.17	0.16
South Carolina	0.17	0.15
Mississippi	0.17	0.15
Indiana	0.17	0.15
Alabama	0.16	0.14

[1]Worker is assumed to be married, with a nonworking spouse, and two children. Dependents' allowances are included where applicable. Worker is assumed to be jobless for one-fourth of the year. Low-wage worker is defined as having annual earnings of $11,400 a year, or an hourly wage rate of $5.50. High-wage worker is defined as having annual earnings of $44,812, four times the 1986 poverty threshold for a family of four. Federal income taxes and social security payroll taxes are calculated at 1988 rates. All calculations were first made on an annual basis and then divided by 52 to convert to weekly replacement rates. UC benefit levels are those available in January 1988.

[2]Puerto Rico and the Virgin Islands are excluded because they do not pay U.S. federal income taxes. However, UC benefits are taxable in those jurisdictions under the applicable tax rates, which would be analogous to state income tax laws in the 50 states.

Source: U.S. Congress, House, Committee on Ways and Means, *Background Material and Data on Programs within the Jurisdiction of the Committee on Ways and Means* (Washington, D.C.: U.S. Government Printing Office, 1989), Table 23, pp. 508–511.

longed. The average value of all employee benefits per employee in 1987 was $10,708.[3]

RELATIVELY SMALL PROPORTION OF UNEMPLOYED RECEIVING BENEFITS

The most serious defect in unemployment insurance (UI) programs at the present time is the relatively small proportion of unemployed workers who receive

---

[3]Research Center, Economic Policy Division, U.S. Chamber of Commerce, *Employee Benefits, 1988 Edition* (Washington, D.C.: U.S. Government Printing Office, 1988), p. 5.

benefits. Although about 97 percent of all wage and salary workers are covered by UI programs, only a small fraction of the total unemployed at any time receives UI benefits. *In 1988, only about one in three unemployed workers received benefits in an average month* (see Table 15-3). The record is not much better during business

TABLE 15-3 Number and Proportion of Unemployed Workers Receiving Unemployment Insurance Benefits 1955–1988

YEAR	NUMBER OF UNEMPLOYED (THOUSANDS)	NUMBER NOT RECEIVING BENEFITS (THOUSANDS)	PERCENT RECEIVING BENEFITS	UNEMPLOYMENT RATE
1955	2,852	1,453	49.1%	4.4%
1956	2,750	1,427	48.1	4.1
1957	2,859	1,288	54.9	4.3
1958	4,602	1,829	60.3	6.8
1959	3,740	1,880	49.7	5.5
1960	3,852	1,781	53.8	5.5
1961	4,714	1,720	63.5	6.7
1962	3,911	1,965	49.8	5.5
1963	4,070	2,097	48.5	5.7
1964	3,786	2,033	46.3	5.2
1965	3,366	1,916	43.1	4.5
1966	2,875	1,746	39.3	3.8
1967	2,975	1,705	42.7	3.8
1968	2,817	1,630	42.1	3.6
1969	2,832	1,655	41.6	3.5
1970	4,093	2,023	50.6	4.9
1971	5,016	2,408	52.0	5.9
1972	4,882	2,690	44.9	5.6
1973	4,365	2,572	41.1	4.9
1974	5,156	2,598	49.6	5.6
1975	7,929	1,943	75.5	8.5
1976	7,406	2,417	67.4	7.7
1977	6,991	3,057	56.3	7.1
1978	6,202	3,517	43.3	6.1
1979	6,137	3,554	42.1	5.8
1980	7,637	3,789	50.4	7.1
1981	8,273	4,848	41.4	7.6
1982	10,678	5,846	45.3	9.7
1983	10,717	6,012	43.9	9.6
1984	8,539	5,630	34.1	7.5
1985	8,312	5,580	32.9	7.2
1986	8,237	5,545	32.7	7.0
1987	7,425	5,089	31.5	6.2
1988	6,701	4,589	31.5	5.5

Note: Unemployment insurance coverage data for 1985–88 do not include beneficiaries for Puerto Rico and the Virgin Islands; the data are consistent with the unemployment data which also do not include these areas. Data before 1985, however, are from historical tables that do include include Puerto Rico and the Virgin Islands in the tabulation of unemployment insurance beneficiaries, but not in the tabulation of the unemployed. The pre-1985 data thus slightly overstate the percentage receiving benefits in those years.

Source: Isaac Shapiro and Marion E. Nichols, Center on Budget and Policy Priorities, *Unprotected: Unemployment Insurance and Jobless Workers in 1988* (Washington, D.C.: Center on Budget Policy Priorities, 1989), Table I, p. 2.

TABLE 15-4   Payment of Unemployment Benefits by the States in 1988

STATE	NUMBER NOT RECEIVING BENEFITS	PERCENTAGE RECEIVING BENEFITS	RANK	UNEMPLOYMENT RATE IN 1988
Alabama	103,800	23.7%	38	7.2%
Alaska	11,200	51.5	3	9.3
Arizona	82,700	20.4	43	6.3
Arkansas	60,400	29.8	27	7.7
California	415,500	44.1	9	5.3
Colorado	82,200	24.6	36	6.4
Connecticut	30,700	40.9	14	3.0
Delaware	6,600	39.8	15	3.2
District of Columbia	8,900	47.9	5	5.0
Florida	252,300	17.3	51	5.0
Georgia	147,900	20.1	45	5.8
Hawaii	9,300	41.9	11	3.2
Idaho	16,200	42.2	10	5.8
Illinois	283,900	27.6	32	6.8
Indiana	119,800	20.1	45	5.3
Iowa	48,600	27.5	34	4.5
Kansas	41,100	32.6	21	4.8
Kentucky	105,400	21.3	41	7.9
Louisiana	166,800	20.2	44	10.9
Maine	12,900	41.3	13	3.8
Maryland	82,400	25.1	35	4.5
Massachusetts	44,000	57.3	2	3.3
Michigan	232,300	33.2	20	7.6
Minnesota	60,000	36.2	18	4.0
Mississippi	74,100	22.8	39	8.4
Missouri	102,200	30.9	25	5.7
Montana	18,700	30.6	26	6.8
Nebraska	20,400	29.5	28	3.6
Nevada	20,600	31.4	23	5.2
New Hampshire	12,100	19.1	48	2.4
New Jersey	78,700	47.8	6	3.8
New Mexico	41,800	22.6	40	7.8
New York	192,600	46.2	7	4.2
North Carolina	81,900	32.3	22	3.6
North Dakota	10,500	34.2	19	4.8
Ohio	229,300	28.4	29	6.0
Oklahoma	83,000	18.7	50	6.7
Oregon	49,700	39.4	16	5.8
Pennsylvania	171,700	41.6	12	5.1
Rhode Island	4,500	72.0	1	3.1
South Carolina	54,600	28.1	30	4.5
South Dakota	11,100	20.6	42	3.9
Tennessee	93,600	31.2	24	5.8
Texas	488,100	19.4	47	7.3
Utah	26,600	28.1	30	4.9
Vermont	4,000	50.2	4	2.8
Virginia	97,300	18.9	49	3.9
Washington	77,700	44.9	8	6.2
West Virginia	56,400	23.8	37	9.9
Wisconsin	67,000	39.1	17	4.3
Wyoming	10,900	27.6	32	6.3

Source: Isaac Shapiro and Marion E. Nichols, Center on Budget and Policy Priorities, *Unprotected: Unemployment Insurance and Jobless Workers in 1988* (Washington, D.C.: Center on Budget Priorities, 1989), Table II, p. 6.

recessions. During the trough of the severe 1981–1982 recession (November 1982), only 49 percent of the unemployed received benefits. This compares with a peak of 81 percent of the unemployed who received UI benefits in April 1975 and a low point of about 26 percent in October 1987.[4] In contrast, foreign countries generally compensate a much higher percentage of unemployed workers. For example, in August 1984, Germany, Japan, and Sweden compensated for over 60 percent of their unemployed, while the comparable figure for the United States was only 31 percent.[5]

In addition, there is wide variation among the individual states (see Table 15-4). In five states (Florida, New Hampshire, Oklahoma, Texas, and Virginia), fewer than one in five unemployed workers received benefits in 1988. Florida had the lowest percentage with only 17 percent of the workers receiving benefits in an average month. Only four states (Alaska, Massachusetts, Rhode Island, and Vermont) paid benefits to more than half of the unemployed workers.

Reasons for the Decline

A recent study by Mathematica Policy Research, Inc., prepared for the U.S. Department of Labor provides valuable information on the reasons for the decline in the proportion of unemployed workers who receive benefits. To estimate the proportion of unemployed who received benefits, Mathematica used a measure called the UI claims ratio. The *UI claims ratio* is the ratio of average weekly UI benefit claims under state programs during a quarter to the state's average total unemployment during the quarter. The UI claims ratio has also declined significantly from 0.492 in the 1950s to 0.347 in the 1980s (see Table 15-5).

Table 15-6 summarizes the major reasons for the decline in the UI claims ratio for 1980 through 1986. A large part of the total decline can be explained by more restrictive and tighter state eligibility requirements and administrative practices, especially in the states with insolvent trust fund accounts. These restrictive changes include increased monetary eligibility requirements and a reduction in the maximum potential duration of benefits (8 to 15 percent); an increase in disqualifying income denials (2 to 10 percent); and changes in other nonmonetary eligibility requirements (3 to 11 percent).

Changes in federal UI policy also accounted for a relatively large part of the decline in the UI claims ratio. These changes included a more restrictive extended benefits program (discussed later) and the partial taxation of UI benefits prior to the Tax Reform Act of 1986. In particular, the partial taxation of UI

---

[4]U.S. Congress, House, Committee on Ways and Means, *Background Material and Data on Programs within the Jurisdiction of the Committee on Ways and Means* (Washington, D.C.: U.S. Government Printing Office, 1988), p. 330.

[5]U.S. Congress, House, Committee on Ways and Means, *Background Material and Data on Programs within the Jurisdiction of the Committee on Ways and Means* (Washington, D.C.: U.S. Government Printing Office, 1987), p. 329.

**TABLE 15-5 Ratio of State UI Weeks
Claimed to Total Unemployment
1948–1986**

	CLAIMS RATIO
1948–49	0.489
1950–59	0.492
1960–69	0.426
1970–79	0.413
1980–86	0.347
Overall Mean	0.428

Note: Data are averages of quarterly figures.

Source: *An Examination of Declining UI Claims during the
1980s* (Princeton, N.J.: Mathematica Policy Research, Inc.,
1988), Table 1.1, p. 3.

benefits accounted for between 11 to 16 percent of the total decline. It is argued
that the after-tax value of UI benefits has declined significantly because of the
taxation of benefits; thus, there is less financial incentive for unemployed workers to apply for benefits.

Other reasons for the decline in the UI claims ratio include shifts in the
geographic distribution of unemployment and a decline in manufacturing un-

**TABLE 15-6 Major Reasons for the Decline in Unemployment Insurance
Claims Ratio, 1980–1986**

	PERCENT OF DECLINE EXPLAINED
1. *Changes in State UI Policy*	
—Increased monetary eligibility require- ments and reductions in the maximum po- tential duration of benefits	8 to 15%
—Increases in disqualifying income denials	2 to 10%
—Changes in other nonmonetary eligibility requirements	3 to 11%
2. *Changes in Federal UI Policy*	
—More restrictive extended benefits program	7%
—Partial taxation of benefits	11 to 16%
3. *Economic Effects*	
—Shifts in the geographic distribution of un- employment	16%
—Decline in manufacturing unemployment relative to total unemployment	4 to 18%
4. *Changes in Unemployment*	
—More accurate measure of unemployment	1 to 12%

Note: The total change explained exceeds 100 percent for the high-range estimates. This
result occurs because a number of estimates are made separately, and the interactions
among the effects are not fully accounted for by this procedure.

Source: *An Examination of Declining UI Claims during the 1980s: Final Report* (Princeton,
N.J.: Mathematica Policy Research Inc., 1988), pp. xii–xiii, 119–20.

employment relative to total unemployment. With respect to the latter reason, employment in manufacturing has declined while jobs in the services industries have expanded sharply. The result is a relative decline in manufacturing unemployment relative to total unemployment. Workers employed in manufacturing are more likely to belong to labor unions, and unions traditionally have encouraged unemployed workers to file for UI benefits. In contrast, workers in the services industry are less likely to be unionized or may be monetarily ineligible for benefits. Thus, they are less likely to apply for benefits. The Mathematica study estimated that the decline in manufacturing employment explained 4 to 18 percent of the decline in the UI claims ratio for 1980 through 1986.

Finally, a more accurate measure of unemployment explained 1 to 12 percent of the total decline in the UI claims ratio. If unemployment had been measured more accurately in previous decades, the UI claims ratio would have been lower, and the decline in the UI claims ratio during the 1980s would have been less pronounced.[6]

Violation of Social Insurance Principles

The fact that only a small proportion of unemployed workers receives benefits in an average month violates one of the most fundamental principles of social insurance—*broad coverage of workers against well-defined social risks, including the risk of unemployment.* Since only a small proportion of the total unemployed receives benefits at any time, the effectiveness of state UI programs in reducing economic insecurity from unemployment can be seriously questioned. In particular, the effectiveness of regular UI programs and the extended benefits program in reducing poverty for long-term unemployed workers has declined sharply. For example, unemployment benefits and other government benefits in 1976 reduced poverty rates for persons unemployed 40 to 52 weeks by 21 to 23 percentage points. However, in 1983, poverty rates for a similar group of long-term unemployed were reduced by only 14 to 16 percentage points by the payment of unemployment benefits and other benefits.[7]

GREATER DIFFICULTY IN OBTAINING EXTENDED BENEFITS

Another serious problem is that extended benefits are more difficult to obtain. Under the federal-state permanent extended benefits program, a maximum of 13 additional weeks of benefits can be paid to unemployed workers who exhaust their regular benefits. However, a change in the 1981 law made it more difficult

[6]Mathematica Policy Research, Inc., *An Examination of Declining UI Claims during the 1980s: Final Report* (Princeton, N.J.: Mathematica Policy Research, Inc., 1988), p. x.

[7]Isaac Shapiro and Marion E. Nichols, *Unprotected: Unemployment Insurance and Jobless Workers in 1988* (Washington, D.C.: Center on Budget and Policy Priorities, 1989), p. 15.

for unemployed workers to receive extended benefits. A substantially higher level of unemployment in a state is now required before extended benefits can be paid. The 1981 amendments eliminated the national "on" indicator which triggered the payment of extended benefits when a national insured unemployment rate (IUR) equaled or exceeded 4.5 percent. As we noted in Chapter 14, the IUR is the ratio of UI claims to total employment covered by UI. The IUR is substantially below the total unemployment rate because many unemployed workers have not met the waiting period and other eligibility requirements, are not covered for UI benefits, or have exhausted their benefits.

The state's IUR is now used to trigger extended benefits, and it is substantially higher than the national IUR used earlier to trigger extended benefits. As we noted in Chapter 14, extended benefits can only be paid when the state's 13-week IUR is 20 percent higher than its average weekly rate over the corresponding 13-week period during the last two years and is at least 5 percent. In addition, a state at its option can trigger the program when its current 13-week average IUR reaches 6 percent. All but 13 states have adopted the second optional trigger.

The state's IUR is badly flawed as a measure of long-term unemployment within the state. After unemployed workers exhaust their benefits, they are no longer counted in the computation of the insured unemployment rate. Thus, states with severe long-term unemployment problems can have a relatively low IUR. If the state's total unemployment rate remains unchanged, but the number of unemployed who exhaust their unemployment benefits increases, the state's IUR can actually fall.[8] As a result, at the present time, if a state has a regional recession and high unemployment, workers experiencing long-term unemployment may be ineligible for extended benefits. In 1988, ten states with troubled economies had high unemployment rates (Alabama, Alaska, Arkansas, Kentucky, Louisiana, Michigan, Mississippi, New Mexico, Texas, and West Virginia). Unemployment rates ranged from 10.9 percent in Louisiana to 7.2 percent in Alabama.[9] *Despite the high unemployment rates in those states, no state had an activated extended benefits program during the first week of January 1988.* Thus, extended benefits could not be paid to the long-term unemployed in those states.

HARSH DISQUALIFICATIONS

Another problem is the harsh disqualification provisions that exist in many states. Most states have tightened their disqualification provisions in recent years, which aggravates the problem of economic insecurity for many unemployed workers. *Of the 14.6 million workers who were "monetary eligible" for initial*

---

[8]U.S. Congress, House, Committee on Ways and Means, *Reform of the Unemployment Compensation Program,* Hearing before the Subcommittee on Public Compensation and Unemployment Compensation, 100th Cong., 1st sess., December 14, 1987, p. 242.

[9]See Table 15-4.

unemployment benefits in fiscal 1988, 23.5 percent were disqualified. This figure is broken down as follows:[10]

6.3%	Voluntarily quit without good cause
5.9	Not able or available for work
3.8	Fired for misconduct on the job
0.3	Refusing suitable work
7.2	Other disqualifying acts

The disqualification can be for a temporary period or for the entire period of unemployment. The states justify the withholding of benefits for a *temporary period,* such as six to eight weeks, on the grounds that the unemployed worker is initially responsible for the unemployment. However, after a reasonable period, it is assumed that the worker's continued unemployment is the result of adverse labor market conditions and that he or she is then considered to be involuntarily unemployed. Thus, based on this viewpoint, benefits should be denied for an initial period that does not exceed the average duration of unemployment in normal periods (six to eight weeks).

However, disqualification for the *entire period of unemployment* is based on the concept that the worker voluntarily becomes unemployed with no immediate job opportunities; consequently, the worker must accept the full consequences of a voluntary quit even if he or she experiences long-term unemployment because of an unexpected recession.

In addition, extended benefits will also be denied to an individual during the entire period of unemployment if he or she has been disqualified from receiving regular state benefits because of a voluntary quit, discharge for misconduct, or refusal of suitable work. Extended benefits are denied even though the disqualification is subsequently lifted with respect to the payment of state benefits prior to reemployment. However, the individual could receive extended benefits if the disqualification is lifted because he or she became reemployed and met the state's normal work or wage requirements.

EXHAUSTION OF BENEFITS

Another serious problem is the relatively large number of claimants who exhaust their regular benefits and are still unemployed. During periods of normal or low unemployment, about 20 to 25 percent of the claimants exhaust their regular benefits. During periods of high unemployment, this percentage increases sharply. For example, in 1975—a period of relatively high unemployment—about 38 percent of the claimants exhausted their regular benefits.[11]

---

[10]*Background Material and Data on Programs within the Jurisdiction of the Committee on Ways and Means,* 1989, p. 448.

[11]National Commission on Unemployment Compensation, *Unemployment Compensation: Final Report* (Washington, D.C.: U.S. Government Printing Office, 1980), Table 4, p. 62.

The maximum duration of regular benefits is 26 weeks in most states. *However, the maximum duration is not available to all claimants because the duration of benefits generally varies with the amount of past earnings or employment.* In some states, the average unemployed worker can expect to receive 26 weeks of regular benefits, but in others, it is considerably shorter. Thus, even in good times, large numbers of claimants exhaust their regular benefits and are still unemployed. For example, in 1988, a year of relatively low unemployment, 1.8 million beneficiaries exhausted their regular benefits.[12]

The National Commission on Unemployment Compensation recommends that state unemployment insurance programs should pay regular benefits for at least 26 weeks to workers with a strong current attachment to the labor force. If implemented, this recommendation would provide greater economic security to unemployed workers, especially those who are unemployed because of technological change, permanent shifts in demand, plant relocations, and declining industries.

INADEQUATE TRUST FUND RESERVES

Another serious problem is that most states have inadequate trust fund reserves for paying benefits during a severe recession. As a result, many states will be unable to pay unemployment benefits in a future recession without substantial borrowing from the federal government.

One commonly used measure to estimate the adequacy of the unemployment reserve account is known as the "high-cost multiple" (sometimes called the "reserve-ratio multiple"). The high-cost multiple is calculated by first computing the ratio of current net trust fund reserves to total wages earned in insured employment in the current year. This figure is then divided by the ratio of the highest amount of total state benefit payments experienced previously in any 12 consecutive months to total wages in insured employment during those 12 months. Thus, we have the following formula:

$$\text{High-cost multiple} = \frac{\text{Ratio of current net trust fund reserves to total wages earned in insured employment in the current year}}{\text{Ratio of highest state benefit payments during 12 consecutive months to total wages in insured employment during those 12 months}}$$

A value of one means that if total potential benefit liabilities increase at the same rate as total wages in insured employment, the state's current reserve

---

[12]*Background Material and Data on Programs within the Jurisdiction of the Committee on Ways and Means,* 1989, Table 12, p. 495.

balance can support 12 months of payments at the highest unemployment rate historically experienced.[13] The U.S. Department of Labor has recommended that the states should have a high-cost multiple between 1.5 and 3.0. A state that meets the 1.5 standard would have net unemployment reserves 1.5 times greater than the fund's historically worst 12-month benefit period and would be able to pay benefits for at least 18 months during a recession without borrowing. However, at the beginning of 1987, the overall system had a high-cost multiple of only 0.44, which meant that reserves would last only about five months during a severe recession. Although 39 states had adequate unemployment reserve accounts in 1969 based on the high-cost multiple measures, only two states (Mississippi and South Dakota) had adequate reserve accounts in 1986.[14]

States with inadequate reserve accounts can borrow from the Federal Unemployment Account. In 1983, about half of the states had to borrow to continue benefit payments to unemployed workers. A state has between 22 and 34 months to repay a loan without penalty. If a state fails to make loan repayments on time, employers operating in the state are subject to penalty taxes in the form of an automatic reduction in the Federal Unemployment Tax Act (FUTA) tax credit. The credit reduction is at least 0.3 percent per year and accumulates until the loan is repaid in full. The penalty taxes essentially represent involuntary repayments of state loans and escalate with the duration of delinquency. However, total penalty taxes often can be substantial and can be viewed as a form of "loan sharking" by the federal government.

For example, Pennsylvania owed the Federal Unemployment Account about $203 million at the beginning of 1989. However, employers in Pennsylvania in 1989 must pay a surcharge that will more than double the amount owed by the state. Under the rates assessed in 1989, Pennsylvania employers must pay about $475 million in unemployment taxes and penalties which exceed the amount owed by $272 million.[15] The excessive overpayments can place a severe financial burden on employers, can restrict the amount of capital available for economic development in the state, and can retard recovery by the state during a recession.

SIZE OF THE TAXABLE WAGE BASE

One proposal for raising additional revenue is to increase the size of the federal taxable wage base. Originally, all covered wages and salaries were subject to the Federal Unemployment Tax Act. However, the federal taxable wage base was reduced to the first $3,000 of each covered worker's earnings in 1939 (effective

---

[13]General Accounting Office, *Unemployment Insurance: Trust Fund Reserves Inadequate* (Washington, D.C.: U.S. General Accounting Office, 1988), pp. 26–27.

[14]Ibid., p. 3.

[15]Statement of Hon. William J. Coyne, *Reform of the Unemployment Compensation Program*, p. 257.

1940), which was the same wage base that applied to Social Security. The wage base was later increased to $4,200 in 1972, to $6,000 in 1978, and to $7,000 in 1983. However, despite increases in the wage base over time, taxable wages as a proportion of total wages nationally have declined from 93 percent in 1940 to 33 percent in March 1988. If the taxable wage base had been indexed for the increase in wages since 1947, the current federal wage base would be $22,097 instead of $7,000.[16] Taxable wages as a proportion of total wages will continue to decline, especially during inflationary periods when wages are rising, if the taxable wage base remains constant.

A higher federal taxable wage base is considered necessary for several reasons. First, failure of the states to increase the taxable wage base as total wages rise is a major reason for the inadequate financing that exists in most states. Unemployment benefits are related to wages, and an increase in wage levels over time results in an increase in unemployment insurance benefits, and thus in liabilities. However, if a state fails to increase its wage base as wages rise, the unemployment reserve account does not keep pace with the increase in liabilities. The result is a shortage of funds during a severe recession.

Second, a higher taxable wage base reduces inequities among employers in the financing of benefits. Some high-wage employers pay unemployment taxes on only a small proportion of their total payrolls, whereas others may pay taxes on 80 percent or more of total payroll. A higher taxable wage base would force the high-wage employers to pay a relatively larger share of total benefit costs.

Third, a higher taxable wage base increases the capacity of the states to raise additional revenues for more adequate unemployment benefits and program improvements.

Finally, the present narrow wage base tends to limit the effectiveness of experience rating. A higher base would widen the range within which experience rating could operate and, thus, make possible a more meaningful differentiation among employers.

As an alternative to increasing the taxable wage base, *tax rates* could be increased. However, the burden of an increase in tax rates falls heavily on low-wage employers, while a large proportion of total payroll paid by high-wage employers escapes taxation. In addition, the tax rates may appear to be excessively high, which can result in negative political or psychological effects.

The National Commission on Unemployment Compensation believes that the federal taxable wage base should be increased every two years to generate additional revenues to pay unemployment benefits and administrative expenses; to reflect increased liabilities over time (since wages are rising); and to minimize inequities in a low, constant wage base. To accomplish these goals, the federal taxable wage base should be equal to 65 percent of the national average

---

[16]*Background Material and Data on Programs within the Jurisdiction of the Committee on Ways and Means,* 1989, p. 462.

annual wage. However, since the taxable wage base would be substantially increased under this proposal, the National Commission recommends that the higher wage base should be gradually increased.

REDUCTION IN THE EFFECTIVENESS OF EXPERIENCE RATING

Another defect is that the effectiveness of experience rating has declined significantly over time. Experience rating was designed to allocate the cost of UI benefits to employers responsible for the unemployment and to encourage firms to stabilize their employment. These objectives are not being met at the present time. *The financing of benefits has shifted away from a system of individual employer responsibility to a largely socialized system in which firms with high unemployment are subsidized heavily by firms with more stable employment.*[17] An audit of 12 states by the U.S. Department of Labor showed that in 1983, firms with high unemployment received $1.6 billion of subsidies from firms with low unemployment. Stable industries such as retailing, finance, and services were heavily subsidizing unstable industries such as manufacturing and construction. For example, for each dollar of UI tax contributions collected from construction and manufacturing, about $3.40 in benefits were paid to unemployed workers within those industries.[18]

The degree of experience rating has also declined over time. Table 15-7 indicates the degree to which benefits are charged to positive-balance employers. The proportion of benefits charged to employers in nine states with positive balances in their reserve accounts declined from 51 percent in 1970 to 36 percent in 1983. The remaining benefits either were charged to negative-balance and inactive employers or not charged at all to employers because of specific exemption by state law or agency procedure (such as disqualifications, overpayments, combined wage claims, and the state's share of extended benefits). The cost of benefits not charged to employers responsible for the unemployment can be viewed as the subsidized or socialized costs of unemployment.

The degree of experience rating has declined because of (1) relatively low maximum tax rates charged to firms, (2) writing off past benefit charges from the benefit payment history used to determine the employer's tax rate, (3) relatively low taxable wages in most states in which only a fraction of total payroll is experience rated, (4) using alternative tax schedules when reserves are relatively low that typically impose the greatest tax increase on employers with favorable employment, and (5) noncharging of benefits to certain employers.[19]

---

[17]U.S. Department of Labor, Office of Inspector General, *Financing the Unemployment Insurance Program Has Shifted from a System Based on Individual Employer's Responsibility towards a Socialized System* (Washington, D.C.: Office of Inspector General, U.S. Department of Labor, 1985), pp. ii–iv.

[18]Ibid., p. iv.

[19]Ibid., pp. v–vi.

TABLE 15-7 **Proportion of Unemployment Benefits Charged to Employers with Positive Balances in Their Experience-Rating Accounts 1970–1983**

YEAR	CA	CO	IN	MO	NJ	NY	SC	WV	WI	TOTAL (A)
1970	53%	49%	—	—	49%	—	39%	37%	47%	51%
1971	54	50	—	—	50	47%	45	43	59	58
1972	52	53	—	—	42	49	—	40	55	48
1973	51	55	—	—	35	39	—	36	48	43
1974	44	42	64%	—	28	38	—	27	45	39
1975	43	35	70	45%	30	34	—	26	36	38
1976	39	21	42	36	30	28	—	24	39	33
1977	37	26	41	31	21	27	—	21	53	36
1978	40	24	45	32	23	24	—	22	—	46
1979	41	39	47	35	26	27	—	19	—	36
1980	43	38	51	36	30	30	—	24	—	35
1981*	42	42	50	33	33	29	33	21	28	35
1982*	40	31	41	30	31	32	44	22	25	34
1983*	33	26	31	34	32	37	41	24	19	36

—Information not available.

*Data for rate year 1983 (all states) and rate years 1981 and 1982 (South Carolina and Wisconsin) were calculated from computer applications.

(A) The percentage was derived from the information available by taking the total benefits paid that were charged to active positive employers and dividing this by the total benefits paid.

Source: U.S. Department of Labor, Office of Inspector General, *Financing the Unemployment Insurance Program Has Shifted from a System Based on Individual Employer's Responsibility towards a Socialized System* (Washington, D.C.: U.S. Department of Labor, Office of Inspector General, 1985), p. 18.

CONTEST OF CLAIMS BY EMPLOYERS

Another problem with experience rating is that low-cost employers have a financial incentive to contest some claims to prevent the claims from being charged to their reserve accounts. However, high-cost firms with negative balances in their reserve accounts may have little financial incentive to contest a claim. Once a high-cost firm pays the maximum rate allowed by law, the marginal cost of laying off additional workers is relatively low since the additional benefits paid do not result in higher tax rates. Thus, because of the subsidy received from low-cost firms, high-cost firms paying the maximum rate have less financial incentive to contest claims or stabilize their employment. The Department of Labor study found that firms paying maximum UI tax rates were less likely to file benefit appeals than firms paying less than the maximum rate.[20] As stated earlier, negative-balance employers paying maximum tax rates have little or no financial incentive to contest improper claims or to stabilize their employment.

---

[20]Ibid., p. 31.

REINSURANCE

Another important issue is whether a national reinsurance plan should be established to protect the state unemployment insurance programs from insolvency during periods of high unemployment. A national reinsurance fund would be established to indemnify the states during periods of high unemployment in which the state's unemployment account is being rapidly depleted.Whenever a state's benefit costs became excessive, part or all of the excess costs would be pooled nationally through the reinsurance fund.

Several arguments are presented for a national reinsurance plan. First, the plan would protect the state's unemployment insurance program from a catastrophic loss because of excessive unemployment. Recent recessions have resulted in a substantial increase in benefit costs, which depleted the unemployment reserves of many states and threatened the solvency of others. A national reinsurance plan would protect the state from a catastrophic loss in such situations.

Second, the costs of high unemployment in certain states would be shared more equitably over the entire nation. Because of the nature of the state's economy, certain states have a much higher level of cyclical unemployment than others. For example, Michigan has a relatively higher unemployment rate than does Nebraska because of the former's susceptibility to the cyclical automobile industry. No matter how hard it tries, Michigan cannot reduce its unemployment rate to the relatively low level that Nebraska enjoys. Thus, it is argued that cyclical unemployment should not fall entirely on an individual state that experiences more of it. A reinsurance fund, therefore, can spread the excess cost of cyclical unemployment more equitably over the nation.

Finally, it is argued that a reinsurance fund would reduce the states' dependence on loans from the federal government and make it unnecessary for an individual state to enact an emergency surtax in the middle of or immediately following a severe recession.

DECLINE IN THE EFFECTIVENESS OF UI AS AN AUTOMATIC STABILIZER

Another defect is that the countercyclical impact of unemployment insurance as an automatic stabilizer has declined substantially over time. Unemployment insurance benefits act in a powerful countercyclical manner to moderate business recessions. *However, recent evidence indicates that the countercyclical effects of unemployment insurance are about 40 percent less than the earlier stimulus provided throughout the 1960s and 1970s.*[21]

---

[21]Statement of Gary T. Burtless in *Reform of the Unemployment Compensation Program*, p. 125.

The reduced countercyclical effects can be explained by at least three reasons. First, relatively fewer unemployed persons now receive unemployment benefits. Second, the countercyclical effects provided by the extended benefits program have been significantly reduced, since the insured unemployment rate is no longer a reliable trigger mechanism to trigger extended benefits during a severe recession. Finally, the taxation of benefits also reduces the countercyclical impact of UI benefits.[22]

IMPROVING UNEMPLOYMENT INSURANCE

The National Commission on Unemployment Compensation has made numerous recommendations to improve the federal-state unemployment insurance programs. Some important recommendations include the following:

1. MAXIMUM WEEKLY BENEFITS STANDARD.   Each state should pay a maximum weekly benefit that is at least two-thirds of the state's average weekly wage in covered employment in the preceding year.

2. WAGE REPLACEMENT RATE.   The weekly benefit amount that is below the state maximum should replace at least 50 percent of the individual's average weekly wage.

3. DURATION OF BENEFITS.   Each state should provide benefits for at least 26 weeks in a benefit year for those workers with a strong attachment to the labor force during their base period.

4. ELIGIBILITY REQUIREMENTS.   There should be a minimum qualifying requirement of at least 14 weeks of work during the base period, but not more than 39 weeks for 26 weeks of benefits.

5. DISQUALIFICATIONS.   There should be no disqualification for a *voluntary quit with good cause,* including compelling family obligations and sexual harassment. Any disqualification for misconduct should be limited to misconduct related to the claimant's employment, and the duration of the penalty should be *variable,* depending on the severity of the offense. Finally, there should be no reemployment and earnings requirement for any disqualifying act.

6. COVERAGE.   Agricultural workers should be covered on the same basis as other workers. Household workers should be covered if the employer pays a worker quarterly wages of $50 or more (rather than $1,000).

7. LONG-TERM UNEMPLOYMENT.   A permanent federal supplementary extended benefits program should be established that would provide additional benefits to individuals who have exhausted both regular and extended benefits. Regular, extended, and supplementary benefits would be paid for a maximum

---

[22]Ibid., pp. 124–125.

of 52 weeks, or up to 65 weeks during periods of high unemployment in the nation or state. In addition, a *lifetime reserve* should be established for older workers age 60 and over who have at least 40 quarters of OASDI coverage and are currently eligible for unemployment insurance benefits.

8. MORE ADEQUATE FINANCING. The federal taxable wage base should be gradually increased to 65 percent of the nation's average annual wage in covered employment. In addition, each state should develop a specific solvency plan to finance benefits over a business cycle and to maintain adequate reserves to accomplish that objective.

9. REINSURANCE FUND. A national reinsurance fund should be established that would pay part of a state's excess unemployment costs whenever benefit costs exceed a certain percentage of taxable payroll.

10. NO TAXATION OF UNEMPLOYMENT BENEFITS. Another recommendation is that unemployment insurance benefits should not be subject to federal income taxes.

SUGGESTIONS FOR ADDITIONAL READING

BURGESS, PAUL L., AND JERRY L. KINGSTON. *An Incentive Approach to Improving the Unemployment Compensation System*. Kalamazoo, Mich.: W. E. Upjohn Institute for Employment Research, 1987.

MATHEMATICA POLICY RESEARCH, INC. *An Examination of Declining UI Claims during the 1980s*. Princeton, N.J.: Mathematica Policy Research, Inc., 1988.

NATIONAL COMMISSION ON UNEMPLOYMENT COMPENSATION. *Unemployment Compensation: Final Report*. Washington, D.C.: National Commission on Unemployment Compensation, 1980.

————. *Unemployment Compensation: Studies and Research*, Vols. 1–3. Washington, D.C.: National Commission on Unemployment Compensation, 1980.

REJDA, GEORGE E., AND KYUNG W. LEE. "State Unemployment Compensation Programs: Immediate Reforms Needed," *The Journal of Risk and Insurance*, Vol. 56, No. 4 (December 1989), pp. 649–669.

REJDA, GEORGE E., AND DAVID I. ROSENBAUM. "Insuring the Risk of Unemployment Privately," *The Journal of Insurance Issues and Practices*, Vol. 13, No. 1 (January 1990).

————. *Unemployment Insurance and Full-Cost Experience Rating: The Impact on Employment*, Working Paper No. 88–1070. Lincoln: Economics Department, University of Nebraska, 1988.

SAFFER, HENRY. "The Effects of Experience Rating on the Unemployment Rate," *Unemployment Compensation: Studies and Research*, Vol. 2. Washington, D.C.: National Commission on Unemployment Compensation, 1980.

SHAPIRO, ISAAC, AND MARION E. NICHOLS, CENTER ON BUDGET AND POLICY PRIORITIES. *Unprotected: Unemployment Insurance and Jobless Workers in 1988*. Washington, D.C.: Center on Budget and Policy Priorities, 1989.

TORRENCE, WILLIAM D., AND GEORGE E. REJDA. "Short-Time Compensation Plans As a New Employee Benefit," *Benefits Quarterly*, Vol. 3, No. 3 (Third Quarter 1987), pp. 7–16.

U.S. CONGRESS, HOUSE, COMMITTEE ON WAYS AND MEANS. *Background Material and Data on Programs within the Jurisdiction of the Committee on Ways and Means*. Washington, D.C.: U.S. Government Printing Office, 1989. This volume is published annually and provides valuable data on current unemployment compensation programs.

————. *Background Material and Data on Programs within the Jurisdiction of the Committee on Ways and Means*. Washington, D.C.: U.S. Government Printing Office, 1987.

————. *Reform of the Unemployment Compensation Program*. Hearing before the Subcommittee on Public Compensation and Unemployment Compensation, 100th Cong., 1st sess., December 14, 1987.

U.S. DEPARTMENT OF LABOR, EMPLOYMENT AND TRAINING ADMINISTRATION, UNEMPLOYMENT INSURANCE SERVICE. *Comparison of State Unemployment Insurance Laws*. Washington, D.C.: U.S. Government Printing Office, 1989. The volume is periodically updated.

————. *An Evaluation of Short-Time Compensation Pro-*

grams. Washington, D.C.: U.S. Government Printing Office, 1986.

U.S. DEPARTMENT OF LABOR, OFFICE OF INSPECTOR GENERAL. *Financing the Unemployment Insurance Program Has Shifted from a System Based on Individual Employer's Responsibility towards a Socialized System.* Washington, D.C.: U.S. Department of Labor, Office of Inspector General, 1985.

U.S. GENERAL ACCOUNTING OFFICE. *Unemployment Insurance: Trust Fund Reserves Inadequate.* Washington, D.C.: U.S. General Accounting Office, 1988.

VROMAN, WAYNE. *The Funding Crisis in State Unemployment Insurance.* Kalamazoo, Mich.: W. E. Upjohn Institute for Employment Research, 1986.

POVERTY AND PUBLIC ASSISTANCE

Although economic growth and expanding employment over time have reduced poverty in the United States, millions of Americans are still poor. Since they cannot attain a reasonable standard of living with respect to food, housing, clothing, and other necessities, they experience considerable economic insecurity.

It is important to reduce the remaining poverty in the United States for several reasons. First, poverty causes economic insecurity not only to the poor but to the entire economy, since the undesirable byproducts of poverty include disease, crime, drug abuse, family tensions, and immorality. Second, poverty impairs the quality of life for individual human beings; it deprives people of not only material goods but also human dignity. Finally, poverty results in lost production because of the waste of human resources.

Public assistance programs are used to meet the problem of poverty in the United States. The benefits are paid only upon the demonstration of need and the fulfillment of strict eligibility requirements. Their basic function is to provide cash income, medical care, and other services to the needy aged, blind, disabled, families with dependent children, and other poor groups. In this chapter, we shall analyze the problem of poverty and the role of public assistance programs in meeting it. In particular, we shall consider the following areas: (1) problem of poverty, (2) nature and reasons for public assistance, and (3) basic characteristics of major public assistance programs.

PROBLEM OF POVERTY

Meaning of Poverty

Poverty can be defined as an insufficiency of material goods and services, whereby the basic needs of individuals or families exceed their means to satisfy them. An individual and family require food, clothing, medical care, housing, and other necessities. The family's basic needs depend on the number and ages of the family members, their place of residence, and their condition of health. The family's ability to meet its basic needs depends on current money income, past savings, property ownership, and access to credit. When the individual or family cannot satisfy certain minimum needs, such individuals or families are living in poverty.

Absolute Poverty. Poverty can be measured on an absolute basis. The Bureau of the Census has computed several poverty thresholds for different-size families to determine the extent of absolute poverty in the United States. The various thresholds are adjusted for differences in family size, sex of the family head, number of children, and annual changes in the Consumer Price Index. Individuals and families whose cash incomes are below the poverty thresholds are counted as poor. The poverty threshold in 1987 was $5,909 for an unrelated individual under age 65 and $11,611 for a four-member family.[1]

Table 16-1 shows the number of persons living in poverty and the poverty rate for selected years based on the poverty thresholds. *In 1987, 32.5 million people, or 13.5 percent of the population, were counted poor.* This represents a significant reduction in absolute poverty since 1959. The decline has been due largely to economic growth and to government transfer payments from social insurance, public assistance, and other welfare programs. In particular, economic growth and full employment are especially important in reducing poverty. A tight labor market increases the money wages of the working poor and allows them to work their way out of poverty; economic growth provides better employment opportunities for the unemployed poor and for those with low-paying or part-time jobs; and full employment reduces the unemployment rates for skilled workers to relatively low levels, which makes firms more willing to train poorly qualified people for skilled jobs.

Relative Poverty. Poverty can also be measured on a relative basis—that is, relative to the goods and services that the nonpoor receive. Although their absolute money income may increase over time, some persons may consider themselves poor if the goods and services they can purchase are relatively fewer than those purchased by the more affluent groups.

One rough measure of relative poverty is to determine the share of

---

[1]U.S. Congress, House, Committee on Ways and Means, *Background Material and Data on Programs within the Jurisdiction of the Committee on Ways and Means* (Washington, D.C.: U.S. Government Printing Office, 1989), Table 1, p. 941.

TABLE 16-1   Number of Persons in Poverty and
the Poverty Rate for Individuals:
Selected Years

YEAR	NUMBER POOR (MILLIONS)	POVERTY RATE (PERCENT)
1959	39.5	22.4%
1965	33.2	17.3
1967	27.8	14.2
1969	24.1	12.1
1971	25.6	12.5
1973	23.0	11.1
1975	25.9	12.3
1977	24.7	11.6
1979	26.1	11.7
1981	31.8	14.0
1983	35.3	15.2
1985	33.1	14.0
1987	32.5	13.5

Source: U.S. Congress, House, Committee on Ways and Means, *Background Material and Data on Programs within the Jurisdiction of the Committee on Ways and Means* (Washington, D.C.: U.S. Government Printing Office, 1989), Table 2, pp. 944–945.

income received by the lowest 20 percent of the families. The following shows the percentage share of family income received by each fifth (quintile) of the families in 1973 and 1987.[2] *The share of family income received by the lowest 20 percent of the families actually declined between 1973 and 1987. The share received by the top 20 percent increased during the same period.* Thus, income equality has not been significantly reduced over time, and the relative position of low-income families has not improved. Thus, although absolute poverty has declined, this is not true of relative poverty.

	1973	1987
Lowest fifth	5.0%	4.1%
Second fifth	11.1	10.2
Middle fifth	16.9	16.4
Fourth fifth	24.1	24.4
Highest fifth	42.9	44.9

Poverty-Stricken Groups.   The principal poverty groups in the United States are the aged, blacks, persons of Hispanic origin, children, families headed by women with children, the working poor, and the homeless.[3]

---

[2]*Background Material and Data on Programs within the Jurisdiction of the Committee on Ways and Means,* 1989, Table 27B, p. 987. The data are adjusted for inflation and family size. For details, see ibid., pp. 984–987.

[3]The principal source of poverty data is *Background Material and Data on Programs within the Jurisdiction of the Committee on Ways and Means,* 1989, pp. 939–982.

1. AGED.   In 1987, 3.5 million persons ages 65 and over, or 12.2 percent of the aged, were living in poverty.

2. BLACKS.   Blacks are often poor because of high unemployment and underemployment rates, inadequate education, inferior educational facilities, and discriminatory hiring practices. In 1987, 9.7 million blacks, or 33 percent of the black population, were counted poor.

3. PERSONS OF HISPANIC ORIGIN.   Persons in this group are often poor because of language and cultural problems, high unemployment rates, inadequate education and work skills, and employment in low-paying jobs as laborers, service workers, or domestics. In 1987, 5.5 million persons of Hispanic origin, or 28 percent, were living in poverty.

4. CHILDREN.   The poverty rate for children under age 18 is especially high. In 1987, the poverty rate for black children was about 46 percent; for white children, about 16 percent; and for children of Hispanic origin, about 40 percent.

Moreover, the poverty rate for children in the United States is much higher than that of many industrial nations. Based on the period 1979–1981, the poverty rates for children in eight countries are as follows:[4]

United States	17.1%
Australia	16.9
United Kingdom	10.7
Canada	9.6
West Germany	8.2
Norway	7.6
Sweden	5.1
Switzerland	5.1

Although the poverty rates are based on 1979–1981 data, experts believe that the relative position of the United States has changed little, if at all, since that time.

5. FAMILIES HEADED BY WOMEN WITH CHILDREN.   The poverty rate for persons in female-headed families with children and no husband present was about 47 percent in 1987.[5] The unusually high incidence of poverty for female-headed families can be explained by the substantial increase in divorce, separation, and children born outside of marriage. As long as family breakup and the number of children born outside of marriage continue to increase, the incidence of poverty for this group will also increase.

6. THE WORKING POOR.   A persistent myth that people are poor because they refuse to work is demolished once the empirical data are analyzed. In 1987,

---

[4]*Background Material and Data on Programs within the Jurisdiction of the Committee on Ways and Means*, 1989, Table 13, p. 956.

[5]Ibid., Table 12, p. 954.

60 percent of all poor families with children were families in which someone worked during the year. Twenty-five percent of all poor families with children had families with one or more full-time worker equivalents.[6] Working poor families are among the most vulnerable of the poor and are always struggling to pay their bills.

 7. HOMELESS. The homeless are another group that experiences great poverty and economic insecurity. The number of homeless people in the United States is estimated to be somewhere between 560,000 and 680,000 persons.[7]

 Who are the homeless? In one study, researchers found that 77 percent of the homeless were single. However, 8 percent of the homeless were adults in families, and 15 percent were children. *Children now represent the fastest growing subpopulation of the homeless population. Furthermore, 88 percent of the heads of homeless families are women.*[8] The increase in homeless families headed by women can be explained largely by the increase in single women with children and the lack of affordable housing for that group.

 In addition, many homeless are alcoholics or drug addicts. Other homeless have serious mental problems. The number of mentally ill homeless people has increased partly because of a policy of deinstitutionalization by which mental patients are released from mental institutions into the community. Community support often is inadequate, and as a result, many former mental patients end up homeless.

 Criticism of Poverty Statistics. Poverty statistics are subject to serious criticism. First, it is argued that the true poverty rate is overstated because income-in-kind is not considered in the official statistics. Income-in-kind refers to the value of food stamps, subsidized housing, medical care, and other subsidies that many poor people receive. Depending on how in-kind benefits are counted, the Census Bureau estimates that the poverty rate for 1987 could be somewhere between 8.5 percent and 11 percent rather than the official 13.5 percent. Moreover, the reduction in poverty from in-kind benefits is especially pronounced for the aged who may have a poverty rate as low as 2.1 percent rather than the official 12.2 percent.[9]

Causes of Poverty

The precise causes of poverty are not completely known. Three theories, however, have gained some acceptance in the professional literature.[10]

---

[6]Ibid., p. 949. A full-time worker equivalent equal to one is defined as 1,750 hours of work during the year (35 hours weekly for 50 weeks) up to 2,080 hours of work during the year (40 hours weekly for 52 weeks).

[7]Ibid., p. 1060.

[8]Ibid.

[9]*The Wall Street Journal,* September 1, 1988, p. 16.

[10]Robert J. Lampman, *Ends and Means of Reducing Income Poverty* (Chicago: Markham, 1971), pp. 36–37.

The random events theory states that individual or families are poor because of events largely beyond their control. For example, a person may become disabled, or die prematurely, which results in poverty for the family; the family may break up from a divorce or desertion; there may be a decrease in demand for the services of people working in certain occupations or living in certain areas or regions; the family's business may end in bankruptcy. These and other events are generally beyond the control of the individual or family and help to explain the high incidence of poverty among aged widows, disabled persons, and the long-term unemployed.

The social barriers theory states that society follows formal or informal policies that cause poverty and make it difficult for the poor to escape from poverty. In other words, certain institutions or practices existing in the United States tend to perpetuate poverty. For example, racial discrimination is a social barrier that helps to explain poverty among certain minority groups. Discrimination in housing, artificial employment barriers by craft labor unions, preemployment hiring tests, and the requirement of a high school diploma are other institutional practices that perpetuate poverty, especially for the hard-core unemployed. Finally, the alienation and social isolation of the poor from the rest of the community often result in a distinct culture of poverty among them.

The personal differences theory states that people are poor because of personal characteristics that make them different from the majority. For example, people are poor because of inadequate education and work skills, low productivity, poor motivation and work habit, mental or physical disabilities, lack of salable skills, alcoholism, drug addiction, or character defects.

Attacking Poverty

The major approaches and proposals for reducing poverty in the United States include expansionary monetary and fiscal policies to promote rapid economic growth and full employment, area and regional redevelopment, employment and training programs for the disadvantaged, housing and rent subsidies for the poor, food stamps, home energy assistance programs, school lunch programs, public health services for children, social insurance programs, public assistance programs, and numerous others. It is beyond the scope of the text to analyze each of these programs in detail.[11] However, it is worthwhile to examine the effectiveness of social insurance and welfare programs in reducing poverty.

Antipoverty Effects of Social Insurance and Welfare Programs. One method of evaluating the effectiveness of an antipoverty program that provides income is to estimate the number of people who would be counted poor without that particular source of income. The additional number who are counted poor provides an estimate of the number who are removed from poverty by that income source.

Table 16-2 provides an estimate of the antipoverty effects of social insur-

---

[11]For a discussion of the various programs for attacking poverty, see Sar A. Levitan, *Programs in Aid of the Poor,* 5th ed. (Baltimore, Md.: Johns Hopkins University Press, 1985).

TABLE 16-2 Antipoverty Effectiveness of Social Insurance and Welfare Programs for All Individuals in Families or Living Alone 1987

	NUMBER OF POOR INDIVIDUALS (MILLIONS)	POVERTY RATE (PERCENT)
Cash income only before any government transfers	49.7	20.6%
Plus Social Security and other social insurance programs	34.4	14.3
Plus means-tested cash transfers (official definition)	32.5	13.5
Plus food and housing benefits	29.0	12.0
Less federal taxes	30.4	12.6

Source: Calculated from U.S. Congress, House, Committee on Ways and Means, *Background Material and Data on Programs within the Jurisdiction of the Committee on Ways and Means* (Washington, D.C.: U.S. Government Printing Office, 1989), Table 16, pp. 962–963.

ance programs and other welfare programs for 1987. Welfare programs such as public assistance that require a needs test are frequently referred to as *means-tested cash transfers.*

Table 16-2 shows that before any government transfer payments, 49.7 million people would have been counted poor in 1987. *However, the addition of cash payments from Social Security and other social insurance programs removed 15.3 million people from poverty. The poverty rate fell sharply from 20.6 percent to 14.3 percent.* Thus, Social Security and other social insurance programs are extremely effective for reducing poverty.

The addition of means-tested cash transfers (such as income from public assistance programs) removed an additional 1.9 million people from poverty. Adding in food and housing benefits removed an additional 3.5 million from poverty. However, federal tax policy (income and payroll tax) added 1.4 million to the poverty rolls.

Conclusions. Social Security and other social insurance programs are extremely effective in reducing poverty. Social insurance programs also are vastly superior to means-tested cash transfer programs, such as public assistance and other welfare programs. The effectiveness of social insurance programs over welfare programs can be shown as follows:[12]

	NUMBER OF INDIVIDUALS REMOVED FROM POVERTY IN 1987 (MILLIONS)	PERCENT OF INDIVIDUALS REMOVED FROM POVERTY IN 1987
Social Security and other social insurance programs	15.3	30.8%
Means-tested cash transfers, food, and housing benefits	5.4	10.8

[12]*Background Material and Data on Programs within the Jurisdiction of the Committee on Ways and Means,* 1989, Table 16, pp. 962–963.

Moreover, unlike welfare programs, social insurance programs do not require a means or needs test.

This concludes our discussion of the poverty problem. Let us next examine public assistance programs and their characteristics in greater detail.

NATURE OF PUBLIC ASSISTANCE

Public assistance programs are welfare programs that provide income, medical care, and other services to poor individuals and families to help meet their basic living needs, when age, illness, disability, divorce, family breakup, or other factors beyond their personal control interfere with individual initiative in providing for necessities.

Basic Characteristics

Public assistance programs have several characteristics that distinguish them from social insurance. First, various benefits are provided to poor individuals and families whose income, assets, and available sources of support fall below some officially determined standard of need. The benefits consist of (1) cash payments, (2) medical care, and (3) social services, such as counseling on family problems, assistance in getting a job or better housing, referral to community resources, and homemaker services.

Second, welfare applicants must demonstrate a needs test. Applicants must show that their income and assets are below some officially defined standard. The benefits are never automatically paid on the basis of an earned right, and they are adjusted to the individual's or family's financial resources and needs.

Third, the benefits are generally financed out of the general revenues of government rather than from specific earmarked taxes. Federal grants-in-aid are available to the states to help finance the costs of the joint programs.

Finally, because of the discretionary needs test and stringent eligibility requirements, public assistance benefits are often difficult to predict in advance. For these reasons and because of the stigma of charity attached to the receipt of benefits, most people do not consider the availability of public assistance benefits in their economic security plans.

Reasons for Public Assistance

Public assistance programs are necessary for several reasons. First, they provide cash payments, medical care, and social services to poor persons and families who are not covered under social insurance or other public programs.

Second, public assistance is used to provide supplemental income to people whose benefits from social insurance or other public programs are inadequate, to those with small or nonexistent financial resources, and to those whose special needs require income supplements or services.

Third, some individuals and families are unable to attain a minimum standard of living because of physical, psychological, or emotional problems. In these cases, public assistance benefits help compensate for these and other adverse economic forces that are beyond their control or understanding.

Finally, public assistance is used because of society's philosophy toward the poor. Because of personal factors or character defects, some persons are unable or unwilling to work and contribute to society. Although they are unproductive, society does not necessarily cast these persons aside as worthless. Society must always assist its less able members to become productive if possible, but the dignity and true worth of a human being are seldom measured only in monetary and economic terms. For this reason, society is unwilling to permit the poor to starve, and public assistance is used to provide a subsistence level of living to poor persons who can meet certain eligibility requirements.

TYPES OF PUBLIC ASSISTANCE PROGRAMS

There are four major public assistance programs in the United States: (1) Supplemental Security Income for aged, disabled, and blind people; (2) Aid to Families with Dependent Children; (3) Medicaid; and (4) General Assistance.

Supplemental Security Income

The Supplemental Security Income (SSI) program for the aged, disabled, and blind is a federal program that pays monthly cash benefits to needy aged, disabled, and blind people who have limited income and assets. The payments can be paid to disabled or blind children, regardless of their age, to adults, and to persons who have never worked.

Federal Minimum Income Guarantee. As of January 1990, all poor aged, disabled, and blind persons with no other source of income are guaranteed a monthly income of at least $386 for an individual and $579 for couples. Not all persons receive these amounts. Some people receive less because of their own income. Some receive more because the state may supplement the SSI payments (discussed later). In addition, the monthly SSI benefits are automatically adjusted each year based on the increase in the Consumer Price Index.

Eligibility Requirements. Certain eligibility requirements must be met to receive SSI benefits. SSI applicants must (1) be aged, disabled, or blind; (2) meet a needs test; and (3) fulfill other eligibility requirements.

1. BE AGED, DISABLED, OR BLIND. An aged applicant must be at least age 65 or over to receive benefits. A disabled or blind person must fulfill the definition of disability or blindness. The definition of disability is similar to the definition used in the disability income portion of the OASDI program, but no waiting period is required. Persons age 18 or over are considered disabled if they have a

physical or mental impairment that prevents them from doing any work for at least 12 months or that is expected to result in death. Disabled children under age 18 may be eligible for benefits if the physical or mental impairment is comparable in severity to an impairment that would prevent an adult from working and is expected to last at least 12 months or result in death.

Also, regardless of age, blind persons may be eligible for SSI benefits if their vision is no better than 20/200 or if they have a visual field of 20 degrees or less with the best corrective eyeglasses. If a person's visual impairment is not severe enough to be classified as blind, he or she may still qualify for SSI benefits as a disabled person.

A state agency contracts with the Social Security Administration to determine if a person is disabled or blind according to law. The state agency reviews the evidence concerning the person's mental or physical condition, including reports from physicians, hospitals, clinics, and institutions where treatment has been provided. Finally, if an SSI recipient is considered disabled, he or she must accept vocational rehabilitation services if they are offered.

2. MEET A NEEDS TEST. SSI applicants must also meet a needs test. A national, uniform needs test is used to determine eligibility for SSI benefits. The needs test considers both financial assets and income. *Financial assets are limited to a maximum of $2,000 for an individual and $3,000 for a couple.*

In determining eligibility, a home is not counted, regardless of its value. Also excluded are personal and household goods with an equity value of up to $2,000, an automobile with current value of up to $4,500, and up to $1,500 in burial funds ($3,000 for a couple). The cash value of life insurance contracts with a face value of $1,500 or less also is not counted. However, the cash value of life insurance contracts exceeding $1,500 must be counted as a financial asset.

The applicant's income is also considered in determining the amount of the monthly SSI benefit. Included are cash, checks from work earnings, OASDI benefits, annuities, and items received in lieu of cash, such as food or shelter. Food stamps, however, are excluded income. Also, a certain amount of income is disregarded in determining the amount of the SSI benefit. The following amounts can be disregarded:

  a. The first $20 of monthly income from virtually any source is not counted (such as OASDI benefits, but not need-tested income such as a veteran's pension). Income in excess of the first $20 (other than work earnings) usually reduces the amount of the SSI benefit.
  b. The first $65 of monthly earned income, plus one-half of the remainder, is also excluded in determining the amount of the SSI benefit.
  c. For blind and disabled persons, the earnings needed to achieve self-support and pay work expenses associated with the disability are also disregarded. For example, the earnings of a blind person used for transportation expenses to and from work are not counted.

If an unmarried child living at home is under age 18, the parents' assets and part of their income are considered to be the child's property and income.

An allowance is made for the parents' work and living expenses and for other children living at home. After these amounts are deducted from the parents' income, the remainder is used to determine if the child meets the income requirements.

The average monthly federally administered payment in December 1988 was $188 for the aged, $306 for the blind, and $294 for the disabled.[13]

3. FULFILL OTHER ELIGIBILITY REQUIREMENTS. Other eligibility requirements must also be met. First, the SSI applicant must be a citizen of the United States or an immigrant who is lawfully admitted or present for permanent residence.

Second, persons who are residents or inmates in public institutions are generally ineligible for SSI benefits. However, there are several important exceptions to this general rule. If the person is in a public or private institution (such as a nursing home), and the state's Medicaid program is paying for more than half the cost of care, a monthly payment of up to $30 can be paid to the person for personal needs. Also, SSI benefits can be paid to persons in a publicly operated community residence that serves no more than 16 persons and to persons who are residents in a public institution primarily to attend an approved educational or vocational training program. Finally, temporary residents of public emergency shelters for the homeless may be eligible for SSI benefits for up to six months in any nine-month period.

If an eligible person is living in the household of another person and receives in-kind support and maintenance, the SSI benefit is reduced one-third. An example would be an adult disabled son or daughter who is living in the parents' home and receives support from them. The rationale for this reduction is that SSI recipients are receiving unearned income in the form of food and shelter. Rather than determining the actual value of the unearned income, which can be complex, the law reduces the benefits by one-third. Table 16-3 shows the maximum income allowed for federal SSI benefits in 1989 for persons receiving only Social Security and those receiving only earned income.

State Supplementation. Prior to the enactment of the SSI program, several states paid public assistance benefits that exceeded the federal minimum guarantee. Under SSI, these states must supplement the benefits for those beneficiaries who otherwise would have had their benefits reduced by the transition to the new program. The states also have the option of paying additional supplements to all public assistance recipients or to selected categories of SSI recipients.

Whether the supplement is mandatory or optional, the states can either administer the supplemental program themselves or arrange to have the benefits paid by the Social Security Administration. In the latter case, the Social Security Administration assumes the administrative costs and is reimbursed by the states for the amount of the supplemental payments.

---

[13]*Social Security Bulletin,* Vol. 52, No. 3 (March 1989), p. 32.

TABLE 16-3   Maximum Income for Eligibility for Federal SSI
Benefits 1989

	RECEIVING ONLY SOCIAL SECURITY		RECEIVING ONLY WAGE INCOME	
	Monthly	Annually	Monthly	Annually
Individual	$388	$4,656	$ 821	$ 9,852
Couple	573	6,876	1,121	14,292

Source: U.S. Congress, House, Committee on Ways and Means, *Background Material and Data on Programs within the Jurisdiction of the Committee on Ways and Means* (Washington, D.C.: Government Printing Office, 1989), Table 3, p. 676.

Financing.   The federal SSI cash payments and the administrative costs of federally administered state supplements are financed entirely by the federal government out of its general revenues. The costs of the supplemental benefits are paid by the states.

An estimated 4.6 million persons received federally administered SSI payments in 1990. Of that number, 1.4 million were aged, and 3.2 million were blind or disabled.[14]

Administration.   The SSI program is administered by the federal government. The Social Security Administration is responsible for the determination of eligibility and benefit amounts and the payment of the monthly SSI checks. As we stated earlier, if the state desires, the Social Security Administration will also administer the state's supplemental payments program.

Aid to Families with Dependent Children

One of the most controversial public assistance programs is Aid to Families with Dependent Children (AFDC). The original Social Security Act of 1935 provided federal grants to states to help poor children whose need was based on the death or incapacity of a parent or on a parent's continued absence from the home. AFDC programs now provide benefits to poor children and to one or two adults caring for the children because of the parent's death, mental or physical incapacity, unemployment, or continued absence from the home.

The AFDC program has changed significantly over time. The most recent changes are due largely to the Family Support Act of 1988.

Eligibility Requirements.   To become eligible for AFDC benefits, applicants must meet strict eligibility requirements. *First, the child must be poor and living with a parent or close relative;* one exception is that payments can be made on

---

[14]*Background Material and Data on Programs within the Jurisdiction of the Committee on Ways and Means,* 1989, Table 11, p. 695.

behalf of a child living in an approved foster home if the child was eligible for or was receiving benefits prior to placement in the home.

Second, the child must be under a certain age. Under the law, AFDC benefits can be paid to dependent children to age 18 or, at the state's option, through age 18 if the child is a full-time student in a secondary or technical school and is expected to complete the program before age 19. Payments to all other children age 18 and over are prohibited.

Third, a strict needs test must be satisfied. The needs test takes into consideration the applicant's financial resources, earned income, and other sources of income and support. The following is a summary of the principal factors that are considered in determining need:

1. LIMITS ON RESOURCES. The states must consider any property or financial resources available to the child or adult in determining eligibility for AFDC benefits. *The maximum amount of nonexcluded family resources is now limited to $1,000 per family.* However, the value of the family home and one automobile can be excluded in determining the amount of family resources. The value of the automobile is limited by regulations. In 1989, an equity of $1,500 was permitted. The states can also exclude basic items essential for daily living, such as clothing and furniture.

2. LIMITS ON INCOME. Eligibility for AFDC benefits is limited to families with *gross incomes* that do not exceed 185 percent of the state's current standard of need. For example, a family of three in Nebraska with a current monthly need standard of $364 would be dropped from the AFDC rolls if gross monthly income exceeds $673.40. In addition, for purposes of determining the family's gross income, the state has the option of disregarding the earned income of a dependent child who is a full-time student for up to six months.

In addition, if a stepparent lives with an AFDC family in a state that does not have a general applicability law (a law that holds a stepparent legally responsible to the same extent as a natural or adoptive parent), the income of a stepparent that exceeds a certain amount must also be counted in determining AFDC eligibility. However, if a state has a general applicability law, the same AFDC regulations and laws that apply to natural or adoptive parents also apply to stepparents.

3. LUMP-SUM PAYMENTS IN EXCESS OF THE STANDARD OF NEED. If a family receives a lump-sum payment (such as life insurance proceeds) that exceeds its standard of need in the month of receipt, the family is ineligible for AFDC benefits for that month. Also, any amount that exceeds the initial month's standard of need would be divided by the monthly need standard, and the family generally would be ineligible for benefits for the number of months resulting from that calculation.

4. INCOME OF PARENTS OF A MINOR PARENT. For purposes of determining AFDC eligibility for a minor parent and dependent child, the income of the parents or legal guardian of the minor parent must be counted when all parties

are living in the same household. For example, if an unwed teen-age mother and her son are living in the home of her parents, the parents' income must be counted in determining AFDC eligibility and benefits for the teen-ager.

Finally, another eligibility requirement is that the *custodial parent or relative must assign all rights to child-support payments to the state*. However, the first $50 collected each month must be paid to the AFDC family as a child-support disregard. AFDC mothers must also cooperate with welfare officials in establishing the paternity of a child born outside of marriage and in obtaining child-support payments from the father.

Amount of AFDC Payments. Under the AFDC program, each state determines its own standard of need, and the family's income is compared with this standard. Various budgets for different classifications of poor families are established, which include an allowance for food, clothing, shelter, utilities, and other necessities. Theoretically, the monthly AFDC cash payment is the difference between the family's standard of need and the amount of family income. However, in most states, the actual cash benefit paid is below the state's standard of need because of statutory and administrative limits on maximum benefits and the failure of many states to keep their need standards up-to-date based on current living costs.

To encourage AFDC recipients to work, a certain amount of earned income can be disregarded when the cash benefits are computed. The states are required to disregard the following amounts of work earnings:

1. WORK EXPENSES. Under the Family Support Act of 1988, the first $90 of monthly earnings from full-time employment is disregarded to reflect work expenses and taxes. Under previous law, the disregard for work expenses was only $75.

2. $30 AND ONE-THIRD RULE. The next $30 of monthly earnings plus one-third of the remainder are also disregarded in determining the benefit amount for a period of up to four consecutive months. After the four months, only the first $30 of earned income is disregarded for an additional eight months (or a total of 12 months).

3. CHILD CARE. Under the Family Support Act of 1988, up to $175 for each child for day care can also be disregarded ($200 for a child under age 2). Under previous law, only a maximum of $160 monthly for each child could be disregarded. Application of these rules can be illustrated by the chart on page 383.

Work Requirements. The Family Support Act of 1988 created a new work program for AFDC families called Job Opportunities and Basic Skills (JOBS). The states are required to establish a JOBS program so that poor families with children can obtain education, training, and employment to avoid long-term dependency on welfare.

AFDC recipients are required to participate in the JOBS program. Those who refuse to register for work or training can lose their benefits. The programs

	FIRST 4 MONTHS	NEXT 8 MONTHS
Gross earnings	$600	$600
Disregards:		
Work expenses	− 90	− 90
$30 monthly	− 30	− 30
One-third of remainder	−160	− 0
Child care for one child		
age 5	−175	−175
Net countable income	$145	$305
AFDC benefits:		
$420 payment standard	$275	$115
$364 payment standard	$219	$ 59

include education, job training, unpaid work in the community and other work-experience programs, and assistance in finding a job. However, certain persons are not required to register. Exempt from registration are persons who are (1) ill, disabled, or old, (2) needed in the home because of the illness or incapacity of another family member, (3) parents caring for a child under age 3 (or, at the state's option, age 1), (4) employed 30 hours or more weekly, (5) children under age 16 or full-time students in an elementary, secondary, or vocational school, (6) women in the second trimester of pregnancy, and (7) residing in an area where the program is not available.

The states are required to provide child care if such care is necessary for an individual's employment. Transportation and other work-related expenses that are necessary for a participant to participate in the program must also be provided. If a parent finds a job and is no longer eligible for cash assistance, the states must provide child care for one year on a sliding fee scale after a parent leaves the welfare rolls. The states must also provide Medicaid coverage for one year to families who leave welfare for work. However, the states at their option can impose an income-related premium for the second six months of that year.

AFDC for Unemployed Parents. AFDC benefits are also available in two-parent families in which the principal wage earner is unemployed (AFDC-UP). Beginning October 1, 1990, all states must provide AFDC benefits to two-parent families in which the principal wage earner is unemployed. Prior to that date, only 26 states provided AFDC-UP benefits; these states are required to maintain their present programs. Those states that are required to enact new AFDC-UP programs have the option of limiting benefits to 6 months out of each 12 months. All states, however, must continue to provide Medicaid coverage even during those months in which cash benefits are not paid.

In addition to the needs test, other eligibility requirements must be fulfilled. First, eligibility is limited to two-parent families in which the *principal earner* is unemployed. The principal earner is the parent with the highest earnings in the past two years who is unemployed. Second, AFDC-UP applicants must not be working more than 100 hours monthly.

AFDC Emergency Assistance.   Most states provide emergency assistance in crisis situations to poor families with children, such as an AFDC family made homeless by a fire. The basic AFDC budget does not take this contingency into account, and there is no allowance in the basic grant to cover emergency situations. Under the Emergency Assistance Program, the states can provide emergency assistance for a short period to families with dependent children. The aid may be cash payments, medical care, payments in kind, or vendor payments for a wide variety of needs, including food, utilities, rent, and other necessities.

Family Support Act of 1988.   To reduce long-term dependency on welfare, Congress enacted the Family Support Act of 1988. The new law significantly overhauls the state AFDC programs. The major provisions are summarized as follows:

1. CHILD SUPPORT AND PATERNITY ESTABLISHMENT.   The new law requires that legally due child support payments from a parent be deducted automatically from the parent's wages, even if the parent is not in arrears. The states must also meet federal standards to establish paternity of a child.

2. JOBS PROGRAM.   As we noted earlier, the states are required to establish a JOBS program for AFDC recipients. The JOBS program must include certain activities: education, job skills training, job readiness, job development, and job placement. In addition, the states must include at least two of the following activities: group and individual job search, on-the-job training, work supplementation (subsidized jobs), and community work experience or other approved work experience.

The states are required to target families in which a parent was a teenager when the children were born or other persons who are likely to become long-term welfare recipients.

3. SUPPORTIVE SERVICES AND TRANSITIONAL BENEFITS.   The states must guarantee child care to AFDC recipients participating in the JOBS program. Child care must also be provided for one year on a sliding fee scale to participants who leave welfare for a job. Transportation and work expenses must also be covered to enable AFDC recipients to participate in the JOBS program. Finally, Medicaid benefits must be provided for one year after a participant leaves welfare for a job. At the state's option, an income-related premium can be imposed for the last six months of that year on families with earnings (less necessary child care expenses) above the federal poverty level.

4. OTHER PROVISIONS.   The states also have the option of requiring minor parents to live with their parents in order to qualify for AFDC.

Also, as we noted earlier, all states must enact AFDC-UP programs that provide benefits to two-parent families in which the principal wage earner is unemployed.

Finally, beginning in fiscal 1994, a parent in each AFDC-UP family must work at least 16 hours weekly in a workfare job. The state has the option of allowing parents under age 25 who have not completed high school to use an education activity to satisfy the requirement.

Financing. The AFDC program is financed jointly by the federal government and the states. The amount of federal matching varies among the states depending, within limits, on the state's per capita income. The federal government's share can range from 50 percent to 79.61 percent; the percentage paid is inversely related to state per capita income. The federal government pays more than 70 percent in 11 states. The federal government also pays 50 percent of the administrative costs of the programs in all states.

Medicaid

Medicaid is a joint federal-state program that provides medical assistance to poor families with dependent children, the aged, the blind, the disabled, and other poor groups. All states now have Medicaid programs. (One state, Arizona, participates in the Medicaid program under a demonstration project that provides certain services to the poor.)

Eligible Groups. A large number of groups are eligible for Medicaid coverage. It is beyond the scope of the text, however, to discuss all of the groups that the states must or can cover. However, for sake of convenience, three major categories can be established: (1) mandatory categorically needy, (2) optional categorically needy, and (3) medically needy.

1. MANDATORY CATEGORICALLY NEEDY. Certain groups must be covered on a mandatory basis as categorically needy. In general, all persons receiving cash payments under a categorical program must be covered. This includes all AFDC recipients and, beginning October 1, 1990, all AFDC-UP two-parent families in which the principal earner is unemployed.

In addition, most SSI recipients are also covered. However, the state has considerable discretion in covering the aged, blind, and disabled under Medicaid: (1) all SSI recipients can be covered, (2) all SSI recipients who meet a separate state determination for Medicaid can be covered, or (3) the aged, blind, and disabled who meet eligibility standards more restrictive than those required under SSI can be covered.

Other groups must be covered on a mandatory basis. These groups include pregnant women who meet the state's income and resource requirements but are not receiving cash payments; children under age 7 who meet the income and resource standards; pregnant women and infants through age 5 with incomes below 133 percent of the federal poverty line; and coverage of Medicare cost-sharing charges for Medicare beneficiaries with incomes below the poverty line (below 95 percent of the poverty line in 1991 and 100 percent in 1992 and later).

Finally, beginning April 1, 1990, all states are required to extend Medicaid coverage for 12 months to families who lose cash benefits because of work earnings under the JOBS program.

2. OPTIONAL CATEGORICALLY NEEDY.   The states have the option of extending categorically needy coverage to certain other groups who are not actually receiving cash payments. For example, the states may elect to cover all or reasonable categories of individual under age 21 (or at the state's option under 20, 19, or 18) who meet the definition of a dependent child. Reasonable categories include children living in two-parent families, children living in privately subsidized foster care, or children living in an intermediate-care facility.

The states also have the option of extending categorically needy coverage to pregnant women and infants under age 1 who have incomes up to 185 percent of the federal poverty guidelines. However, a premium related to income could be imposed.

3. MEDICALLY NEEDY.   The states can also elect to provide Medicaid coverage to the medically needy. In general, the medically needy are persons who are not receiving cash payments under the categorical programs (AFDC, AFDC-UP, SSI), and their incomes are sufficient for their basic living needs but insufficient for paying their medical bills. The medically needy include the following groups: (1) persons who except for their income and assets would fall into one of the categories now covered by the state, or (2) persons whose income and assets exceed the standards established for the categorically needy.

The states with medically needy programs can impose a needs test based on income and assets. The income and asset standards, however, must be based on family size, uniform for all individuals within a covered group, and reasonable. In addition, for purposes of federal matching payments, the income standard cannot exceed $133\frac{1}{3}$ percent of the maximum payment to a family of similar size under the state's AFDC program.

Finally, many persons qualify as medically needy only after they reduce their income and/or resources to the required level. This process is known as a "spend down," which allows applicants to deduct medical expenses from their income for purposes of determining eligibility. For example, if the state's income standard is $350, and the applicant has monthly income of $400, he or she would be required to incur $50 in medical expenses (spend down) to become medically eligible for Medicaid. In 1989, 39 jurisdictions had medically needy programs.[15]

Needs Test.   Medicaid applicants must meet a needs test to receive benefits. The Medicaid income and resource limits for AFDC and SSI recipients and other categorically needy persons generally are the same as those esablished by the state for the receipt of cash benefits under the category or assistance to which the applicant is characteristically related.

Qualifying for Medicaid is not easy. For example, assume that an applicant for Medicaid is in a nursing home. If he or she disposes of financial assets at

---

[15]Ibid., p. 1131.

less than fair market value (such as by a gift to children) within 20 months before applying for Medicaid, eligibility can be postponed.

In addition, in the past the life savings of many couples have been exhausted in those cases where one spouse is in a nursing home and the other spouse is at home. Couples have been forced to exhaust their savings to qualify initially for Medicaid and then had to use most or all of their combined income to pay for the nursing home to maintain eligibility. As a result, many couples concealed their financial assets or obtained a divorce under which the court divided the assets. This result was due to the Medicaid principle of requiring recipients to pay as much as possible of the nursing home bill before Medicaid paid anything.[16] The states are required to allow nursing home residents to keep $30 monthly in income for personal needs. However, until recently, the amount of income that the spouse at home could keep depended on the state in which the couple resided.

A recent change in the Medicaid law is aimed at reducing the problem of impoverishment of a spouse at home. For purposes of establishing *initial eligibility* in those cases where one spouse is in an institution and the other is at home, a new rule applies. After excluding certain assets (such as the home), the total value of the couple's assets is determined. The spouse remaining in the community is permitted to retain half of the assets, subject to a minimum of $12,000 and a maximum of $60,000.

In addition, the spouse living at home is allowed to keep at least part of the couple's combined income based on the federal poverty level for a two-member family.

In 1991, the amount of protected income for the spouse in the community is 133 percent of the federal poverty threshold and 150 percent in 1992. As a result, fewer spouses in the community will be financially destitute if the other spouse is in a nursing home.

Basic Services. The Medicaid program must provide at least the following basic services:

1. Inpatient hospital services and outpatient hospital services
2. X-ray and laboratory services
3. Rural health clinic services
4. Skilled nursing home services for adults
5. Physicians' services
6. Family planning services and supplies
7. Home health services for any eligible person entitled to skilled nursing home services
8. Certain screening, diagnostic, and treatment services for eligible children
9. Nurse and midwife services

---

[16]Robert M. Ball with Thomas N. Bethell, *Because We're All in This Together, The Case for a National Long-Term Care Insurance Policy* (Washington, D.C.: Families U.S.A. Foundation, 1989), pp. 32–33.

The states also have the option of providing other medical services, such as private-duty nursing, clinic services, dental services, physical therapy, prescribed drugs, dentures, prosthetic devices, eyeglasses, intermediate-care facility services, and others. However, the state may require the payment of a normal deductible and coinsurance for an optional service.

If the state elects to cover the medically needy, it has considerable flexibility in determining the types of medical services to be provided to them. Not all of the required services listed earlier have to be provided. Nominal premiums or fees may also be required for any service offered to the medically needy.

Financing.   Medicaid plans are financed jointly by the federal government and the states. A formula is used to determine the federal share of a state's payments for Medicaid services. Under the current formula, the federal share ranges from 50 to 83 percent, depending on the state's per capita income. The formula provides a higher percentage of federal matching funds to states with low per capita incomes and a lower percentage of federal matching funds to states with high per capita incomes.

The federal government generally pays 50 percent of the administrative costs in all states. However, for certain services and programs, the authorized rate is higher.

General Assistance

General Assistance (GA) is a residual welfare program provided by state and local communities to poor persons and families who are ineligible for help under federally aided public assistance programs. In a few states, GA is also used to help people who receive inadequate benefits from federally aided programs to meet their basic needs. GA is often the only welfare program available to temporarily or permanently unemployed people who are ineligible for unemployment insurance benefits or whose benefits are inadequate or exhausted. Some states, however, refuse to help a family with an employable person in the household except in defined emergency situations.

The state and local GA programs are generally more limited in the amount and duration of assistance than are the federally aided assistance programs. In some states, GA programs provide only emergency or short-term aid; in others, assistance is limited to specific situations; a few states limit the length of time that the poor can receive help; and in many states, limitations on GA benefits and services are established from time to time because of insufficient funds.

General Assistance programs are financed either from state and local funds or from local funds alone. They are especially sensitive to the business cycle; the number of recipients aided tends to increase during recessions.

SUGGESTIONS FOR ADDITIONAL READING

AXINN, JUNE, AND MARK STERN. *Dependency and Poverty: Old Problems in a New World.* Lexington, Mass. D. C. Heath and Company, 1988.

DANZIGER, SHELDON H., AND DANIEL H. WEINBERG, EDS. *Fighting Poverty: What Works and What Doesn't.* Cambridge, Mass.: Harvard University Press, 1986.

GOODWIN, LEONARD. *Causes and Cures of Welfare.* Lexington, Mass.: Lexington Books, 1983.

KAMERMAN, SHEILA B., AND ALFRED J. KAHN. *Mothers Alone: Strategies for a Time of Change.* Dover, Mass.: Auburn House Publishing Co., 1988.

LEVITAN, SAR A. *Programs in Aid of the Poor,* 5th ed. Baltimore, Md.: Johns Hopkins University Press, 1985.

LEVITAN, SAR A., RICHARD S. BELOUS, AND FRANK GALLO. *What's Happening to the American Family?* Baltimore, Md.: Johns Hopkins University Press, 1988.

LEVITAN, SAR A., AND ISAAC SHAPIRO. *Working But Poor.* Baltimore, Md.: Johns Hopkins University Press, 1987.

MULROY, ELIZABETH A., ED. *Women as Single Parents: Confronting Institutional Barriers in the Courts, the Workplace, and the Housing Market.* Dover, Mass.: Auburn House Publishing Co., 1988.

SAWHILL, ISABEL V. "Poverty in the U.S.: Why Is It So Persistent?" *Journal of Economic Literature,* Vol. 26, No. 3 (September 1988), pp. 1073–1119.

"Social Security Programs in the United States," *Social Security Bulletin,* Vol. 52, No. 7 (July 1989), pp. 2–79.

U.S. BUREAU OF THE CENSUS, CURRENT POPULATION REPORTS, SERIES P-60, No. 164-RD-1. *Measuring the Effect of Benefits and Taxes on Income and Poverty: 1986.* Washington, D.C.: U.S. Government Printing Office, 1988.

U.S. CONGRESS, CONGRESSIONAL RESEARCH SERVICE. *Medicaid Source Book: Background Data and Analyses.* A Report for the Use of the Subcommittee on Health and the Environment of the Committee on Energy and Commerce. Washington, D.C.: U.S. Government Printing Office, 1988.

U.S. CONGRESS, HOUSE, COMMITTEE ON WAYS AND MEANS. *Background Material and Data on Programs within the Jurisdiction of the Committee on Ways and Means.* Washington, D.C.: U.S. Government Printing Office, 1989. This volume is published annually and provides up-to-date information on public assistance and welfare programs in the United States.

U.S. CONGRESS, SENATE, COMMITTEE ON FINANCE. *Data and Materials Related to Welfare Programs for Families with Children.* Washington, D.C.: U.S. Government Printing Office, 1987.

17

PUBLIC ASSISTANCE PROBLEMS AND ISSUES

Politicians, economists, welfare officials, and the tax-paying public are increasingly concerned about the effectiveness of public assistance programs, and outright hostility and resentment toward welfare recipients are common. At the present time, it is difficult to find another public income maintenance program that rivals public assistance in its unpopularity and general unacceptance by most taxpayers.

In this chapter, we shall critically examine some current problems and issues associated with public assistance programs. Most problems and issues center on the Supplemental Security Income program (SSI) and the highly controversial Aid to Families with Dependent Children (AFDC) and Medicaid programs. In particular, we shall consider the following areas: (1) SSI problems and issues, (2) the AFDC welfare crisis, (3) Medicaid problems and issues, and (4) welfare reform proposals.

SSI PROBLEMS AND ISSUES

The Supplemental Security Income program provides a guaranteed monthly income to needy aged, disabled, and blind persons who have limited financial resources and whose incomes fall below certain standards. Several important problems and issues are associated with the present program.

Lack of Knowledge about SSI

A serious defect is that many poor aged, blind, and disabled persons are not receiving SSI benefits because of lack of knowledge about the program. *It is estimated that one-third to one-half of all eligible aged, blind, and disabled persons are not enrolled in SSI.*[1] In addition, the participation of the aged poor in SSI has declined significantly over time. In 1975, about 76 percent of the elderly poor participated in the SSI program; in 1987, only about 58 percent of the elderly poor were participating.[2]

Many poor eligible individuals are not participating in the SSI program because of lack of knowledge about the program. Although the Social Security Administration conducts outreach campaigns by press releases, radio, questions and answers for the media, and speech material to local SSA offices, millions of poor Americans lack knowledge about the program. Other poor people like the working poor mistakenly believe they are ineligible because they have a low-paying job. Still others are functionally illiterate and cannot fill out the required forms. Finally, others are embarrassed by applying for "charity," especially middle-class older people who are having financial problems.[3]

Finally, large numbers of disabled children under age 18 are not receiving SSI benefits. Many disabled children do not receive SSI because their impairments do not fit any of the listed impairments by SSA; the children are too young to be tested for an impairment; or the list of impairments is out of date. Also, unlike adults, disabled children are not given individual functional assessments. The result is that some disabled children are not eligible for SSI.[4]

Inadequate SSI Benefits

Another defect is that SSI benefits generally are inadequate for many recipients. Although SSI payments are adjusted automatically for inflation each year, the total benefits including food stamps often fall short of providing a decent standard of living. This is particularly true for recipients with no work earnings. Moreover, the total value of SSI payments, food stamps, and the $20 monthly income disregard as a percentage of the poverty line has declined over time. *Maximum federal SSI payments, the value of food stamps, and the $20 income disregard as a percentage of the poverty line for an eligible individual fell from 91 percent in 1975 to an estimated 84 percent in 1989. For a couple, the combined benefits as a percentage of the*

---

[1]Spencer Rich, "Ignorance, Fear Keep Millions Off Welfare," *Washington Post,* June 26, 1989.

[2]U.S. Congress, House, Committee on Ways and Means, *Background Material and Data on Programs within the Jurisdiction of the Committee on Ways and Means,* 1989, Table 12, p. 696.

[3]Rich, "Ignorance, Fear Keep Millions Off Welfare."

[4]*Press Release No. 11,* Subcommittee on Human Resources, Committee on Ways and Means, U.S. House of Representatives, April 27, 1989.

poverty line declined from 106 percent to about 100 percent during the same period.[5] However, many SSI recipients do not receive food stamps. For this group, the percentages cited earlier would be considerably lower.

When state supplements are included, the combined benefits may approach more closely the poverty line. *However, only about 42 percent of SSI recipients receive state supplements.*[6] Moreover, the state supplements paid by most states are low. The median state supplement in January 1989 for aged persons with no countable income and living independently was only $36 for an individual and $60 for a couple. *In real terms, the median value of state supplements declined 48 percent for an aged individual and 53 percent for a couple for the period July 1975–January 1989.*[7] The major reason for the decline is that the $20 income disregard is not indexed for inflation. Thus, for many SSI recipients, economic insecurity is still present despite state supplementation.

No Periodic Adjustment for Income Disregards

For purposes of determining eligibility and the amount of SSI benefits, a certain amount of income can be disregarded. The purpose of the income disregards is to provide a higher total income to SSI recipients who also receive OASDI cash benefits. Thus, SSI recipients receive some recognition for contributing to the OASDI program.

At the present time, there is no periodic adjustment in the amount of income that can be disregarded. As we noted earlier, there is a $20 monthly disregard for unearned income, which has not been increased since the program's inception in 1974. However, inflation has seriously eroded the real value of the $20 limit, especially if OASDI benefits are also being received. Income most frequently disregarded under the $20 limit is monthly income from the OASDI program. However, when there is a cost-of-living increase, persons who receive both SSI and OASDI benefits receive less than the full increase in the cost of living. This result occurs because the increase in OASDI benefits is offset by the static limitation on unearned income in the SSI program. Since the $20 disregard is not adjusted for the cost of living, the individual's total income is increased by less than the full increase in the cost of living. Although the actual amount of benefits lost is not great, over a period of time it can be substantial.

The National Commission on Social Security recommended earlier that the $20 monthly disregard should be increased to $40 and adjusted annually for increases in the cost of living.[8] Thus, indexing the $20 disregard will assure a full cost-of-living increase to persons who receive both SSI and OASDI benefits.

---

[5]*Background Material and Data on Programs within the Jurisdiction of the Committee on Ways and Means, 1989,* Tables 6 and 7, p. 689.

[6]Ibid., p. 680.

[7]Ibid., Tables 24 and 25, pp. 716–717.

[8]National Commission on Social Security, *Social Security in America's Future, Final Report of the National Commission on Social Security, March 1981* (Washington, D.C.: National Commission on Social Security, 1981), p. 253.

In addition, the first $65 of monthly earned income plus one-half of the remainder are also disregarded for purposes of computing SSI benefits and eligibility. However, the $65 earned-income disregard has not been updated since the program's inception. The National Commission on Social Security also recommended that the earned-income disregard should be indexed annually based on the percentage increase in wages. Thus, the real value of the earned-income disregard would be maintained by indexing.

One-Third Reduction Rule

Another issue is the one-third reduction in SSI payments if the recipient is living in the household of another person. The purpose of this reduction is to take into consideration the value of room and board received by the SSI recipient. This reduction makes it unnecessary for welfare officials to make a costly and individual determination of the room-and-board value, and it also avoids the problem of an invasion of privacy.

The National Commission on Social Security and the 1979 Advisory Council on Social Security have both recommended elimination of the one-third reduction rule. It is argued that the one-third reduction may discourage some families from taking a relative into the home to live. The rule could also result in placing aged parents or disabled children in institutions where the cost is paid by the Medicaid program. In addition, some SSI recipients are reluctant to move in with relatives (where they may receive better care) because of the significant reduction in benefits. Finally, the one-third reduction falls disproportionately and heavily on aged SSI recipients of Hispanic origin who customarily live with other family members.

AFDC PROBLEMS AND ISSUES

Most criticisms of welfare center on the controversial Aid to Families with Dependent Children program. Numerous problems and issues are associated with present AFDC programs.

Family Breakup and Children Born
Outside of Marriage

The heart of the AFDC welfare crisis is the increased trend toward family breakup and the number of children born outside of marriage, which then requires financial support for the dependent children. Figure 17-1 indicates the basis of eligibility of AFDC children who became eligible for benefits in fiscal 1987. *Thirty-five percent of the AFDC children became eligible for benefits because of divorce or separation of the parents, which reflects the enormous problem of family breakup in the United States. Fifty percent of the AFDC children became eligible for benefits because the parents were not married, which reflects the growing problem of children born outside of*

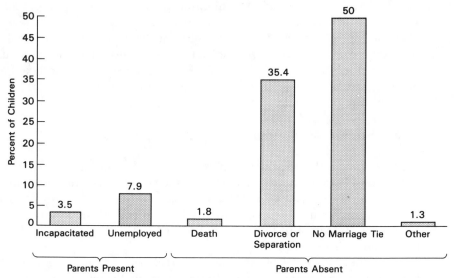

FIGURE 17-1   Percentage Distribution of AFDC Recipient Children, Basis of Eligibility, Fiscal 1987

Source: U.S. Congress, House, Committee on Ways and Means, *Background Material and Data on Programs within the Jurisdiction of the Committee on Ways and Means,* (Washington, D.C.: U.S. Government Printing Office, 1989) Table 22, p. 563.

marriage. Only a relatively small proportion of children were deprived of financial support because of death, physical or mental capacity, or unemployment of the parents.

Although divorce and separation help explain the sharp increase in female-headed families with children, the problem of children born outside of marriage must also be recognized. *About one out of every four children born in 1987 was born to an unmarried mother.*[9] In the vast majority of cases, the children are in the custody of the mother, and the father is absent from the home. It may be difficult for the mother to work because of family responsibilities, and the absent father often pays little or no child support. As a result, the family is forced to apply for AFDC benefits in order to survive. Clearly, the increase in female-headed families with children born outside of marriage is an important contributing factor to the AFDC welfare crisis.

Finally, if the present trend continues, an increased number of children will spend part or all of their early years in female-headed families, especially children in minority families. *It is estimated that white children born in 1980 can be expected to spend 31 percent of their childhood years with one parent. Black children can be expected to spend 59 percent of their childhood years with one parent.*[10] Thus, unless the

---

[9]"Advance Report of Final Mortality Statistics," National Center for Health Statistics, June 29, 1989, Table 18.

[10]U.S. Congress, Senate, Committee on Finance, *Data and Materials Related to Welfare Programs for Families with Children* (Washington, D.C.: U.S. Government Printing Office, 1987), p. 65.

problem of divorce, separation, and children born outside of marriage is reduced, the AFDC rolls are not likely to decline sharply in the near future.

Inadequate AFDC Benefits

Another limitation of AFDC programs is that the monthly cash benefits are inadequate for most AFDC recipients, and maximum AFDC payments vary sharply among the states. As of January 1989, maximum state payments to a one-parent AFDC family of three persons with no countable income ranged from $118 in Alabama to $809 in Alaska. The median AFDC payment was only $360. Moreover, the combined benefits in most cases do not bring the family up to the poverty line. *As of January 1989, maximum AFDC benefits and food stamps for a one-parent family of three persons were below the poverty line in all states. Median combined benefits were only 73 percent of the 1988 poverty threshold.*[11]

In addition, many states do not meet the full standard of need that they themselves define. Because of the critical problem of insufficient state revenues, many states place statutory limits on the maximum monthly benefits that can be paid, so welfare recipients are often paid benefits that are less than their full need. *In January 1989, 31 states paid maximum AFDC benefits to a one-parent family of three persons that did not meet their full standard of need.*[12]

Finally, even if a state pays AFDC benefits equal to the full standard of need, AFDC recipients are not assured of a reasonable standard of living. Many states have need standards that are unrealistically low, or the standards are not periodically adjusted for inflation. For example, Nebraska pays AFDC benefits that meet the full standard of need for all families. But the standard of need is set at such a low level that economic insecurity is still present even though the family's full need is theoretically met. To illustrate, in 1989, a three-member AFDC family in Nebraska with no other source of income is considered to have a monthly need standard of $364. However, in most communities, decent housing alone will cost at least $350 monthly, which leaves only $14 for food, clothing, and other necessities. Thus, despite the full payment of need, an AFDC family with no other source of income is exposed to great economic insecurity.

Work Disincentives

Although the Family Support Act of 1988 is designed to encourage AFDC recipients to work, present programs contain provisions that discourage working. The most important work disincentive is the $30 plus one-third disregard referred to earlier. Under present law, the $30 plus one-third disregard is allowed only for a maximum period of four months. After four months, only $30 monthly can be disregarded for an additional eight months. *This means that after four months, the recipient will lose one dollar of cash benefits for each dollar in excess of the work expense, $30 monthly, and child care disregards. This amounts to a marginal tax rate*

---

[11]*Background Material and Data on Programs within the Jurisdiction of the Committee on Ways and Means,* 1989, Table 9, pp. 539–540.
[12]Ibid.

of 100 percent on earnings in excess of the total disregards. Thus, after four months, there is a strong disincentive to work, since earnings in excess of the total disregards will result in a substantial loss of cash benefits.

In addition, the AFDC-UP program also has an important work disincentive. The program may discourage part-time work, since benefits may be lost if a part-time worker works more than 100 hours monthly.

Dependency on Welfare

An extremely important issue is the length of time a family spends on welfare. Although many families are on the AFDC rolls for relatively short periods, other families are dependent on welfare for long periods of time.

Length of Time on Welfare. It is important to make a distinction between persons who have only a "single spell" of welfare and those who have "multiple spells." *Although most AFDC spells are relatively short, most persons enrolled in the AFDC program at any point in time are in the midst of spells that will last at least eight years.*[13] This important point can be illustrated by Table 17-1 which is based on a 1983 study of AFDC families. The study showed that about half of the AFDC spells lasted two years or less, and 62 percent lasted less than four years (see first two columns in Table 17-1). However, the preceding figures fail to take into account that multiple spells on the AFDC program are common (about one-third of all welfare spells are followed by subsequent spells).[14] If multiple spells on AFDC are considered, the average length of time on welfare is altered considerably (see last two columns of Table 17-1). *The data show that while a significant proportion of all persons beginning their first AFDC spell are enrolled for fewer than two years (30 percent) or fewer than four years (50 percent) the majority of recipients at any point in time will spend at least eight years on welfare (65 percent).*

The preceding paradoxical result can be explained more clearly by a simple example. Assume that a hospital has 13 beds in which 12 beds are occupied the entire year by 12 long-term patients; the other bed is used by 52 short-term patients, each of whom stays exactly one week. A hospital census on any given day would show that 92 percent of the patients (12/13) are experiencing a long-term spell of hospitalization. However, when the entire year is considered, short-term use clearly dominates—of the 64 patients in the hospital, 81 percent (52/64) spend only one week in the hospital. A similar situation applies to AFDC: although the AFDC population at any point in time is composed predominantly of long-term users, the typical recipient is a short-term user.[15]

Welfare Dependency of Teen-age Mothers. Teen-age pregnancy is a serious national problem at the present time. *Of all white babies born to teen-age*

---

[13]Ibid., p. 582.
[14]Ibid.
[15]Ibid., p. 583.

TABLE 17-1   Distribution of Length of Time on AFDC (in percent)

	SINGLE-SPELL ANALYSIS		MULTIPLE-SPELL ANALYSIS	
EXPECTED TIME ON AFDC	Persons Beginning a Spell	Persons on AFDC at a Point in Time	Persons Beginning First AFDC Spell	Persons on AFDC at a Point in Time
1 to 2 years	48%	14%	30%	7%
3 to 4 years	14	10	20	11
5 to 7 years	20	25	19	17
8 or more years	17	50	30	65
All	100%	100%	100%	100%

Source: U.S. Congress, House, Committee on Ways and Means, *Background Material and Data on Programs within the Jurisdiction of the Committee on Ways and Means* (Washington, D.C.: U.S. Government Printing Office, 1989), Table 31, p. 582. Totals may not equal 100 percent because of rounding.

mothers ages 15–19 in 1986, 48 percent were born outside of marriage. Of all black babies born to teen-age mothers ages 15–19 in 1986, 90 percent were born outside of marriage (see Table 17-2).

Since unmarried teen-age mothers typically lack high-paying job skills and caring for their children makes working difficult, most unmarried teen-age mothers cannot support themselves and apply for AFDC. The risk, however, of long-term dependency on welfare for these mothers is great. A large proportion of unmarried teen-age mothers will be on welfare for an extended period. *One estimate is that over 40 percent of the unmarried women who enter the AFDC system at age 25 or less with a child under age 3 will spend 10 years or more on welfare.*[16] The new JOBS program is targeted primarily at this group to reduce the problem of long-term dependency. The JOBS program will be discussed in greater detail later in the chapter.

Going Off Welfare.   It is also important to identify those events that are associated with the termination of AFDC benefits. A 1985 study showed the following events were significant in ending an AFDC spell.[17]

Marriage	35%
Increased earnings of female head or other family members	26
Transfer income increased	14
Children leave parental home	11
Other	14
	100%

Two factors clearly stand out in ending welfare dependency: marriage and work earnings. Just as divorce contributes to welfare spells, marriage of a single

---

[16]Ibid., p. 587.

[17]Ibid., Table 35, p. 587.

**TABLE 17-2   Percent of All Live Births
Occurring Outside of Marriage,
by Age of Mother and Race of Child, 1986**

AGE OF MOTHER	ALL RACES	WHITE	BLACK
15 to 19 years	60.8%	48.1%	90.0%
15 years	85.7	75.4	97.9
16 years	76.8	64.9	96.4
17 years	67.4	55.6	93.4
18 years	59.1	47.0	89.1
19 years	49.4	37.5	83.3
20 to 24 years	28.7	19.6	66.1

Source: U.S. Congress, House, Committee on Ways and Means, *Background Material and Data on Programs within the Jurisdiction of the Committee on Ways and Means* (Washington, D.C.: U.S. Government Printing Office, 1989), Table 9, p. 841.

female family head is associated with the ending of an AFDC spell. Thirty-five percent of the terminations occurred when the female head became a wife. In addition, 26 percent of the terminations occurred because of the increased earnings of the female head or other family member. This clearly reflects the importance of a job, job skills, and basic education in ending welfare. The remaining terminations occurred when transfer income increased (14 percent), the household no longer contained a child under 18 (11 percent), or other factors prevailed (14 percent).

MEDICAID PROBLEMS AND ISSUES

Numerous problems and issues are associated with present Medicaid programs, including incomplete coverage of the poor, rapid escalation in Medicaid costs, and the lack of alternatives to long-term care in nursing homes.

Incomplete Coverage of Poor Persons

Medicaid programs were initially enacted to provide medical assistance to poor individuals and families. This objective has not been completely met at the present time. A study of Medicaid by the Urban Institute showed that a large number of eligible persons are not participating in Medicaid programs. *One-third of all noninstitutionalized, low-income persons who were eligible for Medicaid in 1986 were not enrolled.*[18]

Many poor persons are not covered by Medicaid because they lack knowledge about the program; others are not participating in the categorical cash assistance programs and therefore are not covered; still others have difficulty in filling out the required forms and fail to qualify. In addition, eligibility

[18]Rich, "Ignorance, Fear Keep Millions Off Welfare."

standards vary widely among the states, and there are no uniform national standards. In particular, many working poor families fail to qualify even when the family head earns only minimum wages and household income is below the poverty line. In many states, the incomes of the working poor are too low to maintain a decent standard of living but too high to qualify for Medicaid. Also, their employers often do not provide group health insurance coverage. The result is that many working poor families experience considerable economic insecurity because of heavy medical bills.

Substantial Increase in Medicaid Costs

Medicaid costs are increasing at an alarming rate. In recent years, total state and federal spending on Medicaid programs has risen nationally from $30 billion in fiscal 1981 to an estimated $67 billion in fiscal 1990, or a sharp increase of 123 percent.[19]

Several reasons explain the sharp increase in costs. First, a major reason is the increased cost of care in nursing homes. The costs of providing care in skilled and intermediate nursing facilities have escalated sharply in recent years, which has caused Medicaid costs to skyrocket.

Second, most states have moved in the direction of covering more needy groups, which has also caused a substantial increase in Medicaid costs. Finally, the overall adverse impact of price inflation in health care costs has also contributed to the rise in Medicaid costs.

The financial burden of Medicaid programs on the states has been especially heavy. Medicaid costs account for a substantial proportion of state spending on welfare programs. However, because of a fiscal crisis, difficulties in raising new public revenues, reduction in federal funding, and taxpayer revolt against payment of new and higher taxes, the states have found the financial burden of Medicaid programs to be most severe.

Because of the substantial escalation in Medicaid costs, many states are reimbursing doctors, hospitals, and nursing homes at less than their full costs. As a result, many physicians do not want to treat new welfare patients, and nursing homes may limit the number of welfare patients they will accept. Many states also are extremely slow in reimbursing hospitals and other health care providers, which has resulted in an increased number of lawsuits against the states. Finally, because of cutbacks in spending on Medicaid by the federal government and the states, hospitals and other health care providers have shifted billions of dollars of unreimbursed costs to private cash-paying patients. Since these patients generally are covered by group health insurance, many employers have been faced with significantly higher annual increases in their group health insurance premiums as a result of the cost shifting.

To control Medicaid costs, the states have introduced a wide variety of cost-control techniques, including prospective payment systems (PPS); maxi-

---

[19]*Background Material and Data on Programs within the Jurisdiction of the Committee on Ways and Means,* 1989, Table 11, pp. 1139–1140.

mum limits on the amounts paid for specific medical services; establishment of health maintenance organizations (HMOs) and preferred provider organizations (PPOs); more stringent eligibility requirements; and competitive bidding by providers of health care services.

Lack of Adequate Alternatives to Nursing Home Care

Another important Medicaid issue is the lack of adequate alternatives to long-term care in nursing homes. About 1.3 million aged 65 and older, or 5 percent of the elderly, resided in nursing homes in 1985. When broken down by age, nearly half were age 85 or older.[20] The cost of long-term care in a skilled nursing facility or home is staggering. Many skilled nursing facilities charge $3,000 or more for each month of care. A typical aged patient will spend down his or her financial assets for nursing home care or, if a needs test can be satisfied, apply for medical assistance under the Medicaid program. It is clear, however, that a disproportionate amount of total Medicaid spending is spent on care in nursing homes for a small fraction of the elderly. *Although the elderly account for only 14 percent of all Medicaid beneficiaries, they account for 37 percent of all Medicaid outlays. Two-thirds of Medicaid expenditures for the elderly go to nursing homes.*[21]

Alternatives to nursing home care must be developed quickly, since the proportion of aged persons in the total population will increase sharply in the future. The National Commission on Social Security recommends that a separate program should be created to provide home health services, other than acute care and hospital care, to needy persons who require long-term care. Thus, the need for long-term institutional care in nursing homes would be reduced. Aged persons would also benefit from such a program, since they generally prefer to remain in their homes rather than go to nursing homes. Some suggestions to keep aged persons in their homes include visiting nurses, home health services, homemaker and other in-home services, meals on wheels, adult day care, residential or boarding home care, and minor remodeling for handicapped persons.

WELFARE REFORM PROPOSALS

Many critical observers believe that monumental welfare reforms are necessary to overcome the limitations of public assistance and reduce welfare dependency. Several worthwhile recommendations for welfare reform have been made. They include the following: (1) negative income tax, (2) workfare, (3) greater enforcement of child support payments, and (4) programs to reduce family breakup.

---

[20]Ibid., p. 232.
[21]Robert M. Ball with Thomas N. Bethell, *Because We're All in This Together, The Case for a National Long-term Care Insurance Policy* (Washington, D.C.: Families U.S.A. Foundation, 1989), p. 31.

Negative Income Tax

Many economists have proposed negative income tax (NIT) plans as a technique for reducing poverty. NIT plans are income maintenance programs that would pay cash income to individuals or families whose incomes are below certain levels.

NIT plans have three common features: (1) the cash payment would be based on family income, size, and composition; (2) the major eligibility test would be a comparison of the family's income with the break-even level of income determined for that type of family; and (3) the family's income would be taxable, but the marginal tax rate would be substantially less than 100 percent. For example, if the break-even level of income is set at $5,000 for a four-member family, a marginal tax rate of 50 percent results in a basic allowance of $2,500. As the family's income increases, the NIT payments decline as illustrated by the following:

EARNED INCOME	NIT PAYMENT	TOTAL INCOME
None	$2,500	$2,500
$1,000	2,000	3,000
2,000	1,500	3,500
3,000	1,000	4,000
4,000	500	4,500
5,000	0	5,000

Arguments for the Negative Income Tax.   The arguments offered in support of an NIT plan are based on the implicit assumption that it can overcome many inherent defects now found in public assistance programs.

1. INEFFECTIVENESS OF PRESENT PROGRAMS.   It is charged that present public income maintenance programs do not reach many of the hard-core poor. Because of the categorical nature of the programs, millions of poor people receive little or no financial assistance from public assistance programs. The working poor, in particular, who generally receive few benefits from existing programs, would benefit much more from an NIT plan.

2. MORE EFFICIENT IN REDUCING POVERTY.   NIT supporters argue that this technique is more efficient than are present programs in reducing poverty, since it would do something that present programs do inefficiently: *it would place cash immediately in the hands of the hard-core poor.*

3. INADEQUACY OF PUBLIC ASSISTANCE BENEFITS.   As we have seen, public assistance benefits are below the poverty line in most states, so many welfare recipients find it extremely difficult to attain even a minimum level of economic security. An NIT plan is considered necessary either to replace or to supplement public assistance benefits.

4. LOSS OF JOBS BY CYBERNETICS AND AUTOMATION.   Supporters of an NIT plan or guaranteed minimum income plan argue that millions of jobs are being destroyed by cybernetics and automation and that, consequently, every person should be guaranteed enough income to live in decency and dignity.

5. LESS COSTLY TO TAXPAYERS. Under some proposals, an NIT plan would replace many existing welfare programs, including public assistance, farm price-support programs, unemployment insurance, veterans' benefits, and others. Proponents of NIT argue that having one program replace the present "hodgepodge" of programs would place income in the hands of the poor more cheaply than at present, since many welfare programs overlap and duplicate each other.

Arguments against the Negative Income Tax. Those who are critical of the NIT approach to poverty reduction offer the following counterarguments:

1. REDUCTION OF WORK INCENTIVES. The major argument against the NIT is that work incentives are reduced. If NIT benefits are paid to poor individuals or families, some recipients may prefer receiving the subsidy rather than working. It was believed earlier that NIT payments would not significantly reduce work incentives. However, several research studies indicate that this conclusion may be invalid. The results of four NIT experiments indicate that NIT payments can reduce work incentives, and for some groups, the disincentives to work are strong.[22]

The four NIT experiments were conducted in New Jersey and Pennsylvania (1968–1972); rural areas in Iowa and North Carolina (1970–1972); Seattle and Denver (1970–1978); and Gary, Indiana (1971–1974). In each experiment, an experimental group received NIT payments, while a control group did not receive any payments. The difference in work efforts between the two groups was then measured. Table 17-3 summarizes the results of the four NIT experiments.

The four tests provide strong evidence that hours of work are reduced by NIT payments. The disincentive to work for husbands ranged from about 1 percent to 8 percent. The disincentive effects for wives were much stronger, ranging from about 2 percent to about 55 percent. For female-headed households in Gary and Seattle-Denver, the disincentive effects were also strong, ranging from about 12 percent to about 28 percent. In these experiments, NIT payments were paid to the experimental group, while the control group received AFDC payments; the results indicate that NIT payments have also reduced work efforts relative to existing AFDC programs.

2. NEGLECT OF THE FUNDAMENTAL CAUSES OF POVERTY. Another counterargument is that an NIT plan would treat the symptoms of poverty, but not its causes, which include inadequate education, lack of marketable skills, physical and mental disabilities, low productivity, poor motivation, and large families. Emphasis on employment and training programs, these critics say, is a superior although slower alternative to NIT.

3. PROBLEMS OF COST AND ADMINISTRATION. The NIT approach may be an expensive substitute for existing public income maintenance programs, since,

---

[22]A summary of the NIT experiments can be found in Robert A. Moffitt, "The Negative Income Tax: Would It Discourage Work?" *Monthly Labor Review,* Vol. 104, No. 4 (April 1981), pp. 23–27.

TABLE 17-3 Average Differences in Weekly Hours between Control and Experimental Groups in Four Test Areas

AREA AND SOURCE OF ESTIMATE	HUSBANDS		WIVES		FEMALE HEADS OF FAMILIES	
	Absolute Difference	Percentage Difference	Absolute Difference	Percentage Difference	Absolute Difference	Percentage Difference
New Jersey-Pennsylvania						
U.S. Department of Health, Education and Welfare:[1]						
White	−1.9	5.6	−1.4	30.6	—	—
Black	0.7	2.3	0.1	2.2	—	—
Spanish-speaking	−0.2	0.7	−1.9	55.4	—	—
Hall:[2]						
White	−2.4[a]	7.1	−1.5[a]	32.8	—	—
Rural (nonfarm)						
U.S. Department of Health, Education and Welfare and Bawden[3]						
North Carolina blacks	−2.9[a]	8.0	−5.2[a]	31.3	—	—
North Carolina whites	2.1	5.6	−2.2	21.5	—	—
Iowa whites	−0.5	1.2	−1.2	20.3	—	—
Seattle-Denver						
Keeley and others:[4]	−1.8[a]	5.3	−2.1[a]	14.6	−2.6[a]	11.9
Gary						
Moffitt[5]	−1.6	4.7	0.2	3.7	−2.0[a]	27.8

[1]See *Summary Report: New Jersey Graduated Work Incentive Experiment* (U.S. Department of Health, Education and Welfare, 1973).
[2]See Robert Hall, "Effects of the Experimental Negative Income Tax on Labor Supply," in Joseph A. Pechman and P. Michael Timpane, eds., *Work Incentives and Income Guarantees* (The Brookings Institution, 1975).
[3]See *Summary Report: Rural Income Maintenance Experiment* (U.S. Department of Health, Education and Welfare, 1976).
[4]See Michael Keeley, Philip Robins, Robert Spiegelman, and Richard West, "The Labor Supply Effects and Costs of Alternative Negative Income Tax Programs," *Journal of Human Resources* (Winter 1978), pp. 3–36.
[5]See Robert A. Moffitt, "The Labor Supply Response in the Gary Income Maintenance Experiment," *Journal of Human Resources* (Fall 1979), pp. 477–487.
[a]Significant at 10 percent level (15 percent for New Jersey Department of Health, Education and Welfare estimate).
Note: Hours differences are regression adjusted for differences between experimental control group members in years of education, age, and similar variables.
Dashes indicate data not available.

Source: Robert A. Moffitt, "The Negative Income Tax: Would It Discourage Work?" *Monthly Labor Review*, Vol. 104, No. 4 (April 1981), Table 1, p. 24.

under some plans, NIT benefits would be paid to families above the poverty line to expand work incentives. If the guaranteed benefit is set at some poverty line, and if the percentage of earnings by which benefits are reduced is sufficiently low to preserve work incentives, large amounts of benefits may go to nonpoor, middle-income families.

4. NONREPLACEMENT OF PRESENT WELFARE PROGRAMS. Another argument is that an NIT plan would not replace existing welfare programs. To

preserve incentives, most NIT plans provide for payments that fill only some fraction of the poverty gap, so some families might still be poor after receiving payments. In particular, NIT benefits to the aged and to AFDC families might be inadequate because of the need to preserve incentives for other groups, such as the working poor. Thus, critics say, poverty would still exist despite the adoption of an NIT plan, and public assistance programs would still be needed.

5. ADVERSE EFFECT ON WAGES.   A final counterargument is that, because guaranteed income payments would be supplements to the wages earned by low-income groups and would in effect subsidize the working poor, the question arises as to whether the payments would also subsidize marginal employers. These employers could remain in business by paying the low wages made possible by the guaranteed income payments made to the lower-income groups.

Workfare

Under this approach, employable welfare recipients are expected to work in public or private employment, and the concept of workfare is substituted for welfare. The Family Support Act of 1988 created a new work program for AFDC recipients called Job Opportunities and Basic Skills (JOBS). Under the JOBS program, eligible AFDC recipients must register for work and training. To make it easier for AFDC recipients to work, the states are required to provide child care, medical assistance, and transportation.

Arguments for Workfare.   Several arguments are presented in support of the position that employable AFDC recipients should be required to work. The major arguments are summarized as follows:

1. WORK IS THE KEY TO ENDING WELFARE DEPENDENCY.   Critics of the present system argue that work is the key element in ending dependence on welfare. They argue that the payment of cash benefits based on need, which is the essence of public assistance, has not worked but has actually encouraged greater dependence on welfare. This is particularly true of single teen-age mothers who may be on the AFDC rolls for long periods of time.

To reduce welfare dependency, numerous states have enacted workfare programs. The results so far are encouraging. For example, in Ohio, workfare programs have resulted in a 17 percent reduction in AFDC cases in four years and a 60 percent reduction in male-headed AFDC-UP cases.[23] In Massachusetts, the Employment and Training Program has placed more than 55,000 welfare recipients in jobs, and 75 percent of them have gone off welfare.

2. THE PRESENT SYSTEM HAS NOT IMPROVED THE STATUS OF THE POOR.   It is also argued that the present system of cash payments has not improved the

---

[23]Bradley R. Schiller, "As States Show, Workfare Gets Job Done Fast," *The Wall Street Journal,* June 28, 1988, p. 28.

dignity, status, and quality of life for the poor and that dependence on welfare only aggravates and compounds their misery. The payment of welfare benefits isolates the poor from the rest of society, and the stigma associated with the benefits only humiliates and further degrades the recipients. On the other hand, work is considered rewarding, and income would be received in a dignified way in accordance with the national work ethic.

3. SOCIAL VALUES HAVE CHANGED.   Proponents of compulsory work for welfare recipients argue that social values have changed since the first AFDC programs were established by the Social Security Act of 1935 and that payment of cash benefits to AFDC mothers to enable them to remain at home to care for their children is no longer valid. The labor force currently consists of a high proportion of working mothers, many of whom must now work to support their families. Thus, it is considered unfair and inequitable to pay welfare mothers to stay home and care for their children; employable welfare mothers should be expected to work just like working mothers who are not on welfare.

Arguments against Workfare.   Several counterarguments are advanced against the concept of compulsory work for welfare recipients. They include the following:

1. WORKFARE IS FORCED LABOR.   It is argued that workfare is a form of slave labor and is demeaning. This is particularly true of community work-experience programs in which eligible AFDC recipients can be required to work in unpaid public employment in return for their AFDC benefits.

Critics argue that welfare mothers should not be forced to work against their will. In many cases, the jobs available to welfare recipients pay relatively low wages, and the family's financial position may not be significantly improved even when the mother works full time. The AFDC grant is reduced; higher amounts must be paid for food stamps; higher rent must be paid for public housing; and child day care facilities are in short supply. As a result, many welfare mothers have no strong personal incentives to enter the labor force.

2. WORKFARE IS COSTLY TO ADMINISTER.   Another argument is that certain workfare programs are costly to administer and that financially distressed states lack the funds to administer new programs. For example, under the community work-experience programs, employable AFDC recipients can be required to work off their welfare grants. But supervisors and administrators have to be appointed; the state must pay for transportation and work-related expenses, and child care facilities must also be provided. For these reasons, workfare is costly to implement and administer.

3. UNEMPLOYMENT MAY INCREASE.   It is argued further that forcing welfare recipients to enter the labor market will only increase the amount of unemployment in severely depressed areas. Since many communities have above-average unemployment rates, unemployment in these areas will only worsen under the workfare approach.

Increased Enforcement of Child-Support Payments

Another suggestion for holding down welfare costs is increased enforcement of child-support payments. It is argued that the states should make greater efforts to locate absent fathers and force them to meet their child-support obligations. It is also argued that present AFDC regulations are punitive, since the objective is to force welfare mothers to work by reducing or eliminating their benefits. Thus, the effect of present law is the punishment of welfare mothers and their children. *However, in far too many cases, absent fathers are not punished at all for failure to live up to their financial obligations. This is especially true of males who have fathered one or more children outside of marriage. In many cases, these fathers simply ignore child-support obligations.* In 1985, approximately 4.4 million women with children present under age 21 were entitled to receive child-support payments from absent fathers. *Of that number, slightly more than half did not receive any child-support payments or received less than the full amount.*[24]

As a result of 1975 legislation, the federal-state Child Support Enforcement Program has been created to assist the states in locating absent parents who are delinquent with their child-support obligations. Under this law, the states are required to designate an agency to collect child-support payments from delinquent parents even if their children are not on welfare.

In addition, the states must withhold overdue child-support payments from paychecks; collect overdue payments from state income tax refunds (federal tax refunds may also be withheld by the IRS); establish procedures for imposing liens against property for overdue payments; require a bond or other security from parents who have a pattern of nonpayment; extend paternity statutes of limitation to age 18 of the child; and expedite the legal procedures for hearing support cases.

The Family Support Act of 1988 also contains provisions that should result in an increase in child-support payments. The new law requires automatic payments from the wages of an absent parent, even if the payments are not in arrears. In addition, the law strengthens the procedures for establishing paternity so that absent fathers can be identified and forced to support their children.

If the child-support provisions are enforced more strongly by the states, absent parents would be forced to assume greater financial responsibility. Moreover, child-support programs can be highly cost effective since about four dollars are collected for each dollar spent.[25]

Finally, there is great potential for holding down welfare costs if the states make greater efforts to locate and force absent fathers to live up to their family responsibilities. Leonard Hausman and Robert Lerman estimate that, if absent fathers whose locations are known were forced to contribute $15 weekly for each child, about $2.3 billion could be collected on behalf of AFDC children. If only half the remaining fathers were located and forced to make the same $15

---

[24]*Background Material and Data on Programs within the Jurisdiction of the Committee on Ways and Means,* 1989, Table 2, p. 633.

[25]Ibid., Table 4, p. 639.

weekly payment, an additional $1.3 billion would be received.[26] More important, by locating and forcing absent fathers to live up to their child-support obligations, especially fathers of children born outside of marriage, the long-run effect may be a reduction in illegitimacy, divorce, and desertion rates. Also, society would be giving greater recognition to the fact that absent fathers are partly responsible for the AFDC welfare crisis and should be required to help reduce the magnitude of the problem.

Programs to Reduce Family Breakup

We noted earlier that the heart of the AFDC welfare crisis is an increase in family breakup, divorce, and children born outside of marriage. Thus, another welfare reform proposal is the development of new programs to keep families together and to reduce the number of children born outside of marriage.

Numerous approaches have been suggested to reduce divorce and desertion rates and the number of broken families, but it is beyond the scope of this text to analyze each proposal in detail. However, some worthwhile approaches include the following: (1) many churches now require couples to take mandatory classes on marriage and family life before they can be married; (2) before a divorce is granted, the couple would be required to receive mandatory counseling from a qualified marriage counselor; and (3) churches and communities should develop new programs that emphasize the sanctity of marriage and the importance of intact families to society. *Finally, with respect to the problem of teen-age pregnancy, it is argued that high school sex-education courses should not be taught without a discussion of moral principles and that the courses should stress the moral importance of abstinence from premarital sex.*

SUGGESTIONS FOR ADDITIONAL READING

BALL, ROBERT M., WITH THOMAS N. BETHELL. *Because We're All in This Together, The Case for a National Long-Term Care Insurance Policy.* Washington, D.C.: Families U.S.A. Foundation, 1989.

DANZIGER, SHELDON H., AND DANIEL H. WEINBERG, EDS. *Fighting Poverty: What Works and What Doesn't.* Cambridge, Mass.: Harvard University Press, 1986.

FORD FOUNDATION. *The Common Good, Social Welfare and the American Future.* New York: Ford Foundation, 1989.

GUERON, JUDITH M. "Work and Welfare: Lessons on Employment Programs." *The Journal of Economic Perspectives,* Vol. 4, No. 1 (Winter 1990), pp. 79–98.

OTTEN, ALAN L. "Deceptive Picture: If You See Families Staging a Comeback, It's Probably a Mirage," *The Wall Street Journal,* September 25, 1986, p. 1, 19.

SAWHILL, ISABEL V. "Poverty in the U.S.: Why Is It So Persistent?" *Journal of Economic Literature,* Vol. 26, No. 3 (September 1988), pp. 1073–1119.

SCHILLER, BRADLEY R. "As States Show, Workfare Gets Job Done Fast," *The Wall Street Journal,* June 28, 1988, p. 28.

U.S. CONGRESS, HOUSE, COMMITTEE ON WAYS AND MEANS. *Background Material and Data on Programs within the Jurisdiction of the Committee on Ways and Means.* Washington, D.C.: U.S. Government Printing Office, 1989.

U.S. CONGRESS, SENATE, COMMITTEE ON FINANCE. *Data and Materials Related to Welfare Programs for Families and Children.* Washington, D.C.: U.S. Government Printing Office, 1987.

---

[26]Leonard Hausman and Robert Lerman, "The Trouble with Workfare," *The Wall Street Journal,* April 10, 1981, p. 18.

18

ECONOMICS OF SOCIAL INSURANCE PROGRAMS

The OASDI and unemployment insurance programs are extremely important in providing workers with some protection against certain social risks. These programs, however, also have an important macroeconomic impact on the economy. They affect economic stability and growth, influence the redistribution of income, and help in maintaining consumption and aggregate demand. In addition, the incidence and burden of social insurance payroll taxes have an economic impact that must also be considered.

In this chapter, we shall examine some economic effects of the OASDI and unemployment insurance programs. In particular, we shall consider the following areas: (1) the fiscal impact of the OASDI trust funds; (2) the effects of the OASDI program on economic stability and growth, redistribution of income, and consumption and saving; (3) the incidence and burden of OASDI taxes; and (4) the economic impact of unemployment insurance.

ECONOMIC IMPACT OF THE OASDI PROGRAM

Both OASDI tax contributions and benefits are extremely important in the total federal budget. OASDI and other social insurance contributions are the second most important source of revenue to the federal government, next only to individual income taxes. In fiscal 1991, social insurance taxes and contributions are estimated to total $417 billion, or about 37 percent of the total budget revenues.[1] Likewise, the OASDI cash benefits are a leading federal expenditure. Thus, it is important to analyze the economic impact of the OASDI program on the economy. Let us begin by examining the role of the OASDI trust funds in the unified budget.

Trust Funds in the Unified Budget

From 1968 to 1985, OASDI income and outgo were included in the federal unified budget. In 1983, legislation was enacted to remove the Social Security program from the unified budget beginning in fiscal 1993. However, the Gramm-Rudman-Hollings law was enacted in 1985 and required the federal government to have a balanced budget by fiscal 1993.[2] The Gramm-Rudman-Hollings law also required that the OASDI trust funds should be taken off budget beginning in fiscal 1986. However, for purposes of determining whether the deficit-reduction targets are being met, the OASDI trust fund operations must be counted in the federal budget through fiscal 1993. Thus, the OASDI income and outgo are now counted to determine the size of any federal deficit or surplus.

As we noted earlier in Chapter 6, OASDI trust fund assets have increased substantially in recent years, and the substantial excess of income over outgo has had an enormous impact on the federal budget. As a result, certain economic issues have emerged: (1) including the OASDI trust funds in the computation of the unified budget deficit understates considerably the size of the true deficit, (2) the huge increase in the OASDI trust funds may result in undue liberalization of benefits, and (3) the sizable OASDI annual excess of income over outgo presents a unique opportunity to increase national saving in the United States. We have already discussed these issues in Chapter 6, and additional treatment is not needed at this point.

Economic Stability

It is also important to determine whether the OASDI program contributes to economic stability.[3] This involves consideration of the relationship and OASDI tax collections to benefit payments, legislative changes in the benefit and tax schedules, and trust fund deficits and surpluses.

---

[1]U.S. Congress, House, Committee on Ways and Means, *Background Material and Data on Programs within the Jurisdiction of the Committee on Ways and Means* (Washington, D.C.: U.S. Government Printing Office, 1989), Table 6, p. 1218.

[2]Balanced Budget and Emergency Deficit Control Act of 1985.

[3]For an extensive analysis of the economic effects of OASDI, see Henry J. Aaron, *Economic Effects of Social Security* (Washington, D.C.: The Brookings Institution, 1982); Joseph A. Pechman, Henry J. Aaron, and Michael K. Taussig, *Social Security: Perspectives for Reform* (Washington, D.C.: The Brookings Institution, 1968), pp. 173–212, and Tax Foundation, *Economic Aspects of the Social Security Tax* (New York: Tax Foundation, 1966), pp. 51–54.

OASDI Taxes. From a countercyclical viewpoint, OASDI tax collections should automatically decline during recessions, thereby making available relatively more funds for consumption and investment purposes. Likewise, during expansionary periods, OASDI tax collections should automatically increase, thereby siphoning off funds that would otherwise be used for private consumption and investment.

Based on this analysis, OASDI payroll tax is a poor automatic stabilizer. Although it does not exert perverse effects on the economy by increasing automatically during recessions, nevertheless it does not respond in a sensitive way to changes in business activity. In contrast to the federal income tax, actual OASDI tax collections provide little evidence of increasing automatically during expansions and decreasing during recessions.

In addition, the contribution of OASDI tax collections to economic stability is often hindered by poorly timed payroll tax increases and increases in the taxable wage base. Because of legislative tax schedules that extend many years into the future, the tax rates may increase automatically during recessions. For example, in 1937, a 2 percent tax on payrolls became effective five months before the beginning of a severe business recession. Tax rate increases also went into effect during the 1953–1954 recession, shortly before the beginning of the 1957 and 1960 recessions, and during the slowdown in economic growth in 1967. In addition, payroll tax rates were also increased in 1981 and 1982, and the taxable wage base was also increased. During this latter period, the United States was experiencing one of the most severe recessions in its history. Thus, it can be concluded that the OASDI payroll tax is a relatively poor automatic stabilizer, since it is not sensitive to declines in business activity.[4]

OASDI Benefits. OASDI benefits contribute to economic stability during business recessions for two reasons. First, some older unemployed workers retire early during recessions, since good jobs are not available, and the benefits they receive help to cushion the loss of work earnings. Second, OASDI benefits generally tend to increase during recessions because of the automatic cost-of-living provisions, which tends to offset somewhat the initial deflationary effect of a tax rate increase.[5]

However, the effectiveness of OASDI benefits as an automatic stabilizer is reduced somewhat during the inflationary periods. Under the automatic provisions, the benefits increase automatically during periods of rapid inflation—and this is the wrong time, in terms of desirable countercyclical policy. Such as increase is justified, however, when the major function of the OASDI program is considered. Its primary function is the maintenance of income to the aged and other beneficiaries; the automatic stabilizer function is secondary.

---

[4]Pechman et al., *Social Security,* pp. 183–184.
[5]Ibid.

Using the OASDI Program as a Countercyclical Tool. Although policymakers cannot ignore the long-run fiscal impact of the OASDI program, it is questionable whether tax rates, benefits, and the earnings base should be frequently changed because of short-run countercyclical considerations. Some social insurance scholars seriously question the desirability of using the program as a countercyclical tool.[6] *First, the financing of the program may be jeopardized.* A sound social insurance program must have a definite plan for the financing of benefits, and arbitrary changes in tax rates for fiscal policy purposes could seriously weaken its financial soundness. For example, if a severe recession requires the reduction of OASDI payroll taxes over an extended period, there would arise the danger of generating insufficient revenues for maintaining the financial solvency of the program. Moreover, frequent manipulation of payroll tax rates upward and downward might be psychologically disturbing to the insured population and would make it difficult for employers to make rational business decisions.

Second, taxes are difficult to adjust upward and downward with great speed. Congress is slow to enact tax increases, and even tax reductions may take a considerable amount of time to accomplish. Thus, adjustment of OASDI tax rates to business cycle conditions might be difficult to achieve in time for it to do any good.

Finally, use of the OASDI program for this purpose implies adjustments in the benefit level. However, a downward adjustment of benefits because of countercyclical considerations would be undesirable from the standpoint of sound social insurance policy. In particular, such an adjustment would reduce to poverty many of the aged who are now kept above that level only by the amount of their OASDI benefits. Thus, it may be undesirable to use the OASDI program as a short-run countercyclical tool.

Redistribution of Income

The OASDI program is a system of public transfer payments that leads to a redistribution of income, since the relative share of benefits received by some groups differs from their relative share in the financing of benefits. In particular, the lower-income groups receive proportionately larger benefits compared with their contributions, since the benefit formula weights the benefits heavily in their favor; large families receive relatively higher survivor and retirement benefits than do single persons; the currently retired aged are receiving benefits whose actuarial value substantially exceeds the actuarial value of their contributions; and subsequent benefit increases to retired OASDI recipients also result in the receipt of large amounts of unearned income. The combined effect of these factors is a redistribution of income.

---

[6]Robert J. Myers, "The Past and Future of Old-Age, Survivors, and Disability Insurance," in William G. Bowen, Frederick H. Harbison, Richard A. Lester, and Herman M. Somers, eds., *The Princeton Symposium on the American System of Social Insurance: Its Philosophy, Impact, and Future Development* (New York: McGraw-Hill, 1968), p. 101.

Types of Redistribution.   Two major forms of income redistribution are present in the OASDI program.[7] The first is *interbracket income transfers,* by which income is transferred from higher to lower income groups; the benefits received by lower-income groups are a higher proportion of their average taxable incomes than those of workers with higher incomes. Second, *intergeneration transfers* transfer income from one age group to another; in particular, income is transferred from the younger workers in the labor force to the aged who have retired and are receiving benefits whose actuarial value exceeds the value of their contributions.

Using OASDI for a Greater Redistribution of Income.   Some people believe that the OASDI program should be emphasized more heavily to achieve a greater redistribution of income in the United States. Two major arguments are advanced to support this position. *First, it is argued that a greater redistribution of income under the OASDI program can significantly reduce the remaining poverty in the United States.* The OASDI program has a powerful antipoverty impact on the economy. A recent Congressional Budget Office Study showed that if government transfer payments (including OASDI) had not been paid, the poverty rate in 1987 would have been 20.6 percent. However, the payment of social insurance benefits, primarily OASDI benefits, reduced the poverty rate sharply downward to 14.3 percent.[8] (Note, however, that in addition to social insurance and OASDI payments, the payment of public assistance and other means-tested benefits reduced the poverty rate to the official rate of 13.5 percent in 1987.)

Second, it is argued that the OASDI program can be effectively used to reduce income inequality in the United States. A recent study by the Bureau of the Census revealed that social insurance benefits are more powerful in reducing income inequality than is the federal income tax.[9] This can be illustrated by the Gini index, which is a common measure of income inequality (a value of zero indicates perfect equality of income). In a recent study, the Bureau of the Census computed 12 different definitions of income to measure the incremental effect of government transfer payments (including OASDI) and taxes on the distribution of income and prevalence of poverty in 1986. Although the federal income tax is commonly regarded as progressive, it had a relatively minor impact on the redistribution of income in 1986. *The study showed that the federal income tax reduced the Gini index from 0.500 to 0.486, or a reduction of only 3 percent.*[10] In contrast, the

---

[7]Elizabeth Deran, "Some Economic Effects of High Taxes for Social Insurance," in U.S. Congress, Subcommittee on Fiscal Policy of the Joint Economic Committee, *Old Age Income Assurance, A Compendium of Papers on Problems and Policy Issues in the Public and Private Pension System; Part III, Public Programs,* 90th Cong. 1st sess. (Washington, D.C.: U.S. Government Printing Office, 1967), pp. 196–197. See also Tax Foundation, *Economic Aspects,* pp. 48–49.

[8]*Background Material and Data on Programs within the Jurisdiction of the Committee on Ways and Means,* 1989, Table 16, pp. 962–963.

[9]U.S. Bureau of the Census, Current Population Reports, Series P-60, No. 164-RD-1, *Measuring the Effect of Benefits and Taxes on Income and Poverty: 1986* (Washington, D.C.: U.S. Government Printing Office, 1988).

[10]Ibid., Table B, p. 5.

reduction in income inequality from nonmeans-tested government transfer payments (OASDI, Railroad Retirement, unemployment insurance, workers' compensation, and veterans' payments) was much greater. *The payment of social insurance benefits (plus veterans' payments) reduced the Gini index from 0.483 to 0.434 or a reduction of 10 percent.*[11] Thus, social insurance benefits are much more powerful in reducing income inequality than is the federal income tax.

Arguments against Greater Redistribution of Income. Several powerful arguments, however, are advanced against a greater redistribution of income under the OASDI program. *First, the social insurance principle of relating OASDI benefits to average earnings would be weakened further.* The lower-income groups would be receiving benefits that have little or no relation to their average earnings and the tax contributions paid on these earnings.

Second, a greater redistribution of income under OASDI would increase the welfare element in the program and dilute even more the individual-equity element. It is argued that if the welfare element is substantially increased, then the present system of payroll financing is objectionable. OASDI should be financed more equitably by general revenues, since payroll taxes are not based on the ability to pay.

Finally, it is argued that greater consideration should be given to the principle of individual equity rather than social adequacy in the payment of benefits. The payment of OASDI benefits is now based largely on the social adequacy principle by which lower-income groups receive relatively higher benefits than do the middle- and upper-income groups. However, it is argued that the OASDI program is a social insurance program for all Americans and is not designed only for the poor. Consequently, greater emphasis on individual equity would result in relatively higher benefits for middle- and upper-income persons than is now the case. Therefore, the OASDI benefit formula should not be further skewed or weighted more heavily in favor of the lower-income groups, and the redistribution of income under the OASDI program should not be increased.

Consumption and Saving

The OASDI program also has important macroeconomic effects on the level of aggregate demand in the economy, consumption, and saving.

Consumption and Aggregate Demand. According to economic theory, the initial short-run impact of a new social insurance program financed by payroll taxes is deflationary, since disposable income, and hence consumption spending, is reduced by the amount of the taxes. However, after a time lag, most tax contributions are paid out as benefits, and if the group receiving the transfer payments has a *higher marginal propensity to consume* than has the group on which the taxes are levied, the overall impact is expansionary. For example, assume that

---

[11]Ibid.

the working population under age 65 has a marginal propensity to consume of 0.75. Assume also that disposable income for this group is reduced by $100 because of a social insurance payroll tax, with this sum transferred to the aged and other low-income groups with a marginal propensity to consume of 0.90. The working population under age 65 reduces its consumption expenditures by $75 as a result of the $100 reduction in its disposable income. But the low-income groups gain $100, and their consumption increases by $90. Thus, the net gain in consumption spending is $15.

Based on this example, one is tempted to conclude that a greater re-distribution of income under OASDI is desirable in order to shift the consumption function upward. Economists generally believe, however, that a redistribution of income from the upper- to the lower-income groups will not appreciably affect consumption spending, since empirical research on the consumption function indicates that differences in both the short-run and long-run marginal propensity to consume for the various income groups are not great.

In addition, it should be noted that the influence of the marginal propensity to consume, and any resulting multiplier effects, on consumption and spending is limited to only the *initial change in disposable income* for both the upper- and lower-income groups. If both OASDI payroll taxes and benefits are increased, a permanent redistribution of income occurs in the direction of greater equality. Once this happens, the *average propensity to consume,* rather than the marginal propensity, will govern.[12] Since the average propensity to consume is higher for the lower-income groups, the OASDI program could be considered expansionary.

Other factors also suggest that, on balance, the OASDI program is probably expansionary. Business firms with monopoly pricing powers may shift all or part of their portion of the OASDI payroll tax forward to the public in the form of higher prices. Also, since the excess of tax contributions over benefits paid is invested by the trust funds in government bonds, and the Treasury spends the sums it receives from the trust funds, the effects are expansionary, especially when a sizable proportion of government expenditures are used to finance war goods, as in recent years. Finally, labor unions may press for higher money wages because of the higher OASDI taxes. The combined effects of these factors probably make the OASDI program expansionary in the long run.

Effects of OASDI on Private Saving. Many economists believe that the OASDI program depresses private saving and capital formation. However, the effect of the OASDI program on private saving is a difficult and complex problem to analyze. As we noted earlier in Chapter 6, the OASDI program can both depress and increase private saving, but the net effect is difficult to determine. First, the OASDI program can depress private saving, since the need to save for retirement is reduced; in effect, Social Security wealth reduces the need to save

---

[12]Wallace C. Peterson, *Employment and Economic Growth,* 4th ed. (New York: W. W. Norton, 1978), p. 189.

and accumulate personal wealth. Second, the OASDI program can increase private saving; the OASDI program encourages early retirement and indirectly stimulates saving, since a person who retires early must provide for a longer retirement period. *Thus, the early retirement effect works in the opposite direction from the wealth replacement effect.*

Numerous researchers have attempted to estimate the effect of the OASDI program on private saving, but the studies are largely inconclusive (see Table 18-1).[13] Martin Feldstein argues that the OASDI program has substantially reduced personal savings and capital formation in the United States.[14] However, in a paper presented at the annual meeting of the American Economics Association, researchers in the Social Security Administration maintained that his computer program contained a fundamental flaw, and when corrected, his study would show that the OASDI program did not depress personal saving.[15] However, after correcting the error and introducing new evidence, Feldstein again concluded that the Social Security program has reduced private saving. However, after examining Feldstein's new evidence, Lesnoy and Leimer concluded that the new evidence provided only weak empirical support that the Social Security program reduced private saving.[16]

In summary, the impact of the Social Security program on private saving is inconclusive. The various time series studies on the impact of Social Security on private saving can be criticized on several grounds. We have already discussed these reasons earlier in Chapter 6, but they bear repeating. *First, the studies often fail to consider that persons can save for purposes other than retirement, such as going on a vacation or buying a new car.* Thus, even if saving for retirement is reduced by Social Security, saving for other purposes can dilute that negative effect.

Second, the life-cycle model that is frequently used to explain personal saving may be inadequate. As we noted earlier in Chapter 6, the life-cycle model assumes that individuals have a clear and accurate vision of their economic future, which takes into consideration lifetime earnings, interest rates, family composition, consumption tastes, and other factors. Individuals then make rational and complex decisions concerning their lifetime spending and saving. However, many economists are skeptical that individuals are willing or even able to make these complex decisions.[17]

---

[13]An excellent analysis of the various research studies concerning savings and investment can be found in George F. Break, "The Economic Effects of the OASI Program," in Felicity Skidmore, ed., *Social Security Financing* (Cambridge, Mass.: M.I.T. Press, 1981), pp. 59–71. See also Selig D. Lesnoy and Dean R. Leimer, "Social Security and Private Saving: Theory and Historical Evidence," *Social Security Bulletin*, Vol. 48, No. 1 (January 1985), pp. 14–30.

[14]See Martin Feldstein, "Social Security, Induced Retirement, and Aggregate Capital Formation," *Journal of Political Economy* (September–October 1974), pp. 906–926.

[15]See Dean R. Leimer and Selig D. Lesnoy, *Social Security and Private Saving: A Reexamination of the Time Series Evidence Using Alternative Social Security Wealth Variables,* Working Paper 19, Prepared for presentation at the 1980 Annual Meeting of the American Economics Association, Social Security Administration, Washington, D.C., August 21, 1980.

[16]See Lesnoy and Leimer, "Social Security and Private Saving: Theory and Historical Evidence," pp. 19–28.

[17]Ibid., pp. 16–17.

TABLE 18-1 Empirical Studies of the Effects of Social Security on Saving

AUTHORS	DATA SET	SOCIAL SECURITY VARIABLES	FINDINGS
Barro 1978	Macro time series, 1929–1940, 1947–1974	Gross Social Security wealth; benefits per recipient times proportion of labor force covered	No effects
Barro and MacDonald 1979	16 industrialized countries, 1951–1960	Benefits per recipient	Inconclusive
Boskin and Robinson 1980	Macro time series, 1929–1940, 1947–1974	Gross and net Social Security wealth; benefits per recipient times ratio of covered workers to total labor force	Significant negative effect
Darby 1979	Macro time series, 1929–1940, 1947–1974	Gross and net Social Security wealth; benefits per recipient times proportion of labor force covered times population; OASI taxes	Negative or zero
Feldstein 1974	Macro time series, 1929–1940, 1947–1971	Gross and net Social Security wealth	Significant negative effect
Feldstein 1977	15 industrialized countries, 1954–1960	Benefits per recipient; eligibility ratio; age of system	Support for extended life-cycle model; negative saving effects
Feldstein 1979	Macro time series, 1929–1940, 1947–1974	Gross Social Security wealth	Significant negative effect
Feldstein 1979	12 industrial countries, 1969–1975	Benefits per recipient; benefit replacement ratio; age of system	Support for extended life-cycle model; negative saving effects
Feldstein 1980	Macro time series, 1930–1940, 1947–1977	Social Security wealth	Significant negative effect
Feldstein and Pellechio 1979	Federal Reserve Board, Survey of Financial Characteristics of Consumers, 1963; households headed by insured males, 55–64	Net Social Security wealth	Significant negative effect
Kopits and Gotur 1980	14 industrial countries, 1969–1971	Benefits per recipient; Social Security taxes; age of system	Positive saving effects
	40 developing countries, 1969–1971	Benefits per recipient; Social Security taxes; age of system	No effects
Kotlikoff 1979	Theoretical model of equilibrium steady state capital stock	Social Security tax and benefit rates	Potentially large negative effects on capital stock

(continued)

TABLE 18-1 (*Continued*)

AUTHORS	DATA SET	SOCIAL SECURITY VARIABLES	FINDINGS
Kotlikoff 1979	1966 National Longitudinal Survey of Men, ages 45–49	Lifetime Social Security wealth increments	No effect
		Accumulated value of employee and employer taxes paid per household	Negative effect
Leimer and Lesnoy 1980	Macro time series, 1930–1940, 1947–1974	10 variants of gross, and 11 variants of net, Social Security wealth based on Feldstein and Leimer-Lesnoy algorithms	No significant negative effects. Some significant positive effects for post-war period.
Munnell 1974	Macro time series, 1900–1971	Social Security wealth	Support for extended life-cycle model
		Employee and employer taxes	Negative saving effects

Source: George F. Break, "The Economic Effects of the OASDI Program," in Felicity Skidmore, ed., *Social Security Financing* (Cambridge, Mass.: Massachusetts Institute of Technology, M.I.T. Press, 1981), Table 2.5, pp. 66–67.

Third, the studies also fail to consider that the children may have to support their aged parents if the Social Security program did not exist. Thus, personal saving by the children could decline because of the need to spend additional income to support the parents.

Fourth, the studies also fail to consider that in the absence of Social Security, massive public assistance programs would probably be needed and would have to be financed by taxes, which would also reduce private saving.

Moreover, even if the total evidence shows that the Social Security program reduces private saving (and the time series evidence does not completely support this conclusion by any means), the next question that must be answered is the magnitude of the reduction. Once again, the various studies conflict. *Thus, the negative impact (if any) of the Social Security program on capital formation is still an open question.*

Burden of Social Security Taxes

Since social insurance taxes are the second most important source of federal revenues, ranking only behind the personal income tax, it is also important to analyze the economic burden of payroll taxes.

Incidence of the Social Security Tax. Tax incidence refers to the final resting place of the tax. Since the Social Security tax is levied on the payrolls of almost all occupations and industries, the employee's portion of the total tax is borne entirely by the worker. He or she generally cannot escape paying it by changing occupations or by shifting it to someone else.

However, employers attempt to shift their portion of the Social Security tax to someone else. The employer's portion of the total tax may be shifted backward to the workers in the form of lower wages; it may be shifted forward in the form of higher prices, which reduce real wages; or labor-saving machinery may be substituted for human labor as social insurance payroll taxes increase. Thus, economists generally believe that labor as a group pays most or all of a payroll tax in the long run.

Some earlier research studies support the hypothesis that all payroll taxes, whether paid by employers or employees, are absorbed by labor in the form of lower wages.[18] Firms generally take the view that the Social Security tax is part of the total compensation paid to labor and that a payroll tax increase does not make labor more productive, but only increases the employer's cost. If a payroll tax is increased, a firm may attempt to reduce employment at the given wage, which includes the payroll tax. If the total labor supply is inelastic with respect to small wage changes, as it is generally assumed, the same number of workers can remain employed only if their wages fall by the amount of the tax. In a cross-section analysis of countries with relatively higher employer taxes, John Brittain found that the imposition of a payroll tax tends to reduce wages by roughly the amount of the tax.[19] What usually happens in practice is that money wages do not actually fall, but the firm recoups the higher OASDI tax by granting lower wage increases than it would without the tax, thus shifting the employer's portion to labor.

However, other research studies suggest that not all of the employer's portion of the payroll tax is shifted backward. In a simulation study concerning the incidence of a payroll tax, John Hambor concluded that only about 80 percent of the employer's tax is shifted backward to the workers.[20]

In addition, an earlier study of tax incidence by Daniel Hamermesh showed that little more than one-third of the employer's Social Security contributions is shifted backward to labor.[21] The remainder must either be passed on to consumers (owners of capital and labor services) in the form of higher product prices or be borne entirely by the owners of capital. He also believes that even if the payroll taxes are borne by labor in the long run, a large part of any payroll tax increase will be borne initially by capital for some time. Thus, for public

---

[18]For a critique of the current research studies concerning the incidence of social insurance payroll taxes, see Congress of the United States, Congressional Budget Office, *The Changing Distribution of Federal Taxes: 1975–1990* (Washington, D.C.: Congressional Budget Office, 1987), pp. 20–23. See also John A. Brittain, *The Payroll Tax for Social Security* (Washington, D.C.: The Brookings Institution, 1972), Chaps. 2 and 3, and Joseph A. Pechman, *Federal Tax Policy,* rev. ed. (New York: W. W. Norton, 197), pp. 176–178.

[19]John. A. Brittain, "The Incidence of Social Security Payroll Taxes," *The American Economic Review,* Vol. 59, No. 1 (March 1971), pp. 110–125.

[20]John C. Hambor, "Econometric Models and the Study of the Economic Effects of Social Security," *Social Security Bulletin,* Vol. 47, No. 10 (October 1984), p. 7.

[21]Daniel S. Hameresh, "New Estimates of the Incidence of the Payroll Tax," *Social Security Bulletin,* Vol. 42, No. 7 (July 1979), p. 39.

policy purposes, the effects of payroll tax increase on the economy must be analyzed from the viewpoint of its effect on profits, regardless of the long-run distribution of the burden.

Regressive or Progressive? A tax is progressive if the ratio of taxes to income (the effective tax rate) rises as income rises, regressive if the ratio of taxes to income falls as income rises, or proportional if the ratio is constant at all income levels. It is commonly believed that the Social Security payroll tax is a regressive tax that falls heavily on the low-income groups. A recent simulation study on the distribution of taxes by the Congressional Budget Office casts doubt on this proposition.[22] Table 18-2 shows the impact of various federal taxes on total family income (based on population deciles) under the 1977, 1984, and 1988 tax laws. Figure 18-1 provides similar information but only for social insurance taxes.

The effective tax rates shown are based on the assumption that the workers bear both the employee and employer portions of the total payroll tax. In addition, it is also assumed that the corporate income tax is allocated to capital income.[23]

The effective social insurance tax rates shown in Table 18-2 and Figure 18-1 increased between 1977 and 1988 for all income groups, which reflected the sharp increase in the combined employer-employee Social Security tax rate from 11.7 percent to 15.02 percent. In addition, the taxable wage base also increased from $16,500 to $45,000 during this same period. Thus, the effective social insurance tax rate has increased over time.

In addition, as we noted earlier, it is commonly believed that social insurance taxes, especially the Social Security tax, is a regressive tax. *However, based on the 1988 tax law and total income, the effective social insurance tax rates are progressive through the eighth income decile ($45,752 in nominal dollars for 1988) and then regressive thereafter* (see Figure 18-1). The effective social insurance tax rates declined for families in the highest income groups because Social Security taxes are paid only on part of their earned income and because earnings are a smaller share of their total income.[24]

Burden of Social Insurance Taxes on Family Income. The simulation study by the Congressional Budget Office also provides valuable information on

---

[22]See *The Changing Distribution of Federal Taxes: 1975–1990.*

[23]Because of disagreement among economists concerning the incidence of the corporate income tax, the Congressional Budget Office study allocated the corporate income tax in two ways. Under the first alternative, the corporate income tax is allocated to capital income (net rents, interest, dividends, and realized capital gains). This is considered the standard treatment if the supply of investment capital is fixed, such as in an economy where the savings rate is relatively fixed, and the domestic capital markets are isolated from the international markets. In alternative two, the corporate income tax is allocated to employee compensation. This is considered appropriate if the supply of capital is highly responsive to taxes and other prices, such as in a world economy where the capital markets are interdependent. The effective tax rates shown in Table 18-2 and Figure 18-1 are based on the assumption that the corporate income tax is allocated to capital income (alternative one). For additional details, see *The Changing Distribution of Federal Taxes: 1975–1990*, p. xiv and pp. 22–23.

[24]*The Changing Distribution of Federal Taxes: 1975–1990*, p. 45.

TABLE 18-2 Effective Federal Tax Rates by Population Deciles: 1977, 1984, and 1988 Tax Laws (Corporate Income Tax Allocated to Capital Income)

DECILE[a]	INDIVIDUAL INCOME TAX	SOCIAL INSURANCE TAXES	CORPORATE INCOME TAX	EXCISE TAXES	ALL TAXES
			1977		
First[b]	−0.5%	3.6%	1.5%	3.7%	8.3%
Second	0.0	4.2	1.6	3.3	9.1
Third	1.8	6.2	2.2	2.1	12.3
Fourth	4.3	7.4	2.3	2.0	16.1
Fifth	6.3	8.0	2.3	1.6	18.2
Sixth	7.8	8.1	2.2	1.5	19.6
Seventh	9.2	8.4	1.9	1.3	20.9
Eighth	10.5	8.1	1.8	1.2	21.7
Ninth	11.7	7.5	2.3	1.1	22.6
Tenth	17.0	4.2	7.6	0.7	29.5
Top 5 percent	18.8	3.0	9.7	0.6	32.5
Top 1 percent	23.2	1.2	14.5	0.3	39.2
All Deciles[c]	11.1	6.5	3.9	1.3	22.8
			1984		
First[b]	−0.4%	4.4	0.7	5.6	10.3
Second	0.3	5.0	0.8	2.6	8.7
Third	2.8	7.5	1.0	2.0	13.4
Fourth	4.8	8.3	1.3	1.7	16.1
Fifth	6.3	8.9	1.3	1.4	18.0
Sixth	7.8	9.4	1.3	1.2	19.6
Seventh	8.7	9.6	1.3	1.1	20.7
Eighth	9.7	10.0	1.2	1.0	22.0
Ninth	10.9	9.7	1.3	0.9	22.8
Tenth	15.1	5.6	3.7	0.5	24.8
Top 5 percent	16.3	4.1	4.6	0.4	25.4
Top 1 percent	18.8	1.7	6.2	0.2	26.9
All Deciles[c]	10.6	8.0	2.1	1.0	21.7
			1988		
First[b]	−0.8%	5.0	1.1	4.5	9.7
Second	−0.4	5.9	1.0	2.1	8.6
Third	1.7	8.6	1.3	1.6	13.3
Fourth	4.1	9.4	1.6	1.4	16.5
Fifth	5.9	9.8	1.6	1.1	18.5
Sixth	7.2	10.4	1.6	1.0	20.2
Seventh	8.3	10.5	1.7	0.9	21.4
Eighth	9.0	10.9	1.6	0.8	22.3
Ninth	10.4	10.6	1.7	0.8	23.4
Tenth	15.5	6.0	4.7	0.4	26.6
Top 5 percent	16.9	4.4	5.7	0.4	27.4
Top 1 percent	19.7	1.8	7.7	0.2	29.3
All Deciles[c]	10.4	8.7	2.7	0.9	22.7

[a]Ranked by size family income.
[b]Excludes families with zero or negative incomes.
[c]Includes families with zero or negative incomes not shown separately.

Source: Congress of the United States, Congressional Budget Office, *The Changing Distribution of Federal Taxes: 1975–1990* (Washington, D.C.: Congressional Budget Office, 1987), Table 7, p. 47.

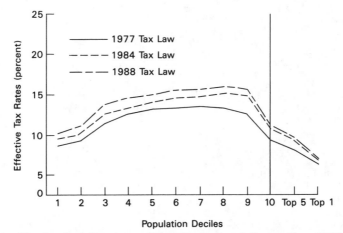

FIGURE 18-1   Effective Social Insurance Tax Rates by Population Deciles: 1977, 1984, and 1988 Tax Laws (Corporate Income Tax Allocated to Capital Income)

Note: Families are ranked by the size of family income. Because family income includes the family's share of the corporate income tax, the ordering of families depends on the allocation of corporate taxes. The lowest decile excludes families with zero or negative incomes. The effective tax rate is the ratio of taxes to family income in each income class.

Source: Congress of the United States, Congressional Budget Office, *The Changing Distribution of Federal Taxes: 1975–1990* (Washington, D.C.: Congressional Budget Office, 1987), Figure 6, p. 44.

the burden of social insurance taxes on family income. Table 18-3 shows the share of federal taxes paid by each income group (based on population deciles) under the 1977, 1984, and 1988 tax laws. The relative burden of social insurance taxes on the low-income groups has not increased over time. *The bottom fifth of the family income groups (first and second deciles) paid 2.2 percent of the total social insurance in 1977. This figure declined to 2.0 percent in 1988.* In contrast, the upper-income groups are now paying a much larger share of total social insurance taxes, largely because of the significant increase in the Social Security taxable wage base in recent years. *The top fifth of the family income groups (ninth and tenth deciles) paid 38.8 percent of the total social insurance taxes in 1977. This figure increased to 44.1 percent in 1988.* Thus, the upper-income groups are now paying a relatively higher proportion of total social insurance taxes.

ECONOMIC IMPACT OF UNEMPLOYMENT INSURANCE

Analysis of the economic impact of unemployment insurance requires a consideration of both its primary and secondary objectives. As explained in Chapter 14, the primary objective is to assist the worker during short-term involuntary unemployment by the payment of weekly cash benefits by which the worker's purchasing power can be maintained, and the secondary objective is to promote economic stability. Thus, two major areas of unemployment insurance must be analyzed: (1) its effectiveness in maintaining purchasing power, and (2) its effectiveness in promoting economic stability.

TABLE 18-3 Share of Federal Taxes Paid by Each Income Group, by Population Decile (Corporate Income Tax Allocated to Capital Income)

DECILE[a]	FAMILY INCOME Before Tax	FAMILY INCOME After Tax	FEDERAL TAXES PAID Individual Income	FEDERAL TAXES PAID Social Insurance	FEDERAL TAXES PAID Excises	FEDERAL TAXES PAID Corporate Income	FEDERAL TAXES PAID All Taxes
			1977				
First[b]	1.1%	1.3%	−0.1%	0.6%	3.2%	0.4%	0.4%
Second	2.5	2.9	0.0	1.6	6.6	1.0	1.0
Third	3.9	4.4	0.6	3.7	6.6	2.2	2.1
Fourth	5.4	5.9	2.1	6.2	8.5	3.3	3.8
Fifth	7.1	7.5	4.0	8.6	8.8	4.2	5.6
Sixth	8.7	9.1	6.1	10.8	10.1	5.0	7.5
Seventh	10.6	10.9	8.8	13.6	11.3	5.3	9.7
Eighth	12.9	13.1	12.3	15.9	12.4	6.0	12.3
Ninth	16.2	16.2	17.1	18.5	14.2	9.5	16.1
Tenth	31.9	29.1	48.9	20.3	17.8	62.8	41.3
Top 5 percent	21.5	18.9	36.5	10.0	9.5	54.0	30.4
Top 1 percent	9.2	7.2	19.2	1.7	2.1	34.3	15.8
All Deciles[c]	100.0	100.0	100.0	100.0	100.0	100.0	100.0
			1984				
First[b]	0.9	1.0	0.0	0.5	4.7	0.3	0.4
Second	2.3	2.6	0.1	1.4	5.6	0.9	0.9
Third	3.6	4.0	0.9	3.4	7.0	1.8	2.2
Fourth	5.0	5.4	2.3	5.3	8.0	3.0	3.7
Fifth	6.5	6.8	3.9	7.3	8.7	4.0	5.4
Sixth	8.2	8.4	6.1	9.7	9.5	5.0	7.5
Seventh	10.1	10.3	8.4	12.2	10.7	6.4	9.7
Eighth	12.6	12.6	11.6	15.9	12.1	7.3	12.8
Ninth	16.3	16.0	16.8	19.7	14.1	10.1	17.1
Tenth	35.0	33.6	49.9	24.5	17.8	61.1	40.1
Top 5 percent	24.3	23.2	37.6	12.5	9.8	52.6	28.5
Top 1 percent	11.8	11.0	20.9	2.4	2.6	34.6	14.6
All Deciles[c]	100.0	100.0	100.0	100.0	100.0	100.0	100.0
			1988				
First[b]	0.9	1.0	−0.1	0.5	4.5	0.3	0.4
Second	2.2	2.6	−0.1	1.5	5.5	0.9	0.8
Third	3.6	4.0	0.6	3.5	6.7	1.7	2.1
Fourth	5.0	5.4	2.0	5.4	7.9	2.9	3.6
Fifth	6.5	6.8	3.7	7.3	8.4	3.8	5.3
Sixth	8.1	8.4	5.7	9.7	9.4	4.9	7.3
Seventh	10.0	10.2	8.0	12.1	10.7	6.3	9.5
Eighth	12.5	12.5	10.9	15.7	12.1	7.2	12.3
Ninth	16.1	16.0	16.1	19.6	14.3	9.9	16.7
Tenth	35.7	33.9	53.2	24.5	18.6	61.7	41.9
Top 5 percent	25.1	23.5	41.0	12.7	10.3	53.0	30.4
Top 1 percent	12.5	11.5	23.8	2.5	3.5	35.4	16.2
All Deciles[c]	100.0	100.0	100.0	100.0	100.0	100.0	100.0

[a]Ranked by size of family income.
[b]Excludes families with zero or negative incomes.
[c]Includes families with zero or negative incomes not shown separately.

Source: Congress of the United States, Congressional Budget Office, *The Changing Distribution of Federal Taxes: 1975–1990* (Washington, D.C.: Congressional Budget Office, 1987), Table B-1, p. 70.

Maintenance of Purchasing Power

As we noted earlier, the primary objective of unemployment insurance is to pay weekly cash benefits to workers who are involuntarily unemployed so that they can maintain their purchasing power and previous standard of living. To maintain purchasing power during a period of unemployment, it is generally agreed that the weekly benefits should restore at least 50 percent of the worker's average weekly wage. However, in most states, unemployment benefits generally are insufficient for maintaining the purchasing power and standard of living of most unemployed workers. Studies made some years ago found this to be true, and the current situation is not much better.[25] The 50 percent replacement rate is a reasonable standard, but it is not being met nationally at the present time. *The ratio of average weekly benefits to average weekly wages in the United States has remained roughly constant at 35 percent since 1971; during the third quarter of 1988, the average replacement rate was only 34 percent.*[26]

Although the national average weekly replacement rate provides a rough measure of benefit adequacy, it provides no information about individual states and income earners. However, a recent study by the House Ways and Means Committee provides valuable information on the adequacy of benefits for both low-wage and high-wage earners in the individual states on both a before-tax and after-tax basis.[27] In general, on an after-tax basis, the 50 percent standard is being met in virtually all states for low-wage earners. *As of January 1988, the ratio of after-tax unemployment benefits to after-tax earnings for low-wage earners ranged from 44 percent in North Dakota to 80 percent in Massachusetts.*[28] With the exception of Tennessee and North Dakota, all states paid benefits to low-wage unemployed workers that replaced at least 50 percent of their average weekly earnings.

A different conclusion emerges, however, when high-wage earners are considered. *As of January 1988, the ratio of after-tax benefits to after-tax earnings for high-wage earners ranged from a low of 16 percent in Alabama to a high of 37 percent in Massachusetts. No state met the 50 percent standard.* In half of the states, the after-tax replacement rate for the high-wage earner was 25 percent or less.

Based on the preceding analysis, unemployment benefits are inadequate for the majority of unemployed workers who are not low-wage earners. As a result, most unemployed workers will be unable to maintain their consumption

---

[25]See Joseph M. Becker, *The Adequacy of the Benefit Amount in Unemployment Insurance* (Kalamazoo, Mich.: W. E. Upjohn Institute for Employment Research, 1961), and Richard A. Lester, *The Economics of Unemployment Compensation* (Princeton, N.J.: Princeton University Industrial Relations Section, 1962).

[26]*Background Material and Data on Programs within the Jurisdiction of the Committee on Ways and Means,* 1989, Table 17, p. 499.

[27]A low-wage earner is assumed to earn $5.50 hourly ($11,400 annually), while a high-wage earner is assumed to earn four times the 1986 poverty threshold for a family of four ($44,812 annually).

[28]*Background Material and Data on Programs within the Jurisdiction of the Committee on Ways and Means,* 1989, Table 23, pp. 508–511.

and previous standard of living based only on the unemployment benefits paid. During periods of extended unemployment, many unemployed workers will be forced to deplete their savings or go heavily into debt. Thus, the effectiveness of unemployment insurance in helping unemployed workers maintain their consumption and previous standard of living during periods of extended unemployment can be seriously questioned.

Economic Stability

For a desirable countercyclical effect, unemployment benefits should increase sharply during business downswings and decline markedly during upswings, and unemployment tax rates should not increase during recession periods. Thus, a correct evaluation of unemployment insurance as an automatic stabilizer requires an analysis of both benefits and taxes during upswings and downswings.

Unemployment Benefits. Unemployment benefits respond in a sensitive way to cyclical declines. An earlier study of four postwar business cycles between 1948 and 1964 indicated that, during three of the four downswings, approximately 24 to 28 percent of the decline in national income was offset by an increase in unemployment benefits.[29] More recently, during the severe recession years of 1981 and 1982, unemployment benefits have also increased in a sensitive manner. State unemployment benefits increased from $13.3 billion in 1981 to $20.6 billion in 1982, or an increase of about 55 percent.[30] Thus, unemployment insurance is a powerful automatic stabilizer during business downswings.

However, despite their quick response to cyclical downswings, unemployment benefits are not as responsive to business upswings. From the viewpoint of desirable short-run fiscal policy, unemployment benefits should decline sharply as the economy recovers. However, the evidence indicates that unemployment benefits tend to lag during the initial period of economic recovery. The benefits tend to remain high during the initial stages of recovery and turn downward only several months after the lowest point of the cycle has been reached. Thus, their stimulative impact is carried into the expansion phase of the next cycle.

Finally, the effectiveness of unemployment insurance as an automatic stabilizer has declined in recent years. As we noted earlier in Chapter 15, the countercyclical effects of unemployment insurance are about 40 percent less than the stimulus provided earlier during the 1960s and 1970s. The countercyclical impact has been reduced significantly since relatively fewer unemployed persons now receive benefits; the stimulus from the extended benefits program has been reduced since the insured unemployment rate (IUR) is not a reliable

---

[29]George E. Rejda, "Unemployment Insurance as an Automatic Stabilizer," *The Journal of Risk and Insurance*, Vol. 33, No. 2 (June 1966), pp. 195–208.

[30]*Social Security Bulletin*, Vol. 52, No. 10 (October 1989), Table M-34, p. 65.

mechanism for triggering the payment of extended benefits; and the taxation of benefits has reduced the purchasing power of the benefits.[31]

Unemployment Taxes.   The behavior of unemployment insurance tax collections and tax rates must also be examined when the countercyclical effects of unemployment insurance are analyzed. A common belief is that the experience-rating provisions in state unemployment insurance laws aggravate cyclical downswings by increasing taxes at the wrong time. An increase in unemployment results in an increase in unemployment benefits, which decreases the size of the state's account in the unemployment insurance trust fund. Thus, employer contribution rates must go up, and the increased tax burden aggravates the business cycle downswing.

Research studies suggest that this view of experience rating is incorrect and that unemployment taxes have actually been stabilizing rather than destabilizing during postwar business cycles. One study of the cyclical behavior of absolute unemployment taxes and the average employer contribution rate during four postwar cycles shows that absolute unemployment taxes tended to move in a desirable countercyclical manner—declining (or increasing less rapidly) during cycle downswings and increasing during cycle upswings.[32] In addition, the empirical evidence indicates no clear-cut cyclical tendency for the average employer contribution rate to increase significantly during downswings.

Palomba also concludes that unemployment tax collections and experience rating are stabilizing. In his study of four postwar cycles, he found that unemployment collections behaved in a stabilizing rather than destabilizing fashion during all four periods, even though the degree of stability they imparted was small.[33]

Experience Rating and Economic Stability.   In Chapter 14, we examined the reasons why experience rating may not be destabilizing. These reasons bear repeating.

First, experience rating may not be destabilizing during recessions, because of the time lag between an increase in unemployment in the firm and higher employer contribution rates. Owing to the time lag and the relative shortness of our postwar recessions, the recession may be over before the higher tax rates have to be paid. Thus, employer contribution rates do not immediately increase for firms during periods of recession.

Second, during periods of high unemployment, workers are laid off, so taxable payrolls tend to decline (or increase less rapidly), and the absolute unemployment taxes paid by the firms on behalf of the laid-off workers are eliminated. The result is that absolute

---

[31]Statement of Gary T. Burtless in U.S. Congress, House, Committee on Ways and Means, *Reform of the Unemployment Compensation Program,* Hearing before the Subcommittee on Public Assistance and Unemployment Compensation, 100th Cong., 1st sess., December 14, 1987, pp. 124–125.

[32]Rejda, "Unemployment Insurance," pp. 195–208.

[33]Neil A. Palomba, "Unemployment Compensation Program: Stabilizing or Destabilizing?" *Journal of Political Economy,* Vol. 76 (January–February 1968), pp. 91–100.

unemployment taxes tend to decline during recessionary periods (or else increase less rapidly) in a desirable countercyclical manner.

Finally, employer contribution rates generally have only a minor influence in reducing the stabilizing effect of unemployment benefits. The benefits tend to stimulate aggregate demand in the economy, but their stimulative effects are reduced somewhat by the dampening effects of employer contribution rates. Higher employer contributions after a period of unemployment (after a lag of one to two years) increase a firm's unit costs. If the firm increases its prices to offset these higher unit costs, real disposable income is reduced, thus partially offsetting the stabilizing effect of unemployment benefits. But the magnitude of this effect is minor; one study showed that in the long run, employer contribution rates reduce by only about one-fourth the effectiveness of state unemployment benefits as an automatic stabilizer.[34]

SUGGESTIONS FOR ADDITIONAL READING

AARON, HENRY J. *Economic Effects of Social Security.* Washington, D.C.: The Brookings Institution, 1982.

BERNHEIM, DOUGLAS B. AND LAWRENCE LEVIN. "Social Security and Personal Saving: An Analysis of Expectations." *The American Economic Review, Papers and Proceedings,* Vol. 79, No. 2 (May 1989), pp. 97–102.

BROWNING, EDGAR K. "Pechman's Tax Incidence Study: A Note on the Data," *The American Economic Review,* Vol. 76 (December 1986), pp. 1214–1218.

———. "Tax Incidence, Indirect Taxes and Transfers," *National Tax Journal,* Vol. 38 (December 1985), pp. 525–534.

CONGRESS OF THE UNITED STATES, CONGRESSIONAL BUDGET OFFICE. *The Changing Distribution of Federal Taxes: 1975–1990.* Washington, D.C.: Congressional Budget Office, 1987.

GARNER, C. ALAN. "The Social Security Surplus–A Solution to the Federal Budget Deficit?" *Economic Review,* Federal Reserve Bank of Kansas City (May 1989), pp. 25–39.

HAMBOR, JOHN C. "Econometric Models and the Study of the Economic Effects of Social Security," *Social Security Bulletin,* Vol. 47, No. 10 (October 1984), pp. 3–8.

KOITZ, DAVID S. *The Social Security Surplus: A Discussion of Some of the Issues.* CRS Report for Congress. Washington, D.C.: Congressional Research Service, November 21, 1988.

LESNOY, SELIG D., AND DEAN R. LEIMER. "Social Security and Private Saving: Theory and Historical Evidence," *Social Security Bulletin,* Vol. 48, No. 1 (January 1985), pp. 14–30.

MYERS, ROBERT J. "Social Security and the Federal Budget: Some Mirages, Myths, and Solutions," *Journal of the American Society of CLU and ChFC,* Vol. 43, No. 2 (March 1989), pp. 58–63.

PECHMAN, JOSEPH A. *Who Paid the Taxes, 1966–85?* Washington, D.C.: The Brookings Institution, 1985.

REJDA, GEORGE E. "Social Security and the Paradox of the Welfare State," *The Journal of Risk and Insurance,* Vol. 37, No. 1 (March 1970), pp. 17–39.

———. "Unemployment Insurance as an Automatic Stabilizer," *The Journal of Risk and Insurance,* Vol. 33, No. 2 (June 1966), pp. 195–208.

TAX FOUNDATION, WASHINGTON, D.C. "Social Security Tax: How Regressive?" *Federal Tax Policy Memo* (July–August 1988).

U.S. BUREAU OF THE CENSUS. Current Population Reports, Series P-60, No. 164-RD-1, *Measuring the Effect of Benefits and Taxes on Income and Poverty: 1986.* Washington, D.C.: U.S. Government Printing Office, 1988.

UNITED STATES GENERAL ACCOUNTING OFFICE. *Social Security, The Trust Fund Reserve Accumulation, the Economy, and the Federal Budget.* Washington, D.C.: United States General Accounting Office, 1989.

VROMAN, WAYNE. *An Interindustry Analysis of Payroll Tax Incidence.* Report to the U.S. Department of Health and Human Services, Washington, D.C., June 1986.

---

[34]Wayne G. Vroman, *Macroeconomic Effects of Social Insurance on Aggregate Demand,* U.S. Department of Health, Education and Welfare, Social Security Administration, Office of Research and Statistics, Staff Paper No. 2, July 1969, pp. 72–73.

19

INCOME MAINTENANCE
PROGRAMS
FOR SPECIAL GROUPS

The preceding chapters have focused primarily on the OASDI program, unemployment insurance, and worker's compensation as the major public income maintenance programs for providing economic security to workers and their families. However, there are separate income maintenance programs for special groups that can be classified as both social insurance and government retirement and insurance programs. In this chapter, we shall analyze the major income maintenance programs for the following special groups: (1) veterans, (2) railroad workers, (3) federal civilian employees, (4) state and local government employees, and (5) victims of violent crimes.

VETERANS

Congress has always been generous to people who have served in the armed forces during both wartime and peacetime periods. Veterans are currently eligible for a wide variety of programs and benefits to help them readjust to civilian life, to reward them for the patriotic defense of their country, to provide cash income to disabled veterans, and to provide compensation payments to their survivors. The various programs include cash income payments for service disabilities, pensions for nonservice-connected disabilities, educational and training allowances, dependents' benefits to the survivors of deceased veterans, hospital and nursing care in military hospitals, domiciliary and restorative care, prosthetic appliances, and outpatient medical and dental care. Other benefits are unemployment insurance for ex-service members, loans for the purchase of homes, job placement preference, vocational rehabilitation, and many others.[1]

Many programs have the major objective of assisting the veteran's readjustment to civilian life. Since most recently discharged veterans have served during the war in Vietnam, it is worthwhile to examine some problems that can cause economic insecurity for Vietnam-era veterans.

Unemployment Problems

The unemployment rate for male Vietnam-era veterans ages 30–34 was 6.5 percent in July 1989. The corresponding rate for nonveterans in the same age group was only 3.9 percent.[2] Many Vietnam-era veterans lack high-priority job skills, and the 1981–1982 recession caused considerable unemployment.

In addition, many Vietnam-era veterans have a serious drug or alcohol addiction problem, while others suffer from severe psychiatric disorders because of their Vietnam War experience. Veterans can receive medical and psychiatric treatment in Veterans Administration hospitals for these problems. However, despite treatment, drug and alcohol addiction and psychotic disorders make regular employment extremely difficult for some Vietnam-era veterans.

Reducing Unemployment for Vietnam-Era Veterans

The U.S. Department of Labor administers a number of programs to assist eligible unemployed veterans. They include the following:

- Job training
- Vocational rehabilitation for service-disabled veterans
- Unemployment compensation for ex-service members
- Veterans' reemployment rights
- Vocational rehabilitation program for veterans with individual unemployability ratings
- Vocational training for pension recipients
- Public information program to inform employers of the advantages in hiring veterans

These programs aim specifically at the unemployment problems of veterans and are designed to place veterans in meaningful jobs.

---

[1] A current description of veterans' benefits can be found in Veterans Administration, Department of Veterans Benefits, *A Summary of Veterans Administration Benefits*, VA Pamphlet 27-82-2 (September 1988); and "Social Security Programs in the United States," *Social Security Bulletin*, Vol. 52, No. 7 (July 1989), pp. 52–55.

[2] *Employment and Earnings*, Vol. 36, No. 8 (August 1989), p. 16.

Inadequate Educational and Vocational Skills

Because some Vietnam veterans have inadequate skills, they often find themselves at a competitive disadvantage in an economy that places a premium on education and training. Educational assistance earlier was provided to Vietnam-era veterans under the Educational Assistance (noncontributory GI bill) program. To be eligible, the veteran had to have at least 181 days of continuous active-duty service after January 31, 1955, and before January 1, 1977. A veteran attending school full time in an approved educational institution received $376 monthly if single, $510 with two dependents, and $32 monthly for each additional dependent.

For persons entering military service after December 31, 1976, but before April 1, 1987, educational assistance was available under the Post-Vietnam Veterans' Educational Assistance Act (VEAP). Under the program, the federal government contributed $2 for every $1 contributed by the service member. The service person contributed between $25 and $100 monthly up to a maximum of $2,700. The maximum entitlement under the VEAP program was 36 months, or the number of months of contribution, whichever was less.

Finally, the Montgomery GI bill established a new education benefits program for persons entering the military after June 30, 1985. Service persons entering active duty can elect to have their basic pay reduced by $100 monthly for the first 12 months of service. When discharged, the service person is entitled to benefits that amount to $300 monthly for 36 months. However, this applies only to service persons who serve a minimum of three years or who serve two years and join a selective reserve.

Disabled Veterans

Two major income maintenance programs are available for disabled veterans: (1) compensation for service-connected disabilities and (2) pensions for nonservice-connected disabilities. Veterans disabled from an injury or disease *that occurs on active duty* are eligible for monthly cash payments. The benefits are based on the degree of disability. In early 1989, the payments ranged from $73 monthly for a 10 percent disability to $1,468 for a 100 percent disability. Additional amounts can be paid to severely disabled veterans, such as those with multiple amputations. Dependents' allowances can also be paid if the disability has a rating of at least 30 percent.

A monthly pension can also be paid for a *nonservice-connected disability* if the veteran is totally and permanently disabled and can satisfy a needs test. The pension is based on financial need, and an income test is used to determine eligibility. In addition, pensions can also be paid to eligible surviving spouses and children of veterans who have died from nonservice-connected disabilities. However, the pension is paid only if the surviving spouse or dependent children have annual incomes that do not exceed certain limits.

Dependency and Indemnity Compensation

Dependency and Indemnity Compensation (DIC) is a program that pays monthly cash benefits to surviving spouses, children, and dependent parents of veterans who die while on active duty or training or as a result of a service-connected disability. The monthly DIC payments to the surviving spouse are based on the last pay rate of the deceased service person or veteran. Additional benefits can be paid to children under age 18, to disabled children, to children between ages 18 and 23 attending school full time, and to dependent parents. In addition to the regular benefits, special allowances can be paid to the surviving spouse and parents if they require regular aid and attendance of another person. Except for benefits paid to dependent parents, no needs test is used to determine eligibility for DIC payments.

DIC benefits can also be paid to surviving spouses and children of veterans whose cause of death is not related to military service. To qualify, the veteran immediately before death must have a total service-connected disability for 10 or more years or have a disability that lasted continuously for at least five years after the veteran's discharge from service.

RAILROAD WORKERS

Separate social insurance programs are established for railroad workers and their families. Protection is provided for retirement, disability, death, unemployment, and sickness. Railroad workers are currently covered for social insurance benefits under two important programs: (1) the Railroad Retirement Act and (2) the Railroad Unemployment Insurance Act. In addition, occupational disabilities are covered under the Federal Employer's Liability Act.

Railroad Retirement Act

The Railroad Retirement Act evolved out of the early pension plans established by the railroads, some of which dated back to the nineteenth century. Before the enactment of the Social Security Act, a majority of railroad employees were covered by these pension plans. Because of the severe depression of the 1930s, however, many plans experienced critical financial problems, and federal assistance was sought. Congress responded by enacting the Railroad Retirement Act in 1934, but the act was subsequently declared unconstitutional. A second attempt in 1935 resulted in only limited protection for railroad workers, largely because the tax provisions were declared unconstitutional by a lower court. Finally, the 1937 amendments resulted in a compromise that was acceptable to both employers and employees. The act has been amended several times since its inception.

Types of Benefits. Covered railroad workers are eligible for numerous benefits, including retirement annuities, survivor annuities, disability benefits, and Medicare.[3]

1. EMPLOYEE ANNUITY. A basic requirement for a regular retirement annuity is 10 years of creditable railroad service. A *regular annuity* can be paid at age 65 if the worker has at least 10 years of creditable service. An employee with 10 to 29 years of service can receive a full annuity at age 65 and can retire as early as age 62 with reduced benefits. An employee with 30 or more years of service can receive a full annuity at age 62 and can retire as early as age 60 with reduced benefits.

The regular retirement annuity is calculated under a two-tier formula. The *tier I benefit* generally is calculated in the same manner as OASDI benefits and is based on both railroad retirement credits and any nonrailroad OASDI credits. In effect, the tier I benefit is the equivalent of an OASDI benefit.

The *tier II benefit* of a regular annuity is computed under a separate formula and is based only on railroad service. It is the equivalent of a private pension that is paid in addition to OASDI benefits. The tier II benefit is equal to seven-tenths of 1 percent of the employee's average monthly earnings (using the tier II tax base) in the 60 highest months of earnings multiplied by the number of years of service. The tier II component is reduced by 25 percent of any employee vested dual benefit amount due.

Both benefits are adjusted for inflation. The tier I benefit is increased automatically for the cost of living at the same time and by the same percentage as OASDI benefits. However, the tier II benefit is increased annually by only 32.5 percent of the CPI increase.

In addition to tier I and tier II benefits, an additional amount (called *vested dual benefits*) can also be paid if the worker qualified for both Railroad Retirement and OASDI benefits before 1975, meets certain vesting requirements and has a *current connection* with the railroad industry.[4]

A *supplemental annuity* can also be paid in addition to the regular annuity. The supplemental annuity can be paid at age 65 if the worker has at least 25 years of railroad service and has a current connection with the railroad industry. The supplemental annuity can be paid as early as age 60 if the employee has at least 30 years of railroad service. The supplemental annuity is not available to new entrants after September 1981.

Finally, regular and supplemental annuities cannot be paid unless the employee stops working for a railroad or the last nonrailroad employer he or she has worked for before retirement.

---

[3] A description of railroad retirement and survivor benefits can be found in U.S. Railroad Retirement Board, *Railroad Retirement and Survivor Benefits for Railroad Workers and Their Families* (Chicago: U.S. Railroad Retirement Board, 1989); and "Social Security Programs in the United States," pp. 58–61. This section is based on these sources.

[4] An employee who works for a railroad in at least 12 months in the 30-month period immediately preceding retirement meets the current condition requirement.

2. SPOUSE AND SURVIVOR ANNUITIES.   Annuities can also be paid to the spouse of a railroad employee and to surviving dependents under certain conditions. They include the following:

a. The spouse of a retired employee is eligible for an annuity at age 62 if the retired employee is at least age 62 and has 10 to 29 years of service. The benefits are reduced for early retirement if the spouse retires before age 65.

b. The spouse of a retired employee is eligible for an annuity at age 60 if the retired employee is age 60 or older and has at least 30 years of service. The spouse's annuity is reduced if the railroad employee retires before age 62.

c. A spouse of an employee who qualifies for a regular annuity can receive a spouse's annuity at any age if he or she is caring for the employee's child under age 16 (or a child who becomes disabled before age 22).

d. A special minimum-guarantee provision applies in which families of railroad workers will not receive less in monthly benefits than they would have received if the railroad earnings were covered only by the OASDI program.

Annuities can also be paid to widows and widowers, children, and certain other dependents. If there are no survivors immediately eligible for benefits, a lump-sum benefit is paid to the deceased railroad worker's estate. Survivor benefits are payable only if the deceased railroad worker had at least 10 years of service and a current connection with the railroad industry. If the deceased employee is not so insured, survivor benefits are paid under the OASDI program.

3. DISABILITY BENEFITS.   A *disability annuity* can be paid to a railroad worker at any age who is permanently disabled for *all regular work* and has at least 10 years of railroad service.

A disability annuity can also be paid for an *occupational disability* at age 60 if the employee has at least 10 years of railroad service, or at any age with at least 20 years of service, when the employee is permanently disabled for his or her *regular railroad occupation*. In addition, a current connection with the railroad industry is also required. A full five-month waiting period is required before disability annuity payments can begin.

4. MEDICARE BENEFITS.   Railroad workers are also eligible for Medicare benefits on the same basis as other persons now covered by the OASDHI program. Thus, railroad employees are eligible for both Hospital Insurance and Supplementary Medical Insurance.

Coordination of Social Security and Railroad Retirement.   We noted earlier that retirement annuities under the Railroad Retirement Act require at least 10 years of credited service. Survivor annuities require at least 10 years of credited service and a current connection with the railroad industry. If these requirements are not met, the employee's railroad retirement credits are transferred to the Social Security Administration and are treated as OASDI credits. Thus, the OASDI benefit that is paid is based on both railroad and nonrailroad work earnings.

Financing.   The benefits are financed by employer and employee contributions, investment income on the trust fund, transfers from the OASDI program under the financial interchange provisions, and a government subsidy for windfall vested dual benefits.

Railroad retirement taxes are now coordinated with Social Security taxes and increase automatically when Social Security taxes are increased. In 1990, the tax on employees and employers each was 7.65 percent on the first $51,300 of earnings. In addition, both employers and employees pay additional taxes to finance tier II benefits. In 1990, the tier II tax rate for employees was 4.90 percent, and the employer rate was 16.10 percent on the first $38,100 of earnings. The tax receipts are credited to the Railroad Retirement Account, and any amounts not needed for current benefits and expenses are invested in government securities. The investment income from government securities is another source of income.

Supplemental annuities are financed by a special cents-per-hour tax paid entirely by the railroads. The tax is based on work-hours paid for in the railroad industry at a rate determined quarterly by the Railroad Retirement Board.

The cost of windfall vested dual benefits for workers who qualified for both railroad retirement and OASDI benefits before 1975 is financed by a government subsidy from the federal government out of general revenues. Windfall vested dual benefits have been eliminated by the 1974 amendments with respect to future service.

Financial Interchange.   We noted earlier that all retirement and survivor benefits paid on behalf of railroad workers with fewer than 10 years of railroad service are paid by the OASDI program. A financial interchange is used to coordinate the railroad retirement program with OASDI. The provision is designed to place the OASI and DI trust funds in the same position they would have been in if railroad employment had been covered by the Social Security Act. Under the terms of the financial interchange, the railroad retirement program is credited with the additional benefits and administrative expenses that the OASDI program would have had to pay on the basis of railroad earnings. The OASDI program is then credited with payroll taxes that would have been accrued on the basis of covered railroad earnings. During fiscal 1988, about $2.5 billion was transferred from the OASDI program to the Railroad Retirement Account under the financial interchange agreement.[5]

Financial Status of the Railroad Retirement System.   One of the most important financial factors affecting the solvency of the Railroad Retirement System is the number of employees in the railroad industry. Railroad employ-

---

[5]U.S. Congress, House, Committee on Ways and Means, *Background Material and Data on Programs within the Jurisdiction of the Committee on Ways and Means* (Washington, D.C.: U.S. Government Printing Office, 1989), Table 4, p. 1197.

ment has declined significantly from 532,000 employees in 1980 to about 305,000 in 1989, or a decline of about 43 percent.[6] Although the trust funds currently have a reserve of about $8 billion, the continuing decline in railroad employment may result in a cash flow problem in the future. The 1989 report to Congress by the Railroad Retirement Board indicates that, barring a sudden decline in railroad employment, the program should not experience any cash flow problems during the next 20 years. However, the long-term financial solvency of the program is questionable if railroad employment continues to decline more than moderately.[7]

Railroad Unemployment Insurance Act

Railroad workers were originally covered for unemployment benefits under the state unemployment insurance programs. Coverage under state laws later proved impractical, largely because of the problem of providing equitable benefits to the employees who worked in several states and also because of the reports that had to be filed by employers in each state in which business was conducted. Also, railroad workers wanted larger benefits than the state unemployment insurance plans provided. As a result, a separate program of unemployment insurance was established for railroad employees in 1938. In 1946, the program was extended to provide cash payments for sickness and special maternity benefits.

Unemployment and Sickness Benefits. Unemployment benefits can be paid to a qualified worker who meets certain eligibility requirements. Sickness benefits are payable to a railroad worker who is disabled from illness or injury. Benefits can also be paid to female employees who cannot work because of pregnancy, childbirth, or miscarriage.

To qualify for unemployment benefits, the worker must be unemployed, must register for work, and must be able, ready, and willing to work. In addition, he or she must have earned qualifying wages. A new benefit year is established each July 1 for unemployment and sickness benefits. To qualify in the benefit year beginning July 1, 1990, a worker must have base year earnings of at least $1,775 in calendar 1989. No more than $710 of earnings can be counted for any one month. If the worker has no railroad service prior to the base year, he or she must have worked at least five months for a railroad during the base year. Finally, an unemployed worker is disqualified for various periods if he or she refuses suitable work, fails to follow instructions to apply for work or to report to an employment office, leaves work voluntarily without good cause, makes a false or fraudulent statement to obtain benefits, or participates in a strike in violation of the Railway Labor Act.

---

[6]Railroad Retirement Board.

[7]*Background Material and Data on Programs within the Jurisdiction of the Committee on Ways and Means,* 1989, p. 1201.

Benefit Amount. The benefit amount depends on the worker's daily wage rate and earnings in the base year and on the length of unemployment or sickness. A claimant normally is paid benefits for up to 10 days during each two-week claim period. The daily benefit is based on a schedule in the law, or on 60 percent of the daily wage, subject to a minimum benefit of $12.70 and a maximum of $31. Thus, the maximum normal benefit for a 14-day period is $310. An initial waiting period of 14 days must be satisfied for the first claim for unemployment or sickness in a benefit year.

The benefits can be paid for a maximum of 26 weeks for unemployment or sickness, but the total benefits paid cannot exceed the worker's creditable earnings in the base year. Extended benefits can be paid for an additional 13 to 26 weeks if the regular benefits are exhausted. Two groups of workers can receive extended benefits. A worker with at least 15 years of service can receive extended benefits for an additional 26 weeks. A worker with 10 to 14 years of service can receive extended benefits for a maximum of 13 additional weeks.

Financing. The unemployment and sickness benefits program is financed by a payroll tax paid only by the railroads. For calendar 1989, the payroll tax rate is 8 percent of taxable payroll for all railroads except certain public commuter railroads. The tax rate is applied to the first $710 of monthly earnings for each employee. The basic unemployment and sickness payroll tax rate paid by railroad employers will be experience rated for each railroad in the future.

The payroll taxes are deposited into two separate accounts. An amount equal to 0.65 percent of taxable payroll is deposited into the Railroad Unemployment Insurance Administration Fund and is used for administrative purposes. The remainder is deposited into the Railroad Unemployment Insurance Account and is used to pay benefits.

Occupational Disability

Railroad workers are not covered for workers' compensation but, instead, are covered under the Federal Employers Liability Act (FELA), enacted in 1908. FELA benefits are not based on the liability-without-fault principle that is used in workers' compensation; the disabled railroad worker must prove negligence to collect for the injury. Proof of negligence, however, had been made easier, because the employer common law defenses have been either abolished or modified. The railroad cannot use the assumption-of-risk doctrine or the fellow servant rule to defeat the injured worker's claim for damages, and contributory negligence does not defeat the worker's claim, but merely reduces it.[8]

---

[8]Herman Miles Somers and Anne Ramsey Somers, *Workmen's Compensation* (New York: John Wiley, 1954), p. 318.

FEDERAL CIVILIAN EMPLOYEES

Federal civilian employees are covered by numerous income-maintenance programs, which provide them with a high degree of economic security. Eligible employees can receive benefits from the Civil Service Retirement System (CSRS), Federal Employees Retirement System (FERS), unemployment insurance, workers' compensation, and group life and health insurance.

Civil Service Retirement System

The Civil Service Retirement System (CSRS) is an important retirement program for federal civilian employees. The program was enacted in 1920 on behalf of federal employees who were forced to retire because of old age or disability, and it has been liberalized many times since its inception.

Coverage.   CSRS now covers virtually all permanent federal civilian employees who were hired before 1984. However, for new federal employees, the basic retirement program is the Social Security program instead of the CSRS. The Social Security Amendments of 1983 extended Social Security coverage to federal employees hired after 1983, including employees hired in the executive, legislative, and judicial branches. The Social Security program now covers current employees of the legislative branch who were not participating in the CSRS as of December 31, 1983, all members of Congress, the president and vice-president, federal judges, and other executive-level political appointees of the federal government.

Federal employees hired after 1983 are covered under the new Federal Employees Retirement System (FERS). The FERS program will be discussed later in the chapter.

Types of Benefits.   CSRS provides retirement, disability, and survivor benefits and lump-sum refunds under certain conditions.

1. RETIREMENT ANNUITY.   A *retirement annuity* can be paid to a worker at age 62 with 5 years of service, at 60 with 20 years, and as early as 55 with 30 years. Except for certain employees (such as air traffic controllers), there is no mandatory retirement age.

The retirement benefit depends on the worker's length of service and average salary during the highest three consecutive years of federal service. The basic annuity for most employees is $1\frac{1}{2}$ percent of average salary for the highest three consecutive years of service for each of the first five years of service, plus $1\frac{3}{4}$ percent of such pay for the next five years of service, plus 2 percent of such pay for each remaining year of service. The maximum retirement benefit is 80 percent of the worker's highest three-year average salary. The retirement benefits are annually adjusted for cost-of-living increases based on changes in the Consumer Price Index (CPI).

If a worker with fewer than five years of service leaves federal employment, a refund of the contributions into the system is paid. Interest is also paid if the terminating employee has one or more years of service. A worker with five or more years of service can elect to receive either (1) a refund of the contributions made without interest or (2) a deferred retirement annuity payable at age 62.

2. DISABILITY ANNUITY. A *disability annuity* can be paid to a disabled worker with at least five years of service. The definition of disability is more liberal than that found in the OASDI program. *A worker is considered disabled if he or she is unable to perform efficiently and satisfactorily the duties of the position occupied or the duties of a similar position. It is unnecessary for the applicant to be disabled for all kinds of work.*

The disability benefit is computed based on the same procedure used to calculate retirement benefits. However, there is a minimum disability benefit of 40 percent of the worker's highest three-year average salary (or, if less, the annuity that would be paid if the employee continued working until age 60 with the same highest three-year average salary). Also, the benefit is not reduced because of age if the worker retires because he or she is disabled. Finally, disability benefits are also annually adjusted for inflation based on the CPI.

3. SURVIVOR BENEFITS. A *survivor annuity* can be paid to the surviving spouse and children of a government employee who dies while in active service. For a survivor annuity to be paid, the surviving spouse must have been married for at least nine months prior to the employee's death (or, if less than nine months, be a parent of a child born of the marriage). The survivor annuity can be paid to the surviving spouse regardless of his or her age or presence of eligible children. However, the benefits cease if the spouse remarries before age 55.

A survivor annuity can also be paid to dependent unmarried children under age 18 (or under age 22 if in school) or to unmarried children over age 18 who are incapable of self-support because of a mental or physical disability that began before age 18.

Finally, a worker who retires can elect an annuity option with a survivor benefit payable to a widow or widower, in which case the retirement benefit is reduced. The widow or widower of a retired employee normally will receive 55 percent of the amount that the employee chooses as a base for the survivor annuity.

Financing. CSRS is financed by employee-employer contributions and by government appropriations. Covered federal employees contribute 7 percent of their basic salary; congressional employees, law enforcement personnel, and firefighters contribute $7\frac{1}{2}$ percent; and members of Congress contribute 8 percent. A matching contribution is also made by the government agency for which the employees work. The federal government pays the remaining costs out of general revenues. General revenues are used to pay (1) the interest on the existing unfunded liability of the system, (2) the cost of allowing credit for military service, (3) the cost of changes in the system, and (4) any residual cost remaining. All contributions are deposited in the Civil Service Retirement and Disability Fund, and the amounts not needed for benefits and expenses are invested in government securities.

In addition, federal employees covered under the Civil Service Retirement System are also required to pay the hospital insurance contribution rate under Medicare (1.45 percent in 1990). Thus, the combined rate for 1990 is 8.45 percent.

Federal Employees Retirement System Act of 1986

The Federal Employees Retirement System Act of 1986 created a new retirement system for federal employees hired after 1983. The new program became effective on January 1, 1987.

The Federal Employees Retirement System (FERS) is a defined benefit pension plan that supplements compulsory coverage under the OASDI program. In addition, FERS participants can contribute up to 10 percent of their earnings into a tax-deferred thrift savings plan, with partial matching by the federal government.[9]

Retirement Annuities. The new program provides for four types of retirement benefits. They are summarized as follows:

1. UNREDUCED RETIREMENT BENEFIT. An *unreduced retirement benefit* can be paid at age 62 with five years of service, at age 60 with 20 years of service, or at the minimum retirement age with 30 years of service. The minimum retirement age will gradually increase from age 55 to age 57 based on the worker's year of birth. The minimum retirement age will increase in the same manner as the normal retirement age under OASDI increases from age 65 to age 67, beginning in 2003 and ending in 2027.

Employees who retire at the minimum retirement age with 30 years of service or at age 60 with 20 years of service receive both an annuity and an annuity supplement. The annuity supplement is equal to the estimated OASDI benefits based on covered earnings in federal service. The annuity supplement ends at age 62 when OASDI benefits become payable.

2. REDUCED RETIREMENT BENEFITS. *Reduced retirement benefits* can be paid at the minimum retirement age to workers who have completed 10–29 years of service. The benefit is reduced 5 percent for each year under age 62. No annuity supplement is paid under these circumstances.

3. INVOLUNTARY SEPARATION. Employees who are *involuntarily separated* from federal service (except for misconduct or delinquency) can retire at age 50

---

[9]The new federal program is discussed in some detail in Wilmer L. Kerns, "Federal Employees Retirement System Act of 1986," *Social Security Bulletin*, Vol. 49, No. 11 (November 1986), pp. 5–10. The author drew heavily on this source in preparing this section.

with a minimum of 20 years of service, or at any age with 25 years of service. An unreduced annuity is paid from the time of separation, and an annuity supplement is also paid from the minimum retirement age to age 62.

4. UNREDUCED DEFERRED VESTED ANNUITY. An *unreduced deferred vested annuity* is the fourth retirement annuity. A previously separated civilian employee with at least five years of service at separation can elect to receive an unreduced annuity at age 62 (or age 60 with 20 years of service and at the minimum retirement age with 30 years of service). However, if a previously separated employee has 10 to 29 years of service, a reduced benefit can be paid at the minimum retirement age.

The unreduced retirement annuity amount is 1 percent of the worker's average pay based on the three highest consecutive years of federal service (not necessarily calendar years) multiplied by the number of years of service. For workers retiring at age 62 or older with 20 or more years of service, the percentage is 1.1 percent.

Survivor Benefits. Survivor benefits can also be paid to eligible survivors. The major survivor benefits are the following:

1. DEATH OF A CURRENT EMPLOYEE. If a current employee (not an annuitant) dies after completing 18 months of service, the surviving spouse receives a lump-sum benefit of $15,000, plus the higher of half of the worker's basic annual pay or half of the average high three years of pay.[10] If the current employee had at least 10 years of service, an annuity equal to 50 percent of the employee's accrued unreduced retirement annuity is also paid. These benefits are paid in addition to OASDI benefits and federal group life insurance.

2. DEATH OF A FORMER EMPLOYEE. If a former employee (not an annuitant) with a right to a deferred annuity dies, the surviving spouse may elect to receive either the employee's accrued contributions plus interest or a 50 percent annuity. The lump-sum benefit discussed in item one is not paid.

3. DEATH OF AN ANNUITANT. To provide for an annuity to a surviving spouse, the annuity of the married retiree is automatically reduced 10 percent unless both spouses sign a waiver of this requirement. If an annuitant dies, the surviving spouse receives 50 percent of the employee's unreduced annuity plus (if not eligible for OASDI benefits) a supplement payable to age 60. The lump-sum payment in item one is not paid.

An annuity can also be paid to a surviving unmarried child of a deceased annuitant (or deceased federal employee with at least 18 months of service) until age 18 or until June 30 of the school year in which a full-time student reaches age 22. An annuity can be paid to a disabled child at any age if the child became

---

[10]The $15,000 death benefit is annually adjusted for inflation based on the increase in the CPI less 1 percent.

disabled before age 18. The annuity paid to a surviving child is reduced by any OASDI child's benefits that are payable.

Disability Benefits. A disability annuity can be paid to a disabled worker who meets the definition of disability and has at least 18 months of civilian service. *The definition of disability is the same definition used in the CSRS program; that is, because of disease or injury, the worker is unable to render useful and efficient service in his or her current position.* In addition, the applicant must not refuse any reasonable offer of reassignment to a vacancy in the same agency for which the applicant is qualified if the position has the same grade level and is within the applicant's commuting area.

Thrift Savings Plan. The new retirement program also provides for a tax-deferred thrift savings plan. The federal government automatically contribute 1 percent of a covered worker's annual salary into a thrift savings plan. FERS participants can also contribute up to 10 percent of their salary into the thrift plan. The federal government matches the contribution dollar for dollar up to the first 3 percent of salary and then 50 cents per dollar for the next 2 percent. Thus, the maximum federal contribution is 5 percent of annual salary.

The thrift contributions can be invested in three types of investments: (1) government securities, (2) a fixed-income fund that yields a fixed rate of return over a set period of time, and (3) a stock index fund that reasonably represents equity markets in the United States.

Active employees cannot withdraw funds from the thrift account. However, a loan can be obtained for certain purposes, such as purchasing a primary residence, medical expenses, educational expenses, or financial hardship. Loans are limited to the amount of employee contributions and the earnings on the contributions.

Financing. The Federal Employees Retirement System is financed by payroll taxes and by government appropriations. The combined OASDHI and FERS tax rate in 1990 is 8.45 percent (7.65 percent for OASDHI and 0.80 percent for FERS). The combined rate is applied to the same taxable wage base used in the OASDHI program. The rate that applies to earnings above the OASDHI wage base is 0.80 percent, which goes to FERS. Additional amounts are also contributed by the federal government out of general revenues.

Unemployment Insurance

In addition to CSRS and FERS benefits, federal employees are also eligible for unemployment insurance. When federal employees are laid off or have their appointments terminated, they are eligible for unemployment benefits similar to those provided workers in private industry. They are covered under the various state unemployment insurance programs, with the weekly benefit and duration of benefits determined by the provisions of the states in which they work. The costs of unemployment benefits, however, are paid by the federal government.

Workers' Compensation

Federal civilian employees are covered for workers' compensation benefits under the Federal Employees Compensation Act. The benefits, which include disability income, medical care, and death benefits to survivors, are substantially more liberal than are those in many state programs. The benefit amounts are significantly higher; there are no limits on the duration of benefits; full medical expenses are paid; and generous death benefits are paid to the survivors of deceased employees.

Group Life and Health Insurance

Group life insurance is also provided to federal employees through the Federal Employees Group Life Insurance (FEGLI) program. Federal employees age 35 or younger receive an amount of life insurance equal to two times the basic insurance amount.[11] This multiple decreases by 0.10 each year, so that at age 45 and older, an employee has life insurance protection equal to one time the basic insurance amount. In addition, subject to maximum limits that affect only high-paid employees, federal employees can also purchase additional optional amounts of life insurance up to five times their annual salary.

The federal government also sponsors a number of health insurance programs for its employees, including basic health protection and major medical coverages. The government pays a portion of the premium, and the employee pays the remainder through payroll deduction. There is no single program. Federal employees have a choice of numerous carriers, some of which offer high-option and low-option benefits.

STATE AND LOCAL GOVERNMENT EMPLOYEES

The majority of state and local government employees are covered by public retirement plans maintained by state and local governments. In addition, separate retirement plans are often established for schoolteachers, firefighters, and police officers. About 72 percent of all state and local government employees are also covered under the OASDI program.

State and local retirement plans have increased in importance in recent years because of an increase in government employment and a growing emphasis on employee benefit plans. Thus, because of their substantial growth, public

---

[11]The basic insurance amount is computed by rounding the employee's annual salary up to the next higher multiple of $1,000 and adding $2,000.

retirement plans are extremely important in the economy. Most workers are affected, either as plan participants or as taxpayers who must support the programs, and the sizable pension fund assets and investment practices have a significant impact on the capital markets.

Benefits

State and local governments provide numerous benefits to covered workers. Retirement and disability benefits are usually provided. Retirement benefits are usually based on the worker's highest three-to-five-year average salary, and a benefit equal to 1.5 or 2.0 percent of average salary for each year of service is commonly provided.[12] Also, retired workers generally have the option of electing a smaller annuity at retirement to provide a survivor annuity to a surviving spouse. A few plans provide for an automatic increase in retirement benefits based on the Consumer Price Index. Other plans use the variable annuity approach to protect the purchasing power of the benefits. Finally, some state legislatures periodically adjust the retirement benefits to compensate retired workers for the loss of real income during a period of rapid inflation.

In addition, sick leave plans, early retirement and disability retirement, group life insurance, group health insurance, and group disability income benefits are commonly provided. Also, many government units have deferred compensation plans in which the worker's salary is voluntarily reduced, and the contributions paid into the plan receive favorable federal income tax treatment. Finally, unemployment insurance benefits and workers' compensation are commonly provided to most government employees.

Financing

Public retirement programs are financed from government contributions, investment income, and employee contributions. With the major exception of plans covering police officers and firefighters, most state and local retirement plans require the employees to contribute. Employees typically contribute at a rate of 5 to 7 percent of salary. In many plans, employee contributions are made with before-tax dollars, which provides favorable income tax treatment. In addition, many plans allow the employees to invest their pension contributions in a wide variety of investments, such as a fixed income fund, common stock growth fund, or money market fund.

Financing Problems and Issues

Public retirement programs present several important problems and issues that center on the following areas: (1) higher pension costs, (2) inadequate funding of some plans, and (3) investments of pension funds.

---

[12]"Social Security Programs in the United States," p. 57.

Higher Pension Costs. Pension costs in many jurisdictions have increased substantially over time. Most state and local governments are having difficulty in raising additional public revenues to fund these costs, and because of taxpayer resistance to higher taxes, many public pension plans are seriously underfunded.

The pension-increased costs are due to several factors. An increase in government employment over time has increased pension costs; higher wage and salary levels of government employees have added to costs; the proportion of public employees who are covered has increased; pressures from public labor unions have led to the liberalization of many plans (especially very low retirement ages); and the critical problem of the loss of purchasing power from inflation has led to the addition of cost-of-living benefits to many plans. The result of these factors has been an increase in legislative appropriations, increases in employer contributions, and the drawing down of pension reserves, which has aggravated the underfunding problem that currently exists in many plans.

Inadequate Funding of Some Plans. Although many public retirement plans operate on a sound financial basis, the degree of funding is inadequate in others. Because of budgetary problems and inadequate contributions, a substantial accrued liability has developed in many plans. In particular, many pension plans for police officers and firefighters are having severe financial problems. These plans generally are not completely funded but operate on a pay-as-you-go basis. As a result, pension costs have appeared to be low for several decades but have gradually increased to relatively high levels, and these higher costs have resulted in difficult budget problems for local governments.[13]

Investments of Pension Funds. Another issue involves the accumulation and investment of pension funds. State and local pension plan assets are substantial. In 1988, assets and reserves totaled about $513 billion, up about 177 percent since 1980.[14]

The substantial increase in public pension assets is important in at least three respects. First, public pension funds are becoming an increasingly important source of private capital. In the past, public state and local retirement funds have accounted for a relatively small proportion of the amounts saved when compared with commercial banks, savings and loan institutions, and insurance companies. However, the recent rapid growth of public pension assets and increased investment earnings has changed the situation. Consequently, public retirement plans can be expected to play an increasingly important role in the capital markets in the future.

Second, pension fund managers are investing relatively more of their funds in corporate stocks and bonds, with government securities receiving less

---

[13]Robert J. Myers, *Social Security,* 3rd ed. (Homewood, Ill.: Richard D. Irwin, 1985), p. 942.
[14]American Council of Life Insurance, *1989 Life Insurance Fact Book Update* (Washington, D.C.: American Council of Life Insurance, 1989), p. 24.

emphasis. The increased emphasis on corporate securities may result in a greater impact on the private investment markets in the future and may also lead to the dangerous situation of increased government influence on private corporations.

Finally, the rapid increase in public pension assets and the increasing role of investment income will require a higher level of investment skills on the part of the plan managers, especially since the investment objective of maximum return is the goal of the fund. The need for competent professional investment managers of pension plan assets will create many challenges for state and local plans in the future.

CRIME VICTIM COMPENSATION PROGRAMS

The states are becoming increasingly concerned about the victims of violent crimes who suffer serious physical injuries. Most states now have some type of crime victim compensation program to compensate innocent crime victims. Crime victim compensation programs pay benefits to innocent crime victims who are physically injured from violent crimes to their dependents if death occurs.

Rationale of Crime Victim Compensation Programs. Crime victim compensation programs are based on two fundamental philosophies. *The first is that the government has the primary responsibility for preventing crime; therefore, it should compensate crime victims for those offenses it fails to prevent.* The second is an ethical argument and involves welfare consideration. *It states that people in need are entitled to public aid by the state, especially those who are needy because of events beyond their control.* Thus, crime victims or their survivors are entitled to assistance if they suffer serious financial hardship as a result of the crime. This second philosophy is particularly important for the poor, since many violent crimes occur in poverty areas, and the crime victims there are the least able to absorb the costs of serious physical injuries.

Basic Characteristics. Crime victim compensation programs have certain basic characteristics involving eligibility requirements, benefits, and financing.[15]

1. ELIGIBILITY REQUIREMENTS. Crime victim compensation programs have several eligibility requirements. *First, only innocent crime victims are compensated.* A person generally is not eligible for compensation if he or she is (1) criminally responsible for the crime or (2) is an accomplice to the crime.

---

[15]A discussion of the basic characteristics of crime victim compensation plans can be found in George E. Rejda and Emil E. Meurer, Jr., "An Analysis of State Crime Compensation Plans," *The Journal of Risk and Insurance,* Vol. 42, No. 4 (December 1975), and Emil E. Meurer, Jr., "Violent Crime Losses: Their Impact on the Victim and Society," *The Annals of the American Academy of Political and Social Science,* Vol. 443 (May 1979).

Second, the programs pay compensation only if the crime victim is physically injured or dies. The term "victim" usually means a person who suffers bodily injury or death as a direct result of a crime.

Third, a double recovery provision is typically provided. Thus, if part of the victim's medical bills is paid by insurance or other sources, the amount paid is deducted from the victim's claim under the crime victim compensation program.

Fourth, the program may provide that the state is subrogated to the extent of any compensation paid to the victim and to any claim that the victim has against the offender as a result of the crime. Thus, in those instances when an offender is caught, convicted, and able to pay a judgment, the state can recover the amount of compensation paid to a victim.

Fifth, the state programs typically do not compensate victims for crimes involving property loss, such as stolen cars or television sets. The states do not act as property insurers.

Finally, many states require a needs test. In these states, crime victims are ineligible for compensation unless the crime results in financial hardship. The purpose of the needs test is to hold down program costs and ensure that the state's limited financial resources are spent only on those crime victims who are most in need.

2. BENEFITS. Benefits generally are paid only for personal injury or death. The benefits typically include payment of unreimbursed medical expenses, lost earnings, and legal fees incurred in setting a claim before the state's crime victim compensation board. If a crime victim dies, benefits can be paid to dependents. A funeral allowance is typically paid plus payment for the loss of support, which usually is reduced by the amount of any life insurance paid. Finally, many states also compensate "good Samaritans" who are injured while assisting crime victims.

To receive benefits, the crime victims must report the crime to the police and file a claim within a limited time period. Also, the victims must cooperate with the police and be willing to testify.

3. FINANCING. The programs typically are financed primarily by general revenues appropriated by the state legislatures; some states provide for additional financing by imposing fines on convicted criminals.

Problems and Issues. Although crime victim compensation programs reduce financial hardship among crime victims, they have serious defects that interfere with their effectiveness. First, relatively few victims of violent crimes receive benefits for their injuries. The small percentage aided can be explained by the fact that many crime victims are unaware that crime compensation programs exist and that some states require a financial hardship test that must be satisfied before benefits can be paid.

Second, although a relatively large proportion of crime victims are assaulted by spouses or other relatives, injuries inflicted by members of the victim's family generally are not compensated.

Third, many states require a needs test before the benefits are paid. In effect, crime victims are treated as second-class citizens. If violent crime is considered a serious social problem, which few would dispute, then crime compensation programs should cover the masses to provide some protection against this important social risk. A needs test defeats this objective. Crime compensation programs should follow the social insurance principle of the payment of benefits based on right rather than a needs test such as that found in public assistance.

Finally, considerable research is necessary to improve the programs. Accurate data must be made available regarding the number of victims made destitute by crimes, the proportion of claims denied, the financial experience of the programs, and the extent to which crime compensation benefits are reduced by payments from other sources.

SUGGESTIONS FOR ADDITIONAL READING

BJORKMAN, SHARON. *Public Pensions: A Legislator's Guide.* Denver, Colo.: National Conference of State Legislatures, 1985.

ENNIS, RICHARD M. "Is a Statewide Pension Fund a Pension or a Cookie Jar? The Answer Has Implications for Investment Policy," *Financial Analysts Journal* (November–December 1988), pp. 21–47.

KERNS, WILMER L. "Federal Employees' Retirement System Act of 1986," *Social Security Bulletin*, Vol. 49, No. 11 (November 1986), pp. 5–10.

LONGMAN, PHILLIP. "Railroad Pension System's Tunnel Vision," *The Wall Street Journal*, February 2, 1989, p. A10.

MEURER, EMIL E., JR. "Violent Crime Losses: Their Impact on the Victim and Society," *Annals of the American Academy of Political and Social Science*, Vol. 443 (May 1979), pp. 54–62.

THE NATIONAL UNDERWRITER COMPANY. *Federal In-surance Benefits*, 1988 ed. Cincinnati, Ohio: The National Underwriter Company, 1988.

REJDA, GEORGE E., AND EMIL E. MEURER, JR. "An Analysis of State Crime Compensation Plans," *The Journal of Risk and Insurance*, Vol. 42, No. 4 (December 1975).

"SOCIAL SECURITY PROGRAMS IN THE UNITED STATES," *Social Security Bulletin*, Vol. 52, No. 7 (July 1989), pp. 2–79.

U.S. RAILROAD RETIREMENT BOARD. *Railroad Retirement and Survivor Benefits for Railroad Workers and Their Families.* Chicago, Ill.: U.S. Railroad Retirement Board, 1989.

U.S. RAILROAD RETIREMENT BOARD. *Unemployment Benefit Handbook for Railroad Employees.* Booklet UB-10, September 1989.

WHITE, JAMES A. "Public Pension Funds Increase Pressure in Deciding Roles of Firms They Invest In," *The Wall Street Journal*, May 15, 1989, p. A6.

INDEX

INDEX OF AUTHORS

INDEX OF SUBJECTS